Internet
Literacy

FOURTH EDITION

Internet Literacy

FOURTH EDITION

Fred T. Hofstetter

University of Delaware

McGraw-Hill
Irwin

Boston   Burr Ridge, IL   Dubuque, IA   Madison, WI   New York   San Francisco   St. Louis
Bangkok   Bogotá   Caracas   Kuala Lumpur   Lisbon   London   Madrid   Mexico City
Milan   Montreal   New Delhi   Santiago   Seoul   Singapore   Sydney   Taipei   Toronto

McGraw-Hill
Irwin

INTERNET LITERACY

Published by McGraw-Hill/Irwin, a business unit of The McGraw-Hill Companies, Inc., 1221 Avenue of the Americas, New York, NY, 10020. Copyright © 2006 by The McGraw-Hill Companies, Inc. All rights reserved. No part of this publication may be reproduced or distributed in any form or by any means, or stored in a database or retrieval system, without the prior written consent of The McGraw-Hill Companies, Inc., including, but not limited to, in any network or other electronic storage or transmission, or broadcast for distance learning.

Some ancillaries, including electronic and print components, may not be available to customers outside the United States.

This book is printed on acid-free paper.

1 2 3 4 5 6 7 8 9 0 QPD/QPD 0 9 8 7 6 5

ISBN 0-07-226061-0

Executive editor: *Paul Ducham*
Editorial assistant: *Alaina Grayson*
Marketing manager: *Sankha Basu*
Senior media producer: *Victor Chiu*
Project manager: *Laura Griffin*
Production supervisor: *Debra R. Sylvester*
Coordinator freelance design: *Artemio Ortiz Jr.*
Photo research coordinator: *Ira C. Roberts*
Photo researcher: *Keri Johnson*
Senior media project manager: *Rose M. Range*
Developer, Media technology: *Brian Nacik*
Cover design: *Artemio Ortiz Jr.*
Typeface: *10/12 Minion Pro*
Compositor: *Interactive Composition Corporation*
Printer: *Quebecor World Dubuque Inc.*

Information has been obtained by McGraw-Hill/Irwin from sources believed to be reliable. However, because of the possibility of human or mechanical error by our sources, McGraw-Hill/Irwin, or others, McGraw-Hill/Irwin does not guarantee the accuracy, adequacy, or completeness of any information and is not responsible for any errors or omissions or the results obtained from the use of such information.

Library of Congress Cataloging-in-Publication Data
Hofstetter, Fred T. (Fred Thomas), 1949–
    Internet literacy / by Fred T. Hofstetter.—4th ed.
        p. cm.
    Includes bibliographical references and index.
    ISBN 0-07-226061-0 (alk. paper)
    1. Internet literacy—Textbooks. I. Title.
TK5105.875.I57H65 2006
004.67′8—dc22
                                        2005050530

www.mhhe.com

Dedication

This book is dedicated to the memory of the four people who made my childhood special: Aunt Irene, Uncle Guy, and Grandma and Grandpa Jones. Never was a child shown more love, caring, and devotion. I wish every child could be so fortunate as to have such super relatives.

In Memoriam Amantem

Irene Trenor Landerman, 1899–1969

Guy N. Landerman, 1896–1965

Benjamin F. Jones, 1896–1971

Margaret E. Trenor Jones, 1904–1996

Brief Contents

Contents

PART TWO　Getting On the Internet　　　　　　　　　　　　**41**

Chapter 3　　　　**Getting Connected**　　　　　　　　　　　　_42_

PART SIX   Using Multimedia on the Internet   327

Introduction

Internet is the buzzword of the millennium. Never before has a technology spread so rapidly. Never has an invention enabled so many people to do so many things—things that are strategically important to life in the information society. So strategic that being able to use the Internet has become a basic skill. So important that understanding the Internet and knowing how to communicate over it have become a literacy.

Internet literacy is what this book is about. The goal is to provide a course of study that will enable students to acquire the conceptual background and the online skills needed to become Internet literate. An important feature of this book is the way it avoids unnecessary jargon and computer terms. By focusing on the tasks that an Internet literate person should be able to accomplish, and by using software that makes those tasks easy to accomplish, this book provides a course of instruction that any college student, adult learner, or motivated high school student can successfully complete. Working through this book will enable students to use the Internet in their daily lives and become intelligent consumers of information.

Another key feature is the way this book teaches the student how to create Web pages and publish them on the World Wide Web. After learning how to use Internet search engines to conduct research, students complete a Web page creation tutorial that steps through the process of online writing and documenting Internet resources with proper bibliographic style. Thus, the student becomes a creator and a publisher, not just a consumer, of the Internet. Along the way, the student creates a home page and a Web page résumé. Several students have reported that putting their résumé on the Web helped them find jobs.

The course is organized into seven parts. Part One defines the Internet and explains how it is changing the world. After defining the basic Internet services of electronic mail, listserv, newsgroups, chat, instant messaging, videoconferencing, FTP, multimedia streaming, the World Wide Web, RSS, and blogging, the book explains how they are being used across a broad range of industries to provide people with important new capabilities, including telecommuting, home shopping, online learning, government services, and interactive television. Especially relevant to college students are the sections on teaching, learning, and interconnected scholarship.

Part Two covers the logistics of getting connected to the Internet. Students learn about Internet service providers and how to connect via telephone modems, Ethernet, ISDN, DSL, satellite, or cable modems. Then the students go online and learn how to surf the Net using a World Wide Web browser. The tutorial teaches the theory of surfing without getting too technical. By learning the principles of surfing, students learn how to go places and find things that casual users are unlikely to discover.

In Part Three, students learn how to communicate over the Internet, first through electronic mail, and then via listservs, newsgroups, and forums. Step-by-step tutorial exercises allow students to practice key concepts and develop online skills. A chapter on Internet etiquette covers rules, courtesies, and ethics that all users should observe when communicating online.

Part Four is a tutorial on how to use Internet search engines to find things online via subject-oriented searches, keyword searching, natural language searches, and metasearching. Students learn how to search scholarly databases of refereed articles as well as more general sources. In addition to searching for text, students learn how to conduct multimedia searches for pictures, animations, audio, and video. A special section on peer-to-peer file sharing sensitizes students to the ethics of sharing copyrighted works over the Internet.

In support of online writing, students learn the proper bibliographic style for citing Internet resources. MLA, APA, and CMS styles are covered. Because almost anyone can learn how to publish information on the Web, this book encourages the students to question the source and evaluate the information before citing it.

In Part Five, students learn how to establish a presence on the Internet by creating Web pages and mounting them on the World Wide Web. A chapter on Web page creation strategies helps students choose the proper tool for the task at hand. A chapter on Web page design teaches screen design principles and shows how to lay out Web page elements effectively. Then students learn how to create a home page and a Web page résumé and publish documents on the Web. By linking their home page to their résumé and to other online resources, students experience how hyperlinks can create a world of interconnected scholarship.

Part Six brings the students' Web pages to life by showing how to use multimedia on the Internet. After making a waveform audio recording, students learn how sounds, movies, and animations can be linked to Web pages and made to play via different kinds of multimedia controllers and streaming technologies. Then the book provides access to a large number of multimedia creation tools for making active Web pages.

Even though the Internet has already become an essential part of life in the information society, the Net still is in many ways an emerging technology that is inspiring debates about how it should evolve and become regulated. Accordingly, Part Seven gets the students involved in planning for the future of the Internet by discussing and debating the societal issues of equity, privacy, security, protectionism, censorship, decency, copyright, and Fair Use. Then students learn about the emerging technologies of the multimedia backbone, Internet talk radio, the real-time streaming protocol, artificial intelligence, voice recognition, text-to-speech conversion, image recognition, robots, intelligent agents, videoconferencing, Internet phone services, Webcasting, virtual reality, wireless communications, digital hubs, and Internet PCs.

The book concludes by showing students how to use the Internet for continued learning about the exciting new products that will be invented during the coming decades. The best listservs, newsgroups, and Web sites for keeping up with this fast-paced field are identified, and students learn how to subscribe for free. On both Windows and Macintosh platforms, students learn how to subscribe freely to software update services and security newsletters that provide ongoing advice to keep computers protected from viruses, worms, spyware, malicious code, and crackers.

World Wide Web Site

Accompanying this book is an Internet Literacy Web site. It is called the *Interlit* Web site—*Interlit* stands for Internet Literacy. The address of the site is http://www.udel.edu/interlit. It provides quick and easy access to all of the Internet resources and examples referred to in this textbook. In addition to making it easy to find things, the *Interlit* Web site can help save you money, because almost all of the resources it uses are available free of charge.

Icons coordinate what you read in this book with what you will find at the *Interlit* Web site. When you see an icon in the margin of this text, you will know that you can go to the *Interlit* Web site for quick and easy access to that item. For example, in the Web page creation tutorial, where the book provides a layout analysis of exemplary Web pages, the *Interlit* Web site provides hot links that enable you to visit the exemplars and try them out.

End-of-Chapter Exercises

Throughout the course, end-of-chapter exercises provide practical, hands-on assignments for students to complete outside of class. The instructor can adjust the depth and rigor of the course by deciding which assignments to require. Highly motivated students can go ahead and complete all of the exercises, to harness the full potential of the Internet.

Situated Case Projects

At the end of the exercises in each chapter is a special section containing situated case projects. These projects are called situated because they present the student with real-world problems. The student imagines being employed in a small company or school that is planning how to use the Internet to improve daily operations. After completing each chapter, the student applies its content to solving a real-world need or problem related to the use of information technology in the workplace. The case projects are optional and need not be done in sequence. For a quick course about the Internet, the case projects can be skipped. Longer courses can use some or all of the cases to deepen understanding by immersing students in the solution of real-world problems in the workplace. Appendix B contains an outline of the situated case projects.

Basic Windows and Macintosh Tutorials

At six strategic locations in this book, Windows and Macintosh tutorials have been provided for inexperienced students who may need help completing basic computing tasks. The tutorials are presented at the point where students will first need them. For students or instructors who want to locate the basic Windows and Macintosh tutorials at other times, Appendix C shows where to find them.

What You Will Need to Use This Book

Internet Literacy works on both Windows PCs and Macintoshes with all of the leading Web browsers, including Microsoft Internet Explorer, Netscape Navigator, Safari, and Mozilla Firefox. In order to complete the exercises and tutorials in this book, the student will need to have access to a Web browser that is running on a Windows PC or a Macintosh. The student also will need an Internet account that provides the basic Internet services of e-mail, newsgroups, FTP, and the Web. Students who do not already have Internet access should refer to Part Two of this book, which provides a detailed explanation and comparison of the options for getting connected to the Internet. While high-speed connections work best, all of the exercises in this book can be completed via modem over an ordinary telephone line.

Internet Toolkit

By working through the tutorial exercises in this book, the student will acquire a toolkit full of utilities for authoring Web pages, manipulating images, recording and editing sound, creating animations, and maintaining a Web site. Appendix A lists the utilities used in this book. Any of these utilities that the student does not already have can be downloaded from the *Interlit* Web site. Utilities are provided for both Windows and Macintosh computers.

Dreamweaver, FrontPage, and Mozilla Downloads

In the Web page creation tutorial that begins in Chapter 18, you will have your choice of using either Macromedia Dreamweaver, Microsoft FrontPage, or Mozilla Nvu. If you do not already own a copy, you can get a free trial version by following these links:

Dreamweaver: www.macromedia.com/software/dreamweaver/download

FrontPage: www.microsoft.com/office/frontpage/prodinfo/trial.mspx

Mozilla Nvu: www.nvu.com

If you plan to use the trial version of Dreamweaver or FrontPage, please understand that it will expire after the trial period. You should therefore not install it until you are actually ready to begin working on the exercises in Chapter 18. The Mozilla download, on the other hand, will not expire. As open source software, the Mozilla Nvu program is freely downloadable, so you do not need to pay anything if you decide to keep using it.

If do not know how to decide which software to use, read Chapter 15, which discusses Web creation strategies and provides more information on Macromedia Dreamweaver, Microsoft FrontPage, and Mozilla Nvu.

Acknowledgements

I have many people to thank for making this project possible, but most of all, I want to acknowledge my students, who inspired this book through their enthusiastic participation in the experimental courses that were the precursors to what we now know as *Internet Literacy*. I learn more from my students than from anyone else, and I look forward to every class, not so much to teach, as to learn.

University of Delaware Research Professor L. Leon Campbell provided valuable service as the author's "intelligent agent" on the Internet. Almost daily, Leon sent the author information about issues, trends, and new developments gleaned from his extensive surfing of the network. Leon is a valued friend and colleague.

Pat Sine, Director of the Office of Educational Technology at the University of Delaware, provided invaluable service as the technical editor for this book. I am grateful for Pat's expertise, dedication, and numerous contributions.

Dr. Primo Toccafondi, coordinator of the University of Delaware's degree programs in Southern Delaware, helped the author teach Internet Literacy in a distance learning format. I will always be grateful to Toc for his many suggestions and helpful comments on drafts of the text, as well as for his camaraderie. Making new friends is one of the lifelong rewards of working on projects like this one.

While working at PBS, David Collings made substantial contributions to a distance learning format that uses this textbook to deliver an Internet Literacy course over the Web. I am grateful to David for his insight and dedication to making courses available online.

Rhonda Sands of McGraw-Hill served as this book's first-edition editor, Jodi McPherson edited the second edition, Dan Silverburg did the third, and Don Hull edited this fourth edition. I thank Rhonda, Jodi, Dan, and Don for their many contributions, both editorial and otherwise. I am especially grateful to Don for the thorough manner in which he conducted external reviews of this text prior to its publication. I want to thank the following reviewers for their many insights and suggestions:

Michael Anderson, *ECPI College of Technology*

Dr. Donna Austin, *Louisiana State University–Shreveport*

Ron Berry, *Northeast Louisiana University*

Dr. Gary Buterbaugh, *Indiana University of Pennsylvania*

Carolyn Walsh Carter, *Milligan College*

Tim Eichers, *Northern Virginia Community College*

Bret Ellis, *Brigham Young University, Hawaii Campus*

Lew Garrett, *Alvin Community College*

Toby Gustafson, *University of California, Riverside*

Daris Howard, *Ricks College*

Robert Hubbard, *Albertus Magnus College*

Tim Kennedy, *Bellevue Community College*

Jennifer Laiger, *California State University, Monterey Bay*

Roger Lee, *Houston Community College*

Mike Michaelson, *Palomar College*

Anita Philipp, *Oklahoma City Community College*

Pratap P. Reddy, *Raritan Valley Community College*

Jerry Ross, *Lane Community College*

Lauran Sattler, *Ivy Tech State College*

Kala Chand Seal, *Loyola Marymount University*

Nanette Stillwell, *Pitt Community College*

Robert Youngblood, *Arizona State University*

Internet
Literacy

FOURTH EDITION

PART ONE
UNDERSTANDING THE INTERNET

CHAPTER 1

Definitions

CHAPTER 2

How the Internet Is
Changing the World

What do you want the Internet to be?

—Nortel Networks TV advertisement

Many people have a cloudy understanding of the Internet. Technical network diagrams often use the symbol of a cloud to represent large portions of the Internet, rather than depicting all the switches, routers, signal boosters, and wiring that wind their way across the Net. This cloud is not meant to imply, however, that the Internet is elusive or hard to understand.

This part of the book will enable you to see through the clouds by defining what the Internet is, describing what you can do with it, and demonstrating how it is changing the world.

1

DEFINITIONS

After completing this chapter, you will be able to:

- Define the Internet, describe how large it is, and find out how fast it is growing.

- List and define the 10 basic Internet services of e-mail, listserv, newsgroups, chat, instant messaging, videoconferencing, File Transfer Protocol (FTP), the World Wide Web, the Rich Site Summary (RSS), and blogging.

- Explain what is meant by client-server computing.

- Define the role played by the transmission control protocol (TCP) and the Internet Protocol (IP) in the TCP/IP protocol suite.

- Understand the Internet naming system of domains and subdomains.

- Provide a brief history of the Internet, explaining how it grew from its humble origins into the worldwide network that we enjoy today.

- Technical terms can scare people. Especially when computers are involved, technical terms can make things so hard to understand that people may shy away from learning how to do things that really are quite simple. This book purposefully avoids unnecessary jargon. The goal is to enable you to take advantage of the wonderful resources on the Internet without having to learn a lot of technical terms. There are certain terms, however, that an Internet literate person must know. This chapter defines those terms.

What Is the Internet?

U.S. Department of Defense

The **Internet** is a worldwide connection of more than 285 million computers that use the Internet Protocol (IP) to communicate. The Internet Protocol was invented for the Advanced Research Projects Agency (ARPA) of the U.S. Department of Defense. The goal was to create a decentralized network that would continue to function if a bomb destroyed one or more of the network's nodes; information would get rerouted automatically so it could still reach its address. As a result of this bomb-proof design, any user on the Internet can communicate with any other user, regardless of their locations.

Figure 1-1 illustrates the web that is formed by the interconnections of computers on the Internet in the United States. Nearly 200 countries and territories around the world are similarly connected to the Internet, forming a worldwide telecommunications network.

Who Is Using the Internet?

America Online

People from all walks of life are using the Internet. Business professionals, stockbrokers, government workers, politicians, doctors, teachers, researchers, students, monks, kids, elderly people, soldiers, parents, entertainers, police, social workers, pilots, waiters, disk

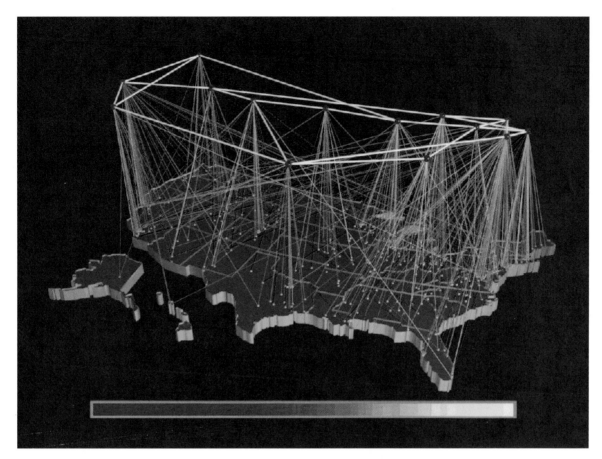

Figure 1-1 This image is a visualization study of traffic on the Internet. The traffic volume range is depicted from purple (zero bytes) to white (100 billion bytes). Move your eye along the white lines to get a sense of how very high-speed lines called the backbone carry Internet traffic to distribution points that route the packets toward their destinations.

Source: "NSFNET T1 Backbone and Regional Networks." Rendered by Donna Cox and Robert Patterson, National Center for Supercomputing Applications/University of Illinois.

jockeys, and movie stars—virtually everyone who wants to succeed in the information society is using the Internet.

According to the CIA's World Factbook, 604.1 million people were online worldwide in August 2003. To find out how many people are online today, follow the *Interlit* Web site links to the Internet usage surveys.

How Fast Is the Internet Growing?

Nielsen Media Research

Figure 1-2 shows how fast the Internet is growing. The number of pages on the Web has increased dramatically from about 300 million in 1998 to more than three billion in 2003. According to Nielsen Media Research, the number of people who are banking online nearly doubled, from 13 million in 2001 to 23.2 million in 2003. For more information, follow this book's Web site links to the Nielsen NetRatings and to Hobbes' Internet Timeline.

What Are the Internet Services?

What people do on the Internet is organized according to services defined by protocols that specify how information moves across the Net. The most popular services include electronic mail (e-mail), listserv, newsgroups, chat, videoconferencing, File Transfer Protocol (FTP), multimedia streaming, the World Wide Web, the Rich Site Summary (RSS), and blogging. Figure 1-3 shows that you have access to all these services when you are connected to the Internet.

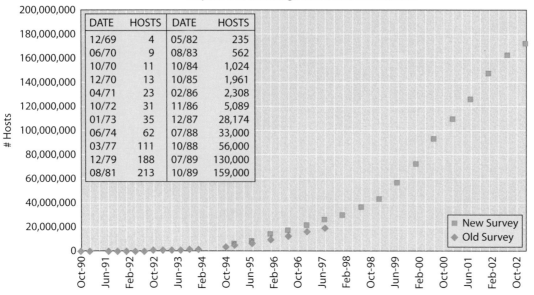

Hobbes' Internet Timeline Copyright ©2003 Robert H Zakon
http://www.zakon.org/robert/internet/timeline/

DATE	HOSTS	DATE	HOSTS
12/69	4	05/82	235
06/70	9	08/83	562
10/70	11	10/84	1,024
12/70	13	10/85	1,961
04/71	23	02/86	2,308
10/72	31	11/86	5,089
01/73	35	12/87	28,174
06/74	62	07/88	33,000
03/77	111	10/88	56,000
12/79	188	07/89	130,000
08/81	213	10/89	159,000

Figure 1-2 How fast the Internet is growing.

Source: Hobbes' Internet Timeline at http://www.zakon.org/robert/internet/timeline/#Growth. Used by permission of Robert H. Zakon.

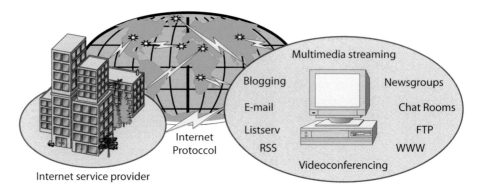

Figure 1-3 An Internet Protocol (IP) connection provides you with access to Internet services all over the world.

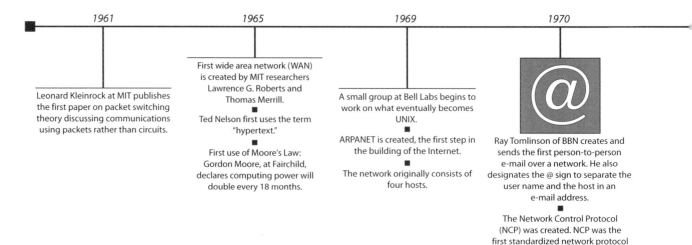

1961

Leonard Kleinrock at MIT publishes the first paper on packet switching theory discussing communications using packets rather than circuits.

1965

First wide area network (WAN) is created by MIT researchers Lawrence G. Roberts and Thomas Merrill.

■

Ted Nelson first uses the term "hypertext."

■

First use of Moore's Law: Gordon Moore, at Fairchild, declares computing power will double every 18 months.

1969

A small group at Bell Labs begins to work on what eventually becomes UNIX.

■

ARPANET is created, the first step in the building of the Internet.

■

The network originally consists of four hosts.

1970

@

Ray Tomlinson of BBN creates and sends the first person-to-person e-mail over a network. He also designates the @ sign to separate the user name and the host in an e-mail address.

■

The Network Control Protocol (NCP) was created. NCP was the first standardized network protocol used by ARPANET.

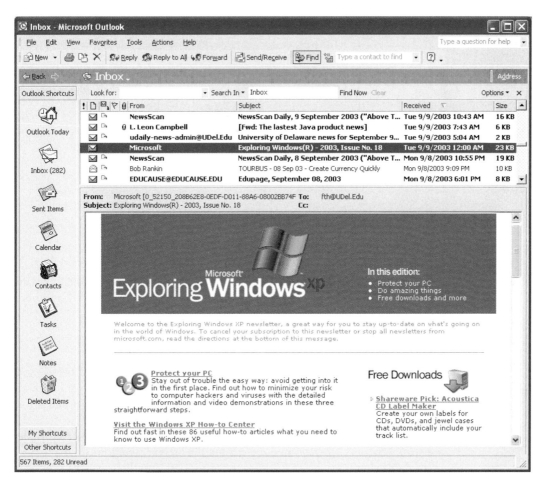

Figure 1-4 E-mail clients, such as the Microsoft Outlook program shown here, display the incoming queue of e-mail messages in your Inbox. When you click a message to select it, the client displays the message and provides you with options to reply, forward, file, or delete the message.

Electronic Mail

The most often used Internet service is electronic mail, which is also known as **e-mail.** Every registered user on the Internet has an e-mail address. E-mail is a great way to communicate, because it avoids the delays caused by playing telephone tag. As depicted in Figure 1-4,

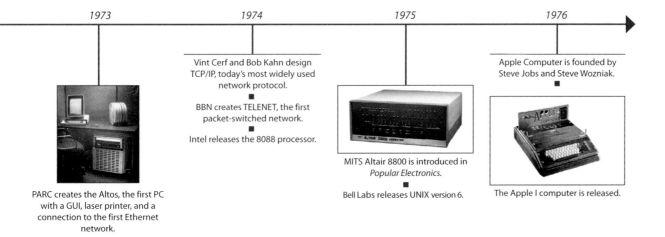

1973 — PARC creates the Altos, the first PC with a GUI, laser printer, and a connection to the first Ethernet network.

1974 — Vint Cerf and Bob Kahn design TCP/IP, today's most widely used network protocol.
BBN creates TELENET, the first packet-switched network.
Intel releases the 8088 processor.

1975 — MITS Altair 8800 is introduced in *Popular Electronics*.
Bell Labs releases UNIX version 6.

1976 — Apple Computer is founded by Steve Jobs and Steve Wozniak.
The Apple I computer is released.

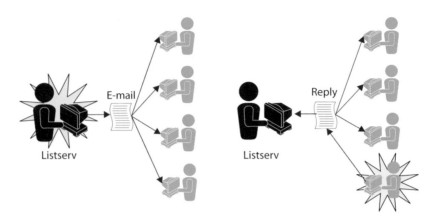

Figure 1-5 Listservs distribute messages to people whose names are on an electronic mailing list. When you send a message to a listserv, everyone on the list receives a copy via e-mail.

mail queues up in your Inbox, and you read and respond to it at your convenience. Many users read their electronic mail several times a day. You will learn how to use advanced electronic mail features in Chapter 6.

Listserv

Listserv stands for "list server" and is built on top of the e-mail protocol. Listservs work like electronic mailing lists, sending e-mail messages to people whose names are on the list. You join a listserv by e-mailing a message to it, saying you want to subscribe. Most listservs also let you subscribe by filling out a Web form at the listserv's Web site. After you subscribe, whenever someone sends e-mail to the listserv, you receive a copy in your e-mail. Likewise, when you send e-mail to the listserv, everyone on the listserv receives a copy of your message, as depicted in Figure 1-5. Thus, listserv is a simple way for groups of people to communicate with one another through e-mail.

There are thousands of listservs on the Internet. Listservs are used, for example, to deliver many of the Internet's ezines (electronic magazines) via e-mail. You will learn how to find out about listservs and join them in Chapter 7.

Newsgroups

A more highly organized way for groups of people to communicate is through **Usenet,** which is an electronic bulletin board service consisting of newsgroups, newsfeeds, and newsreaders. Once you subscribe to a newsgroup, you use a newsreader to access the group's newsfeed.

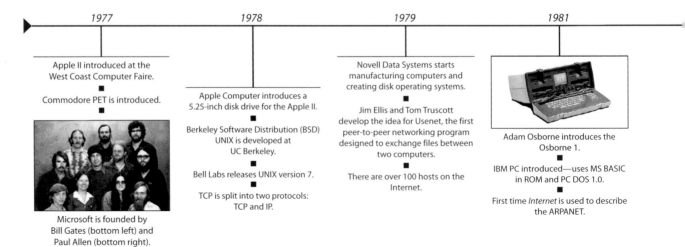

1977

Apple II introduced at the West Coast Computer Faire.

Commodore PET is introduced.

Microsoft is founded by Bill Gates (bottom left) and Paul Allen (bottom right).

1978

Apple Computer introduces a 5.25-inch disk drive for the Apple II.

Berkeley Software Distribution (BSD) UNIX is developed at UC Berkeley.

Bell Labs releases UNIX version 7.

TCP is split into two protocols: TCP and IP.

1979

Novell Data Systems starts manufacturing computers and creating disk operating systems.

Jim Ellis and Tom Truscott develop the idea for Usenet, the first peer-to-peer networking program designed to exchange files between two computers.

There are over 100 hosts on the Internet.

1981

Adam Osborne introduces the Osborne 1.

IBM PC introduced—uses MS BASIC in ROM and PC DOS 1.0.

First time *Internet* is used to describe the ARPANET.

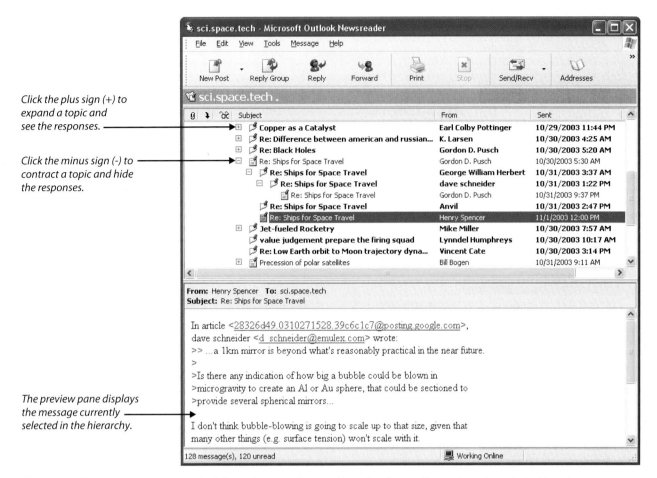

Click the plus sign (+) to expand a topic and see the responses.

Click the minus sign (-) to contract a topic and hide the responses.

The preview pane displays the message currently selected in the hierarchy.

Figure 1-6 Usenet newsgroups organize information according to a hierarchy of topics. You navigate through the hierarchy via onscreen controls that enable you to scroll up or down and expand or contract the menu of messages to reveal something that interests you.

Figure 1-6 shows how information in the newsfeed is organized according to topics. In addition to reading information on existing topics, you can add your own comments and create new topics, thereby participating in a virtual conference on the Internet.

Do not be confused by the use of the word *news* in the term *newsgroup*. Although some newsgroups are devoted to what is traditionally known as news, a newsgroup can contain discussions on any topic. In Chapter 8, you will learn how to find out what newsgroups exist and how to join them.

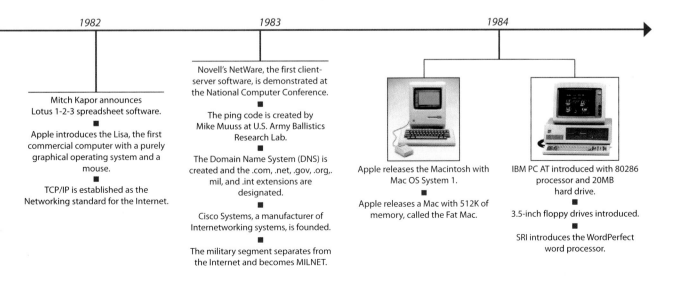

1982

Mitch Kapor announces Lotus 1-2-3 spreadsheet software.
■
Apple introduces the Lisa, the first commercial computer with a purely graphical operating system and a mouse.
■
TCP/IP is established as the Networking standard for the Internet.

1983

Novell's NetWare, the first client-server software, is demonstrated at the National Computer Conference.
■
The ping code is created by Mike Muuss at U.S. Army Ballistics Research Lab.
■
The Domain Name System (DNS) is created and the .com, .net, .gov, .org,. mil, and .int extensions are designated.
■
Cisco Systems, a manufacturer of Internetworking systems, is founded.
■
The military segment separates from the Internet and becomes MILNET.

1984

Apple releases the Macintosh with Mac OS System 1.
■
Apple releases a Mac with 512K of memory, called the Fat Mac.

IBM PC AT introduced with 80286 processor and 20MB hard drive.
■
3.5-inch floppy drives introduced.
■
SRI introduces the WordPerfect word processor.

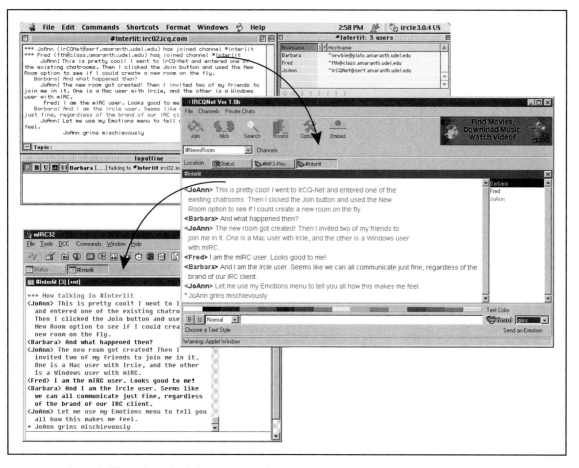

Figure 1-7 Several different brands of clients support the Internet's chat protocol. Here you see a conversation in progress between three users who are using a Windows client, a Macintosh client, and a browser-based Java client.

Chat

A very popular form of real-time communications is **chat,** which enables people to converse with one another over the Internet. As you type a message on your computer keyboard, the people you are chatting with see what you type almost immediately, and you can simultaneously see what they type in reply. Figure 1-7 shows a conversation in progress. Users with microphones and speakers can speak verbally to one another if their chat software supports audio.

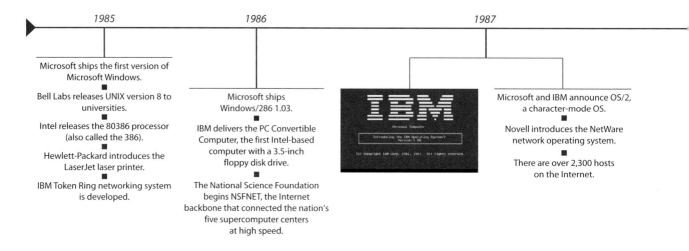

1985

Microsoft ships the first version of Microsoft Windows.

Bell Labs releases UNIX version 8 to universities.

Intel releases the 80386 processor (also called the 386).

Hewlett-Packard introduces the LaserJet laser printer.

IBM Token Ring networking system is developed.

1986

Microsoft ships Windows/286 1.03.

IBM delivers the PC Convertible Computer, the first Intel-based computer with a 3.5-inch floppy disk drive.

The National Science Foundation begins NSFNET, the Internet backbone that connected the nation's five supercomputer centers at high speed.

1987

Microsoft and IBM announce OS/2, a character-mode OS.

Novell introduces the NetWare network operating system.

There are over 2,300 hosts on the Internet.

By clicking this arrow, you can change your status from online to offline in case you want to hide from your buddies.

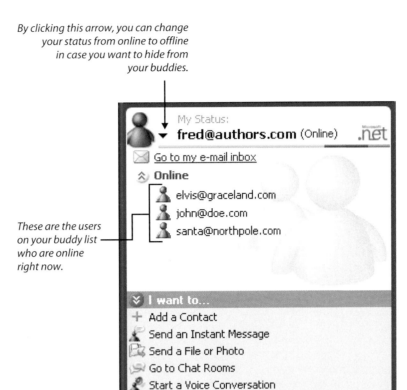

These are the users on your buddy list who are online right now.

Figure 1-8 Buddies can IM each other through instant messaging.

The conversations take place in virtual spaces called chat rooms or channels; each chat room or channel is a different conversation that is going on. There are thousands of chat rooms where you can join a conversation, or you can create your own chat room. In Chapter 9, you will learn how to find and enter existing chats or create your own free chat room.

Instant Messaging

Most people have a circle of friends or working associates with whom they like to keep in close contact. A service called **instant messaging (IM)** enables you to do that. Figure 1-8 depicts how you can put your friends on a buddy list that identifies who is allowed to contact you. When someone on your buddy list asks to talk with you, an instant message appears

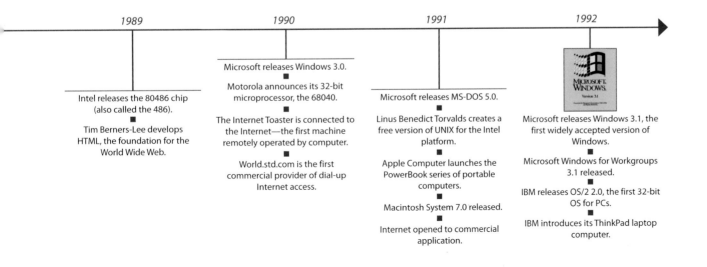

1989

Intel releases the 80486 chip (also called the 486).

Tim Berners-Lee develops HTML, the foundation for the World Wide Web.

1990

Microsoft releases Windows 3.0.

Motorola announces its 32-bit microprocessor, the 68040.

The Internet Toaster is connected to the Internet—the first machine remotely operated by computer.

World.std.com is the first commercial provider of dial-up Internet access.

1991

Microsoft releases MS-DOS 5.0.

Linus Benedict Torvalds creates a free version of UNIX for the Intel platform.

Apple Computer launches the PowerBook series of portable computers.

Macintosh System 7.0 released.

Internet opened to commercial application.

1992

Microsoft releases Windows 3.1, the first widely accepted version of Windows.

Microsoft Windows for Workgroups 3.1 released.

IBM releases OS/2 2.0, the first 32-bit OS for PCs.

IBM introduces its ThinkPad laptop computer.

on your screen, letting you know that someone wants to chat, something just happened that you wanted to know about, or an important message just arrived in your e-mail.

Instant messaging has become so popular that its acronym "IM" has become a verb, which is pronounced *eye-emm*. To IM someone means to send them an instant message over the Internet. Chapter 9 covers instant messaging in more detail.

Videoconferencing

Videoconferencing is the use of a video camera and a microphone to enable people conversing over the Internet to be able to see and hear each other. Because of the higher bandwidth or data rate required to transmit video over the Internet, videoconferencing has not yet become as popular as text-only chat. As data rates increase, however, more people will be able to participate in videoconferences. Chapter 3 explains your options for connecting to the Internet at different data rates, and Chapter 9 describes the leading videoconferencing programs.

FTP

FTP stands for **File Transfer Protocol.** It is the standard method for transferring files over the Internet from one computer to another. "FTP" can be used as a verb as well as a noun. For example, if you want someone to send you a file, you can ask them to FTP it to you. FTP comes in handy, especially when files are too large to attach to an e-mail message.

Figure 1-9 shows how the author used FTP to transfer this book's chapters to McGraw-Hill for production and publication. You will learn how to use FTP in Chapter 7.

Multimedia Streaming

Streaming is the digital transmission of multimedia content in real time over the Internet. Streaming enables a large multimedia file to begin playing as soon as your computer has received enough of the information to begin playing it, without waiting until it all downloads. Instead of swamping your hard drive with all the data in the file, your computer stores in a memory buffer only the amount of data needed for the media to continue playing. Once played, the data is erased from the buffer. Thus, broadcasters can use multimedia streaming to send out copyrighted material without fear that it will be reproduced.

Many radio stations, for example, use real-time streaming to broadcast shows live over the Internet. Television networks often archive important video streams after the broadcast,

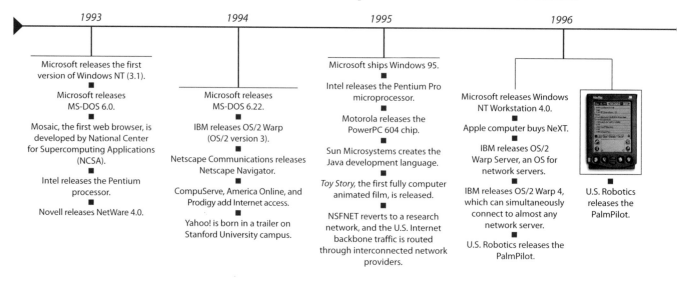

The right pane shows this book's folder on McGraw-Hill's FTP server.

The left pane shows the Word processor files on the author's computer.

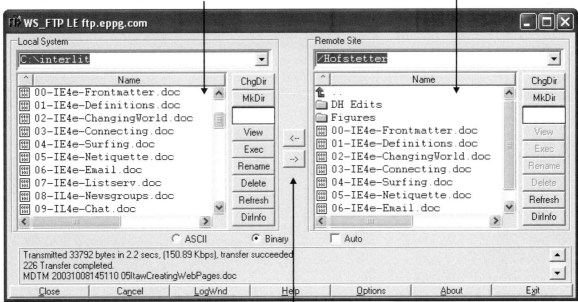

The author clicks this button to FTP a file from his computer to McGraw-Hill.

Figure 1-9   FTP transfers files over the Internet from one computer to another.

enabling you to access the broadcast stream later if you were unable to view the show live. The CNN Web site at www.cnn.com, for example, has links you can click to play video streams of the day's leading news broadcasts. Chapter 10 covers multimedia streaming and plugs you in to the key multimedia resources on the Internet.

World Wide Web

Invented by Tim Berners-Lee in 1989, the **World Wide Web** (WWW) is a networked hypertext system that allows documents to be shared over the Internet. Developed at the European Particle Physics Center (CERN) in Geneva, Switzerland, the Web's original purpose was to let researchers all over the world collaborate on the same documents without needing to travel anywhere physically.

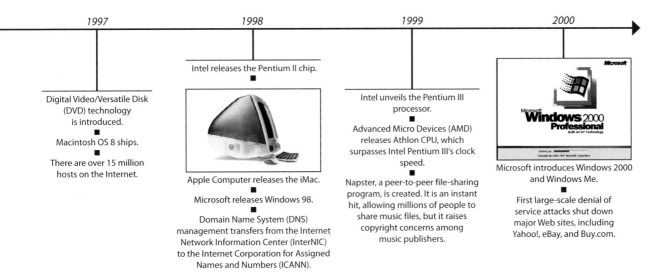

1997

Digital Video/Versatile Disk (DVD) technology is introduced.
■
Macintosh OS 8 ships.
■
There are over 15 million hosts on the Internet.

1998

Intel releases the Pentium II chip.
■

Apple Computer releases the iMac.
■
Microsoft releases Windows 98.
■
Domain Name System (DNS) management transfers from the Internet Network Information Center (InterNIC) to the Internet Corporation for Assigned Names and Numbers (ICANN).

1999

Intel unveils the Pentium III processor.
■
Advanced Micro Devices (AMD) releases Athlon CPU, which surpasses Intel Pentium III's clock speed.
■
Napster, a peer-to-peer file-sharing program, is created. It is an instant hit, allowing millions of people to share music files, but it raises copyright concerns among music publishers.

2000

Microsoft introduces Windows 2000 and Windows Me.
■
First large-scale denial of service attacks shut down major Web sites, including Yahoo!, eBay, and Buy.com.

The word **hypertext** was coined by Ted Nelson in 1965 and refers to text that has been linked. When you click a linked word, your computer launches the object of that link. The links give the text an added dimension, which is why it is called *hyper*.

When the Web was released in 1991, it was purely text-based. In 1993, the National Center for Supercomputer Applications (NCSA) released Mosaic, a graphical user interface that made the Web extremely easy to use. Thanks to Mosaic, Web pages could contain pictures, with links to audio and video as well. This led to the Web's becoming the most popular service on the Internet. As depicted in Figure 1-10, the Web enables you to follow links to documents and resources all over the world.

In 1994, Netscape Communications Corporation was started by some of Mosaic's developers, and over the next few years, a program called Netscape Navigator became the most popular Web browser. Microsoft also created a Web browser called Microsoft Internet Explorer, which now ships as part of Windows. The popularity of Netscape Navigator and Microsoft Internet Explorer diminished the need for Mosaic, and in 1997, the NCSA quietly discontinued work on it, opting instead to work on other advanced Internet technologies. In the meantime, Netscape and Microsoft grew their browsers into suites of programs that enable users to access almost all the Internet's services and resources without needing any other software.

In 2003, Netscape provided startup funding for the Mozilla Foundation to create open-source versions of the Netscape products. Open source means that the source code is available to the general public free of charge. Software developers can make improvements to the code and submit them to the Mozilla Foundation for inclusion in the open-source code base. Open-source products based on the Netscape code include a browser called Firefox and a Web-page editor called Nvu, which is one of the programs featured in the Web creation part of this book.

World Wide Web Consortium

You can learn more about the history of the Web by following the *Interlit* Web site links to the **W3C (World Wide Web Consortium),** which coordinates the research and development of new standards and features for the Web. By following the links to Tim Berners-Lee, you can read papers about the past, present, and future of the Web written by the person credited with inventing the Web.

Rich Site Summary (RSS)

The World Wide Web has become so popular that it has spun off some Internet services of its own. One of these Web-inspired services is **Rich Site Summary (RSS),** which is an XML format for syndicating the content of a Web site in a form that can be registered with

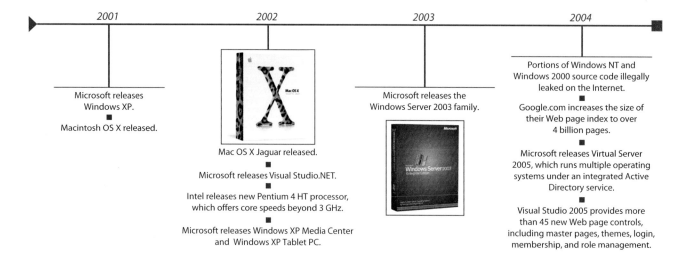

| 2001 | 2002 | 2003 | 2004 |

Microsoft releases Windows XP.
■
Macintosh OS X released.

Mac OS X Jaguar released.
■
Microsoft releases Visual Studio.NET.
■
Intel releases new Pentium 4 HT processor, which offers core speeds beyond 3 GHz.
■
Microsoft releases Windows XP Media Center and Windows XP Tablet PC.

Microsoft releases the Windows Server 2003 family.

Portions of Windows NT and Windows 2000 source code illegally leaked on the Internet.
■
Google.com increases the size of their Web page index to over 4 billion pages.
■
Microsoft releases Virtual Server 2005, which runs multiple operating systems under an integrated Active Directory service.
■
Visual Studio 2005 provides more than 45 new Web page controls, including master pages, themes, login, membership, and role management.

Figure 1-10 The World Wide Web is the most popular service on the Internet. The U.S. Department of State uses the Web to communicate all over the world via printed text, audio, and video.

an RSS publisher. Other sites can subscribe to the Web site in order to access the RSS feed and display its content onscreen. RSS has become a very popular format for distributing news headlines, project updates, and events listings. Figure 1-11 shows how the NASA site uses RSS to provide users quick access to news headlines. By clicking a headline, the user can follow links to more detailed information. Behind the scenes at the NASA site, the XML file shown in Figure 1-12 contains the newsfeed. Comparing these two figures will provide you with insight into how RSS works. RSS is just one example of how the eXtensible Markup Language (XML) can add functionality to the Web. You will learn more about this kind of markup in Chapter 17.

Blogging

As the Web becomes a mass market utility, new ways of using the Web are emerging to address the needs and preferences of the masses. One of the most popular ways of using the Web is blogging. The term **blog** is short for Web log, which is a Web-accessible log

The breaking news content displayed here …

Figure 1-11   NASA uses RSS to feed breaking news into its Web site. Compare the breaking news shown here to the RSS feed in Figure 1-12.

written by an individual who wants to chronicle activity related to a given topic that is often personal. "Blog" can be used as a noun to refer to what gets written or as a verb that means the act of writing these kinds of messages. Through blogging, people are essentially keeping their diaries online. The mass-market appeal of blogging teaches us that people like to make these kinds of diaries public.

In response to this mass-market appeal, a wide range of blogging tools have arisen. At sites such as www.blogger.com, you can create your own public blogs. You also can license blogging tools for private use, such as to keep track of a worker's progress toward meeting a project milestone or target date. Figure 1-13 shows how the campaign to reelect President Bush used a blog to chronicle their activities. For a list of blog directories, go to Google or Yahoo! and search for "blog directory." For tools, search for "blog tools."

What Is Client-Server Computing?

Client-server computing is an important concept on the Internet. Think about what the Internet is: a worldwide connection of millions of computers. Think about what these computers do: they send and receive information. That is what client-server computing is

… comes from the RSS newsfeed shown here.

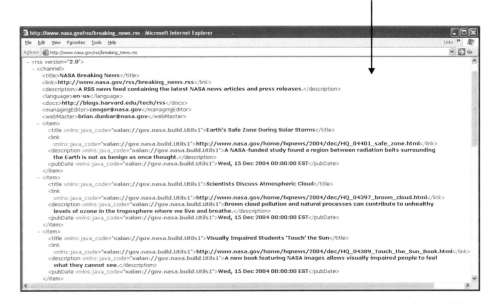

Figure 1-12   This is the RSS breaking news feed at the NASA Web site. Anyone who has an RSS reader can subscribe to this feed at **www.nasa.gov/rss.**

all about. When a computer sends information, the computer is a server. When a computer receives information, the computer is a client. The term *client-server computing* refers to the manner in which computers exchange information by sending it (as servers) and receiving it (as clients).

In client-server networks, end-user workstations are called *clients* because they primarily receive information. For example, when you surf the World Wide Web with a browser such as Microsoft Internet Explorer, your computer is a client, because you are receiving information from other computers on the World Wide Web. The computers that are devoted primarily to sending information are called *servers;* computers devoted to serving Web pages are called *Web servers.*

Sometimes a server needs to obtain additional information in order to answer a request from a client. At the moment when the server requests information from another computer, the server becomes a client. When the server obtains the information it needs, it routes the information back to you, fulfilling its role as your server.

You will encounter the terms *client* and *server* a lot. The key to understanding them is to remember that client means "receive" and server means "send." If you play tennis, this will be easy to remember, because when you serve a tennis ball, you send it—hopefully very fast—to your opponent!

What Is TCP/IP?

On the Internet, information gets transmitted from place to place in logical units called packets. In order to send these packets to the right place in the correct order, two protocols are required. The first protocol, which is called *TCP,* handles the routing. The second protocol, which is called *IP,* governs the addressing. Because both protocols are needed to make the Internet work, the Internet is said to use the **TCP/IP** protocol suite. Let us take a closer look at what TCP and IP do. TCP stands for the **Transmission Control Protocol,** which defines the rules and procedures for transmitting information across the Internet. The information gets transmitted in packets.

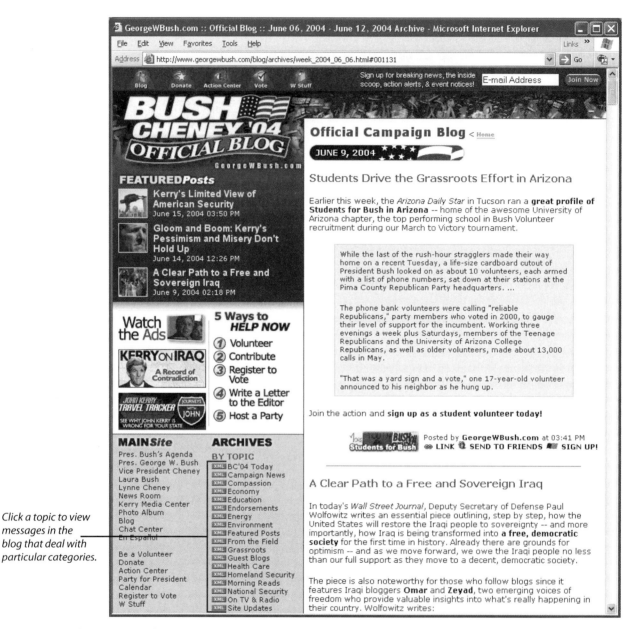

Figure 1-13   When you visit a blog, you scroll down to peruse the entries, which appear in reverse chronological order. Pictured here was the official blog of the campaign to reelect President George W. Bush. Democratic candidates Wesley Clark, Howard Dean, John Kerry, and Dennis Kucinich also used blogs in their campaigns.

If a message is too long to fit in one packet, the data gets divided into more than one packet. Each packet contains addressing that identifies which computer sent the packet and which computer will receive it. The packets also contain sequencing information that specifies the order in which they must be reassembled when the packets arrive at their destination.

IP stands for **Internet Protocol,** which defines the addressing system TCP uses to transmit packets over the Internet. Every computer on the Internet has a unique Internet Protocol (IP) address. Each packet of information that gets transmitted over the Internet contains the IP address of the computer that sent it and the IP address of the computer to which it is being sent. An IP address consists of four numbers separated by periods. The numbers are 8-bit bytes that range in value from 0 to 255. The smallest address is 0.0.0.0 and the largest is 255.255.255.255. The number of IP addresses this scheme allows is 256^4, which is 4,294,967,296. This provides room for adding more computers as the network grows.

The format of an IP address that has four 8-bit bytes separated by periods is known as **dotted quad notation.** When the Internet was invented, people thought dotted quad notation would provide enough unique addresses for every computer to have its own IP address. The proliferation of computers all over the world, however, will eventually exceed this number. A new version of IP addressing, called IPv6, will have eight numbers instead of four, and each number will be a 16-bit value ranging from 0 to 65,535. The number of IP addresses this scheme allows is $65,536^8$, which is a huge number that provides thousands of addresses per square meter of the earth's surface. Why are so many new addresses being created when the world will most likely never have that many computers? One of the reasons is to permit computers to contain multiple interfaces, with each interface having a unique IPv6 address. IPv6 is being used in a new version of the Internet called Internet2, which is one of the emerging technologies you will study later in this book in Chapter 26.

What Are Domains and Subdomains?

IP addresses can be hard to remember. For example, the Web server at the Library of Congress has the IP address 140.147.249.7. The Smithsonian is at 160.111.252.106. The U.S. Patent and Trademark Office is at 151.207.245.67. If you had to remember numbers like these, the Internet would not be very user-friendly.

To make IP addresses easier for human beings to remember, a **domain name system (DNS)** was invented to permit the use of alphabetic characters instead of numbers. For example, instead of having to remember that the Library of Congress is at 140.147.249.7, you can use its domain name, www.loc.gov. The Smithsonian is www.si.edu, and the U.S. Patent and Trademark Office is www.uspto.gov. Thus, DNS is a method of resolving names that humans understand into IP addresses that the network understands.

A complete DNS address is called a **fully qualified domain name (FQDN).** Fully qualified domain names have the following format:

hostname.registered-domain-name.top-level-domain

In the United States, the top-level domain (TLD) normally consists of one of the following:

.aero	aerospace
.biz	business
.com	commercial
.coop	cooperatives
.edu	educational
.gov	government
.info	public use information
.int	international treaty organizations
.mil	military
.museum	museums
.name	individual's names
.net	network support centers
.org	other organizations
.pro	professionals

In the rest of the world, top-level domains are usually country codes, such as *fr* for France. The domain refers to the network to which a computer is connected, and the host name refers to the computer itself. For example, in the domain name www.louvre.fr, which is the World Wide Web server at the famous Louvre museum in Paris, the top-level domain *fr* indicates that the server is located in France, the domain *louvre* tells you that the server is on the Louvre's network, and the host name *www* identifies this computer as the Louvre's World Wide Web server.

ICANN

The Internet Corporation for Assigned Names and Numbers (ICANN) is in charge of the coordination of domain names, IP address numbers, and protocol parameter and port numbers. Registering a domain name costs so little that many users are beginning to register their own domain names on the Internet. If your family name has not already been registered as a domain name, for example, you should consider grabbing it before someone else registers it. To find out whether you can register your family name and to find out how little it will cost to do so, follow these steps:

- Browse to www.verisign.org. This brings you to the ICANN-accredited registrar for .com and .net domains. If you want to choose a different registrar, go to www.icann.org and follow the link to the registrar of your choice.

- At the Verisign site, you'll find a domain registration blank into which you can type any name to find out whether it has been taken. Enter the domain you want to register, such as your last name, into this blank. It will not cost you anything to find out if the name is taken.

- Check the boxes corresponding to your choice of top-level domains.

- When you click the submit button, Verisign responds by telling you whether the name is taken. If the name is available, you will be offered an opportunity to register it.

- If you want to reserve a domain name for future use, you can register the name without yet having an IP address to connect it to.

ICANN has established a process for creating new top-level domain names. Several new names are being considered. You can find out the status by following this book's Web site link to ICANN.

Brief History of the Internet

The Internet originated when the **Advanced Research Projects Agency (ARPA)** of the United States Department of Defense began a network called **ARPANET** in 1969. Its goal was to support military research about how to build a network that could continue to function in the midst of partial outages that could be caused by bomb attacks. Instead of giving the network the responsibility for routing the information, the computers on the network shared equally in the responsibility for ensuring that the communication was accomplished. The messages were divided into packets that wound their way through the network on an individual basis. Each packet contained some information and the address of the destination to which it was to be delivered. If one of the computers along the way stopped functioning, such as in a bomb attack, the packets would automatically find an alternate route to their destinations. Thus, every computer on the network was treated as a peer. That is why, to this day, no computer on the Internet is more important than any other, and no one computer is in charge.

During the 1970s, universities began using the Internet Protocol to connect their local networks to the ARPANET. Access to the Pentagon's computers on the ARPANET was tightly controlled, but university computers were permitted to communicate freely with one another. Because the IP software was public-domain and the basic technology made joining the network relatively simple, the Internet became more diverse. Joining the Internet did not cost much, because each local network simply paid for its connection to the nearest node. As the network grew, it became more valuable as it embraced larger user populations, social groups, and resources. Diversity posed security risks, however, and in 1983 the military segment broke off and became **MILNET.**

In 1986, the National Science Foundation (NSF) began the **NSFNET,** a backbone that connected the nation's five supercomputer centers at high speed. NSF upgraded the network repeatedly, setting a blistering pace for technical advancement. In 1991, NSF lifted the restriction that prohibited commercial entities from using the backbone. By 1994, the NSFNET was carrying 10 trillion bytes of Internet traffic per month. In 1995, NSFNET reverted to a research network, and the U.S. Internet backbone traffic is now routed through interconnected network providers.

During the late 1990s, use of the Internet exploded as costs declined, access increased, and new companies such as amazon.com, ebay.com, and yahoo.com pioneered the commercial potential of the Internet. When this book went to press, online ad spending in the United States had grown to $9.5 billion annually. By the time you read this, online business-to-business (B2B) activity is projected to top $6.3 trillion annually.

To support this kind of growth, attempts to expand and speed up the Internet continue. A consortium of research universities is working in partnership with industry and government to create an even faster network named **Internet2.** The White House has pledged financial support to help build it. To learn more, follow this book's Web site link to Internet2. For a complete chronology of the Internet, follow the link to Hobbes's Internet Timeline.

exercises

Note: Many of this book's exercises direct you to click links at the *Interlit* Web site. The address of the *Interlit* Web site is www.udel.edu/interlit.

1. Find out the domain name of the computer network at your school or place of work. If you have an e-mail address on that network, the domain name will be the part of your e-mail address after the @ sign. For example, if your e-mail address is SantaClaus@toymakers.northpole.com, the domain name is toymakers.northpole.com.

2. How well-connected are the people in your life? How many of your friends and relatives have access to the Internet? What about your school or workplace: Do you have convenient access to the Internet there? How about your home—do you have Internet access at home? Do you believe that having access to the Internet should be a high priority for anyone planning to succeed in the twenty-first century?

3. How many e-mail addresses do you have? It is possible for a person to have more than one e-mail address. You might have one e-mail address that you use for work or school, for example, and another e-mail address that you use when communicating with friends and family. Anyone can get an e-mail address from one of the free Web-based e-mail services such as Microsoft's hotmail at www.hotmail.msn.com. List your e-mail addresses and tell briefly what you use each one for. Note: If you do not have an e-mail address, follow the *Interlit* Web site links to free e-mail services, where you can get a free e-mail account.

4. How large is the Internet today? When this book went to press, just over 285 million computers were using the Internet Protocol (IP) to communicate. To find out how much the Internet has grown since then, follow the *Interlit* Web site links to one of the Internet surveys. Tell how large the Internet is today, and state which survey you used to obtain this data. Also tell which kind of data you think best measures how large the Internet is.

5. Match the Internet services on the left with the description of what they enable you to do.

_____ e-mail   a. Participate in an online conference consisting of hierarchically organized topics and subtopics.

_____ listserv   b. Transfer a file from one computer to another.

_____ instant messaging   c. Converse with one or more people in real time over the Internet.

_____ Usenet newsgroups   d. Web-accessible chronicle of activity related to a given topic that is often personal.

_____ chat

          e. A global hypertext system.

_____ stream

          f. An XML format for syndicating the content of a Web site in a form that can be registered with a publisher. Other sites can subscribe to the Web site in order to access the feed and display its content onscreen.

_____ FTP

          g. Send an e-mail message to a single address that routes the message to a list full of people.

_____ World Wide Web

          h. Send a message to an individual.

_____ Rich Site Summary

          i. Contact your buddies whenever they are online to chat or trade files.

_____ blog

          j. Begin watching a video without first having to download it completely to your computer.

SITUATED CASE PROJECTS

Case 1: Planning Internet Services

At the end of each chapter in this book, a situated case project provides the student an opportunity to put the chapter's contents to practical use in a workplace situation. Each case has the same number as the chapter in which it appears.

Imagine that you are employed in a school or small company that is planning its information technology infrastructure. Your employer has asked you to consider the basic Internet services and plan how they can function in the workplace to improve productivity and communication of the employees on a daily basis. Submit your plan in the form of a matrix. To create the matrix, follow these steps:

1 Use your word processor to make an outline of the basic functions of your school or business.

2 Consider how each function in the outline could make use of one or more of the basic Internet services you studied in this chapter.

3 Using the table feature of your word processor, create a matrix that lists the 10 basic Internet services across the top and the functions in your outline along the side.

4 In each cell of the matrix, put a checkmark if the Internet service in that column can help achieve the task in that cell's row.

This matrix constitutes a functional analysis that will inform how and where your school or company will apply the different Internet services in the workplace. Save the matrix on your hard drive. If your instructor has asked you to hand in the matrix, make sure you put your name at the top of the matrix, then save it on disk or follow any other instructions you have been given for submitting this assignment.

2

HOW THE INTERNET IS CHANGING THE WORLD

After completing this chapter, you will be able to:

- ■ **Describe how the Internet is changing the world by means of a process called convergence.**

- ■ **Give reasons for the recent mega-mergers in the communications field.**

- ■ **Tell what percentage of the population is telecommuting.**

- ■ **Gauge the extent to which commercial advertising is paying for services available "for free" on the Internet.**

- ■ **Know where the hottest shopping sites are on the Net.**

- ■ **Explain how online shopping and banking are creating a cashless society.**

- ■ **Understand how government officials and politicians are using the Internet.**

- ■ **Define information warfare and learn how the Department of Defense is preparing to defend against it.**

- ■ **Realize how the Internet is revolutionizing the publishing industry.**

- ■ **Quote the latest Nielsen statistics on how the Internet is competing with television for people's free time.**

- ■ **Share the vision of how the Web is capable of hosting an interconnected world of research and scholarship.**

- ■ **Understand how the Net provides educators with a powerful medium for more actively involving students in the teaching and learning process.**

● If you had to summarize in one word how the Internet is changing the world, that word would be **convergence.** Figure 2-1 illustrates how all of our traditional ways of communicating are converging into a networked supermedium on the Internet.

No matter how you want to encode your message—whether through text, image, video, audio, print, or speech—you can communicate it digitally over the Internet. Convergence is the process of unification that digitalization causes by enabling all the world's traditional ways of communicating to work over a common communications medium on the Internet. Digitalization is changing the kind of world we live in. It is becoming an instantaneously connected world that is highly productive and knows no bounds.

Figure 2-1   The forces of digitalization are converging traditional forms of communication into a networked supermedium on the Internet.

Because the Net cannot see racial differences, age, sex, or physical disabilities, it does not show favoritism. It does perhaps discriminate against the unconnected, because in an information society, to be cut off from the network is to be disenfranchised. **Digital divide** is a term used to refer to the barriers faced by the unconnected. Chapter 25 will explore the digital divide and other societal issues related to the Internet.

Corporate Mergers and Alliances

Bane, Bradley, and Collis (1995:2) compare the forces of digitalization to the gravity of a wormhole in *Star Trek,* pulling recognizable industries through it and merging them into newly converged companies. Indeed, these forces have caused an unprecedented number of mergers and alliances as corporations jockey for position in the converged world. Viacom's $48.9 billion buyout of CBS, for example, merged a movie studio, cable networks, the Blockbuster video chain, and the UPN and CBS television networks.

Why are media companies forming alliances with computer vendors? Because they want to grow their markets by offering digital information and entertainment services that can be displayed either on a TV set or on a computer screen. NBC partnered with Microsoft, for example, to create the MSNBC network at www.msnbc.com, which uses the brand power of a TV network to transition people to become online users. Motorola bought cable set-top box maker General Instrument for $11.4 billion, positioning Motorola to become a leading manufacturer of equipment for both cable TV and wireless Internet services. To set the stage for launching a new travel-oriented cable TV company, USA Networks purchased the travel Web site Expedia.com.

Telecommuting

For a large percentage of the population, the Internet is becoming the workplace. Because tens of millions of workers have Internet access at home, the home is a potential place to work online. As depicted in Figure 2-2, telecommuting is the act of working from home by using computers, dial-up modems or broadband network connections, and fax machines

Figure 2-2   Telecommuting is the act of working from home by using computers, dial-up modems or broadband network connections, and fax machines.

to perform work that formerly required a person to travel physically to work. According to TeleWork America (2000) survey results, there were 16.5 million teleworkers in the United States in the year 2000. Of workers not telecommuting, 39 percent expressed an interest in working from home, and 13 percent said the ability to telework would be an important decision in accepting another job. An In-Stat/MDR survey estimates that by the year 2008, there will be 51 million teleworkers in the United States, with 14 million working full-time at home (*The Age,* 21 Jul 2004). Look to see these estimates reflected in the next U.S. census, which tracks the number of Americans who are telecommuting.

By reducing the need for people to drive to work, telecommuting results in fewer automobiles on highways. In addition to relieving traffic congestion, this improves air quality by reducing the number of cars emitting pollutants. To hasten the adoption of telecommuting, the Environmental Protection Agency and the Department of Transportation have established a voluntary National Standard of Excellence for employer-provided commuter benefits that not only reduce pollution but also lower expenses and taxes for employers and employees alike. For more information, follow the *Interlit* Web site link to EPA telecommuting programs.

Business and Advertising

The Internet has become a mass-market utility, and businesses are using it to advertise and market their products. To attract users who will see their ads, commercial Web sites are offering an increasingly wide range of free Internet services. For example, to expand the popularity of its Web site, Yahoo! wanted to offer free Web space, so it bought the popular GeoCities community and Web-hosting site for $5 billion. As a result, you can go to www.yahoo.com and follow the link to GeoCities to get a free Web site. Other free services at Yahoo! include keeping your address book, photo album, and personal calendar, which can send you e-mail reminders as important dates approach.

If you follow the links to My Yahoo, you can set up a personal Yahoo home page, including weather reports for your favorite cities, stock quotes for your stock portfolio, news reports from your favorite newsfeed, show times at local movie houses, and scores from your favorite sports teams. As if all this were not enough, you can also use Yahoo to get driving instructions, search the yellow pages, go shopping, read and post classified ads, and get a personal Web-based e-mail account. By the time you read this, more free services will be at Yahoo, all intended to make you spend more time there. Every time you use one of these services, you will see one or more ads. Thus, the frequency with which you visit the site increases the value of the commercial advertising you see there.

More pervasive forms of Internet advertising seek to capture your attention while you're browsing. So-called pop-under ads persist onscreen in their own windows after you close the Web site that created them. Saunders (2001) reports that pop-under ads can backfire, however, because consumers are quick to click to eliminate the unwanted window. Pop-up ads, on the other hand, are more than twice as likely to engage users in shopping, because these ads appear on top of the window the user is trying to look at. The user must move or close the pop-up ad in order to see what it is hiding. During the process of dismissing the pop-up, the user is likely to notice what is in it. Pop-under ads are not visible until the user closes the main window. Once the main window is gone, users are quick to delete a pop-under ad without paying much attention to it.

Online Shopping

The goal of all this advertising is not just to get you to see the ads; vendors also want you to purchase products over the Net, which is changing how the world shops. Instead of wearing yourself out trekking from store to store, trying to find the size and style you like, and then waiting in line to pay for it, teleshopping services let you shop from home. In 2003, 49 percent of new car buyers reported that their buying decisions were influenced by the Internet, which affected significantly the make and model purchased. This was up 9 percent from the year before, when 40 percent of new car buyers felt this way (J.D. Power and Associates, 2003). During the 2004 holiday shopping season, online sales jumped to $8.8 billion, a 24 percent increase over the previous year (CNET news.com, Dec 30, 2004).

According to market research firm TNS Interactive (2001), 57 percent of adults in the United States shopped online in 2001, representing a 50 percent growth from the year before. The most popular items are books, clothes, and music. The most frequent reason given for not wanting to shop online is the fear of providing credit-card information over the Web. As the financial industry works to improve security, the number of online shoppers will continue to increase. Follow the *Interlit* Web site links for evaluations and rankings of online shopping sites. To find out if there are any consumer complaints against your potential shopping sites, follow the link to the Better Business Bureau Online.

Online Banking and Investing

The Internet is changing the face of business. Online shopping and banking are creating a cashless society by eliminating the need for printed money. When this book went to press, more than 27 million Americans were paying their bills online. If you still write checks by hand, follow the *Interlit* Web site links to learn how you can pay bills online through AOL, Yahoo, American Express, or Citibank.

During the past few years, online brokers have captured a third of the retail investor market. By following the *Interlit* Web site links, you can visit some of the more popular online brokerages, including Charles Schwab, E*trade, Fidelity, Ameritrade, Morgan Stanley Online, and Quick & Reilly. In addition to investing online, you can use the Web to help manage your portfolio. At Yahoo Finance, for example, you can track the value of each stock or mutual fund in your portfolio. If a stock goes down in value, you can read news reports explaining why. Research informs you of recommended stocks, and profiles give insight into the nature of the business and financial summaries of the company.

At InfoBeat Finance, you can subscribe to news alerts for the companies in which you are invested. If late-breaking events affect the value of one of your investments, you receive an e-mail message informing you of the news, hours before it appears in the newspapers. To learn more about investing online, follow the *Interlit* Web site links to Yahoo Finance, InfoBeat Finance, and the Gomez Scorecard site, where you will find ratings of online banks and brokerages and other consumer services.

Figure 2-3 You can download tax forms at the Internal Revenue Service Web site.

Government and Politics

U.S. Government Consumer Information Center

Internal Revenue Service

Government officials have turned increasingly to the Internet for solutions to problems inherent in governance. The Net makes services more widely available and enables municipalities to respond more quickly to emergencies and disasters. You can access a wealth of information by following the *Interlit* Web site links to the U.S. Government Consumer Information Center in Pueblo, Colorado. At the Internal Revenue Service Web site pictured in Figure 2-3, you can learn about the tax code, download tax forms, and file your income tax return over the Internet.

Videoconferencing and the Internet provide ways for politicians to reach, canvass, and broaden their constituencies. The Internet has become so important in getting elected to public office that almost every political candidate has a Web site. For example, Figures 2-4 and 2-5 show the Democratic and Republican Web sites, respectively. For an index of political candidate Web sites, follow the *Interlit* Web site links to Political Candidates.

Information Warfare and Homeland Security

DARPA

The United States relies heavily on the Internet. Perhaps as devastating as a nuclear attack would be an electronic invasion of the computer networks without which this country would grind to a halt. Such a form of electronic attack is known as **information warfare.**

Figure 2-4   The Democratic National Committee Web site. http://www.democrats.org.

Figure 2-5   The Republican National Committee Web site. http://www.rnc.org.

To protect against a global large-scale attack on the Internet, the Pentagon has prepared a failsafe whereby the Department of Defense could disconnect its entire global network from the Internet if security threats arise that warrant so doing.

As president of the United States, George Bush Senior criticized the CIA for being so slow to issue reports that the White House learned more about world developments by watching commercial TV. The government now uses the Internet to provide officials with newsfeeds from online news services such as cnn.com and msnbc.com.

Especially challenging is the use of the Internet by terrorists who hide secret messages in graphics, video, or audio files. The process is called *steganography,* from the Greek word for hidden writing. A terrorist arrested for planning to blow up the U.S. Embassy in Paris, for example, communicated with the Al Qaeda terrorist organization through pictures posted on the Internet.

To intercept messages from terrorists and criminals, the FBI is using a system called **Carnivore** that can scan the Internet's e-mail traffic, looking for key words and phrases related to terrorist plots and criminal investigations. Messages containing suspicious content get routed to an FBI agent to investigate. The **USA PATRIOT Act,** signed into law in October 2001 in the aftermath of the 9/11 attacks on America, gives the federal government wide latitude in using Internet surveillance systems, including Carnivore and its successors. For more information about the use of information technologies in defense applications, follow the *Interlit* Web site links to Carnivore, the USA PATRIOT Act, and the Defense Advanced Research Projects Agency (DARPA).

Electronic Publishing

Newslink

During the past decade, virtually every newspaper has created a Web site. By following the *Interlit* Web site link, you can peruse the Newslink index of more than 4,000 online newspapers, magazines, broadcasters, and news services. The Internet enables people to go online and quickly see headlines and search through articles printed in the newspapers. Most of the news services keep online archives of past stories, making the Web a valuable resource for searching past as well as current events. News programs broadcast by cable news services, such as CNN and MSNBC, often refer you to their Web sites for more in-depth coverage or to conduct public opinion polls. People who are online frequently can subscribe to a news service that e-mails you when important news breaks.

Electronic book (eBook) technology enables publishers to sell books in an electronic format. Consumers download the eBook into a portable reading device, such as a Palm Pilot or a PocketPC. Not only does the eBook become as portable as a printed book; it also overcomes one of the greatest disadvantages of books printed on paper. How many times have you been frustrated by trying to find a quote or a passage you know you read in a certain book, but try as you might, you just cannot find it? The eBook solves this problem by rendering books in a full-text searchable format.

Besides purchasing eBooks from commercial publishers, you can also create eBooks of your own. If you have Microsoft Word, for example, you can create an eBook with the Microsoft Reader Add-In. The free service eBook Express enables you to create eBooks online from almost any text document. These books are formatted according to the Open eBook standard, which provides an industrywide format for eBooks. The Open eBook standard is based on XML, which stands for eXtensible Markup Language. Electronic books contain hidden XML codes that enable eBook viewers to display the books and provide users with a rich set of reading features. The XML section of Chapter 17 takes you behind the scenes and shows you how the markup works. For more information about electronic books, follow the *Interlit* Web site links to Microsoft Reader, eBook Express, and Open eBook.

Television and Entertainment

The Internet is competing with television for people's free time. According to a Nielsen survey, the turn of the century marked the point at which more than half of U.S. households had obtained Internet access. Nearly 144 million people in the United States logged on to the Internet during July of 2000, for example. A survey of 3,000 households indicated that these users were spending an average of 10 hours a month online, up 26 percent from the year before (*Financial Times,* 18 Aug 2000). According to the Pew Internet & American Life Project (2005), 37 percent more Americans were logging on habitually in 2004 than in 2000.

TV Guide

As you might expect, the Internet can also help you find what is worth viewing on television. At www.tvguide.com, for example, you will find the leading independent TV entertainment guide on the Internet. You can create and search free TV listings by day, time, program category, or specific channel up to seven days in advance, in either a traditional grid or a scroll-down list format. So-called top picks, movie picks, and sports picks recommend what is worth viewing on TV.

MSN TV

Microsoft's MSN TV (formerly called WebTV) is making substantial progress toward making television more interactive. Interactive TV merges the Internet and television so you can participate in your favorite shows. On *Wheel of Fortune* and *Jeopardy,* for example, you can play along and match wits with other contestants. While watching *Judge Judy,* you can vote in live polls taken during the show. Tens of thousands of people are participating. During a recent NFL football game, the referees made a disputed call. The announcers invited the TV audience to log on to the program's Web site and cast a vote either agreeing or disagreeing with the call. Within five minutes, more than 75,000 viewers had voted. MSN TV receivers are sold at Wal-Mart, Best Buy, and Circuit City. For the latest information, follow the *Interlit* Web site links to MSN TV.

Teaching and Learning

The benefits of computer-based learning are well-documented by Professor James Kulik (1985, 1986, 1991, and 1994) and his associates at the University of Michigan. During the past 25 years, Kulik has analyzed hundreds of controlled experiments on the effectiveness of computer-based learning. Overall, the findings indicate that average learning time has been reduced significantly (sometimes by as much as 80 percent), and achievement levels are more than a standard deviation higher (a full letter grade in school) than when computers are not used.

The Internet is enabling educators to make use of computer-based learning strategies online. By linking universities, colleges, schools, and homes into a worldwide network, the Internet is helping to break down the distinctions between grade levels. The Internet is enabling students of all ages to collaborate on worldwide projects, share discoveries, and develop strategies for acquiring knowledge in a social context.

It is difficult for a teacher to provide this kind of environment for each student in a traditional classroom. Since there is only one teacher for many students, it is physically impossible for a teacher to support each student's individual needs. The World Wide Web helps by providing students with an interconnected world of knowledge to explore. Screen capture and downloading enable students to collect what they discover and construct a framework for organizing and understanding. Since the learner is portrayed as an active processor who explores, discovers, reflects, and constructs knowledge, the trend to teach from this perspective is known as the constructivist movement in education.

Breeding Fruit Flies

Suppose you are a biology student learning the laws of genetic inheritance. As illustrated in Figure 2-6, the Virtual FlyLab lets you breed fruit flies, formulate hypotheses, and run statistical procedures, creating a framework for discovering and validating genetic laws. FlyLab is part of a suite of Web-based applications called Biology Labs On-Line. Other programs in the suite include DemographyLab, in which students investigate how differences in population size,

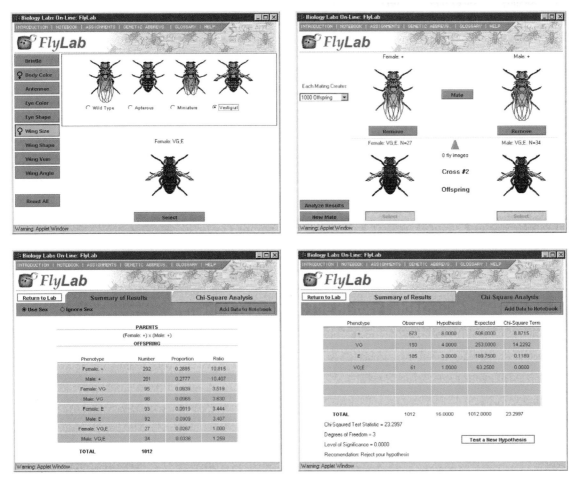

Figure 2-6   The Virtual FlyLab lets you breed fruitflies and explore the laws of genetic inheritance.

age-structure, and age-specific fertility and mortality rates affect human population growth; LeafLab, which has students measure photosynthetic rates of leaves by carbon dioxide assimilation while investigating how photosynthetic rates change as a function of light intensity, light quality, temperature, and ambient carbon dioxide; EvolutionLab, in which students investigate the process of adaptation by natural selection by manipulating various parameters of a bird species, such as initial mean beak size, variability, heritability, and population size, and various parameters of the environment such as precipitation and island size; as well as CardioLab, EnzymeLab, HemoglobinLab, MitochondriaLab, PedigreeLab, and TranslationLab. To learn how to subscribe to the Biology Labs On-Line, and to get a free trial, follow the *Interlit* Web site link to Biology Labs On-Line.

Downloading Economic Indicators and Forecasts

Imagine an economics student who is studying macroeconomics. Instead of relying on static information printed in a textbook, the student can browse to a site such as Economy. com and download the latest economic indicators and forecasts. Figure 2-7 shows how the

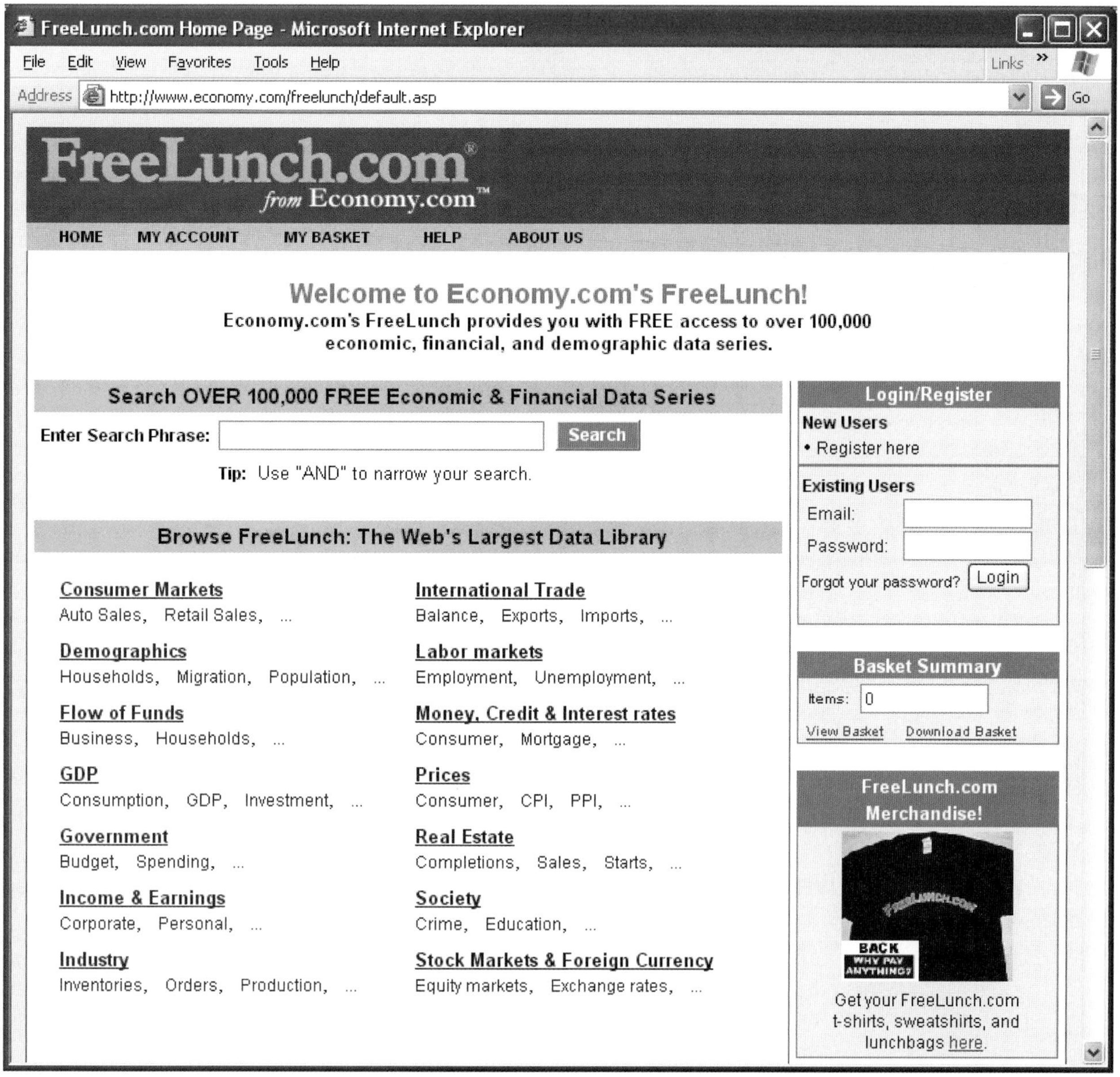

Figure 2-7   Economics databases available for free download in the FreeLunch section of the Economy.com Web site.

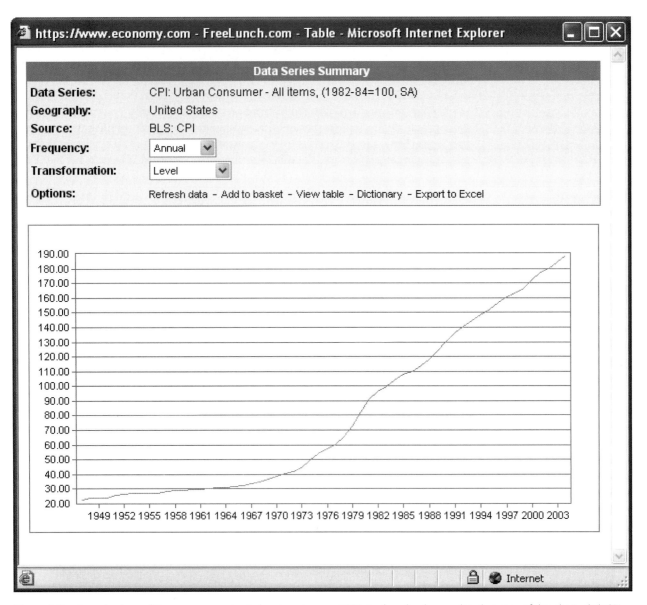

Figure 2-8   Annual values of the consumer price index since January 1947. To download an updated version of this chart, click CPI under Prices at **www.economy.com/freelunch**.

student can ask to see reports for production, consumption, interest rates, exchange rates, GDP, income, labor, prices, exports, imports, and real estate. In Figure 2-8, for example, a student who is analyzing inflation and learning about the consumer price index has asked to see an annual summary of consumer prices. The Export to Excel option enables the student to download the data into a spreadsheet for further manipulation.

Visualizing Chemical Models

One of the most difficult problems in teaching chemistry is to help students visualize the structure of chemical models. In a textbook, students are limited to a static photo showing only one position. On the Web, using active technologies such as Sun's Java, students can rotate chemical models by clicking and dragging with a mouse. For example, Figure 2-9 shows different stages in the rotation of a model of a benzene molecule on a Java Web page. To try this and other chemical models on the Web, follow the *Interlit* Web site link to the Java Molecule Viewer.

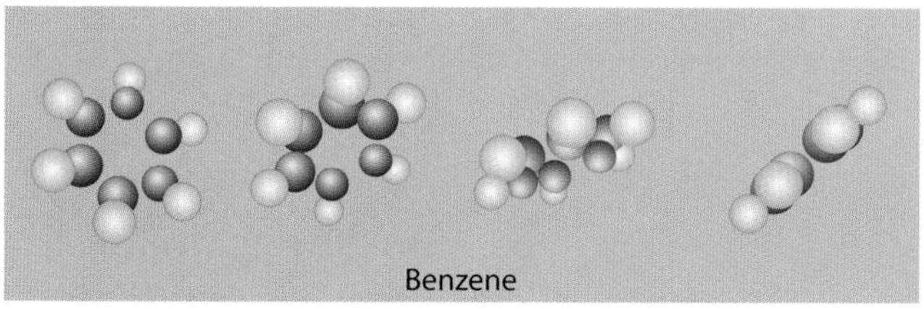

Benzene

Figure 2-9 Java rotations of a model of a benzene molecule. Rotating the chemical model leads the user to discover that the centers of the six carbon atoms and six hydrogen atoms in benzene are coplanar.

Studying Science via the Internet

Science teachers are using the Internet to provide students with collaborative learning experiences, access to scientific databases, and virtual visits to science laboratories. Reporting on the New Jersey Networking Infrastructure in Education project, Friedman, Baron, and Addison (1996) cite several compelling examples of science study via the Internet. Students gather samples from local pond water, measure chemical characteristics, examine organisms, and share observations with peers over the Internet. An ocean weather database that tracks ships at sea enables students to calculate the speed and direction of oceangoing vessels and predict arrival times.

The New Jersey Networking Infrastructure in Education project has won a major grant to update and continue its many science education projects. Figure 2-10 shows how the online catalog links to the National Science Standards and NCTM math standards each project supports. All of these projects and more are linked to the *Interlit* Web site. For the latest information, follow the *Interlit* Web site link to the New Jersey Networking Infrastructure in Education.

Virtual Tokamak Reactor Simulation

A fascinating virtual field trip awaits you at the Internet Plasma Physics Education Experience (IPPEX) Online. Figure 2-11 shows how students can run the same nuclear reactor simulation that Princeton University scientists use to determine optimal settings for tokamak fusion reactors. By following the *Interlit* Web site link to IPPEX Online, you can control the virtual tokamak reactor, which downloads and runs as a Java applet on your computer.

Global Schoolhouse Projects

The Global Schoolhouse

The Global Schoolhouse (GSH) has been a leader in collaborative learning since the project started in 1984. It began as the Free Educational Mail (FrEdMail) Network and in 1990 became the Global SchoolNet Foundation. In 1993, with a grant from the National Science Foundation, GSN created the Global Schoolhouse Web site. Its purpose is to provide a living curriculum that makes the world a laboratory. In pursuit of this goal, the Global Schoolhouse has used the Web to establish a community in which students learn and interact with fellow students all over the world. Global Schoolhouse projects include:

Field Trips	Students share their discoveries during real-life field trips, while distant classrooms follow along.
GeoGame	Help students learn about our world, its maps, and its people.
Classroom Conferencing	Use video conferencing to connect cultures, classrooms, and communities so that students around the world can learn together.
Conversion Tools	Links to map resources, language translators, measurement converters, currency and time zone converters, and postal zip codes
Online Expeditions	Follow real explorers as they travel to interesting and exotic locations.
Newsday	Involve your students in international affairs with Newsday newswire. They will create their own newspaper based on articles submitted by global student correspondents.
Classroom Conferencing	Use video conferencing to connect cultures, classrooms, and communities so that students around the world can learn together.

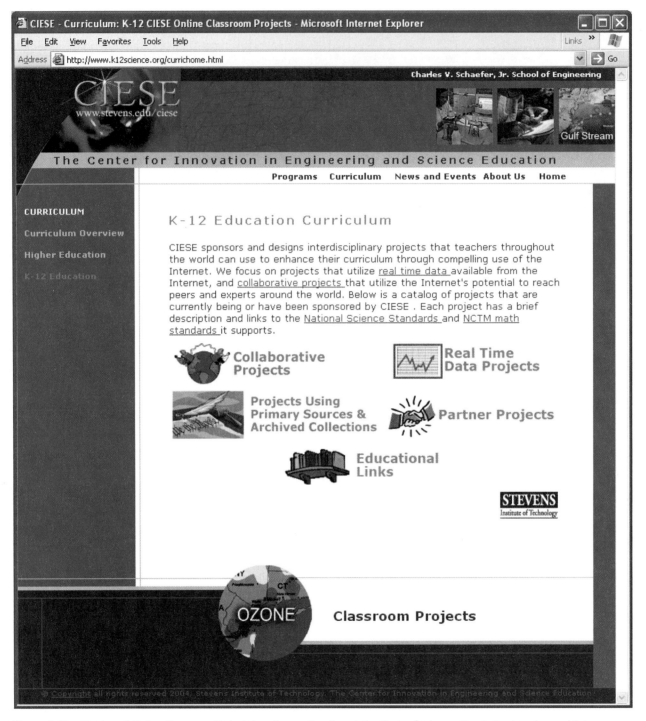

Figure 2-10   Catalog of Online Classroom Projects in science education at the Center for Innovation in Engineering and Science Education in the New Jersey Networking Infrastructure in Education.

Figure 2-12 shows an online collaboration called Journey North, for example, in which students study wildlife migration and seasonal changes, and use e-mail and discussion groups to track the emergence of spring across the globe. Students make observations in their own locations, report their findings to the central database, and learn lessons from the conglomeration of each other's data. Instructional strategies include classroom lessons, challenge questions, and live online interaction between students in classrooms and scientists in the field. Lessons include tracking the seasonal migration of humpback

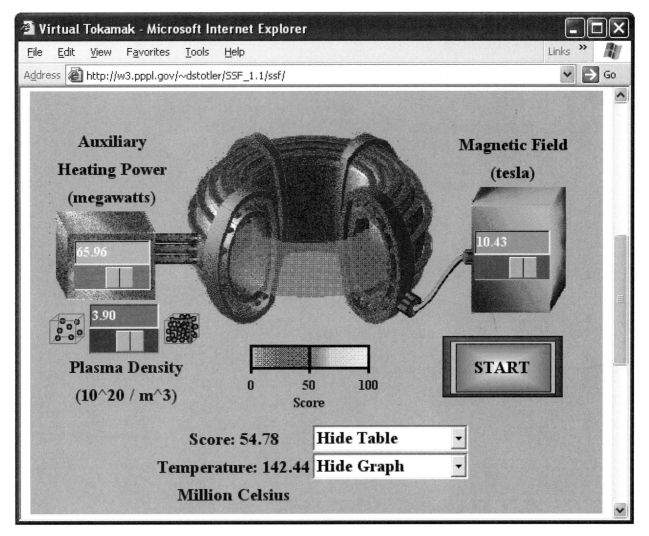

Figure 2-11   By manipulating the sliders that control the plasma density, heating power, and magnetic field, you can learn how these parameters interact, and develop an intuitive feel for the process scientists go through in designing tokamak reactors.

whales and the manatee. More than 400,000 students in 11,000 classrooms participated in the 2004/2005 Journey North program.

Live WebCams at the Discovery Channel

The Discovery Channel offers educators and students an innovative set of tools for integrating current events into the classroom. At www.discovery.com you can see the science behind the awesome fury of a live volcano, for example, and check out an interactive map of America's volcanic hotspots. A tour of the galaxies accompanies a tutorial about the universe and space exploration. Figure 2-13 shows how live WebCams let you look in on live action shots of animals, people, and places. Discovery Channel is very quick to integrate instruction around current events. A tragic crash of the Concorde, for example, became an example for a high-speed flight tutorial that appeared within a few days of the crash.

National Educational Technology Standards

To enable schools to take advantage of the benefits of technology in education, the Department of Education (DOE) has created an Office of Educational Technology (OET) that coordinates many educational technology projects funded by the U.S. government.

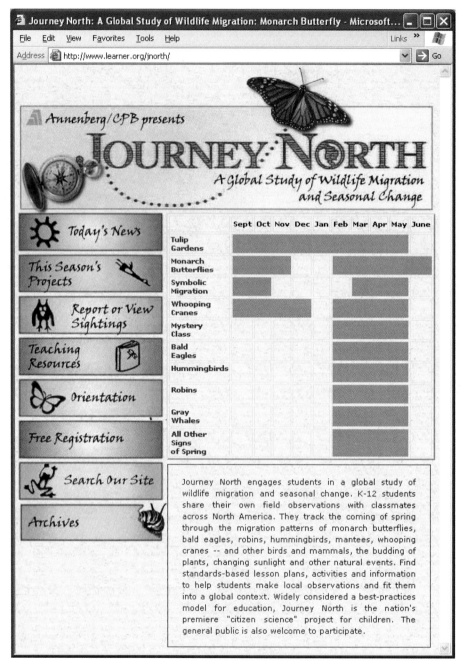

Figure 2-12   Journey North is an online collaboration in which students participate in a global study of wildlife migration.

By following the *Interlit* Web site link to the OET, you can peruse the guide to education programs, read the National Education Technology Plan, and search hundreds of research syntheses, reports, and studies from contracts and grants funded by the DOE. Also linked to the *Interlit* Web site are the Federal Resources for Educational Excellence (FREE), which are the result of more than 30 federal agencies working together to make hundreds of federally supported teaching and learning resources easier to find.

Teachers and school administrators will be particularly interested in the National Educational Technology Standards (NETS) Web site, which defines standards for integrating technology into the curriculum and for preparing teachers to use technology. The NETS project is publishing an innovative series of books full of ideas and sample lesson plans

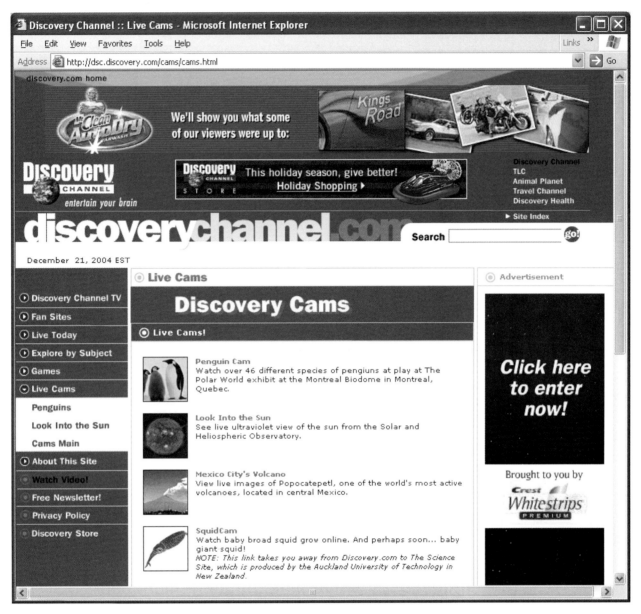

Figure 2-13 Live WebCams at the Discovery Channel. http://dsc.discovery.com/cams/cams.html.

that teachers can use to combine technology with curriculum. The series contains books devoted to teaching with technology in prekindergarten through grade 2, grades 3–5, grades 6–8, and for social studies in grades 9–12. New titles are in preparation. There are also books that provide administrators with guidance in aligning their schools with the technology standards. For the latest, follow the *Interlit* Web site links to NETS.

Interconnected Scholarship

The Internet affords researchers an unprecedented opportunity to create an interconnected world of scholarship. Imagine having every scholarly paper mounted on the World Wide Web, with hypertext links that put you just a mouse click away from calling up the source materials referenced in the article. Such was the dream of Tim Berners-Lee when he began making plans to create the Web back in the early 1980s. At that time, the tools for creating Web pages were primitive, however, and mounting documents on the Web required technical skills that exceeded what the average scholar had the time to learn and use. Happily, there now are Web page creation utilities for the world's most popular word processors—Microsoft Word and Corel WordPerfect. After just a few mouse clicks, scholars can create Web pages out of any research paper.

Some journals are making full-text versions of scholarly papers freely available on the Web. In Chapter 11, you learn how to use a scholarly search engine to perform keyword searches to locate papers on topics that interest you. There are many scholarly papers, however, that are not available on the Web. I believe that all scholars whose research papers are not available on the Web should assume the responsibility of using their word processor's Web publishing tool to mount their papers on the Web. Then the Web crawlers will find the papers and index them into the Internet's search engines. Automatically, a world of interconnected scholarship arises.

By helping everyone who reads this book learn how to create Web pages and mount them on the Web, it is hoped that the Web page creation tutorial in Part Five will contribute to making the world of interconnected scholarship happen sooner rather than later.

Ubiquity

Wireless technologies are making it possible for people to access the Internet almost anywhere. Through the Wireless Application Protocol (WAP), financial brokerages such as Charles Schwab enable you to access your account and trade stocks via your mobile phone. Microsoft provides mobile phone access to its Hotmail service, which enables people to send and receive e-mail over the Web. Communications giant Ericsson has created a mobile phone with a color screen that enables people to view pictures and animations in a format called *multimedia mobile messaging* (MMS).

By the time you read this book, wireless Internet services will probably be available in your city or neighborhood. The emerging technologies part of this book in Chapter 26 will provide more information about the wireless protocols that permit people to access the Internet from cell phones, pagers, and tablet PCs.

Patron Saint of the Internet

This chapter has dealt with how the Internet is changing the world. In concluding this chapter, it seems appropriate to mention how the Vatican is considering naming a patron saint to watch over users and programmers. The top candidate is Isidore of Seville, who died in 636 on April 4, which now is his feast day. He was chosen because of the database tree-like structure of his *Etymologies,* which is a 20-volume encyclopedia dealing with medicine, mathematics, history, and theology. For the latest news on the Vatican's progress toward naming Isidore officially, follow the *Interlit* Web site links to Patron Saint of the Internet.

exercises

1. Give examples of how the Internet has affected (*a*) the nation as a whole, (*b*) your local community, and (*c*) your personal life.

2. In your chosen career or profession, would telecommuting be appropriate? How would it help or hinder your work?

3. This chapter described how the Internet is changing the world through mergers and alliances, telecommuting, home shopping, interactive television, online government services, electronic publishing, and computer-based learning. How else do you see the Internet changing the world?

4. Compare the advantages and disadvantages of online shopping as you see them. What impact will online shopping have on traditional stores and shopping malls?

5. How are your state and local governments using the Internet? Do your local politicians have Web sites? Does your state have kiosks in public places to provide better access to government services? If so, what services are available through kiosks in your state?

6. Think of an example showing how a computer helped you learn something. What was the subject matter? What role did the computer play? Did you learn better because of the computer? Why or why not?

7. How do you believe the Internet will affect the future of schooling? For example, do you believe that if the Information Superhighway could serve all the nation's educational software to children at home, there would be no further need for schools as we know them? Are there any aspects of schooling that technology cannot replace?

8. Figure 2-8 showed a forecast of the consumer price index. Go to www.economy.com/freelunch and look up the actual figure for the current year. What is the consumer price index for the year in which you are doing this exercise?

9. Of all the different kinds of occupations you can think of, which ones need the Internet the most? The least? What is your chosen occupation? Why will you need to know about the Internet to do well in your line of work?

10. Follow the *Interlit* Web site link to WebCam Central, WebCamWorld, or one of the other WebCam directories you will find there. Check out some of the live WebCams you will find on the Web. What is the most interesting WebCam you found? What is its URL? Why did it interest you?

SITUATED CASE PROJECTS

Case 2: Evaluating Online Procurement Options

At the end of each chapter in this book, a situated case project provides the student an opportunity to put the chapter's contents to practical use in a workplace situation. Each case has the same number as the chapter in which it appears.

No matter what school or business you work for, there most likely is a need to procure supplies and materials to support daily operations. Imagine that your employer has asked you to visit the online shopping site at www.amazon.com and recommend whether it can be used for online procurement at your workplace. In formulating your recommendation, consider these issues:

❶ *Security.* Is the online shopping site reputable, and does it have strong security measures in place? What documentation is provided to support this claim?

❷ *Payment.* Does the site let users register more than one credit card, so the user can separate personal purchases made on a personal credit card from workplace purchases made on a corporate credit card?

❸ *Shopping carts.* Does the site have an e-mail shopping cart feature whereby employees can put desired items into a shopping cart and e-mail the cart to an officer of your company to make the purchase of the items in that cart?

❹ *Limits.* What will be the limit on spending by each person, and how will you enforce that limit or audit the spending?

❺ *Privacy.* Does the shopping site keep private the names and e-mail addresses of its shoppers?

Use your word processor to write your recommendation in the form of a brief statement indicating whether you recommend using amazon.com, followed by a bulleted list of the reasons why you have recommended for or against using Amazon. In this list, address the issues of security, payment, shopping carts, and spending limits, plus any other issues or concerns you noted while evaluating Amazon's security measures and operating procedures. If you work at a school, for example, you might comment on the search engine at Amazon for locating books and the next-day shipping option for getting items in stock delivered quickly. Also consider the available of third-party stores with which Amazon has partnerships, and whose products appear in store categories at the site. Save the recommendation on your hard drive. If your instructor has asked you to hand in the recommendation, make sure you put your name at the top, then save it on disk or follow the other instructions you may have been given for submitting this assignment.

PART TWO
GETTING ON THE INTERNET

CHAPTER 3

Getting Connected

CHAPTER 4

Surfing the Net

On the Internet, there is no there.

—Anna Paquin, MCI Commercial

Almost everyone reading this book has already been on the Internet. You have probably already surfed the Web, for example, and you may consider yourself pretty good at surfing. But do you know the most cost-effective way to connect to the Internet from your locale? Do you understand the theory of surfing well enough to truly glide across the Net and find things quickly?

This part of the book will enable you to get more out of the Internet by helping you understand how best to connect and surf the Net.

3

GETTING CONNECTED

After completing this chapter, you will be able to:

- ■ Understand the purpose and function of an Internet service provider (ISP).

- ■ Find out who the ISPs are in your locale.

- ■ Compare the advantages and disadvantages of the different transport mediums, including plain old telephone lines, high-speed broadband cable, digital telephone lines, satellites, and television cable.

- ■ Decide the best way to connect, given your particular circumstances.

- ■ Understand how the TCP/IP protocol connects your computer to the Internet and sends information in packets over the Net.

● In order to get connected to the Internet, you need three things. First, you need to subscribe to an Internet service provider. Second, you need a communications medium through which information can pass to and from your computer. Third, you need a TCP/IP connection from your computer to the Internet. This chapter will help you accomplish all three.

Internet Service Providers

Most users get their Internet connection from an **Internet service provider (ISP).** An ISP is a networking company that connects you to the Internet and provides you with Internet services, including access to the World Wide Web, e-mail, listserv, chat, and newsgroups.

In the past, some ISPs charged an hourly fee. If you use the Internet a lot, however, paying by the hour can be very expensive. Listed here are four of the most popular ISPs, all of which provide unlimited dial-up usage for a flat fee of about $24 per month.

America Online

America Online

America Online, also known as AOL, is the largest Internet service provider. The number of AOL subscribers has skyrocketed to 32 million users. Each user gets up to seven e-mail accounts and an allotment of 2MB of personal Web space for each account. AOL uses a channel style of presentation to make it easy to navigate its many offerings. A huge amount of AOL content is not otherwise available on the Internet. Parental controls enable parents to limit access to adult content. To find out more about AOL, go to www.aol.com.

AT&T WorldNet

AT&T WorldNet Service

AT&T WorldNet Service provides fast, reliable Internet access nationwide. You get six e-mail accounts, each of which has 10MB of personal Web space. For more information about AT&T WorldNet Service, go to www.att.net.

Microsoft Network

Microsoft Network (MSN)

The Microsoft Network (MSN) provides up to nine e-mail accounts, the MSN Messenger service for talking with your friends online, and up to 30MB of space for your photos and personal Web pages. To find out more about the Microsoft Network, go to www.msn.com.

EarthLink

EarthLink

In 2000, EarthLink merged with Mindspring to become the nation's second largest ISP (Bloomberg News, 2000). Its partnership with the Snap! Portal provides EarthLink users with an intuitive user interface. Every user gets an allotment of web space with a personal start page including an e-mail indicator, a search engine, headline news, stock quotes, weather, and personal reminders. You can find EarthLink on the Web at www.earthlink.net.

Regional and Local Networks

Starpower

By looking up "Internet Services" in the yellow pages of your telephone directory, you will probably find some regional and local ISPs listed in addition to the nationwide service providers discussed so far. For example, a regional ISP called *Starpower* offers Internet services in Washington, DC; northern Virginia; and Maryland. Starpower also can provide telephone and cable TV services. To contact Starpower, go to www.starpower.net.

The List

An excellent source for finding out about other ISPs in your area is on the Web at thelist. internet.com.

School and College Networks

Schools and colleges commonly operate computer networks that provide Internet services for free to their faculty, staff, and students. If you are lucky enough to belong to such a user community, your local school or college serves as your ISP. Because these services are free, however, the resources are sometimes inadequate to meet the demand, and it is not uncommon for members of school and college networks to also subscribe to one of the commercial ISPs. Some campuses have even negotiated deals with commercial ISPs to get a lower price for individuals to subscribe to the commercial service.

User Satisfaction

Consumer Search

J.D. Power & Associates ranks ISPs in terms of customer satisfaction. In a 2004 survey of 9,400 residential customers, EarthLink scored highest in both dial-up and broadband services. Following EarthLink in the dial-up ranking are Juno/NetZero, AT&T WorldNet, and BellSouth, respectively. In broadband, EarthLink is followed by Verizon, Road Runner, and a tie between BellSouth and Cox, respectively. For the latest rankings of Internet service providers, follow the *Interlit* Web site link to the Consumer Search review of Internet service providers.

Transport Medium

The transport medium is the physical connection over which information travels on the Internet. Very high-speed transmission lines carry the backbone of the Internet across the country and over the world. Most often these backbone lines are fiber-optic cables or copper transmission lines. The major ISPs have very high-speed connections to the Internet's backbone.

The physical connection between your computer and your ISP is often the most critical part of the transport medium, because it determines the bandwidth of your connection

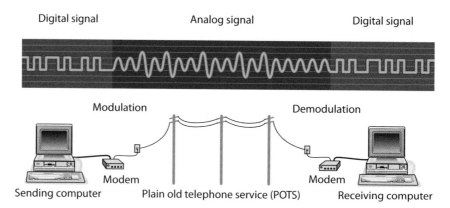

Digital signal   Analog signal   Digital signal

Modulation   Demodulation

Modem   Modem

Sending computer   Plain old telephone service (POTS)   Receiving computer

Figure 3-1   Follow the signal to see how modems work by modulating the computer's digital signal into an analog signal that can be transmitted over plain old telephone service (POTS) to your ISP, where the signal is demodulated into a digital signal.

to the Net. Most Internet connections use wires or cables you can see and touch. It is also possible to use wireless connections such as cell phones and satellites that communicate via radio signals. Depending on the medium you choose, you need to have specific hardware installed in your computer to handle the communication.

Telephone Modems

The most common means of connecting to the Internet from home is via plain old telephone service, also known as *POTS*. To communicate with the Internet over an ordinary telephone line, your computer must have a modem. The term **modem** is a combination of the terms *mo*dulate and *dem*odulate, which describe how your computer sends and receives digital information over analog phone lines. Modems are so popular that most computers being sold today come with modems built in. Other models require the addition of external modems that connect to your computer's serial port or modem cards that plug into one of your computer's expansion slots. Figure 3-1 contains a block diagram that describes how modems work.

Modems have gotten steadily faster as computer technology has advanced. Modem speed is important because it determines how long you have to wait for information to arrive. Modem speed is often expressed in units known as **bits per second (bps)** or **kilobits per second (Kbps).** A kilobit is a thousand bits. Common speeds are 14,400 bps (14.4 Kbps), 28,800 bps (28.8 Kbps), 33,600 bps (33.6 Kbps), and 56,000 bps (56 Kbps). For example, information traveling at 14,400 bps takes twice as long to arrive as it would at 28,800 bps.

Just because you have a superfast modem, such as 56 Kbps, does not necessarily mean information actually travels that fast to and from your computer. The telephone lines and the equipment (routers and switches) the lines pass through on their way to your ISP may preclude your superfast modem from using its highest speed. Many modems have built-in compression and decompression features that enable them to pack information more tightly in the communication packets, thereby achieving an actual transmission rate higher than their advertised data rate. This feature only works, however, for data that have not already been compressed.

Ethernet

The invention of **Ethernet** (pronounced *ee-thur-net*) in Bob Metcalfe's Harvard Ph.D. thesis in 1973 was a data communications breakthrough that fueled the explosion of local area networks (LANs) throughout academia and industry. Ethernet networks transmit data at high speed, typically up to 10 **megabits per second (Mbps).** (Mega means a million, so 10 megabits means 10 million bits.) At Ethernet speeds, a file that takes 10 minutes to transmit over a 14.4 Kbps modem arrives in just 1 second. Actual downloading times may vary, depending on compression schemes, network traffic, and the number of users sharing the Ethernet.

10 Gigabit Ethernet Alliance

If you work at a school or company that has its PCs connected to the Internet at high speeds, chances are the communications medium is an Ethernet. At first, Ethernet required the use of coaxial cable, the kind of wire used in cable TV. Now there is a so-called **10BaseT** Ethernet that can use category 5 (**CAT 5**) twisted-pair telephone wiring. A faster **10/100BaseT** Ethernet can move data at rates up to 100 megabits per second. There is also a 10 gigabit Ethernet standard known as **10GbE.** Officially ratified in the summer of 2002, the 10GbE standard uses fiber optics to push Ethernet into speeds ranging up 10 **gigabits per second (Gbps).** The prefix *giga* means billion; a gigabit is one billion bits and 10 Gbps is therefore 10 billion bits per second.

ISDN

ISDN stands for **Integrated Services Digital Network.** It is the digital telephone system the regional Bell companies are installing in most of the United States; when this book went to press, about 80 percent of the country could get ISDN.

ISDN signals are carried over two or more 64-Kbps (64,000 bits per second) circuit-switched channels to carry voice and data and a lower-speed packet-switched channel that carries control signals. The Basic Rate Interface (BRI) service of ISDN is 144 Kbps, made up of two 64-Kbps data channels and one 16-Kbps control channel. The Primary Rate Interface (PRI) service uses 23 data channels and a 64-Kbps control channel to boost the data rate to 1,544 Kbps (1.544 Mbps), which is capable of real-time videoconferencing in addition to more traditional data services.

To use ISDN to connect to the Internet, you need to contact both your local telephone company and your Internet service provider to find out whether ISDN is available in your area and to make sure your ISP supports it. ISDN lines cost more than ordinary phone lines, so be prepared to pay more for the higher data rate.

Cable Modems

A **cable modem** is a network adapter used to connect PCs to TV cables in neighborhoods where cable TV companies offer Internet services over TV cables. Cable modems are potentially faster than telephone modems because TV cables, being coaxial, are capable of carrying high-speed Ethernet signals in addition to conventional television signals. The term **broadband** is used to refer to this type of connection that carries multiple channels of information over a single cable.

To find out if cable modems are available in your neighborhood, follow the *Interlit* Web site link to the cable modem zip code search.

DSL, SDSL, and ADSL

DSL stands for **Digital Subscriber Line,** which is a broadband method of connecting to the Internet over existing telephone lines. There are two kinds of DSL: synchronous and asynchronous. Synchronous DSL (SDSL) supports the same high-speed data rate for both upstream and downstream traffic. Asynchronous DSL (ADSL) lowers the cost of DSL connections by using a high-speed data rate for downloads but a slower rate for uploads. Download speeds range from 384 Kbps to 8 Mbps, and upload speeds range from 128 Kbps to 1 Mbps. The faster the speed, the higher the cost.

The typical home user spends a lot more time downloading than uploading. When you click to play a movie, for example, very little information goes up from your computer to the movie site to trigger the playing of the movie. When the movie comes down to your PC, on the other hand, the amount of bandwidth required is huge. ADSL models itself after this trend of home users downloading much more information than they upload. Another advantage of ADSL is that you can use the same telephone line for voice as well as data transmissions. SDSL, on the other hand, cannot operate simultaneously with voice transmissions on the same wire.

When this book went to press, DSL was available in about 75 percent of the United States. To find out whether you can get DSL at your home or business, follow the *Interlit* Web site link to the DSL area code search and use the menus to find out if access is available in your locale, and how much it costs to connect at different speeds. Be prepared to see some pretty high prices for the faster speeds.

To learn more about DSL and compare the relative merits of SDSL and ADSL, follow the link to the DSL Resource Center.

Satellite

Where cable or DSL is not available, satellite Internet service is an attractive alternative in areas that have a clear view of the southern sky. Like ADSL, satellite Internet service has a faster download than upload speed. Typical transmission speeds are 500 Kbps downstream and 150 Kbps upstream. In extremely bad weather, the speeds can decline due to the obstructed view. Whereas most DSL vendors permit subscribers to connect more than one computer, satellite providers normally restrict usage to a single computer per subscription. To learn more, follow this book's Web site links to satellite Internet providers.

Transmission Control Protocol

As you learned in Chapter 1, the complete, formal name for the protocol that connects computers to the Internet is TCP/IP. IP stands for Internet Protocol, and TCP stands for Transmission Control Protocol.

True to its name, TCP governs how information gets transmitted in packets over the Internet. If the information is too large to fit in a single packet, multiple packets get sent. TCP takes care of dividing the information into packets, routing the packets to their destination, and assembling the information when it arrives. If the packets arrive out of sequence, TCP puts them back together in the right order. TCP can even detect when errors occurred on the transmission line to alter the information, in which case TCP asks for the errant packets to be retransmitted.

TCP/IP is built in to the Windows and Macintosh operating systems. If you have Windows or a Mac, you have TCP/IP. When you connect your computer to the Internet via your chosen ISP, your computer will automatically use TCP/IP to route your information over the Net.

Comparing the Ways to Connect

To summarize the many alternatives presented in this chapter, Table 3-1 compares the different ways to connect to the Internet. By studying this comparison, you should be able to select an option that suits your needs and budget.

To test the bandwidth your connection actually provides, follow the *Interlit* Web site link to the bandwidth meter.

Table 3-1 Internet connection comparison matrix

Transport Medium	Time to Download 100 KB Picture	Time to Download 900 KB Audio	Time to Download 10 MB Movie	Estimated Monthly Communications Cost
14.4 Kbps Modem	55 seconds	500 seconds	93 minutes	$23
28.8 Kbps Modem	28 seconds	250 seconds	46 minutes	$23
33.6 Kbps Modem	24 seconds	214 seconds	40 minutes	$23
56 Kbps Modem	14 seconds	128 seconds	24 minutes	$23
128 Kbps ISDN	6 seconds	56 seconds	10 minutes	$35
256 Kbps DSL	3 seconds	28 seconds	5 minutes	$129
500 Kbps Satellite Downstream, 159 Kbps Upstream	1.6 seconds	14.4 seconds	2.6 minutes	$70
1.5 Mbps DSL	0.54 second	4.8 seconds	54 seconds	$309
1.5 Mbps ADSL Downstream, 128 Kbps Upstream	0.54 second	4.8 seconds	54 seconds	$49
3 Mbps Cable Modem	0.27 second	2.4 seconds	27 seconds	$35–50

Note: Cable modem speeds vary, depending on the number of simultaneous users of the local cable network.

Prepaid Internet Cards

Computer users who travel may be interested in prepaid Internet calling cards. Offered by Sprint and AT&T, the prepaid Internet cards let you purchase a number of hours of Internet connection time in advance of using it.

The prepaid Internet card also may be of interest to people who seldom connect to the Internet and wish to avoid paying a regular monthly fee. The prepaid Internet market is expected to grow from $10 million in 2001 to $280 million in 2005. To learn more, follow the *Interlit* Web site links to prepaid Internet cards.

Direct Connections

An Internet connection that is always on is called a **direct connection.** To use the Internet over a direct connection, you simply begin using the client software with which you wish to access the Internet. Of the various ways this chapter has presented for connecting to the Internet, the following provide you with a direct connection:

- Ethernet
- ISDN
- Cable modem
- DSL
- Satellite

Connections that are not direct, on the other hand, require you to do something special to get connected. To use a dial-up connection, for example, you must dial up to your ISP to get connected.

Sometimes even a direct connection can stop working. When hurricane Isabel hit the mid-Atlantic United States, for example, my ISDN line was out of service for several days.

To work online in the meantime, I used a modem to dial up, which enabled business to continue, albeit at a lower speed. Many users with direct connections keep a prepaid Internet card on hand for emergency use during such outages.

exercises

1. Who is the primary regional ISP in your area, and how much does that ISP charge per month for Internet service? To help answer this question, check the yellow pages of your phone book under Internet services, and go to www.thelist.com to find out which ISPs are listed under your area code.

2. Follow the *Interlit* web site links to the DSL lookup site, and find out whether DSL is available in your area code. If DSL is available, what data rates are available in your neighborhood, and what do they cost?

3. Contact your cable TV company to find out if cable modems are available. If so, how much does it cost to get connected, and what is the ongoing cost? If your cable TV company tells you cable modem service is not available, follow the *Interlit* web site link to the Cable Modem Area Code Search to find out if any other companies offer cable modems in your area.

4. Survey 10 or more of the homes in your neighborhood to find out how they are connected to the Internet. List the kinds of connections you find (such as dial-up modems, ISDN, cable modems, satellite, or DSL), and tell what percentage of your neighbors use each type of connection. If any of your neighbors are not connected, include on your list the percentage of homes you surveyed that are not on the Internet.

SITUATED CASE PROJECTS
Case 3: Connectivity Planning

At the end of each chapter in this book, a situated case project provides the student an opportunity to put the chapter's contents to practical use in a workplace situation. Each case has the same number as the chapter in which it appears.

In order for the employees of a company or school to work online, they need to be able to connect to the Internet. Imagine that you work for a small company or school that has decided to begin permitting its employees to do some of their work from home. Your employer has asked you to recommend the best method or strategy for your fellow employees to connect from home so they can telecommute over the Internet. In developing this recommendation, you will need to consider the following factors:

 Time. How many hours per week will the typical employee spend telecommuting?

2 *Bandwidth.* Does your school or company require high bandwidth for some or all of its computing activities? How would higher bandwidth impact worker productivity?

3 *Geography.* Can each employee connect from home to an Internet service provider without incurring long distance charges?

 Cost. In almost every school or company, you need to stay within a budget. Refer to the cost comparison in Table 3-1, and consider the cost of the telecommunication solutions you recommend.

Use a word processor to type your telecommuting recommendation in the form of a brief essay describing the network strategy that seems appropriate for your co-workers to connect to the Internet from home. If your instructor has asked you to hand in the recommendation, make sure you put your name at the top, then save it on disk or follow any other instructions you may have been given for this assignment.

4

SURFING THE NET

After completing this chapter, you will be able to:

- Define what it means to surf the Net.

- Select a Web browser and use it to go surfing.

- Recognize the elements of a uniform resource locator (URL).

- Know how to go to any URL on the World Wide Web.

- Visit some of the most exciting sites on the World Wide Web.

- Define the concepts of linking and browsing.

- Define the concepts of a Web page, a home page, and a default page.

- Manipulate a window by sizing, scrolling, hiding, maximizing, and switching among multiple windows.

- Navigate using the browser's buttons and shortcut keys.

- Go to different levels of a Web site by manipulating its URL.

- Avoid distractions and stay focused on the purpose for which you visited a Web site.

- Bookmark your favorite Web sites for quick recall whenever you want to visit them again.

- Know how to create more screen space to display the maximum amount of a Web page inside your browser window.

● Most of the people reading this book have probably already had their first surfing experience. Many may consider themselves adept at surfing, and some could even be addicted to it.

Whether or not you have surfed the Net, studying the concepts in this chapter will enable you to become a better surfer than if you "just do it." If you have become addicted, the techniques you learn here will help you gain control over the Net instead of allowing it to control you.

What Is Surfing?

In telecommunications, the term **surf** means to browse by going from place to place in search of something that interests you. On TV, you surf by changing channels continually until you find a program you want to watch; this is known as *channel surfing*. On the Net, surfing means to use a program called a *browser* to go from site to site in search of information that interests you.

The most popular place to surf on the Internet is the World Wide Web. As you learned in Chapter 1, the Web is a worldwide hypertext system that interconnects millions of documents.

The connections are made through links, which can be textual or graphical. A **link** is a hot spot that, when selected, triggers the object of the link. You select the link by clicking on the word or picture that triggers it. Progressively clicking through the Web by triggering the links that interest you is known as **browsing,** a term synonymous with surfing the Net.

What Is a Browser?

The program you run when you surf the Web is called a **browser.** Because you surf the Web to receive content, the browser is an example of client software. As this book proceeds, you will learn how to use a browser not only to surf Web pages but also to search for and download pictures, audio, and video content. You will learn how to configure the browser to display multimedia content by using the plug-in of your choice. To keep your computer safe, you will also learn how to configure the browser's security settings to protect your computer from Internet attacks.

Selecting a Web Browser

Microsoft makes a browser called **Internet Explorer (IE)** that is preinstalled on most computers running the Windows operating system. Internet Explorer comes in both desktop and handheld versions. The handheld version is called Pocket Internet Explorer and runs under Windows CE on the Pocket PC family of handheld computers. Users who do not have Internet Explorer can download it freely from www.microsoft.com/windows/ie, where the latest updates are also available. If you have trouble downloading the browser, ask your Internet service provider to help you get a setup disk that will install the browser for you.

On the Macintosh, an important Web browser change occurred in 2003. Before then, the default browser was the Macintosh version of Internet Explorer. In 2003, however, Microsoft announced that it was discontinuing work on the Macintosh version of IE. Apple now produces its own Web browser, which is called **Safari** and ships on every Macintosh as the default Web browser. Macintosh users can download the latest version or get updates at www.apple.com/safari. To run Safari, Macintosh users need to be running the Mac OS X operating system.

Another popular Web browser is **Firefox,** which is an enhanced browser built upon open source code from the Netscape Navigator browser. The term **open source** refers to software for which the source code is available to the general public free of charge. Anyone can download the source code, use it freely, and make enhancements. People who make enhancements to Firefox can submit them to the Mozilla Foundation, which maintains the official master copy of the Firefox software. You can download the Windows, Linux, or Macintosh version of Firefox from www.mozilla.org.

Using a Web Browser

Before you can start using a Web browser, you must accomplish two tasks:

- You must have a computer that is connected to the Internet according to the Transmission Control Protocol/Internet Protocol (TCP/IP). Chapter 3 describes how to get such a connection through an ordinary dial-up phone line, an ISDN digital phone line, a cable modem, a Digital Subscriber Line (DSL), a satellite modem, or a high-speed broadband network.

- If the browser is not installed on your computer, you must install it. Many ISPs provide new users with a CD containing a Web browser. Follow the installation instructions that came with your browser. If you do not have a browser, you can download Firefox from www.mozilla.org, or you can download Internet Explorer from www.microsoft.com/windows/ie. Both of these downloads are free.

With your computer connected to the Internet, you can start your Web browser and get ready to surf. Typically you start your Web browser by double-clicking one of these icons:

Internet Explorer   Mozilla Firefox   Safari   Netscape

Mozilla Firefox is a trademark of the Mozilla Foundation.

Understanding URLs

Every place you can go on the Web has an address known as a **URL,** which stands for uniform resource locator. Most often the resources are hypertext documents, but they also can be pictures, sounds, movies, animations, or application software. URLs also can bring up newsgroups, chat rooms, search engines, and real-time audio and video streams.

Elements of a URL

A URL can have several parts, which always appear in this order:

- Protocol
- Server name
- Port number (optional)
- Filename (optional)
- Anchor (optional)

Here is what the different parts of a URL mean:

protocol	Protocols include http, ftp, mailto, and news; the most popular protocol is http, which stands for *hypertext transfer protocol.* Every Web page's URL begins with http.
server name	The server name is the Internet address of the computer or file server on which the resource resides.
port number	Port numbers rarely appear in URLs because almost every file server is on the Web's default port, which is port 80.
filename	The filename is the name the file has on the server. If the file is in a folder or subfolder on the server, the filename includes the path to the file as well as the name of the file. If a URL that begins with http does not contain a filename, the default filename (usually index.html) gets served.
anchor	The anchor is a named bookmark within an HTML file. Anchors are optional. If a URL does not contain an anchor, the browser begins display at the start of the file.

The following analysis shows how the various parts of a URL get combined into a specific address on the World Wide Web. This example is the URL for the professional experience section of my résumé.

http://www.udel.edu:80/fth/resume.html#professional

protocol	**http**
port	**80**
server name	**www.udel.edu**
filename	**fth/resume.html**
anchor	**professional**

In most cases, a URL simply consists of a protocol, a server name, and a filename, such as http://www.udel.edu/fth/resume.html.

Web Sites

Every hypertext document on the World Wide Web resides on one of the computers connected to the network. The place where the hypertext document is stored on that computer is known as its **Web site.** Every Web site has a URL.

For example, Sony's Web site is http://www.sony.com. CNN's Web site is http://www.cnn.com. IBM is at http://www.ibm.com. Microsoft is http://www.microsoft.com. Do you notice the similarity in these corporate Web site addresses? Almost every company in the world has a Web site address in the form of http://www.*company_name*.com.

Because http is the default protocol for Web pages, the browsers let you skip typing http:// at the beginning of an http Web address. The URL www.cnn.com will take you to the same place as http://www.cnn.com, for example. You only need to type the protocol if it is not http.

Web Pages

Like books, each site on the Web consists of one or more pages. Each page at a Web site is known as a **Web page.** Unlike the pages in books, however, Web pages can contain more information than you can see at once. Scrollbars let you move the page up and down inside your browser window, which displays the text and graphics on the Web page.

Every Web page has a URL. For example, the URL of my résumé is http://www.udel.edu/fth/resume.html. By analyzing this URL, you can see that this Web page is stored in the *fth* folder (*fth* are my initials) at the University of Delaware's Web site. The filename of the Web page is *resume.html*. The filename extension *html* is the standard format used for documents on the Web. HTML stands for *h*ypertext *m*arkup *l*anguage. You will learn HTML in the Web page authoring tutorial in Part Five of this book.

Surfing Concepts and Techniques

Surfing the Net is a lot more involved than channel surfing a television. Instead of just flipping through the relatively limited number of channels available on a TV, surfing the Net enables you to navigate a world full of interconnected information, discover new sites you did not know about, keep track of where you have been so you can easily get there again, and download things that interest you. By practicing the surfing concepts and techniques presented here, you can master the art of navigating the Net so you can get where you want quickly and accomplish your purpose for going there. Even if you consider yourself an accomplished surfer, studying these concepts will probably teach you some new techniques that will make you even more productive in surfing the Net.

Entering URLs

Oftentimes you will have been given a specific URL or Web address that you want to go to. For example, you may have seen an ad for a Sony product that told you to go to the Web site www.sony.com for more information. To go there (or to any other site for which you know the URL), you simply type the URL into your Web browser's address or location field, and press the ⌷Enter⌷ key. If your browser's address or location field is not visible, follow the steps in Table 4-1 to get it on your screen.

Table 4-1 How to go to a URL

Firefox	Internet Explorer
▶ If the URL field is not visible, pull down the View menu and click Toolbars→Navigation Toolbar.	▶ Internet Explorer calls the URL field the Address field. If this field is not visible, pull down the View menu, select Toolbars, and if the Address Bar is not checked, select the Address Bar to display it.
▶ Click once inside the URL field to position your cursor in it.	▶ If the URL field still is not visible, click your right mouse button on the Toolbar and select Address Bar.
▶ Type the URL you want to go to. In this example, type www.sony.com.	▶ Click once inside the URL field to position your cursor in it.
▶ Press `Enter`.	▶ Type the URL you want to go to. In this example, type www.sony.com.
	▶ Press `Enter`.

To activate the URL field so you can type a URL into it, click once inside the URL field to position your cursor there. Erase any URL that might be there currently by dragging your mouse over the URL to select it, then press the `Delete` key to delete it. Or you can just position your cursor at the end of the URL and backspace over the URL to delete it. Now press `Enter`. Your browser takes you to the Sony site.

Home Pages

Home is a relative concept. For example, a person from London considers England to be home. To fly to Hawaii, that person takes off from London's Heathrow Airport. When someone from Los Angeles flies to Hawaii, however, the plane takes off from the Los Angeles airport. So it is on the Web, where your **home page** is your taking-off point. Many people create their own home page, to which they link documents and resources they want people who visit their home page to be able to access. Almost every company has a home page, as do government offices, schools, and colleges. Home pages organize the information at that site and help you access it. If you were considering going to graduate school at Princeton University, for example, you could find out a lot about it by going to their home page at www.princeton.edu.

A huge mass of information is out there on the Net. Other people's home pages help you make sense out of their stuff. Eventually, after you complete the Web page creation tutorial in Part Five, your home page will organize your stuff and help other people make sense out of it.

Default Pages

If you go to a Web site without requesting a specific document, you will view that site's **default page.** For example, when you went to www.sony.com, you were taken to the default page of the Sony site. The default page is often the home page of the company or person who owns the site. In Part Five, you will learn how to make your home page function as the default startup page for your Web site.

Scrolling Pages

Unlike books, Web pages can contain more information than you can see all at once. When a Web page contains more information than can fit on the screen, a scroll bar will appear. A **scroll bar** is a control that lets you move the contents of a window up or down to reveal more information.

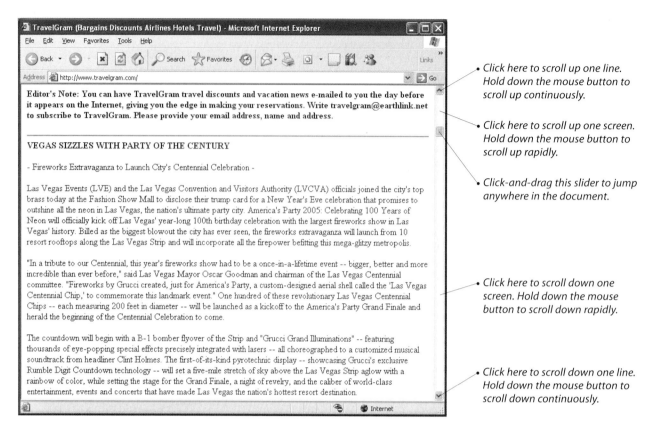

Click here to scroll up one line. Hold down the mouse button to scroll up continuously.

Click here to scroll up one screen. Hold down the mouse button to scroll up rapidly.

Click-and-drag this slider to jump anywhere in the document.

Click here to scroll down one screen. Hold down the mouse button to scroll down rapidly.

Click here to scroll down one line. Hold down the mouse button to scroll down continuously.

Figure 4-1   Using a scroll bar to reveal different parts of a Web page, http://www.travelgram.com.

Figure 4-1 shows where to click on a scroll bar in order to move the window's contents line by line or screen by screen, or to skip to any part of the page. A good Web page on which to practice scrolling is the TravelGram International Travel Newsletter at http://www.travelgram.com. Go there now. Remember that you do not need to type the entire URL; you can get there by simply typing www.travelgram.com into your browser's URL field and pressing Enter. Now practice the scroll bar techniques in Table 4-2 using the scroll bar you will find at the right edge of your browser's window.

Links

Links are perhaps the most important surfing concept, because without links, there would be no Web! Links form the pathways that interconnect the documents and resources on the Web. You activate a link by clicking it. There are two kinds of links: hypertext and hypergraphic.

HYPERTEXT LINKS

A **hypertext·link** consists of one or more words that you click to trigger the events that are linked to the text. Hypertext links are also known as **hot words,** because they make things happen when you click them. So you can tell which words are hot, the hypertext links are underlined or printed in a different color than the rest of the text. Usually, links you have not visited are colored blue, and visited links are dark pink. When you move your cursor over a hypertext link, the cursor shape changes from an arrow to a hand pointer.

You can change the default color of the hot words by modifying your browser's preferences. To change the color of the hypertext links in Firefox, pull down the Tools menu, choose Options, click Fonts & Colors, and click the color swatches for Visited Links and Unvisited Links. In Internet Explorer, pull down the Tools menu, choose Internet Options, click

Table 4-2 How to use a vertical scroll bar

▶ You will find the scroll bar at the right edge of the window. The scroll bar consists of a down-arrow, an up-arrow, and a slider.

▶ Click the down-arrow at the bottom of the scroll bar a few times. Notice how each click moves the document down one line. Now hold down the mouse button on the down-arrow to scroll down continuously.

▶ Click the up-arrow at the top of the scroll bar a few times. Notice how each click moves the document up one line. Now hold down the mouse button on the up-arrow to scroll up continuously. Keep the mouse button pressed until you get back up to the top of the document. *Note:* If you have a Macintosh with OS X, both the up- and down-arrows are at the bottom of the scroll bar.

▶ Click on the area of the scroll bar above the down-arrow. Each time you click this part of the scroll bar, the document moves down one screen. Notice how the slider moves to indicate how far down the document you are.

▶ Click on the area of the scroll bar below the up-arrow. Each time you click this part of the scrollbar, the document moves up one screen, and the slider moves to indicate how far up the document you are.

▶ Finally, practice dragging the slider to jump to different places in the document. To drag the slider, position your mouse on it, then hold down the mouse button while you move the slider up or down. When you release the mouse button, the document jumps to the new position. Practice dragging the slider to the bottom, middle, and top of the document.

Colors, and click the color swatches for Visited Links and Unvisited Links. Even though you can change the colors, however, it is recommended that you not modify them unless you have a special reason for doing so.

Sometimes the color selections you make have no effect on the colors you see on a Web page. That is because the Web page author may have preset the hypertext links to specific colors that you cannot change. Unless the author has preset the colors on the Web page, the color preferences you choose will take effect.

HYPERGRAPHIC LINKS

A **hypergraphic link** is a graphical hot spot that you click to trigger the events that are linked to the image onscreen. The image can range in size from a small icon to a large picture.

Well-designed Web pages make it obvious where to click to make different things happen. Poorly designed pages can be confusing if they're not clear on what will happen when you click a link. In Part Five, you will learn how to design Web pages that make it clear what will happen when the user clicks a link.

Figure 4-2 shows a Web page with an interesting combination of hypertext and hypergraphic links. Its URL is http://www.loc.gov. Point your browser there (to "point" your browser means to go to the URL) and try clicking the different hypertext and hypergraphic links.

IMAGE MAPS

An image may have more than one hot spot; if so, clicking different parts of the image triggers different links. Consider the question being asked in Figure 4-3. The user is being asked to click Middle C on a piano keyboard. The image has triggers on the region of the keyboard below C, above C, and on Middle C itself. Depending on where the user clicks, the appropriate feedback is given.

Figure 4-4 maps the triggers in Figure 4-3. The technique used to map multiple triggers onto an image is known as an **image map.** In Part Five, you learn how to create image maps.

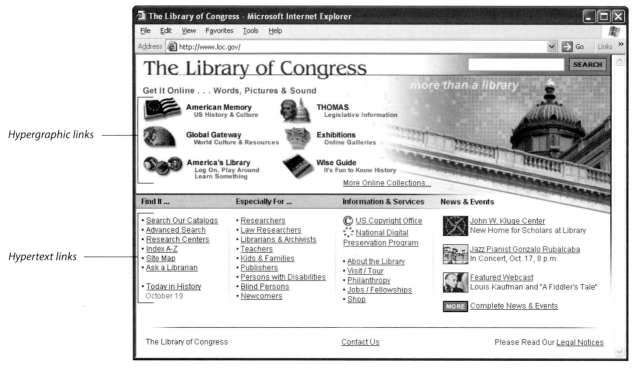

Figure 4-2   This Web page contains both hypertext and hypergraphic links. When you move your mouse over these links, notice that your cursor changes shape to indicate that you are hovering over a hot spot.

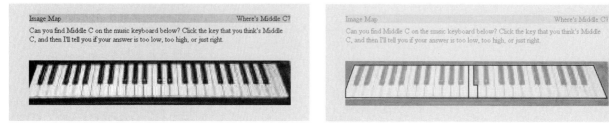

Figure 4-3   The student is asked to click Middle C on a music keyboard.

Figure 4-4   Mapping of the triggers in Figure 4-3.

Navigation Buttons

At the top of your browser you should see a row of navigation buttons with names such as Forward, Back, Home, and Stop. Figure 4-5 shows how the buttons appear in Firefox, and Figure 4-6 shows the navigation buttons in Internet Explorer. If these navigation buttons are not showing on your screen, you can make them visible by following the steps in Table 4-3.

One of the most useful navigation buttons is the Back button. If you end up someplace you did not want to go, clicking the Back button will return you to the page from which you triggered the ill-chosen link. Conversely, the Forward button will move you ahead to pages that you visited previously during your current browsing session. Right-clicking on back or forward pops out a menu that shows the whole path you covered, and you can click a site to jump directly to it. *Note to Macintosh users:* On a Mac, you trigger the menu by holding down Ctrl during the click or by holding down the mouse button until the menu pops out.

Any time you want to return to your browser's default home page, just click the Home button. If you want to change your browser's default home page, follow the steps in Table 4-4.

Use the Stop button if you want to interrupt your browser. Sometimes it may appear as though the Internet has gotten stuck after you click on a trigger to go somewhere. If you wait for a while with no response, try clicking the Stop button to cancel the request, and then click the trigger

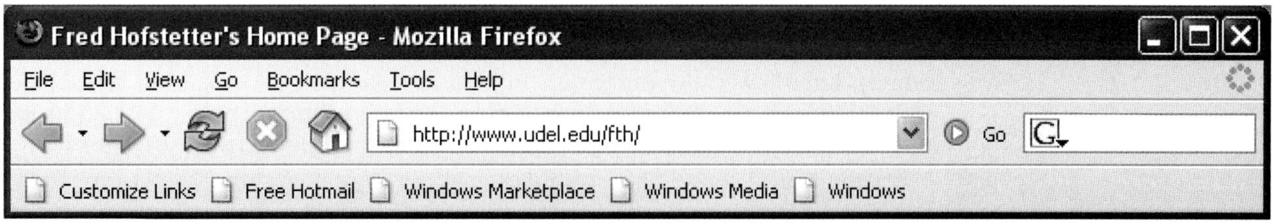

Figure 4-5 Navigation buttons in Firefox. You can change the appearance of these buttons by pulling down the Tools menu and choosing Themes.

Figure 4-6 Navigation buttons in Internet Explorer.

Table 4-3 How to make your browser's navigation buttons visible

Firefox	Internet Explorer
▶ Pull down the View menu.	▶ Pull down the View menu and choose Toolbars.
▶ Choose Toolbars→Navigation Toolbar.	▶ If Standard Buttons is not checked, choose Standard Buttons.
▶ If the navigation buttons still do not appear, right-click the toolbar and choose Navigation Toolbar.	▶ If the navigation buttons still do not appear, right-click the toolbar and choose Standard Buttons.

Table 4-4 How to change your browser's default home page

Firefox	Internet Explorer
▶ If you have Windows, pull down the Tools menu, choose Options, and click the General tab, if it is not already selected.	▶ Pull down the Tools menu and choose Internet Options.
▶ If you have a Macintosh, pull down the Firefox menu, choose Preferences, and click the General icon.	▶ Click the General tab, if it is not already selected.
▶ In the Home Page group's Location field, enter the URL of the desired home page.	▶ In the Address field, type the URL of your desired home page.
▶ Click OK to close the dialog.	▶ Click OK to close the dialog.

again. This will usually get things moving again. Another use of the Stop button is to cancel a process that is taking too long. For example, you may have clicked a trigger to download a movie that could take more than an hour to arrive over a slow Internet connection. Clicking the Stop button interrupts the download so you do not have to wait an hour.

Manipulating URLs

You can play some tricks with URLs to help find information. For example, suppose you have been told to go to the URL http://www.microsoft.com/windows/ie/enthusiast/default. mspx for a list of tips to help you learn more about the features of Internet Explorer. You find the list helpful, and you are curious what else is available at this site. By progressively stripping off the subfolder names of the path to the original document you were given, you can go to the higher levels of the Web site, and use them as surfing-off points. For example, http://www.microsoft.com/windows/ie/ takes you to a menu of other links related to Internet Explorer. Stripping off the last part of the URL (i.e., /ie) and trying http://www.microsoft.com/windows/ brings up a list of feature articles related to Windows technologies. Going all the way back to http://www.microsoft.com takes you to the Microsoft default page.

It is easy to manipulate URLs in this manner by using your browser's URL field. Click once in the field, position your cursor at the end of the URL, and backspace to erase the last part of the URL. If your browser's URL field is not visible, follow the steps in Table 4-1 to make it appear. Click once inside the URL field to position your cursor there, erase anything that already appears in the field, type the URL http://www.loc.gov/exhibits/flw/flw03.html and press Enter to go there. Then complete the following exercise, which will help you learn how to manipulate a URL:

- Position your cursor at the end of the URL field and use the backspace key to erase the last part of the URL, which is /flw03.html. Press Enter. Your Web browser displays the Web page of the manipulated URL.

- Once again, position your cursor at the end of the URL field, and use the backspace key to erase the last part of the URL, which is /flw. Press Enter to go to the manipulated URL.

- Repeat this process for each part of the URL until all you have in the URL field is http://www.loc.gov—this is the URL of the Library of Congress Web server. LOC stands for Library of Congress.

Stripping off parts of the URL in this manner normally brings you to the home page of the Web site where the page resides. Taking a look at the site's home page takes you to the source of the information, which can help you judge how reliable the information is. Remember that anyone can publish pages to the Web. If you discover that one page about airplanes, for example, came from the Smithsonian's air and space museum, while another page came from a four-year-old child learning how to build paper airplanes, you would consider the page from the Smithsonian to have greater authority. Going to the source of the information also can help you find related information available at the site and correct errors in the URL if the original file could not be found.

Partial URLs

Many people are unaware of one of the greatest time-savers in typing URLs. Both Firefox and Internet Explorer allow you to type partial URLs. A partial URL is a shortened form of a complete URL, which the browser automatically expands into a complete URL. For example, the complete URL of the Weather Channel is http://www.weather.com, but you do not need to type all of that to get there. Follow these steps to learn how to use partial URLs:

- Begin by typing the complete URL http://www.weather.com into your browser's URL field, and press Enter. Your browser takes you to the Weather Channel. Now click Home to return to your browser's home page.

- Repeat the process, but this time, only type www.weather.com and press Enter. Notice how your browser automatically fills in the http:// for you and takes you to the Weather Channel. Almost every Web address begins with http://, and by not having to type that specifically, you can save a lot of time. Click Home to return to your browser's home page.

- Now try weather.com to see if your browser still takes you to the Weather Channel.

- Finally, try typing the single word weather. Where does your browser take you now?

Table 4-5 How to resize and position a window

Desired Window Movement	Windows	Macintosh
Maximize the window	Double-click the title bar or click the ▢ icon.	Click the ◯ icon in the upper-left corner of the window.
Unmaximize the window	Double-click the title bar or click the ▣ icon.	Click the ◯ icon in the upper-left corner of the window.
Size the window	Click and drag the corners or the sides of the unmaximized window.	Click and drag the lower-right corner of the unmaximized window.
Move the window	Click and drag the title bar of the unmaximized window.	Click and drag the title bar of the unmaximized window.

Coping with "404: File Not Found" Errors

The Web is a work in progress. People are adding new Web pages and revising things all the time. Sometimes these changes can cause URLs that worked previously to become invalid. If you get a "File Not Found" error, try manipulating the URL by removing the last part of it. Start by removing the filename, and see if the URL takes you somewhere useful. If that does not work, try removing the folder names. By progressively stripping off the filename and then the folders, you can usually get the URL to take you to a Web page from which you can browse to what you need.

Sizing and Positioning Your Browser Window

Normally, when you surf the Net, you will want your browser's window to be full screen so you will be able to view the maximum amount of the document you are reading. There are times, however, when you will want the browser to be less than full screen. For example, you might want to have two browser windows open simultaneously so you can do side-by-side comparisons of the information at different Web sites. Table 4-5 shows how to size and position a window.

Get your Web browser running, and practice the steps in Table 4-5. Make your window fill the screen; then make it small. Size the window to make it long and narrow, then short and wide. With practice, you will form your own personal habits for how large or small you prefer your windows to be for different purposes.

Working with Multiple Windows

Windows and the Macintosh are both multitasking operating systems. That means you can have more than one task running at a time. If you are writing a term paper, for example, you can have your word processor running at the same time as your Web browser. When you get an idea from surfing the Web, you can quickly switch to your word processor and make a note of that idea.

To work with multiple windows, you need to know how to make a particular window become visible when you want to view it, and how to hide the window when you want something else on your screen. Table 4-6 shows how to do this.

Try working with multiple windows now. Get your Web browser running, then hide it. Now get your word processor running, and hide it. Follow the instructions in Table 4-6 to make your Web browser visible again. Now make your word processor become visible. Avoid the temptation to relaunch the running program; you want to make the running copy of the program become visible, not start a new instance of the program.

Table 4-6   How to hide and reveal a window

Desired Window Movement	Windows	Macintosh
Hide a window	Click the window's ▬ icon.	Click in a different window or window shade, or click an item in the Dock.
Show a hidden window	Hold down the Alt key and press Tab until the window's icon appears.	Click the window's icon in the Dock.

Focusing on a Purpose

When doing research out on the Web, you need to remain focused on the reason why you are browsing. A whole world of interconnected information is available to you, and it is loaded with distractions. Novices invariably surf off into unintended directions and spend hours pursuing things off course. Sometimes this can be fun and adventurous, but if it becomes habitual, you will waste a lot of time.

Be mindful of the purpose for which you are using the Net, and try to remain focused. If you avoid the distractions, you can usually find what you are looking for quickly.

Distractions to Avoid (or to Enjoy)

Mass-market retailers have discovered the potential of the Internet to advertise products. Many Web sites sell advertising space. When you visit a site that contains commercial advertising, you will likely encounter a "tickler" in the form of an attractive graphic enticing you to click and launch the ad, as illustrated in Figure 4-7. Since the tickler usually appears on screen first, you may be tempted to click on the ad before your information arrives.

Instead of clicking on the ad, you need to discipline yourself to wait until your information appears. Although the ads can be fun, and sometimes you will want to click one, you need to be careful not to form a habit of meandering. Your time is limited, and you need to use it wisely. It is better to form the habit of not surfing off into unintended directions, and make such an adventure the exception, rather than the rule. This is getting harder to do because the commercial Web sites have databases that keep track of your likes and dislikes and buying habits. If you go to one of the Web's search engines and search for something related to automobiles, for example, the next ad you see will most likely be something related to cars. Try to stay focused on your purpose for conducting the search, and avoid the temptation to become distracted by the ads.

Bookmarking Your Favorite Sites

Web browsers have built-in support for bookmarks, which make it quick and easy for you to take note of your favorite Web pages and return to them later on. In a Web browser, a **bookmark** is a pointer to a Web page that enables you to jump directly to that page, without having to navigate the Web to get there.

As you surf the Net and become familiar with the wealth of resources available, you will begin to favor certain sites over others. To save time getting to your favorite sites, you can bookmark them. To bookmark a site, follow the steps in Table 4-7.

To jump to any site that you bookmarked, simply pull down your browser's Bookmark menu and select the bookmark you want. Your browser will take you to the bookmarked Web page. If you later decide you want to delete a bookmark, pull down your browser's Bookmark menu, right-click (Windows) or control-click (Macintosh) the bookmark to pop out the quick menu, and choose delete.

Figure 4-7   Advertising on the Net entices you to click the ad to launch a commercial product presentation,
http://www.miamiherald.com, January 3, 2005.

Source: Reprinted by permission of *The Miami Herald.*

Table 4-7   How to bookmark a Web page

Firefox	Internet Explorer
▶ Browse to the page you want to bookmark.	▶ Browse to the page you want to bookmark.
▶ Pull down the Bookmarks menu and chooose Bookmark This Page.	▶ Pull down the Favorites menu.
▶ If you have Windows, click OK.	▶ Click Add to Favorites.
▶ If you have a Macintosh, click Add.	▶ Click OK.

Table 4-8   How to create a bookmark folder

Firefox	Internet Explorer
▶ Pull down the Bookmarks menu and choose Manage Bookmarks; the Bookmarks Manager dialog appears as shown in Figure 4-8.	▶ Pull down the Favorites menu and choose Add to Favorites; the Add Favorite dialog appears.
	▶ Click the Create In button to expand the dialog to appear as shown in Figure 4-9.

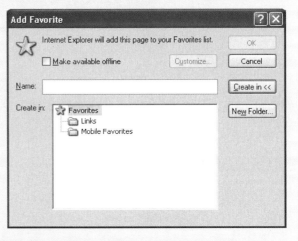

Figure 4-8   Firefox Bookmarks Manager dialog.

Figure 4-9   Internet Explorer Add Favorite dialog.

Firefox	Internet Explorer
▶ Click the New Folder button or pull down the File menu and choose New Folder; the New Folder Properties dialog appears.	▶ Click the New Folder button to make the Create New Folder dialog appear.
▶ In the Name field, type the name you want the new folder to have.	▶ In the Folder Name field, type the name you want the new folder to have.
▶ Click OK to close the Folder Properties dialog, and then close the Bookmark Manager.	▶ Click OK to close the Create New Folder dialog.
▶ To bookmark a Web site in a folder, pull down the Bookmarks menu, choose Bookmark This Page, and use the Create In menu to select the desired folder. If you have a Windows, click OK; if you have a Macintosh, click Add.	▶ Click OK to close the Add Favorite dialog.
	▶ To bookmark a Web site in a folder, pull down the Favorites menu, choose Add to Favorites, click Create In, select the desired folder, and click OK.

Using Bookmark Folders

You can organize your bookmarks in folders. This is recommended if you have a lot of bookmarks so you can organize them according to topics. You might make a folder called SearchEngines, for example, to hold bookmarks to your favorite search engines. Similarly, you might create a folder called Shopping in which you bookmark your favorite shopping sites. To create a bookmark folder, follow the steps in Table 4-8.

Retracing Your Steps: The History Folder

Both Firefox and Internet Explorer remember your most recently visited sites and make it possible for you to jump back to a previous site without having to press the Back button repeatedly to back through the sites one by one. To jump back to a site you previously visited, follow the steps in Table 4-9.

Auto Completion

Some browsers have a feature called auto completion. If you begin typing into the browser's URL field the address of a Web site that you visited previously, the browser auto-completes the entry to save you time. If you do not mean to go exactly to the address that gets auto-completed, just keep on typing, and the auto-completed address adjusts to what you type.

Table 4-9 How to jump back to a site previously visited

Firefox	Internet Explorer
▶ Pull down the Go menu; your most recently visited Web sites will be listed there. ▶ Select the site you want to jump to, and your browser will take you there.	▶ Click the History button; a History pane opens up to provide a visual display of the sites you visited. ▶ Click a category in the history to expand it, then click a Web site to go there. ▶ If you want to hide the history, click the close icon in the upper-right corner of the history pane.

Table 4-10 How to increase the browser's viewing area

Firefox	Internet Explorer
▶ Pull down the View menu, choose Toolbars, and see if the Navigation Toolbar is checked; if so, click Navigation Toolbar to free the screen space used by the navigation buttons. (To reverse this, choose View→Toolbars→Navigation Toolbar.) ▶ Pull down the View menu, choose Toolbars, and see if the Bookmarks Toolbar is checked; if so, click Bookmarks Toolbar to turn it off. (To reverse this, choose View→Toolbars→Bookmarks Toolbar.) ▶ Pull down the View menu and see if the Status Bar is checked; if so, click Status Bar to free the screen space used by the Status Bar. (To reverse this, choose View→Status Bar.)	▶ Pull down the View menu, choose Toolbars, and see if the Standard Buttons are checked; if so, click Standard Buttons to turn the buttons off. ▶ Pull down the View menu, choose Toolbars, and see if the Address Bar option is checked; if so, click Address Bar to turn it off. ▶ Pull down the View menu and see if the Status Bar is checked; if so, click Status Bar to turn it off. ▶ To turn the toolbars back on, pull down the View menu, select Toolbars, and click the toolbars to turn them back on. ▶ To turn the status bar back on, pull down the View menu and select Status Bar.

When you begin typing a Web address you visited previously, some browsers will pop out a menu of similar addresses you visited. If you see the address you want in the menu, just click the address to go to it.

Creating More Screen Space

No matter how large your computer screen is, you will sometimes wish it were larger so more information would fit into it. You can play a couple of tricks to increase the viewing area of your Web browser. First, and most obvious, maximize the size of your browser window by following the instructions provided in Table 4-5. A more subtle trick is to turn off some of the options that make your browser use extra screen space. For example, turn off the display of the URL field to save a little screen space and increase the viewing area inside the browser. Turning off the navigation buttons frees even more screen space. You can still navigate by using your browser's shortcut navigation keys, or you can turn the navigation buttons back on again when you want them to reappear. Table 4-10 shows how to do these things according to your brand of browser.

Visiting Selected Web Sites

Having studied the browsing principles and techniques presented so far in this chapter, now you are ready to go out on the Net and do some serious surfing. The remainder of this chapter consists of an illustrated tour of recommended Web sites.

Following the instructions provided in Table 4-1, How to go to a URL, you should visit each one of these sites using the URL printed alongside the name of each site. You will probably want to bookmark most of these sites, to make them easy for you to visit subsequently. To bookmark a site, follow the instructions provided in Table 4-7, How to bookmark a Web page.

CNN

At www.cnn.com you will find the Cable News Network (CNN) Web site. Figure 4-10 shows how it presents a menu of local, national, and world news; sports and weather information; and special features including health, style, and travel. Be sure to scroll down

Figure 4-10   The Cable News Network site at www.cnn.com, January 3, 2005.

to see information that does not appear all at once on your screen. This is a large Web page that you need to scroll in order to reveal it all. Click on your interests and become informed.

Amazon.com

Fulfill your shopping fantasies at www.amazon.com. Here you will find a wide range of products, as illustrated in Figure 4-11. If you do not find the item you want by browsing through the list of products, use the Search feature to find the product you want. For other shopping sites, follow the *Interlit* Web site links to reviews and rankings of online stores. Amazon is featured here because, when this book went to press, Amazon was the highest rated site for general-purpose shopping.

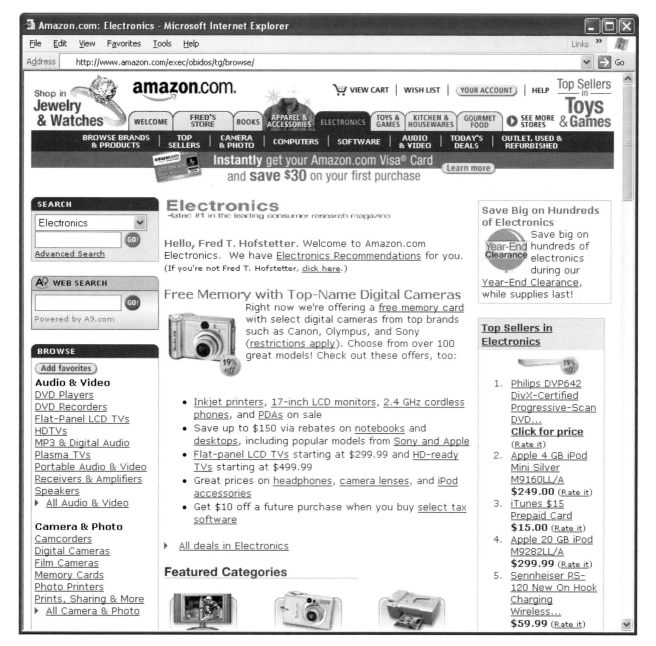

Figure 4-11   You can buy products online or just browse at www.amazon.com.

Figure 4-12   The ESPN site at espn.go.com.

ESPN Sports

At espn.go.com you can find all the latest information about your favorite sport. As illustrated in Figure 4-12, you can choose basketball, hockey, baseball, soccer, golf, football, tennis, auto racing, and more. Be sure to scroll down to peruse all of the sports headlines; this is a large Web page that will not appear on your screen all at once.

NASA Goddard Space Flight Center

How fortunate we are that NASA conducts an outreach program to the schools. At the Goddard Space Flight Center site pictured in Figure 4-13, you can click the Education button to bring up an index of education links. Programs for K–12 include program descriptions and sample lesson materials correlated to the national standards in mathematics, science, and technology education. Higher-education programs

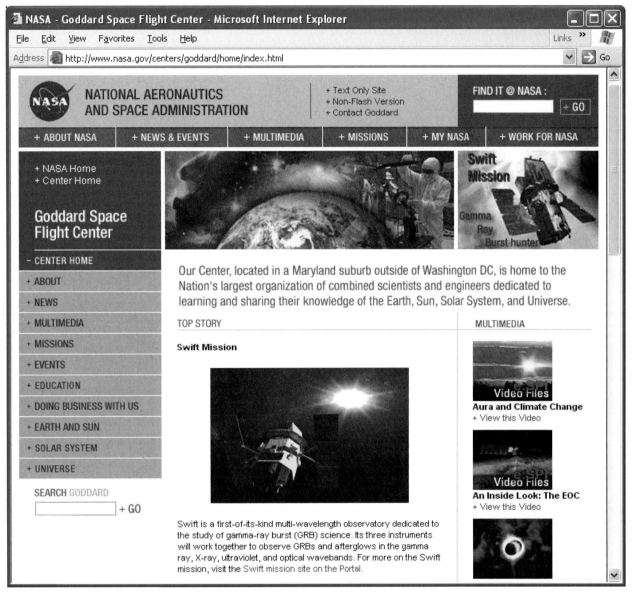

Figure 4-13 The NASA Goddard Space Flight Center at www.nasa.gov/centers/Goddard.

provide support for postdoctoral opportunities and resources. Cool tools include the NASA Technology portal and NASA-TV, which provides real-time coverage of space missions and educational programming to teachers, students, and the general public. You will find the NASA Goddard Space Flight Center on the Web at www.nasa.gov/centers/goddard.

Government Online (THOMAS)

Named after Thomas Jefferson, THOMAS is a Web-based information service of the U.S. Congress. As depicted in Figure 4-14, you can visit the THOMAS site to find out what is happening on the floor of the House and the Senate, check the status of pending bills and legislation, and read the *Congressional Record*. Also online at this site are historical documents and an index of U.S. Government Information Services. You also can find out the e-mail address of any senator or congressional representative, and find out how your

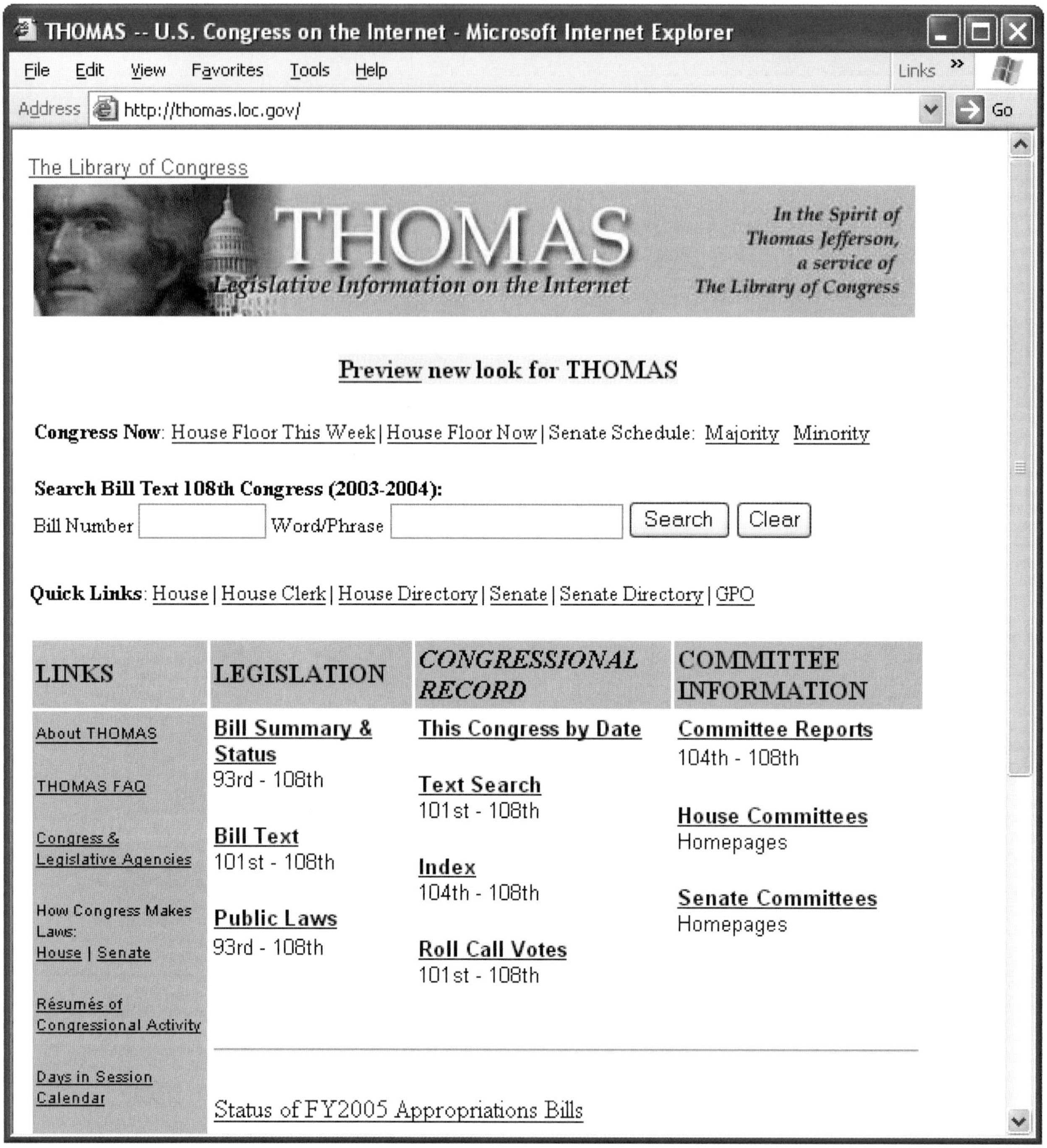

THOMAS -- U.S. Congress on the Internet - Microsoft Internet Explorer

File   Edit   View   Favorites   Tools   Help   Links »

Address   http://thomas.loc.gov/   Go

The Library of Congress

THOMAS
Legislative Information on the Internet

*In the Spirit of
Thomas Jefferson,
a service of
The Library of Congress*

Preview new look for THOMAS

Congress Now: House Floor This Week | House Floor Now | Senate Schedule: Majority   Minority

Search Bill Text 108th Congress (2003-2004):

Bill Number [＿＿＿]   Word/Phrase [＿＿＿＿＿＿＿]   [Search] [Clear]

Quick Links: House | House Clerk | House Directory | Senate | Senate Directory | GPO

LINKS	LEGISLATION	*CONGRESSIONAL RECORD*	COMMITTEE INFORMATION
About THOMAS	**Bill Summary & Status** 93rd - 108th	**This Congress by Date**	**Committee Reports** 104th - 108th
THOMAS FAQ		**Text Search** 101st - 108th	**House Committees** Homepages
Congress & Legislative Agencies	**Bill Text** 101st - 108th	**Index** 104th - 108th	
How Congress Makes Laws: House | Senate	**Public Laws** 93rd - 108th	**Roll Call Votes** 101st - 108th	**Senate Committees** Homepages
Résumés of Congressional Activity			
Days in Session Calendar	Status of FY2005 Appropriations Bills		

Figure 4-14   Located at thomas.loc.gov, THOMAS is operated for the United States Congress by the Library of Congress.

representatives voted on recent legislation. To check how well you are being represented, visit THOMAS at thomas.loc.gov.

Louvre

Figure 4-15 shows how the world-famous *musée du Louvre,* the largest museum in western Europe, is online at www.louvre.fr. Here you will find an electronic version of the *Louvre* magazine, a schedule of cultural activities, a guide to the collections, the history of the buildings, and thousands of images, including the famous *Mona Lisa.* Originally available only in French,

Figure 4-15   The famous *musée du Louvre* is on the Web at www.louvre.fr.

the site now has buttons you can click for different languages, including English, Spanish, and Japanese. There are QuickTime VR (virtual reality) images that let you take 3D walks through parts of the museum. If you try to take one of the VR tours and your computer does not have the QuickTime plug-in, your browser will prompt you to install it, or you can go directly to www.apple.com/quicktime and follow the onscreen instructions to install the latest release of QuickTime, which is available both in Windows and Macintosh versions.

Newspapers

The NewsLink site provides access to the top-25 rated online newspapers, plus more than 18,000 other links to newspapers, magazines, broadcasters, and news services around the world. As you can see from the list of awards along the right margin of Figure 4-16, this is one of the top-rated sites on the Web.

Autobytel

If you are looking to buy or sell a car, you should first go to www.autobytel.com. As illustrated in Figure 4-17, you can research new and used cars by make and category. If you are interested in a minivan, for example, and you do not know which brand you want, Autobytel shows you a picture menu featuring all the brands in your price range, and you can follow the links to compare prices and options for all the different models. If you have a used car to trade in, blue-book values are instantly available to help you negotiate a fair price for your trade. Sites such as autobytel.com can really save you money when you buy or sell a car.

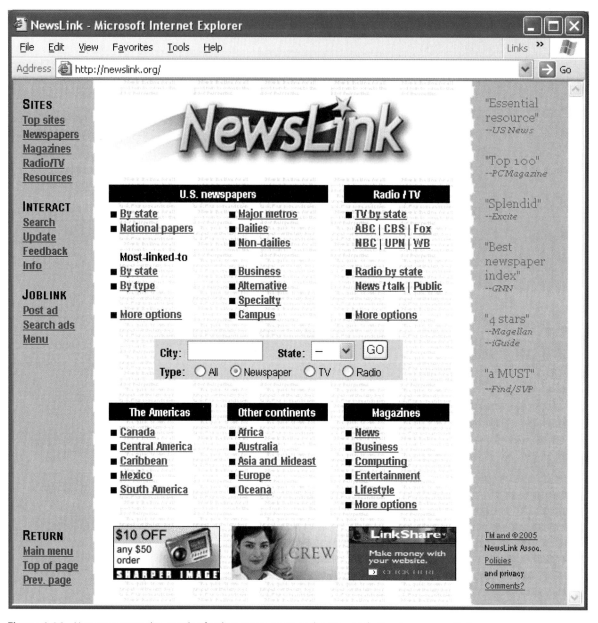

Figure 4-16   You can access thousands of online newspapers at the NewsLink site at www.newslink.org.

Smithsonian

The Smithsonian Institution sponsors many Internet services that provide access to materials from its various museums and research arms. For example, the National Air and Space Museum, the National Museum of American Art, and the National Museum of Natural History are all online. You can search the Smithsonian databases, join discussion groups, and explore information on the Smithsonian's many museums, galleries, research centers, and offices. Figure 4-18 shows how you can access all of these resources on the Web at www.si.edu.

Stock Exchanges

You can find the New York Stock Exchange (NYSE) at www.nyse.com. Designed as an educational tool for investors, students, and teachers, this Web site presents the NYSE in its role as publisher, generator of news, patron of education, sponsor of scholarly

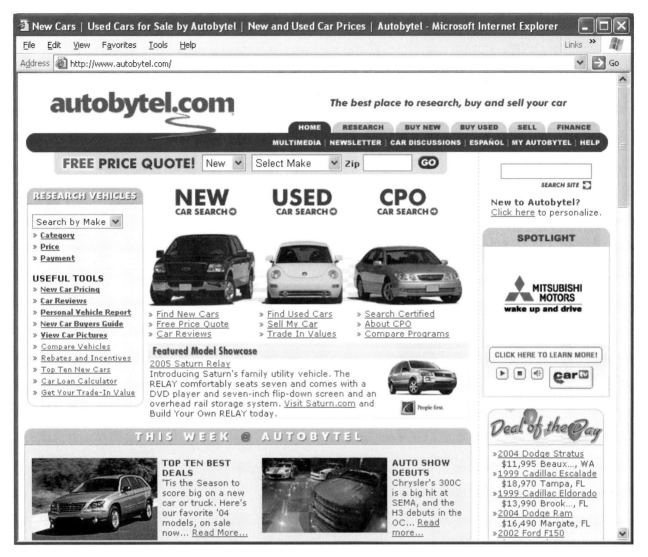

Figure 4-17 New and used car buying and selling at www.autobytel.com.

research, and storehouse of statistical data. Figure 4-19 shows how the NYSE site enables you to begin a tour of the world's largest ($18 trillion global market value) securities market. Also on the Web is the NASDAQ Stock Market, which is at www.nasdaq.com. Figure 4-20 shows how the NASDAQ site lets you enter up to 10 stock symbols and get fast quotes or more detailed InfoQuotes including current prices and company information. If you are using Internet Explorer, you can click the NASDAQ Toolbar button to download the free NASDAQ Toolbar, which is a browser plug-in that appears along with the Internet Explorer toolbar to provide quick access to NASDAQ content and resources.

TERC

TERC is a nonprofit research and development organization committed to improving mathematics and science teaching and learning. Founded in 1965, TERC is internationally recognized for creating innovative curricula, fostering the professional development of teachers, pioneering creative uses of technology in education, helping educators understand and benefit from the results of educational research, and developing equitable

Figure 4-18   The Smithsonian Institution is on the Web at www.si.edu.

opportunities for underserved learners. You can learn more about TERC and the programs it sponsors by going to www.terc.edu. Figure 4-21 shows the TERC home page, which provides a menu of projects for you to peruse.

Weather Channel

Weather is one of life's common denominators because everybody seems to care about it. You can find out the current weather conditions and forecast for almost every city in the United States and in many international cities at the Weather Channel Web site. Figure 4-22 shows how you find it on the Web at www.weather.com. Clicking the name of a city on the forecasts ticker brings up a detailed weather report for that city, complete with local and regional Doppler radar and weather satellite maps.

Figure 4-19   The New York Stock Exchange is on the Web at www.nyse.com.

Figure 4-20   The NASDAQ Stock Market is online at www.nasdaq.com.

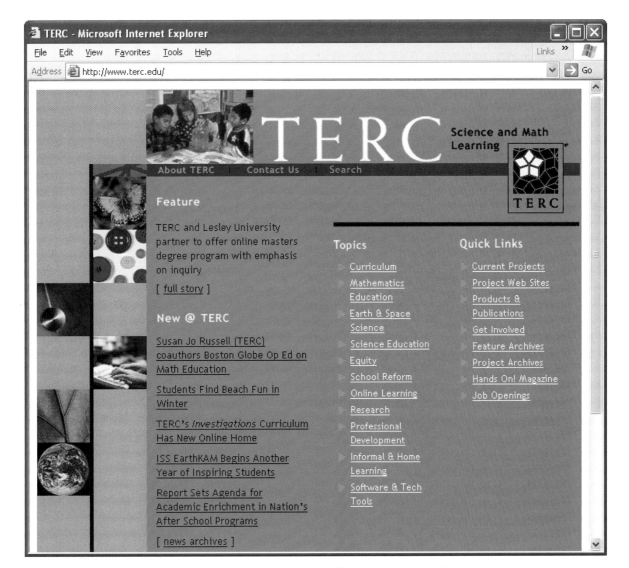

Figure 4-21   Some of the innovative projects you can visit at the TERC site at www.terc.edu.

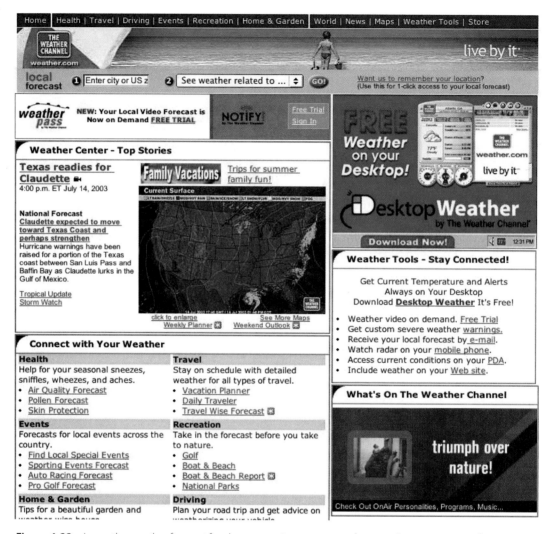

Figure 4-22 Learn the weather forecast for almost any city at www.weather.com. Image courtesy of *The Weather Channel®*.

White House

To kindle your patriotic spirit, visit the White House at www.whitehouse.gov. After reading the top stories, you can use the menus to access the resources in Figure 4-23. In addition to taking a tour and writing e-mail to the president and vice president, you can get briefings on hot topics and the latest federal statistics. Clicking the KIDS link takes you to the White House for Kids, which is intended to help young people become more active and informed citizens. *Warning:* Especially if you have children, you should be aware that the name *whitehouse* is also used on the Net for some rather questionable content. When you tell someone to go to the White House Web site, therefore, make sure you mention specifically the *.gov* top-level-domain name and tell the person to go to www.whitehouse.gov.

MapQuest

If you plan to drive somewhere, you can save time by first getting a map from www.mapquest.com. As illustrated in Figure 4-24, MapQuest not only provides you with maps and driving instructions to and from any address or intersection in the United States, Canada, and Mexico, but it also warns you of any accidents or major delays along the way. You can even get this information en route via MapQuest's wireless services or download the information to your PDA before you leave.

Clicking the KIDS link takes you to the White House for Kids, which is intended to help young people become more active and informed citizens.

Figure 4-23 Resources available at the White House Web site.

Internet Movie Database

Rated by ZDNet as the best movie site on the Web, the Internet Movie Database (IMDb) catalogs more than 400,000 movies and keeps information on over 1.6 million actors and actresses. Figure 4-25 shows how you can visit the database at www.imdb.com, where you can search the database for free, look up movie showtimes, watch trailers, and use message boards to converse with other users about the movies. When you look up a movie, you can ask for recommendations of other movies the database thinks you will also like, based on your viewing habits and preferences.

Finding More Cool Web Sites

There are more than four billion pages you can go to on the World Wide Web. Some are obviously better than others. To help you find the best sites, a company called About.com hires guides and pays them to keep updating and adding new information and links to Web sites in hundreds of different subjects. Figure 4-26 shows the page you get when you go to www.about.com. Notice that it has a list of subject areas. Because the guides who maintain the links are subject-matter experts in their respective fields, going to About.com is a good way to find some of the better Web sites on the Internet. When this book went to press, About.com had 475 guides.

Figure 4-24   Get maps, driving directions, and live traffic reports at www.mapquest.com.

Portals

A **portal** is a Web site whose purpose is to provide access to other Web sites and services on the Internet. Portals organize their links and services in a manner that is appealing to the users. There is a lot of competition among the portals, which want you to keep coming back for more. They are all trying to get you to make their portal be your start page so you will see their ads each time you launch your Web browser. It is the income from the ads that pays for the portals and enables you to have free access.

The owners of the portals know that the more they can make their services match your needs, the more likely it is that you will make their portal be your start page. No two users are exactly the same, however. People have different needs and preferences. Some people like to follow football scores, for example, while others couldn't care less. People who live in New York are interested in East Coast weather, while Californians want West Coast weather reports. Investors want to be able to track the value of some stocks but not others. These kinds of differences among individual users set the stage for the popularity of personal portals.

Personal Portals

A **personal portal** is a Web site that lets users set preferences, which make the portal show the kinds of information the user wants to see, and hide what the user is not interested in. Thus, the personal portal becomes the user's customized launch pad to other sites and

Figure 4-25   The Internet Movie Database at www.imdb.com.

services on the Web. From your perspective, the personal portal is "my" portal. Hence the names *My Yahoo, My Excite,* and *My Lycos* for the personal portals you can set up at Yahoo, Excite, and Lycos, respectively.

MY YAHOO!

My Yahoo!

At Yahoo, for example, the personal portal lets you pick cities for weather reports, track your stock quotes, read your choice of news, find local movie showtimes, and follow your favorite sports teams. To set up a personal portal at Yahoo, go to www.yahoo.com and click the My button, or go to my.yahoo.com.

MY EXCITE

My Excite

My Excite lets you customize your start page with colors, news, stock quotes, sports scores, horoscopes, and your favorite cartoons. To get started, go to www.excite.com and click the link to personalize your start page. After you register, you follow the onscreen instructions that let you click to add, change, or remove content; arrange the layout of your modules; and select a color scheme for your page.

Figure 4-26   Subject-matter experts called guides keep the links and information up-to-date at www.about.com.

MY LYCOS

Lycos advertises its brand of personal portal as "your launch point to the Web." From your personal Lycos page, you can track your stock portfolio, get local weather forecasts, follow your favorite sports teams, see movie showtimes, stay informed of the news you care about, and read your daily horoscope. To set up a personal portal at Lycos, go to www.lycos.com and click My Lycos, or go to my.lycos.com.

In describing these different brands of personal portals, the author has been careful not to advocate for one over the other. If you want to see a comparison of the leading portals reviewed from a design perspective, follow the *Interlit* Web site link to Taking Portals Personally: A Design Review.

Managing Your Web Browser's Cache

When you surf the Web, your browser keeps copies of the most recently visited Web sites in a place on your hard disk called the **cache** (pronounced *cash*). As you navigate back and forth around the Web and revisit one of the sites in the cache, your browser will check to see if the timestamp on the Web site has changed since your local copy was cached. If the site has not changed, the browser redisplays the site from the cache instead of downloading it again. Thus, the cache speeds your use of the Web and reduces traffic on the Net.

How to Manipulate the Cache

If you want to increase the number of pages your cache can hold, it is possible to change the size and location of the browser's cache. You can also purge (i.e., delete) the cache, which you might want to do if you have been reading sensitive information that you would not want someone else using your computer to find. Purging the cache also can fix problems when Web pages do not work properly, especially Web pages with Java, for which purging the cache causes the Java to reload. To manipulate your cache, follow the steps in Table 4-11.

Table 4-11   How to manipulate the cache

Firefox	Internet Explorer
▶ If you have Windows, pull down the Tools menu and choose Options; the Options dialog appears.	▶ Pull down the Tools menu and choose Internet Options; the Internet Options dialog appears.
▶ If you have a Macintosh, pull down the Firefox menu and choose Preferences.	▶ If the General tab is not already selected, click the General tab.
▶ Click the Privacy button to reveal the privacy options. One of the options is the Cache.	▶ The Temporary Internet Files group contains your cache controls. Click the Settings button to make the cache settings appear, as shown in Figure 4-28.
▶ Click the plus-sign (Windows) or arrow (Macintosh) alongside the Cache option; the Cache settings will appear as shown in Figure 4-27.	

Figure 4-27   Firefox cache settings.

▶ You can change the amount of your hard disk that is used for the cache by changing the number of kilobytes (KB) devoted to the cache. Do not change this unless you really want to modify this setting; most users never need to change this.

▶ To clear the cache, click the cache option's Clear button.

▶ When you are done manipulating the cache, click OK to close the Options dialog.

Figure 4-28   Internet Explorer cache settings.

▶ You can change the amount of your hard disk that is used for the cache by dragging the slider. Do not change this unless you really want to modify this setting; most users never need to change this.

▶ To move the cache to a different folder, click the Move Folder button. Do not do this unless you really know what you are doing. Most users never need to change the location of the cache.

▶ To view the contents of your cache, click the View Files button.

▶ Click OK to close the cache settings dialog.

▶ To purge the cache, click the Delete Files button in the Temporary Internet Files group.

▶ Click OK to close the Internet Options dialog.

exercises

These exercises are intended to be done in order, from number 1 through 7, consecutively.

1. Get your Web browser running if it isn't already, and go to the URL http://www.loc.gov/exhibits/gadd/ gadrft.html.

2. Use your mouse to resize the dimensions of the browser window. Notice how the information inside the window flows to fit the shape that you make the window. If you cannot grab the frame of the window and resize it with your mouse, the window might be maximized. Double-click the window's title bar to unmaximize it. If you have trouble, refer to Table 4-5 for help.

3. Make the browser window invisible by minimizing it. Now make the window visible again. If you have trouble doing this, refer to Table 4-6 for help.

4. Practice using the scroll bar to move the document up and down inside your browser window. Fix your eyes on a line of text near the bottom of the screen and practice moving it to the top, and then back down to the bottom of the screen. Practice dragging the scroll button to jump to different parts of the Web page. Drag the button all the way to the bottom to get to the end of the page, then drag it back to the top.

5. Increase your browser's viewing space by turning off the display of the URL field and the navigation buttons. Notice how you can see more of the document when these options are turned off. If you have trouble doing this, refer to Table 4-10 for help.

6. Turn the URL field and the navigation buttons back on. Explore the higher levels of the URL by stripping off items from the end of it. For example, what do you find at http://www.loc.gov/exhibits/gadd? What is at http://www.loc.gov/exhibits? How about http://www.loc.gov?

7. Bookmark the site you are on now. Then go to the URL http://www.amazon.com. After the new screen appears, see if you can return to the site you just bookmarked by accessing it from your browser's bookmark menu. If you have trouble, refer to Table 4-7 for help.

SITUATED CASE PROJECTS
Case 4: Sharing Bookmarks and Favorites

At the end of each chapter in this book, a situated case project provides the student an opportunity to put the chapter's contents to practical use in a workplace situation. Each case has the same number as the chapter in which it appears.

One of the most valuable resources a school or company can have is a list of good, reliable, recommended Web sites where employees can go to accomplish the kinds of tasks typical of the workplace. In this chapter you learned how the browsers have a mechanism for accessing such sites quickly. Internet Explorer calls it Favorites, whereas Firefox calls it Bookmarks. Regardless of what you call it, bookmarks and favorites provide a quick and easy way for users to access Web sites.

Imagine that your employer has asked you to create a common list of bookmarks and favorites that your fellow employees can use to enhance productivity in your workplace. Both Firefox and Internet Explorer have import and export mechanisms for doing this. Follow these steps:

1. Use your Web browser to visit the sites you want included in the list of bookmarks or favorites.

2. While you are at each site, follow the steps in Table 4-7 to bookmark it.

3. Do not be concerned if you feel your list is a little short. You will be able to add more bookmarks later, when you learn to find more appropriate Web sites using search strategies taught later in this book.

4. Follow the steps in Table 4-8 to create folders that organize your bookmarks according to categories.

5 If you have Internet Explorer, follow these steps:

    a. Pull down the File menu and choose Import and Export; the Import/Export Wizard appears.

    b. Click Next to begin the Wizard, and follow the onscreen instructions.

    c. When the Wizard asks what you want to import or export, choose Export Favorites.

    d. When the Wizard asks what folder or subfolder of the favorites you want to export from, click what you want and click Next.

    e. When the Wizard asks where you want to save the exported favorites, click the Browse button to choose the folder of your choice. Your *bookmark.htm* file will be copied into the folder you designate. Click Next.

6 If you have Firefox, follow these steps:

    a. Pull down the Bookmarks menu and choose Manage Bookmarks. The Bookmarks Manager window appears.

    b. In your Bookmarks Manager window, pull down the File menu, and choose Export.

    c. In the Export Bookmark File dialog, choose a folder. Your *bookmarks.html* file will be copied into the folder you choose.

    d. Click Save.

If your instructor has asked you to hand in the exported bookmark file, the file to submit will be named bookmark.htm (Internet Explorer) or bookmarks.html (Firefox). Copy that file to a disk, or follow the other instructions your instructor gave you for submitting this assignment. If you have trouble finding the bookmark file, use the Macintosh Finder or the Windows Start→Search option to locate it. Later in this book, after you learn how to publish files on the Web, you will be able to publish this bookmark file to a location from which your users can easily access it over the Web or import it into their browser's bookmarks or favorites.

PART THREE
COMMUNICATING OVER THE INTERNET

We have got to start meeting this way.

—Lily Tomlin as Ernestine,
WebEx Commercial

The most powerful use of the Internet is for communicating with other users. Never before has a communications medium made it so quick, easy, and cost-effective to communicate with tens of millions of users all over the world. So great is the benefit that the Internet can truly be called a supermedium for communicating.

In this part of the book, you will learn techniques for communicating more effectively via *electronic mail,* which is a store-and-forward type of communications medium between two people; *listserv,* a way of communicating ideas to a specific group of people; *newsgroups,* which are online discussion groups in which the topics are organized hierarchically, allowing users to read and write messages and converse about the topics in a manner comparable to attending a conference; *blogs,* in which you publish a Web-accessible log that other users can read to keep up with what you are doing; *chat rooms* and other real-time environments for carrying on live conversations; and *streaming,* which you can use to tune in to real-time audio and video channels on the Internet.

Before you begin communicating on the Information Superhighway, however, you should learn some of the rules of the road. Therefore, we begin with a discussion of Internet etiquette.

5

INTERNET ETIQUETTE (NETIQUETTE)

After completing this chapter, you will be able to:

- Define the term *netiquette* and explain its derivation.

- Understand what it means to "spam" someone on the Internet, and know what to do if someone spams you.

- Be prepared to protect yourself against unethical users who use e-mail to spread hoaxes and send viruses that can damage your computer or the programs and data it contains.

- Understand the concept of lurking, and know when you should lurk.

- Know what it means to "flame" someone on the Internet.

- Understand the concept of SHOUTING on the Internet and become sensitized to not overdoing it.

- Recognize the more common smileys and other emoticons used on the Internet, and know how to look up the meaning of less common symbols.

- Understand what the more common three-letter acronyms mean, and know where to go on the Web to look up more esoteric acronyms.

- Understand some of the more commonly used Internet jargon, and know where to find a more complete listing of Internet terms and definitions.

● *Netiquette* is a term coined by combining the words "Internet etiquette" into a single name. **Netiquette** is the observance of certain rules and conventions that have evolved in order to keep the Internet from becoming a free-for-all in which tons of unwanted messages and junk mail would clog your Inbox and make the Information Superhighway an unfriendly place to be. This chapter presents the rules for commercial and educational use of the Internet, suggests a way for you to become a good citizen of the Net (network citizens are called *Netizens*), and defines everyday terms and jargon used on the Net.

Netiquette Guidelines

IETF

The Net: User Guidelines and Netiquette

In the "Netiquette Guidelines" section of the *Interlit* Web site, you will find links to the official rules of etiquette and ethics for responsible use of the Internet. Chief among these is RFC 1855, which was developed by the Responsible Use of the Network (RUN) Working Group of the Internet Engineering Task Force (IETF). This document consists of a bulleted list of specifications that organizations can use to create their own guidelines. For example, Arlene Rinaldi's award-winning Netiquette Home Page, which is entitled "The Net: User Guidelines and Netiquette," contains the Netiquette guidelines used at Florida Atlantic

University. The introduction explains how use of the Internet is a privilege, not a right:

> The use of the network is a privilege, not a right, which may temporarily be revoked at any time for abusive conduct. Such conduct would include, the placing of unlawful information on a system, the use of abusive or otherwise objectionable language in either public or private messages, the sending of messages that are likely to result in the loss of recipients' work or systems, the sending of "chain letters" or "broadcast" messages to lists or individuals, and any other types of use which would cause congestion of the networks or otherwise interfere with the work of others.

American Association for Higher Education

Another example of Netiquette guidelines was developed by Frank Connolly in conjunction with the American Association for Higher Education and EDUCAUSE. Connolly's *Bill of Rights and Responsibilities for Electronic Learners* is a succinct and eloquent statement of Netiquette guidelines. To read these guidelines, follow the links to the *Bill of Rights* at the *Interlit* Web site. Also linked to the *Interlit* Web site is a related article by Connolly entitled "Intellectual Honesty in the Era of Computing." The most commonly known Netiquette rules are as follows:

- Use business language and write professionally in all work-related messages.

- Remember that your message may be printed or forwarded to other people.

- Proofread and correct errors in your message before sending it.

- Do not use all capital letters because this connotes shouting.

- Keep in mind that your reader does not have the benefit of hearing your tone of voice and facial clues.

- Remember that the time, date, and reply address are added automatically to your e-mail message; therefore, you do not need to type this information.

- Always include an appropriate subject line in an e-mail message.

- Respond promptly to e-mail.

CPSR

Whenever you use the Internet, you should observe the ethics principles illustrated in Figure 5-1, which lists the Ten Commandments of Computer Use. These principles were

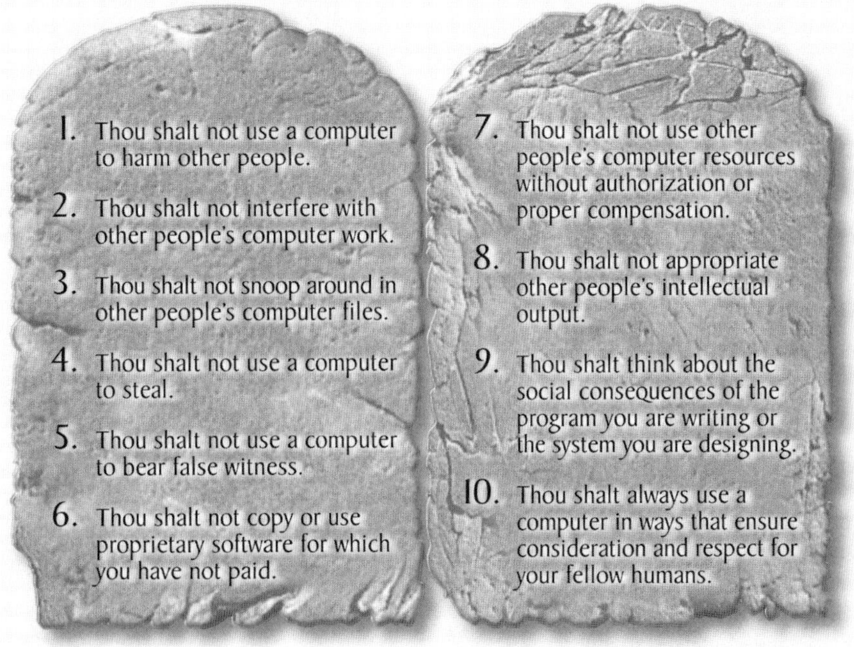

1. Thou shalt not use a computer to harm other people.
2. Thou shalt not interfere with other people's computer work.
3. Thou shalt not snoop around in other people's computer files.
4. Thou shalt not use a computer to steal.
5. Thou shalt not use a computer to bear false witness.
6. Thou shalt not copy or use proprietary software for which you have not paid.
7. Thou shalt not use other people's computer resources without authorization or proper compensation.
8. Thou shalt not appropriate other people's intellectual output.
9. Thou shalt think about the social consequences of the program you are writing or the system you are designing.
10. Thou shalt always use a computer in ways that ensure consideration and respect for your fellow humans.

Figure 5-1 The Ten Commandments of Computer Use.

Source: Computer Ethics Institute at www.cpsr.org/program/ethics/cei.html.

developed by the Computer Ethics Institute in Washington, D.C. Computer Professionals for Social Responsibility (CPSR) maintains a list of other current links to Web sites devoted to computer ethics on the Internet. To peruse them, follow the *Interlit* Web site link to the CPSR computer ethics links.

Spam

On the Internet, the term **spam** refers to unwanted messages posted to newsgroups or sent to a list of users through e-mail. The term can be used either as a verb or a noun. To spam means to send unwanted messages to a list of users on the Internet. Likewise, unwanted messages that you receive are called *spam*.

Perhaps the most obnoxious form of spam is unwanted commercial advertising. The Coalition Against Unsolicited Commercial Email (CAUCE) has done the math, and the outlook is daunting. As CAUCE chairman Scott Hazen Mueller explains, "There are 24 million small businesses in the United States, according to the Small Business Administration. If just one percent of those businesses sent you just one e-mail advertisement a year, that's 657 e-mail advertisements in your inbox each day" (CAUCE, 2001).

To prevent this from happening, Congress enacted the CAN-SPAM Act, which took effect on January 1, 2004. This legislation requires that e-mailed advertising contain a working Unsubscribe link. Furthermore, the CAN-SPAM Act makes it illegal to falsify the From and Subject lines of an e-mail message. For violations, spammers can be jailed for up to five years and fined up to a million dollars. In practice, however, few spammers have been convicted, while the amount of spam has mounted to consume as much as 75 to 80 percent of the typical user's e-mail. As a result, ISPs are looking to technological instead of legislative means of reducing the amount of spam on the Internet. The strategy is to create e-mail authentication technology that would make it harder for spammers to falsify the origin of their messages.

There are other forms of spam besides unwanted commercial advertising. A lot of chain letters, for example, are circulating on the Internet. Chain letters are spam; do not send or forward them. If you get one, you may be tempted to send a message to the originator stating that chain letters are an unethical use of the Internet, and that the sender should be ashamed of so littering the Information Superhighway. Be aware, however, that responding to spam lets the spammer know that your e-mail address is valid, thereby increasing the likelihood that you may receive more spam.

Some useful suggestions for fighting spam are found at the *Interlit* Web site. If you follow the links to "Fight Spam on the Internet," you will find a tutorial entitled "How to Complain to the Spammer's Provider." By following the link to the blacklist of Internet advertisers, you can see the worst offenders and read how they have violated the rules of Netiquette. For the latest on attempts to reduce the amount of spam, follow the links to anti-spam legislation and e-mail authentication technology.

Hoaxes

Some pretty incredible hoaxes have been propagated across the Internet. The hoaxes are designed to prey upon people's fears, desires, and sensitivities to keep the hoax spreading to other users over the Net. An example is the Netscape-AOL giveaway hoax. It got sent all over the Internet via e-mail by the following chain letter:

> Netscape and AOL have recently merged to form the largest internet company in the world. In an effort to remain at pace with this giant, Microsoft has introduced a new email tracking system as a way to keep Internet Explorer as the most popular browser on the market. This email is a beta test of the new software and Microsoft has generously offered to compensate those who participate in the testing process. For each person you send this email to, you will be given $5. For every person they give it to, you will be given an additional $3. For every person they send it to you will receive $1. Microsoft will tally all the emails produced under your name over a two week period and then email

you with more instructions. This beta test is only for Microsoft Windows users because the email tracking device that contacts Microsoft is embedded into the code of Windows 95 and 98.

I know you guys hate forwards. But I started this a month ago because I was very short on cash. A week ago I got an email from Microsoft asking me for my address. I gave it to them and yesterday I got a check in the mail for $800. It really works. I wanted you to get a piece of the action. You won't regret it.

Computer Incident Advisory Capability

Sometimes you may not be sure whether a message is a hoax or not. The major hoaxes are catalogued at the U.S. Department of Energy's Computer Incident Advisory Capability (CIAC) Web site, where you can look to see whether the hoax is a recognized one. For many of the hoaxes, the CIAC will recommend what actions you can take to discourage the spreading of the hoax. To look up a hoax and find out what to do about it, follow the *Interlit* Web site link to the CIAC Internet hoaxes page. Printed there are dozens of hoaxes along with an analysis of how each hoax worked. At the CIAC site you will also find links to Web pages warning you about the major chain letters and viruses that you need to watch out for on the Internet.

Viruses

Some of the more harmful chain letters and hoaxes have transmitted viruses across the Internet. While it is not possible for your computer to catch a virus from an e-mail message directly, the mail message can contain attachments that can give your computer a virus if you open them. One of the most harmful such e-mail viruses was the Love Bug virus. It spread as an attachment to an e-mail message entitled "I Love You" and asked you to open the attachment, which was named LOVE-LETTER-FOR-YOU.TXT.VBS. When you opened the attachment, the virus caused computers using the Microsoft Outlook and Outlook Express e-mail programs to send copies of the message to all of the users in your computer's address book. The messages appear to come from the person who owns the computer, serving as further enticement to open the attachment, since it appeared to come from someone you knew. In addition to spreading itself to your friends, the message also deleted certain kinds of files from your computer and replaced them with more copies of the virus.

The best way to guard against catching a virus through e-mail is never to open an attachment to an e-mail message, especially if the attachment has an executable filename extension such as *.exe, .vbs,* or *.class*. It is also possible for macros in MS Word DOC files and MS Excel XLS files to transmit viruses. Before you open any e-mail attachment, make very sure that the source of the message is one you trust, and that the message actually came from that person. If you have any doubts, follow the *Interlit* Web site link to the antivirus pages to see if the message you received is part of a nationally recognized virus attack.

A message may appear to come from a trusted acquaintance, when in fact it came from a worm. Recently, some viruses spread via e-mail that did not require the recipient to open the attachment. In addition, there are malicious virus programs that mimic the e-mail addresses of people from your address book. It is very important to keep current antivirus protection software on your computer. Most virus scanners have an option to scan incoming mail messages automatically; setting this option can help you avoid opening a malicious message. To keep yourself informed of the latest viruses, follow this book's Web site links to About.com's antivirus site, McAffee's antivirus center, and Symantec's Antivirus Research Center (SARC). You will learn more about protecting your computer from viruses in Chapter 13, which will teach you how to download files from the Internet.

Lurking

To **lurk** means to participate in a conversation on the Internet without responding to any of the messages. You receive and read the messages, but you do not say anything in return. Thus, you are lurking!

It is not unethical to lurk. To the contrary, it is often a good idea to lurk at first. For example, suppose you join a listserv that has been going on for a while. Instead of jumping right in and writing something that may make you seem really out of touch with what is going on, it is smarter to lurk for a while, so you can pick up the gist of the conversation before joining in.

The same guideline applies to newsgroups. Before you begin writing messages in a newsgroup, spend some time looking around at what has been written previously in that newsgroup. When you write something, you want it to sound as though you know what is going on. It is inconsiderate to write messages that waste the time of other users on the Net.

Ditto for chat rooms. When you enter a chat room in which other people are talking, spend some time listening to get the gist of the conversation before you chime in.

Flames

On the Internet, a **flame** is a message written in anger. The term *flame* can be used either as a verb or a noun. To flame someone is to send them an angry message. Angry messages that people send you are known as flames.

You need to be careful, especially if you have a temper. Form the habit of thinking carefully about what you write, and proofread several times before you send the message. Make sure the message truly conveys the emotions you want to communicate. If you are extremely mad and send a hastily written flame, you may regret it later on. When you cool off a few minutes later, you may wish you could tone down the message a little, but it will be too late. The message has already been sent, and unfortunate damage may be done to your relationship with the receiving party.

Firefighters

Sometimes flaming can get out of hand, especially when it occurs in a newsgroup or a listserv with a lot of users. People start sending hotter messages, and things can get ugly. Someone has to step in and write a message intended to restore peace. Because that puts an end to the flames, such peacemakers on the Internet are known as **firefighters.**

SHOUTING

Messages written on the Internet are normally written in lowercase letters, with capital letters appearing only at the start of the first word of each sentence, and on proper nouns, such as the term *Internet*. WHEN YOU WRITE IN ALL CAPS, ON THE OTHER HAND, YOU ARE SHOUTING! **Shouting** means to add emphasis by writing in all capital letters.

In general, you should not shout on the Internet. You already have the full attention of the person reading your message, and you do not need to shout unless you *really* want to add emphasis to something. Shouting is almost always regarded in poor taste, however, so do it sparingly, if at all.

If you hit the ‾Caps Lock‾ key by mistake, everything you enter will be written in all caps. Do not turn on the ‾Caps Lock‾ option unless you really want to shout.

An alternative to writing in all caps is to add emphasis to a word or phrase by surrounding it with asterisks, such as: it is *rude* to shout on the Internet. If the person to whom you are sending the message can read mail formatted as a Web page, you can use the "send as web page" option, which lets you send real boldings, enlarged, and italicized characters in an e-mail message. You will learn how to do this in Chapter 6.

Smileys and Emoticons

One of the problems inherent in text messages is that you cannot see the body language or facial expression of the person sending the message. Not knowing for sure whether something is said in jest can lead people to make false assumptions about the intent of a message. You need to be careful, because miscommunication can cause serious problems.

To give the person reading your message a clue as to what your emotions are, emoticons were devised. **Emoticons** are combinations of a few characters that conjure a facial expression when turned sideways. The most common form of emoticon is the smiley, which conveys a happy facial expression. Turn your book clockwise, and you will see that the characters :) convey a happy face. The smiley often has a nose :-) and sometimes winks ;-) at you. Left-handed people can use a left-handed smile (:, which also can have a nose (-: and can wink (-; at you.

Emoticons are not always happy. For example, :(is a frown, and :-(is a frown with a nose. Someone really sad may be crying :~~(and someone obnoxious may stick out the tongue :-P at you. You can even convey drooling :-P~~ with an emoticon. There are hundreds of these faces. For a more complete list, follow the *Interlit* Web site links to smileys and emoticons.

Three-Letter Acronyms (TLAs)

To shorten the amount of keyboarding required to write a message, some people use three-letter acronyms, which are appropriately known as TLAs. A **three-letter acronym (TLA)** is a way of shortening a three-word phrase such as "in my opinion" by simply typing the first letter of each word, such as *imo*. I'm not a proponent of three-letter acronyms, because life on the Internet is already filled with enough jargon, abbreviations, and technical terms. TLAs are so common, however, that no book about Internet literacy would be complete without mentioning them. Cell phone users, for example, use TLAs to reduce the amount of keypresses required to TXT a message to another phone. Some of the more common three-letter acronyms are

brb	be right back
bbl	be back later
btw	by the way
imo	in my opinion
lol	laughing out loud
j/k	just kidding
oic	oh, I see
ott	over the top (excessive, uncalled for)
thx	thanks

There are also two-letter acronyms, such as

np	no problem
re	hi again, as in "re hi"
wb	welcome back
b4	before

Some of these are more intuitive than others! There are also acronyms with more than three letters, including

bbiaf	be back in a flash
hhoj	ha ha, only joking

imho	in my humble opinion
morf	male or female?
nhoh	never heard of him/her
rotfl	rolling on the floor laughing
ttfn	ta ta for now

NetLingo

For a more complete list of TLAs, follow the *Interlit* Web site link to the NetLingo smiley dictionary.

Jargon on the Net

The New Hacker's Dictionary

Table 5-1 contains a list of terms you are likely to encounter out on the Net. For a more complete list of Internet jargon, follow the *Interlit* Web site and links to the Web's official "Jargon File" site. You also can get a printed copy of the Jargon File, which is called *The New Hacker's Dictionary* (MIT Press, ISBN 0-262-68092-0).

Table 5-1   Commonly used Internet jargon

Technical Term	What It Means
admin	Administrator; the person in charge on a computer
ASCII	American Standard Code for Information Interchange; the file format of a plain-text (*.txt*) file
avatar	An icon or representation of a user in a shared virtual reality
back door	A hole in the security of a system deliberately left in place by designers or maintainers
bandwidth	The volume of information per unit of time that a computer, person, or transmission medium can handle
banner	Opening screen containing a logo, author credits, or copyright notice
baud	Bits per second, a measure of telecommunication speed
BBS	Electronic bulletin-board system
beta	Mostly working, but still under test
bit	Binary digit; a computational quantity that can take on one of two values, such as true and false, or 0 and 1
byte	Eight bits; 1 byte can hold 1 ASCII character (see *ASCII*)
channel	The basic unit of discussion in an IRC (see *IRC*}
channel op or chanop	Someone who is endowed with privileges on a particular IRC channel
cookie	A handle, transaction ID, or other token of agreement between cooperating programs; also, a record of the mouse clicks made by a user at a Web site
cracker	Someone who breaks security or intentionally causes operational problems on a computer system
eBook	A paperless electronic book
egosurfing	Typing your own name as a key word into an Internet search engine
emoticon	A character combination used in e-mail or news to indicate an emotional state; the most famous is the smiley **:)**
FAQ	Frequently asked question; also, a list of frequently asked questions and their answers
firefighter	A peacemaker on the Internet who intervenes to stop a flame war
firewall	Provides security by preventing unauthorized data from moving across a network
flame	To send an e-mail message intended to insult or provoke; also used as a noun to refer to the insulting e-mail message
flame war	An acrimonious dispute conducted via e-mail or newsgroups

Table 5-1   *(continued)*

Technical Term	What It Means
flamer	A person who flames habitually
giga	A billion; abbreviated G, as in GB, meaning a billion bytes, which is also called a *gigabyte*
hacker	A person who enjoys exploring the details of programmable systems and how to stretch their capabilities; someone who can program quickly. Sometimes the term *hacker* is incorrectly used to refer to a programmer who causes trouble intentionally on a network; the proper term for that is *cracker*
IRC	Internet Relay Chat, a worldwide "party line" network that allows one to converse with others in real time in chat rooms on the Internet
ISP	Internet service provider, a company that sells Internet access
kilo	A thousand; abbreviated K, as in KB, meaning a thousand bytes, which is also called a *kilobyte*
lurker	One of the silent majority in an electronic forum who posts occasionally or not at all but reads the group's postings regularly
mega	A million; abbreviated M, as in MB, meaning a million bytes, which is also called a *megabyte*
MMOG	Massively Multi-player Online Games.
MP3	Music file compressed via MPEG audio layer 3
MPEG	Motion Picture Experts Group family of digital video file formats
MUD	Multiuser dimension; also Multiuser dungeon
mudhead	Someone addicted to a MUD
Netiquette	Network etiquette
newbie	Someone new to the network or to a newsgroup
newsgroup	One of Usenet's many discussion groups; see *Usenet*
nick	Short for a nickname; in a chat room, every user must pick a nick
ping	A tiny network message sent by one computer to check for the presence and alertness of another computer
POTS	Plain old telephone service
rave	To persist in discussing a specific topic when other users wish you would drop it
snail mail	Paper mail, as opposed to electronic mail
sneakernet	Term used to refer to transporting data by carrying physical media such as diskettes from one computer to another, instead of transferring the data over the Internet
spam	To send unwanted messages to newsgroups or listservs; also used as a noun to refer to the unwanted messages
surf	To browse the Internet in search of interesting stuff, especially on the World Wide Web
sysadmin	System administrator; the technical support person in charge of a server
TCP/IP	Transmission Control Protocol/Internet Protocol; the wide-area networking protocol that makes the Internet work
txt	To send a text message over a cell phone, as in, "txt me your nick"
URL	Uniform resource locator, an address that identifies a document or resource on the World Wide Web
Usenet	A distributed bulletin-board system hosting more than 10,000 newsgroups
virus	A cracker program that searches out other programs and infects them by embedding a copy of itself in them. When these programs are executed, the embedded virus is executed too, thus propagating the infection
wannabee	A would-be hacker; see *hacker*
yo-yo mode	The state in which the system is said to be when it rapidly alternates several times between being up and being down

E-words and Emoticons Enter *Oxford English Dictionary*

Some people may laugh about the new terms, and some of the expressions are genuinely funny, but the *Oxford English Dictionary* takes them seriously. MP3, digital divide, and eBook, for example, have been entered in the dictionary as official English words. The *Concise Oxford Dictionary* lists expressions such as RUOK, OIC, and KWIM (know what I mean). Also included are the chat room signoffs BCNU and BFN (bye for now). (*USA Today*, 7/12/01; *Interlit* Web site).

exercises

1. Follow the *Interlit* Web site link to the Coalition Against Unsolicited Commercial Email (CAUCE). What is the latest news in their fight against spam? Follow the link to see how you can help and read about joining CAUCE. Do you think you should join the organization? Why or why not?

2. Follow the *Interlit* Web site link to the CIAC hoaxes page and scroll down to read about the latest hoaxes. Which one do you think is the most dangerous to have circulating about the Internet? What kind of damage could it do to the Internet and/or to your computer?

3. Use your favorite word processor to write a mock mail message, which you will not actually send to anyone—this is just for the purpose of the exercise. Now practice SHOUTING in the message. Put different parts of the message in uppercase. Read the message and consider the effect of the shouting. Decide whether and when you should shout in your messages. Remember that since you already have the attention of the person reading your message, you should SHOUT only when such added emphasis is warranted. Again, shouting is generally discouraged on the Internet.

4. Go to one or more of the smiley sites you will find in the smiley section of the *Interlit* Web site, and browse the list of emoticons you will find there. What are your favorite emoticons? Which emoticons do you find too esoteric (that is, too hard to understand) for general use on the Internet? In your answer, identify the emoticons by including both their symbol and their name. For example, if you write about the priest smiley, refer to it as the **+:-) priest smiley.**

5. In the *Interlit* Web site section on TLAs, follow the link to online acronyms. Browse the list of acronyms you find there. Which TLAs do you think an Internet-literate person should know? Which ones are too esoteric for general use on the Internet? In your answer, identify the TLAs by including both their symbol and their meaning. For example, if you write about the laughing out loud TLA, refer to it as **lol laughing out loud.**

6. Go to the Bill of Rights and Responsibilities site by following the links in the "Netiquette" section of the *Interlit* Web site. Read carefully the *Bill of Rights and Responsibilities for Electronic Learners* that you find there. Do you agree with all of the items covered in this Bill of Rights? What do you disagree with? Do you plan to abide by these guidelines? Do you think they leave out anything important? What is not covered that should be?

SITUATED CASE PROJECTS

Case 5: Writing an Acceptable Use Policy

At the end of each chapter in this book, a situated case project provides the student an opportunity to put the chapter's contents to practical use in a workplace situation. Each case has the same number as the chapter in which it appears.

Every school or company that provides computing services to students or employees should have an acceptable use policy that specifies the terms and conditions under which users can access the school or company's computing facilities. Imagine that your employer has asked you to develop an acceptable use policy for your workplace. To create such a policy, follow these steps:

 Make an outline of the concerns, both legal and ethical, that you think need to be included in the acceptable use policy for your school or company. Try to make this list before you proceed to step 2, which could influence or mask some of your initial instincts.

2 Study some examples of acceptable use policies currently in use at workplaces similar to yours. To see some good examples, follow the Chapter 5 *Interlit* Web site link to acceptable use policies.

3 Use your word processor to draft an acceptable use policy for your workplace.

If your instructor has asked you to hand in the acceptable use policy, make sure you put your name at the top, then save it on disk or follow the other instructions you may have been given for submitting this assignment. Later on in this book, you will learn how to convert this document into a Web page that can be published on the school or company Web site.

6

ELECTRONIC MAIL

After completing this chapter, you will be able to:

- ■ Understand what an e-mail account is and know how to get one set up for you.

- ■ Select an e-mail client for use in sending, receiving, and filing e-mail messages.

- ■ Configure your e-mail client so you can begin using e-mail.

- ■ Send, receive, answer, forward, and file e-mail messages.

- ■ Create a signature file that will identify who you are at the end of your e-mail messages.

- ■ Know how to attach files to your e-mail messages.

- ■ Avoid catching harmful viruses that can be transmitted in e-mail attachments.

- ■ Use an address book to keep track of the e-mail addresses of people to whom you send mail.

- ■ Create a mailing list that enables you to send a message to several people at once.

- ■ Search your stored mail messages to find things you have filed for future reference.

- ■ Deal with unwanted mail and detect fake mail IDs.

- ■ Encrypt your mail so only the person receiving it can read it.

- ■ Read your mail with a Web-based e-mail service.

● Electronic mail has revolutionized the way people communicate when they cannot talk in person. No longer must people wait for traditional postal mail delivery, which has become known as "snail mail" due to its comparative slowness. On the Internet, if both the sender and the receiver log on frequently, it is possible to exchange several messages with someone in a single day.

Electronic mail is highly efficient. Compared to other forms of communication, it is probably the greatest time-saver in the world. Because you must initiate the reading of your e-mail by running your e-mail software, you read e-mail only when you decide to do so; thus, e-mail does not interrupt your workday. If you are too busy to read e-mail, or if you are on vacation, your e-mail queues up in your Inbox, waiting patiently for the next time you log on. When you travel, you can dial up and read your e-mail using almost any telephone line anywhere in the world. You can even avoid the need for a phone line if your computer is equipped for wireless communications or if you have a cell phone that supports wireless e-mail. If you have a job in which reading e-mail promptly is important, you can get a wireless e-mail device that alerts you when a message arrives.

Getting an E-mail Account

Before you can begin using e-mail, you must have an **account.** An account enables you to log on to the computer that hosts your e-mail service. The computer that hosts your account is known as your mail server. On the mail server, your account consists of file space where your e-mail queues up waiting for you to read it, and a login procedure that enables you to log on and access your files.

You get the account from your Internet service provider (ISP). Chapter 3 tells you how to select an ISP. When the ISP sets up your account, you will be told the name of your account. Usually this is your own name (such as fred.hofstetter) or your initials (such as fth) or a nickname (such as freddy). If your account name is something impersonal like a number (such as 02737), ask your ISP how to go about changing the number to something more user-friendly. Be careful, because once you choose a name, many computers will not allow you to change it.

In addition to being told the name of your account, you will be given a password that you must enter each time you log on to your account. The password prevents unauthorized users from logging on under your name and gaining access to your mail. Most host computers permit you to change your password. Choose a password that you will remember, but do not select one that is easy to guess, because you do not want someone malicious to guess your password and log on under your name. That person could send offensive mail under your name and cause problems for you. Do not use your first or last name as your password, for example. If you are known to love Corvettes, do not make *Corvette* your password. Choose something unlikely to be guessed. Include a combination of letters, numbers, and special characters. If you ever suspect that someone has guessed your password, change it immediately. Above all, remember your password. ISPs do not like it when you forget your password and they have to reset it for you.

Your ISP also will tell you the IP address of the mail server that hosts your e-mail account. The IP address will be in domain-name format, such as mail.udel.edu. You will need to know all three items—your account name, password, and mail server's IP address—in order to complete the tutorial exercises in this chapter.

Selecting an E-mail Client

The software program that you use to read your e-mail is known as an **e-mail client.** Both Mozilla and Microsoft provide freely downloadable e-mail clients in their Web browser software suites. This chapter contains detailed instructions on how to use the Mozilla Thunderbird and Microsoft Outlook Express e-mail clients. You are free to choose either one for use in this tutorial. If you are an AOL user and you have AOL mail, it is OK to continue using the AOL mail client that is built into your AOL account. AOL users can also install either Mozilla Thunderbird or Microsoft Outlook Express and follow the instructions in this chapter to use them for mail.

Mozilla Thunderbird

Mozilla's e-mail client is called Thunderbird. You can download it freely from www.mozilla.org. After you run the downloaded file to install Thunderbird, you will find Mozilla Thunderbird on the Windows Start→Programs menu. During the installation process, the Thunderbird setup program will ask if you want the Thunderbird launch icon placed on your Windows desktop and quick launch bar. The Thunderbird launch icon appears as follows:

Mozilla
Thunderbird

Microsoft Outlook Express

The e-mail client in Microsoft Internet Explorer is called *Outlook Express*. If the Microsoft Internet Explorer is installed on your computer, you already have Outlook Express. It is possible that your copy of Microsoft Internet Explorer may be set to bring up some other e-mail client, such as Microsoft Office Outlook. If that happens when you work through the exercises in this chapter, you can change mail packages by following these steps:

● Pull down the Microsoft Internet Explorer's Tools menu and choose Internet Options; the Internet Options dialog appears.

● Click the Programs tab.

● Pull down the E-mail menu and choose Outlook Express mail.

● Click OK to close the Internet Options dialog.

Configuring Your E-mail Client

You must configure your e-mail client before you can begin reading mail. Configuring an e-mail client means telling it the essential information it needs to know, such as the IP address of your ISP's mail server and the name of your e-mail account. You can also set preferences that determine whether the mail will get deleted from the host or stay there after the mail gets downloaded to your computer. To configure your e-mail client, follow the steps in Table 6-1.

Table 6-1　How to configure an e-mail client

Mozilla Thunderbird	Microsoft Outlook Express
▶ Get Thunderbird running if it is not already onscreen.	▶ Get Internet Explorer running if it is not already onscreen.
▶ If you have not set up a mail account, the Account Wizard will launch. The wizard will ask you several questions.	▶ ✉ Select the Mail icon to drop the menu down, and select Read Mail.
▶ First, the wizard asks what kind of account you would like to set up. Figure 6-1 shows the choices. Choose e-mail and click the Next button.	▶ If you get a dialog box asking you to select a folder for your mail; select the Inbox folder, unless you want your mail kept somewhere else.
	▶ Since you have not set up Internet Explorer for mail, the Internet Connection Wizard will launch. The wizard will ask you several questions.
	▶ First, the wizard asks for your Internet mail account name, as shown in Figure 6-3. The author typed **Fred T. Hofstetter** here.

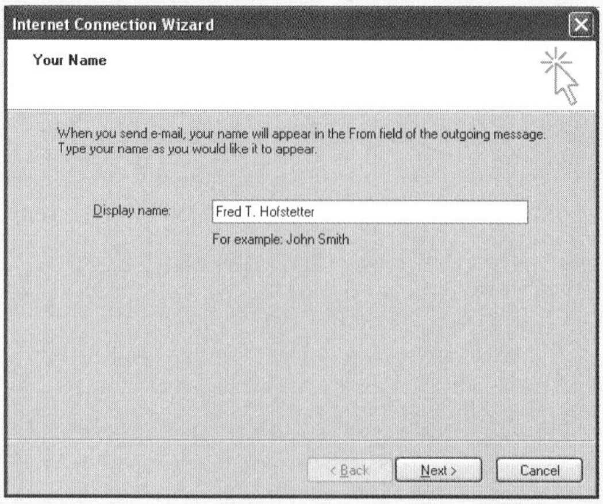

Figure 6-1　The Mozilla Account Wizard helps you configure Mozilla for mail.

Figure 6-3　The Internet Connection Wizard presents a series of five screens that ask you setup questions.

Table 6-1 *(continued)*

Mozilla Thunderbird	Microsoft Outlook Express
▶ Second, the wizard asks you to fill in your name and e-mail address. Your e-mail address is your account name, followed by an @ sign, followed by the domain name of your ISP's host computer. For example, if your account name is SantaClaus and your host computer is northpole.com, you would type **SantaClaus@northpole.com**	▶ Second, the wizard asks for your e-mail address. Your e-mail address is your account name followed by an @ sign, followed by the domain name of your ISP's host computer. For example, if your account name is SantaClaus and your host computer is northpole.com, you should type **SantaClaus@northpole.com** here.
▶ Third, the wizard asks whether you want the mail server to be set up as POP or IMAP. Choose POP if you want your mail to be transferred to your computer, or click IMAP to leave it on the server. Then you enter the name of your incoming mail server and your outgoing mail server, which in the case of Santa Claus would be **mail.northpole.com**. Figure 6-2 shows how Santa would complete this step. *Note:* If you want to learn more about the differences between POP and IMAP, follow the *Interlit* Web site link to POP versus IMAP.	▶ Third, the wizard asks whether you want the mail server to be set up as POP3 or IMAP. Choose POP3 if you want your mail to be transferred to your computer, or click IMAP to leave it on the server. Then you enter the name of your incoming mail server and your outgoing mail server, which in the case of Santa Claus would be **mail.northpole.com**. Figure 6-4 shows how Santa would complete this step. *Note:* If you want to learn more about the differences between POP and IMAP, follow the *Interlit* Web site link to POP versus IMAP.

Figure 6-2 The wizard's Server Information screen.

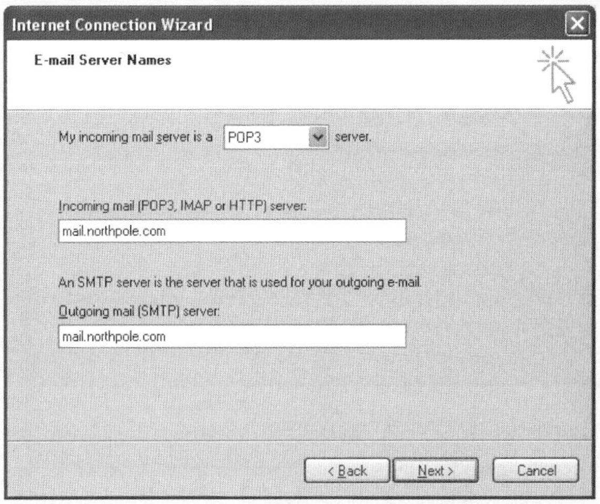

Figure 6-4 The wizard's Mail Server setup screen.

▶ The wizard will ask for your user name. Enter the user account name given to you by your ISP.

▶ The wizard will ask you to enter the name by which you want this account to be known; type the name you want this to be. Santa Claus would type something like **Northpole mail** here, for example.

▶ Finally, the wizard will print a summary of the settings you have entered. If they look OK, click Finish to save the settings. Otherwise, click Back to go back to the setting you want to change.

▶ The wizard will ask you to enter your e-mail logon name and password.

▶ The wizard will ask for your Internet mail account name; type the name you want this to be. Santa Claus would type something like **Northpole mail** here, for example.

▶ Next, the wizard will ask whether you are using a phone line or a network connection; answer accordingly.

▶ If you have multiple connections to the Internet, the wizard will ask what Internet connection to use. You should choose the same connection you made when you configured your Web browser, unless you have a reason for doing otherwise.

▶ When the wizard is done, the Microsoft Internet Explorer will fetch your mail.

Having configured the e-mail client, now you are ready to send and receive mail. Read on.

Table 6-2   How to send e-mail

Mozilla Thunderbird	Microsoft Outlook Express
▶ Get Thunderbird running if it is not already onscreen. The first time you do this, the Account Wizard may appear to help you make sure your preferences are set up correctly. Follow the onscreen instructions as the wizard helps you.	▶ 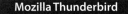 In Internet Explorer, click the Mail icon and choose New Message.
▶ To compose a message to send someone, pull down the Message menu and choose New Message, or click on the Write icon. The Compose window appears as shown in Figure 6-5.	▶ The New Message window appears as shown in Figure 6-6.

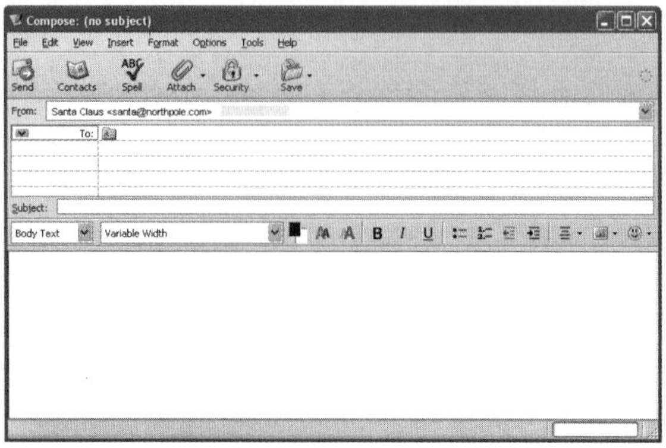

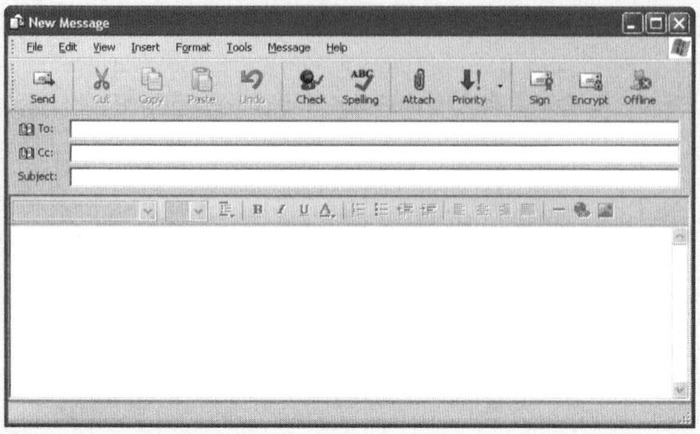

Figure 6-5   Thunderbird Message Composition window.

Figure 6-6   Microsoft Outlook Express New Message window.

▶ Click once in the To field and enter the e-mail address of the person to whom you want to send a message. The first time you do this, send a message to yourself, so you will be sure to have a message waiting to be read in the "Reading Mail" part of this tutorial.

▶ Click once in the Subject field and enter a short phrase telling what this e-mail is about. If this is your first message, you might make the subject read **My first mail message.**

▶ Click in the large blank area beneath the subject field to position your cursor in the composition area. Here is where you type the message you want to send. If this is your first message, type something like **Hello, world! This is my very first e-mail message.**

▶ Click the Send button to send the message.

(Right column, Outlook Express:)

▶ Your cursor will already be in the To field, so enter the e-mail address of the person to whom you want to send a message. The first time you do this, send a message to yourself, so you will be sure to have a message waiting to be read in the "Reading Mail" part of this tutorial.

▶ For the time being, skip the Cc: field.

▶ Click once in the Subject field and enter a short phrase telling what this e-mail is about. If this is your first message, you might make the subject read **My first mail message.**

▶ Click in the large blank area beneath the subject field to position your cursor in the composition area. Here is where you type the message you want to send. If this is your first message, type something like **Hello, world! This is my very first e-mail message.**

▶ Click the Send button to send the message.

Sending Mail

To send someone an e-mail message, follow the steps in Table 6-2. The first time you do this, address the message to yourself, so you will have a message waiting to be read when you learn how to read mail in the next part of this chapter.

Reading Mail

To read your electronic mail, follow the steps in Table 6-3.

Table 6-3 How to read e-mail

Mozilla Thunderbird	Microsoft Outlook Express
▶ Get Thunderbird running if it is not already onscreen. If the Password dialog appears, type your password and click OK.	▶ If you are not already in Outlook Express, click the Internet Explorer Mail icon to drop the menu down, and select Read Mail; the Outlook Express window appears.
▶ To find out if you have new mail waiting for you, click the Get Mail button.	▶ In Outlook Express, select your Inbox by clicking it once. If you chose IMAP when you configured your mail in Table 6-1, your Inbox is a subfolder of the messages folder on your mail server; if you chose POP3, click the Inbox in your Outlook Express folder.
▶ If new mail has arrived, the Inbox window will display a menu of your incoming mail messages, as shown in Figure 6-7.	▶ If new mail has arrived, the Inbox window will display a menu of your incoming mail messages, as shown in Figure 6-8.

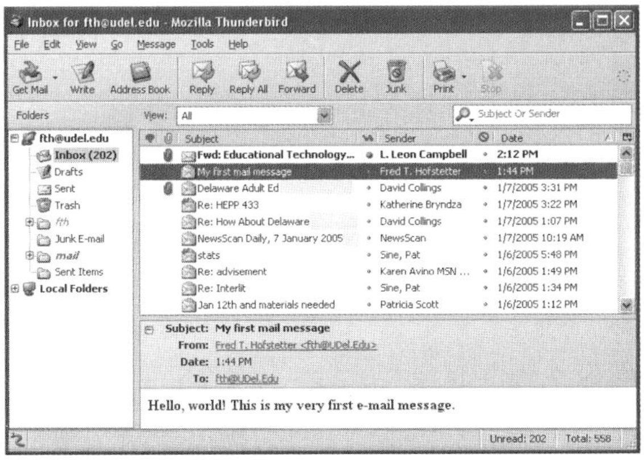

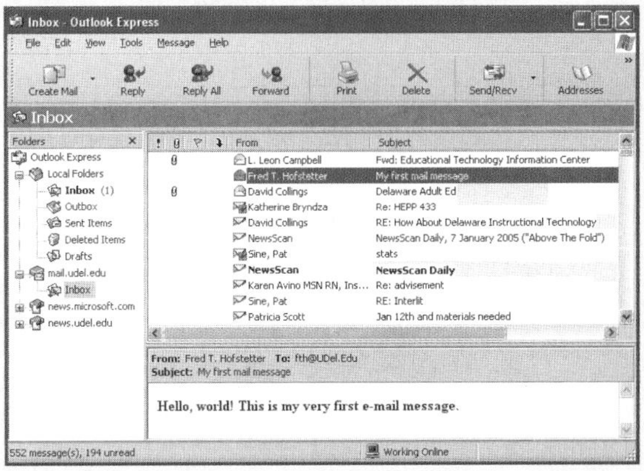

Figure 6-7 The Thunderbird Inbox displays a menu of incoming mail messages.

Figure 6-8 The Outlook Express Inbox displays a menu of incoming mail messages.

▶ To preview a message, click its title once, and the message will appear in the window at the bottom of the screen. To read a message, double-click on its title, and the text of the message will appear in a message window. When you are done reading the message, close the message window.

▶ In your Inbox, the mail message will be marked as having been read. It will stay on your computer unless you delete it.

▶ If you want to delete the message, click on its title once to select it, then click the Delete button.

▶ To preview a message, click its title once, and the message will appear in the window at the bottom of the screen. To read the message, double-click its title; the message will appear in a Message window. When you are done reading the message, close the message window.

▶ In your Inbox, the mail message will be marked as having been read. The message will stay on your computer unless you delete it.

▶ If you want to delete the message, click on its title once to select it, then click the Delete button.

Answering Mail

Once you start using e-mail regularly, you will find that something you will often want to do is respond to a message someone sent you. Instead of having to go through all of the steps needed to send a totally new message, you can simply reply to the message while it is on your screen. To reply to a message, follow the steps in Table 6-4.

Table 6-4 How to reply to an e-mail message

Mozilla Thunderbird	Microsoft Outlook Express
▶ While viewing the message, click the ⬜ Reply button to reply to the sender, or click the ⬜ Reply All button to reply to the sender and all of the recipients.	▶ While viewing the message, click the ⬜ Reply button to reply to the sender, or click the ⬜ Reply All button to reply to the sender and all of the recipients.
▶ A shortcut for replying to the sender is to press Ctrl - R , and to reply to all, press Shift - Ctrl - R .	▶ A shortcut for replying to the sender is to press Ctrl - R , and to reply to all, press Shift - Ctrl - R .
▶ A new message window automatically appears, addressed to the sender. Enter your reply, then send the message as usual.	▶ A new message window automatically appears, addressed to the author. Enter your reply, then send the message as usual.

Table 6-5 How to forward an e-mail message

Mozilla Thunderbird	Microsoft Outlook Express
▶ While viewing the message, click the ⬜ Forward button; a new Message window will appear.	▶ While viewing the message, click the ⬜ Forward button; a new Message window will appear.
▶ In the To field, enter the e-mail address of the person to whom you want to forward the message.	▶ In the To field, enter the e-mail address of the person to whom you want to forward the message.
▶ In the body of the message, enter anything more that you want to send along with the message, such as a few words indicating why you are forwarding this.	▶ In the body of the message, enter anything more that you want to send along with the message, such as a few words indicating why you are forwarding this.
▶ Send the message as usual.	▶ Send the message as usual.

Forwarding Mail

At some point you will receive mail that you want to send a copy of to someone else. Instead of having to go through all of the steps needed to copy and paste the message into a new message window, you can simply forward the message. To forward an e-mail message, follow the steps in Table 6-5.

Filing E-mail Messages

Occasionally you will receive an important message that you want to keep so you can refer to it later on. Instead of deleting it, you can file it. To file an e-mail message means to move it into a folder on your hard drive from the Inbox folder where your incoming mail accumulates. There are three processes to learn related to filing e-mail messages: creating an e-mail folder in which to hold your messages, filing mail into an e-mail folder, and retrieving filed mail whenever you want to read it again.

Creating an E-mail Folder

To file mail, you can create different folders regarding different topics. To create an e-mail file folder, follow the steps in Table 6-6.

Filing Mail into an E-mail Folder

You can file mail in any e-mail folder on your computer. Follow the steps in Table 6-7.

Table 6-6   How to create an e-mail file folder

Mozilla Thunderbird	Microsoft Outlook Express
▶ Pull down the Thunderbird File menu and choose New→New Folder; the New Folder dialog appears as shown in Figure 6-9.	▶ In the Outlook Express Folders pane, click the place where you want to create a folder. For example, click Local Folders.
	▶ Pull down the File menu and choose New→Folder. The Create Folder dialog appears and displays an outline of your file folders as shown in Figure 6-10.

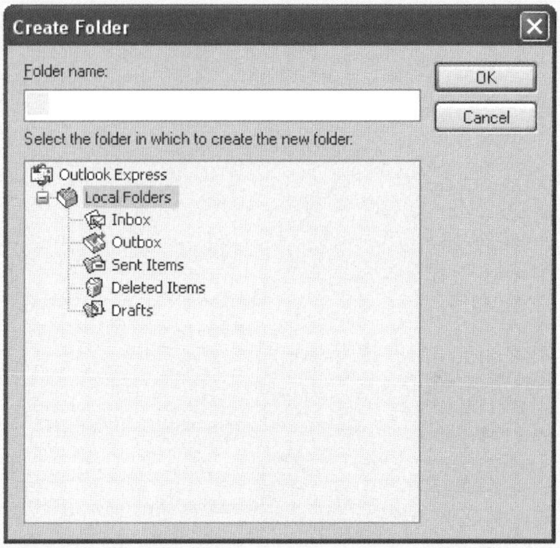

Figure 6-9   The Thunderbird New Folder dialog.

▶ In the Name field, type the name you want the new folder to have.

▶ If you want the new folder to be created as a subfolder of an existing folder, click the arrow to drop down the list of existing folders and select the one in which you want the new folder to reside.

▶ Click OK to create the new folder.

▶ If you ever want to delete a file folder, click its name once to select it, then press the ⌐Delete⌐ key. To remove the folder completely, click to select the Trash folder, then pull down the File menu and choose Empty Trash.

Figure 6-10   The Create Folder dialog in Outlook Express.

▶ Enter a name for the new folder and click on the folder into which you want to insert the new folder. Click on OK.

▶ You will see the new folder in the list on the left of the Outlook Express window.

▶ If you ever want to delete a file folder, click its name once to select it, then press the ⌐Delete⌐ key. To remove the folder completely, pull down the Edit menu and choose Empty "Deleted Items" Folder.

Table 6-7   How to file an e-mail message

Mozilla Thunderbird	Microsoft Outlook Express
▶ Get your Thunderbird window onscreen and select your Inbox. You will see the messages in your Inbox. If there are no messages waiting for you there, click the Get Mail button to see if any mail awaits. If not, you will have to wait until someone sends you mail before you can complete this exercise. One sure way to get mail is to send yourself a message!	▶ Get your Outlook Express window onscreen and select your Inbox. If there are no messages waiting for you there, click the Send and Receive button to see if any mail awaits. If not, you will have to wait until someone sends you mail before you can complete this exercise. One sure way to get mail is to send yourself a message!
▶ There is a Folders pane on the left side of your Inbox. If the folder into which you want to file the message is not showing in the Folders pane, click the plus-sign icons to expand the file tree until the folder is visible.	▶ There is a Folders pane on the left side of your Inbox. If the folder into which you want to file the message is not showing in the Folders pane, click the plus-sign icons to expand the file tree until the folder is visible.
▶ Click and drag the title of the message and drop it into the folder you want to file the message in.	▶ Click and drag the title of the message and drop it into the folder you want to file the message in.

Table 6-8   How to retrieve a filed e-mail message

Mozilla Thunderbird	Microsoft Outlook Express
▶ Get your Thunderbird window onscreen and select your Inbox.	▶ In Outlook Express, click one of the folders shown on the left of the Outlook Express window.
▶ If your mail folders are not visible in the File pane, click the plus-sign icons to expand the file tree until the desired folder is visible.	▶ An Inbox window will appear, displaying the titles of the mail messages filed in this folder.
▶ Click on the name of the folder from which you want to retrieve a filed e-mail message.	▶ To retrieve a message, double-click its title.
▶ An Inbox window will appear, displaying the titles of the mail messages filed in this folder.	
▶ To retrieve a message, double-click its title.	

Retrieving Mail from an E-mail Folder

Filing mail would serve no purpose without a way to retrieve it when you want to refer to it again. To retrieve a filed e-mail message, follow the steps in Table 6-8.

Creating a Signature File

When you send someone an e-mail message, it is nice to include information about yourself, so the person receiving the message will know something about you, such as your street address, where you work or go to school, and your telephone number. To keep from having to enter this information each time you send an e-mail message, you can create a **signature file,** which is a block of text that automatically gets appended to the e-mail messages you originate.

To create a signature file, you use any word processor or text editor to create a text file containing the information you want to have appear at the bottom of your e-mail messages. You should not make the lines in a signature file longer than about 72 characters, otherwise they may wrap when people with small screens read your message, and wrapping will throw off the formatting. Please be aware that it is not good netiquette to have extremely long signature files. Try to keep your signature file short—four to seven lines is about right. When you save the file, make sure you save it in plain text format, in the file folder of your choice. Table 6-9 shows how to create a file folder; follow these steps whenever you need to create a new file folder to hold the files you create. Table 6-10 shows how to create a plain text file. To make your e-mail client automatically attach the signature file to the e-mail messages that you send, follow the steps provided in Table 6-11.

Table 6-9   How to create a file folder

Windows	Macintosh
To create a folder, you use the Windows Explorer. To get the Windows Explorer started, use the Windows Start button. If the Start button is not visible on your screen, hold down CTRL and press ESC, and the Start button will appear. Click the Start button and choose Programs. You will find the Windows Explorer listed either on the Programs menu or on the Programs→Accessories menu. Click on the Windows Explorer to get it running. Figure 6-11 shows how the Windows Explorer provides a visual diagram of how all the files are organized on your computer. You can click on any folder to see a list of the files it contains.	To create a folder on the Macintosh, use the New Folder command in the File menu of the Finder. If you have no programs running, then you are already in the Finder; if you have other programs running, click the Finder icon on the Dock. Figure 6-12 shows how the Finder provides a visual diagram of how all the files are organized on your computer. You can click on any folder to see a list of the files it contains.

Table 6-9   *(continued)*

Windows	Macintosh

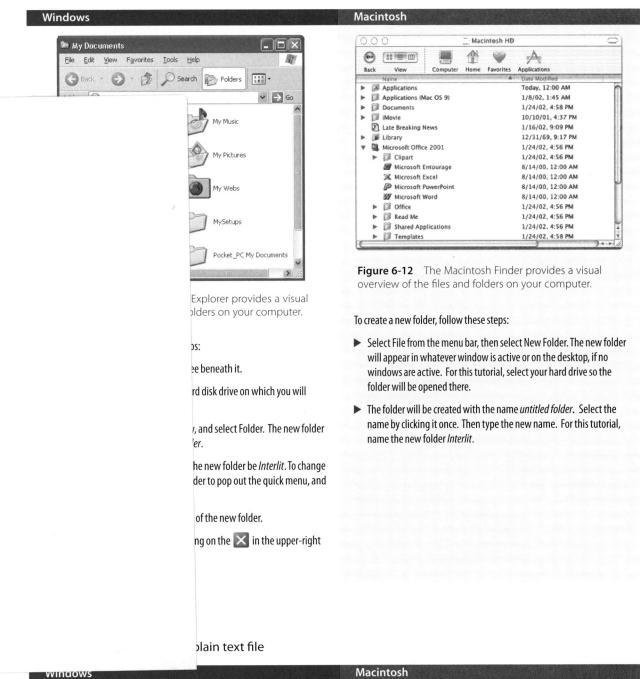

Figure 6-12   The Macintosh Finder provides a visual overview of the files and folders on your computer.

Explorer provides a visual
olders on your computer.

To create a new folder, follow these steps:

ps:

▶ Select File from the menu bar, then select New Folder. The new folder will appear in whatever window is active or on the desktop, if no windows are active. For this tutorial, select your hard drive so the folder will be opened there.

ee beneath it.

rd disk drive on which you will

▶ The folder will be created with the name *untitled folder*. Select the name by clicking it once. Then type the new name. For this tutorial, name the new folder *Interlit*.

, and select Folder. The new folder
er.

e new folder be *Interlit*. To change
der to pop out the quick menu, and

of the new folder.

ng on the ⨯ in the upper-right

lain text file

Windows	Macintosh

▶ Click the Start button, and choose Run to make the Run dialog appear.

▶ Type **notepad** and press ⎡Enter⎤. A Notepad window will appear.

▶ Type the text you want the file to contain. Figure 6-13 contains a model to follow for creating a signature file.

▶ When you are done, pull down the Notepad's File menu and choose Save to make the Save dialog appear. Use the Save dialog to save the file in the folder of your choice.

▶ Double-click the icon for TextEdit.

▶ A window with the name *untitled* will appear.

▶ Type the text you want the file to contain. Figure 6-13 contains a model to follow for creating a signature file.

▶ When you are done, pull down the File menu and choose Save to make the Save dialog appear. Use the Save dialog to save the file in the folder of your choice.

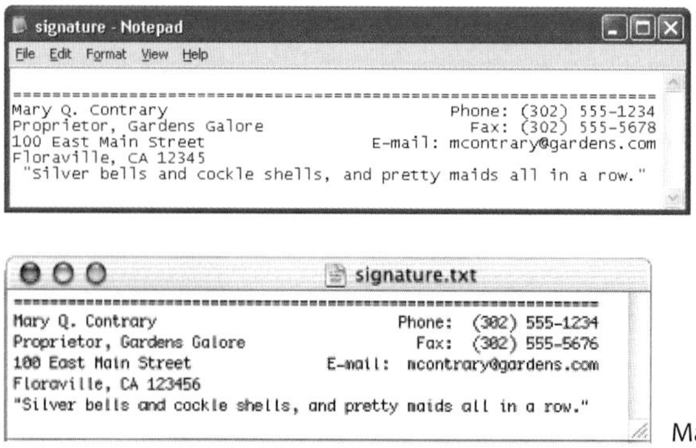

Figure 6-13 A sample signature file showing a person's name, title, address, telephone, fax, e-mail address, and a little saying. When this file gets appended to an e-mail message, the line of equal signs at the top of the file will serve as a divider between the text of the e-mail message and the signature file.

Windows

Macintosh

Table 6-11 How to set up a signature file

Mozilla Thunderbird	Microsoft Internet Explorer
▶ Pull down the Thunderbird Tools menu and choose Account Settings.	▶ In Outlook Express, pull down the Tools menu and choose Options.
▶ The Account Settings dialog appears as shown in Figure 6-14.	▶ When the Options dialog appears, click the Signatures tab; the dialog appears as shown in Figure 6-15.

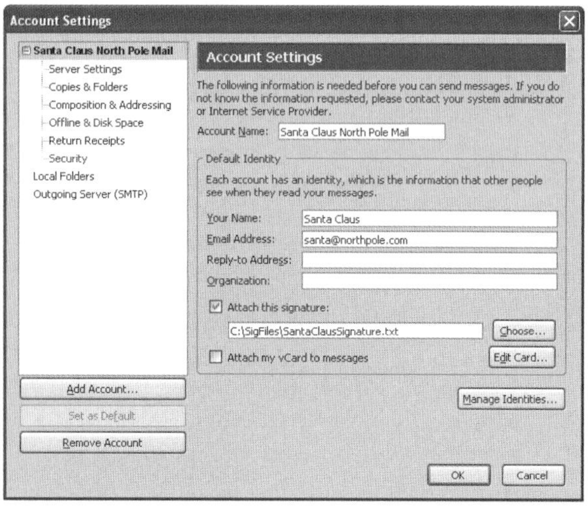

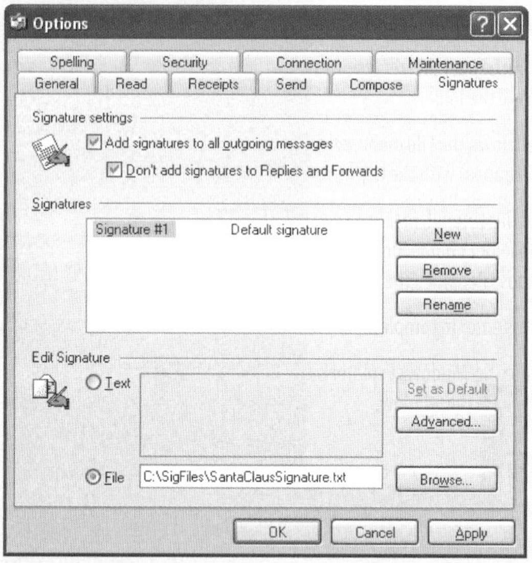

Figure 6-14 The Thunderbird Account Settings dialog.

▶ Click the option to attach this signature.

▶ Enter the complete path/filename of your signature file into the signature file field, or click the Choose button, which will bring up a Choose File dialog that will help you locate the file and enter the filename for you.

▶ Click OK to close the dialog.

Figure 6-15 The Outlook Express Signatures tab in the Options dialog.

▶ Click the New button to add a new signature.

▶ Click the radio button for File. Enter the complete path/filename of your signature file into the Signature File field, or click the Browse button, which will bring up a browse dialog that will help you locate the file and enter the filename for you.

▶ You could also click on the radio button for Text and type or paste your signature file into that space.

▶ You will also want to click on your choices of when to use the signature file.

▶ Click OK to close the Signature dialog; then click OK to close the Options dialog.

Table 6-12   How to attach files to e-mail messages

Mozilla Thunderbird	Microsoft Outlook Express
▶ From your Thunderbird Inbox, click the Write button, and create the mail message to which you want to attach a file.	▶ From Outlook Express, click the Compose Message button and create the mail message to which you want to attach a file.
▶ Before you send the message, click the 📎 Attach button, and, in the menu that pops out, choose File. The Attach File(s) dialog appears.	▶ Before you send the message, click the 📎 Attach File button to make the Insert Attachment dialog appear.
▶ Enter the complete path/filename of the file you want to attach, or use the controls to locate the file and click on its name to enter it into the Filename field.	▶ Enter the complete path/filename of the file you want to attach, or use the controls to locate the file and click on its name to enter it into the Filename field.
▶ Click Open to complete the Attach dialog. The file is now attached to your mail message.	▶ Click Attach to complete the Insert Attachment dialog. The file is now attached to your mail message.
▶ Send the mail message as usual.	▶ Send the mail message as usual.

Eventually, you will want to add to your signature file the address of the World Wide Web home page that you will create in Part Five. You can edit your signature file at any time by using your text editor to open your signature file, change it as you like, and save it again.

Note: If you make a change to your signature file while you have your e-mail software running, the change you make may not take effect right away, because your e-mail client reads the signature file only at the start of the session. To make changes to the signature file take effect, shut down your e-mail client by closing all of your Mozilla or Microsoft Internet Explorer windows, then restart it.

Sending and Receiving Mail Attachments

A mail attachment is a file that you attach to an e-mail message. When you send the message, the attached file gets sent along with it. File attachments can be text documents, pictures, audio recordings, movies, spreadsheets, or virtually any other kind of file that you are accustomed to using on your computer. To learn how to send attached files, follow the steps in Table 6-12.

How to Read an E-mail Attachment

When you read an e-mail message that has one or more files attached, each file will appear as an icon toward the top or bottom of the message. To open the file, simply double-click its icon. If the file is a text document, you will be able to read it. If it is a picture, you will see it. If the file is a song, you will hear it. Before you open any attached files, however, make sure you read the following warning about how to avoid catching viruses from e-mail attachments.

How to Avoid Catching Viruses from E-mail Attachments

You need to be very careful before you open certain kinds of files that you receive as e-mail attachments over the Internet. Especially if the file is an executable module that can run on your computer, it could be carrying a virus that might infect your computer when you open it. A growing number of e-mail messages carry viruses. Antivirus firm Message Labs, for example, detected a virus in one out of every 370 e-mail messages in 2001. This doubled the virus rate of the previous year. (AP/Wall Street Journal, 4 Jan 2002) When this book went to press in 2005, live statistics at ieinternet.com reported that almost 1 in 10 e-mail messages contained a virus.

The rule of thumb used to be: never open an e-mail attachment from someone you do not know. But then came the Melissa and Love Bug viruses, which appeared to originate from people you knew. Instead, these viruses made your friend's e-mail system send you an infected message in such a way that you could not tell that your friend's identity had been faked. The Love Bug was a particularly nasty virus because it deleted and renamed files on your computer, and, if you were using Microsoft Outlook or Outlook Express, it sent copies of the virus to all the people in your address book, making the messages appear to have come from you. The Love Bug propagated all over the Internet, especially among corporate users, and companies lost billions of dollars in wasted time when the virus clogged several commercial networks.

Use extreme caution whenever you open an e-mail attachment, especially if it has an executable filename extension such as .exe, .bat, .class, or .vbs, but executables can be disguised, so always be on guard. Screen savers also can carry viruses, so be wary if anyone e-mails you a screen saver. Even an innocent-looking .html attachment can carry a virus. The Gigger/JS HTML virus, for example, spreads through JavaScript in an HTML attachment. If you open the attachment, the script modifies your AUTOEXEC.BAT file to reformat your hard drive the next time you start your computer.

Be careful when you check the filename of an attachment when you decide whether to open it. Windows hides the filename extension, for example, when filenames are displayed. Some crackers take advantage of this and write viruses with names such as HAPPY.JPG. SCR, which will display onscreen as HAPPY.JPG. It may appear to be a JPG image file, but it carries a vicious virus. To make Windows display the entire filename, get the Windows Explorer running by clicking the Windows Start button and choosing Programs→ Windows Explorer or Programs→Accessories→Windows Explorer. Pull down the Tools menu and choose Folder Options to make the Folder Options dialog appear. Click the View tab and uncheck the option to hide file extensions for known file types.

Because attachments can carry viruses, you need to be careful using the preview option in your mail reader. The preview option can cause certain kinds of attachments to execute. The nasty Nimda worm, for example, spreads through an e-mail attachment disguised as an audio file. To turn off the preview option in Thunderbird, pull down the Inbox window's View menu, choose Layout, and unselect the Message Pane option. To turn off the preview option in Microsoft Outlook Express, pull down the View menu, choose Layout, and uncheck the Preview Pane.

To keep yourself informed of the latest viruses, follow the *Interlit* Web site link to About. com's antivirus site, McAfee's antivirus center, Symantec's Antivirus Research Center (SARC), and CNET's antivirus help site.

Beware of E-mail Hoaxes

Some pretty incredible hoaxes have been propagated across the Internet. The hoaxes are designed to prey upon people's fears and sensitivities or their desires to keep the hoax spreading to other users over the Net. An example is the sulfnbk.exe virus hoax. The message comes from one of your friends telling you that a previous e-mail may have infected your computer with a nasty virus called sulfnbk.exe. The message tells you to delete the file sulfnbk.exe and then send e-mail to all of your friends warning them to do likewise because your messages may have infected their computers.

In reality, the file sulfnbk.exe is part of the Windows operating system. Fortunately, deleting this file does not render your computer inoperable. As it turns out, sulfnbk.exe is needed only to resolve long filename extensions during file recovery operations after a catastrophic system crash.

Computer Incident Advisory Capability

Figure 6-16 shows the sulfnbk.exe hoax message. I will keep secret the name of the distinguished professor who sent it to me. The danger is that someday, such a hoax could entice people to do something that could result in data loss or a computer crash. If you receive a message that you suspect may be a hoax, follow the *Interlit* Web site link to the catalog of hoaxes at the U.S. Department of Energy's Computer Incident Advisory Capability

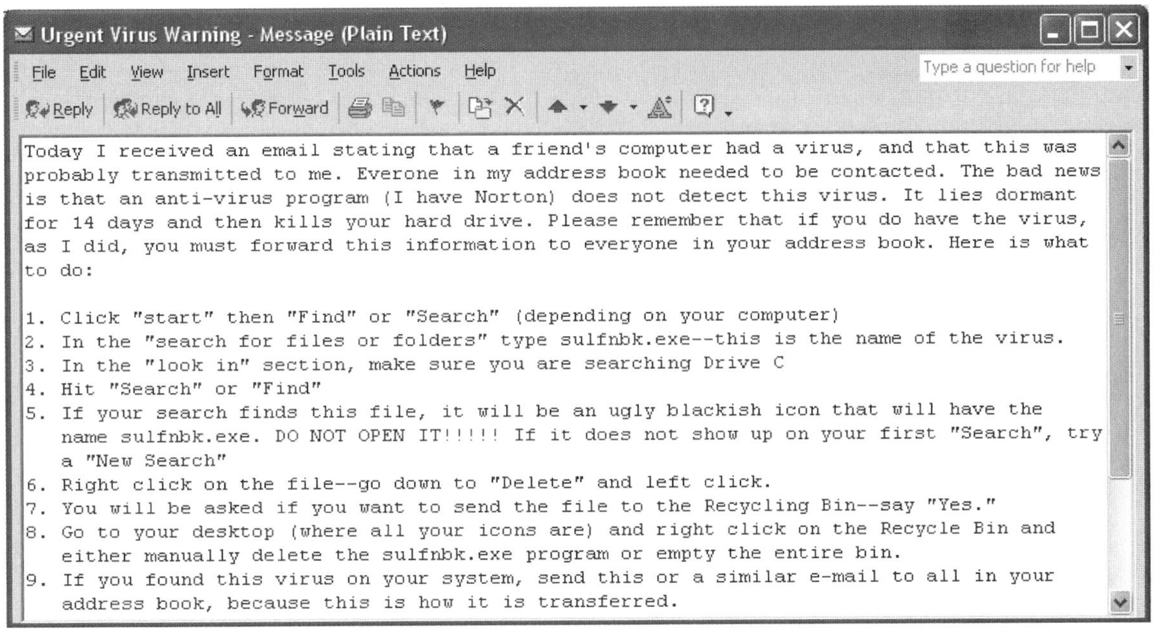

Urgent Virus Warning - Message (Plain Text)

File Edit View Insert Format Tools Actions Help   Type a question for help

Reply   Reply to All   Forward

Today I received an email stating that a friend's computer had a virus, and that this was
probably transmitted to me. Everone in my address book needed to be contacted. The bad news
is that an anti-virus program (I have Norton) does not detect this virus. It lies dormant
for 14 days and then kills your hard drive. Please remember that if you do have the virus,
as I did, you must forward this information to everyone in your address book. Here is what
to do:

1. Click "start" then "Find" or "Search" (depending on your computer)
2. In the "search for files or folders" type sulfnbk.exe--this is the name of the virus.
3. In the "look in" section, make sure you are searching Drive C
4. Hit "Search" or "Find"
5. If your search finds this file, it will be an ugly blackish icon that will have the
   name sulfnbk.exe. DO NOT OPEN IT!!!!! If it does not show up on your first "Search", try
   a "New Search"
6. Right click on the file--go down to "Delete" and left click.
7. You will be asked if you want to send the file to the Recycling Bin--say "Yes."
8. Go to your desktop (where all your icons are) and right click on the Recycle Bin and
   either manually delete the sulfnbk.exe program or empty the entire bin.
9. If you found this virus on your system, send this or a similar e-mail to all in your
   address book, because this is how it is transferred.

Figure 6-16 The sulfnbk.exe virus hoax, as received by the author from a distinguished professor colleague.

(CIAC) Web site, where you can look to see whether the hoax is a recognized one. For many of the hoaxes, the CIAC will recommend what actions you can take to discourage the spreading of the hoax. To look up a hoax and find out what to do about it, follow the *Interlit* Web site link to the CIAC Internet hoaxes page. Printed there are dozens of hoaxes along with an analysis of how each hoax worked. At the CIAC site you will also find links to Web pages warning you about the major chain letters and viruses that you need to watch out for on the Internet.

Beware of Phishing

Phishing is a type of scam in which you receive an e-mail message that appears to come from a legitimate business or financial agency. The e-mail message lures you into clicking a link (the bait) that takes you to a Web site where the scam artist prompts you to fill in personal information such as your social security number, credit card information, and bank account. The scam site can be cleverly disguised to look like the real McCoy.

You need to be careful never to fall for a phishing scam. Never click this kind of link in an e-mail message. Instead, if you want to verify your account information, use your browser to log on to the company's Web site, and follow the legitimate process there to check your account settings. Chapter 25 discusses phishing in more detail in the section on privacy.

Address Books

Before you can send e-mail to someone, you must know the person's e-mail address. To avoid having to look up a person's e-mail address every time, you can record it in an **address book,** which is an index of the e-mail addresses you want to keep for future use. To address an e-mail message to someone in your address book, you simply go into your address book, click the person's name, and choose the Send Mail option. This makes an e-mail composer screen appear with the person's e-mail address already filled in.

Adding a Name to Your Address Book

To add a name to your address book, follow the steps in Table 6-13.

Table 6-13   How to add a name to your address book

Mozilla Thunderbird	Microsoft Outlook Express

▶ Click the Thunderbird 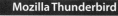 Address Book button; the Address Book window appears as shown in Figure 6-17.

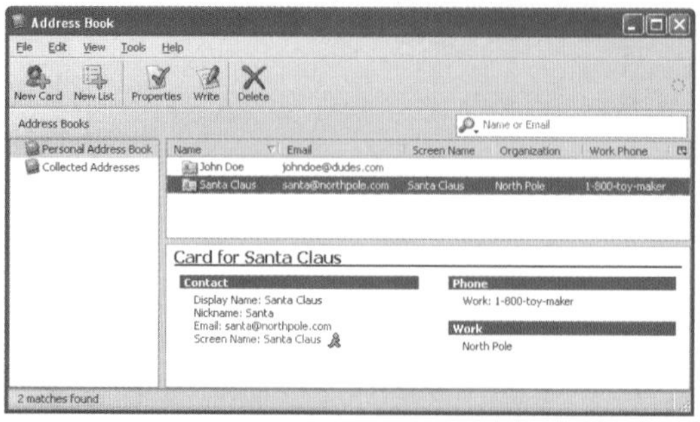

Figure 6-17   Thunderbird's Address Book window.

▶ To add a name, click the New Card button. The New Card dialog appears as shown in Figure 6-18.

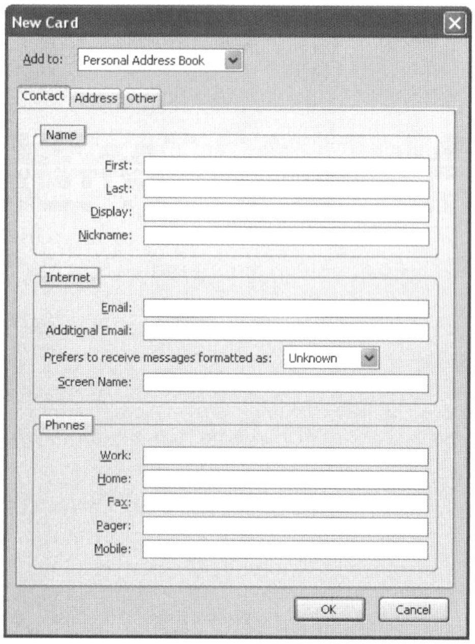

Figure 6-18   Thunderbird's New Card dialog.

▶ In the blanks provided, fill in the person's first name, last name, e-mail address, and a nickname.

▶ If you know the person reads mail with an HTML-enabled e-mail reader, set the Prefers to Receive Messages Formatted option to HTML; otherwise, leave that option set to unknown.

▶ If you want to record the person's phone numbers, fill out the Phones section at the bottom of the dialog.

▶ If you want to include information about the person's street address, click the Address tab and fill out that information.

▶ Click OK to close the New Card dialog, and you will see how the person has been added to your Address Book.

▶ If you ever want to change any of this information, just double-click the user's name in your Address Book.

▶ In Outlook Express, click the Addresses button; the Address Book window appears as shown in Figure 6-19.

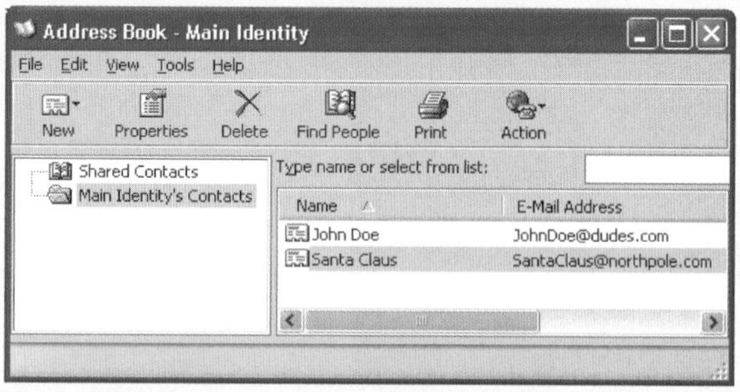

Figure 6-19   The Outlook Express Address Book window.

▶ To add a name, click the New button, and when the menu pops out, click New Contact. The Properties dialog appears as shown in Figure 6-20.

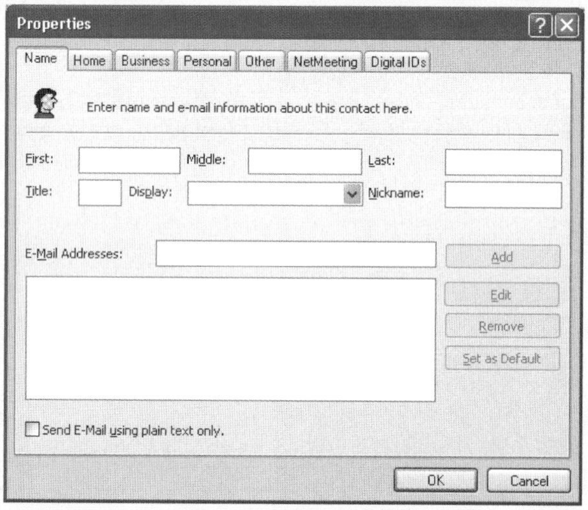

Figure 6-20   The Properties dialog for a new contact.

▶ In the blanks provided, fill in the person's first name, last name, e-mail address, and a nickname.

▶ If you know the person reads mail with a plain text (i.e., non-HTML) mail reader, click the option to send e-mail using plain text only. These days, most people read mail with HTML-enabled mail readers, so leave this option unchecked if you are unsure.

▶ By choosing the other tabs in the Properties dialog, you can add other information such as a home and business address.

▶ Click OK to close the Properties dialog, and you will see how the person has been added to your Address Book.

▶ If you ever want to change any of this information, just double-click the user's name in your address book.

Addressing E-mail to Someone Listed in an Address Book

To address an e-mail message to someone listed in an address book, follow the steps in Table 6-14.

Addressing E-mail to Groups of People

As social beings, it is natural for computer users to want to communicate with groups of people. You might be working on a project at work or at school, for example, and you would like to send a message to all of the people working on that project with you. Instead of having to enter each person's e-mail address each time you want to send the group a message, you can use your address book to create mailing lists consisting of as many users as you like. To create a mailing list, follow the steps in Table 6-15.

To send mail to the people in a mailing list, address the mail to the name of the mailing list, following the instructions provided in Table 6-2.

Table 6-14   How to address mail to someone listed in an address book

Mozilla Thunderbird	Microsoft Outlook Express
▶ From your Inbox window, click the Write button to make the Compose window appear.	▶ From the Outlook Express Inbox window, pull down the Message menu and choose New Message to make the New Message window appear.
▶ Click the Contacts button; the Contacts pane appears on the left side of the Compose window.	▶ In the To and Cc fields you will notice little address book icons at the left. Click the address book icon in the To field to bring up the Select Recipients dialog.
▶ Double-click on the name of the person to whom you want to address the message; the person's name appears in the address part of your message.	▶ Click once on the name of the person to whom you want to address the message.
▶ If you want the message to be sent as a carbon copy or a blind carbon copy, click the down-arrow alongside the To: field, and when the quick menu appears, choose cc: for a carbon copy or bcc: for a blind carbon copy.	▶ Click the To, Cc, or Bcc button, depending on whether you want the person to receive the original message, a carbon copy, or a blind carbon copy.
	▶ Click OK to close the Select Recipients dialogue; the person's name appears in the address part of your message.

Table 6-15   How to create a mailing list

Mozilla Thunderbird	Microsoft Internet Explorer
▶ Click the Thunderbird Address Book button to make the Address Book window appear.	▶ From the Outlook Express menu, click the Addresses button to make the Address Book window appear.
▶ Click the New List button. The Mailing List dialog appears as shown in Figure 6-21.	▶ Click the New button, and when the menu pops out, click New Group. The Properties dialog for the group appears as shown in Figure 6-22.

Figure 6-21   The Mailing List dialog.

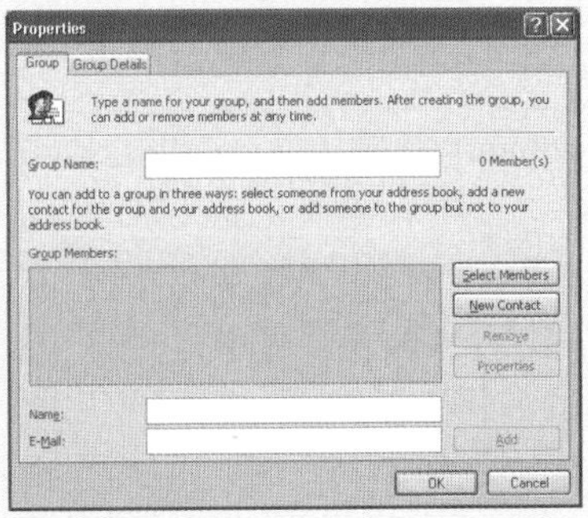

Figure 6-22   The Properties dialog for the new group.

Table 6-15 *(continued)*

Mozilla Thunderbird	Microsoft Internet Explorer
▶ In the blanks provided, fill in the name of the list, a nickname for the list, and a description summarizing the purpose of the list.	▶ Fill in a name for the group.
▶ On the lines in the mailing list, type the e-mail addresses of the users that you want included in this mailing list.	▶ Click the Select Members button to bring up the Select Group Members dialog shown in Figure 6-23.
▶ Click OK to close the Mailing List dialog, and you will see how the mailing list has been added to your Address Book.	
▶ If you ever want to change any of this information, just double-click the mailing list's name in your Address Book.	

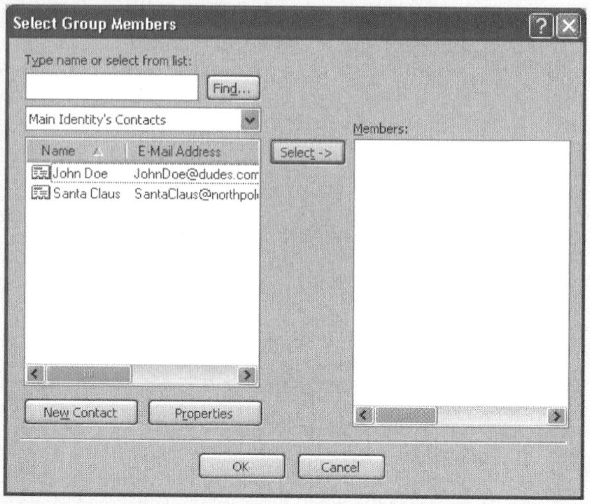

Figure 6-23 The Select Group Members dialog.

▶ Add names from your Address Book to the group by double-clicking on them or by clicking once and then clicking Select. If you want to include someone who is not already in your Address Book, click New Contact and proceed as before.

▶ When you are finished, click OK.

▶ If you ever want to change any of this information, just double-click the group's name in your address book.

Searching E-mail Messages

When you have a lot of accumulated mail, you will eventually lose track of where everything is. Happily, you can search your mail messages to find things. To search an e-mail message, follow the steps in Table 6-16.

Dealing with Unwanted E-mail

The best way to deal with unwanted e-mail is to delete it. If you are tempted to send a reply indicating your disdain for the unwanted mail, think twice before answering. If the message is unwanted commercial advertising, sending a reply will tell the sender that yours is a valid e-mail address, and you may receive even more spam as a result.

If you believe the unwanted mail is illegal, such as a mail message containing child pornographic material or other criminal activity, you can report the transmission by forwarding it to the appropriate authorities. For example, you can find out how to contact your local FBI office at www.fbi.gov. It may help to forward the message to the postmaster at your Internet service provider, informing your ISP of the unwanted activity and asking for it to be stopped. To send mail to your postmaster, assuming your ISP is northpole.com, you would address the mail to *postmaster@northpole.com*.

Table 6-16   How to search e-mail messages

Mozilla Thunderbird	Microsoft Outlook Express

▶ In the 🔍 search field in your Inbox window, type the keyword(s) that your search comprises.

▶ At the left edge of the search field in your Inbox window, click the 🔍 Search button to pull down the search menu and select the kind of search you want to perform. The choices include (1) subject, (2) sender, (3) subject or sender, (4) Entire message, (5) Find in message, or (6) Save search as a folder.

▶ If you choose to save the search as a folder, the Saved Search Folder dialog will appear, as illustrated in Figure 6-24.

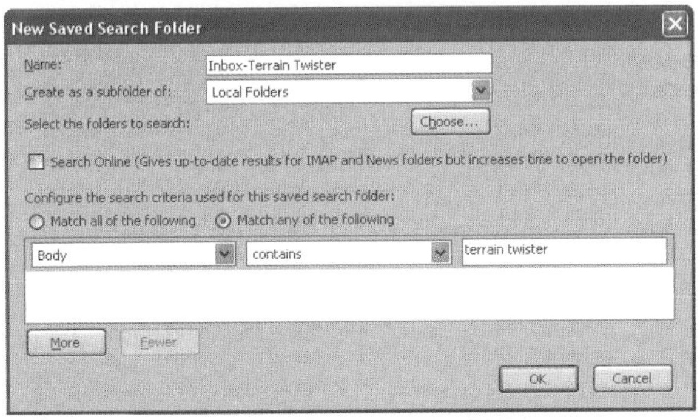

Figure 6-24   The Thunderbird Saved Search Folder dialog.

▶ Use the controls in the top half of the dialog to give the search a name and tell where you want the saved search folder created.

▶ Use the controls in the bottom half of the dialog to configure your search. For example, if you click on the first arrow, you get a menu that lets you choose what part of the mail messages to search. The second arrow sets whether to look for or exclude what you type into the corresponding text field.

▶ Click the More button if you want to define more search criteria.

▶ Click the OK button to start the search.

▶ The results of your search will appear in a file folder located in the place you specified in the top half of the dialog.

▶ From the Outlook Express window, pull down the Edit menu and choose Find→Message; the Find Message dialog appears as shown in Figure 6-25.

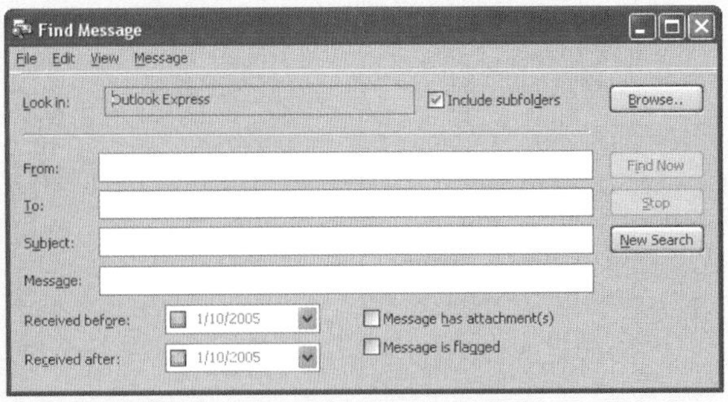

Figure 6-25   The Outlook Express Find Message dialog.

▶ Type the word or phrase that you want to find into the category you want searched; fields are provided for searching the From, To, Subject, or Message categories.

▶ Click Find Now to begin the search.

▶ The results of your search will appear in a list box beneath the search controls.

▶ Double-click an item in the list box to go to it.

Spam Recycling Center

You may also wish to support legislation to stop the unwanted mail, especially if it is unwanted commercial advertising. In that case, follow the *Interlit* Web site link to the Coalition Against Unsolicited Commercial Email (CAUCE) and the Spam Recycling Center. When this book went to press, 33 states had anti-spam laws.

Using Mail Filters

You can block mail from unwanted sources by using mail filters. Table 6-17 shows how to use a mail filter, for example, to block mail coming from any e-mail address that you forbid. You also can block mail by filtering key words in the subject line.

Mail filters also can direct certain messages into a file folder, which helps you organize incoming mail into categories. You could group messages from your superiors, for example, into a folder called Important.

Table 6-17 How to block unwanted messages with a mail filter

Mozilla Thunderbird	Microsoft Outlook Express
▶ From your Inbox window, pull down the Tools menu, and choose Message Filters.	▶ From the Outlook Express window, pull down the Tools menu and choose Message Rules→Mail. *Note:* The Message Rules apply only to POP3 accounts. If you are using IMAP, these instructions do not apply.
▶ In the Message Filters dialog, click the New button to create a new filter. The Filter Rules dialog appears.	▶ When the Message Rules dialog appears, click the New button to create a new rule.
▶ Enter the criteria for the messages you want to block. For example, Figure 6-26 shows how to block junk mail from cyberpromo.com.	▶ The New Mail Rule dialog appears.
	▶ Enter the criteria for the messages you want to block. For example, Figure 6-27 shows how to block junk mail from cyberpromo.com.

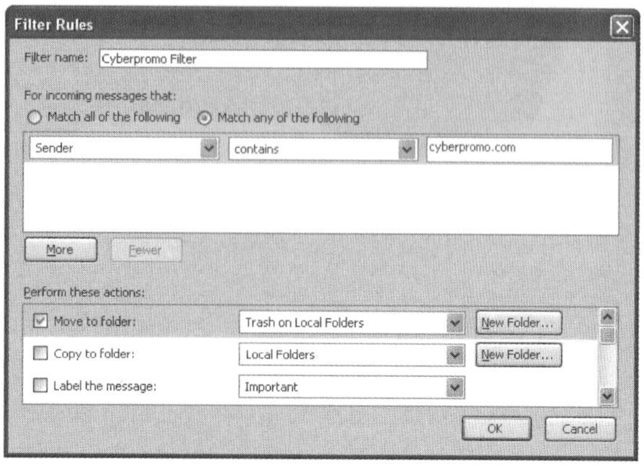

Figure 6-26 The Thunderbird Filter Rules dialog.

▶ Click OK to close the Filter Rules dialog. Your new rule appears in the Mail Filters dialog.

▶ Click the ☒ Close button to close the Mail Filters dialog.

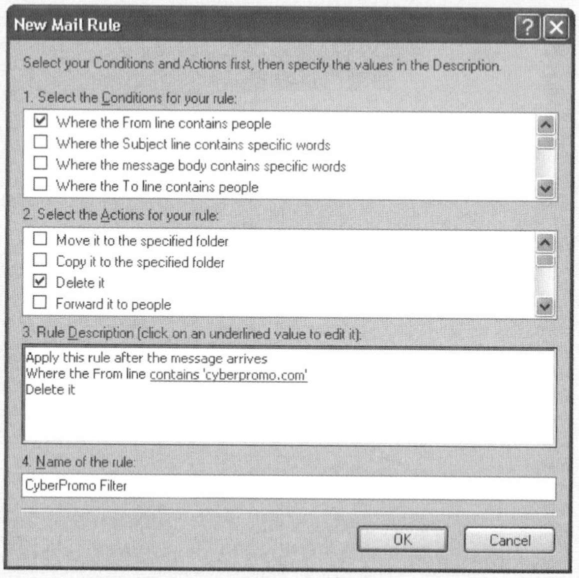

Figure 6-27 The Outlook Express New Mail Rule dialog.

▶ Click OK to close the New Mail Rule dialog. Your new rule appears in the Message Rules dialog.

▶ Click OK to close the Message Rules dialog.

Using Spam Filters

In my workplace, the University of Delaware has a spam filter that computes a spam score when it suspects that an incoming message is spam. When the message arrives in my Inbox, it has a spam score expressed by a string of asterisks in the message title. The more asterisks, the higher the likelihood the message is spam. Here are some examples:

[Spam:************* SpamScore] Very Important!

[Spam:******************* SpamScore] Re:

[Spam:**************** SpamScore] Re: Opportunity of a lifetime

Following the steps in Table 6-17, I can set a mail filter to delete automatically messages whose titles begin with a certain spam score. For example, to delete all messages with a spam score of 12 or higher, I set the filter to block messages beginning with [Spam:***********.

Thunderbird's Junk Mail Filter

Thunderbird has a spam filter called the Junk Mail filter. In your Inbox, Thunderbird displays the Junk icon alongside messages suspected of being spam. The Junk Mail filter has an adaptive mode in which Thunderbird learns to detect spam. You train it by clicking the Junk button to indicate whether or not a given message is spam. On the Thunderbird toolbar, the Junk button appears as follows:

If you receive spam that Thunderbird has not marked as junk, you click the message to select it and then click the Junk button to mark it as spam. If Thunderbird marks a desired message as spam, on the other hand, you click the message to select it and then click the Junk button to unmark it as spam.

To configure Thunderbird's Junk Mail filter settings, pull down Thunderbird's Tools menu and choose Junk Mail Controls to bring up the Junk Mail Controls window. Figure 6-28

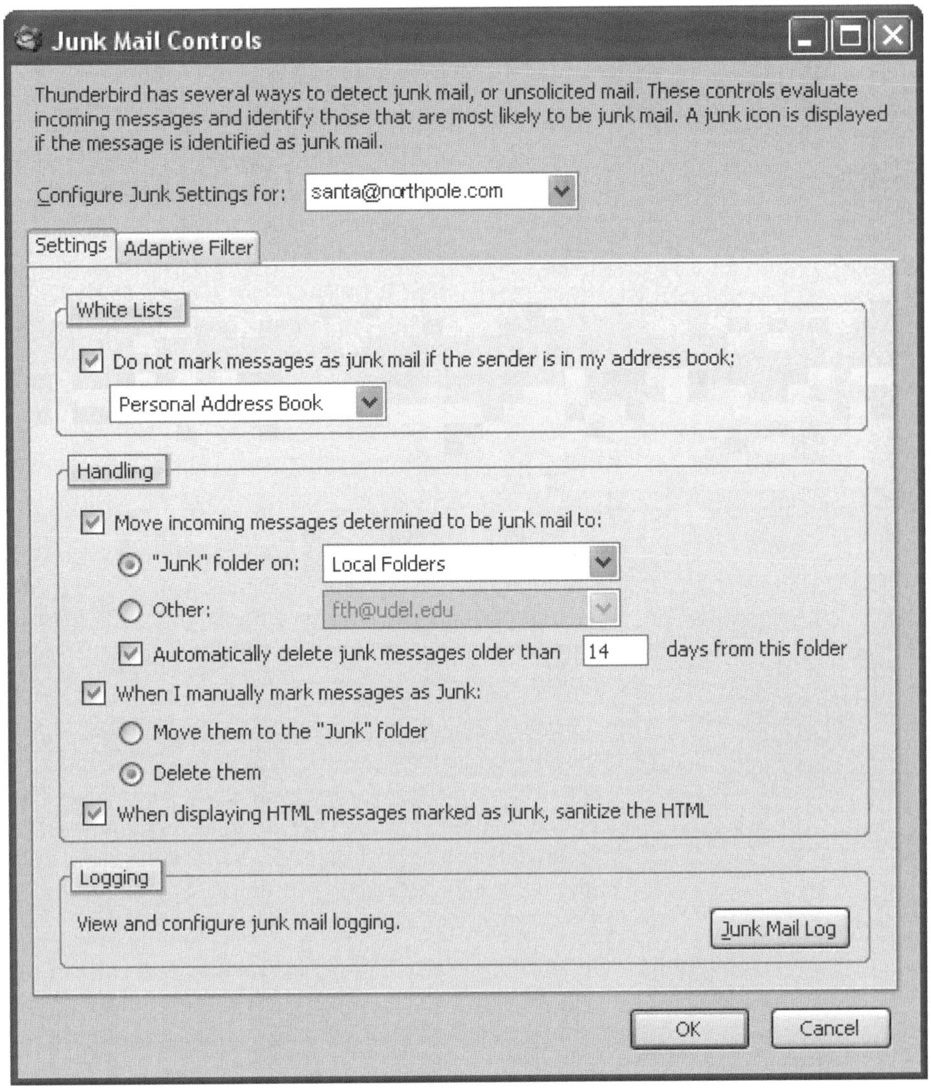

Figure 6-28 The Junk Mail Controls window enables you to customize the manner in which Thunderbird detects and disposes of spam.

Table 6-18 How to detect fake mail IDs

Mozilla Thunderbird	Microsoft Outlook Express
▶ With a message selected, pull down the View menu and choose Headers→All. The complete header information appears at the top of the e-mail message. ▶ To return to viewing normal headers, pull down the View menu and choose Headers→Normal.	▶ With a message selected, pull down the File menu, choose Properties, then click the Details tab. ▶ Click OK to exit the Properties dialog.

shows how the settings enable you to (1) prevent Thunderbird from marking as junk mail sent from someone in your address book, (2) move incoming messages to a junk folder and automatically delete them after a certain number of days, (3) delete messages when you manually mark them as junk, and (4) sanitize the HTML in messages marked as junk. To sanitize means to remove active content and mail attachments capable of transmitting viruses.

Detecting Fake Mail IDs

If you get mail saying it is from someone that you doubt actually wrote the message, such as a message from your boss giving you a million-dollar raise, someone may have used a bogus From field when they sent you the message. You can get more information about where the message came from by revealing the headers of the mail message. To detect a fake mail ID, follow the instructions in Table 6-18. You need to be aware, however, that sophisticated spammers can fake any of the headers except for the last Received header, which identifies the last computer through which the message passed on its way to your Inbox.

Encrypting Your Mail

If you are concerned about privacy, you may want to consider encrypting your e-mail messages. To **encrypt** a message means to run it through an encoder that uses an encryption key to alter the characters in the message. Unless the person wanting to read the message has the encryption key needed to decode it, the message appears garbled.

Consider a simple example of an encryption key "123" that will shift each successive character in the message by 1, 2, or 3 characters in the alphabet. So encrypted, the message *Hello world* appears as *Igomq zptoe*. In practice, encryption keys are much longer, and the encoding process is so complex that you would need a supercomputer to crack the key to an encrypted message. As you will learn in Part Seven, legislation has been created that allows the government to obtain a court order to decode encrypted messages of suspected criminals.

Outlook Express has an ⬚ Encrypt icon that you can click when you want a message to be sent encrypted. To see the encryption settings, pull down the Outlook Express Tools menu, then click Options. In the Options dialog, click the Security tab.

Thunderbird also lets you encrypt your mail. To see the settings, pull down Thunderbird's Tools menu, choose Options, click ⚙ Advanced, and expand the section on Certificates.

In order for this to work properly, however, you need to have a Digital ID, which consists of a public key, a private key, and a digital signature. When you receive a digitally signed message, you can inspect the signature to see where the message came from, who owns the key that signed the message, what certificate authority issued the key, and what algorithms created the signature and the message digest.

VeriSign

Although it is beyond the scope of this book to provide a tutorial on encrypting mail, it is easy to get you started. One of the Internet's primary certificate authorities is VeriSign. Follow the *Interlit* Web site link to VeriSign's e-mail security service for an explanation of how the process works. A detailed tutorial is in Chapter 13 of my more-technical book entitled *Internet Technologies at Work* (McGraw-Hill, ISBN 0-07-222999-3).

E-mail Priorities

Both Mozilla and Microsoft support a priority-setting option that lets you set the priority of an e-mail message. You set this option when you send a message, and when it arrives at its destination, it has a priority flag indicating how important it is. The person receiving the messages can sort them in order of priority and read the most important ones first. To set the priority for an e-mail message, follow the steps in Table 6-19.

Return Receipt Requested

For a really important message, you may want to be sure the person to whom you sent it has received it. To verify the receipt of a message, you can set an option for the person's e-mail client to send you a return receipt when the person opens the message. To request

Table 6-19 How to set the priority of an e-mail message

Mozilla Thunderbird	Microsoft Outlook Express
▶ In the Composition window in which you normally create an e-mail message, there is a Priority setting on the Options menu.	▶ In the New Message window in which you normally create an e-mail message, click the arrow alongside the ⬇! Priority button.
▶ Pull down the Options menu, select Priority, and a menu will pop out giving you the priority choices illustrated in Figure 6-29.	▶ The priority settings pop out, as shown in Figure 6-30.

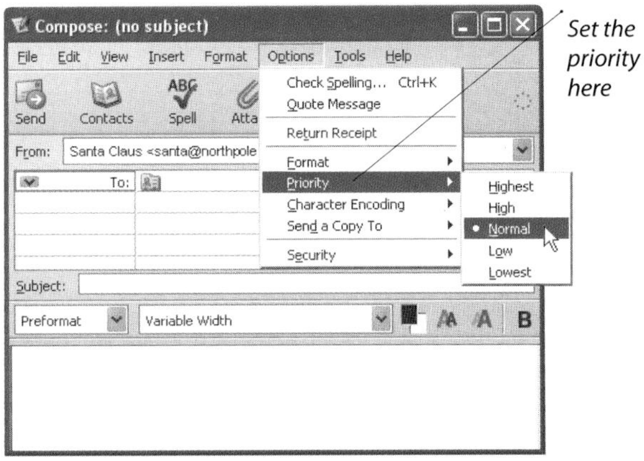

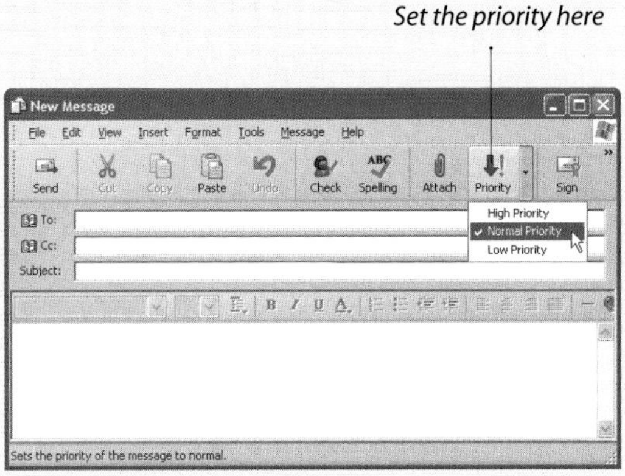

Figure 6-29 The Priority menu.

▶ Click the option you want.

▶ Send the mail as usual.

Figure 6-30 The Priority menu pops out.

▶ Click the option you want.

▶ Send the mail as usual.

Table 6-20   How to set the return receipt requested option

Mozilla Thunderbird	Microsoft Outlook Express
▶ In the Compose window in which you normally create an e-mail message, there is a Return Receipt setting on the Options menu.	▶ In the New Message window in which you normally create an e-mail message, there is a Request Read Receipt option on the Tools menu.
▶ Pull down the Options menu and select Return Receipt, as illustrated in Figure 6-31.	▶ Pull down the Tools menu and select Request Read Receipt, as illustrated in Figure 6-32.

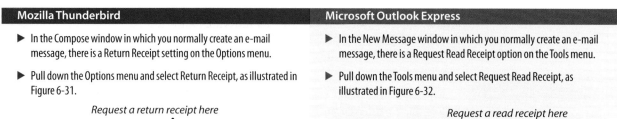

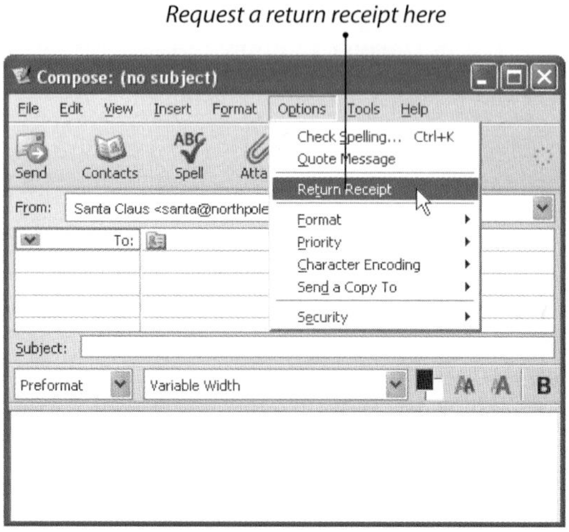

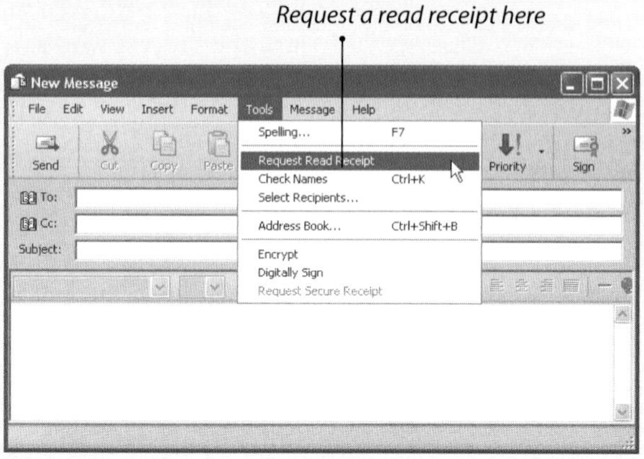

Request a return receipt here

Request a read receipt here

Figure 6-32   The Request Read Receipt option.

Figure 6-31   The Return Receipt option.

▶ Send the mail as usual.

▶ Send the mail as usual.

a return receipt, follow the steps in Table 6-20. *Note*: There is no guarantee that the person who receives the message will choose the setting that acknowledges receipt. Many users, in fact, say no when asked if they want the receipt sent.

Spell Checking

As a final touch, before you send the e-mail message, you may want to spell check it and correct any spelling mistakes.

To spell check an e-mail message with Thunderbird, click the Spell button in the Compose window.

If you are using Outlook Express, click the Spelling button in the New Message window.

Web-Based E-mail

Several Internet service providers make it possible to do your e-mail on the Web, using a browser instead of an e-mail program. Sending and receiving e-mail on the Web is convenient because you can access your e-mail from any computer that has a browser and an Internet connection.

MSN Hotmail

Several Internet portal sites offer Web-based e-mail services. Anyone can register at the portal to receive a free Web-based e-mail account. Then you can read and send mail with your browser. Popular Web-based e-mail services are at hotmail.com and mail.yahoo.com. They include a POP option, which enables you to read the mail delivered via your ISP's mail server. This comes in handy when you travel, for example, because your e-mail can be delivered to any PC connected to the Internet, such as at a public library or an Internet café.

Yahoo Mail

America Online has a Web-based e-mail service that lets AOL users read their AOL mail from their browser, as an alternative to also reading it with the AOL mail program. Microsoft Network users can read their MSN mail with Hotmail. Yahoo operates a Web-based e-mail service called Yahoo Mail. Follow the *Interlit* Web site links to learn more about the Web-based e-mail services available from Hotmail, Yahoo, AOL, and other Web-based e-mail providers.

Sending Mail as HTML

In the Web-page creation part of this book (Part Five), you will learn how to use HTML, which stands for Hypertext Markup Language. HTML enables you to include in a mail message bolding, italics, underlining, colors, fonts, and special symbols that do not get transmitted in plain text messages. If you know that the person to whom you are sending an e-mail message is using an e-mail program that can handle HTML, therefore, you may wish to consider sending the mail as HTML instead of plain text.

E-mail programs that can handle HTML include Thunderbird and Outlook Express. Web-based e-mail programs such as Hotmail and Yahoo Mail also understand the HTML option. On the other hand, if you know that the person reads mail with a text-based e-mail program such as PINE, which is popular on Unix systems, then you should not set the HTML option because HTML mail does not display properly in a text-based e-mail reader. To send mail as HTML, follow the steps in Table 6-21. Note about conserving bandwidth: The HTML option enables you to put pictures in your e-mail messages. Be aware, however, that including pictures in HTML mail messages makes the files considerably larger and therefore longer to send and receive, especially for users with dial-up access.

Table 6-21   How to send mail as HTML

Mozilla Thunderbird	Microsoft Outlook Express
▶ In the Compose window in which you normally create an e-mail message, pull down the Options menu and choose Format.	▶ In the New Message window in which you normally create an e-mail message, the HTML option is one of the choices on the Format menu.
▶ The formatting options pop out as illustrated in Figure 6-33.	▶ Pull down the Format menu and select Rich Text (HTML), as illustrated in Figure 6-34.

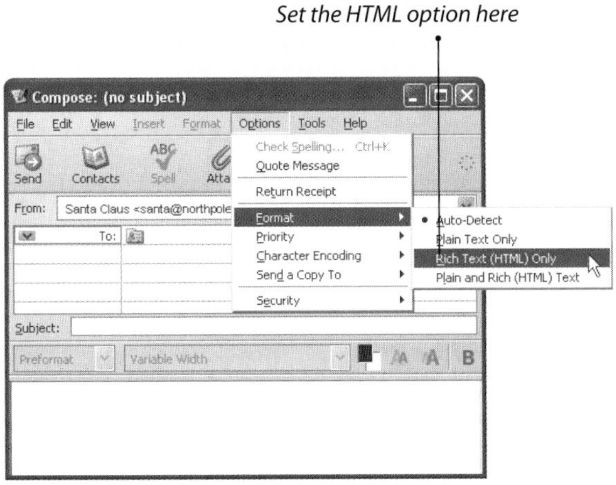

Set the HTML option here

Set the HTML option here

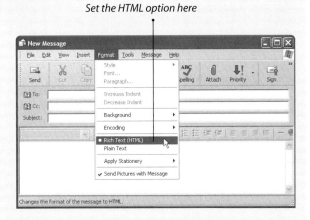

Figure 6-33   The Thunderbird mail format options.

Figure 6-34   The Outlook Express mail format options.

▶ Choose the option to send the mail as Rich Text (HTML), or if you want to send it both as HTML and plain text, choose the option to send as Plain Text and Rich (HTML) Text. This will increase the size of the e-mail message, however, so do this only in cases where you are unsure.

▶ Send the mail as usual.

▶ Send the mail as usual.

exercises

1. Practice sending e-mail messages to yourself. Send yourself one message, then use your e-mail client to get your new mail and see if you can read the message you sent yourself. Then send several messages to yourself without reading them yet. Tell your e-mail client to get your new mail and see whether all of the messages arrive. Notice how each message will bear a time stamp telling when it was written.

2. Find a couple of friends who have e-mail addresses and practice sending and receiving messages with them. Try using the forward feature to forward mail received from one friend to another.

3. Create e-mail file folders named after two of your friends and practice filing the mail they send you into their respective e-mail folders. Later on, use your e-mail reader (Thunderbird or Outlook Express) to go into the e-mail folders and see if you can find the messages you filed there. Does this make it easier to find messages than if you kept them all in the same file?

4. To save time addressing messages to your e-mail friends, enter their e-mail addresses into your address book. Practice sending your friends messages that you address by selecting their names from the address book instead of typing their e-mail addresses. How much time does this save you per message?

5. Reveal the full headers on an e-mail message that someone sends you. What additional information can you glean from the complete headers as to who sent the message and how it got routed to your computer?

6. Follow the *Interlit* Web site link to the voting record of members of Congress to find out whether your congressional representatives are voting the way you want them to. Send e-mail to express your views. Point-and-click e-mail addresses are available for every member of Congress at Yahoo. Follow the *Interlit* Web site link to congressional e-mail addresses, or go to yahoo.com and search for "Congressional e-mail addresses."

7. This chapter warns against viruses that can be transmitted in e-mail attachments. When this book went to press, the most harmful virus that had appeared to date was the Love Bug virus. Follow the *Interlit* Web site link that monitors the latest viruses. What is the name of the latest virus to have appeared to date? How does the virus work; that is, how is it transmitted, what triggers it, and what effect does it have on the user's files or computers? Do you think it is worse than the Love Bug virus? Why or why not?

SITUATED CASE PROJECTS
Case 6: Adopting an E-mail Client

At the end of each chapter in this book, a situated case project provides the student an opportunity to put the chapter's contents to practical use in a workplace situation. Each case has the same number as the chapter in which it appears.

Not all e-mail packages were created equal. They all have their own look and feel, features, advantages, disadvantages, and security issues to contend with. Most companies and schools adopt a common e-mail client and recommend or require that all employees use it when accessing the office mail server. Imagine that you have been charged with recommending an e-mail client for use by your school or company. Consider the following issues in formulating this recommendation:

1 How does the e-mail client look and feel? If you do not have a lot of experience with different e-mail clients, study this chapter's many side-by-side comparisons of Mozilla Thunderbird and Microsoft Outlook Express. Consider which e-mail client appeals to you most.

2 How well does the e-mail client integrate with other software and services used in your school or company?

3 How secure is the e-mail sent or received by this client, and how prone is it to sending or receiving viruses?

4 How much does the e-mail client cost, and can your school or company afford it?

Use a word processor to write up your recommendation in the form of a brief essay describing the e-mail clients you compared and citing the reasons why you chose the one you recommended. If your instructor has asked you to hand in the recommendation, make sure you put your name at the top, then save it on disk or follow the other instructions you may have been given for submitting this assignment.

7

LISTSERV MAILING LISTS

After completing this chapter, you will be able to:

- Describe how listserv mailing lists work through e-mail protocols.

- Find out the names of listserv mailing lists in your discipline or any other subject that interests you.

- Subscribe to a listserv mailing list.

- Know when to lurk on a listserv mailing list.

- Respond to messages received from a listserv.

- Send new messages to a listserv mailing list.

- File messages received from a listserv.

- Unsubscribe from a listserv mailing list.

- Set up your own listserv mailing list on the Internet.

Now that you know how to send and receive electronic mail, you are ready to take advantage of the powerful capabilities of listserv, which is an Internet service that uses e-mail protocols to distribute messages to lists of users. The messages get served to everyone whose name is on the list, hence the name *listserv*.

There are tens of thousands of listserv mailing lists that this chapter will enable you to join. Almost every subject imaginable has a mailing list already set up for people to receive and exchange information about that topic. When someone sends a message containing new information to the mailing list, everyone on the list receives a copy of the message.

Some listserv mailing lists are moderated, meaning that someone screens incoming messages before they are distributed to the list. Most mailing lists are not moderated, however, meaning that you can freely send messages. Some lists are used only to distribute messages from the list's owner to the members of the list, while others let the members of the list participate in the discussion. Listservs can be used to distribute electronic magazines called *e-zines,* in which each new issue gets e-mailed to all the members of the list periodically. At the end of this chapter, you will learn how to set up your own listserv mailing list, through which you could publish your own e-zine, for example.

How to Subscribe to a Listserv Mailing List

Because a listserv uses e-mail protocols that virtually every user of the Internet already knows, listserv is easy to learn and use. There are two ways to subscribe to a listserv mailing list. First, many listservs have a Web page where you sign up by filling out a form

Table 7-1   How to subscribe to a listserv mailing list

▶ Use your e-mail client to create a new message window.

▶ Address the message to the listserv. In this example, address the message to **listserv@listserv.educause.edu**

▶ Leave the subject line blank, and as your message, type:
   SUBSCRIBE Edupage *YourFirstName YourLastName*

▶ Replace *YourFirstName* and *YourLastName* with your first and last names.

▶ Send the message.

that prompts you for your name and e-mail address. When you click the submit button to submit the form, your name gets added to the list. The second way to join a listserv mailing list is to send its host computer an e-mail message saying you want to subscribe. For example, suppose you want to join Edupage, which is a listserv that sends you news about new technology three times each week. To subscribe to Edupage, follow the steps in Table 7-1.

Although most listservs will send you a reply right away because a computer handles the request to subscribe, you may not always receive an instant response. Before too long, however, you will receive an e-mail reply from the server letting you know that you are now subscribed to the Edupage mailing list. Read the first message carefully. If you subscribed via the Web, it may instruct you to send a confirming e-mail message. This confirmation prevents other people from impersonating you and signing you up to the listserv. The first message also normally contains the instructions for how to unsubscribe from the list. Therefore, you may wish to file the first message to save these instructions for future use.

Because hundreds of thousands of people subscribe to Edupage, it is tightly controlled by the people who moderate it. Edupage's purpose is to distribute technology news e-zine style rather than to host discussions via the listserv. Therefore, if you try to post messages to the Edupage listserv after you join it, you will probably receive a reply that Edupage does not enable discussions among the members of the listserv.

Finding Listservs in Your Profession

You can use the Web to find out about listservs across a broad range of disciplines and professions. Click the listserv icon at the *Interlit* Web site, or go to one of the listserv search tools listed in Table 7-2.

Recommended Listserv Mailing Lists

I would like to recommend a few listserv mailing lists to you. These lists deal with technology and focus especially on emerging trends and issues regarding the Internet.

Edupage

Edupage

Instructions for joining Edupage were provided earlier in this chapter in Table 7-1. You can also use the Web signup form at listserv.educause.edu/archives/edupage.html. If you have not already joined Edupage, please do so. It is the best single source for keeping up with what is happening, imho.

Table 7-2 Listserv search tools

Name of Search Tool	Web Address	Logo
TileNet/Lists	tile.net/lists	
Liszt Directory of Email Discussion Groups	lists.topica.com	
CataList Catalog of Listserv Lists	www.lsoft.com/lists/listref.html	

Tourbus

The Internet Tourbus

The best listserv for someone new to the Internet is Tourbus. Two times a week, you will receive in your e-mail a message giving you the scoop on search engines, spam, viruses, cookies, urban legends, and the most useful sites on the Net. When this book went to press, 90,000 users from 130 countries were riding the Tourbus. To subscribe, go to www.tourbus.com and follow the onscreen instructions.

LockerGnome

LockerGnome

At lockergnome.com, you can subscribe to lists that will send you newsletters containing tips, updates, and industry news for Windows, OS X, or Linux users. A list called *Mobile Lifestyle* will send you news of MP3 releases, streaming video sites, online radio stations, media player skins, Webcam pages, DVD reviews, and new multimedia hardware and software. *Tech News Watch* includes the latest technology reviews, press releases, news, subscriber feedback, and stuff that does not fit into any of the other LockerGnome newsletters. To subscribe, go to www.lockergnome.com and follow the onscreen instructions.

Receiving Listserv Messages: Remember to Lurk!

The easiest part of belonging to a listserv is receiving the messages the listserv sends you. The messages sent by the listserv appear automatically in your e-mail inbox, where you read them like any other e-mail message. As illustrated in Figure 7-1, the From field of your e-mail message will indicate that it came from the listserv.

If you join a listserv that allows you to send as well as to receive messages, remember the advice that was provided in Chapter 5 on Netiquette. Before you jump in and start originating your own messages, remember to lurk for a while, reading without responding, until you get the gist of the ongoing conversation. When you start sending messages, make sure each message fits the topic or purpose of the listserv. If the topic does not fit the purpose of the listserv, you should not send it there.

If you do not want the messages from a listserv arriving in your daily e-mail, you can use an e-mail filter to collect them and place them in a separate folder for reading later. Chapter 6 contains instructions for setting up e-mail filters (see Table 6-17).

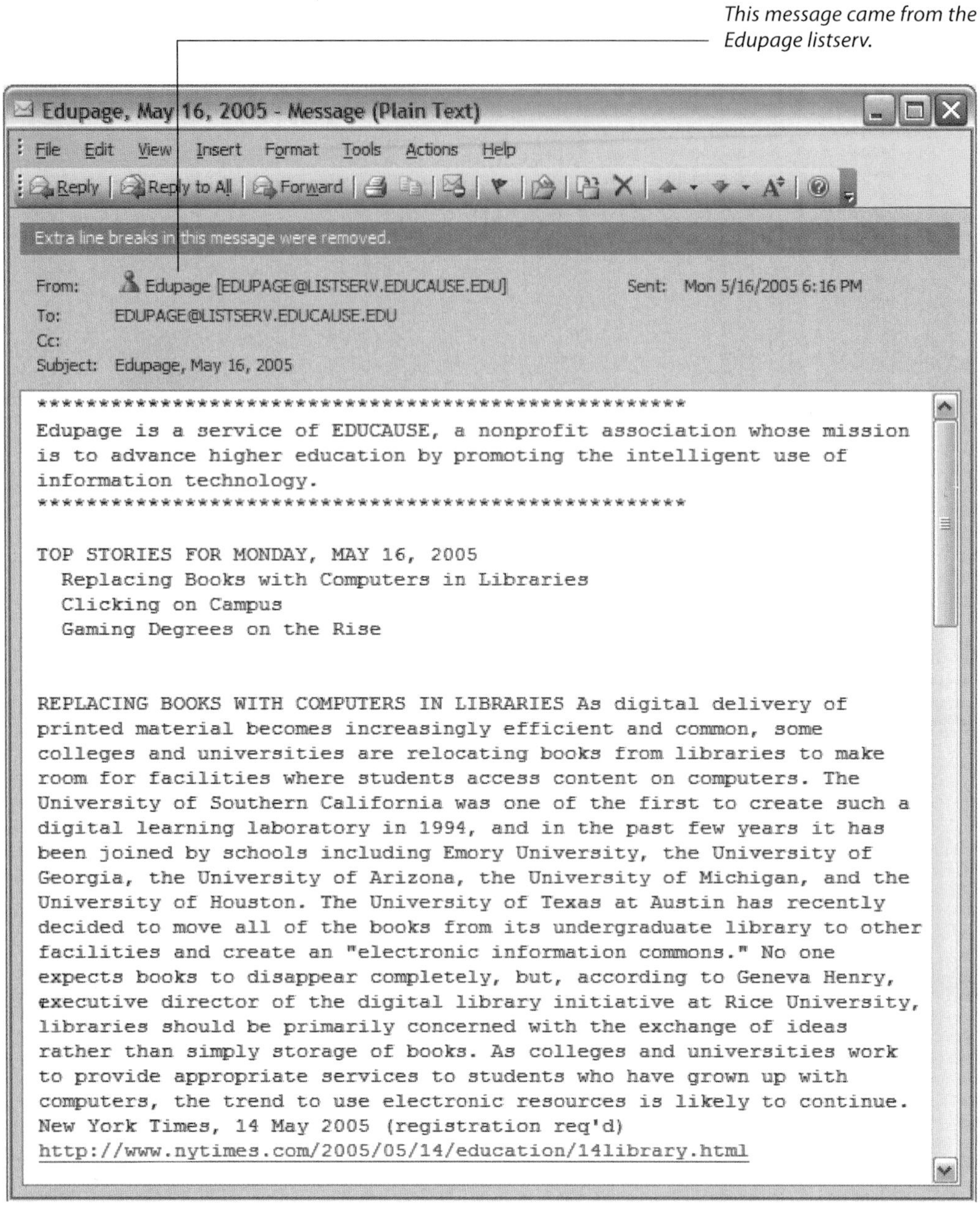

This message came from the Edupage listserv.

✉ Edupage, May 16, 2005 - Message (Plain Text)   _ □ ✕

File   Edit   View   Insert   Format   Tools   Actions   Help

Reply | Reply to All | Forward | 🖨 📋 | ✉ | ⬇ | 📁 📁 ✕ | ⬆ ▾ ⬇ ▾ A⁺ | ⓘ

Extra line breaks in this message were removed.

From: 👤 Edupage [EDUPAGE@LISTSERV.EDUCAUSE.EDU]   Sent: Mon 5/16/2005 6:16 PM
To: EDUPAGE@LISTSERV.EDUCAUSE.EDU
Cc:
Subject: Edupage, May 16, 2005

```
*********************************************************
Edupage is a service of EDUCAUSE, a nonprofit association whose mission
is to advance higher education by promoting the intelligent use of
information technology.
*********************************************************

TOP STORIES FOR MONDAY, MAY 16, 2005
  Replacing Books with Computers in Libraries
  Clicking on Campus
  Gaming Degrees on the Rise


REPLACING BOOKS WITH COMPUTERS IN LIBRARIES As digital delivery of
printed material becomes increasingly efficient and common, some
colleges and universities are relocating books from libraries to make
room for facilities where students access content on computers. The
University of Southern California was one of the first to create such a
digital learning laboratory in 1994, and in the past few years it has
been joined by schools including Emory University, the University of
Georgia, the University of Arizona, the University of Michigan, and the
University of Houston. The University of Texas at Austin has recently
decided to move all of the books from its undergraduate library to other
facilities and create an "electronic information commons." No one
expects books to disappear completely, but, according to Geneva Henry,
executive director of the digital library initiative at Rice University,
libraries should be primarily concerned with the exchange of ideas
rather than simply storage of books. As colleges and universities work
to provide appropriate services to students who have grown up with
computers, the trend to use electronic resources is likely to continue.
New York Times, 14 May 2005 (registration req'd)
http://www.nytimes.com/2005/05/14/education/14library.html
```

Figure 7-1   The From field indicates that an e-mail message came from a listserv.

Responding to a Listserv Message

Responding to a listserv message is easy because the address of the listserv is already in the From field or the Reply field of the listserv message. To respond, simply press your Reply button and enter your response just like you would to send an ordinary e-mail message. Remember that your reply will be sent to lots of people, however, so make sure that what you write pertains to the purpose of the listserv.

If you want to respond only to the individual who sent the message, remember to edit the To field so the reply will go to the sender instead of everyone on the list. It can be embarrassing when a private message intended for an individual gets copied to an entire list full of people.

Sending a New Message to a Listserv

When you join a listserv mailing list, you will be told how to address new messages that you want to send to the list. Since listserv addresses can be technical and hard to remember, it is a good idea to enter this address in your e-mail client's address book so you will not forget it. To send a new message to the listserv, you send e-mail to this address just as if you were sending mail to an individual user. Once again, please remember that your message will be sent to lots of people; make sure it is a proper use of the listserv.

Note: Each listserv has two addresses that you will want to keep track of. First is the listserv address, which is the address to which you send your subscribe command. Second is the list address to use when you want to send messages to everyone on the list. The listserv will tell you this list address in response to your subscribe command.

Filing Messages Received from Listservs

Occasionally you may receive a message from a listserv that you want to file for later reference. Since messages from listservs arrive as e-mail messages, you can click your File button and file them just like any other e-mail message. Refer to Chapter 6 for instructions on how to create an e-mail folder (Table 6-6) and how to file messages in it (Table 6-7).

Pausing a Listserv

If you plan to be away from your computer for a while, such as on a vacation, you may want to send a command to the listserv to make it stop sending messages to you. To pause a listserv, send it the following command in the body of an e-mail message, leaving the subject blank:

SET NOMAIL

To resume the listserv, send the following command:

SET MAIL

Because there are several software packages that listserv owners can use to manage their listservs, not all listservs respond to the same set of commands. If a listserv does not respond to the SET NOMAIL command, for example, you may need to unsubscribe to get the listserv to stop sending you messages and then subscribe again when you want to resume. If the listserv has a Web site, look there for documentation of the features you can use to control the sending of messages.

Finding Out Who Belongs to a Listserv

It is natural to be curious about who belongs to a listserv. When you send messages to a listserv, everyone on the list gets a copy of your message. To find out who is getting a copy, send the listserv the following command in the body of an e-mail message, leaving the subject blank:

REVIEW *listname*

If that does not work, try

WHO *listname*

Replace *listname* with the name of the list. The listserv will respond by e-mailing you a list of its members, unless the list has a privacy policy not to reveal the members of the list.

Note: The REVIEW and WHO commands must be sent to the listserv address, not the list address. If you send a command to the list address, every member of the list will get it; this can be embarrassing, and it marks you as a newbie on the Net.

If the listserv does not respond to the REVIEW and WHO commands, or if you do not know the e-mail address of the listserv, try going to the listserv's Web site and looking there for documentation of the features you can use.

Receiving Messages in Digest Mode

Digest mode is a way of receiving several messages packaged in one e-mail with an index at the top summarizing the subject and sender of each message. If a listserv is full of activity, for example, and sends you several messages a day, you may prefer to receive one digest message instead of many individual messages. To tell a listserv you want to receive the messages in digest mode, send it the following command:

SET *listname* **MAIL DIGEST**

Replace *listname* with the name of the list. The listserv will begin sending you a digest of each day's messages. To end digest mode and make the list send each message in a separate e-mail, send the listserv the following command:

SET *listname* **MAIL**

How to Unsubscribe from a Listserv

Sometimes you join a listserv only to find that its content does not meet your needs, or you get sent so many messages that you just cannot keep up with them. In either case, you will probably want to unsubscribe from the listserv. To unsubscribe, follow the steps in the message you got from the listserv. Many listservs write unsubscribe instructions at the bottom of every message so you can always find out how to unsubscribe.

If you subscribed from a Web site, you can probably fill out a form at the Web site that will unsubscribe you. Otherwise, try sending an e-mail message to the listserv address, which is the address you used when you joined the listserv. Leave the subject line blank, and as your message, type **SIGNOFF** followed by the name of the listserv.

Note: Do not send the signoff message to the list address. Doing so will not unsubscribe you from the list. Rather, your signoff message will go to every member of the list, marking you as a novice who does not fully understand how to use a listserv.

Listserv Archives

Many listservs have archives in which the messages sent to the list are filed. You can read and in many cases search the archives online. You can send listserv commands to see the archives, or if the listserv keeps archives on the Web, you can use your browser to inspect them. There is a Web-based archive of the messages at the Edupage listserv, for example; to see them, follow the *Interlit* Web site link to the Edupage archive. Likewise, there is an archive of the Tourbus listserv; follow the link to the Tourbus archive to see the archived Tourbus messages.

Table 7-3 Listserv commands

Listserv Command	What the Command Does
SUBSCRIBE *listname full_name*	Subscribes you to the list or changes the name under which you were previously subscribed; replace *full_name* with your name.
SUBSCRIBE *listname* ANONYMOUS	Subscribes you to the list anonymously, if the listserv allows that for this list.
REVIEW *listname*	Requests information about a list, including who owns it and who belongs to it.
SET NOMAIL	Makes the listserv stop sending you messages. (To resume, send the command **SET MAIL.**)
RELEASE	Find out information about the listserv software being used to run this listserv, and who maintains the server.
SIGNOFF *listname*	Unsubscribes you from the list.
SET *listname* CONCEAL	Hides your listing from REVIEW.
SET *listname* NOCONCEAL	Lets you be listed by REVIEW.
SET *listname* MAIL DIGEST	Makes the listserv send a day's messages in a single e-mail with a table of contents at the top.
SET *listname* MAIL	Ends digest mode and makes the listserv send you separate messages.
SHOW STATS	Shows statistics about the listserv.
SEARCH *listname keyword1* *<keyword2...>*	Search the listserv archives; for more search options, send the **LISTSERV REFCARD** command.
QUERY *listname*	Queries your set of options on the listserv; use **SET** to change them.
LISTSERV REFCARD	Asks the listserv to e-mail you a reference card listing commands users can send the listserv.

Listserv Command Summary

Table 7-3 contains a summary of some of the commands you can send a listserv. For a more complete list, send the listserv the command **LISTSERV REFCARD.** Remember that if you joined the listserv from the Web, an easier way to send commands may be to click the controls at the listserv's Web site. The trend is to put commands at the listserv's Web site instead of requiring you to send them via e-mail.

Setting Up Your Own Listserv

topica.com

Yahoo! Groups

If you want to set up your own listserv, you can do so for free at a Web site such as topica.com or groups.yahoo.com that offers free list creation. This is one of the perks to keep people coming back to the site where they see the commercial ads that pay for the "free" service. On the other hand, if you want to avoid the commercial ads that will appear on messages sent in a free listserv, you can pay a fee to get an advertisement-free list. You can also check to see if ad-free listservs are available from your ISP.

To set up a listserv that you can get for free, follow the *Interlit* Web site link to setting up your own free listserv.

exercises

1. Following the instructions provided in this chapter, join the following three listserv mailing lists: Edupage, Tourbus, and the LockerGnome list of your choice. Read all three for a while, until you decide which one you like best. Maybe you will want to remain subscribed to all three! But if you do not, unsubscribe from the one(s) you no longer want to receive. Which one(s) did you decide to keep receiving? Explain briefly your reasons for staying on or getting off these three lists.

2. Using one of the listserv search tools listed in Table 7-2, find an unmoderated listserv mailing list that interests you and subscribe to it. Lurk for a while until you get used to the conversation, then try sending your own message to the listserv. Make sure your message fits the stated purpose of the listserv. If it makes sense in the context of the conversation, ask a question in your message, and see whether anyone responds with the information you are seeking. Which listserv did you join? Describe briefly the conversation you joined and tell how you contributed.

3. Send a command to the list you joined in exercise 2 to find out who belongs to the mailing list. If you have trouble doing this, review the listserv commands in Table 7-3. If the listserv does not respond to commands, check its Web site for an option you can click to see who belongs to the list. You can also try sending the listserv a message in which the body contains the single word *help*. Some servers will respond to the *help* request by e-mailing you a help page listing all of the other commands you can send. How many names are on the list? If the listserv does not support listing its members, it is okay to answer this question by saying so.

4. Browse to listserv.educause.edu/archives/edupage.html and choose the option to search the archives of Edupage. In the search field, type the word **virus,** then click the Search button. What is the most recent posting in which the word *virus* appears? In your own words, summarize the news in the posting.

SITUATED CASE PROJECTS
Case 7: Creating a Listserv

At the end of each chapter in this book, a situated case project provides the student an opportunity to put the chapter's contents to practical use in a workplace situation. Each case has the same number as the chapter in which it appears.

Listserv provides any school or company with an easy way of communicating or discussing issues of common concern to fellow employees via e-mail. Imagine that your employer has assigned you the task of creating a listserv for your workplace. To create such a listserv, follow these steps:

① Follow the Chapter 7 *Interlit* Web site links to one of the recommended sites that host listservs on the Web.

② Peruse the site's features and policies. If you do not like what you see, return to step (1) and choose another site.

③ Set up the listserv, following the instructions at your chosen listserv hosting site.

④ Using your word processor, draft an invitation to your fellow employees, inviting them to join the list. In this message, write step-by-step instructions for the employees to follow in joining your list. Save the message on your hard drive.

⑤ Following the step-by-step instructions you wrote in step (4), join the list you created in step (3).

⑥ Test the listserv and make sure it works properly. To test the list, e-mail it a message. Use your e-mail client's "send" feature to send the mail now rather than having it queue in your outbox. Soon the message you sent should appear in your inbox. Open the message to make sure it arrived correctly.

If your instructor has asked you to hand in this assignment, submit the draft invitation you created in step (4). Make sure your name is at the top of the document, then save it on disk or follow the other instructions you may have been given for submitting this assignment.

8

USENET NEWSGROUPS, WEB-BASED FORUMS, AND RSS BLOGS

After completing this chapter, you will be able to:

■ Understand how Usenet newsgroups originated as a grassroots effort by students who wanted a better way to organize conversations over the Internet.

■ Visualize how the hierarchical structure of a newsgroup mirrors the manner in which physical conferences are organized.

■ Use your e-mail reader to list the newsgroups available through your Internet service provider.

■ Subscribe to the newsgroups of your choice.

■ Read and respond to topics in a newsgroup and post new topics that you want to initiate.

■ Understand the difference between moderated and unmoderated newsgroups.

■ Know when it is too late to cancel a message that you have written in a newsgroup.

■ Find out about newsgroups in your field of study or line of work.

■ Understand the difference between newsgroups and Web-based discussion forums.

■ Learn how to create your own Web-based discussion forum on the Internet.

■ Set up a blog to keep an online diary that logs events you want to chronicle online.

■ Configure an RSS reader to feed you news about new content posted at blogs you want to keep up with.

● Wonderful as they may be, e-mail and listserv have some shortcomings. E-mail is a great way for individuals to exchange messages with one another, and listserv makes it easy to send mail to lists of people. But it is not easy to maintain your train of thought in a conversation conducted via e-mail. That is because e-mail queues up in your Inbox on a variety of topics, requiring your mind to shift gears continually as you read mail on different subjects.

Enter the Usenet newsgroup, a resource invented in the late 1970s by students who wanted a better way to converse over the Internet on specific topics. In this chapter, you will learn how Usenet newsgroups enable users to hold virtual conferences over the Internet. You will find out what newsgroups exist in your profession, learn how to join and participate in a newsgroup, and know how to go about creating a new newsgroup. You also will learn about Web-based forums, which enable you to accomplish similar tasks over the Web.

Another form of Web-based communication covered in this chapter is the blog, which enables you to create an online diary that logs events you want to chronicle online. This chapter will enable you to find out what blogs exist, read blogs that interest you, create a blog of your own, and use RSS technology to alert you to new content posted at blogs you want to keep up with.

Computer Conferencing

Usenet newsgroups are based on the concept of computer conferencing. Just as physical conferences are held on different topics around the country, so do Usenet newsgroups concentrate on a given subject. Just as physical conferences consist of a series of meetings dealing with different topics within the subject of the conference, so do newsgroups divide into topics that make it easy for you to participate in the discussion that interests you. The main difference between a physical conference and a newsgroup is that the Internet is bounded neither by time nor by space—anyone can participate in any discussion at any time from any place where there is an Internet connection. Another advantage of newsgroups is that you can participate simultaneously in various discussions of different topics. At a physical conference, on the other hand, you can attend only one session at a time.

For more background on how Usenet started, follow the *Interlit* Web site link to Usenet history.

Universe of Usenet Newsgroups

There are more than 100,000 Usenet newsgroups on the Internet. Newsgroups have dotted names such as rec.bicycles.racing that describe what the groups are about. The different parts of a newsgroup name are separated by periods. The part of the name up to the first dot is known as the prefix. Common prefixes are *news* for newsgroups that actually deal with news, *comp* for discussions about computers, *sci* for science, *soc* for social issues, *talk* for debates on controversial subjects, *rec* for recreation, and *misc* for miscellaneous topics that do not fit into the other categories.

Usenet Hierarchy

Usenet newsgroups are organized hierarchically. Each newsgroup has a list of topics. Under each topic is a list of subtopics. Under each subtopic comes a list of messages that users have written in response to that subject. By traversing this hierarchy with a newsgroup reader, you can quickly go to any part of a newsgroup and participate in the topic of your choice.

Messages written in a newsgroup are called *postings* or *articles*. The articles look like e-mail between one user and another, but instead of just being sent between people, the postings can be read by anyone in the world through a news server that provides access to those newsgroups.

Reading Newsgroups

Both Mozilla Thunderbird and Microsoft Outlook Express have newsgroup readers built in to their mail windows. Both make it easy for you to participate in a newsgroup by clicking on a graphical map that shows the hierarchical outline of topics and subtopics in a newsgroup. Figure 8-1 shows how the hierarchy gets displayed when you read a newsgroup with Thunderbird, and Figure 8-2 shows how Outlook Express displays the same newsgroup.

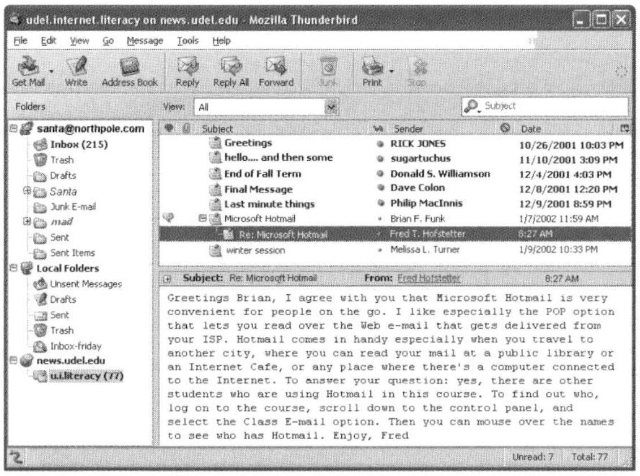

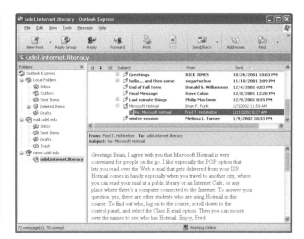

Figure 8-1   How Thunderbird displays a newsgroup.

Figure 8-2   How Outlook Express displays a newsgroup.

Configuring Your Newsgroup Client

Before you can read news, you need to configure your newsgroup client. In order to do this, you need to know the name of your newsgroup server. It will be a domain name; if you were Santa Claus, for example, the newsgroup server would be named something like news.northpole.com. If you do not know the name of your newsgroup server, ask your Internet service provider. Then follow the steps in Table 8-1 to prepare your newsgroup client for reading newsgroups.

Table 8-1   How to configure your newsgroup client

Mozilla Thunderbird	Microsoft Outlook Express
▶ Get Thunderbird running, pull down the Tools menu, and choose Account Settings; the Account Settings dialog appears.	▶ Get Microsoft Internet Explorer running, click the Mail button, and choose Read News.
▶ In the Account settings dialog, click the Add Account button; the Account Wizard appears as shown in Figure 8-3.	▶ Since you have not read news before, the Internet Connection Wizard appears, as shown in Figure 8-4.

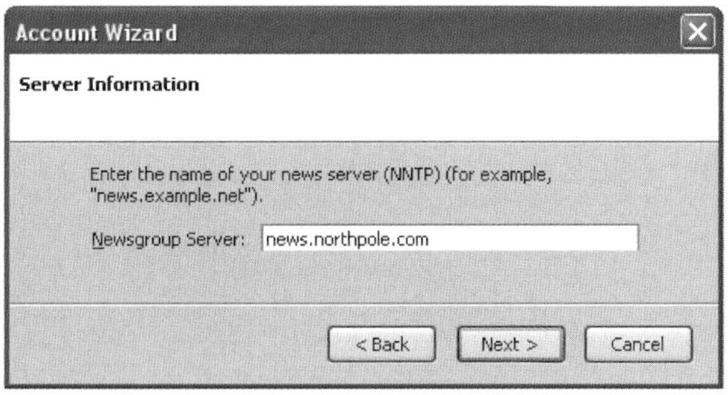

Figure 8-3   The Account Wizard helps you configure your newsgroup account.

- ▶ The first screen of the Account Wizard lets you tell what kind of account you want to create; click Newsgroup account and click Next.

- ▶ The second screen of the wizard asks for your name and e-mail address; fill them in and click Next.

Figure 8-4   The Internet Connection Wizard helps you configure your newsgroup client.

- ▶ The wizard will ask you a series of questions. First, the wizard asks you to type your name as you want it to be displayed when you write a newsgroup message; type your name, then click Next.

Table 8-1   *(continued)*

Mozilla Thunderbird	Microsoft Outlook Express
▶ Screen 3 asks you for the name of your newsgroup server. Type the name of the newsgroup server that you got from your Internet service provider, and click Next.	▶ Second, the wizard asks you to type your e-mail address. Do so, then click Next.
▶ On screen 4, the wizard asks for the name to identify your news account. This is the name that will show up in the account tree on the left side of the Mail window. When you make up this name, include the word *news* to identify this as a newsgroup account.	▶ Third, the wizard asks you to enter your Internet news server name. Type the name of the newsgroup server that you got from your Internet service provider, and click Next.
▶ Screen 5 gives you a chance to review the settings. If anything is wrong, click Back to fix it. Otherwise, click Finish.	▶ Depending on how you are connected to the Internet, the wizard may ask you some other questions; follow the on-screen instructions to answer the questions.
▶ The new account now appears in the Account Settings dialog. Click OK to close the dialog.	▶ When the wizard is done, it will ask you to click Finish to complete the configuration. Click Finish.
▶ To learn how to choose a newsgroup, proceed to the next part of this tutorial, "Choosing a Newsgroup."	▶ The wizard will ask if you want it to view the list of available newsgroups; click Yes. To learn how to choose a newsgroup from this list, proceed to the next part of this tutorial, "Choosing a Newsgroup."

Choosing a Newsgroup

Your Internet service provider subscribes to a number of newsgroups from which you can choose one or more that you would like to read. To get a list of the newsgroups from which you can choose, follow the steps in Table 8-2.

Table 8-2   How to choose a newsgroup

Mozilla Thunderbird	Microsoft Outlook Express
▶ In the account tree on the left side of the Thunderbird Mail window, click to select the news account you created in Table 8-1. Newsgroup options appear in the pane on the right, as shown in Figure 8-5.	▶ In order to select a newsgroup, you need to make Outlook Express list the names of the available newsgroups. If you just ran the Internet Connection Wizard in the previous section of this chapter, the list is already on your screen; proceed to the next step. Otherwise, in Outlook Express, click the ![icon] icon next to the name of your news server in the left-hand column, as shown in Figure 8-7. Then click the Newsgroups button.

First select a newsgroup in the account tree.

Then click Subscribe to Newsgroups.

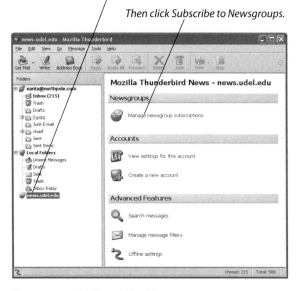

Figure 8-5   The Thunderbird Newsgroup options appear when you select a news account in the account tree.

First select a newsgroup in the account tree.

Then click the Newsgroups button.

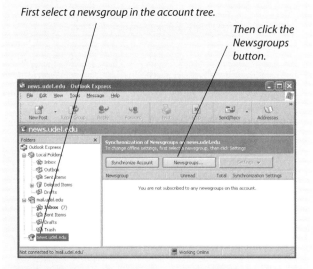

Figure 8-7   Outlook Express displays the newsgroup options.

Table 8-2   *(continued)*

Mozilla Thunderbird	Microsoft Outlook Express
▶ Click the option to Manage Newsgroup Subscriptions, or pull down the File menu and choose Subscribe; the Subscribe dialog appears. At the bottom of the dialog you will see the status as Thunderbird reads the list of newsgroups available at your ISP.	▶ Outlook Express will download all of the available newsgroups and display them for you, as illustrated in Figure 8-8.
▶ When the list has finished loading, you can scroll through it to find a newsgroup you like. You will see the hierarchy of newsgroups, as illustrated in Figure 8-6. You can click the plus signs (Windows) or arrows (Macintosh) to reveal newsgroups in different categories.	

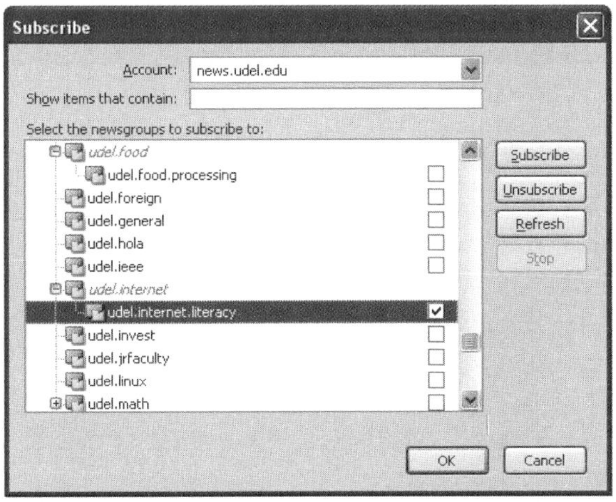

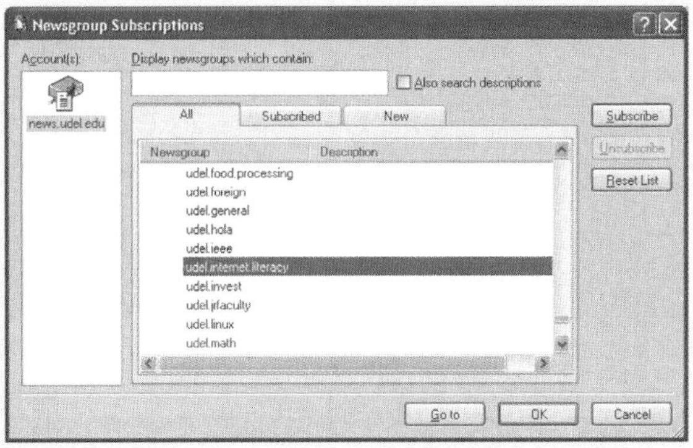

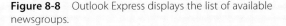

Figure 8-8   Outlook Express displays the list of available newsgroups.

▶ To subscribe to a group, select it by clicking on it, and then click Subscribe.

▶ You can narrow the list by entering a keyword in the box labeled *Display newsgroups which contain*. To get the full list back, just delete the word you entered.

▶ If you want to unsubscribe from a group, you can select it from this list and click Unsubscribe.

▶ To subscribe to a group you already know the name of, start typing the name of the group, and the list will shrink. When you see the one you want, select it by clicking on it, and then click Subscribe.

▶ Click OK when you are done choosing newsgroups.

Figure 8-6   Thunderbird displays the list of available newsgroups.

▶ To subscribe to a newsgroup, click the name of the newsgroup to select it, then click the Subscribe button.

▶ If you are already subscribed to a group, you can unsubscribe by clicking on its name to select it, then click Unsubscribe.

▶ You can narrow the list by entering a keyword in the box labeled *Show items that contain*. To get the full list back, just delete the word you entered.

▶ To subscribe to a group you already know the name of, start typing the name of the group, and the list will shrink. When you see the one you want, select it by clicking on it, and then click Subscribe.

▶ Click OK when you are done choosing newsgroups.

In the list of newsgroups, you will see that the names of newsgroups are grouped by title using compound names such as *rec.sport.basketball.college*. Here, *rec* specifies recreational topics, *sport* specifies a subgroup of recreation, and so on.

Good newsgroups to join first are news.newusers.questions and news.announce.newusers, where you can read the articles about newsgroup technique and Netiquette before you begin posting your own messages to any newsgroups. If you have trouble using newsgroups, you can ask questions in news.newusers.questions.

Reading a Newsgroup

Newsgroups are threaded. Each thread represents a different topic being discussed in the newsgroup. To read a newsgroup, you point and click on the topics and subtopics to navigate to the part of the newsgroup you want to read. Both Mozilla Thunderbird and Microsoft Outlook Express keep track of what topics you have and have not read, so it is easy to tell whether you have already visited part of the newsgroup. It is also possible to display only new messages written to the newsgroup since the last time you read news. To read messages in a newsgroup, follow the steps in Table 8-3.

Responding to a Newsgroup

Responding to a newsgroup is a lot like responding to an e-mail message. The main difference is that instead of being sent to an individual, your response gets posted to the newsgroup. Some newsgroups are moderated, meaning that someone looks over the messages you send to the newsgroup and makes sure the messages fit the purpose of the newsgroup before they get posted to the newsgroup. Many newsgroups are unmoderated, meaning that users can freely write messages without any form of review or censorship.

The rules of Netiquette dictate that when you are first learning how to use newsgroups, you should write your test messages in the newsgroup news.test. Subscribe to news.test now. If you have trouble, refer to the instructions in Table 8-2. Other practice newsgroups are at alt.test and misc.test.

To learn how to respond to a message written in a newsgroup, follow the steps in Table 8-4.

Table 8-3   How to read a newsgroup

Mozilla Thunderbird	Microsoft Outlook Express
▶ In the Thunderbird mail window, if the newsgroup tree is not already expanded, click the plus sign to expand the tree under your newsgroup account to reveal the list of newsgroups to which you are subscribed.	▶ In Outlook Express, double-click the 📰 icon next to your newsgroup server to reveal the list of newsgroups to which you are subscribed.
▶ Click to select the name of the newsgroup you want to read. If the name of the newsgroup you want is not listed, follow the instructions in Table 8-2, which tells how to choose a newsgroup.	▶ Click the name of the newsgroup you want to read. If the name of the newsgroup you want is not listed, follow the instructions in Table 8-2, which tells how to choose a newsgroup.
▶ Your computer will contact your ISP and download a directory of the messages in the newsgroup; then the directory of messages will appear onscreen.	▶ Your computer will contact your ISP and download a directory of the messages in the newsgroup; then the directory of messages will appear onscreen.
▶ If a message has a plus sign alongside it, that means the message has a hierarchy of other messages beneath it; click the plus sign to reveal the hierarchy. Click the minus sign if you want to collapse the hierarchy.	▶ If a message has a plus sign alongside it, that means the message has a hierarchy of other messages beneath it; click the plus sign to reveal the hierarchy. Click the minus sign if you want to collapse the hierarchy.
▶ New messages that you have not read yet will be printed in bold. To read a message, double-click its title. Thunderbird will download the message and display it in a message window.	▶ New messages that you have not read yet will be printed in bold. To read a message, double-click it. Outlook Express will download the message and display it in a message window.
▶ To read the next message in the newsgroup, pull down the Go menu and choose Next. If there are no more messages, the Next option will be inactive.	▶ 🔽 To read the next message in the newsgroup, click the Next button;
▶ Close the message window when you are done reading the message.	▶ 🔼 To read the previous message, click the Previous button.
▶ To read another message in the newsgroup, click the title of the message you want to read.	▶ Close the message window when you are done reading the message.
▶ To help you find your way through the newsgroup, Thunderbird lets you sort the messages in a variety of ways, as shown in Figure 8-9. To sort by subject, click the Subject button; to sort by the sender, click the Sender button; to sort by date, click the Date button.	▶ To read another message in the newsgroup, double-click the message title.
	▶ To help you find your way through the newsgroup, Outlook Express lets you sort the messages in a variety of ways, as shown in Figure 8-10. To sort by subject, click the Subject button; to sort by who sent the message, click the From button; to sort by date, click the Sent button.

Click here to reveal the hierarchical structure of the newsgroup.

Click here to sort by the name of the sender.

*Click here to sort the
newsgroup by date.*

*Click this minus sign
to collapse the
directory listing.*

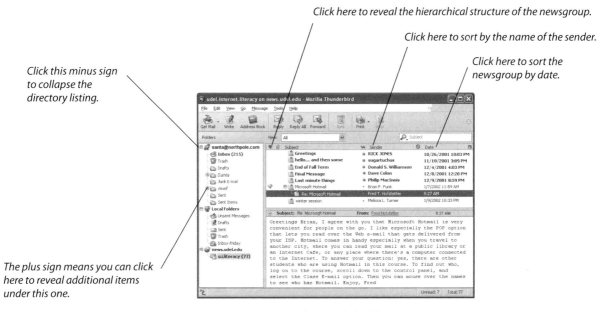

*The plus sign means you can click
here to reveal additional items
under this one.*

Figure 8-9   How Mozilla Thunderbird lets you sort newsgroup messages.

*Click a minus sign to collapse
the directory listing.*

*The plus sign means you can click
here to reveal additional items
under this one.*

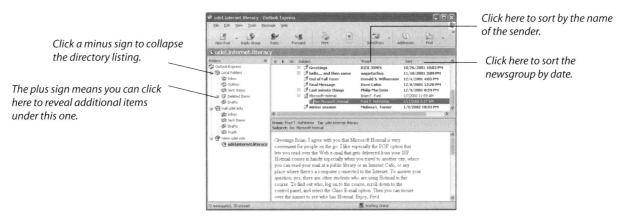

*Click here to sort by the name
of the sender.*

*Click here to sort the
newsgroup by date.*

Figure 8-10   How Outlook Express lets you sort
newsgroup messages.

Table 8-4   How to respond to a message in a newsgroup

Mozilla Thunderbird	Microsoft Outlook Express
▶ 📩 While reading the message in the newsgroup to which you want to respond, click the Reply button. If you also want a copy of your reply to be e-mailed to the sender, click the Reply All button.	▶ 📩 While reading the message in the newsgroup to which you want to respond, click the Reply Group button. If you just want to reply to the author, click the Reply button.
▶ The mail composition window appears with a blank message automatically addressed.	▶ The mail composition window appears with a blank message automatically addressed.
▶ Complete the message as if you were creating an e-mail message.	▶ Complete the message as if you were creating an e-mail message.
▶ 📩 Click the Send button to send the message.	▶ 📩 Click the Send button to send the message.

Creating a New Topic in a Newsgroup

While participating in a newsgroup, you may want to start a conversation on a new topic. To create a new topic in a newsgroup, follow the steps in Table 8-5.

The next time you read the newsgroup, you should find your new topic listed in the newsgroup's hierarchy. If your topic is not there yet, it is possible that the server has not yet processed it, or in the case of a moderated newsgroup, the newsgroup's owner may have disallowed the topic. Netiquette calls for the newsgroup's moderator to send you an e-mail message if your posting gets rejected, to let you know why your message was not accepted into the newsgroup. Beginners need to learn to wait for the message to get posted or rejected instead of resending the message too soon. Give the Internet a day or so to process your message before you resend it because you think it didn't get through.

Deleting a Message from a Newsgroup

Two rules govern the deleting of messages from a newsgroup. First, you can only delete messages that you write. You cannot delete messages written by other users. Second, you should only delete messages to which no one has responded yet. If another user has written a reply in the newsgroup to one of your messages, deleting your message will interrupt the flow of the conversation. To delete a message in a newsgroup, follow the steps in Table 8-6.

Be aware that when you delete a message from a public newsgroup, this will not necessarily prevent it from going around the world, because newsgroups get copied from node to node as they make their way over the Internet. When you delete a message, it gets deleted from your ISP's copy of the newsgroup, but that may be too late to keep it from going around the world. Your cancel message will go around the world to the servers that

Table 8-5   How to create a new topic in a newsgroup

Mozilla Thunderbird	Microsoft Outlook Express
▶ Enter the newsgroup in which you want to create a new topic of conversation. (The first three steps of Table 8-3 told how to enter a newsgroup.)	▶ Enter the newsgroup in which you want to create a new topic of conversation. (The first three steps of Table 8-3 told how to enter a newsgroup.)
▶ Click the Write button; a mail composition window appears with a blank message automatically addressed to the newsgroup.	▶ Click the New Post button; a mail composition window appears with a blank message automatically addressed to the newsgroup.
▶ Complete the message as if you were sending electronic mail.	▶ Complete the message as if you were sending electronic mail.
▶ Click the Send button to send the message	▶ Click the Send button to send the message.

Table 8-6   How to delete a message in a newsgroup

Mozilla Thunderbird	Microsoft Outlook Express
▶ Enter the newsgroup in which you want to delete a message.	▶ Enter the newsgroup in which you want to delete a message.
▶ In the hierarchical listing of messages in the newsgroup, select the message you want to delete by clicking it once.	▶ In the hierarchical listing of messages in the newsgroup, select the message you want to delete by clicking it once.
▶ Press the Delete key on your computer keyboard, or pull down the Edit menu and choose Cancel Message.	▶ Pull down the Message menu and choose Cancel Message. This option will be active only if you are the author of the message.
▶ If Thunderbird cannot delete the message, you will be told why not; otherwise, the message will be deleted from the newsgroup.	▶ If Outlook Express cannot delete the message, you will be told why not; otherwise, the message will be deleted from the newsgroup.

received it, but some servers do not honor cancel messages because some people have abused them by canceling other people's messages. Even if all the servers do delete your message, remember that canceling the message does not remove it from another user's computer if the user downloaded the message before you canceled it.

Communities Formed by Newsgroups

A researcher at Microsoft named Marc Smith is conducting research into the communities that get formed through newsgroups. He has developed a package called Netscan that tracks and stores in a database the structure and dynamics of newsgroup communications. The Netscan analyzer can read this database and generate reports of the activity in selected newsgroups over different periods of time. Mapping tools then summarize the data graphically so you can see the pattern. Figure 8-11, for example, shows a global summary of all of the activity in the highest levels of the Usenet hierarchy. You also can type in the name of any newsgroup and see the Netscan analysis either graphically or in tabular data format. To try your hand at this, follow the *Interlit* Web site link to Netscan.

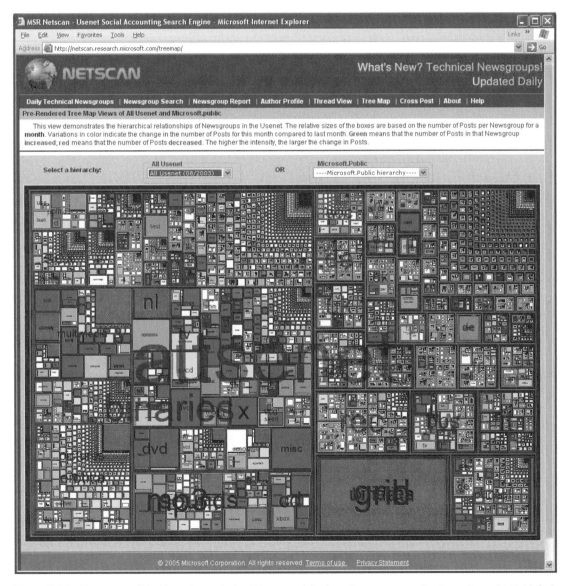

Figure 8-11 Netscan graphical box-plot analysis of Usenet activity. http://netscan.research.microsoft.com/static/default.asp?

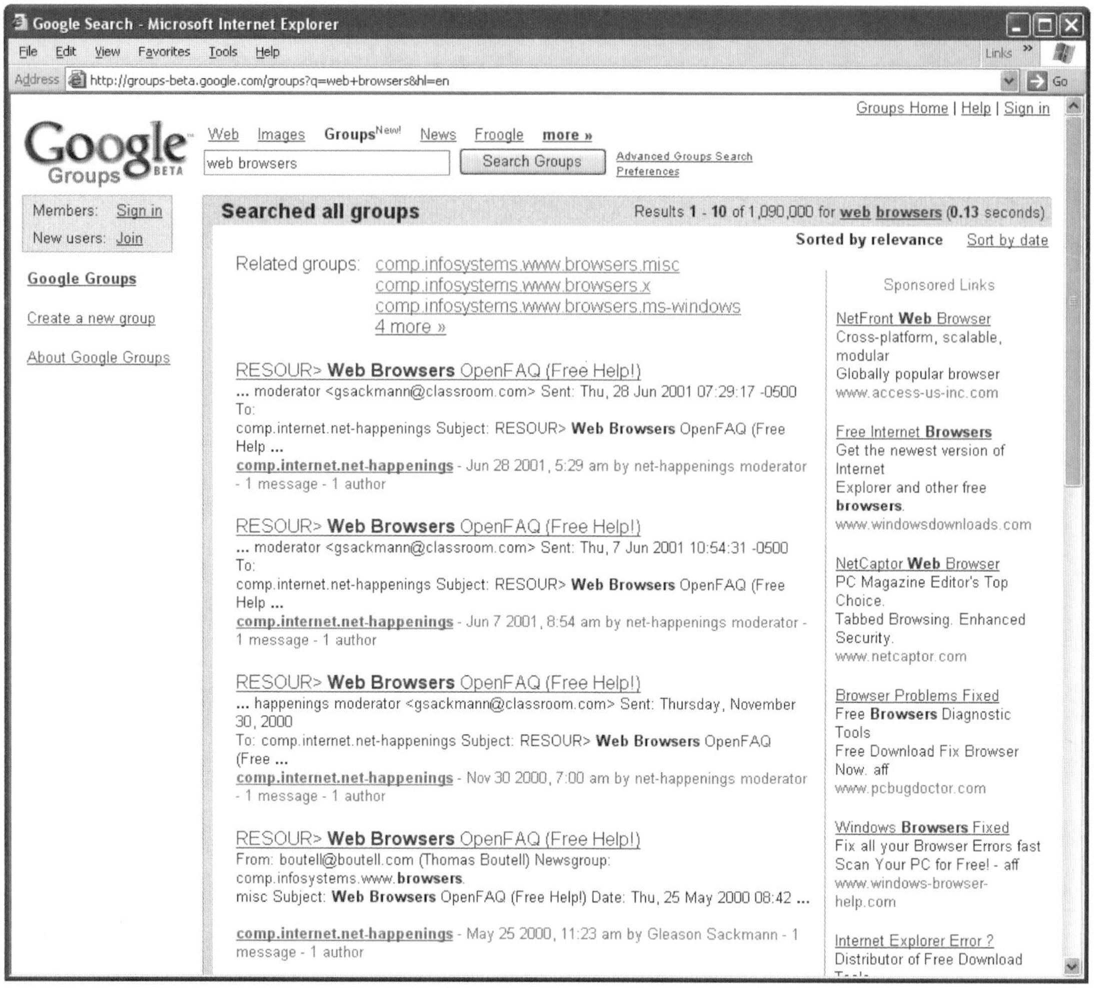

Figure 8-12   You can do a full-text search of newsgroups, topics, and articles by browsing to groups.google.com. Google™ is a trademark of Google Inc.

Finding Newsgroups in Your Profession

CyberFiber Newsgroups

If you follow the link to CyberFiber at the *Interlit* Web site, you will get a comprehensive listing of Usenet newsgroups. Click the subject you are interested in, and an outline of the newsgroups devoted to that topic will appear. To join a newsgroup, just click it, and your browser will automatically subscribe you and take you there.

Google Groups

Another way to find out about newsgroups in your profession is to use the Google Usenet search engine, which can perform full-text searches of the Internet's newsgroups. Chapter 11 provides detailed information on how to use Google to find out about information written in newsgroups. When you find the information you are looking for, Google will identify the name of the newsgroup it came from. Then you can subscribe to that newsgroup to explore more of the information it contains. As illustrated in Figure 8-12, Google finds groups aligned to your topic as well as threads and articles in other groups containing your search words.

Web-Based Discussion Forums

Web-based discussion forums are an alternative to newsgroups. Like newsgroups, forums have discussions that are organized according to topic and subtopic, in which users can participate much like a newsgroup. Unlike newsgroups, however, forums are not cataloged as part of the public Usenet service on the Internet. What you write in a forum, therefore, does not get searched by the Usenet search engine described above.

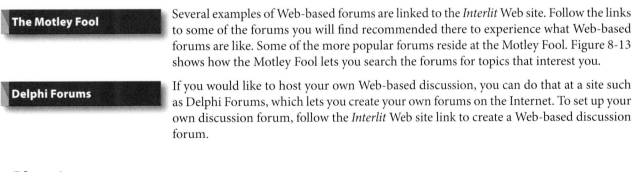

Figure 8-13 The Motley Fool Web-based discussion forum recommends posts in your area of interest. http://boards.fool.com/Index.aspx?ref=topnav.

The Motley Fool

Several examples of Web-based forums are linked to the *Interlit* Web site. Follow the links to some of the forums you will find recommended there to experience what Web-based forums are like. Some of the more popular forums reside at the Motley Fool. Figure 8-13 shows how the Motley Fool lets you search the forums for topics that interest you.

Delphi Forums

If you would like to host your own Web-based discussion, you can do that at a site such as Delphi Forums, which lets you create your own forums on the Internet. To set up your own discussion forum, follow the *Interlit* Web site link to create a Web-based discussion forum.

Blogging

Blogger

As you learned in Chapter 1, blogging is fast becoming one of the most popular ways of using the Web. There are three reasons for its popularity. First, people like to keep diaries full of chronological entries describing events that have taken place. Second, people want to share these logs with a large audience. Third, blogs are very quick and easy to create. People who would become frustrated learning HTML, for example, can easily create a blog, because the blogging tools prompt users to type in their news and click a Submit button to trigger a server-side process that automatically stores the content and creates the HTML needed to display it onscreen. The popular blogging site www.blogger.com refers to this process as "push-button publishing for the people."

The appeal of blogging has created a market for blog authoring tools. You can peruse these tools by following the *Interlit* Web site link to blogging. One of the leading tool providers is blogger.com, which is owned by Google. Taking a look at the tools and services available at blogger.com provides a good overview of the kinds of services that blogging enables. At blogger.com you will find

- A template you fill out specifying where you want your postings to appear and what style they should appear in.

- A form you fill out to make a posting. This form-driven design makes it possible for people who do not know HTML to create blogs. People who do know HTML can use it nonetheless.

- A publish button that, when clicked, FTPs the posting to the site of your choice.

- Free hosting services if you do not already have a Web site.

Reading RSS Channels and Feeds

Depending on who defines it, RSS can stand for different things. In Chapter 1, for example, you learned that RSS stands for Rich Site Summary. In a more technically correct sense, RSS stands for RDF Site Summary, where RDF stands for the Resource Description Framework, which specifies the XML syntax from which RSS is derived. Not everyone likes these highly technical terms, however. Less technical people say that RSS stands for Really Simple Syndication. Whatever you call it, RSS has become very popular because it provides a quick and easy way for Web developers to summarize what is happening at their sites into a feed that can be channeled in to other sites that want to display the news headlines with links to follow for more information.

RSS readers are available for all the major operating systems. Under Windows, popular RSS readers include BlogExpress and SharpReader. On the Macintosh, there is NetNews-Wire. Linux users have an RSS reader called Lifera. The *Interlit* Web site links to these and other popular RSS readers. There is also a Web-based RSS reader called BlogLines that enables you to read RSS feeds from your browser. Firefox users can employ the Live Bookmarks feature to view RSS news and blog headlines in the bookmarks toolbar or bookmarks menu.

RSS files are sometimes called *channels* or *news feeds*. Whatever you call them, they normally have either XML or RDF filename extensions. To subscribe to an RSS feed or channel, you simply copy its link into your RSS reader. You can often find a Web site's RSS feed by looking for the XML icon **XML** alongside a link to such a feed. To copy the link, right-click (Windows) or [Control]-click (Macintosh) this icon to pop out the quick menu; then choose Copy Shortcut or Copy Target Address. To subscribe, paste the link into the appropriate section of your RSS reader. In some readers, you can use your mouse to drag the link from your browser to your RSS reader.

Reading RSS Feeds with Thunderbird

If you have Mozilla Thunderbird, you can use its built-in RSS reader to subscribe to a channel. To read an RSS feed with Thunderbird, follow these steps:

- Pull down Thunderbird's Tools menu and choose Account Settings; the Account Settings dialog appears.

- In the Account Settings dialog, click the Add Account button; the Account Wizard appears.

Mozilla Thunderbird™ is a trademark of the Mozilla Foundation.

Figure 8-14   Thunderbird lets you create an RSS News & Blogs account.

- The first screen of the Account Wizard lets you tell what kind of account you want to create. Figure 8-14 shows that one of the choices is RSS News & Blogs. Choose RSS News & Blogs and click Next.

- The second screen asks for the name to identify your RSS account. This is the name that will show up in the account tree on the left side of the Mail window. When you make up this name, include the word RSS to identify this as an RSS account. I named my account RSS News and Blogs.

- Screen 3 gives you a chance to review the settings. If anything is wrong, click Back to fix it. Otherwise, click Finish.

- The new account now appears in the Account Settings dialog. Click OK to close the dialog.

- The newly created RSS News and Blogs account resides in Thunderbird's File pane. If you do not see it there, expand the file tree to reveal your RSS account.

- Click this account once to select it; the RSS News and Blogs options appear onscreen. Figure 8-15 shows that one of these options is to manage subscriptions.

- Click the option to Manage Subscriptions; the RSS Subscriptions window appears. Figure 8-16 shows that the RSS subscriptions window lets you add, edit, or delete an RSS subscription.

- To add an RSS subscription, click the Add button; the News Feed Properties dialog appears. As illustrated in Figure 8-17, the News Feed Properties dialog prompts you to enter the feed's URL and set whether to show the article summary or load the entire page.

- To obtain the URL of the feed to which you want to subscribe, for example, go to www.syndic8.com and search for a feed that interests you. Figure 8-18 shows that the author searched on the keyword NASA and found the Science@NASA feed. Right-click (Windows) or [Control]-click (Macintosh) the **XML** icon to pop out the quick menu and choose Copy Shortcut or Copy Target Address. This puts the URL into your computer's copy buffer.

Click here to reveal the
RSS News & Blogs options.

Click here to add, delete, or modify
an RSS subscription.

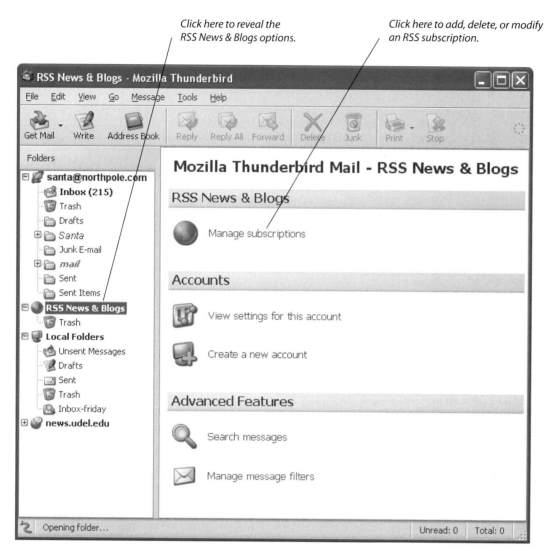

Figure 8-15   Thunderbird's RSS News & Blogs Options.

Your current subscriptions
(if any) appear here.

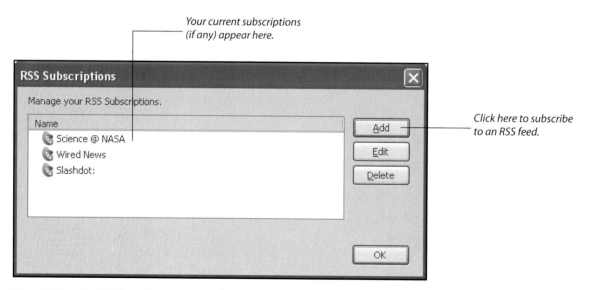

Click here to subscribe
to an RSS feed.

Figure 8-16   The RSS Subscriptions window lets you add, edit, or delete subscriptions.

Enter the RSS news feed's URL here.

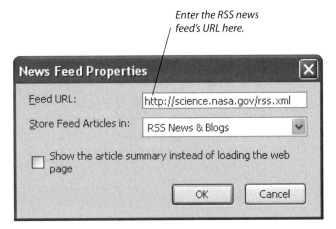

Figure 8-17   Thunderbird's News Feed Properties dialog.

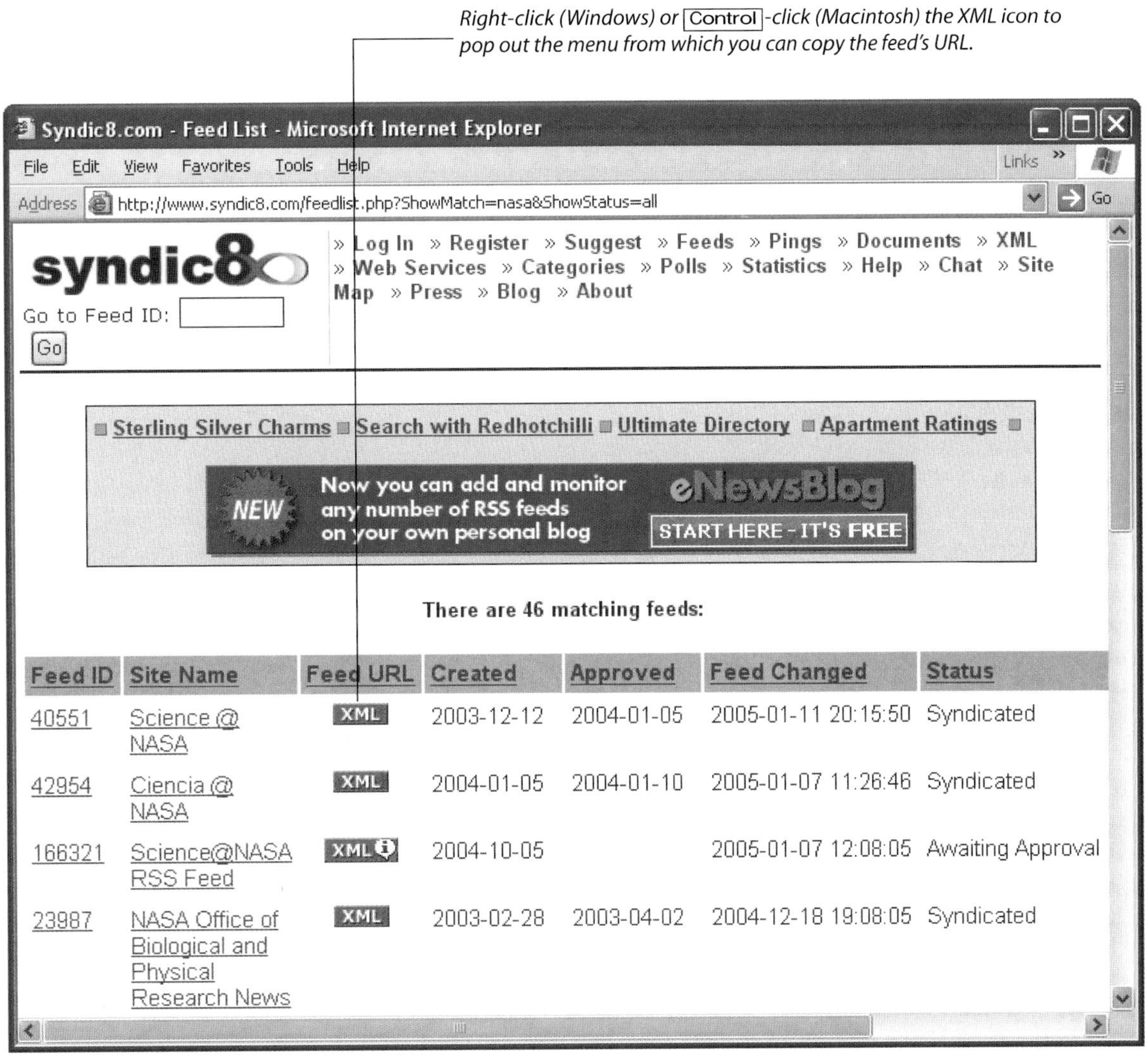

Right-click (Windows) or Control -click (Macintosh) the XML icon to pop out the menu from which you can copy the feed's URL.

Figure 8-18   I searched syndicat8.com on the keyword NASA to find the Science@NASA feed.

- Click to position your cursor in the Feed URL field illustrated in Figure 8-17, and click [Ctrl]-[V] (Windows) or [⌘]-[V] (Macintosh); this pastes the URL from the copy buffer into the Feed URL field.

- Click OK to close the News Feed Properties dialog, then click OK to close the Manage Subscriptions window.

- Notice how the RSS feed's name appears in Thunderbird's File pane under your RSS News & Blogs. Click the feed's name to select it; the feed's current subjects appear onscreen. Double-click any subject to see the corresponding message.

exercises

1. Subscribe to the newsgroups news.newusers.questions and news.announce.newusers and read the articles you find there to learn about newsgroup technique and Netiquette before you begin posting your own messages to any newsgroups. If you have trouble using newsgroups, you can ask questions in news.newusers. questions, but read the introduction first before you write messages of your own.

2. Browse to groups.google.com and perform a search of newsgroups based on topics that interest you. If you are a student, search topics dealing with your major program of study. If you are employed, search on topics related to your line of work. Subscribe to three of the newsgroups and lurk in them for a while. Remember that before you begin to participate in a newsgroup, you should first read a representative selection of articles for a few days before posting your own messages. Your chosen newsgroup may have its own set of accepted guidelines for what constitutes an appropriate posting; you should study those guidelines before posting messages. If you are unable to subscribe to the newsgroup, the reason may be that your ISP does not support it. Ask your ISP to help you subscribe.

3. Of the three newsgroups you joined in exercise 2, which one is most valuable? Why?

4. Following the instructions in Table 8-4, write a response to one of the topics that already exist in your favorite newsgroup. An hour or so later, go back into the newsgroup to find out if your message now appears there for the entire world to see. Because the whole world can see your message, make sure it makes sense in the context of the newsgroup's topic. In which newsgroup did you write your message?

5. Following the instructions in Table 8-5, create a new topic in the newsgroup of your choice. Sometime later, go back into the newsgroup to find out if your new topic now appears in the newsgroup's hierarchical listing of topics. Since the whole world can see your new topic, make sure the topic and the message you wrote to initiate it make sense in the context of the conversation going on in the newsgroup. In which newsgroup did you write your message?

6. Remember that anything you write in a newsgroup will probably remain on the Internet forever. Never write anything in a newsgroup that may embarrass you later on. In Chapter 11, you will learn how prospective employers can use Google to search newsgroups for things written by job applicants. It is possible that writing dumb stuff in newsgroups now could reduce your chance of getting a good job later on.

SITUATED CASE PROJECTS
Case 8: Creating a Discussion Forum

At the end of each chapter in this book, a situated case project provides the student an opportunity to put the chapter's contents to practical use in a workplace situation. Each case has the same number as the chapter in which it appears.

Web-based discussion forums provide one of the most powerful yet easiest ways for the employees of a workplace to communicate on topics of mutual concern. Imagine that your employer has just found out about forums and has asked you to set up a Web-based forum that your fellow employees can use to discuss issues of common concern with your employer. To set up such a forum, follow these steps:

1 Follow the Chapter 8 *Interlit* Web site links to one of the recommended sites that host forums on the Web.

2 Peruse that site's features and policies. If you do not like what you see, return to step 1 and choose another site.

3 Set up the forum, following the instructions at the forum site you chose in steps 1 and 2.

4 Using your word processor, draft an invitation to send your fellow employees, inviting them to join the forum and participate in the discussion. In this message, write step-by-step instructions teaching your co-workers how to participate in the forum. Save the message on your hard drive.

5 Test the forum and make sure it works properly. To test the forum, create a new topic in it. The first message in a forum is normally a welcome message that welcomes users to the discussion and states the forum's purpose.

6 Invite one of your fellow students or co-workers to the forum and ask him or her to write a response to the message you wrote in step 5. Log on to the forum and see if you can read this response properly.

If your instructor has asked you to hand in this assignment, what you will submit is the draft invitation you created in step (4). Make sure your name is at the top of it, then save it on disk or follow any other instructions you may have been given for submitting this assignment.

9

COMMUNICATING IN REAL TIME

After completing this chapter, you will be able to:

- Define the most popular methods for communicating in real time over the Internet.

- Describe how Internet Relay Chat (IRC) organizes conversations into channels.

- Enter Web-based chat rooms on the Internet and engage other users in meaningful real-time conversations.

- Configure an instant messaging (IM) client so you can IM your buddies over the Internet.

- Configure your computer for videoconferencing and participate in conversations that let you see and hear your conversants.

- Understand the purposes of and the distinctions between a MUD, a MOO, a MUSH, and a MMOG.

- Set up your own private chat room on the Internet.

E-mail, listserv, and newsgroups are great ways to communicate, but all three suffer from the lack of real-time interaction between you and the person with whom you are communicating. Historically, real-time communication has occurred either in face-to-face conversation or over the telephone. Now it is also possible to converse in real time over the Internet. If the person you are talking to has a video capture card, you can even see the other person on screen.

This chapter covers five kinds of environments used to communicate in real time over the Internet: chat rooms, instant messaging, whiteboards, videoconferencing, and MUDs (multiuser dimension).

IRC Chat Rooms

Chat rooms are places on the Internet where you can go to talk with other users in real time. Following the metaphor for which this technology is named, you imagine yourself entering a room in which you can converse with other users you will find there.

One of the oldest and most established chat-room protocols is **Internet Relay Chat (IRC),** which consists of several networks of IRC servers that support chat on the Internet. The largest IRC networks are EFnet (the original IRC net, often having more than 32,000 people chatting at once), Undernet, IRCnet, DALnet, and NewNet.

IRC conversations are organized into channels. You can join one or more communication channels and converse with other users who are subscribed to the same channel. EFnet often has more than 12,000 channels. Conversations may be public, allowing everyone in a channel to see what you type, or private between only two people, who may or may not be on the same channel.

mIRC

To connect to an IRC server, you must run an IRC client program. The most popular clients for Windows are mIRC and Trillian. On the Macintosh, the IRC client is Ircle. You can download the client of your choice by following the *Interlit* Web site links to IRC.

Ircle

It is also possible to join an IRC chat through your Web browser. When you enter an IRC chat through your browser, a Java-based IRC client is downloaded automatically, without requiring you to set up anything special in advance.

IRC is not a game. The users you will meet there are real people, and you should treat them with the same courtesy as if you were talking to them in person. You should be aware that it is possible, however, for robots to enter a chat room and lead you to believe they are human.

The *Interlit* Web site links to an IRC Help site. One of its subsites is an IRC Prelude site for people new to chat rooms. Before you begin using Internet Relay Chat, you should follow the links to the IRC Help site and the IRC Prelude site and learn the rules of the road and the principles of IRC Netiquette you will find there. Then you will be ready to visit CityLive, IrCQ-Net, and other chat networks linked to the *Interlit* Web site.

Instant Messaging

Instant messaging (IM) is a real-time communication protocol that lets you send and receive instant messages over the Internet. An instant message is an electronic notification that appears on your computer screen automatically to notify you that an important message just arrived in your e-mail or someone wants to talk with you now or something just happened that you wanted to know about, such as the value of one of your stocks moving up or down on the stock market.

To prevent instant messaging from becoming a free-for-all in which anyone on the Internet could interrupt your work instantly, you use a buddy list to identify the people who are allowed to contact you. When you are online, your buddies can send you instant messages, and you can chat with them live over the Internet. If you are busy working on something that you do not want interrupted by an instant message, however, you can set your busy flag. If someone sends you an instant message while your busy setting is on, the person will be told you are busy, while you continue working uninterrupted.

Instant messaging has become so popular that its acronym *IM* has become a verb, which is pronounced *eye-emm*. To IM someone means to send them an instant message over the Internet.

There are four major brands of instant messaging: ICQ, AOL Instant Messenger (AIM), Microsoft's MSN Messenger, and Yahoo Messenger. When this book went to press, AOL dominated instant messaging with 100 million users worldwide. The AOL-owned ICQ had 68 million users, MSN Messenger had 66 million, and Yahoo Messenger 36 million. According to Nielsen/NetRatings, MSN Messenger had the highest growth rate, having grown 21 percent over the previous year, while Yahoo Messenger grew by 11 percent, and AOL increased 2 percent. In addition to its mass-market popularity, instant messaging is working its way into the workplace. On a typical workday, for example, 21 percent of American workers use IM at work (Pew Internet & American Life Project, 2004).

As audio and video technology progresses, IM clients are beginning to support multimedia. In a multimedia chat, users who have microphones and speakers can talk out loud to each other and hear what the participants are saying. Users with cameras attached to their computers can appear on the screen of the people they are chatting with. Multimedia chat requires a much higher bandwidth than text-based chat, however, and many users do not have fast enough connections for real-time video. Not to worry, because text-based chat offers a lot of functionality for getting your message across. Even if you have a slow connection that does not have enough bandwidth for multimedia, you will be happy to discover how effective a plain text-based chat can be for conversing with other users over the Internet.

When you are deciding which brand of instant messenger to use for your own chatting, you need to consider the fact that the different brands do not interoperate with each other. AOL Instant Messenger chatters, for example, cannot use AIM to chat with Microsoft's MSN Messenger users. When you choose an instant messenger, therefore, you need to use the brand where your friends are or convince your friends to get the brand you choose.

ICQ

ICQ

True to its name, ICQ (pronounced *I Seek You*) is an instant messaging service that lets you contact people you want to chat with on the Internet and create peer-to-peer communication channels that are quick and easy to use. The latest version adds a file-sharing option that lets you set up a folder on your PC in which you can share files with your buddies.

ICQ has a contact list in which you keep the names of the ICQ users with whom you want to be in contact. You can add more friends or business associates to your contact list at any time, or you can remove people when you no longer want them to contact you. Figure 9-1 shows how ICQ displays the names of your buddies who are online. Notice that there is a button you can press to search Google. This is but one of many ways in which instant messaging vendors are extending the scope of what you can do from an IM window. You can use the rich set of send options in Figure 9-2 to send messages, files, Web pages, or greeting cards to your friends. Figure 9-3 shows that you can TXT

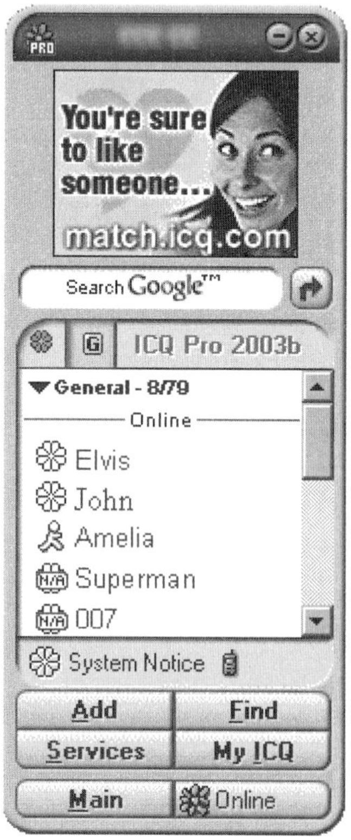

Figure 9-1   ICQ displays the names of your buddies who are online.

Figure 9-2   ICQ has a rich set of send options. To TXT a friend on her mobile phone, click the option to send an SMS message.

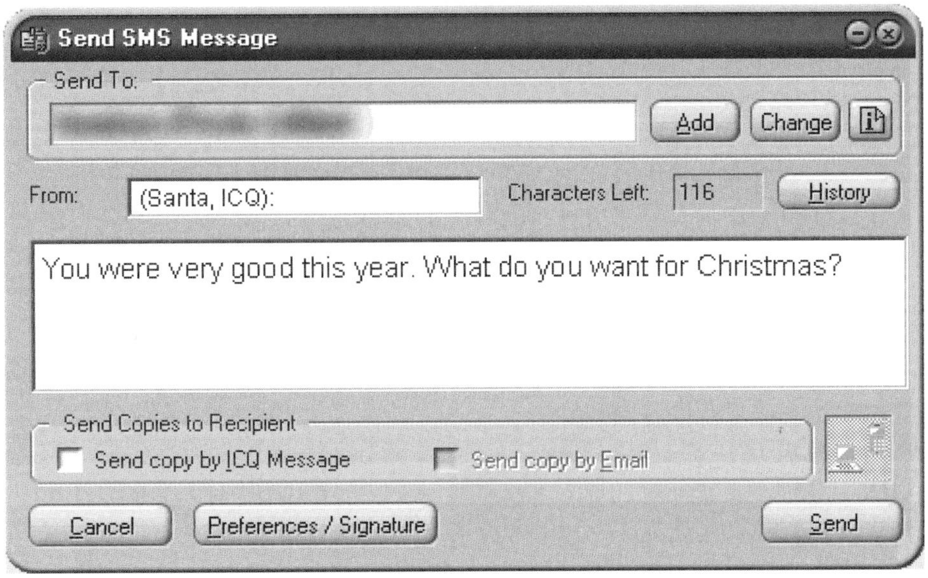

Figure 9-3 When you TXT a message to or from a mobile phone, try to fit what you have to say in a single transmission because avoiding a roundtrip saves transmission time.

your friends via the Short Message Service (SMS), which is a protocol for sending text messages to mobile phones.

When you TXT messages to or from a mobile phone, try to fit what you have to say in a single transmission, instead of sending lots of shorter messages. The sentences illustrated in Figure 9-3, for example, could have been sent in separate messages, but that would have created an extra round trip that would make the transmission take longer than a single message.

ICQ lets you keep a to-do list and set alarms that will remind you to perform a task or help you remember something important, such as your wedding anniversary. When this book went to press, a tool was released that permits ICQ users to communicate with AOL Instant Messenger users. For the latest information, go to www.icq.com.

AOL Instant Messenger

AOL Instant Messenger

As you might expect, AOL, which is the largest Internet service provider, has the largest instant messaging network. AOL subscribers access it via the Buddy List feature. Other users can participate via the AOL Instant Messenger (AIM) product, which is available to anyone, not just AOL members. Especially popular is the AIM Express version, a Web-based AIM client with which you can IM from any Web-connected computer. You can use AIM to accomplish the following tasks over the Internet:

- Receive instant notification when you have mail, your stocks move up or down, or a specific friend or family member comes online.

- Send instant messages.

- Share pictures, sounds, and animation with people on your AIM buddy list.

- Talk live with your friends and family through your computer.

- Chat with friends and family or people with similar interests.

- Stay on top of the news and stocks.

- Use IM Forwarding to deliver messages to your cell phone when you are away from your PC.

This icon indicates that the conversation is encrypted.

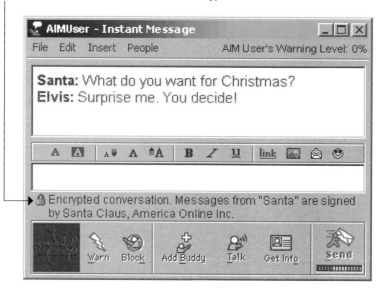

Figure 9-4   AIM gives you the option of encrypting and digitally signing messages that need to be kept private.

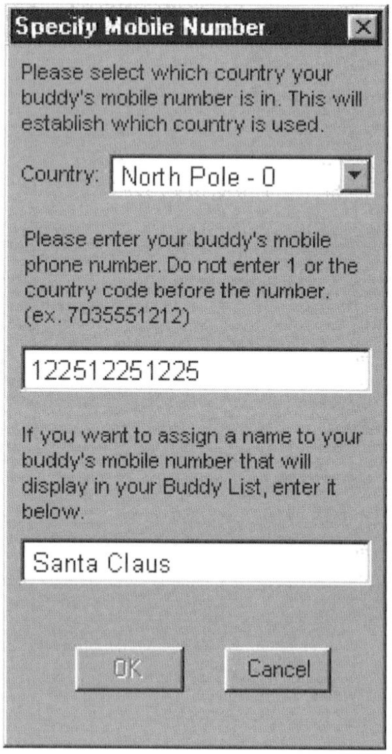

Figure 9-5   AIM lets you send a message to a mobile phone number.

Figure 9-6   Mobile buddies appear in your AIM buddy list.

The latest version of AIM has an encryption feature so you can send encrypted messages and files. The chat in Figure 9-4 is using this encryption option. Notice that the messages are digitally signed.

Figures 9-5 and 9-6 show that you can AIM your mobile buddies. If you assign a name to the mobile phone number, it appears in your buddy list. Hovering over a mobile buddy pops out an alert letting you know how long your buddy has been online. Go to www.aim.com if you want to get started using AOL Instant Messenger.

Microsoft MSN Messenger Service

MSN Messenger Service

Micosoft markets its MSN Messenger Service as a great way to make free phone calls to your friends and family. All you need are a Passport or Hotmail account, a multimedia PC, 28.8 Kbps modem or faster, a sound card, speakers, a microphone, and Internet access. MSN Messenger Service supports the following features:

- *Voice calls with microphones.* Call PC to PC or PC to phone anywhere in the United States or Canada. This feature is not available, however, to users who are behind a firewall or a router that blocks these kinds of binary transmissions.

- *Online status and instant message exchange.* See when your friends are online and exchange instant messages with them. You can chat with up to four friends in the same message window.

- *File sharing.* Trade pictures, music, documents, and more—right from MSN Messenger Service.

- *Reaching beyond computers.* You can send messages to pagers and cell phones.

- *Automatic typing indicator.* To help keep you from interrupting, MSN Messenger Service lets you know when one of your friends is typing a response.

- *Customization.* Change font styles and colors. Choose your own system sounds.

- *Emoticons.* Express yourself with pictures like ☺, ☹, and ☻.

- *Games.* The latest version has free games, including tic-tac-toe and checkers.

- *Information on Demand.* There are tabs to display MSNBC news, weather, and traffic reports.

- *WebCam.* Users with high bandwidth can use a video webcam option powered by Logitech.

Figure 9-7 shows an MSN Messenger chat in progress. In this example, two users have decided to play a game of Tic-Tac-Toe over an aquarium background. Other games include Solitaire Showdown and Mindsweeper Flags.

MSN Messenger has built-in support for COPPA, the Child Online Privacy Protection Act, which allows you to control whether or not your children can use the service. For more information, go to messenger.msn.com.

Yahoo Messenger

Yahoo! Messenger

If you are a Yahoo devotee, you may wish to consider using its brand of instant messenger, which is called Yahoo Messenger. It lets you access information throughout the Yahoo portal, and it supports multiparty voice conference calls with hands-free full-duplex conversation. Full duplex means you can talk and listen at the same time. Users with high bandwidth can use a Super Webcam feature to engage in broadband video messaging at speeds up to 20 frames per second. The search tool enables IM users to look up movie listings and restaurant addresses, which display as clickable links in the chat window. Windows users can download IMVironments that create themed backgrounds for the chat window. One of the IMVironments, for example, lets you get "in the zone" with Britney Spears.

You can also use Yahoo Messenger to send messages to buddies who have mobile phones. Figure 9-8 shows a message being sent from a PC, for example, and Figure 9-9 shows how the message appears on the phone. For more information, go to messenger.yahoo.com.

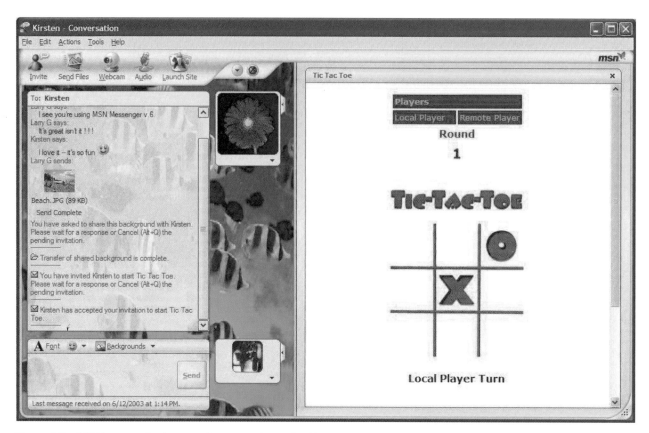

Figure 9-7   MSN lets you play fast-paced games with your buddies.
MSN® Logo reprinted by permission from Microsoft Corporation.

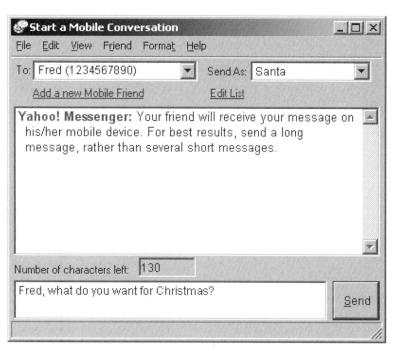

Figure 9-8   When a PC user initiates a mobile phone conversation, Yahoo
Messenger advises that for best results, you should send a long message,
rather than several short messages.

Figure 9-9   On the mobile phone,
the buddy sees the message (top),
chooses to reply (middle), and
answers appropriately (bottom).

Whiteboarding, Audioconferencing, and Videoconferencing

It is not always enough just to see what the other users are typing in a conversation. Sometimes you want to see other information that is on their screen as well. For example, a group of professionals collaborating on an economic model might want the conversants to be able to see a spreadsheet, play what-if games, and work together to evolve the best business plan. Distance-learning students collaborating on a scientific research project could similarly benefit from being able to contribute data from remote locations and view the results on a screen shared across the network. The type of computer program that enables remote users to share a common screen across the network is called **whiteboard** software, and the act of sharing such a screen is called *whiteboarding*.

Audio conferencing adds an aural dimension by enabling you to hear what people are saying into a microphone during a conversation, and with videoconferencing, you can see them as well. Virtually every computer sold today comes with a microphone and speakers that can be used for audio conferencing. For less than $50, you can add a camera to your computer so participants can see as well as hear you during a conference. In a videoconference, each person's PC has a video camera and a microphone attached to video and audio adapters that digitize what the camera sees and the microphone hears. Because digital audio and video transmissions contain many more bits of information than textual communications, you need a faster connection to the Internet than is required for text-based chat. A lot of research and development is being done on compressing audio and video to make them require less bandwidth, however, and hopefully videoconferencing will become more widespread when the cost of transmitting it decreases.

In the meantime, if you try to use more bandwidth than your local communication line can handle, you will notice your service degrade. Some day, as the Internet continues to develop, everyone will probably be able to use audio and video without worrying about bandwidth limitations. Until then, a good rule of thumb is to use text-based chat unless you really need audio and not to use video unless the participants really need to be able to see what you are doing on camera. If you need to use a camera but there is not enough bandwidth for the audio to work uninterruptedly, try turning off the audio channel and use text-based chat in combination with the video. While the video frame may not update very often under these conditions, it will not be as disturbing as an audio channel that keeps dropping out due to low bandwidth. Many corporate intranets, on the other hand, have high-speed connections that permit the use of high-quality videoconferencing. If you are fortunate enough to be on such a LAN, you can enjoy today the full benefits of the emerging videoconferencing technology.

WebEx

WebEx

More than 8,000 companies are using a Web-based whiteboard and videoconferencing service created by WebEx. Based on industry standards for scalable distributed networks, the WebEx platform has grown rapidly because it integrates well with any Web-based environment. Features include the real-time sharing of applications, presentations, or documents as well as Web co-browsing, live chat, record and playback, remote control, and file transfer. Figure 9-10 shows that files and applications on any participant's desktop can be opened and shared in real time during a WebEx meeting. During a meeting, you can use the drawing tools to make annotations that all of the participants will see. Figure 9-11 shows that you click the WebEx Video tab to view live video images of the participants who have cameras.

Because the system is Web-based, WebEx can be used by Windows, Macintosh, and Unix users to collaborate on applications running on different platforms. Spontaneous presenter delegation enables any one of the participants to become the presenter and share applications and data resident on their desktop. For more information, go to www.webex.com.

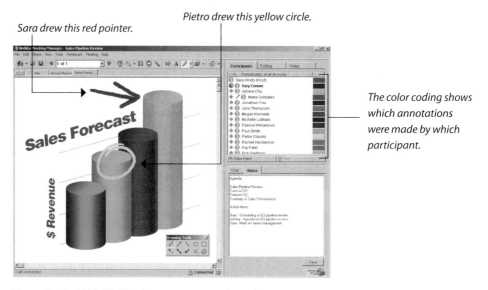

Sara drew this red pointer.

Pietro drew this yellow circle.

The color coding shows which annotations were made by which participant.

Figure 9-10   With WebEx, the presenter can show documents, run applications, and remotely control the participants' computers.

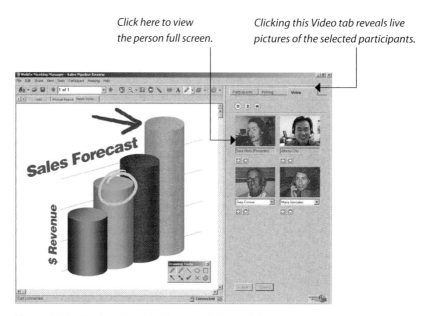

Click here to view the person full screen.

Clicking this Video tab reveals live pictures of the selected participants.

Figure 9-11   To view live video images of the participants who have cameras, you click the WebEx Video tab.

You can experience the power of WebEx first-hand by getting a free demo that is delivered live by WebEx representatives. You do not need a video camera in order to do this. Follow these steps:

- Go to www.webex.com and follow the link to join a live demo.

- You will get a screen asking you to choose a region, such as North America, Europe, Australia, or Asia, click the region that represents your locale.

- You will be given the option of joining a live demo now, which repeats every 30 minutes, or you can sign up for a more detailed overview that is given at a specific date and time. For the purpose of this exercise, choose the option to join a live demo.

- You are served a form on which you must enter your first name, last name, and e-mail address. Fill out that information and click the Join Now button.

- At the prompt to install the WebEx client on your computer, follow the online instructions to install this browser plug-in. On my computer, this installation took three minutes over an ISDN line.

- When the WebEx Meeting Manager appears, follow the onscreen instructions to join the demonstration, and enjoy your journey into videoconferencing!

NetMeeting and LiveMeeting

When this book went to press, Microsoft was in the process of transitioning from NetMeeting to LiveMeeting for its videoconferencing software. Introduced in 1996, NetMeeting worked its way into the Windows operating system, where it became part of Windows 2000 and Windows XP. For earlier versions of Windows, NetMeeting was freely downloadable. Known especially for its integration with the Microsoft Office programs, NetMeeting enabled users to call each other over the Internet, using the H.323 calling protocol. Figure 9-12 shows a NetMeeting session in which three users are discussing the design of a PowerPoint presentation. Each developer sees the whiteboard window, the chat window, and the PowerPoint window. The moderator uses the Online Meeting toolbar to control the meeting.

In 2003, Microsoft purchased a videoconferencing company named Placeware and re-named the product LiveMeeting. By the time you read this, LiveMeeting will be integrated throughout the Microsoft Office suite, much as NetMeeting was in previous versions of Windows. To learn more, go to www.microsoft.com/livemeeting.

MUDs, MOOs, and MUSHes

The term **MUD** has evolved from its earlier game-related meaning of multiuser dungeon to the more general concept of a multiuser dimension. MUDs are synchronous multiuser communication environments that enable participants to take on a persona and create virtual worlds out of their own imaginations. In other words, you invent a character (which could be yourself) and interact with the characters created by other users you will encounter in the MUD. MUDs are anonymous, meaning that you cannot know for sure who owns the characters you will encounter. Thus, MUDs provide environments for playing out fantasies that you could never enact in real life. As in chat rooms, you communicate by typing, thereby creating a textual world. The major advantage of a MUD over a chat room is that the participants have a chance to build a virtual world in which the location, participants, and objects in the environment can all be described, visited, and interacted with.

MUSH stands for *multiuser shared hallucination*. The acronym MUSH was chosen because this kind of environment is thought to be more squishy than a MUD. MUSHes are situated MUDs used for role-playing games that simulate worlds from books and movies or completely original environments.

MOO stands for *MUD, Object-Oriented*. The term **object-oriented** refers to a style of programming in which applications are constructed from reusable code segments known as objects that several programs can share. MOOs enable users to share code segments from one another's characters.

zMUD

From a technical standpoint, MUDs, MOOs, and MUSHes are programs that run on one of the servers connected to the Internet. You enter the multiuser environment through a MUD client, such as zMUD, which has pull-down menus containing features that make it easy to enter and use the MUD. Figure 9-13 shows zMUD in action. Notice how the AutoMapper window shows the context for the conversation that is taking place onscreen. Double-clicking on a room in the map will speedwalk you to that room by taking the shortest path to get you there. To learn more about this and other features, follow the *Interlit* Web site link to zMUD.

The Whiteboard contains shared text and graphics.   The Chat window displays the conversation.

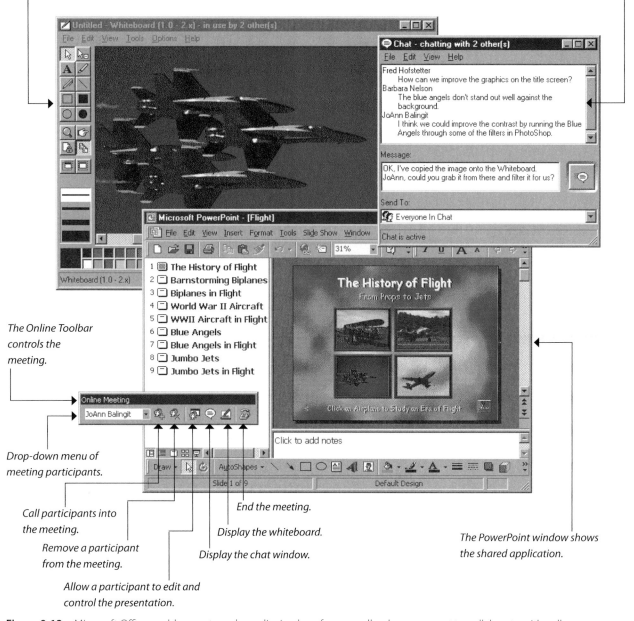

The Online Toolbar controls the meeting.

Drop-down menu of meeting participants.

Call participants into the meeting.

Remove a participant from the meeting.

Allow a participant to edit and control the presentation.

Display the chat window.

Display the whiteboard.

End the meeting.

The PowerPoint window shows the shared application.

Figure 9-12   Microsoft Office enables you to make audiovisual conference calls when you want to collaborate with colleagues over the Internet.

TAPPED IN

Because MUDs, MOOs, and MUSHes originated in game-playing, many schools prohibit their use during peak operating hours. Academic work is beginning to be done in MUDs and MOOs, however, as educators discover their potential for distance education, cooperative learning, and collaboration. An excellent example is TAPPED IN, which is a MOO designed for educational agencies and programs. K–12 teachers and librarians, professional staff, teacher educators, and researchers engage in professional development programs and collaborative activities. TAPPED IN is free, and guests are welcome. To explore it, follow the *Interlit* Web site link to TAPPED IN.

To learn more about MUDs, MOOs, and MUSHes, follow the links at the *Interlit* Web site. The MUD Connector, for example, links to more than 1,700 MOOs and MUDs on the Internet. See also the societal issues discussion in Chapter 25 about how stalking and unwanted sexual advances can occur in MUDs.

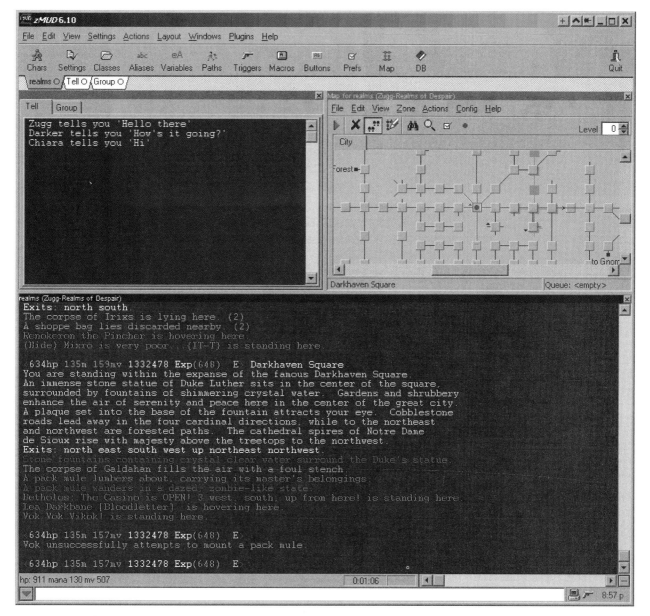

Figure 9-13 zMUD in action.

MMOGs and MMORPGs

A **massively multiplayer online game (MMOG)** is a computer game in which thousands of players can interact simultaneously via the Internet in a virtual game world. As individual users log on and off, the game continues, thereby creating a persistent play space. Characters acquire powers through skillful play. The more powerful the character, the more clout it has in player-to-player combat. Some players profit by selling their powerful characters to less skilled players.

In a **massively multiplayer online role-playing game (MMORPG),** also known as an **RPG,** your character is represented by an avatar, which is a player's graphical representation in the virtual world. Deriving socialization from MUSHes, most RPGs enable players to form groups typically called *clans* or *guilds* that can team up in combat. Examples of RPGs are (1) EverQuest, a Sony Playstation game in which more than 400,000 online players traverse vast continents filled with dragons, wizards, and dungeons; (2) Asheron's Call, a 3D fantasy world inhabited by thousands of players who make friends and seek out perilous

Figure 9-14   Scenes from the U.S. Army's Asymmetric Warfare Environment (AWE). http://www.gamespot.com/2004/04/21/screenindex-6093860.html.

adventures on the Microsoft Network (MSN); and (3) The Sims Online, a simulation in which you create a character called a Sim who can buy, build, and create things and form relationships with other players to enhance your Sim's power and social standing.

Besides fun and games, you may wonder what practical use massively multiplayer games can have. The U.S. Army is developing a MMORPG called Asymmetric Warfare Environment (AWE). By the time you read this, AWE will be training soldiers for urban warfare. The goal is to teach soldiers how to think in a squad-based environment. While soldiers can also role-play and shoot, the goal is to teach them to think more than it is to shoot.

Instead of referring to AWE as a game, the Army calls it a tactical decision aid. Some of the issues covered in AWE include (1) What will a soldier experience in Iraq or Afghanistan? (2) How does a soldier learn to relate to the people there? (3) How do you know who is the enemy? (4) How does a soldier keep a riot from starting when the food runs out? As you might expect, downtown Baghdad is one of the AWE environments. Figure 9-14 illustrates four of AWE's Baghdad scenes. To learn more about AWE and to explore a variety of massively multiplayer gaming environments, follow the *Interlit* Web site links to MMOGs and RPGs.

exercises

1. Download and install one of the instant messengers described in this chapter, such as AOL Instant Messenger, ICQ, Microsoft Messenger, or Yahoo! Messenger. Get one of your friends to do likewise, or find a friend who already is using the brand you chose. When you and your friend are online at the same time, try giving your friend a call, and have a conversation. Then, ask your friend to hang up and call you, so you can experience what it is like to receive as well as make an IM call. After you are finished talking, describe the experience you had. Which IM did you use? Did you have any trouble IMing your friend? Was your friend able to IM you? What improvements, if any, do you think need to be made in the brand of IM you chose to use in this exercise?

2. Go to the *Interlit* Web site, click the IRC Prelude icon, and familiarize yourself with Internet Relay Chat terminology and Netiquette. This will prepare you for the next exercise.

3. Go to one of the Web-based IRC portals featured at the *Interlit* Web site. When you get to the IRC portal, connect to an IRC server, list the channels of conversation, and pick one that interests you. Lurk until you get used to the conversation that is in progress. Then join in and participate. How does this form of communication differ from face-to-face communication? What are the advantages and disadvantages of IRC as compared to face-to-face communication?

4. If you are a Windows user and you do not already have the NetMeeting software on your computer, click the NetMeeting icon at the *Interlit* Web site and download Microsoft's NetMeeting software. Use NetMeeting to conference with one of your fellow classmates or co-workers. What do you see as the advantages of the NetMeeting software? Are there any disadvantages?

5. Go to www.webex.com and follow the link to join a live demo. After you register by filling in your name and e-mail address, you will be prompted to install the WebEx client; follow the online instructions to install this browser plug-in. When the WebEx Meeting Manager appears, follow the onscreen instructions to join the demonstration. Depending on Internet traffic and the speed of your Internet connection, the quality of the video you get may vary. Do you see a smooth video stream, or is it jerky? About how often would you say the frame rate is refreshing? (For comparison purposes, the frame rate of a television program on American TV is 30 frames per second.) Note: You do not need a video camera to complete this exercise.

SITUATED CASE PROJECTS
Case 9: Instant Messaging

At the end of each chapter in this book, a situated case project provides the student an opportunity to put the chapter's contents to practical use in a workplace situation. Each case has the same number as the chapter in which it appears.

When you are working online to complete a project that involves collaborating with other people, you like to be able to contact them quickly when you have a question or need something only they can provide. Instant messaging is one of the best ways to provide this kind of just-in-time connectivity among co-workers online. Imagine that your employer has heard about the way instant messaging can enhance productivity in your workplace. Your employer has asked you to set up an instant messaging environment, try it out with a few of your co-workers, and report back on how the IM panned out. To conduct this IM trial experiment, follow these steps:

1 Study the sample screen diagrams and descriptions of the instant messaging services presented in Chapter 9. Decide which one appeals to you most. Because IM systems are constantly evolving, improving, and getting new features, follow the *Interlit* Web site links to visit the leading IM sites and check out the latest enhancements.

2 Get your own account at the IM provider you selected in step (1).

3 Invite one or two of your classmates or co-workers to get an account at your chosen IM provider.

4 Use your word processor to begin writing up a report on this assignment. Put your name at the top, then write a paragraph telling what IM you chose and why.

5 IM your buddies from step (3) and chat about this assignment. Ask their opinion on how easy it was to get their IM account. Include their assessments in your report. Depending on the brand of IM you chose, you may be able to drag and drop what they say from the IM window into your word processor.

6 Conclude the report by providing your own recommendation on how well IM works for online collaboration between co-workers in your school or company.

If your instructor has asked you to hand in this assignment, save your IM report on disk or follow the other instructions you may have been given for submitting this assignment.

10

STREAMING MEDIA AND SYNCHRONIZED MULTIMEDIA

After completing this chapter, you will be able to:

■ Understand why streaming is an important strategy for delivering multimedia over the Internet.

■ Define streaming and name the different kinds of media that are being streamed over the Internet.

■ Go to Web sites where you can see and hear streaming media in action.

■ Know when and where to download the latest streaming media plug-ins and drivers.

■ Understand how the synchronized multimedia integration language (SMIL) is making it possible to create, publish, and deliver synchronized multimedia content over the Web.

● As you learned in Chapter 2, the process of digitalization is changing the world by converging the world's communications media into a digital data stream that can be delivered over the Internet. No matter what you want to say, and no matter how you want to say it—text, speech, graphics, animation, music, video—it can all be digitized and published to the Web. When a user clicks to trigger your content, it gets delivered over the Internet to the user's Web browser.

When content gets digitized, however, some types of media create larger data files than others. Consider this paragraph, for example. If you type it into a word processor, this paragraph takes up 989 bytes of file space. That is a relatively small amount of data that can be transmitted over the Internet very quickly. Because it is a small amount of data, we say it is low bandwidth, meaning not much time or space is needed to send it over the Web. When the user clicks to see the paragraph, the text appears very quickly. If you read this paragraph aloud and record it with your computer's microphone, on the other hand, the resulting audio file is many times larger. It has higher bandwidth, and it takes longer to transmit over the Internet. Add a webcam to record video while you read into the microphone, and the file becomes very large. Its bandwidth is now so high that the user may lose interest while waiting for the video to arrive and the content to start playing.

Streaming was invented to remove this kind of startup delay and make it possible to transmit real-time audio and video over the Internet. In this chapter, you will learn how multimedia content creators are using streaming to deliver high-bandwidth media quickly and efficiently over the Internet. This enables you to visit Web sites where audio and video recordings are standing by, ready to begin streaming on demand to your computer as soon as you click on them. In addition to playing prerecorded streams, you will also visit real-time sites, such as news channels and radio stations that are playing right now, using streaming media to deliver what is happening right now to your desktop.

Streaming Media

A **stream** is a real-time feed from an audio or video source, encoded in such a way that the media can begin playing steadily without making users wait for the entire file to download to their computers. Streaming media, therefore, is the simultaneous transfer and display of the sound and images on the World Wide Web. Streaming media enables users to watch and listen to a movie while it is being sent to their browsers, for example, instead of waiting minutes or hours to download and then play it.

Streaming media also can be used to broadcast real-time events over the Internet. **Webcasting** is the term used to describe the simultaneous broadcast of a live event over the Web. Webcasting software gives you the option to make an archive, which means to save the Webcast in a computer file from which you can replay the broadcast sometime after the event. On the Web, the commercial news sites such as cnn.com, msnbc.com, cbs.com, and abc.com make news archives available. When you click to play an archive, you see the same video as the audience that viewed the stream live.

When this book went to press, the three most popular platforms for streaming media were Apple QuickTime, Windows Media, and RealNetworks. The following sections describe these three leading products, telling you how to download them and providing links to some exciting demonstrations. There are several other vendors involved in streaming media. If you want to learn about the others, follow the *Interlit* Web site links to other streaming media products.

Apple QuickTime

QuickTime

One of Apple Computer's greatest gifts to the world is QuickTime, which is Apple's brand of multimedia. Originally for the Macintosh only, QuickTime is now one of the finest cross-platform tools available for multimedia creation and delivery. It plugs in seamlessly to the Netscape, Firefox, Internet Explorer, and Safari Web browsers, and it works on Windows as well as Macintosh computers.

Boston's public television station WGBH uses QuickTime to power the WGBH Netcast at broadband.wgbh.org. When you click to begin the Netcast, the QuickTime window launches to display streaming content from WGBH. Figure 10-1 illustrates how the WGBH Netcast takes advantage of QuickTime's ability to embed hyperlinks that enable users to make choices by clicking hotspots in the content.

The QuickTime player is free. For a modest fee, you can upgrade the free player to Quick-Time Pro, which lets you edit audio and video clips as well as play them. To learn more and to download either the free player or the more fully featured QuickTime Pro, follow the *Interlit* Web site link to Apple QuickTime.

Windows Media

Windows Media Player

Microsoft is aggressively pursuing the market for streaming video and has created its own product line of streaming media servers. The player, which is free, is called the Windows Media Player. If you have Windows, there is probably a version of the Windows Media Player installed on your computer. To find out, click your computer's Start button, select Programs, and look under Accessories or Multimedia for the Windows Media Player. To check whether a more recent version is available, follow the *Interlit* Web site link to the Windows Media Player.

Figure 10-2 shows Windows Media in action at the C-SPAN site at www.c-span.org. The user can click to view the live stream from any one of the C-SPAN channels. In addition

Click here to watch the TV broadcast from WGBH in Boston.

Click one of these titles to preview WGBH-produced programs airing on PBS.

Click here to listen to Boston's GBH radio station.

Figure 10-1   QuickTime powers the WGBH Netcast at broadband.wgbh.org.

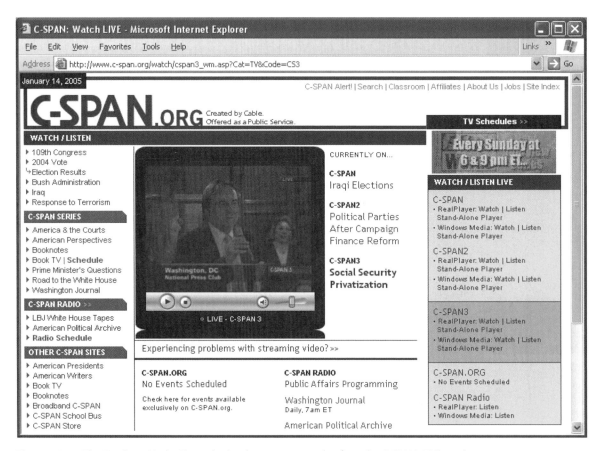

Figure 10-2   The Windows Media Player displays live streaming video from the C-SPAN3 TV broadcast at www.c-span.org.

Figure 10-3   Prime Minister Tony Blair answers a question in a streaming video from the C-SPAN broadcast of the *Prime Minister's Questions.*

to the live feeds, the C-SPAN site hosts a huge library of recorded programs. By following links in the sidebar, you can choose thousands of archived streams. One of my favorites is the *Prime Minister's Questions.* Figure 10-3 shows Prime Minister Tony Blair answering a question in the Windows Media Player.

RealNetworks

RealNetworks

RealNetworks is one of the best-known multimedia streaming companies on the Internet. Its flagship product is the RealPlayer™. According to RealNetworks, the RealPlayer™ can play more than 85 percent of the multimedia content on the Web. It can play CDs, DVDs, and all the major file types. Best of all, the basic player is free.

RealPlayer™ is one of the streaming media formats in which you can watch the C-SPAN streams. Figure 10-4 shows how C-SPAN appears in the RealPlayer™ window. You get public streams such as C-SPAN for free. You pay extra if you want premium sports, news, and entertainment services.

To learn more about RealPlayer™ services, follow the *Interlit* Web site links to RealNetworks and RealPlayer™. RealNetworks has proposed that its streaming protocol become

Figure 10-4   C-SPAN streams into the RealPlayer™.

an Internet standard. The name of the protocol is Real Time Streaming Protocol (RTSP). If you want the technical background, follow the *Interlit* Web site link to the Real Time Streaming Protocol.

Guide to Streaming Videos

About.com

After you have exhausted the links at the vendor sites described above, you may be interested in visiting the About.com guide to streaming videos. There you can access thousands of clips from TV shows and movies. The directory includes new releases, reviews, recommendations, and articles you can read to learn more about streaming video. To click through the directory, follow the *Interlit* Web site link to the About.com Guide to Streaming Videos.

National Public Radio

National Public Radio

One of the author's pet peeves has been the difficulty of receiving National Public Radio (NPR) broadcasts due to his home's distance from the nearest NPR antenna. Now that NPR is streamed on the Web, antennae are no longer an issue. Figure 10-5 shows how the NPR Web site provides not only a 24-hour news stream, but also lets you search via keywords through the NPR archives of online programming. To listen, follow the *Interlit* Web site link to NPR.

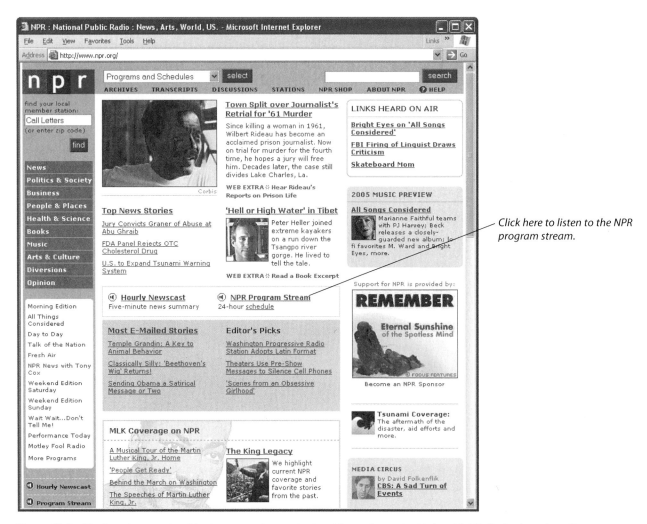

Click here to listen to the NPR program stream.

Figure 10-5   Live broadcasts and archived news can be searched and listened to at the National Public Radio site at http://www.npr.org. Copyright NPR® 2005. This material is used with permission of NPR, Inc. Any unauthorized duplication is strictly prohibited.

Synchronized Multimedia

SMIL

If you ever watched a movie in which the video moved a second or two ahead of the sound, then you know why it is important to synchronize multimedia. To provide a standard way for Web page authors to synchronize different kinds of multimedia events, the World Wide Web consortium (W3C) is creating a language called SMIL (pronounced *smile*), which stands for Synchronized Multimedia Implementation Language. SMIL enables you to create a narrated slide show, for example, in which photos you have taken appear in sync with an audio commentary and provide your users with onscreen controls to pace the presentation.

All three of the multimedia streaming vendors featured in this chapter, including Apple, Microsoft, and RealNetworks, have built support for SMIL into their streaming media players. This support for SMIL makes it possible for users to create narrated slide shows with a wide range of multimedia effects. For some colorful examples, follow the *Interlit* Web site link to the SMIL showcase, where you can click to view SMIL presentations created by Ford Motor Company, the Getty Center, the History Channel, Sony Music, the Sci-Fi Channel, and others.

World Wide Web Consortium

Recently, the World Wide Web Consortium has been working on separating SMIL into modules that Web designers can use to create multimedia Web pages. A language called XHTML+SMIL permits the Web designer to use SMIL animations, timings, and transitions within a conventional HTML page layout. Microsoft has created an implementation of XHTML+SMIL called HTML+TIME, which works with Internet Explorer versions 5.5 and later. True to its name, the most important part of HTML+TIME is the timing module, because that is how you create synchronized multimedia events.

An excellent example of a multimedia event that requires timing is the captioning of a video, which requires you to display onscreen subtitles at precise times in sync with the video. Figure 10-6 shows how I used HTML+TIME to create subtitles for President John F. Kennedy's famous Moon Challenge speech. The timing module makes the captions appear in sync with the video. I used the SMIL <switch> command to check the accessibility

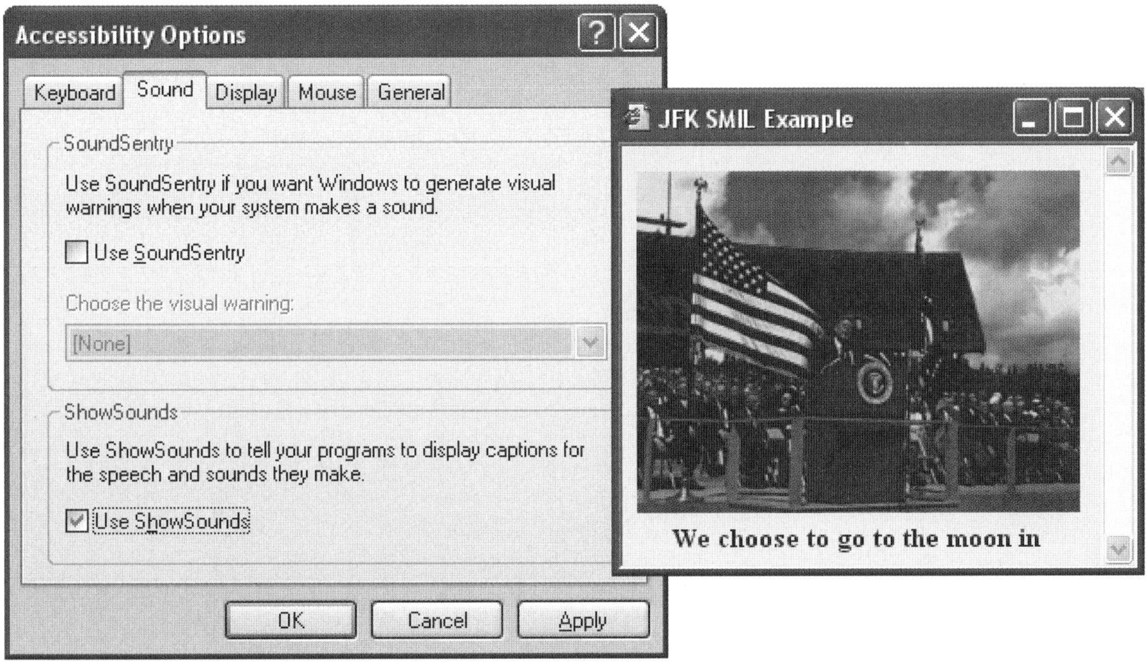

Figure 10-6   The SMIL timing module makes the subtitles appear onscreen in sync with the video. I used the SMIL <switch> command to make the browser display subtitles if the user's accessibility settings have captioning turned on.

settings on the user's PC. If the user has captioning off, the <switch> command turns the captions off. If the user has captioning on, it switches the subtitles on. Thus, SMIL helps the Web author create more accessible Web sites.

To learn more about the status of SMIL, follow the *Interlit* Web site links to the SMIL resources. There you will find a tutorial on how to create your own slide show. There is also a link to the World Wide Web Consortium's SMIL site, where you can find out the latest about the continuing evolution of SMIL.

exercises

1. Go to the National Public Radio site at www.npr.com. Click the option to hear the live broadcast that is airing now. What do you think about the quality of the audio? Does it meet your expectations? *Note:* In order to complete this assignment, your computer will need to have one of the streaming media players that NPR supports. If your computer does not have one of the supported players, follow the link on the NPR page to install the player of your choice.

2. At the NPR site you visited in exercise 1, choose the option to hear one of the archived programs that has been prerecorded. Compare the quality and performance to what you heard in exercise 1. Could you hear any difference? If so, what? Did one of the broadcasts start up more quickly, for example? Did one of the broadcasts have more audible interruptions than the other? Describe any glitches you heard or other problems you encountered.

3. Go to the QuickTime site at www.apple.com/quicktime. If you have not already downloaded and installed the QuickTime Player, do so now. The free version of the player will work fine for this assignment, or you can use the QuickTime Pro version. Then follow the links to play one of the QuickTime TV channels. Which channel did you choose to play? What do you think about the quality of the video you saw? How does it need to be improved? What impact do you believe streaming video technology will have on the future of television?

4. Go to the CNN Web site at www.cnn.com. In the multimedia section of the menu, follow the link to video. Choose the option to view the current newscast. You may be asked how you want to view the video, whether with Windows Media, QuickTime, or RealVideo. With what video player did you watch the newscast? How well did it play? Was the newscast continuous, or were there hiccups or delays? Was the video sharp and clear, or was it blurred and jerky? Did the video play in sync with the audio? Note any other quirks or problems you encountered.

SITUATED CASE PROJECTS
Case 10: Choosing a News Service

At the end of each chapter in this book, a situated case project provides the student an opportunity to put the chapter's contents to practical use in a workplace situation. Each case has the same number as the chapter in which it appears.

It has always been important to stay informed. This is all the more important after the terrorist attacks on America. Internet news services provide an excellent way to stay informed. Imagine that your employer has raised the concern that your co-workers need to keep better informed about current events. Your employer wants you to recommend what online news channel would be best for your co-workers to join and monitor. In developing this recommendation, consider these issues:

❶ Online news is a quickly growing market, and there is a lot of competition among the news sites. By the time you read this, there could be new channels and services available for getting the news online. Follow the Chapter 10 *Interlit* Web site links to the hottest online news services to learn of their latest features.

❷ One or two frontrunners will probably emerge based on the look and feel of the news sites you visit in step (1). Check to see if the frontrunners have e-mail notification services that can send your co-workers an e-mail message in the event of another attack or other national emergency.

3 Also check to see if the news service provides an RSS channel that your organization could put in a news window on your home page. Many online news services provide such a channel to display headlines that, when clicked, display the breaking news stories.

4 Consider the timeliness, quality of reporting, political orientation, breadth of coverage, and reliability of information posted at the site you recommend.

Use a word processor to write up your online news recommendation in the form of a brief essay describing the news services you compared and citing the reasons why you chose the one you recommended. If your instructor has asked you to hand in the recommendation, make sure you put your name at the top of the document, then save it on disk or follow any other instructions you may have been given for submitting this assignment.

PART FOUR
FINDING THINGS ON THE INTERNET

"Stand on the shoulders of giants."

—Google slogan from scholar.google.com

The Internet is the richest source of information on the planet. According to Bergman's (2001) white paper on the deep Web, more than 100,000 searchable databases exist, containing nearly 550 billion documents, 95 percent of which are publicly available.

Just about anything you could ever want to know is available online. Especially for students and scholars conducting research, the Internet is a fantastic resource for finding out what has been done in your field.

While so much information is available online, however, finding what you want to know is not always easy because knowledge gets organized and stored in different ways. To find what you want, you need to understand how the different kinds of search engines work. Then you will be ready to conduct a search that has a better chance of finding what you seek.

Accordingly, this part of the book focuses on helping you find things on the Internet.

11

SEARCHING FOR INFORMATION

After completing this chapter, you will be able to:

- **Conduct subject-oriented searches of World Wide Web directories.**

- **Search by keyword to find what you are looking for.**

- **Perform full-text searches of the Web's full-text indexes.**

- **Use the advanced search syntax to find what you are looking for efficiently.**

- **Perform concept searches based on ideas instead of specific keywords.**

- **Use metasearching to search via several search engines at once.**

- **Know how to get online help from human beings who will conduct searches on your behalf.**

- **Conduct scholarly searches across a broad range of academic disciplines.**

- **Use multimedia search engines to find pictures, audio, and video, in addition to text.**

- **Search Usenet newsgroups to find information in discussions of current research topics.**

- **Learn how to search the Web for people and find the person you are looking for.**

- **Get maps and driving instructions.**

- **Find out about new search engines and improved search strategies.**

● The key to unleashing the research potential of the Internet is to know how to use the search engines. That is what this chapter is about. You will learn how to search subject-oriented directories that organize material according to topic. Then you will learn how to use full-text keyword searching that will enable you to find articles containing specific words or phrases in documents mounted on the Web. A tutorial on the advanced search syntax will refine your searching skills to make you more efficient in finding what you want on the Internet.

You also will learn how to do concept-oriented searching using search engines that can expand an idea into related topics and search them automatically. Metasearching will enable you to use one search engine to search several other search engines for the information you seek, collate the results of the searches, and return the results in a single organized report. You also will learn about human search services that use people to conduct searches. If you have trouble finding something on your own, you can pay a small fee, and a human being skilled at searching will conduct the search for you.

Some disciplines are ahead of others in terms of providing full-text source materials on the Internet, but online indexes make it quick and easy to create bibliographies of material related to topics in any field. This chapter will enable you to use discipline-based academic search engines. You also will learn how to do multimedia searches that can find pictures, audio, and video, in addition to plain text. You will even learn how to search Usenet newsgroups, which provide a rich source of information about current research in many fields.

As you study this chapter, you will notice that certain Web sites are featured in the discussion of each kind of searching. These sites were chosen because they pioneered in the development of the search technique and are considered to be the best in that kind of searching. When you visit one of these featured sites, however, you are likely to find other kinds of searching also available there. Google and Yahoo are the most popular search sites and feature most if not all of the techniques featured in this chapter.

Subject-Oriented Searching of Directories

When you research a topic, it is wise to begin by conducting a subject-oriented search of one or more of the Web's directories. This will tell you how much information is available about your topic as a subject that other people have written about. The subject-oriented directories use a combination of human beings and robots called **spiders** that search the Web continually, organizing what is found into a hierarchical directory of topics. When you conduct a subject-oriented search, the search engine searches this directory and provides you with a list of items related to your topic. To retrieve an item, you simply click it.

Yahoo

Yahoo!

As this book goes to press, Yahoo is the most popular subject-oriented directory. Its Web address is www.yahoo.com. There is also a version for kids at www.yahooligans.com, whose directory indexes materials appropriate for the needs and interests of children. To perform a Yahoo search, follow the steps in Table 11-1.

Keyword Searching

Like subject-oriented directories, keyword search engines have spiders that are constantly combing the Web and feeding information into a database. Instead of organizing the Web according to subject areas, however, keyword search engines let you search for keywords in documents, regardless of the subject of the documents. Therefore, keyword search engines are likely to find more than subject-oriented searches, but what is found may not be as relevant to your subject.

AltaVista

AltaVista

The AltaVista search engine was invented by the Digital Equipment Corporation as the Web's first full-text keyword search engine. Now a freestanding company, AltaVista's Web address is www.altavista.com. AltaVista has been awarded more search-related patents than any other company. According to Digital, AltaVista is the fastest search service available (0.4–0.5 second average response time), with the most up-to-date content (refreshed every 28 days). When this book went to press, AltaVista's index included 350 million Web pages.

Because you are likely to get thousands of hits when you search AltaVista for a keyword, AltaVista sorts the hits according to the relevance or level of importance of the information

Table 11-1   How to perform a Yahoo! search

▶ Point your Web browser at www.yahoo.com—the Yahoo home page appears.

▶ If you want to search all of Yahoo, type your search term(s) into the blank search field and click the Search button.

▶ If you want to search within a Yahoo subject area, scroll down through the subjects listed on the Yahoo home page and click on the subject area you want—the Yahoo subject area page appears.

▶ If subtopics are listed on the subject area page, scroll down through the subtopics and select the one you want. Repeat this process until you have narrowed the subject area of your search.

▶ When you are ready to conduct a search, type your search term(s) into the blank search field.

▶ Click the option to search all of Yahoo or just the subject area you have chosen.

▶ Click the Search button; Yahoo performs the search and displays the items that match your search terms.

▶ Scroll down through the matches to see what Yahoo found. All of the matches are hotlinked; to see an item, click a highlighted word.

▶ If there are more matches to be displayed, you will find "Next 20 matches" printed at the bottom of the search results. Click "Next 20 matches" if you want to see more.

▶ By default, Yahoo combines your search terms with the Boolean AND, which means you will get a match only when all of the search terms are found together in an item. If you want a Boolean OR done instead, click the Advanced Search option that you see printed next to the Search button.

▶ In addition to letting you perform the Boolean OR option by searching for "any of these words," the advanced options also let you search for an exact phrase. I find this very helpful in troubleshooting technical problems. If a computer program gives you a cryptic error message, for example, you can use the Yahoo exact phrase option to search for that reported error. Chances are that someone else has already encountered this error and has written on the Internet about how to solve the problem.

found. This is done through statistical analysis that organizes pages with similar content into groups.

While conducting searches at the AltaVista site, you may notice how the commercial ads that appear onscreen often relate to your keywords. This is done by matching the content of the ads to the concept analysis of your keywords. This kind of concept mapping is used at many commercial search sites. Advertisers pay to have their ads come onscreen when someone conducts a search in the product's concept area.

Advanced Boolean Searching

Boolean logic is named after the nineteenth-century mathematician George Boole, who invented a form of algebra in which all values reduce to either TRUE or FALSE. The Boolean operators AND, OR, and NOT are widely used in computer programming and in search engines to construct queries that narrow a search to find precisely what you are looking for. The simplest form of a Boolean query uses AND to find things that contain two items that must be found together in the same document, such as:

> hot AND cold

Such a search will find fewer documents than the following search, which is less exclusive:

> hot OR cold

The opposite of that search is

> hot AND NOT cold

More complex searches can be done by using parentheses to create more complex queries:

> sunny AND NOT (hot OR cold)

Table 11-2   How to perform an advanced Boolean search at AltaVista

▶ Browse to www.altavista.com—the AltaVista home page appears.

▶ Click the Advanced Search option to make the advanced search screen appear.

▶ Click the option to search with a Boolean expression.

▶ In the Boolean Expression field, type:

"Martin Luther"

Be sure to type the quote signs, which force the search engine to look for the words *Martin* and *Luther* appearing next to each other. Click the Find button and make note of the number of hits you get.

▶ In the Boolean Expression field, type:

"Martin Luther" AND NOT "Martin Luther King"

Click the Find button and make note of the number of hits you get. Can you explain why you get fewer hits than when you searched for "Martin Luther" by itself?

▶ In the Boolean Expression field, type:

"Martin Luther King" AND ("I Have a Dream" OR "Letter from a Birmingham Jail")

Click the Find button. Notice how this search finds documents that mention Martin Luther King and either his famous *I Have a Dream* speech or his *Letter from a Birmingham Jail*.

▶ Almost anything in the world that you want to know is retrievable once you develop skill at using the advanced search syntax. For more information about advanced searching, click the AltaVista Help option and follow the link to free-form Boolean queries using special search terms.

To search for exact phrases, you can use quotation marks, as in

sunny AND NOT ("too hot" or "too cold")

Learning how to conduct a Boolean search will make you very powerful because the Boolean logic enables you to narrow your search down to find just what you are looking for. The best way to learn how to do a Boolean search is to simply try one. To perform a Boolean search with AltaVista, follow the steps in Table 11-2.

Concept Searching

Some users are better at keyword searching than others. Finding the right combination of keywords and logical operators (AND, OR, NOT) to get a search engine to find the kind of information you seek can be time-consuming and tedious. Concept-oriented search engines can help users who have difficulty with keyword searching.

Excite

Excite

Excite is a concept-based search engine that you will find at www.excite.com. It uses a search technology called Excite Precision Search to analyze more than 250 million Web pages in the Excite search index. Evaluations of link authority and Web page popularity combine with text indexing, semantic matching, and link analysis to select the most relevant and popular Web pages that match your search query.

But Excite is much more than a search engine. It also provides customizable newsfeeds and stock reports, shopping and weather, live chats and bookmarks. Quick Tools include a personal address book, a calendar, horoscopes, maps/directions, and yellow pages. Excite also offers a free start page that includes e-mail, clubs, chat, and your own personal portfolio. Perhaps even more than being a search engine, Excite wants to become your personal portal to the Internet. To check out its wide range of Internet services, go to www.excite.com.

Google

Google

The Google search engine adds a new twist to searching by using an automated method that ranks relevant Web sites based on the link structure of the Internet itself. When you conduct a search, Google sorts the results in order of importance, based on how the site is linked to and referred to by other sites. The assumption is that the more a site is linked, the more of an authority it is. Google certainly takes a lot of Web pages into consideration; when this book went to press, Google indexed more than three billion Web pages. To search them, go to www.google.com.

Metasearching

By now you may be getting overwhelmed by the number of different search engines and the subtle distinctions in how they work. **Metasearching** provides an alternative to trying many individual search engines to find the information you seek. Metasearching is the searching of searching, which you perform with a metasearch engine that invokes the other search engines automatically. Behind the scenes, the metasearch engine conducts different kinds of searches for you, collates the results into one list of hits, and reports back to you.

MetaCrawler

MetaCrawler

MetaCrawler conducts searches by sending your queries to several Web search engines, including AltaVista, FindWhat, Yahoo, Ask Jeeves, LookSmart, Google, About, and Overture. MetaCrawler organizes the results into a uniform format and displays them in the order of the combined confidence scores given to each reference by the services that return it. You also have the option of scoring the hits, enabling what is found to be sorted in a number of different ways, such as by date, locale, and organization. MetaCrawler supports the advanced search syntax, which was explained previously in the section on Boolean searching. MetaCrawler is on the Web at www.metacrawler.com.

Dogpile

Dogpile

Research attorney Aaron Flin created Dogpile when he got frustrated finding too few results with subject-oriented directories such as Yahoo, and then trying keyword search engines like AltaVista that returned 30,000 or more documents in response to the same query. Dogpile is a metasearch engine that sends your Web queries to the Internet's top search engines, including Google, Yahoo, AltaVista, Ask Jeeves, About, FAST, FindWhat, and LookSmart. Dogpile also searches FTP sites, newsfeeds, yellow pages, white pages, classifieds, auctions, audio, and image files. You can find Dogpile on the Web at www.dogpile.com.

CNET Search.com

Search.com

CNET's Search.com is a metasearch engine that searches more than 800 engines, including Yahoo, AltaVista, Magellan, Lycos, Inktomi, Direct Hit, and Snap. A special feature is the channel, which lets you customize the search engines used to look for information in different content areas. Channels include categories such as automotive, business, computing, entertainment, government, music, people, shopping, and travel. To search these channels and more, go to www.search.com.

Human-Based Searching

When you do not have time to wade through the tens of thousands of documents that a keyword search engine can return in response to a search, you may wish to consider using a human-based search service. A person skilled in searching published information sources, proprietary databases, and the Internet will find an answer and e-mail you the results.

Ask the Experts

Refdesk.com

Refdesk.com has an Ask the Experts page that connects you to advice from experts who can answer your questions on topics ranging from antiques to whales. The answers come to you from real-world experts who have volunteered to answer your questions. The Ask an Experts page is on the Web at www.refdesk.com/expert.html.

Scholarly Searching

One of the problems with searching for information on the Internet is that the Web is a public resource. Anyone can create a Web page about any topic, regardless of how much (or how little) the Web page author knows about the subject. When you use a search engine like AltaVista to find information about that topic, the results contain a mix of pages written by people who know a lot about what they are talking about along with people who may not know much and may even write misleading or false information.

One way of filtering out the bad information is to use a search engine that restricts itself to scholarly information that has been published in refereed journals.

ERIC

ERIC

ERIC stands for Educational Resources Information Center. The ERIC database includes more than a million abstracts of articles from education journals and other scholarly documents, including books, conference proceedings, symposia, studies, and tests. Figure 11-1 illustrates how you can access ERIC at www.eric.ed.gov, where you can search the database by keyword, author, title, or topic. If you are unsure of your topic, you can use the ERIC thesaurus to select a topic.

About.com

About.com

Formerly known as The Mining Company, About.com takes a unique approach to providing access to scholarly sources. It hires real scholars to serve as guides in more than 700 subject areas. (I was invited to be the educational technology guide, for example, but had to decline due to other writing commitments, such as this book.) The guides at About.com organize the links, keep them updated, write new articles, host discussions and chats, and answer questions online. To find out more and to search your subject area, go to www.about.com.

Britannica.com

Encyclopedia Britannica Online

Britannica.com is a Web-based knowledge and learning center that includes the complete, online version of the *Encyclopaedia Britannica*. The obvious advantage of the online version is that you have access to all the latest information at once, without needing to conduct separate searches through the 32 printed volumes and the annual *Book of the Year*. The online version also includes hundreds of articles not found in the printed encyclopedia, including selected articles from *Newsweek, Discover,* and *The Economist*. There are also thousands of links to Web sites selected by Britannica editors.

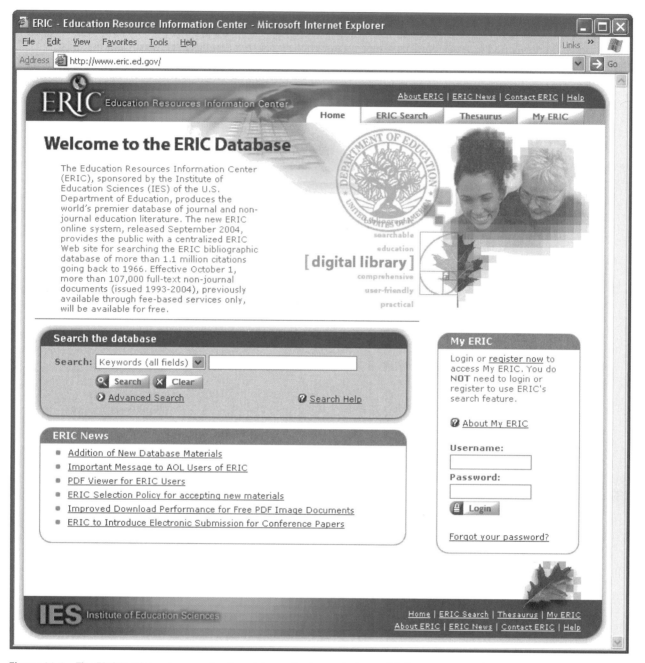

Figure 11-1 The ERIC Database at www.eric.ed.gov lets you freely search the world's largest source of educational information, which contains more than a million abstracts of journal articles and education documents.

To search the *Encyclopaedia Britannica* online, go to www.britannica.com. Although you can search the encyclopedia for free, you must pay a subscription fee in order to view the full text of encyclopedia articles over the Internet. Free trial subscriptions are available that permit you to try out the service before you begin paying for it.

XanEdu

XanEdu offers access via the Web to thousands of publications indexed by ProQuest, which is a global leader in the collection, organization, and distribution of value-added information to researchers, faculty, and students in libraries, government, universities, and schools in more than 160 countries. In addition to providing a search tool for the entire

ProQuest database, XanEdu has created a ReSearch Engine for General Studies, Education, and MBA business majors. These three ReSearch Engines provide access to thousands of the world's best newspapers, magazines, and scholarly journals. The education engine keys these materials to education standards and textbooks. A special section on "Teaching as a Profession" helps teachers keep up with the latest news and issues including school reform, labor issues, and certification standards. For more information, visit www.xanedu.com, where you can get a free trial subscription to try out the service.

Google Scholar

Google Scholar

The hottest news in scholarly searching is the Google Scholar search engine at scholar.google.com. Instead of searching the entire Internet, Google's scholar search looks for your keywords in scholarly literature, including peer-reviewed papers, doctoral dissertations, technical reports, and books. The database indexed by Google Scholar includes articles from academic publishers, professional societies, preprint repositories, and universities. Google Scholar also searches scholarly articles residing in full text out on the Web. Regardless of whether you are a student writing a term paper or a working professional looking for best practices based on scholarly research, Google Scholar is a site you will want to bookmark. To check it out, browse to scholar.google.com.

Multimedia Searches

Multimedia is extremely popular on the Internet. You can find millions of pictures, audio files, animations, and videos to play on your computer. The challenge is to find the ones you are interested in. Happily, most of the search engines provide ways for you to search for multimedia.

Lycos Multimedia

Lycos

At the Lycos Web site at www.lycos.com, you can click the multimedia option, or you can go directly to multimedia.lycos.com. After you enter your key words, select the kind of media you are looking for, and click the Search button, the Lycos search engine returns a list of pictures, movies, streams, or sounds dealing with your topic. You then preview the objects and download the ones you want.

If your intended use of a picture or a sound found on the Internet is not a fair use, you will need to seek copyright permission by contacting the administrator of the Web site where the object was found. Chapter 25 provides detailed information and guidelines regarding the fair use of multimedia.

AltaVista Multimedia

AltaVista Multimedia

AltaVista has a multimedia section where you can search for images, audio, and video. The audio search includes the popular MP3 audio file format for sharing music over the Internet and downloading it to play on your computer or a portable digital audio device. To perform a multimedia search, go to www.altavista.com. Depending on what you are looking for, click Images, MP3/Audio, or Video.

With the Images search, you can look for photos, graphics, or buttons and banners, either in color or in black and white. The audio search lets you specify whether you want MP3, WAV, Windows Media, or Real audio, lasting for more or less than a minute. The video search finds movies lasting more or less than a minute in AVI, MPEG, QuickTime, Windows Media, or Real video formats. You learn about these file formats in the next chapter, which covers the types of files you are likely to find when downloading from the Internet.

Singingfish

Singingfish

Singingfish specializes in the development and delivery of search engines that can find streaming media content on the Web. Included is access to music, news, movies, sports, TV, radio, finance, and live events. Singingfish is a wholly owned subsidiary of Thomson multimedia. To check out their services, or to conduct a multimedia search, go to www.singingfish.com.

Newsgroup Searches

Newsgroups are a rich source of information about current research in progress. Most disciplines have active newsgroups where current research topics are discussed. Some of the keyword-oriented search engines discussed earlier in this chapter have options you can choose to search newsgroups as well as Web pages. For example, AltaVista, Dogpile, Excite, Google, InfoSeek, and Yahoo all provide a newsgroup search option.

Google Groups

At groups.google.com, for example, you can perform keyword searches of information written in more than 700 million Usenet messages over the past 20 years. The search terms can include the names of the people who wrote the messages. You also can search only on a name to get an index of all of the topics and messages a given person may have written in a newsgroup.

Many users have expressed surprise upon learning that now you can search through newsgroups and find out what has been written by specific people about specific topics. Some users consider this to be a retroactive invasion of privacy. If you want to prevent messages you write in newsgroups from being visible to search engines, you must set the x-no-archive flag when you write the message. You can set this flag by making the first line in the body of your message read as follows:

    x-no-archive: yes

File Searches

As you learned in Chapter 1, FTP stands for File Transfer Protocol. There are millions of files you can download to your computer from FTP sites all over the Internet. Many of these files are Web resources that you can find with the Web-based search engines discussed earlier in this chapter. When searching for files, however, you may find it more efficient to use a site that is tuned to searching for downloads.

Download.com

CNET's Download.com is a handy site for finding and downloading useful files to your computer. The file categories include MP3/audio, business/finance, desktop enhancements, development tools, games, Internet, multimedia/design, Web authoring, utilities, and drivers. The menus make it easy to drill down to the file you want to download. There are in-depth reviews and spotlight articles highlighting featured downloads of the day. To peruse the latest list of downloads, go to download.com.

How to Find People

In addition to helping you find Web pages, newsgroups, files, and scholarly documents, the Internet also can help you locate people.

Bigfoot

Bigfoot

Located at www.bigfoot.com, Bigfoot offers a huge catalog of e-mail addresses and white page directories. These catalogs enable you to search for someone's e-mail address or white-page street address.

WhoWhere

WhoWhere

WhoWhere lets you look up e-mail addresses, residential listings, toll-free 800 numbers, and millions of businesses, including maps and directions. Now that WhoWhere has become part of the Lycos network, you will find WhoWhere at www.whowhere.lycos.com.

Switchboard

Switchboard

You can use the Switchboard white pages service to find people and businesses. It handles more than five million lookups for people and businesses each week. You can find Switchboard at www.switchboard.com.

Yahoo People

Yahoo! People

There is a free online white pages search and listing service at people.yahoo.com. You can search by the person's name, city, or state to find out the person's e-mail address or street address. You can also search thousands of public databases with one click to find addresses, property records, licenses, and court records.

Finding Places

Have you ever gotten lost when driving somewhere? Have you encountered road closings or construction delays that you wish you had known about in advance? The next time you plan a trip, treat yourself by getting a map and a list of specific driving instructions before you take to the roads.

MapQuest

MapQuest

You can visit the most popular interactive mapping service on the Web at www.mapquest.com. It enables you to find more than three million locations worldwide, print driving directions, create personalized maps, and download them to a PDA. Live traffic updates are a popular feature that can save you time when roads close or traffic snarls.

As one of the busiest sites on the Internet, MapQuest serves on the average more than 10 million maps per day. MapQuest's tools provide maps and directions tailored to different types of travelers. MapQuest's clients include Yahoo!, Lycos, the National Geographic Society, the American Auto Association, Fodor's, and many yellow page directories. As a personal user of MapQuest, I can attest to the quality and accuracy of its maps and driving instructions. Best of all, MapQuest is free.

Finding Legal Information

If you know where to look, the Web is an excellent source of legal information. By visiting the sites that follow, you will see why the Web has become the legal profession's primary source of news and information.

Law.Com

Law.com

American Lawyer Media (ALM) is one of the leading sources of news and information for the legal industry in the United States. ALM sponsors a Web site at Law.com, which is where many legal professionals go to get their news. The search engine at Law.com enables you to search the wire services for news about current legal cases. You also can read or search the full text of more than 20 legal publications, including *The National Law*

Journal, The American Lawyer, New York Law Journal, and *Legal Times.* To peruse these and other ALM services, go to www.law.com.

FindLaw

FindLaw

True to its name, the FindLaw site enables you to search for all kinds of legal information. It also can match you up with a lawyer, if you need legal help or advice. FindLaw has channels for legal news, professionals, students, businesses, and the public at large. The search engine enables you to perform keyword searches of the U.S. Constitution, the Supreme Court, government sites, legal sites, the legal news channel, a legal dictionary, and an online library of legal articles. To visit the FindLaw site, go to www.findlaw.com.

LexisONE

LexisONE

Sponsored by LexisNexis, the LexisONE Web site brands itself as "The Resource for Small Law Firms." It features a free legal headline news service and provides free keyword searches of the news, case law, and legal forms. In order to perform these free searches, however, you must first register at the site. To do so, go to www.lexisone.com. To find out about other LexisNexis services, go to www.lexisnexis.com.

Index of Collected Search Engines

Search engines are undergoing a lot of research and development on the Internet. By the time you read this, new search engines will be announced that were not available when this book went to press. You can use Yahoo to find the latest information about new search engines and what they do. At www.yahoo.com, go to the section on Computers and Internet, and do a search for the key word *search.*

Search Engine Watch

Another good place to learn about search engines is the Search Engine Watch, where you will find announcements of the latest search services and Web searching tips. Hosted by Internet.com, you will find the Search Engine Watch at searchenginewatch.internet.com.

exercises

1 Use your Web browser to go to www.yahoo.com. Set a bookmark there. In the future, whenever you want to go to Yahoo, you can get there quickly via the bookmark.

2 Use Yahoo to conduct a subject-oriented search for the topic "Martin Luther King" and make a note of the number of items found. You will need this number to conduct the comparison in exercise 4.

3 Use your Web browser to go to www.altavista.com. Set a bookmark there. In the future, whenever you want to go to AltaVista, you can get there quickly via the bookmark.

4 Use AltaVista to conduct a full-text search for the topic "Martin Luther King" and make a note of the number of items found. How does this compare to the number of hits you got when you searched Yahoo in exercise 2? Why did AltaVista find so much more than Yahoo?

5 Use AltaVista advanced search to perform the following searches. How many matches does each search find? Can you explain why these particular searches find progressively fewer matches?

   ■ "Martin Luther" AND NOT "Martin Luther King"

   ■ "Martin Luther King" AND ("I Have a Dream" OR "Letter from a Birmingham Jail")

   ■ "Martin Luther King" AND "Letter from a Birmingham Jail"

6 At the *Interlit* Web site, follow the links to the people-finder search engines listed in the section on how to find people. Look yourself up in the different directories. Does Bigfoot find you? How about WhoWhere? Do you find yourself listed in Switchboard and Yahoo! People Search? How do you feel about being included or excluded from these people finders? If you are not included, and you would like to be, follow the onscreen instructions for getting yourself listed.

7 Use MapQuest to get driving instructions from your home to 1 Times Square in New York City. Does MapQuest know where you live? Can you see any errors in the driving instructions for the roads near your home? What does MapQuest tell you is the total distance from your home to Times Square, and what is the total estimated travel time?

SITUATED CASE PROJECTS
Case 11: Adopting a Search Engine

At the end of each chapter in this book, a situated case project provides the student an opportunity to put the chapter's contents to practical use in a workplace situation. Each case has the same number as the chapter in which it appears.

An important key to the success of any Web site is how quickly surfers can find what they are looking for. Imagine that you work for a school or company that has a large Web site. There are hundreds or thousands of Web pages at the site, and some users have complained that it takes too long to find what they are looking for. Your employer has heard that some of the leading search engines have a search button that you can put on your organization's Web page. When this book went to press, for example, there was a Google button at w3.org, which is the World Wide Web Consortium (W3C) site. The W3C is a huge site, and the Google search button really helps you find what you are looking for. Your employer wants you to look into which search button would work best at your school or company Web site. In selecting a search engine, consider these issues:

1 Does the search engine work well for the kinds of information stored at your site?

2 How much does it cost to license the search button to put at your site? Is it free, or is a licensing fee required?

3 Will the search engine push commercial ads onto your user's screens? If so, will your school or company accept that? Some schools, for example, have policies against displaying ads onscreen. If ads are not suitable in your workplace, check to see if there is a version that does not display ads, and find out the cost of the ad-free version.

4 Are any resources or system-related tasks required on your Web server, or is everything handled by the third-party search engine site?

Use a word processor to write up your search button recommendation in the form of a brief essay. Describe the search engines you compared, citing their comparative advantages or disadvantages for use in your workplace. Be sure to mention whether the one you recommend comes free or costs money, and mention any work your local server administrator may need to do to support the search button. If your instructor has asked you to hand in the recommendation, make sure you put your name at the top of the document, then save it on disk or follow any other instructions you may have been given for submitting this assignment.

12

COMMONLY FOUND INTERNET FILE TYPES

After completing this chapter, you will be able to:

- **Recognize the commonly found Internet file types.**

- **Understand how browsers launch different plug-ins and helper applications to play certain types of files.**

- **Explain why MIDI files occupy so much less file space than waveform audio files.**

- **Understand the concept of a markup language.**

- **Know the difference between the GIF and JPEG graphics formats.**

- **Understand why the audio/video interleave (AVI) file format was designed to give audio the priority when a computer does not have enough processing time to show all of the frames of a movie.**

- **Explain the difference between lossy and lossless compression methods.**

- **Understand how animated GIFs can bring a Web page to life.**

- **Explain the concept of JavaScript.**

- **Understand the purpose of Adobe's Portable Document Format.**

- **Know the rule search engines use to decide whether to include or exclude active server pages (ASP) files from a search.**

- **Avoid the common pitfall of changing a filename extension when you rename a file.**

● When you use an Internet search engine to find something, the information is almost always returned in the form of a file. The way in which the file is organized is known as its format. File formats vary according to the kind of information being transmitted and its intended use. It is important for you to recognize the commonly found Internet file types, for two reasons. First, you will want to know what the file contains, whether it is text, image, audio, video, animation, or data. Second, knowing the file type enables you to make the right choice in selecting a tool to view, manipulate, interpret, or modify the contents of the file.

When you access a file from the World Wide Web, for example, your Web browser takes a look at the file and, based on the type of file that it is, decides how to handle it. If the file is a Web page, for example, it will display in your browser's window. If the file is a movie, on the other hand, your browser will probably launch a plug-in or a helper application to play it. Later on, in the chapter on multimedia, you will learn how to change the file handlers if you want your browser to use a different player for a certain type of file. Let us begin by learning about the text file types.

Text Formats

There are three families of text formats: plaintext, hypertext, and word processor files. **Plaintext** means just that—the text and nothing but the text. **Hypertext** contains the text intermingled with standardized codes called *tags* that determine how the text is to appear and which words in the text serve as triggers that launch things when clicked. Word processors like Microsoft Word and WordPerfect use proprietary formatting to encode the text and its properties, including font, size, margins, borders, headings, and pagination.

TXT (Plaintext)

Plaintext files are identified by the filename extension *.txt*. When you see a filename such as *history.txt,* for example, you know by its *.txt* filename extension that it is a plaintext file. In computer jargon, plaintext files are known as ASCII files. *ASCII* (pronounced *askee*) stands for American Standard Code for Information Interchange. Every text editor and word processor has an option for reading and writing files in ASCII format. Sometimes the format is called *plaintext* or *DOS text* instead of ASCII text.

Because plaintext files are so common on the Internet, every Web browser needs to be able to display them. Both Mozilla Firefox and Microsoft Internet Explorer have this ability built in. For more information about ASCII files, follow the *Interlit* Web site link to ASCII.

HTML (Hypertext)

HTML stands for hypertext markup language. Files in HTML format have the filename extension *.html* or *.htm*. **HTML** is the most prevalent file format on the World Wide Web, because most Web pages are encoded in HTML. True to its name, an HTML file contains the text that gets displayed on a Web page, along with special codes known as **markup** that define (1) how the text should appear onscreen, (2) which words in the text are hyper, and (3) what gets triggered when the user clicks the hypertext. For example, Figure 12-1 shows how a Web page displays an HTML file, and Figure 12-2 shows how the same file appears when viewed with a text editor. The codes inside <brackets> are the markup that tells the Web browser how to interpret the text. You will learn more about the HTML codes in the Web page creation tutorial in Part Five of this book. To visit the official Web site where the latest HTML specification is found, follow the *Interlit* Web site link to HTML.

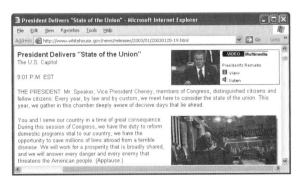

Figure 12-1 The State of the Union Address as viewed with a Web browser.

Figure 12-2 The State of the Union Address as viewed with a text editor.

Microsoft Word

DOC (Microsoft Word) and WPD (WordPerfect)

There are many word processor formats. The most common are Microsoft Word's DOC format and WordPerfect's WPD format. *DOC* stands for *document,* and *WPD* stands for *WordPerfect document.* Web browsers do not usually contain built-in support for word processor file formats. Instead, your browser calls upon a helper application to display the file upon demand. You will learn more about helper applications in Chapter 23.

Portable Document Format (PDF)

Adobe PDF

To provide a way to digitize printed text into a format that can be viewed on any computer platform, Adobe created the **Portable Document Format (PDF),** for which the filename extension is *.pdf.* You create PDF files with a program called Adobe Acrobat. If you have a lot of pages to scan, you can use a sheet feeder to speed the scanning process. Through optical character recognition (OCR) software, Acrobat can create from scanned documents machine-readable text that is full-text searchable.

Acrobat's capabilities go beyond text, however. If you have Adobe Acrobat, you can create a PDF file from any computer application that can print. To create a PDF version of a PowerPoint presentation or an MS Word document, for example, you simply pull down the File menu, choose Print, and select Adobe Acrobat as your printer. PDF files are popular on the Web because they retain the look of the original document, and you can set an option that prevents users from editing the text.

You view PDF files with the Adobe Acrobat Reader, a free plug-in that any user can get from the Adobe Web site. If you configure the Acrobat Reader as the helper application for viewing PDF files in your Web browser, then your browser will launch Acrobat automatically whenever you follow a link to a PDF file. You will learn how to configure helper applications in Chapter 23.

You will make some pretty amazing discoveries when you use the Adobe Acrobat Reader to view a PDF document. Because you are looking at what appears to be pictures of the original document, you do not expect to be able to select, copy, paste, and search for text as you could on a regular Web page. You will be pleasantly surprised to find, however, that all of these functions are available unless the author disabled them. Perhaps your biggest surprise will come when you choose to print the document. Instead of printing the bitmap version of the image you see on screen, Acrobat prints the document using the fonts on your printer. As a result, the printed version may appear better than the original.

To learn more about the PDF file format, and to see some examples of *.pdf* files in action, follow the *Interlit* Web site links to Adobe Acrobat and Portable Document Format.

Image Formats

The computer industry has produced so many graphics formats (more than 30 at last count) that there is no true standard across the industry. Table 12-1 lists a few of the more popular graphics file formats and describes what they are used for. On the Web, however, there are only two file formats that every Web browser can be guaranteed to support: GIF and JPEG. The latest browsers also support PNG, a newer format described below.

GIF

GIF stands for **Graphics Interchange Format.** Invented by CompuServe for use on computer networks, GIF is highly efficient. Instead of containing the RGB (red, green, blue) value of every pixel (picture element) in the image, a GIF file contains a table defining the different pixel patterns found in the image, with pointers into the table indicating where the patterns go onscreen. It is important to understand that although GIF files are

Table 12-1 The most common computer graphics formats

Filename Extension	Intended Purpose
.bmp	Windows bitmap. The .*bmp* file is the most efficient format to use with Windows.
.gif	Graphics Interchange Format. Invented by CompuServe for use on computer networks, GIF is the most prevalent graphics format for images on the World Wide Web.
.pcd	Kodak's Photo CD graphics file format; contains five different sizes of each picture, from "wallet" size to "poster" size.
.jpg or **.jpeg**	JPEG image, named for the standards committee that formed it: Joint Photographic Experts Group. Intended to become a platform-independent graphics format, this is arguably the best choice for publishing full-color photographs on the Web.
.pict	An older Macintosh graphics format.
.png	Portable Network Graphics format. Pronounced *ping,* PNG is the patent and license-free format approved by the W3C (World Wide Web Consortium) to replace the patented GIF format. Because the PNG format is not yet fully supported by all browsers, Web authors typically convert graphics to GIF or JPEG for use on Web pages.
.tga	Truevision Targa format; *tga* stands for Targa, which is a video capture board.
.tif	TIFF file; stands for Tagged Image File Format. Known as "the variable standard" because there are so many kinds of TIFF subformats.
.wpg	WordPerfect graphics format.

compressed, none of the original information in the graphic gets lost in the compression process. The decompressed image you see on screen is exactly the same as the one that got compressed into the GIF file. Because nothing gets lost, this kind of encoding process is known as **lossless** compression. GIF files, however, are limited to a palette of 256 colors; if you need more than 256 different colors in a picture, you should use the JPEG format (see below). For more information about how GIF compression works, follow the *Interlit* Web site links to GIF.

JPEG

JPEG (pronounced *Jay-peg*) stands for **Joint Photographic Experts Group,** which is the name of the international standards committee that created it. JPEG was invented as a platform-independent graphics format. JPEG images can contain millions of colors, whereas GIF images are limited to a palette of 256 colors. If you are creating a photo in which color is important, therefore, you should use the JPEG format. GIF is for simpler images such as icons or logos.

JPEG uses a lossy compression algorithm to reduce the amount of space it would otherwise require to store images with millions of colors. **Lossy** means that some of the image data can become lost, depending on how much compression is used when the image gets saved. JPEG compresses the image by dividing it into tiny cubes and averaging the color values within the cubes. Most people are unable to notice the tiny cubes in the image. One of the settings you can vary when saving a JPEG image is the size of the cubes. The larger the cubes, the more compression you will get, but the cubes will also be more noticeable.

PNG

The World Wide Web Consortium is working on a new graphics format called **Portable Network Graphics (PNG).** The goal is to create a fast, lossless, patent-free file format that can handle pictures containing up to 48 bits of color information per pixel. The screen

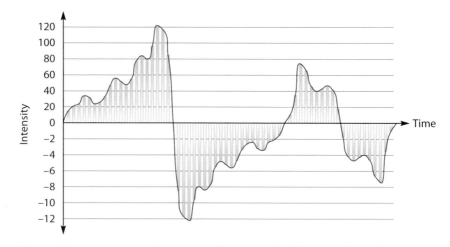

Figure 12-3   A waveform in the process of being sampled; the vertical lines show the points at which samples are taken.

captures and logos in this book, for example, were transmitted in PNG format from my PC to the publisher's typesetter. You can monitor the progress of the creation of this new file format by following the *Interlit* Web site links to PNG.

Waveform Audio Formats

Every sound has a waveform that describes its frequency, amplitude, and harmonic content. Waveform audio digitizers capture sound by sampling this waveform thousands of times per second; the samples are stored in a computer file. Figure 12-3 shows a waveform in the process of being sampled. For each sample, a number gets written into the corresponding waveform audio file. The number tells how far the sample rises above or falls below the zero amplitude line. When you click to play the file, the samples play back through your computer's sound chip, and you hear the waveform audio. Waveform audio can be transmitted over the Net in several file formats.

WAV

On computers running Windows, the native waveform audio filename extension is *.wav,* which stands for waveform. When the Web started, you needed helper applications to play audio, because the first browsers lacked built-in support for *.wav* files. Happily, all the major browsers now contain native support for playing *.wav* files, on Macintosh as well as Windows operating systems. For more information about the WAV format, follow the *Interlit* Web site links to Waveform Audio.

RA and RAM

RealAudio

Real-time audio streaming used in Internet radio broadcasts requires a special file format optimized for real-time transmission over the Internet. The RealAudio filename extensions are *.ra* and *.ram,* which stands for RealAudio metafile. A RealAudio metafile is a text file that contains the Web address (URL) of a RealAudio file. RealAudio files cannot be referenced directly by the Web page because this would cause them to be downloaded in their entirety before playback. In order for a RealAudio file to be played in real time, it must be played through a RealAudio player and served by a RealAudio server. To accomplish this, there must be a link between the Web server and the RealAudio server. The link is contained in the metafile. For more information about the RealAudio file formats, follow the RealAudio links at the *Interlit* Web site.

AIF, AIFF, AIFC

AIFF stands for Audio Interchange File Format. Apple invented this file format to create and play audio files on the Macintosh. AIFC is a compressed version; the C stands for compressed. When you find an AIF file on the Web, chances are it was recorded on a Macintosh. For more information about the AIF file formats, follow the *Interlit* Web site links to AIF.

MP3

mp3.com

MP3 is one of the most popular audio formats on the Internet. **MP3** stands for MPEG audio layer 3. It is an audio file format that uses an MPEG audio codec to encode (compress) and decode (decompress) recorded music. MP3 can compress a CD audio track into a substantially smaller file requiring significantly less bandwidth (about 10 percent) to transmit over the Internet, without degrading the original sound track's quality.

To download a free MP3 player, find MP3 Web sites, and create MP3 files from your favorite audio CD, follow the *Interlit* Web site links to MP3. If you do not personally own the CD and/or if the MP3 files are not for your own personal use, please observe the copyright and fair use guidelines presented in Chapter 25. Because the MP3 technology makes copyright violation so easy, the kind of software used to create an MP3 file from an audio CD is called a **ripper.** Please be aware, however, that MP3 has many legitimate uses on the Web. Some recording artists are choosing to distribute their own songs in the MP3 format, for example, and some hit songs have appeared in MP3 format first before being distributed on CD. Little-known artists use MP3 as a way to gain fans who may eventually want to hear them in concert or buy their CDs.

MIDI Synthesizer Format (MID)

Musical Instrument Digital Interface (MIDI) is a music synthesizer file format that requires very little bandwidth to transmit because the sound chip inside your multimedia PC does the work of generating the waveform you hear. What gets transmitted is the performance information required for your computer's sound chip to play the music. Accordingly, a MIDI file consists of a stream of codes that tells your computer when to turn notes on and off, how loud to make them, what instrument should make the sound (such as trumpet, flute, or drum), and whether to bend the notes or add other special effects. Compared to the amount of storage required for waveform audio recordings, MIDI takes up so little space that it is a very popular format for transmitting music over the Internet. MIDI files have a *.mid* filename extension.

There are some incredible indexes of MIDI files that you can listen to at the *Interlit* Web site. Follow the links to the MIDI archives, and you will get a list of indexes that contain thousands of songs in a wide variety of styles, ranging from classical to modern, and funk to rock. You also will find music listed by artists, from Abba to Frank Zappa. You need to realize, however, that MIDI does not record the singer's voice. Thus, you will hear the synthesized music, but you will not hear the lyrics.

AAC, M4A, M4P

Apple's popular iTunes service uses the file format AAC, which stands for Advanced Audio Coding. Under the cover, this is the audio format used in MPEG-4. MPEG is discussed below in the section on video formats. Protected iTunes downloads have the filename extension M4P where P stands for Protected, meaning that the download contains a digital rights management scheme that prevents unauthorized users from playing the file without paying for it. Downloads that are not protected have the filename extension M4A, which stands for MPEG-4 Audio.

Table 12-2 Video compression schemes

Method	How It Works
YUV subsampling	Divides the screen into little squares and averages color values of the pixels in each square.
Delta-frame encoding	Shrinks data by storing only the information that changes between frames; for example, if the background scene does not change, there is no need to store the scene again.
Run-length encoding	Detects a "run" of identical pixels and encodes how many occur instead of recording individual pixels.

WMA

True to its name, Windows Media Audio (WMA) is Microsoft's file format for streaming audio. The WMA encoder can compress audio to match various bandwidth requirements. If you have a slow Internet connection, for example, you can listen to a low-bandwidth stream containing more highly compressed audio. The WMA encoder also can use high-fidelity settings that create compact disc quality sound. Music downloading services typically use the high-fidelity settings. The WMA file format supports digital rights management (DRM); if a song contains DRM, users who have not paid for the song cannot listen to it.

Video Formats

When a movie is digitized into a computer file, the digital data stream is enormous. To conserve file space and thereby reduce the bandwidth required to transmit the movie, the video gets compressed, down to as little as 1/200th of its original size. One or more of the video compression schemes explained in Table 12-2 may be used.

AVI

Windows Media

The most common video format in the Windows world is Microsoft's AVI, which has the *.avi* filename extension. **AVI** stands for audio/video interleave, a clever scheme in which audio frames are interleaved with the video. The sound track plays without interruption because the audio always takes priority. Then your computer shows as many frames of video as it has time to process. If it is too late to show a given frame, the player just skips it and goes on to the next frame. Because the audio has priority, you get the aural illusion of uninterrupted playback.

MOV and QT

Quick Time

One of Apple Computer Corporation's greatest gifts to the field of multimedia is the QuickTime audio/video format. QuickTime is so robust and popular that it exists in both Macintosh and Windows formats. Because of its cross-platform capabilities, QuickTime has become very popular on the Internet. The filename extensions of QuickTime movies are *.qt* and *.mov*. For the latest information, go to www.apple.com/quicktime.

ASF and WMV

Advanced Streaming Format (ASF) is a multimedia streaming format invented by Microsoft. ASF files that contain audio and video typically have the filename extension. *wmv,* which stands for Windows Media Video. Internally, the file structure of an ASF file is basically the same as a WMV file. ASF files that contain only audio typically have the Windows Media Audio (WMA) filename extension discussed earlier in this chapter.

MPG, MPEG, and MPE

Motion Picture Experts Group

MPEG is emerging as the digital video standard for the United States and most of the world. **MPEG** stands for Motion Picture Experts Group, the International Standards Organization committee that created the standard. Endorsed by more than 70 companies, including IBM, Apple, JVC, Philips, Sony, and Matsushita, MPEG compresses video by using a discrete cosine transform algorithm to eliminate redundant data in blocks of pixels on the screen. MPEG compresses the video further by recording only changes from frame to frame; this is known as delta-frame encoding. MPEG is expected to become the digital video standard for compact discs, DVD, cable TV, direct satellite broadcast, and high-definition television (HDTV).

Four versions of MPEG have been worked on:

- **MPEG-1** is the noninterlaced version designed for playback from CD-ROMs.

- **MPEG-2** is the interlaced version intended for the all-digital transmission of broadcast-quality TV. Adopted by the U.S. Grand Alliance HDTV specification, the European Digital Video Broadcasting Group, and the Digital Versatile Disc (DVD-ROM) consortium, MPEG-2 features surround sound. RCA's DirecTV service uses MPEG-2.

- **MPEG-3** was to be the HDTV version of MPEG, but then it was discovered that the MPEG-2 syntax could fulfill that need by simply scaling the bit rate, obviating need for the third phase.

- **MPEG-4** is a low-bit-rate version of MPEG that is being invented for transmitting movies over mobile and wireless communications.

For more information, follow the *Interlit* Web site links to MPEG.

RM

RealNetworks

One of the greatest challenges on the Internet is to deliver to your player full-motion video in an uninterrupted real-time data stream. First to market with a product that does that was RealNetworks, which is the same company that brought you the RealAudio technology discussed earlier in this chapter. The name of the product is RealVideo, and the filename extension is *.rm,* which stands for Real metafile.

RealVideo follows the **real-time streaming protocol (RTSP)** that RealNetworks invented for streaming audio and video over the Internet. To read about this and other technical details, follow the *Interlit* Web site link to RTSP.

Animation Formats

Animation is the use of a computer to create movement on the screen. There are several ways to bring Web pages to life through animation. Discussed here are four methods that progress in order from simple to complex.

Animated GIFs

Animated *GIF* is a special kind of GIF file (known as GIF89a) that may contain multiple images that are shown in a sequence at specific times and locations on the screen. A looping option causes your Web browser to keep showing the frames in the GIF file continually, and as a result, you see an animation onscreen. Animated GIFs are very efficient because they are only downloaded once, then cached from your hard drive as your browser loops the images. There is a collection of animated GIFs that demonstrates how effective this very simple approach to animation can be. To see the demos, follow the *Interlit* Web site links to Animated GIFs.

JavaScript

Netscape

Java is a programming environment that can be used to create little applications known as **applets** that can be downloaded along with a Web page. One of the main uses of applets is to make Web pages animated. Ordinarily, it requires a high level of programming skill to create an applet in Java. Netscape invented a scripting language called **JavaScript,** however, that greatly simplifies the process. Instead of writing native Java code, you call scripts that can perform some of the same functions as a Java applet with much simpler coding. For a demonstration of the kinds of animations that JavaScript can create, follow the JavaScript links at the *Interlit* Web site. You also will find links to more information about JavaScript, including a tutorial on using JavaScript and a comparison that points out the differences between Java and JavaScript. It should be noted that JavaScript can be used for more than just animations. It also can be used to perform calculations, make comparisons, interact with the user through forms, and make information persist as the user moves from page to page.

QuickTime

QuickTime

Apple Computer Corporation offers a plug-in whereby QuickTime movies can be embedded as animation objects on Web pages. All the major browsers support this plug-in. To see some examples of Web pages containing QuickTime animations, follow the *Interlit* Web site links to QuickTime.

Flash

Flash

Created by Macromedia, Flash is a multimedia development tool that lets designers and developers integrate video, text, audio, graphics, and animations with Web forms to create so-called rich client applications. According to Macromedia, 97 percent of the world's Internet-enabled desktops have Flash installed. The Flash player is free. To learn more, follow the *Interlit* Web site link to Flash Player At a Glance.

Shockwave

Shockwave

Macromedia's Director is the undisputed leader in multimedia animation. Breakthrough products such as BrØderbund's *Living Books* series of animated storybooks and the recording artist Sting's fantastic double CD-ROM *All This Time* were created with Director. Shockwave is a free player that enables animations created with Director to plug in to Web pages. Shockwave can deliver e-merchandising applications and rich-media multiuser games. For a demonstration, follow the *Interlit* Web site link to Shockwave. If Shockwave is not already on your computer, your Web browser will prompt you and help you install it.

Active Server Pages (ASP) Formats

Microsoft ASP.NET

Microsoft invented **Active Server Pages (ASP)** files as a special type of document that permits Web pages to contain scripts that execute on the server at run time to provide so-called active content onscreen. A simple example would be a script that displays the current date and time on a Web page at the moment it is being served. More involved scripts can perform calculations, query databases to display a catalog of products, show which products are in stock, and allow the user to make a purchase. Active Server Pages have the *.asp* filename extension. Microsoft subsequently invented a more powerful version called ASP.NET in which active server pages have the filename extension *.aspx*.

Search engines typically include ASP files in searches when there are no variables included in the URL. If the URL contains variables, on the other hand, the search engine assumes that the file relies on the execution of a script to render the content, in which case it cannot be indexed because its content is not static. *Note:* You can tell whether a URL contains variables by looking to see if there are one or more question marks in it. The question marks delimit the names and values of the variables.

Avoiding the Pitfall of Renaming Filename Extensions

When you access the different types of files described in this chapter, you may occasionally be prompted to save the file on your computer's hard drive. When you save the file, a dialog box will appear containing the name of the file and the folder in which it will be saved. You can use the Save dialog to select or create a different file folder, and you can even change the name of the file. Be careful, however, not to rename the filename extension. If the filename extension is *.wav,* for example, do not change it to *.mid.* Remember that your computer looks at the filename extension to determine what application will be used to handle the file. Renaming the filename extension will only confuse your computer when you try to access the file.

Beginners will sometimes believe that renaming a filename extension reformats the file. It does not. Renaming a filename extension from *.gif* to *.jpeg,* for example, does not convert the file into the *.jpeg* format. In order to change the format of the file, you need to use a graphics editor. In Chapter 19 you learn how to use a graphics editor to convert images into different formats.

exercises

1. One of the most important concepts in the hypertext markup language (HTML) file format is the way it specifies how text and graphics flow with respect to each other, depending on the size and shape of the window in which the file is viewed. Follow the *Interlit* Web site link to Lewis Carroll's famous story *Through the Looking Glass* and experiment with resizing your browser's window. Notice how the text and graphics of the story adjust themselves automatically to the size and position of the window.

2. Imagine a situation in which you have a MIDI file and a waveform audio recording of a symphony orchestra playing the same piece of classical music. What will be the main difference you hear between the two files? Which file will take more time to transfer from the Web to your computer? To help you answer these questions, there is a Waveform audio file and a MIDI file for you to compare at the *Interlit* Web site. Follow the links to MIDI versus Wave, and listen to the two files. Both files are the same size, 17 kilobytes. Which one lasts longer? How do you explain the difference in the length of the music you hear, when the file size is the same? Which example sounds better to you?

3. Give one example of when you might use each one of the following techniques to animate a Web page. Make sure the example you give is appropriate to the technique in terms of authoring time and visual effect.
   - Animated GIF
   - QuickTime
   - Shockwave

4. What is the most important difference between the documents you view onscreen when you use your Web browser to view an HTML file as opposed to a PDF file? Under what circumstances is it better to use a PDF file than an HTML file?

SITUATED CASE PROJECTS
Case 12: Handling Commonly Found File Types

At the end of each chapter in this book, a situated case project provides the student an opportunity to put the chapter's contents to practical use in a workplace situation. Each case has the same number as the chapter in which it appears.

As you learned in this chapter, there are many types of files that users are likely to encounter on the Internet. Imagine that your employer has assigned you the task of assessing how well the computers in your school or company handle the commonly found Internet file types. Your employer wants you to try accessing these file types from a typical computer deployed at your workplace, report any problems you encounter, and recommend what needs to be done to the computers in your workplace to enable your co-workers to access these kinds of files. To create this assessment, follow these steps:

1 Go to a typically configured computer at your school or company and get the Web browser running on that computer.

2 Browse to the Episode 12 section of Chapter 12 at the *Interlit* Web site. Episode 12 contains links to different kinds of files that are typically found on the Internet.

3 Follow each link and observe how your computer handles the type of file to which the link goes.

4 Use your word processor to keep a log of each kind of file you visit. In this log, make note of any problems you encounter. For example, if you get a message telling you that some kind of special software needs to be downloaded to the computer to handle a certain type of file, make a note in your log identifying the name and location of the recommended download.

Use a word processor to write up your file-handling assessment in the form of a brief essay. Identify the name and location of the computer you used during this test. Include the log that identifies each kind of file you visited and what happened when you followed its link. Conclude your assessment with a summary of what steps need to be taken to enable the computers in your workplace to handle any file types that were not handled properly. If your instructor has asked you to hand in this report, make sure you put your name at the top of the document, then save it on disk or follow any other instructions you may have been given for submitting this assignment.

13

DOWNLOADING FROM THE INTERNET

After completing this chapter, you will be able to:

- Download text and graphics from the Internet.

- Download audio and video resources from the Internet.

- Download data files and software from the Internet.

- Make sure the downloaded file has the correct filename extension for the type of file it is.

- Install self-extracting archives that you download from the Internet.

- Safeguard against downloading viruses that can be harmful to your computer.

In the past, prior to the creation of the graphical user interface that is used in the Netscape, Mozilla, Safari, and Internet Explorer Web browsers, downloading files required you to know how to use a complicated set of commands for connecting to the computer that hosts the file and FTPing the file to your computer. These commands were so complicated that only technically inclined users were able to download files from the Internet.

Happily, the graphical user interface has made it so easy to transfer files that you no longer need to know a single FTP command to download a file. In this chapter, you learn how to download text, graphics, audio, video, data, and software from the Internet. To safeguard against catching viruses from the files you download, this chapter concludes by teaching you how to install a virus scanner and set it to scan incoming as well as outgoing files.

Downloading Text from the Internet

The quickest way to download text from the Internet is to copy the text onto your computer's clipboard, from which you can paste the text into any other window on your screen. All of the leading browsers let you copy text onto your computer's clipboard. To download text this way, follow the steps in Table 13-1.

Note: Because this is the standard way to copy and paste text in the Windows and Macintosh operating systems, the technique taught in Table 13-1 will come in handy any time you want to copy text from one application to another.

Downloading Images from the Internet

The quickest way to download an image from the Internet is to use your Web browser's option for saving the image to a file. When you save the image to a file, you will have the option of changing its name. If you change the filename, make sure that you keep the

Table 13-1   How to download text via the clipboard

Windows	Macintosh
▶ Use your browser to display the text you want to download.	▶ Use your browser to display the text you want to download.
▶ Click and drag your mouse over the text you want to copy; the selected text will appear highlighted. If you want to select all of the text on the Web page, pull down the browser's Edit menu and choose Select All.	▶ Click and drag your mouse over the text you want to copy; the selected text will appear highlighted. If you want to select all of the text on the Web page, pull down the browser's Edit menu and choose Select All.
▶ Press the Windows Copy keys Ctrl - C or pull down the Edit menu and choose Copy.	▶ Press the Macintosh Copy keys ⌘ - C or pull down the Edit menu and choose Copy.
▶ If the application into which you want to paste the text is not already running, get it running now.	▶ If the application into which you want to paste the text is not already running, get it running now.
▶ Position your cursor at the spot in the window to which you want to paste the text.	▶ Position your cursor at the spot in the window to which you want to paste the text.
▶ Press the Windows Paste keys Ctrl - V or pull down the application's Edit menu and choose Paste.	▶ Press the Macintosh Paste keys ⌘ - V or pull down the application's Edit menu and choose Paste.

Table 13-2   How to download an image from the Internet

▶ Use your browser to display the image you want to download.

▶ Right-click (Windows) or control-click (Macintosh) on the image you want to download, and a menu will pop out. On a Mac, you can also trigger the menu by holding down the mouse button until the menu pops out.

▶ The popout menu provides you with options you can do with the image; choose the option to "Save image as . . ." or "Save picture as . . ." The Save As dialog appears.

▶ In the Filename field, you will see the name of the file that this image has on the Internet. You can change the name if you want, but make sure you leave the filename extension the same as in the original.

▶ You can use the Save As dialog to navigate to a different drive or folder on your computer, or you can type a complete path onto the beginning of the filename, to specify exactly where you want the image file to be saved on your computer.

▶ Click the Save button when you are ready to save the file.

filename extension the same as the original filename's, because that is how other programs recognize it as the type of file it is. For example, if the image you are saving is in GIF format, make sure the filename extension on the file to be saved is *.gif*. If the image you are saving is in JPEG format, make sure the filename extension on the file to be saved is *.jpg*. Renaming the filename extension of a *.gif* file to *.jpg* does not change the format of the file. If you want to change the format of the file, you must use a file-conversion program such as Paint Shop Pro (Windows) or Graphic Converter (Macintosh), which you will learn how to use in Chapter 19. To download an image from the Internet, follow the steps in Table 13-2.

Downloading Audio and Video from the Internet

Downloading audio and video is similar to downloading graphics. You right-click (Windows) or control-click (Macintosh) on the link that triggers the audio or video, and the Save As dialog appears. Detailed instructions are provided in Table 13-3.

Table 13-3 How to download audio and video from the Internet

- ▶ Use your browser to display the link that triggers the audio or video you want to download.

- ▶ Right-click (Windows) or control-click (Macintosh) on the trigger. A popout menu will provide you with options you can do with the object linked to the trigger; choose the "Save link as" or "Save target as" option to make the Save As dialog appear.

- ▶ In the Filename field, you will see the name of the file that this object has on the Internet. You can change the name if you want, but make sure you leave the filename extension the same as in the original.

- ▶ Click the Save button when you are ready to save the file.

Downloading Software and Data from the Internet

To download software and data from the Internet, you should begin by reading any special instructions that might appear onscreen explaining what will happen when you trigger the download. Almost all of these instructions fall into one of three categories: documents, archived files, and self-extracting archives. Each kind is discussed in turn as follows.

Documents

When a document is linked to a Web page, you have two options. You can either click to view the document or, if you want to download it, you can right-click (Windows) or control-click (Macintosh) the link to pop out the menu that lets you save the document on your computer. The biggest problem beginners report is knowing where to save the downloaded document. If you have Windows, a good place is the folder called My Documents or My Downloads. On the Macintosh, beginners normally download a document onto the desktop, from which you can move it later to another folder if you want to file it away.

To download the document that your Web browser is currently displaying, you pull down the browser's File menu, choose Save As, and use the Save dialog to save the file to a folder on your computer's hard drive. As always, please remember not to alter the filename extension when you save the file. If the file has a *.doc* filename extension, for example, do not change it to a *.txt* filename extension. Remember that your computer looks at the filename extension to determine what application will handle the file. Renaming the filename extension will confuse your computer when someone tries to access the file.

Archived Files

A popular method of distributing software and data over the Internet is via archived files. An **archive** is a container into which one or more files have been compressed to save space and packed into a single file that can be transmitted easily over a network. When you receive such a file, you need to use an extractor to unpack the archive and restore its contents onto your computer. On the Windows operating system, the archive format is called ZIP. When a Windows user downloads an archive, it has the *.zip* filename extension. Windows XP contains built-in support for zipping and unzipping archives. To open a ZIP file with Windows XP, you simply open it with My Computer or Windows Explorer.

PKZIP FOR WINDOWS

Windows users who do not have Windows XP normally unpack a ZIP archive by opening it with PKZIP for Windows. Figure 13-1 shows how PKZIP for Windows displays the contents of the zipped file. Then, following the instructions on the Web page from

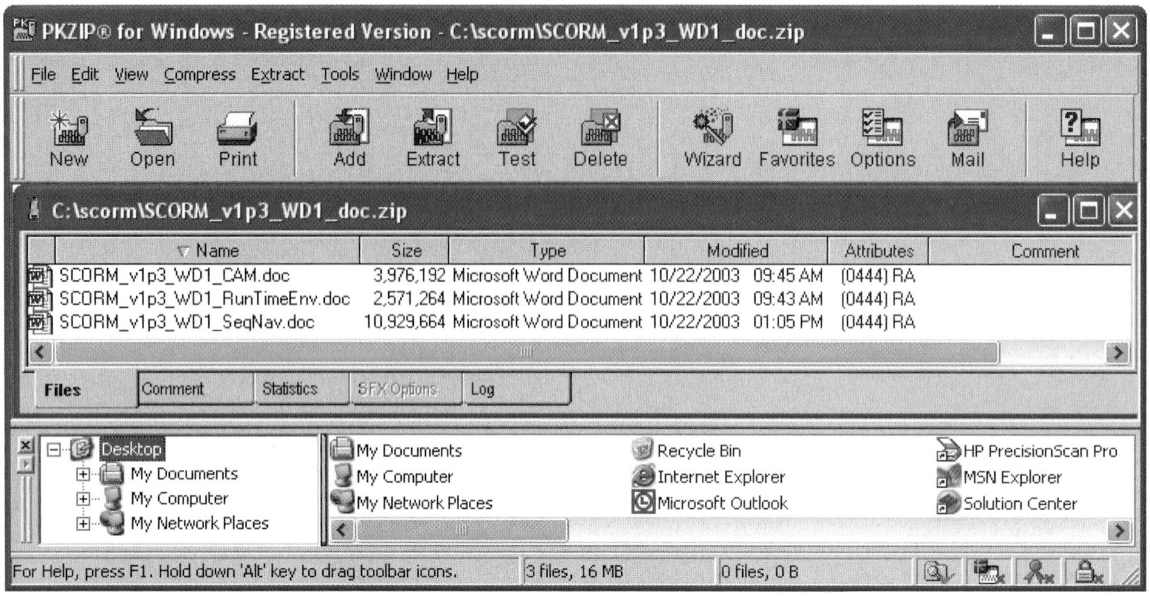

Figure 13-1 PKZIP for Windows displays the contents of the zipped file.

which you downloaded the ZIP file, you install the files to your computer by running the *install.exe* or *setup.exe* file listed in the contents.

PKZIP for Windows is **shareware,** meaning that you can download it for free, try it out for a limited time period (usually 30 to 60 days), and then, if you decide to keep using it, pay a reasonable fee (usually $29 to $39) to the vendor. To download a copy of PKZIP for Windows, follow the *Interlit* Web site link to PKZIP.

STUFFIT EXPANDER FOR THE MACINTOSH

Stuffit Expander

On the Macintosh, archives are handled with a freeware program from Aladdin Systems called Stuffit Expander, which is also available for Windows. True to its name, Stuffit Expander can extract files from archives you download from the Internet. If you are using a Macintosh and you do not have Stuffit Expander, you should download it by following the *Interlit* Web site link to Stuffit Expander.

When you ask Stuffit Expander to expand a file, it opens a new folder on the desktop and decompresses each file into that folder. Figure 13-2 shows that as the files are expanded, a status bar displays the status of the decompression. When Stuffit Expander is done extracting the files, many applications will be ready to run by clicking their icon in the new folder. Others will create an install program that must be run separately to set up the application.

In OS X, many applications are distributed in the disk image (DMG) format. The archives typically have the double filename extension *.dmg.sit*. When an OS X user downloads

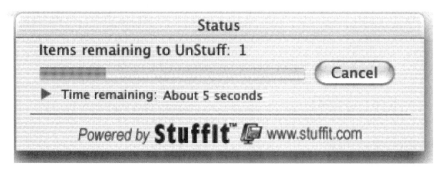

Figure 13-2 Stuffit Expander displays a status bar while it extracts archived files on the Macintosh.

Table 13-4 How to start a program if its icon is not visible

Windows	Macintosh
▶ Click the Start button and choose Run to make the Run dialog appear.	▶ 🔍 Get Sherlock running by pressing ⌘-F or pull down the File menu and choose Find File.
▶ Click the Browse button; the Browse dialog appears.	▶ Set the option to search for Applications, enter the name of the program you are looking for, and click the 🔍 Find button to make your computer find the file.
▶ Use the browse controls to select the filename of the program you want to run.	▶ Double-click the file to run it.
▶ Click Open; the filename of the program to be run appears in the Open field of the Run dialog.	
▶ Click OK to run the file.	
▶ If you are unable to locate the file using this method, click the Windows Start button and use Find→Files to locate the file. Then double-click the file to run it.	

such an archive, Stuffit Expander automatically decompresses the file and puts the DMG folder on your desktop. To install the application, you open the DMG folder and drag the program into your Applications folder. To launch the application, you double-click its icon in your Applications folder. If you want a quick launch icon on your Dock, simple drag the icon from the Applications folder to the Dock. After you get the application running, you can drag the DMG file and the SIT file into the trash to save disk space.

Self-Extracting Archives

Another popular method of distributing software and data on the Internet is via self-extracting archives. A **self-extracting archive** is a compressed file into which the files that comprise an application or set of data have been packed. You download the archive file to your computer. Then you run the archive, which unpacks the files and stores them on your computer.

Most of the downloads you will find at the CNET download.com site, for example, are distributed in self-extracting archives. When you click to download one of them, your browser will prompt you whether you want to save the archive to disk or open it directly from the Web. If you choose the option to save it to disk, a Save dialog will appear. Use the Save dialog to save the archive in your computer's *temp* folder. Then you run the self-extracting archive. If the archive's icon is not visible, follow the steps in Table 13-4, which shows how to start a program if its icon is not visible.

To conserve space on your computer's hard disk, after you run the self-extracting archive, you can delete it from your computer's *temp* folder.

Safeguarding against Viruses

When you open files that you get from the Internet, you run the risk of infecting your computer with viruses that may attach or embed themselves in certain kinds of files. The most vulnerable types of files are the executables, which cause code to run on your computer. Before you download an executable file, you need to check carefully the source from which you are downloading it. If the file is coming from a reputable site, such as Microsoft or Mozilla or CNET Download.com, the file is most probably virus-free. The executable filename extensions to be most careful about are *.exe, .bat, .vbs,* and *.class*. It is also possible for macros to transmit viruses in *.doc* and *.xls* files.

Set your antivirus software to scan automatically all incoming and outgoing mail and file transfers. It is important to remove viruses promptly, because letting them remain on your computer can cause disruptive things to happen, such as files disappearing, unwanted messages coming onscreen, software acting strangely, and even your entire hard disk losing its contents. Make sure your virus scanner is up-to-date so it will recognize the latest viruses. When a new virus hits the Net, updates are normally available within the day, and you should install the update promptly. For the latest information about viruses and how to remove them from your computer, follow the antivirus links at the *Interlit* Web site.

exercises

1. Get your favorite word processor or text editor running on your computer. If you do not have a word processor, follow the instructions in Table 6-10 to get Notepad or TextEdit running on your computer. Use your Web browser to display one of your favorite Web pages. Practice copying and pasting text from the Web page into your word processor or text editor window. If you have trouble, refer to the instructions in Table 13-1.

2. There are lots of interesting icons at the *Interlit* Web site. Use your Web browser to go to the *Interlit* Web site and download one of the icons to your computer. If you have trouble, refer to the instructions in Table 13-2. If you change the filename before you save the file, make sure the filename extension of the file you save matches the filename extension of the original. Now use the Windows Explorer or the Macintosh Finder to locate the file, and double-click the file to launch it. If the image appears properly, you have succeeded in learning how to download images to your computer. *Note:* If your computer tells you there is no program available to display the image, follow the steps in Chapter 19 to install either Paint Shop Pro (Windows) or Graphic Converter (Macintosh).

3. There is a touchy-mood MIDI file at the *Interlit* Web site, provided courtesy of the Ensoniq Corporation, makers of some of the world's finest MIDI gear. To hear the song, click *touchy.mid*. Download this file onto your computer so you can listen to it whenever you want, whether or not your Web browser is running. If you have trouble downloading the MIDI file, refer to the instructions in Table 13-3. Now get a program running that can play MIDI files, such as the Windows Media Player or the Macintosh QuickTime Player. Use this program to open and play the MIDI file you downloaded. If the song plays properly, you have succeeded in learning how to download audio files to your computer.

4. Depending on whether you are using Firefox, Internet Explorer, Netscape Navigator, or Safari, click your browser's icon in the Chapter 13 exercises section of the *Interlit* Web site. This takes you to the Web site from which you can download new versions of your browser. Check to see if a new version is available. If so, follow the onscreen instructions to download and install the update. If you are an Internet Explorer user and you would like to explore what life is like on the other side of the tracks, download the Firefox browser and take it for a test drive. Likewise, if you are a Safari user, give Firefox a try. How do the two browsers compare? Which one do you like best? Why do you feel that way? How would you recommend that Firefox improve its browser? How could Safari or Internet Explorer be improved?

SITUATED CASE PROJECTS
Case 13: Choosing Antivirus Software

At the end of each chapter in this book, a situated case project provides the student an opportunity to put the chapter's contents to practical use in a workplace situation. Each case has the same number as the chapter in which it appears.

Schools and companies can lose a lot of time and money when viruses strike. It is critically important for both the servers and the client computers in your workplace to be protected from viruses. Imagine that you work for a school or company that has recently undergone a bad virus attack. Your employer wants to prevent such an attack from happening again. Your employer has asked you to recommend the brand of antivirus software that should be installed on all of the machines at your workplace. You also have been asked to look into protecting the computers your fellow employees have at home, to minimize the risk that employees might inadvertently transmit to the workplace a virus from their home computer. In recommending antivirus software for use in your school or company, consider these issues:

 Dangerous viruses can spread quickly across the Internet. The antivirus software you recommend should have an update service that automatically updates the virus definitions when new viruses come on the Net.

❷ Home computers need to be protected as well as machines in the workplace.

3 If there is a mix of Windows and Macintosh machines in the workplace and in your co-workers' homes, you will need to consider virus protection for both brands of operating systems. Also consider other operating systems that may be used on your workplace network.

4 Viruses can be caught both coming and going. Consider whether the antivirus software you are considering can scan outgoing as well as incoming messages.

5 Consider all the ways information can come and go, including e-mail, IM, FTP, and peer-to-peer file sharing. Check to see whether the antivirus software you are proposing scans all these ways of transmitting viruses.

6 New ways of transmitting viruses may have been discovered or invented since this book went to press. Follow the Chapter 13 *Interlit* Web site links to the virus alert centers to see if any new transmission modes have arisen.

Use a word processor to write up your virus scanner recommendation in the form of a brief essay. Report the brand names of the virus scanners you considered, identify the one you recommend for adoption in your workplace, and explain the reasons why you selected it instead of the others. If your instructor has asked you to hand in the report, make sure you put your name at the top, then save it on disk or follow the other instructions you may have been given for submitting this assignment.

14

BIBLIOGRAPHIC STYLE FOR CITING INTERNET RESOURCES

After completing this chapter, you will be able to:

■ Explain the differences among APA, MLA, and CMS styles.

■ Know when to use APA, MLA, or CMS style.

■ Cite Internet resources in APA, MLA, or CMS style.

■ Use the Fair Use guidelines to determine whether your use of a copyrighted work is fair.

● Scholarly writing is not done in a vacuum. Instead of writing only about your thoughts on a topic, you conduct research to find out what other people have discovered and documented. When you write your paper, you refer to this research to support your assertions or to compare them with another point of view.

To provide a standard way of presenting and documenting references to scholarly material, style guides have been created. This chapter demonstrates how to cite Internet resources according to the three most popular style guides.

APA, MLA, and CMS Style Guides

The three most popular style guides are the **American Psychological Association (APA)** method, the **Modern Language Association (MLA)** style, and the *Chicago Manual of Style* **(CMS).** All three use in-text citations rather than footnotes at the bottom of the page to refer to scholarly references. Because Web documents are not paginated, in-text citations are particularly suited to Web documents. Imagine trying to print footnotes at the bottom of each screen of a Web document; it just wouldn't work. Due to different screen resolutions and font sizes, you could never be sure where the bottom of the screen would be, so you would not know where to put the footnotes. Plus, the user can scroll a Web document to any position of any page, which would throw off the footnoting. It is fortunate, therefore, that the three most popular style guides use in-text citations appropriate for use on Web pages.

At the *Interlit* Web site, you will find examples of a term paper written in APA, MLA, and CMS styles. When you write a term paper, you should emulate one of these styles. The APA style is normally used for papers written in psychology classes and the social sciences. The MLA style is often used for papers written in English courses and the humanities. The CMS style is used across a broad range of disciplines; this book, for example, is written in CMS style.

Unless your instructor, publisher, or employer tells you to use a specific style guide, it does not really matter whether you choose APA, MLA, or CMS style. What's important is that you follow an established style guide consistently to enable people who read your paper to locate the sources you cite.

Citing Internet Resources in APA Style

American Psychological Association

In the APA section of the *Interlit* Web site, you will find resources related to APA style. Among them is a sample term paper written in APA style. If you study that term paper, you will notice that in the body of the text, there are citations in parentheses, such as (Hofstetter, 2002, p. 2). These citations refer to references typed at the end of the paper, where the person reading it can find out publication information about the sources you cited. The APA guidelines for creating citations call for you to identify the author and the date inside the parentheses, and, if you are quoting something in the article, you also give the page number. If an electronic document does not have page numbers, then you cite the paragraph number if the paragraphs are numbered in the document, or you cite the heading and the number of the paragraph following it, such as

(Myers, 2000, ¶ 5)

(Beutler, 2000, Conclusion section, para. 1)

At the end of the sample APA term paper at the *Interlit* Web site, you will notice that some of the references have been linked to other documents on the Web. When a reference that you cite is available online, you should link the URL of that reference to the online resource, to provide someone reading your article quick and easy access to the online reference. Printed here are the guidelines for citing Web documents in APA style. Other aspects of the APA style are documented in the *Publication Manual of the American Psychological Association*. To obtain a copy, follow the *Interlit* Web site link to APA Style Guidelines.

INDIVIDUAL WORKS

Author/editor. (Year, month day). *Title* (edition) [Type of medium]. Producer (optional). Retrieved month day, year, from source.

Example: Hofstetter, F. T. (1999, June 23). Emerging Technology and the Future of Education. Retrieved January 18, 2005, from http://www.udel.edu/fth/necc.

PARTS OF WORKS

Author/editor. (Year, month day). Title. In *Source* (edition) [Type of medium]. Producer (optional). Retrieved month day, year, from source.

Example: Shirley, W. (No date). A Brief Introduction to the Music of Aaron Copland. In *Aaron Copland Collection* [Online]. Library of Congress. Retrieved January 18, 2005, from http://memory.loc.gov/ammem/achtml/acintro00.html.

JOURNAL ARTICLES

Author. (Year, month day). Title. *Journal Title* [Type of medium], *volume*(issue), paging or indicator of length. Retrieved month day, year, from source.

Example: Kresh, D. (2000, June). Offering High Quality Reference Service on the Web. *D-Lib Magazine* [Online], 6(6), 20 paragraphs. Retrieved January 18, 2005, from http://www.dlib.org/dlib/june00/kresh/06kresh.html.

NEWSPAPER ARTICLES

Author. (Year, month day). Title. *Newspaper Title* [Type of medium], paging or indicator of length. Retrieved month day, year, from source.

Example: Barry, D. (1999, October 24). The War on Tobacco: Where there's smoke, there's money. *Miami Herald* [Online], 9 paragraphs. Retrieved December 11, 1999, from http://www.miamiherald.com/content/archive/living/barry/1999/docs/oct24.htm.

OTHER FORMS OF ONLINE COMMUNICATION

For other forms of online communication, such as newsgroups, Web sites, and listservs, provide as much of the following information as you can, in the order specified.

Author. (Year, month day). *Title*. [Type of medium]. Retrieved month day, year, from source.

Example: Ritchie, Collin. (1997, July 2). *Emulating PRINT & COPY in a JAVA Applet.* [Newsgroup]. Retrieved July 9, 1977, from news://msnews.microsoft.com/microsoft.public.java.visualj++.

Citing Internet Resources in MLA Style

Modern Language Association

In the MLA section of the *Interlit* Web site, you will find resources related to MLA style. Among them is a sample term paper written in MLA style. If you study that term paper, you will notice that in the body of the text, there are citations in parentheses, such as (Hofstetter, 2002, p. 2). These citations refer to references typed at the end of the paper, where the person reading it can find out publication information about the sources you cited. The MLA guidelines for creating citations call for you to identify the author and the date inside the parentheses, and, if you are quoting something in the article, you also give the page number. If an electronic document does not have page numbers, then you cite the paragraph number if the paragraphs are numbered in the document, or you cite the heading and the number of the paragraph following it, such as

(Myers, 2000, ¶ 5)

(Beutler, 2000, Conclusion section, para. 1)

At the end of the sample MLA term paper at the *Interlit* Web site, you will notice that some of the references have been linked to other documents on the Web. When a reference that you cite is available online, you should link the URL of that reference to the online resource, to provide someone reading your article quick and easy access to the online reference. Printed here are the guidelines for citing Internet resources in MLA style. Other aspects of the MLA style are documented in the *MLA Style Manual and Guide to Scholarly Publishing*. To obtain a copy, follow the *Interlit* Web site link to MLA Style Manual.

INDIVIDUAL WORKS

Author/editor. *Title of Individual Work.* Edition statement (if given). Publication information (Place of publication: publisher, date), if given. *Title of Electronic Work.* Medium. Information supplier. Access date <electronic address>.

Example: Hofstetter, Fred T. *Emerging Technology and the Future of Education.* 23 June 1999. 18 January 2005 <http://www.udel.edu/fth/necc>.

PARTS OF WORKS

Author/editor. "Part title." *Title of Print Version of Work.* Edition statement (if given). Publication information (Place of publication: publisher, date), if given. *Title of Electronic Work.* Information supplier. Access date <electronic address>.

Example: Shirley, Wayne. "A Brief Introduction to the Music of Aaron Copland." *Aaron Copland Collection.* Library of Congress. 18 January 2005 <http://memory.loc.gov/ammem/achtml/acintro00.html>.

JOURNAL ARTICLES

Author. "Article Title." *Journal Title.* Volume.Issue (Year): paging or indicator of length. Access date <electronic address>.

Example: Kresh, Diane. "Offering high quality reference service on the Web." *D-Lib Magazine* 6.6 (2000): 20 pars. 18 January 2005 < http://www.dlib.org/dlib/june00/kresh/06kresh.html>.

NEWSPAPER ARTICLES

Author. "Article Title." *Newspaper Title.* Date, Edition (if given): paging or indicator of length. Access date <electronic address>.

Example: Barry, Dave. "The War on Tobacco: Where there's smoke, there's money." *Miami Herald.* 24 Oct. 1999. 9 paragraphs. 11 December 1999 <http://www.miamiherald.com/content/archive/living/barry/1999/docs/oct24.htm>.

OTHER FORMS OF ONLINE COMMUNICATION

For other forms of online communication, such as newsgroups, Web sites, and listservs, provide as much of the following information as you can, in the order specified.

Author. "Title." (Year). Medium. Access date <electronic address>.

Example: Ritchie, Collin. "Emulating PRINT & COPY in a JAVA Applet." (1997). Newsgroup. 9 July 1997 <news://msnews.microsoft.com/microsoft.public.java.visualj++>.

Citing Internet Resources in CMS Style

Chicago Manual of Style

In the CMS section of the *Interlit* Web site, you will find resources related to CMS style. Among them is a sample term paper written in CMS style. If you study that term paper, you will notice that in the body of the text, there are author-date citations in parentheses, such as (Hofstetter 2002, 2). These citations refer to references typed at the end of the paper, where the person reading it can find out publication information about the sources cited in the paper. The CMS guidelines for creating author-date citations call for you to identify the date inside the parentheses, and, if you are quoting something in the article, you also give the page number. If an electronic document does not have page numbers, then you cite the paragraph number if the paragraphs are numbered in the document, or you can cite the heading and the number of the paragraph following it, such as

(Myers 2000, ¶ 5)

(Beutler 2000, Conclusion section, para. 1)

At the end of the sample CMS term paper at the *Interlit* Web site, you will notice that some of the references have been linked to other documents on the Web. When a reference that you cite is available online, you should link the URL of that reference to the online resource, to provide someone reading your article quick and easy access to the online reference.

INDIVIDUAL WORKS

Author/editor. *Title.* Type of medium. Subordinate responsibility (optional). Edition. Publication information (Place of publication: publisher, date, date of update/revision). Date of citation. Series (optional). Notes (optional). URL (accessed date).

Example: Hofstetter, F.T. *Emerging Technology and the Future of Education.* PowerPoint presentation. 23 June 1999. http://www.udel.edu/fth/necc (accessed 18 January 2005).

PARTS OF WORKS

Author/editor (of host document). Title (of host document). Type of medium. Subordinate responsibility (of host document) (optional). Edition. Publication information (place of publication: publisher, date, date of update/revision), if given. Date of citation. Chapter or equivalent designation (of part). Title (of part). Location within host document. Notes (optional). URL (accessed date).

Example: Shirley, W. "A Brief Introduction to the Music of Aaron Copland." In *Aaron Copland Collection.* http://memory.loc.gov/ammem/achtml/acintro00.html (accessed 18 January 2005).

JOURNAL ARTICLES

Author. Year. Article Title. *Journal Title,* issue information. URL (accessed date).

Example: Kresh, D. 2000. Offering High Quality Reference Service on the Web. *D-Lib Magazine* [journal online], 6, no. 6, 20 paragraphs. http://www.dlib.org/dlib/june00/kresh/06kresh.html (accessed 18 January 2005).

NEWSPAPER ARTICLES

Author. Year. Article Title. *Newspaper Title,* issue information, paging or indicator of length. URL (accessed date).

Example: Barry, Dave. 1999. The War on Tobacco: Where there's smoke, there's money. *Miami Herald,* 24 Oct. 1999, 9 paragraphs. http://www.miamiherald.com/content/archive/living/barry/1999/docs/oct24.htm (accessed 11 December 1999).

OTHER FORMS OF ONLINE COMMUNICATION

For other forms of online communication, such as newsgroups, Web sites, and listservs, provide as much of the following information as you can, in the order specified.

Author. Title. Type of Medium. Date. URL (accessed date).

Example: Ritchie, Collin. "Emulating PRINT & COPY in a JAVA Applet." In Visual J++ News [Newsgroup online]. Written July 2, 1997. news://msnews.microsoft.com/microsoft.public.java.visualj++ (accessed 9 August 1997).

Fair Use Guidelines for Internet Resources

The Internet is a brave new world in which debates about copyright and **Fair Use** are ongoing. Suppose you find a diagram or an illustration on the Internet that you would like to present on screen. Are you permitted to put the picture into your multimedia application? What about poems and songs, animations and movies that you find on the Internet—are you permitted to include them in your multimedia creations?

Consortium of College and University Media Centers

To provide guidance in what is fair, the Consortium of College and University Media Centers (CCUMC) has issued a set of guidelines for the educational fair use of new media. These guidelines have been endorsed by a broad range of publishers and educational institutions. The recommendations provided here are based on the CCUMC guidelines. The full text of the guidelines is available at the *Interlit* Web site; follow the links to the Fair Use Guidelines.

Downloading

According to the CCUMC guidelines, students are permitted to download into term papers certain portions of copyrighted works. These portions include

- Up to 10 percent or 1,000 words of a text, whichever is less. Special rules apply to poetry; see section 4.2.2 of the guidelines for details.

- Not more than 5 images by an individual artist or photographer; for anthologies, not more than 10 percent or 15 images, whichever is less.

- Up to 10 percent but never more than 30 seconds of music, lyrics, and music video.

- Up to 10 percent of motion media or three minutes, whichever is less.

- Up to 10 percent or 2,500 fields or cell entries, whichever is less, from a copyrighted database or data table.

If you are not a student or an educator, however, or if you are engaging in a profit-making activity, you may not qualify for Fair Use. Refer to the CCUMC guidelines for detailed information on who qualifies. When in doubt, always request permission from the person or agency holding the copyright to the resource you wish to include.

Whenever you include a portion of a copyrighted work, you should always document the source with an in-text citation at the point where the object appears in your paper, and you must include a bibliographic reference at the end of the paper. If an image includes a copyright notice that is part of the bitmap of the image, it is unethical to remove the copyright notice from the image.

Linking

An alternative to downloading an Internet resource into your term paper is to link to its URL instead. For example, suppose you want a picture of the *Mona Lisa* to appear as an illustration in your term paper. There is a beautiful image of the *Mona Lisa* at the Louvre Web site. Instead of downloading the image to your computer and making it part of your term paper locally, you could link to the image's URL, thereby saving disk space on your computer. This could cause problems, however, if the Louvre Web site is down when someone is reading your paper, or if the Louvre changes the URL of the *Mona Lisa* image.

When you include portions of Internet resources in a term paper, therefore, you will probably want to download those portions to your computer and put them into the same folder your term paper is in. Thus you can work with local resources that you control and eliminate the risk of something preventing the original copy from being found, thereby creating a hole in your term paper. Figures 14-1 and 14-2 show what the browsers do when images on a Web page cannot be found.

Please understand that regardless of whether you decide to link or download the picture, you still must follow the CCUMC Fair Use guidelines for educational multimedia.

Citation Machine

| Citation Machine |

If you are using MLA or APA style, you will find the Citation Machine to be a useful tool. In three simple steps, the Citation Machine automatically generates both bibliographic references and in-text citations. You simply (1) click the type of resource you want to cite, (2) fill out a Web form with information from your resource, and (3) click Make Citations to generate your citation. The Citation Machine returns the bibliographic reference and the parenthetical in-text citation in both MLA and APA style. The Citation Machine is a free service of David Warlick's Landmark Project. To try it out, follow the *Interlit* Web site link to the Citation Machine.

This icon appears in the place of the missing image.

This icon appears in the place of the missing image.

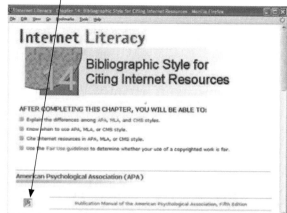

Figure 14-1   Microsoft Internet Explorer displays an icon when an image is missing from a Web page.

Figure 14-2   Mozilla Firefox displays an icon when an image is missing from a Web page.

exercises

1. Go to www.usatoday.com and find a newspaper article that interests you. Following the style guidelines presented in this chapter, write a bibliographic reference to the article in APA, MLA, and CMS styles.

2. After you complete exercise 1, tell which style you would prefer to use in your own writing, and state why you like it better than the others.

3. Imagine yourself applying for a job and wanting to send your employer a copy of a multimedia term paper you wrote as a student. Suppose the term paper contains a copyrighted picture that you included as a Fair Use. Do the Fair Use guidelines permit you to include the copyrighted picture when you submit the paper as a writing sample while applying for a job? To find out, follow the *Interlit* Web site link to the Fair Use Guidelines for Educational Multimedia.

4. For a work to be in the common or public domain means that it is publicly available and free of copyright restrictions. Suppose you find an article on the Internet that does not bear the copyright symbol. Can you safely assume that the article is in the common domain? Before you answer this question, follow the *Interlit* Web site link to the Fair Use Guidelines for Educational Multimedia and read especially Section 6.2.

SITUATED CASE PROJECTS
Case 14: Bibliographic Referencing and Copyright Guidelines

At the end of each chapter in this book, a situated case project provides the student an opportunity to put the chapter's contents to practical use in a workplace situation. Each case has the same number as the chapter in which it appears.

Schools and companies may have different reasons for wanting to adopt bibliographic referencing and copyright guidelines. Schools want students to learn how to document their sources so people reading term papers and articles can refer to the source materials cited in the documents. Companies, on the other hand, have legal reasons for needing to document carefully the source of materials used in the conduct of research and daily operations. A company that begins using a method or process that is later patented, for example, may be liable to pay royalties or get sued if it cannot prove that the method or process was in common use prior to the filing of the patent.

Related to this is the issue of copyright. If a school or company is sued for a copyright violation, the court may ask to see evidence that an honest effort was made to inform employees of the copyright law and any applicable Fair Use guidelines. Imagine that your employer has become aware of these issues and has asked you to recommend which style of referencing should be used by employees in your workplace. Your employer also wants you to develop a copyright policy statement to inform all employees of the rules and regulations related to copyright and, if applicable, Fair Use in your workplace. In responding to your employer, consider these issues:

1 Your co-workers may already be using a bibliographic style they like very much. Consult with your co-workers and find out what bibliographic style they are using, if any.

2 Consider the fact that certain styles are used more in some disciplines than others. In recommending a style, consider the nature of your school or business.

3 You can recommend more than one style if you feel it is not appropriate to use just one. Keep in mind, however, that adopting more than one style will require that your organization's technical writers and proofreaders will need to know multiple styles.

4 In your proposed copyright policy, make sure you provide the links to the U.S. Copyright law, the Fair Use guidelines, and the Digital Millennium Copyright Act. The current versions of those links are provided in Chapter 14 of the *Interlit* Web site. Being able to prove that a company has proactively made its employees aware of these laws can be very important in a copyright infringement case.

5 In writing your copyright policy statement, be sure to emphasize that when in doubt, ask permission before using a copyrighted work or a portion of a work that is not clearly covered by Fair Use.

Use a word processor to write up your answer to this assignment in the form of a two-part essay. Tell what bibliographic style you recommend and briefly state the reason for choosing it for use in your workplace. Then type the Copyright Policy statement that you recommend your employer distribute to all of your co-workers. If your instructor has asked you to hand in this assignment, make sure you put your name at the top of the document, then save it on disk or follow any other instructions you may have been given for submitting this assignment.

PART FIVE
CREATING WEB PAGES

"If you can dream it, you can do it."

—Adobe Slogan

Learning how to create a Web site is one of the most empowering skills you will ever learn. Because the Internet is ubiquitous, Web page creation gives you a worldwide reach that enables you to communicate your message virtually everywhere. This tutorial on creating Web pages has a topic that will interest almost everyone: creating a résumé that you can use to apply for a job. Creating a résumé on the Web may provide you with a strategic advantage because you will be able to give prospective employers the World Wide Web address of your résumé. This shows you have network savvy that can benefit an employer in an information society.

On the Web, your résumé will be presented in color with hypertext links that make it quick and easy to read and to find information. You will be able to print your résumé from the Web; the printed version will be neatly typeset with professional-looking fonts, headings, graphics, and bulleted lists of your qualifications and accomplishments.

You also will learn how to create your home page, which is the Web page that establishes your identity on the Web. By linking things to your home page, you will create a hierarchy that makes it easy for people to access resources you put on the Web. For example, one of the things you will link to your home page is your Web page résumé. Later on, you will be able to link multimedia term papers that you publish on the Web. Thus, your home page will provide potential employers with convincing examples of your online writing skills, and your term papers will contribute to the world of interconnected scholarship.

15

WEB PAGE CREATION STRATEGIES

After completing this chapter, you will be able to:

- **Explain the three basic approaches to creating Web pages.**

- **Know when to use an HTML editor, an HTML translator, or a WYSIWYG tool.**

- **Understand how HTML editors work, and be able to find HTML editors on the Web.**

- **Realize how HTML translators can save time when you need to create a Web page from a word-processed document, a spreadsheet, a database, or a presentation.**

- **Learn what WYSIWYG stands for and understand the concept of WYSIWYG editing.**

There are three ways to create Web pages. First, you can use an HTML editor to create a Web page by working directly with the hypertext markup language, in which all Web pages are encoded. This method provides you with a good understanding of how HTML works, but it is technical. Second, you can use the "Save as Web Page" option to convert word-processed documents into Web pages. This is the most productive way to create Web pages from term papers and other forms of scholarly writing. Third, you can use a what-you-see-is-what-you-get (WYSIWYG) editor to create Web pages through a graphical user interface that lets you enter text and graphics directly onto the screen exactly as you want them to appear. As you create the screen, the WYSIWYG editor automatically generates the HTML codes that make the Web page.

HTML Editors

As you learned in the previous chapter, Web pages are encoded in the hypertext markup language (HTML). This language consists of the text of the Web page, plus special codes called **tags** that mark up the text. The tags determine how the text will flow onto the screen, whether it will contain pictures and where they will appear, and what will happen when the user triggers items linked to the document. An editor that lets you create Web pages by working directly with the HTML tags is known as an **HTML editor.** The advantage of creating Web pages with an HTML editor is that it gives you more control over the Web page than WYSIWYG editors and HTML translators, which create the HTML for you. The disadvantage is that for less technically inclined authors, editing HTML tags can seem tedious and time-consuming. The latest versions of the HTML editors, however, contain helpful drop-down menus that enable you to choose tags from a list as you type your code.

HomeSite™

HomeSite™ is a popular HTML editor for creating Web pages under the Windows operating system. As shown in Figure 15-1, HomeSite lets you edit the HTML in one window and view how it will appear on the Web in another. HomeSite™ is a product of Macromedia,

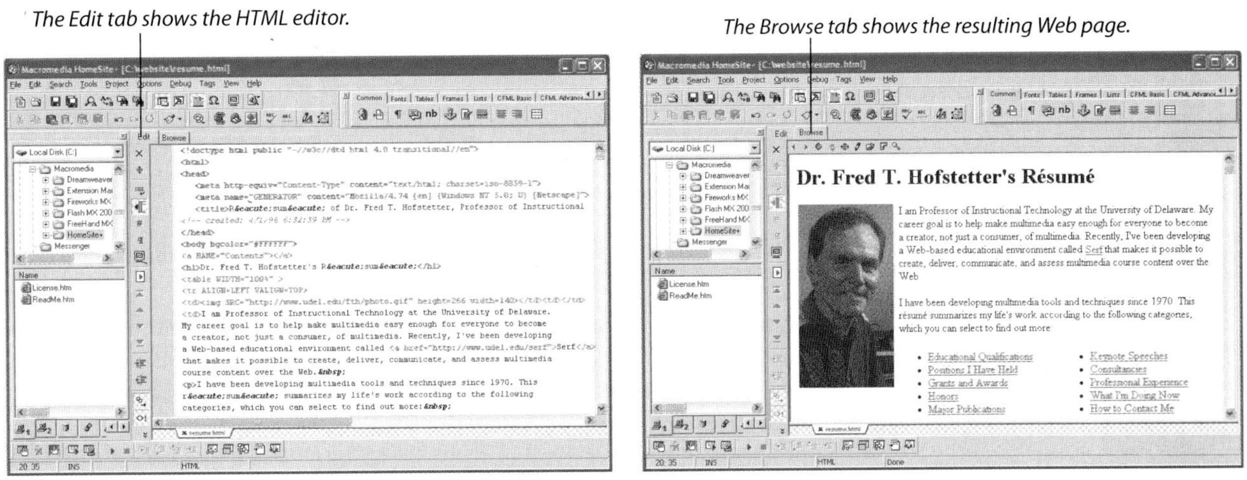

The Edit tab shows the HTML editor.

The Browse tab shows the resulting Web page.

Figure 15-1 HomeSite™ lets you edit the HTML source code in the Edit window. To see the resulting Web page, you click the Browse tab.

which sells it as a stand-alone package or in bundles with Macromedia's Dreamweaver software. For more information, follow the *Interlit* Web site link to HomeSite, where you can get a 30-day free trial version.

BBEdit

BBEdit

On the Macintosh, the most popular HTML editor is Bare Bones Edit (BBEdit). As illustrated in Figure 15-2, BBEdit uses menus and buttons to make it easy to input HTML tags, choose colors, and enter special symbols. For more information, follow the *Interlit* Web site link to BBEdit, where you can get a free demo version.

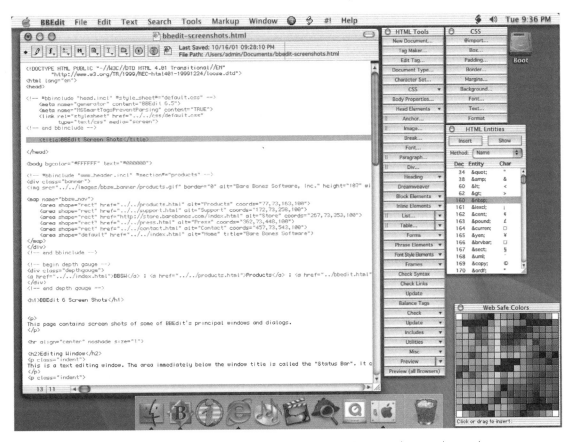

Figure 15-2 BBEdit uses menus and buttons to make it easy to input HTML tags, choose colors, and enter special symbols.

Other HTML Editors

There are dozens of other HTML editors that help you create Web pages by working directly with HTML tags. For information about the others, follow the *Interlit* Web site links to the Google and Yahoo directories of HTML editors.

HTML Translators

An **HTML translator** is a tool that can convert an existing document into the HTML format. Microsoft Word, Excel, Access, and PowerPoint have HTML translators built in. If you have an existing document that you want to turn into a Web page, the most efficient way to create the page is to pull down the File menu and choose the Save as HTML or Save as Web Page option. These options are built in to the latest versions of Word, Excel, Access, and PowerPoint.

Microsoft Word

Microsoft Word

Microsoft Word is a word processor that has an HTML translator built in. After you create a document with MS Word, you can easily translate it into a Web page. Simply pull down the File menu and choose Save as Web Page. This will create an HTML version of your document that has the *.htm* filename extension. To see what the translated document will look like on the Web, you can use the browser's File menu to open the file you just saved.

Microsoft Excel

Microsoft Excel

Imagine being able to publish your spreadsheets to the Web. You can do this with Microsoft Excel. Simply pull down the File menu and choose Save as Web Page. This will create an HTML version of the spreadsheet that has the *.htm* filename extension. To preview what the spreadsheet will look like on the Web, you can use your Web browser's File menu to open the HTML version you just saved. The information in your spreadsheet lines up neatly formatted in rows and columns on the Web page. HTML table tags are used to create the rows and columns. You will learn how to create tables with HTML in Chapter 20.

Microsoft Access

Microsoft Access

Access is the name of the database program in Microsoft Office. To create a Web page version of a data table, you select the table to view it, then pull down the File menu and choose Export. When the Export dialog appears, set the Save as Type field to HTML Documents. Then click the Save button. This will create an HTML version of the data table that has the *.htm* filename extension. To preview how the data will appear on the Web, you can use your Web browser's File menu to open the HTML version you just saved. In Chapter 22, you learn how to publish the file to the Web.

PowerPoint

Microsoft PowerPoint

Microsoft's presentation software is called PowerPoint. It has a very powerful Web page creation capability. When you choose the option to save a presentation as a Web page, PowerPoint goes through your presentation and creates a separate HTML file for each one of your slides. The filename of your first slide is the name of your presentation followed by the *.htm* file extension. The HTML files for the rest of your slides get placed into a supporting folder that also includes any sounds and graphics used in your presentation. When

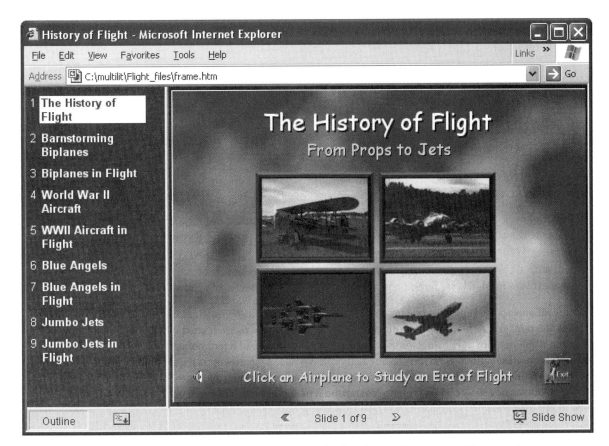

Figure 15-3   PowerPoint creates Web pages that have a menu that lets the user jump to any slide at any time.

you view the presentation with a Web browser, a menu of your slides appears alongside the startup screen, as shown in Figure 15-3. To navigate, the user can either click items on your presentation screen or use the menu to go to any slide at any time.

WYSIWYG Editors

WYSIWYG is an acronym that stands for **what you see is what you get.** WYSIWYG editors let you create Web pages by typing your text directly onscreen, where it appears exactly as it will look on the Web. To change a font, size, color, or other text attribute, you select the text you want to change, then click a button or icon that makes the change. You do not need to know the HTML tags, which the WYSIWYG editor inserts into the document automatically, depending on what you do with the WYSIWYG controls.

Dreamweaver

Macromedia Dreamweaver

This part of the book began by quoting the Adobe slogan, "If you can dream it, you can do it." The title of Macromedia's Dreamweaver software plays on this theme by implying that you can weave your Web via graphical tools that can do a lot of the work for you. Figure 15-4 shows how Dreamweaver appears onscreen. For authors who are less technically inclined, using a WYSIWYG tool such as Dreamweaver is preferred to using a tag-oriented HTML editor. When you work with WYSIWYG tools, however, you do not have as much control over the appearance of the Web page as when you work directly with the HTML tags. To overcome this limitation, Dreamweaver provides an option that lets you edit the tags directly. Figure 15-4 shows a Split view in which Dreamweaver

Display the WYSIWYG Design view.

Split the screen to display both the Code and the Design.

This is the Code window.

Display the Code view.

This is the Design window.

The Properties window enables you to edit aspects of the selected element.

The Reference tab puts at your fingertips all the documentation you will need.

The Files tab makes it easy to find resources that you can drag and drop onto your page.

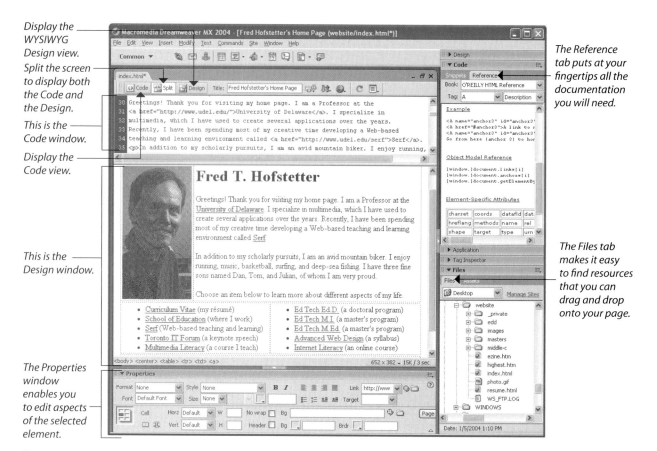

Figure 15-4 Dreamweaver lets you view the WYSIWYG Design view, the Code view, or both views simultaneously. Illustrated here is the Split view, which displays both views onscreen.

simultaneously displays both the Code window and the WYSIWYG window. Any change you make in the Code window takes effect immediately in the WYSIWYG window, and vice versa. Thus, Dreamweaver provides you with the best of both worlds. You can get a free trial version by following the *Interlit* Web site link to Dreamweaver.

Microsoft FrontPage

Microsoft FrontPage

Designed for use with Microsoft Office, FrontPage is a Web page editor that combines a WYSIWYG tool with an HTML editor. You can use the WYSIWYG tool to create a Web page in one window, and, at any time, you can switch to an HTML window that lets you view and edit the HTML tags. Changes you make in the HTML window take effect instantly in the WYSIWYG window, and vice versa. Figure 5-5 shows a Web page being edited by Microsoft FrontPage. You can get a free trial version by following the *Interlit* Web site link to FrontPage.

Nvu

Nvu

Nvu (pronounced *N-view* or *new-view*) is a WYSIWYG Web page editor that is the open-source replacement for the former Netscape Composer program used in previous editions of this book. One of the improvements is Nvu's inclusion of a site manager. Whereas Composer was a single-page editor, Nvu lets you manage an entire site. Figure 15-6 shows that Nvu displays the Site Manager window alongside the Web page editor. You can edit your Web page in the Preview window as well as the Normal and HTML windows. Editing

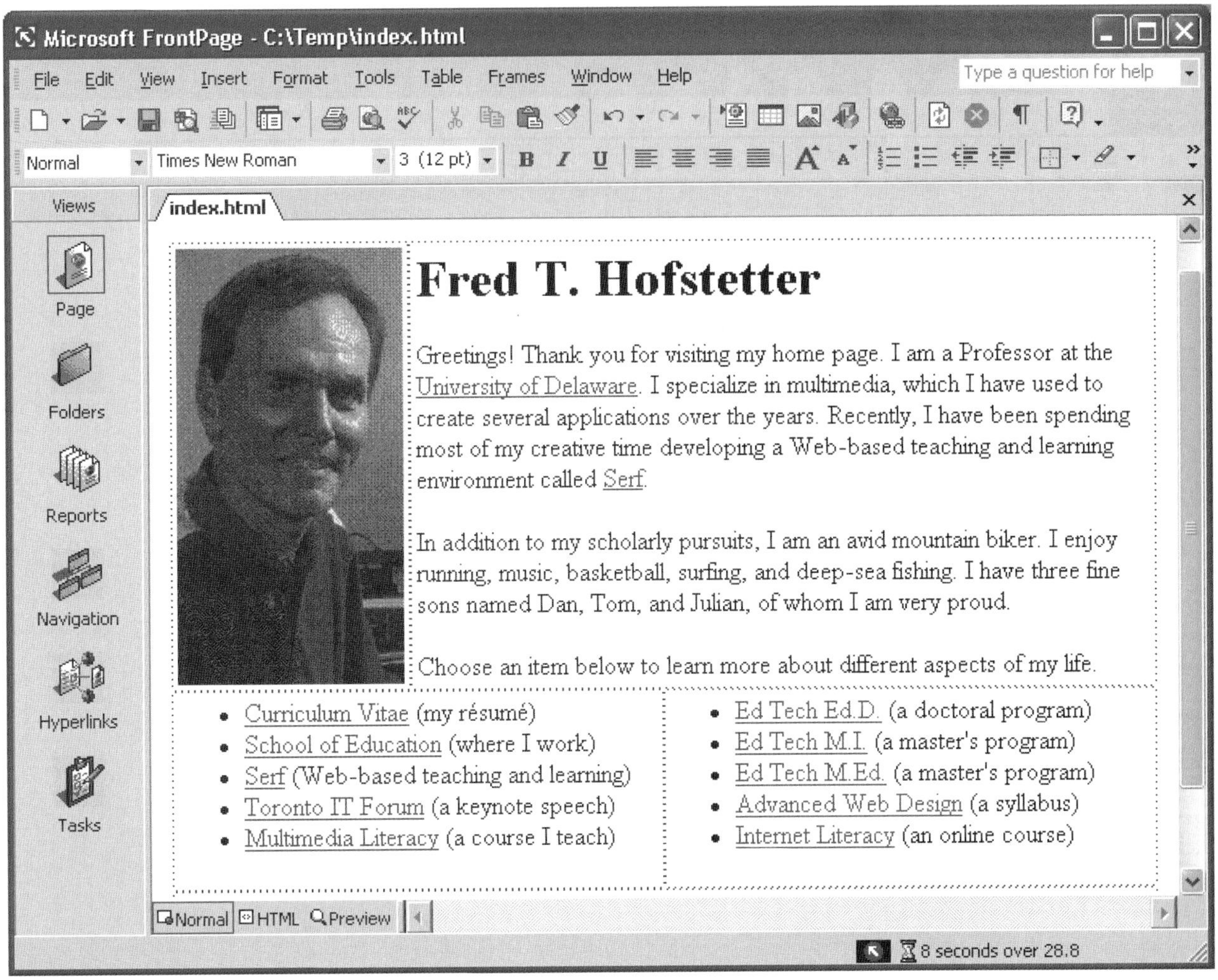

Figure 15-5   Microsoft FrontPage is editing my home page. At any time, I can click the HTML button to view the code, or I can click the Preview button to see how the page will appear on the Web.

in the preview window makes what you type appear just as it will when viewed in a Web browser, hence the term *what you see is what you get* (WYSIWYG).

As an open-source program, Nvu is freely downloadable. There are versions for Windows, Macintosh, and Linux. You can download the version appropriate for your computer by following the *Interlit* Web site link to Nvu.

Choosing a Web Page Editor

The tutorial in this book will introduce you to the concept of WYSIWYG editing by teaching you how to use either Dreamweaver, FrontPage, or Nvu. Because the book teaches all three of these tools, you need to decide which tool you will use. If your school or workplace has already adopted Dreamweaver, you may decide to learn Dreamweaver so you can use the software installed at your site. If your site has a FrontPage license, on the other hand, you may use FrontPage. If you prefer open-source software that is freely downloadable, Nvu is an excellent choice.

In this book's exercises, the Dreamweaver, FrontPage, and Nvu programs can be used interchangeably. Figure 15-6, for example, shows Nvu editing the same page that FrontPage is editing in Figure 15-5, as is Dreamweaver in Figure 15-4.

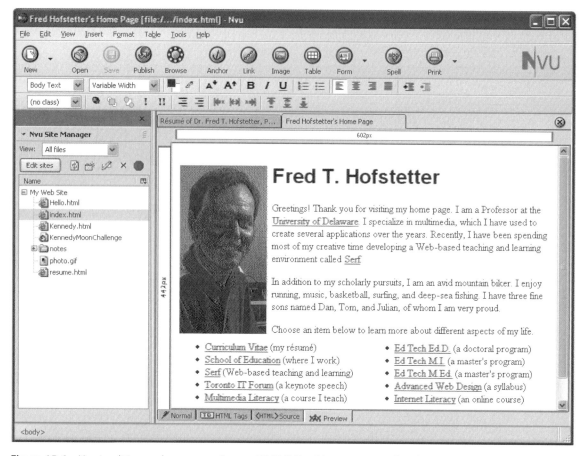

Figure 15-6 Nvu is editing my home page. For true WYSIWYG editing, you can make editorial changes in the Preview window shown here. You can also edit the HTML code in the HTML Source window.

If you are not sure which tool you want to start with, just begin reading the tutorial. After you compare the side-by-side instructions that show how each tool works, you will get a clearer idea of which one suits you better. Read on.

exercises

1. In your own words, describe when it is best to use an HTML editor, a WYSIWYG tool, or an HTML translator to create a Web page.

2. Follow the *Interlit* Web site link to the list of HTML editors. How many editors do you find listed there? What are the three top-rated HTML editors?

3. Follow the *Interlit* Web site link to HomeSite. What is the version number of the latest update? What is the hottest new feature you see advertised for the latest update?

4. Use Microsoft Word or WordPerfect to open a document you have written recently, such as a term paper or an essay. Pull down the File menu and choose the option to Save as Web Page or Save as HTML. When the Save dialog appears, save the Web page in your computer's *temp* folder. Name the file whatever you want, but make careful note of what you name it. You could name it *translated,* for example, since the file will contain the HTML translation of your document. The filename extension will be either *.htm* or *.html*. Now get your Web browser running. Pull down the File menu, choose Open, and open the file you just saved. If you followed the suggestion in this exercise, and if the letter of your hard drive is C, the filename will either be *c:\temp\translated.htm* or *c:\temp \translated.html*. Compare how the document appears in your browser to how it looks in your word processor. Can

you see any differences? If so, what are they? Did anything happen in the translation process that you would like to change in the Web page version of your document? If so, what would you like to change? You will be able to make changes in your HTML documents after you complete this book's Web page creation tutorial. Read on.

SITUATED CASE PROJECTS
Case 15: Web Page Creation Strategy

At the end of each chapter in this book, a situated case project provides the student an opportunity to put the chapter's contents to practical use in a workplace situation. Each case has the same number as the chapter in which it appears.

When employees can create their own Web pages and publish them to the Web, a school or company becomes much more efficient in posting and sharing information. Hyperlinking enables the Web page author to link items on the page to other information that a co-worker, student, or customer might be expected or encouraged to access as related information. Search engines enable users to search via keyword for any other page at the site to which they have access. This kind of information publishing, linking, and search capability is the very reason Tim Berners-Lee gives for inventing the Web back in 1989. In his 1989 proposal for creating the Web, Berners-Lee (1989, ¶ 5) said his goal was to help his co-workers keep track of things in a large project. Imagine that your employer wants to empower your co-workers to take advantage of the power of publishing, linking, and searching school or company information on the Web. Your employer wants you to recommend a Web page creation strategy that is appropriate for your workplace. In developing a recommendation for the best approach for your school or company to take in creating Web pages, consider these issues:

1 *Technical support.* How much technical support is available to co-workers in your school or company? If your company has an IT organization with a support staff that helps employees troubleshoot technical problems, you may be able to recommend a more technical solution than for a small company or school that does not have a lot of technical support staff, if any.

2 *Other software products.* Take into account other software products that your school or company is already using. If all your co-workers are using Microsoft Office, for example, that might direct your choice toward a FrontPage solution. If your school or company has adopted Firefox as its standard browser, on the other hand, Nvu may be the obvious choice.

3 *Training.* How will your co-workers learn how to use the Web page creation software you recommend? If you recommend FrontPage, Dreamweaver, or Nvu, for example, you could use the Web page creation tutorial in this book as training material.

Use a word processor to write up your answer to this assignment in the form of a two-part essay. In the opening paragraph, tell what Web page creation strategy you recommend and briefly state the reason for choosing it for use in your workplace. Then write another paragraph or two describing the other approaches you considered, and state your reasons for rejecting them. Conclude your recommendation with a paragraph describing how empowering you feel your recommended strategy will be, and give examples of a few ways in which creating Web pages in this manner will empower your co-workers and improve operations in your workplace. If your instructor has asked you to hand in this assignment, make sure you put your name at the top, then save it on disk or follow the other instructions you may have been given for submitting this assignment.

16

WEB PAGE DESIGN

After completing this chapter, you will be able to:

- Identify the basic elements that constitute a Web page.

- Explain the uses and general appearance of the elements of a Web page.

- Begin thinking about the design of your Web page résumé and how to make it engaging and informative.

- Arrange text in the proper size, color, and font on a Web page.

- Choose an appropriate background color and understand how foreground text colors interact with background screen colors.

- Arrange pictures on the screen either as background images or design elements for text to flow around.

- Make text stand out against a background photo.

- Adopt a common look and feel for your Web pages.

● There are two primary factors to consider in World Wide Web page design: how the page will look and how the user will interact with it. This chapter presents the elements you will use to design your Web page résumé.

Web Page Elements

World Wide Web pages consist of elements defined in the HTML language that is used to create Web pages. As you will see in Figures 16-1 to 16-9, these elements include

- headings
- paragraphs
- horizontal rules
- lists
- images
- backgrounds

- bookmarks
- links
- special characters
- tables
- frames

Headings

As illustrated in Figure 16-2, there are six HTML **heading** styles, numbered from H1 to H6. The smaller the number, the bigger the heading. H1 is the biggest or most important heading, and H6 is the smallest. Headings can be left justified, centered, or right justified. While it is possible to create the same visual effect as a heading style by simply enlarging

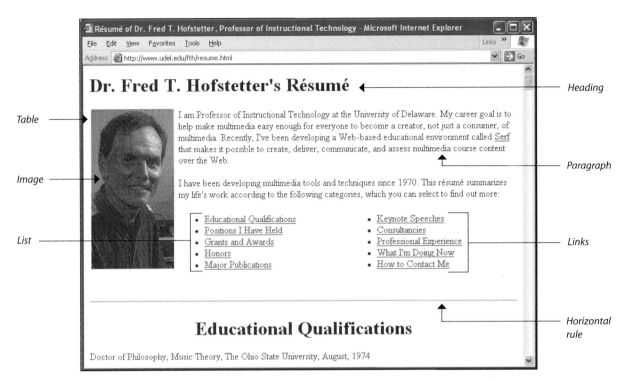

Figure 16-1 Web page elements in action on the author's Web page résumé.

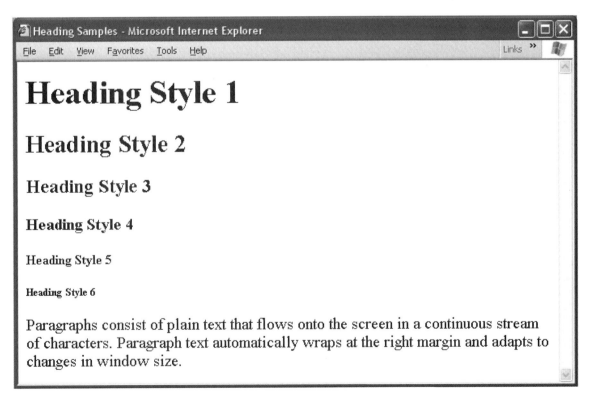

Figure 16-2 Heading styles and paragraphs.

and bolding the text, you can use heading styles to create a structure within a document that programs such as Microsoft Office can use to generate an outline or a table of contents. Therefore, it is a good idea to form the habit of using heading styles for the headings of sections and subsections within a Web page.

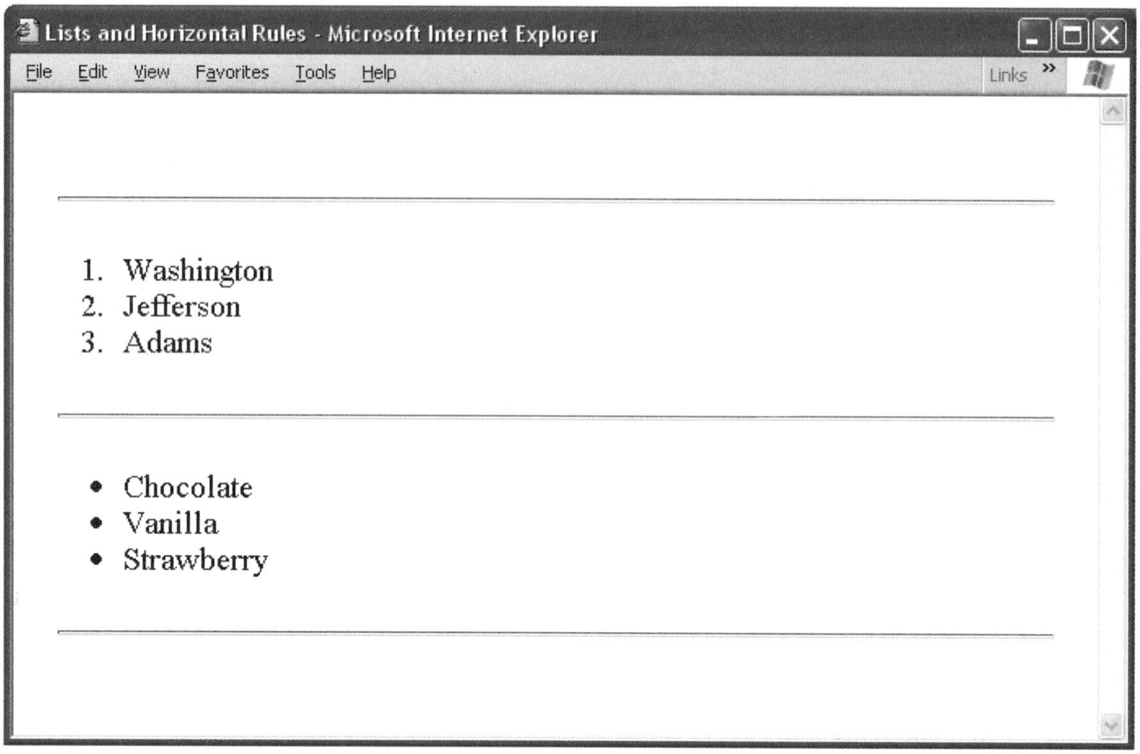

Figure 16-3 Horizontal rules and lists help organize and delimit information on a Web page.

Paragraphs

Paragraphs consist of plaintext that flows onto the screen in a continuous stream of characters. Paragraph text automatically wraps at the right margin and adapts to changes in window size.

Horizontal Rules

A **horizontal rule** is a design element used to create dividers between sections of a Web page. As illustrated in Figure 16-3, horizontal rules appear with a neat three-dimensional effect. It is possible to vary the length, thickness, and shading of a horizontal rule, but the default settings look pretty good.

Lists

Lists can be ordered or unordered. In an **ordered list,** the items are numbered automatically; in an **unordered list,** the items are bulleted. Figure 16-3 shows an example of both types of lists.

Images

Images enhance the visual appeal of Web pages. Images can be left justified, right justified, or centered on the screen. Text can be made to flow around the left or the right side of an image, as illustrated in Figure 16-4.

Backgrounds

Backgrounds can be filled with a solid color, or you can tile a bitmap into the background to create a textured appearance. It is important to choose a background that does not

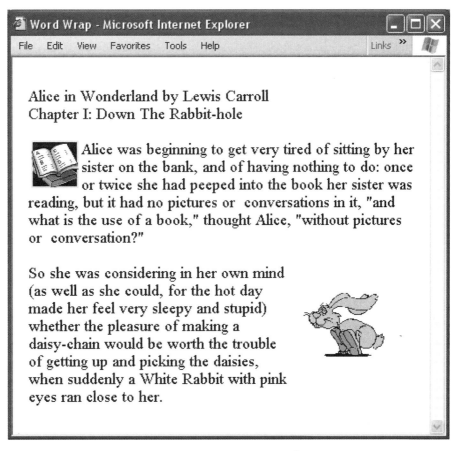

Figure 16-4   Text can flow around the left or the right side of an image.

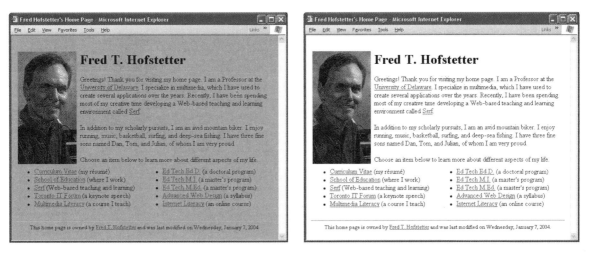

Figure 16-5   When the Web started, the default background color was defined as gray, as illustrated on the left. Notice how much harder it is to read the text when it appears on the gray background as compared to the white background illustrated on the right.

detract from the readability of the text. For this reason, black text on a white background is the most popular color choice on the Web.

When the Web started, the first browsers made the default background color gray. When the default black text color displays on a gray background, the screen is not as readable as black text on a white background, which provides better contrast. Figure 16-5 compares the black-on-gray color combination to the more readable black-on-white color scheme.

Bookmarks

A **bookmark** is a named anchor to which you can link a hot word or menu item to provide a way for the user to jump around to different places within a Web page. For example, you might create a bookmark anchor named "education" at the start of the education section of your résumé. In your résumé's bulleted table of contents, you would link the education bullet to the bookmark anchor named "education" to provide a quick way of jumping to your educational qualifications.

Links

Links are the most essential element in Web design, because links create webs. Without links, there would be no webs! On World Wide Web pages, links can be textual or pictorial. Any word or picture on the screen can be linked to any resource on the Web. Most **links** connect you to other Web pages or bookmarks on the current Web page, as shown in Figure 16-6. As you will learn in Chapter 23, however, any multimedia file or application can be the object of a link on the World Wide Web. For example, your term papers, scholarly publications, software, and multimedia applications can all be mounted on the World Wide Web and linked to your résumé so potential employers can review samples of your work. It is also common to find e-mail addresses linked to Web pages in a so-called mailto link; when you click the mailto link, an e-mail window opens, addressed to the person whose address is in the mailto. You learn how to create mailto links in Chapter 18.

Click here to jump to a named anchor bookmark further down on this Web page.

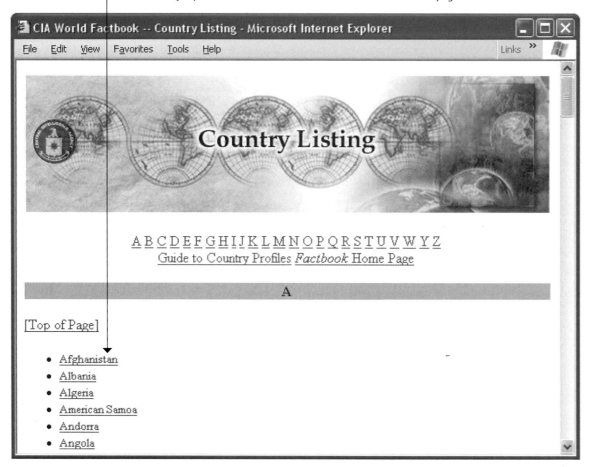

Figure 16-6   Named anchors work like bookmarks to provide easy access to sections within a Web page.

Special Characters

Web pages can contain special symbols such as the Greek characters used in scientific notation, as well as mathematical functions, operators, delimiters, accents, arrows, and pointers.

Tables

Normally, the text of a Web page flows evenly onto the screen, aligning itself automatically with the left and right edges of your browser's window. The **table** is a design element that provides a way of dividing the screen into rectangular regions into which you can lay out text and graphics on a Web page. Text flows inside the rectangles of the table, creating a columnar appearance much like the columns of text that appear in printed newspapers. Graphics also can be made to flow into tabular columns. The borders of the rectangles in the table can be visible, creating onscreen dividing lines between the table elements, as shown in Figure 16-7, or the border can be invisible, as illustrated in Figure 16-8.

When HTML was invented, there was no support for tables, and Web pages looked pretty much the same in terms of design and layout. HTML was enhanced to provide this support, and today, tables are the most powerful way of positioning items on a Web page to create more interesting designs. In Chapter 20, you will get a lot of practice using tables to lay out Web pages.

Frames

Have you ever seen a TV that supports a feature called *picture in a picture?* While viewing one television program full-screen, you can watch another program in a smaller onscreen window. On Web pages, frames serve a similar purpose. The term **frame** refers to the border that appears around windows on your screen. When you learned how to resize your Web browser in Chapter 4, you did so by clicking and dragging its window frame.

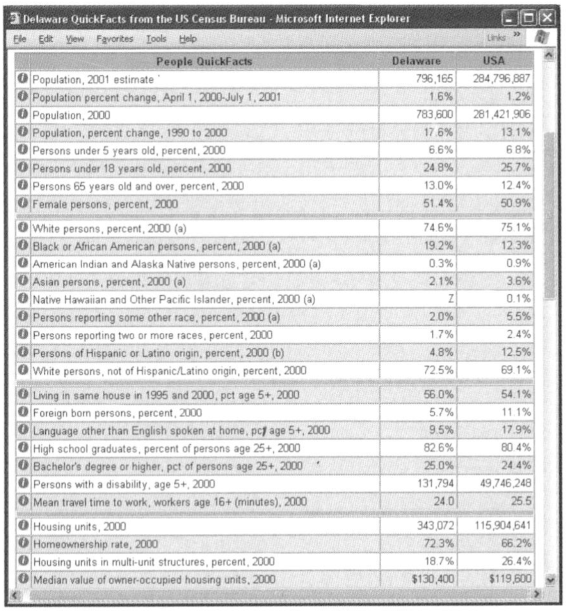

Figure 16-7 Making the borders of the table visible helps the user follow data across the table.

Figure 16-8 Invisible borders permit a table to govern subtly the positioning of Web page elements.

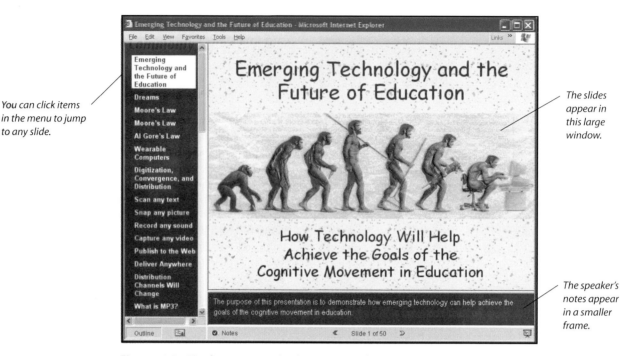

You can click items in the menu to jump to any slide.

The slides appear in this large window.

The speaker's notes appear in a smaller frame.

Figure 16-9   This frameset provides three windows for viewing and controlling a PowerPoint presentation on the Web.

When Web pages contain frames, more than one window appears on your Web page, and you can interact with the information in the windows independently.

You can try out frames for yourself by following the *Interlit* Web site link to the presentation entitled "Emerging Technology and the Future of Education." This presentation was authored in Microsoft PowerPoint. The Web version was created by PowerPoint's Save as Web Page feature. Figure 16-9 shows how the Save as Web Page feature uses frames to provide you with three windows in the Web browser. The big window shows the slides. The window on the left displays an outline of the presentation. The window at the bottom displays the speaker notes that go with each slide.

Screen Design Principles

The hands-on tutorial in this part of the book teaches you how to create a Web page résumé. You will learn how to flow text onto the screen, create bulleted lists, and link items in the list to the different parts of your résumé. Then you will learn how to put pictures on the screen, either as backgrounds that appear behind the text or as design elements around which text flows. Before you begin, it is important to understand a few principles of Web page design that will help you make good layouts for your screens.

Layout

As you learned earlier in this chapter, Web pages consist of several design elements, including headings, paragraphs, horizontal rules, lists, images, backgrounds, bookmarks, links, special characters, tables, and frames. The relationship among these elements on the screen is called **layout.** When you create a Web page, you should plan its layout so your content is presented with good balance. Think of dividing the screen into regions, of which some will be pictorial, with others consisting of blocks of text. You also must think about how the user will interact with your screen so you can include the appropriate navigational buttons and hypertext links.

Figures 16-10 through 16-15 analyze the screen layouts of some example Web pages. Notice how some rely heavily on text, while others are more graphical. All of the sample screens provide intuitive ways to navigate that make these Web pages user-friendly. Chapter 20 will show you how to use tables to lay out Web pages in rectangular regions such as these.

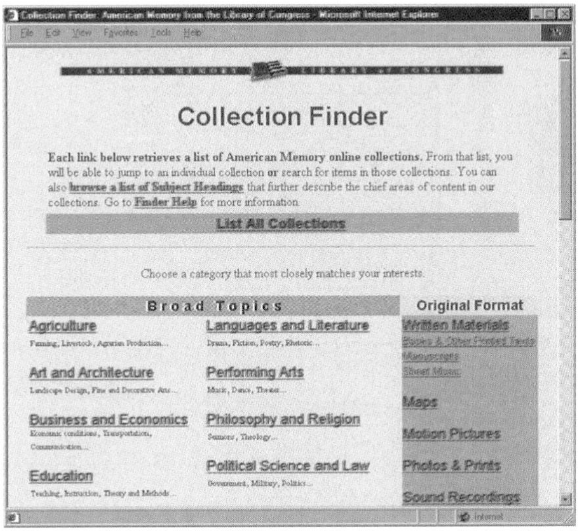

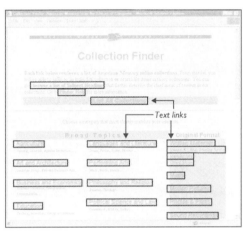

Figure 16-10 Textual screen design.

Figure 16-11 Layout analysis of Figure 16-10.

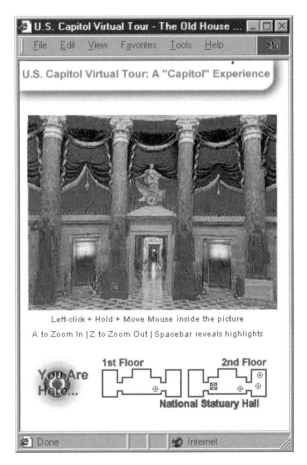

Figure 16-12 Graphical screen design.

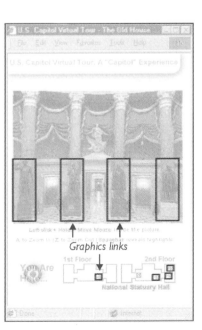

Figure 16-13 Layout analysis of Figure 16-12.

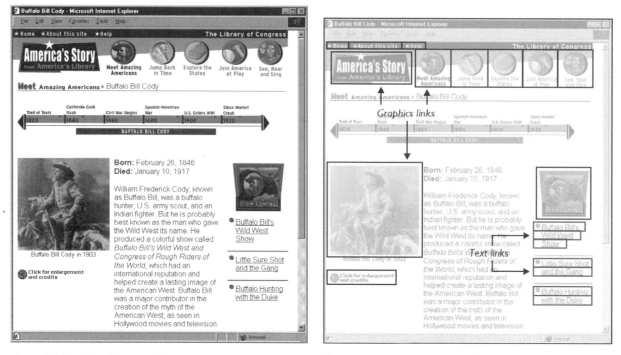

Figure 16-14   Mixed screen design.

Figure 16-15   Layout analysis of Figure 16-14.

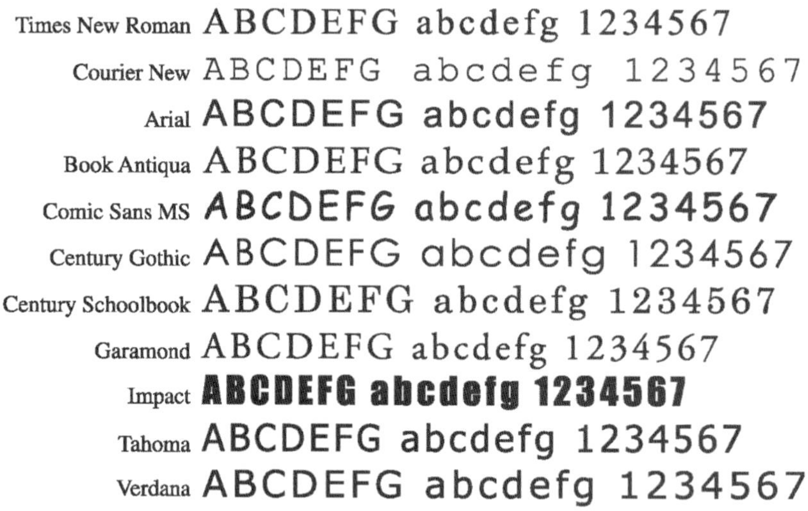

Times New Roman ABCDEFG abcdefg 1234567

Courier New ABCDEFG abcdefg 1234567

Arial **ABCDEFG abcdefg 1234567**

Book Antiqua ABCDEFG abcdefg 1234567

Comic Sans MS **ABCDEFG abcdefg 1234567**

Century Gothic ABCDEFG abcdefg 1234567

Century Schoolbook ABCDEFG abcdefg 1234567

Garamond ABCDEFG abcdefg 1234567

Impact **ABCDEFG abcdefg 1234567**

Tahoma ABCDEFG abcdefg 1234567

Verdana ABCDEFG abcdefg 1234567

Figure 16-16   Fonts used on the Web.

Font Selection

Most Web browsers support the fonts listed in Figure 16-16. Web pages can either set these fonts specifically or leave the choice of the font up to the user. When no font is specified, the browser displays text in the default font. Most users have the default font set to Times New Roman. The Arial font, however, is generally considered to be more readable on Web pages.

All of the fonts illustrated in Figure 16-16 are proportionally spaced except for Courier. Proportional spacing means that fat letters like *m* and *w* take up more space than thin letters like *l* and *i*. Normally you will want to use a **proportional font,** because proportional spacing is easier to read than nonproportional fonts. However, if you want to make columns of text line up precisely on the screen, such as in a spreadsheet, you will need

Times New Roman

Proportional fonts are pleasing to the eye; their characters are varied in width and easier to read. You cannot use spaces to achieve vertical alignment:

Sales:	$100,000	$85,000	$43,614
Taxes:	54,521	3,425	6,921
Fees:	231,947	41	324
Total:	$386,468	$88,466	$50,859

```
Courier New
```

Nonproportional, or monospaced, fonts are regimented and somewhat graceless, but make vertical alignment much easier:

```
Sales:    $100,000   $85,000    $43,614
Taxes:      54,521     3,425      6,921
Fees:      231,947        41        324

Total:    $386,468   $88,466    $50,859
```

Figure 16-17 Comparison of proportional and nonproportional spacing.

to use the nonproportional Courier font. Figure 16-17 illustrates the difference between proportional and nonproportional spacing.

Times and Arial are the most popular proportionally spaced fonts. The primary difference between the Times and Arial fonts is that Times has serifs, whereas Arial does not. A **serif** is a decorative line stemming at an angle from the upper and lower ends of the strokes of a letter. Figure 16-18 compares a few characters from the Times and Arial fonts, pointing out the serifs in the Times font.

Much of the fancy, stylized text you see on the Web is actually a graphic that was made from a font on a graphic artist's computer. The *Interlit* Web site links to some cool sites where you can make fancy text for use in banners and other places where you might want highly stylized text. In Chapter 19, you learn how to put these kinds of images onto your Web pages.

Text Sizing

Text size is measured in points, which tell how high the text is. In print media, a point is one-seventy-second (1/72) of an inch. On a typical computer screen, a point is about the height of a single pixel. Because monitors come in different sizes, the actual size of the text varies somewhat, depending on the physical height of the screen. Figure 16-19 illustrates different **point sizes** used on the Web.

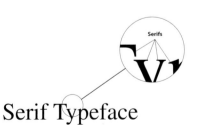

Serif Typeface

Sans Serif Typeface

Figure 16-18 Comparison of Times New Roman and Arial fonts. Notice that Times has serifs, while Arial does not.

4 Point

8 Point

10 Point

12 Point

14 Point

16 Point

20 Point

24 Point

36 Point

Figure 16-19 Comparison of point sizes. The higher the point size, the larger the font.

Background Color	Recommended Foregrounds	Foregrounds to Avoid
White	Black, DarkBlue, Red	Yellow, Cyan, LightGray
Blue	White, Yellow, Cyan	Green, Black
Pink	Black, White, Yellow, Blue	Green, Red, Cyan
Red	Yellow, White, Black	Pink, Cyan, Blue, Green
Yellow	Red, Blue, Black	White, Cyan
Green	Black, Red, Blue	Cyan, Pink, Yellow
Cyan	Blue, Black, Red	Green, Yellow, White
LightGray	Black, DarkBlue, DarkPink	Cyan, Yellow
Gray	Yellow, White, Blue	DarkGray,
DarkGray	Cyan, Yellow, Green	Red, Gray
Black	White, Cyan, Green, Yellow	DarkRed, DarkCyan
DarkBlue	Yellow, White, Pink, Green	DarkGreen, Black
DarkPink	Green, Yellow, White	Black, DarkCyan
DarkRed	White, LightGray, Yellow	Black, DarkBlue,
Brown	Yellow, Cyan, White	Red, Pink, DarkGreen
DarkGreen	Cyan, White, Yellow	DarkBlue, DarkRed
DarkCyan	White, Yellow, Cyan	Brown, Blue, Cyan

Figure 16-20   Recommended color combinations and colors to avoid.

Foreground versus Background Colors

You can select from a wide range of colors for the text and the background of a Web page. Some color combinations work better than others. Figure 16-20 illustrates recommended color combinations as well as colors to avoid.

There are sites on the Web where you can see what different color combinations look like. To explore different foreground/background combinations, follow the *Interlit* Web site links to Color Pickers. As you explore the use of colored backgrounds, keep in mind that the most readable combination is black text on a white background. You will want the bulk of your text to be readable, so save the razzle-dazzle colors for special effects.

Photographic Backgrounds

Exercise care when placing text on photographic backgrounds. Some photos are so busy that text placed atop them is difficult to read. Bolding can improve the readability of text placed on photographic backgrounds. Figure 16-21 illustrates text printed on top of a background photo in different colors and sizes, with and without bolding. Notice how the color combinations with greater contrast are more readable than the colors that blend.

Tiled Backgrounds

A **tiled background** is a graphical effect created when a bitmap smaller than the screen is drawn repeatedly up, down, and across the screen until the entire screen surface has been covered. As illustrated in Figure 16-22, a tiled background can create a special effect on a Web page. You must be careful, however, to select a tile that does not interfere with the readability of the text printed on top of it.

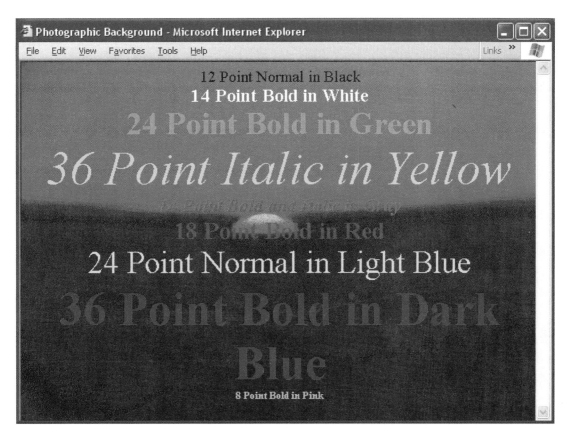

Figure 16-21 Sizing, bolding, and coloring affect the readability of text on a photographic background.

Figure 16-22 Example of a seamless tile in the background of a Web page. The tile image is 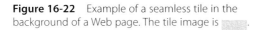.

Figure 16-23 A bad tile that is not seamless and interferes with the readability of the text. The tile image is .

Tiles should be seamless, meaning that when the bitmap replicates itself up and down the screen, you cannot perceive the edges of the bitmap or detect a regular interruption in the pattern caused by the edges of the bitmap not fitting against each other smoothly. Figure 16-23 shows an example of a bad tile, in which you can clearly see a rectangular interruption around the edges of the bitmap. It is also difficult to read the text on top of this tile, making it a doubly bad choice on a Web page.

Navigational Icons

Some Web pages contain navigational icons that give the user the option to page forward or backward, go to a menu, or return to a home page. Navigational icons normally work best when they appear lined up in the same region of the screen instead of scattered about the screen. Try to position the icons in a logical order. For example, it is logical to place the page-back icon in the lower left corner of the screen and the page-forward icon in the lower right. Here is a suggested sequence of icons that gives the user the option to page back, return to the menu, go to a home page, or page forward:

Scrolling

When you design a Web page, keep in mind that the user can scroll up and down through the information that is in it. Imagine what the user will see on each screen of your Web page document and plan the layout accordingly. If your document is long, consider splitting it into smaller pages. If the page must be long, provide navigation options periodically in the midst of the document instead of putting them only at the end. Otherwise, the user will have to scroll all the way down to find the navigation options.

When you have a long page, organize it into sections divided by horizontal rules and put the navigation options at the end of each section. You will learn how to do this in Chapter 18 by providing navigation options at the end of each section of your Web page résumé.

As a general rule, it is best to keep the front page of a Web site short if you can, and use it to provide links to the longer pages. My home page at www.udel.edu/fth is very short, for example, and some of the documents it links to are quite long.

User Friendliness

Web pages must be easy to use. When you plan your layout and decide where you will place pictures and text on your screen, make sure you include navigational buttons, icons, or hypertext to clarify what the navigational options are and where the user should click to navigate.

Word your hypertext links to make it clear what will happen when the user triggers them. Descriptive phrases are better than single words. A descriptive phrase such as "table of contents" tells what will come onscreen when the link is clicked. Try to avoid the temptation to include the word "click" in your instructions. Telling users to click this to go here and click that to go there gets old after a while and sounds overly technical.

Iconic navigation is often more effective than words, takes up less screen space, and works better with international audiences because the icons can be understood regardless of what language the user speaks.

Be consistent. If you adopt navigational icons, use them consistently throughout your Web site. If you use hypertext navigation, be consistent in how you word the directions.

Consistency

Avoid the temptation to demonstrate every trick you know when you design a Web page. Keep it simple. Do not make every screen look and work a different way. Rather, adopt a common look and feel so the user will be able to navigate through your Web site intuitively.

It is frustrating to use a Web page with mixed metaphors and icons that change their meaning on different screens. Be consistent.

Layout Analysis of a Web Page Résumé

Figure 16-24 contains a layout analysis of a Web page résumé. Notice how the text, fonts, sizes, and colors enhance the readability of the text. Each item in the menu serves as a hypertext that links to different sections of the résumé. The navigation options at the end of each section make it clear how to move around on the page. The common look and feel of each section makes it easy for a prospective employer to find out about your job skills and work experience.

Figure 16-24 Layout analysis of a Web page résumé. This is my résumé, which you can visit on the Web at **www.udel.edu/fth/resume.html**. The HTML tutorial in Chapter 18 will step you through the process of creating your own Web page résumé, which will come in handy whenever you are looking for a job.

exercises

1. Using the design elements presented in this chapter, plan the layout of your Web page résumé. Think about the menu choices you will want to provide prospective employers who visit your Web page to find out about your experience and qualifications. Include this menu as one of the design elements in your résumé. Possible menu items include:

    - Educational Qualifications
    - Work Experience
    - Computer Skills
    - Grants and Awards
    - Honorary Societies

    - Professional Association Memberships
    - Publications
    - Software
    - Presentations
    - How to Contact Me

    If you are just starting out, you may not have this many items, but remember not to be shy on a résumé. Think about all the things you have done, the part-time jobs you have had, the organizations for which you have volunteered, the sports teams on which you have played, and the clubs you joined. You probably have more things to list on a résumé than you can think of at first. You do not want to go overboard, however, because a résumé should be succinct, but if you cannot fill a screen or two, think harder about what you have done in life.

2. Since it is possible to link any document, audio, picture, movie, or software application to your Web page, you will be able to link your résumé to examples of your work to prove your worth to a prospective employer. What examples would you like to link to your résumé? Include these links in the design of your résumé.

3. There is a knack to writing hypertext in such a way that the wording makes it clear what will happen when the user triggers the link. Write three examples of text containing a word or a phrase that, when clicked, takes the user to your home page.

4. Draw three different ways of providing an icon that moves forward to the next screen of an application.

SITUATED CASE PROJECTS
Case 16: Adopting a Common Look and Feel

At the end of each chapter in this book, a situated case project provides the student an opportunity to put the chapter's contents to practical use in a workplace situation. Each case has the same number as the chapter in which it appears.

Whether or not the Web page author is aware of it, every Web page has a certain kind of look and feel. If the look and feel are consistent from page to page, co-workers and others who visit the site frequently get used to looking in certain places on the page to find such things as menus, link bars, headlines, different kinds of content, and navigation buttons. If the look and feel are not consistent from page to page, the user must spend more time finding where things are on the page. This is inefficient at best and can be frustrating as well. Imagine that your employer has decided that your school or company Web site needs to adopt a common look and feel. Your employer has asked you to create a design specification recommending a common look and feel for Web pages created in your workplace. In creating this design spec, address the following issues:

❶ *Templates.* What kinds of pages do your co-workers typically create? The pages probably fall into a few basic types, such as home pages for different projects or products, search pages for finding things, catalog pages for listing products for sale, and document pages containing reports, product information, or scholarly papers.

❷ *Design elements.* What are the design elements that are likely to appear on the kinds of pages identified in step (1)? Make an outline that lists the basic kinds of pages typically used in your workplace. Under each kind, list the design elements that appear on that kind of page. Consider all the different elements that can appear on your workplace Web pages, such as banners, menus, search buttons, quick links, news feeds, headlines, navigation buttons, pictures, icons, logos, prose, products, catalogs, advertisements, and bibliographies.

3 *Positioning.* Add to the outline created in step (2) an indication of where each element will go on the Web page. If you are not sure where things should go, visit some Web sites of organizations like yours and study their Web page designs. If you have FrontPage, you can look at the built-in templates there. Pull down the File menu, choose New→Page, and click the option to see the templates. As you click each template, a preview pane shows the layout. There is also a template gallery at http://office.microsoft.com/en-us/templates. Surf these templates and visit other Web sites in your industry or subject matter to get more design ideas.

4 *Navigation.* Include in your design spec a strategy for placing navigational elements at consistent places onscreen.

Use a word processor to write up your answer to this assignment in the form of a three-part essay. In the first part, describe the overall approach you recommend. Mention the three or four basic kinds of templates you feel your school or company needs. In the second part, present the outline of design elements that will typically appear on each template. Conclude by describing where onscreen these design elements will appear. If you are graphically inclined, you can use your word processor's table feature to create a prototype of the screen designs you envision. Otherwise, you can describe the layout prosaically. Make sure you specify where the navigational elements will be onscreen. If your instructor has asked you to hand in this assignment, put your name at the top, then save it on disk or follow any other instructions you may have been given for submitting this assignment.

17

HOW HTML WORKS

After completing this chapter, you will be able to:

- **Explain the concept of a markup language.**

- **Realize that different Web browsers may display the same HTML somewhat differently.**

- **Understand the two HTML tag formats.**

- **Define the families of HTML tags.**

- **Recognize the HTML tags used in creating a résumé.**

- **Understand the relationship between HTML, SGML, and XHTML.**

HTML is the markup language used to create hypertext documents for the World Wide Web. HTML stands for *h*ypertext *m*arkup *l*anguage. The key to understanding how HTML works is to know what it means to mark up a text. This chapter explains the concept of a markup language, defines the families of HTML tags, and identifies the tags that you will use in creating your Web page résumé.

If you are not a technical person, you may be concerned that it is too complicated to learn these tags, and you will never be able to create a Web page on your own. Do not worry about this. You do not need to memorize the tags presented in this chapter. When you create your Web page résumé in the next chapter, you will use a WYSIWYG tool that inserts the tags automatically for you. Why then, you may ask, do you need to know about the tags at all? Because sometimes you do need to work at the level of the HTML code to create a special effect or to insert a command that a certain tool may not yet handle.

Understanding Markup

To **mark up** a text means to insert special codes called tags into the text. The *tags* control how the text appears on a Web page. For example, compare Figures 17-1 and 17-2. In Figure 17-1, you see how a text appears on a Web page; notice the different-sized headings, the paragraphs, and the list of bulleted items. In Figure 17-2, you can see the HTML tags that mark up the text. By comparing these two figures, you can begin to understand how HTML controls the appearance of text on the Web. Notice how the HTML tags always appear <inside> brackets.

HTML Tag Formats

There are two HTML tag formats: paired tags and single tags.

Paired tags come in pairs that consist of a **start tag** and a **stop tag.** Headings are an example of paired tags. For example, to make the words *Internet Literacy* appear in the

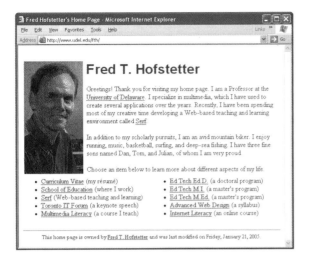

Figure 17-1 This is how my home page appears on the Web.

Figure 17-2 This is the HTML source code that creates my home page. The codes in <brackets> are the HTML tags that mark up the text.

largest style of heading, you would mark them up as follows:

<h1>**Internet Literacy**</h1>

<h1> is the start tag, and </h1> is the stop tag. The words between them will appear in heading style h1, which is the largest of the six heading styles. You can tell a start tag from a stop tag because the stop tag always has a slash, as in </h1>.

Single tags function on their own with no stop tag. For example, the tag <hr> makes a line known as a "horizontal rule" appear on your Web page; there is no stop tag for a horizontal rule.

Taxonomy of HTML Tags

There are more than a hundred HTML tags. Learning that many tags may seem like a foreboding task. You can simplify the process, however, if you realize that the tags can be thought of in families devoted to accomplishing similar tasks. The following taxonomy groups the HTML tags into 12 families:

- **Page structure tags** provide a framework for the document as a whole. They identify that the document is encoded in HTML and provide titling, framing, and header information that defines the structure of the file.

- **Block-style tags** control the flow of text into blocks on the screen. The most common block style is the paragraph.

- **Logical font-style tags** include styles for abbreviations, acronyms, citations, and quotations.

- **Physical font-style tags** let you create text that is blinking, bold, italic, subscripted, superscripted, or underlined.

- **Heading tags** let you create headings in six different levels or sizes of importance.

- **Lists and miscellaneous tags** let you create numbered lists, bulleted lists, menus, directories, horizontal dividing lines, and line breaks.

- **Form tags** let you create input fields, buttons, and selection boxes for gathering information from the user.

- **Table tags** let you define tables that present data in neat rows and columns.

- **Character entities** provide a wide range of Greek characters and special symbols used in mathematical and scientific notation.

- **Anchor/link tags** let you create bookmarks, hypertext, and hyperpictures and link them to any resource or file on the World Wide Web.

- **Image tags** let you insert figures, center or align pictures with the left or right margin, flow text around images, or place little icons inline in the midst of your text.

- **Object tags** provide a means for defining a way to interact with plug-ins, media handlers, and Java applets, which are little applications that get downloaded to your computer along with a Web page.

Tags Used in the Web Page Creation Tutorial

Table 17-1 defines the HTML tags used in this book. These tags are all a standard part of HTML, and they will work with all the leading Web browsers, including Mozilla Firefox, Microsoft Internet Explorer, Safari, and Netscape Navigator.

Table 17-1   HTML tags used in the Web page creation tutorial

HTML Tag Syntax	Use on Web Page
\<html\> and **\</html\>**	These tags define the beginning and end of an HTML document. Your Web pages will always begin with the **\<html\>** start tag and end with the **\</html\>** stop tag.
\<head\> and **\</head\>**	The headers of your HTML file will appear between these tags.
\<title\> and **\</title\>**	The title of your HTML file goes between these tags, which in turn go between the header tags.
\<body\> and **\</body\>**	The body of your HTML file goes between these tags.
\<h1\> and **\</h1\>**	You will use these heading tags at the beginning of your résumé to make your name appear in the most important heading style.
\<p\> and **\</p\>**	The **\<p\>** tag marks the beginning of a new paragraph. The stop tag **\</p\>** is optional. The **\<p\>** tag will always begin a new paragraph, whether or not a **\</p\>** tag marks the end of the paragraph.
\<ul\> and **\</ul\>**	These unordered list tags will mark the beginning and end of the table of contents in your résumé.
\<li\> and **\</li\>**	The list item tag will mark each item in your table of contents.
\<hr\>	The horizontal rule tag makes the neat three-dimensional dividing lines on Web pages.
\<a name="*name***"\>** **\</a\>**	*A* stands for *anchor*. An anchor tag with a name parameter creates names for the bookmarks in your résumé.
\<a href="*url***"\>** **\</a\>**	*Href* stands for *hypertext reference*. An anchor tag with an href parameter creates hypertext links.
\<img src="*filename***"\>**	The image tag places pictures on your Web page.
\<body background="*filename***"\>** **\</body\>**	The background parameter of the body tag tiles an image into the background of your Web page if you want to give your résumé a textured appearance.
\<table\> and **\</table\>**	Table cells go between these tags.
\<tr\> and **\</tr\>**	Create a row in a table; *tr* stands for table row.
\<td\> and **\</td\>**	Create a data cell inside a row of a table; *td* stands for table data.

Versions of HTML

HTML has progressed through several versions, each of which added new functionality to what you can do on a Web page. When HTML was invented, the Web was a text-only medium used to display simple text documents onscreen. To keep the markup simple enough for beginners to learn, HTML did not require all of the structural elements defined by its parent language, which is the **Standard Generalizable Markup Language (SGML).** According to SGML, for example, every begin tag needs some kind of logical ending. In early versions of HTML, however, several elements did not have end tags. The list item tag <li>, for example, did not have a corresponding end tag </li>. Moreover, SGML requires that the order of the tags adhere to the document's defined structure. If a bold italicized phrase begins, for example, with <strong> <em> it must end with </em> </strong> and not </strong> </em>. Early versions of HTML permitted both kinds of endings.

Such loose encoding, however, does not lend itself to the kind of structure needed to transition the Web into an application model, in which servers exchange data in a disciplined manner. Enter **XML,** which stands for **eXtensible Markup Language.** True to its name, XML enables you to extend a document's structure by defining new tags. This was not possible in HTML. Another difference between XML and HTML is that XML adheres to the structural rules of SGML. Every begin tag must have an ending, and the order in which the tags close must follow the structure of the document's definition.

More than a billion Web pages have been created with HTML. The vast majority of these pages contain loose encodings that do not follow the strict rules of SGML. As a result, these pages will not validate in XML tools that require tags to follow the document's definition. To solve this problem, the W3C created a new language called **XHTML.** True to its name, XHTML includes most of the classic HTML codes, but they appear in the context of an XML schema (hence the X in XHTML) that XML tools can understand.

Pages authored in XHTML will render not only on the Web but also on pagers, PDAs, cell phones, tablet PCs, and other devices that are following the new XML-based wireless protocols. XHTML pages also can be mined by XML tools as data that can be used in server-to-server and business-to-business applications. XHTML further enables you to use the **eXtensible Stylesheet Language (XSL)** to transform a document from one format into another, such as from an HTML Web page into a PDF document. Finally, XHTML makes it possible for you to use other XML languages on your Web page, such as the Synchronized Multimedia Integration Language (SMIL), which you read about in the Synchronized Multimedia section of Chapter 10.

In this book, the HTML tags you will be learning follow the XHTML specification. To visit the official Web site where the HTML and XHTML specifications are found, go to www.w3.org/MarkUp.

exercises

1. Compare the advantages and disadvantages of the evolutionary nature of HTML. What is good about designing the language so that new tags can be added to it? Are there disadvantages to developing a language this way?

2. Think about the taxonomy of HTML tags provided in this chapter. What capabilities do you think the World Wide Web should have that are not included in this taxonomy?

3. Follow the links to W3C at the *Interlit* Web site and read how the consortium oversees the continued evolution of HTML. What mechanism is provided by the W3C for you to request new features to be added to HTML and XHTML?

4. Follow the links to W3C at the *Interlit* Web site and have a look at the new initiatives listed there. Of the new activities you find announced at the W3C site, which one is most interesting to you? Why are you most interested in it?

SITUATED CASE PROJECTS
Case 17: Planning XML Web Services

At the end of each chapter in this book, a situated case project provides the student an opportunity to put the chapter's contents to practical use in a workplace situation. Each case has the same number as the chapter in which it appears.

One of the hottest things happening on the Web right now is the creation and implementation of a new protocol enabling servers to communicate with each other via XML. The new protocol is called SOAP, which stands for Simple Object Access Protocol. SOAP enables computer applications to communicate and share data over the Internet, regardless of operating system, device, or programming language. One program running on a computer in one location on the Web can send a SOAP request that is handled by another program running somewhere else on the Web. End users never see the raw SOAP transmissions, which are encoded in XML and look rather technical. Instead, the SOAP transmissions run in the background between the computers and servers that will eventually render the result as an HTML page for display on the user's screen.

Without getting too technical, you can get an idea how this works by considering that in just two weeks, Dollar Rent-A-Car was able to interface the reservation system running on its IBM mainframe with an airline partner's UNIX servers. When a user books a flight and clicks the option to rent a car, Dollar Rent-A-Car's IBM system makes the reservation automatically, based on the user's flight times and destination on the airline's UNIX server. All the user sees is a simple HTML page that makes the reservation quick and easy. Behind the scenes, however, many other transactions happen via SOAP.

Because the SOAP transmissions happen over the same HTTP transport mechanism that the Web uses, services that get provided via SOAP are known as Web Services. For each XML Web Service, there is an XML document called a Web Services Description Language (WSDL) that describes how another program or computer can use the service. XML Web Services are registered through an online yellow-pages mechanism called Universal Discovery Description and Integration (UDDI) so potential users can find Web Services easily.

Imagine that your superior has heard of Web Services and has asked you to look into the new technology, find out what it can do, and recommend how your school or company should be planning to use Web Services. In developing your recommendation, follow these steps:

1 Follow the Chapter 17 *Interlit* Web site links to learn more about XML Web Services. Read the definition first, then visit the XML Web Services showcase. You will see how Web Services are already being used across a broad range of business, government, industry, and education.

2 Think about the computer applications used at your school or company. How do they interact now? How could your daily operations be enhanced if these applications could communicate with each other?

3 Use your word processor to write a paragraph describing how you envision Web Services being used in the IT infrastructure of your workplace. Cite any relevant examples of similar applications you found in step (1) when you toured the XML Web Services showcase.

4 Underneath the paragraph you wrote in step (3), list the relevant applications or processes that run on your computer network today, and tell how you envision them using XML Web Services to enhance current operations.

5 Conclude by writing a paragraph or two describing new applications or capabilities you foresee that could increase worker productivity or provide better service to end users.

If your instructor has asked you to hand in this assignment, make sure you put your name at the top, then save your XML Web Services report on disk, or follow any other instructions you may have been given for submitting this assignment.

18

CREATING YOUR WEB PAGE RÉSUMÉ

After completing this chapter, you will be able to:

- **Create a file folder for your Web pages.**

- **Use Dreamweaver, FrontPage, or Nvu to create a new HTML file.**

- **Enter your own content into the Web page.**

- **Create new paragraphs on a Web page.**

- **Make lists on a Web page.**

- **Put pictures on a Web page.**

- **Tile a background onto a Web page.**

- **Create named anchor bookmarks on a Web page.**

- **Create links to named anchor bookmarks.**

- **View the Web page with your favorite Web browser.**

- Now that you know how HTML works, you are ready to put your new knowledge to work. This chapter takes you through all the steps needed to build your own online résumé with text, graphics, and links to other Web pages.

Making a File Folder for Your Web Pages

When you create a Web site, you begin by creating the file folder in which the Web pages will reside. The name of the folder for this tutorial is *website;* you should create the *website* folder now. Follow these steps:

- If you have Windows, click the Start button, choose Programs→Accessories, open the Windows Explorer, navigate to the root of your hard drive, pull down the Explorer's File menu, choose New→Folder, type **website,** and press Enter.

- If you have a Macintosh, select File from the Finder's menu bar, then select New Folder. The folder will be created with the name *untitled folder.* Select the name by clicking it once, then type the new name **website** and press Enter.

Selecting a Web Page Creation Tool

The Web page creation tutorial in this part of the book can be completed with either Dreamweaver, FrontPage, or Nvu. If your school or workplace has already adopted Dreamweaver, you may decide to learn Dreamweaver so you can use the software installed at your site. If your site has a FrontPage license, on the other hand, you may use FrontPage. If you prefer open-source software that is freely downloadable, Nvu is an excellent choice.

If you do not already have the tool of your choice, you can get a free trial version by following these links:

Dreamweaver	www.macromedia.com/software/dreamweaver/download/
FrontPage	www.microsoft.com/office/frontpage/prodinfo/trial.mspx
Nvu	www.nvu.com

Running the Web Page Creation Software

The first step in creating a new Web page is to get your Web page creation software running. Depending on your chosen brand of Web page editor, double-click one of the following launch icons. If the launch icon is not visible, refer to Table 13-4 for help running a program when you cannot see its icon.

Dreamweaver   Frontpage   Nvu

Starting a New Web Page

Now that you have your Web page creation software running, you can start creating a Web page. Follow the steps in Table 18-1.

Inspecting the HTML Code of a Web Page

When you start a new Web page, something interesting happens behind the scenes. Your Web page editor automatically creates a minimal amount of HTML code that defines a blank page. Out of curiosity, you may take a look at this HTML code. To inspect the HTML code of a Web page, follow the steps in Table 18-2.

Creating the Page Title

The page title is the name that will appear in the browser's title bar when people visit your Web page on the Internet. The title is also used by many Web search engines, so you will want to make sure the title identifies the primary purpose of your Web page by including keywords you want search engines to find. To create the page title, follow the steps in Table 18-3.

Writing the Heading

Since this Web page is your résumé, you will want to start it with a heading that includes your name in big, bold letters at the top of the Web page. The largest heading style is the **<h1>** style. To create a heading, follow the steps in Table 18-4.

Do not confuse the heading you just entered with the document title that you entered previously in this tutorial. The heading will appear on your Web page, while the document title will appear in the Web browser's title bar. It is fine for both the heading and the title to be the same, such as *Santa Claus's Résumé*.

Saving the File

Whenever you make a change to a file that you want to keep, you should save the file. Do so now by following the steps in Table 18-5.

Table 18-1 How to start a new Web page

Dreamweaver

▲ When you launch Dreamweaver, it displays a menu of startup options. To start a new Web page, choose the option to Create New HTML. If you ever need to create another page, pull down the File menu, choose New, click Basic Page, select HTML, and click the Create button.

▲ The Dreamweaver window appears as shown in Figure 18-1.

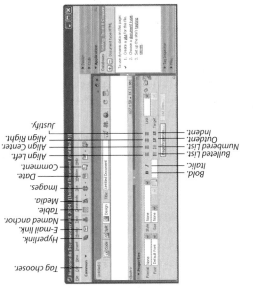

Tag chooser.
Hyperlink.
E-mail link.
Named anchor.
Table.
Media.
Images.
Date.
Comment.
Align Left.
Align Center.
Align Right.
Justify.
Bulleted List.
Numbered List.
Outdent.
Indent.
Italic.
Bold.

Figure 18-1 The Dreamweaver window.

▲ If the toolbars pictured in Figure 18-1 are not visible, pull down the View menu, choose Toolbars, and turn on the Insert toolbar. To make the side panels appear or disappear, pull down the View menu and choose Show Panels or Hide Panels.

▲ If you mouse over one of the Dreamweaver buttons and pause, leaving your mouse stationary for a moment, a tooltip pops out explaining what the button is. Do not click any buttons yet, but do explore what the different buttons are by mousing over each one and holding your mouse still to pop out the tooltip.

▲ Notice the Properties window at the bottom-left of Figure 18-1. This is a very handy Dreamweaver feature because it lets you see the properties of the element you are editing.

FrontPage

▲ FrontPage automatically starts a new page. If you ever need to create another one, click the ▢ New Page button. *Note:* If you click the arrow next to the New Page button, you will get a menu that provides other choices. For now, all you need to click is the New Page button, not the arrow beside it.

▲ The FrontPage window appears as shown in Figure 18-2.

Create a new Web page.
Open an existing file.
Save the file.
Search for a keyword.
Publish the site.
Folder list.
Print the page.
Preview in browser.
Spell check.
Cut.
Copy.
Paste.
Format Painter.
Undo.
Redo.
Insert Component.
Insert Table.
Insert Layer.
Insert Picture from File.
Drawing.
Insert hyperlink.
Refresh.
Stop.
Show/hide formatting.
Show layer anchors.
Help.

Change the style.
Change the font.
Toggle a pane.
Change the font size.
Bold.
Italic.
Underline.
Align left.
Center.
Align right.
Justify.
Increase font size.
Decrease font size.
Numbered list.
Bulleted list.
Decrease indent.
Increase indent.
Outside borders.
Highlight color.
Font color.

Figure 18-2 The Microsoft FrontPage window.

▲ If the toolbars pictured in Figure 18-2 are not visible, pull down the View menu, choose Toolbars, and turn on the Standard toolbar and the Formatting toolbar. To make the Task Pane appear or disappear, pull down the View menu and choose Task Pane.

▲ If you mouse over one of the FrontPage buttons and pause, leaving your mouse stationary for a moment, a tooltip pops out explaining what the button is. Do not click any buttons yet, but do explore what the different buttons are by mousing over each one and holding your mouse still to pop out the tooltip.

Nvu

▲ Nvu automatically starts a new page. If you ever need to create another one, click the ◯ New Page button.

▲ The Nvu window appears as shown in Figure 18-3.

Create a new page.
Open a local file.
Save the file locally.
Publish the file.
Preview in browser.
Insert named anchor bookmark.
Insert link.
Insert image.
Insert table.
Insert Form.
Spell Check.
Print this page.

Change the style.
Change the font.
Foreground color.
Background color.
Highlight color.
Smaller font size.
Larger font size.
Bold.
Italic.
Underline.
Numbered list.
Bulleted list.
Align left.
Center.
Align right.
Justify.
Indent.
Outdent.

Figure 18-3 The Nvu window.

▲ If the toolbars pictured in Figure 18-3 are not visible, pull down the View menu and choose Show/Hide→Composition Toolbar and Show/Hide→Format Toolbar.

▲ If you move over one of the Nvu buttons and pause, leaving your mouse stationary for a moment, a tooltip pops out explaining what the button is. Do not click any buttons yet, but do explore what the different buttons are by mousing over each one and holding your mouse still to pop out the tooltip.

Table 18-2　How to inspect the HTML code of a Web page

Dreamweaver	FrontPage	Nvu

Dreamweaver

▶ Each new page created by Dreamweaver contains a minimal amount of HTML code. You cannot see the HTML code in the Design view of the Dreamweaver window, which only shows what will appear onscreen when the user views your Web page with a browser. Since you have not entered anything onto the Web page yet, the Dreamweaver screen appears blank.

▶ To inspect the HTML code that is in your page so far, click the Code button at the top of the page's window, or pull down the View menu and choose Code.

▶ The HTML code appears in the Dreamweaver window, as shown in Figure 18-4. Here you can see what happened when the new page was created. The nice thing about a WYSIWYG editor is that it takes care of creating the HTML code for you automatically, so you do not need to worry about it. This tutorial will ask you to inspect the HTML from time to time, however, so you will realize what is going on behind the scenes as you create your Web page résumé.

This tells you what version of HTML is being used.
The tags <html> and </html> mark the beginning and end of the document.
<head> and </head> mark the document's heading.
<body> and </body> mark the body of the document.

Figure 18-4　A new Web page displayed in the HTML Code view.

▶ When you are done inspecting the HTML codes of your new Web page, click the Design button, or pull down the View menu and choose Design, and read on.

FrontPage

▶ Each new page created by FrontPage contains a minimal amount of HTML code. You cannot see the HTML in the normal FrontPage window, which only shows what will appear onscreen when the user views your Web page with a browser. Since you have not entered anything onto the Web page yet, the screen appears blank.

▶ To inspect the HTML code that is in your page so far, click the HTML Code tab at the bottom of the window. The HTML Code window appears, as shown in Figure 18-5.

The tags <html> and </html> mark the beginning and end of the document.
<head> and </head> mark the document's heading.
<body> and </body> mark the body of the document.

Figure 18-5　A new Web page displayed in the HTML Code window.

▶ The HTML Code window shows what went on behind the scenes when FrontPage created the new page for you. The nice thing about a WYSIWYG editor is that it takes care of creating the HTML code for you automatically, so you do not need to worry about it. This tutorial will ask you to inspect the HTML from time to time, however, so you will realize what is going on behind the scenes as you create your Web page résumé.

▶ When you are done inspecting the HTML codes of your new Web page, click the Design tab at the bottom of the window, and read on.

Nvu

▶ Each new page created by Nvu contains a minimal amount of HTML code. You cannot see the HTML code in the normal view of the Nvu window, which only shows what will appear onscreen when the user views your Web page with a browser. Since you have not entered anything onto the Web page yet, the Nvu screen appears blank.

▶ To inspect the HTML code that is in your page so far, click the HTML Source tab at the bottom of the window. *Note:* If the HTML Source tab is not visible, pull down the View menu and choose Show/Hide→Edit Mode Toolbar.

▶ The HTML code appears in the Nvu window, as shown in Figure 18-6. Here you can see what happened when the new page was created. The nice thing about a WYSIWYG editor is that it takes care of creating the HTML code for you automatically, so you do not need to worry about it. This tutorial will ask you to inspect the HTML from time to time, however, so you will realize what is going on behind the scenes as you create your Web page résumé.

This tells you what version of HTML is being used.
The tags <html> and </html> mark the beginning and end of the document.
<head> and </head> mark the document's heading.
<body> and </body> mark the body of the document.
*
 is a break tag.*

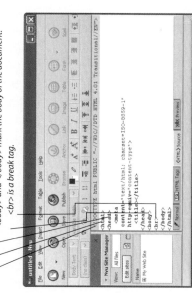

Figure 18-6　A new Web page displayed in the HTML Source view.

▶ When you are done inspecting the HTML codes of your new Web page, click the Normal tab, and read on.

Table 18-3   How to create the page title

Dreamweaver	FrontPage	Nvu

Dreamweaver

▲ Click to position your cursor inside the Title field at the top of the document window, as illustrated in Figure 18-7.

Type your Web page's title here.

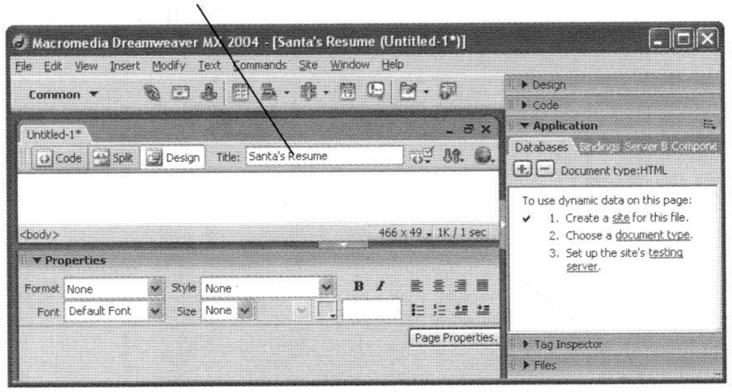

Figure 18-7   The Title field is at the top of Dreamweaver's document window.

▲ At first, the Title field will say "Untitled Document." Replace that with an appropriate title for this Web page. If your name is Santa Claus, for example, you might type **Santa's Resume,** since this Web page will be your résumé.

▲ If you click the Code tab to inspect your HTML code, you will see how the page title has been added to the <head> section of your Web page.

▲ Now it is time to enter some text onto your Web page. Click the Design tab, and read on.

FrontPage

▲ Right-click anywhere in the white space of the page to pop out the quick menu and choose Page Properties; the Page Properties dialog appears as shown in Figure 18-8.

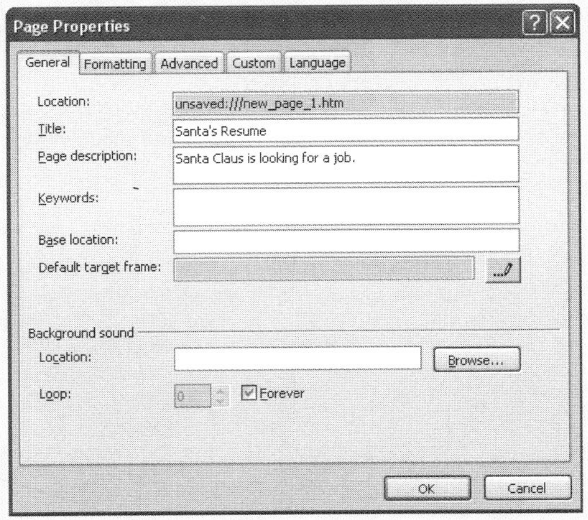

Figure 18-8   The FrontPage Page Properties dialog.

▲ At first, the Title field will say "New Page 1." Replace that with an appropriate title for this Web page. If your name is Santa Claus, for example, you might type **Santa's Resume,** since this Web page will be your résumé.

▲ In the Page description field, type a brief description of what this page is. If your name is Santa Claus, for example, you might enter **Santa Claus is looking for a job.**

▲ Click OK to close the Page Properties dialog.

▲ If you click the Code tab to inspect your HTML code, you will see how the page title has been added to the <head> section of your Web page.

▲ Now it is time to enter some text onto your Web page. Click the Design tab, and read on.

Nvu

▲ If you are not already in Normal view, click the Normal tab.

▲ Pull down the Format menu and choose Page Title and Properties; the Page Properties dialog appears as shown in Figure 18-9.

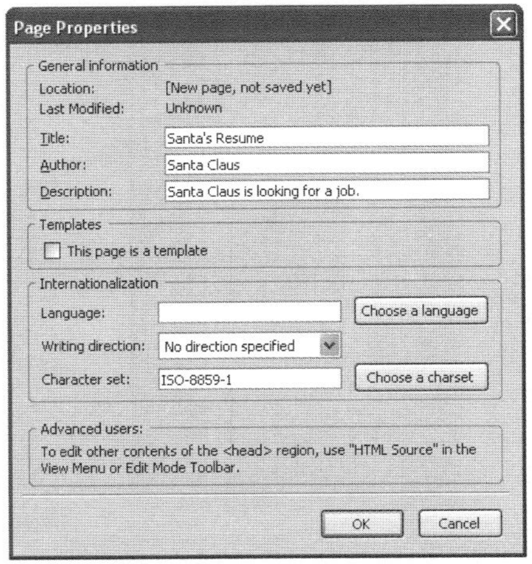

Figure 18-9   The Nvu Page Properties dialog.

▲ In the title field, enter an appropriate title for this Web page. If your name is Santa Claus, for example, you might type **Santa's Resume,** since this Web page will be your résumé.

▲ In the Author field, type your name, since you are the author of this Web page.

▲ In the Description field, type a brief description of what this page is. If your name is Santa Claus, for example, you might enter **Santa Claus is looking for a job.**

▲ Click OK to close the Page Properties dialog.

▲ If you click the HTML Source tab to inspect your HTML code, you will see how the page title has been added to the <head> section of your Web page.

▲ Now it is time to enter some text onto your Web page. Click the Normal tab, and read on.

Note: If the HTML Source and Normal tabs are not visible, pull down the View menu and choose Show/Hide→Edit Mode Toolbar. From now on, this tutorial will assume that the Edit Mode toolbar is onscreen.

Table 18-4　How to write a heading

Dreamweaver	FrontPage	Nvu
▲ Type your heading onto your Web page. For example, if your name is Santa Claus, you would type **Santa Claus's Resume**	▲ Type your heading onto your Web page. For example, if your name is Santa Claus, you would type **Santa Claus's Resume**	▲ Type your heading onto your Web page. For example, if your name is Santa Claus, you would type **Santa Claus's Resume**
▲ With your cursor positioned any place on the line of text you just typed, pull down the Format menu and choose Heading 1, as shown in Figure 18-10.	▲ With your cursor positioned any place on the line of text you just typed, pull down the Style menu and choose Heading 1, as shown in Figure 18-11.	▲ With your cursor positioned any place on the line of text you just typed, pull down the Style menu and choose Heading 1, as shown in Figure 18-12.

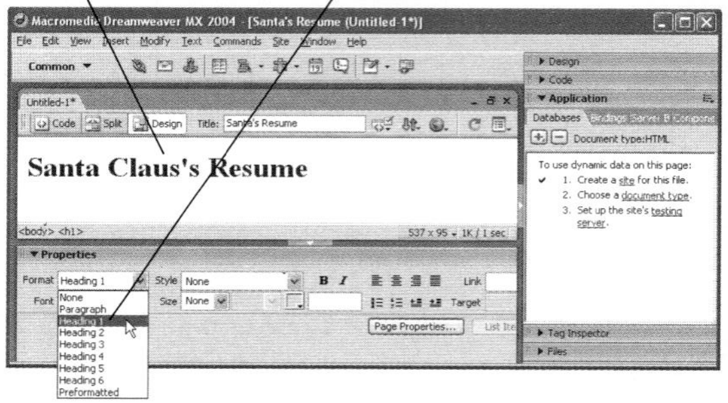

Type the heading here.　_The format setting._

Figure 18-10　Writing a heading in Dreamweaver.

▲ The text changes to the large, bold style of Heading 1.

▲ To inspect your HTML and see the result of typing the heading, click the Code tab to make the HTML Code window appear. Notice how your heading appears inside **<h1>** and **</h1>** tags.

▲ Click the Design tab, and read on.

The style setting.　_Type the heading here._

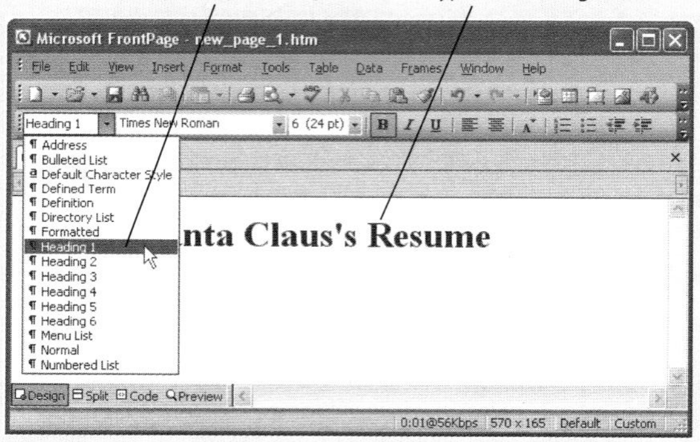

Figure 18-11　Writing a heading in Microsoft FrontPage.

▲ The text changes to the large, bold style of Heading 1.

▲ To inspect your HTML and see the result of typing the heading, click the Code tab to make the HTML Code window appear. Notice how your heading appears inside **<h1>** and **</h1>** tags.

▲ Click the Design tab, and read on.

The style setting.　_Type the heading here._

Figure 18-12　Writing a heading in Nvu.

▲ The text changes to the large, bold style of Heading 1.

▲ To inspect your HTML and see the result of typing the heading, click the HTML Source tab to make the HTML window appear. Notice how your heading appears inside **<h1>** and **</h1>** tags.

▲ Click the Normal tab, and read on.

Table 18-5 How to save a Web page file

Dreamweaver	FrontPage	Nvu
▲ Pull down the File menu and choose Save, or press `Ctrl`-`S`, the shortcut key for Save.	▲ Click the [icon] Save button, or pull down the File menu and choose Save.	▲ Click the [icon] Save button, or pull down the File menu and choose Save.
▲ The first time you save a file, the Save As dialog will appear, as illustrated in Figure 18-13.	▲ The first time you save a file, the Save As dialog will appear, as illustrated in Figure 18-14.	▲ The first time you save a file, the Save Page As dialog will appear, as illustrated in Figure 18-15.

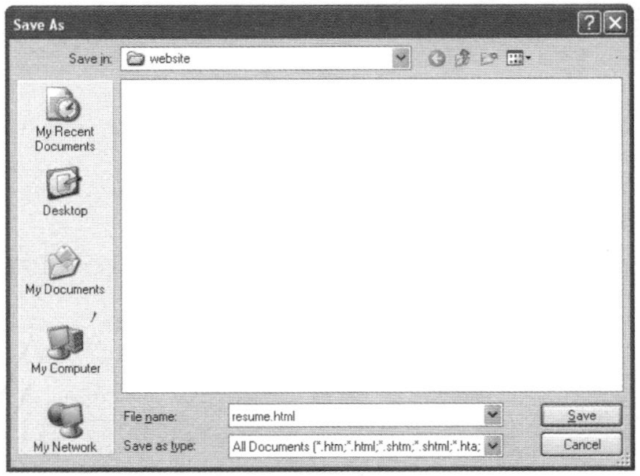

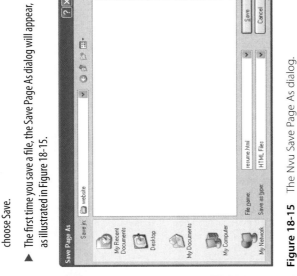

Figure 18-13 The Dreamweaver Save As dialog.

▲ Save this file in the *website* folder that you created at the beginning of this chapter. Since this file is your résumé, you should name it *resume.htm*. Thus, assuming your hard drive is C, the filename will be *c:\website\resume.htm*.

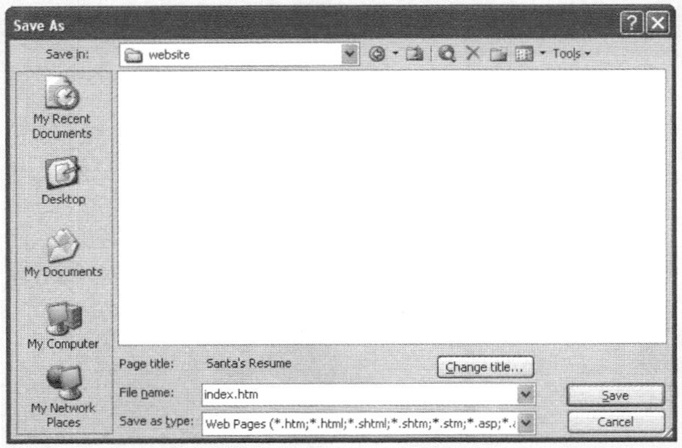

Figure 18-14 The FrontPage Save As dialog.

▲ Save this file in the *website* folder that you created at the beginning of this chapter. Since this file is your résumé, you should name it *resume.htm*. Thus, assuming your hard drive is C, the filename will be *c:\website\resume.htm*.

Figure 18-15 The Nvu Save Page As dialog.

▲ Save this file in the *website* folder that you created at the beginning of this chapter. Since this file is your résumé, you should name it *resume.html*. Thus, assuming your hard drive is C, the filename will be *c:\website\resume.html*.

Inspecting Your New Web Page with a Browser

While you are creating a new Web page, you will want to have a look at it with a Web browser from time to time so you can see how it is going to appear on the Web. Even though the editor is supposed to be WYSIWYG, not all things look exactly the same in a browser as they do in the editor. To preview a Web page with a browser, follow the steps in Table 18-6.

Entering the First Paragraph

Now you are ready to type the first paragraph of your résumé. Mouse to the spot on the screen right after the heading on your Web page and press Enter . If you mistakenly press Enter in the midst of the heading, instead of at the end of it, you can pull down the Edit menu and choose Undo to fix the mistake.

Now you are ready to type a few sentences about yourself, as an introduction to your résumé. Do not be bashful: a résumé should begin with a strongly stated summary of your professional qualifications and career goals. Figure 18-16 shows how I began my résumé.

Repeat the steps in Table 18-6 to take another look at your Web page in the browser window. Notice how the paragraph you typed appears beneath the heading of your résumé.

Starting a New Paragraph

To make a new paragraph, follow the steps in Table 18-7.

Table 18-6   How to preview a Web page with a browser

Dreamweaver	FrontPage	Nvu
▶ Click the ⊕▾ Preview in Browser button.	▶ Click the 🔍 Preview in Browser button.	▶ Click the ✷ Browse button.
▶ If the file has not been saved, Dreamweaver will prompt you to save it before you preview it.	▶ If the file has not been saved, FrontPage will prompt you to save it before you preview it.	▶ If the file has not been saved, Nvu will prompt you to save it before you preview it.
▶ Click the ⊕▾ Preview in Browser button again, or press the F12 function key, to have a look at your Web page in the browser window. Notice how the title you entered appears in the browser's title bar and the heading appears at the top of your Web page.	▶ Click the 🔍 Preview in Browser button again to have a look at your Web page in the browser window. Notice how the title you entered appears in the browser's title bar and the heading appears at the top of your Web page.	▶ Click the ✷ Browse button again to have a look at your Web page in the browser window. You may get a message warning you that an external application must be launched. If so, click the Launch Application button.
▶ After you are done looking at your Web page with your Web browser, close the browser window; the Dreamweaver window will reappear.	▶ After you are done looking at your Web page with your Web browser, close the browser window; the FrontPage window will reappear.	▶ When the browser displays your Web page, notice how the title you entered appears in the browser's title bar and the heading appears at the top of your Web page.
▶ If you want to preview your page in more than one brand of Web browser, click the ⊕▾ Preview in Browser button to drop down the menu and choose Edit Browser List to make the Preferences window appear. Click the plus sign to add a browser. If you need more detailed instructions, click the Help button.	▶ You also can preview the page by clicking the Preview tab at the bottom of the FrontPage window; after you are done previewing the page, click the Normal button to return to normal editing. Note, however, that the Preview tab does not contain the full feature set of the browser. You, therefore, should preview the page in the browser occasionally as you are creating the page.	▶ After you are done looking at your Web page with your Web browser, close the browser window; the Nvu window will reappear.
		▶ You also can preview the page by clicking the Preview tab at the bottom of the Nvu window; after you are done previewing the page, click the Normal button to return to normal editing. Note, however, that the Preview tab does not contain the full feature set of the browser. You, therefore, should preview the page in the browser occasionally as you are creating the page.

I am Professor of Instructional Technology at the University of Delaware. My career goal is to help make multimedia easy enough for everyone to become a creator, not just a consumer, of multimedia. Recently, I have been developing a Web-based educational environment called Serf that makes it possible to create, deliver, communicate, and assess multimedia course content over the Web.

Figure 18-16   How I began my résumé.

Table 18-7   How to start a new paragraph

Dreamweaver	FrontPage	Nvu
▶ In the Dreamweaver window, position your cursor at the place you want the new paragraph to start and press Enter. This creates white space that will appear between the two paragraphs.	▶ In the FrontPage window, position your cursor at the place you want the new paragraph to start and press Enter. This creates white space that will appear between the two paragraphs.	▶ In the Nvu window, position your cursor at the place you want the new paragraph to start and press Enter twice. This creates white space that will appear between the two paragraphs.
▶ Now type another paragraph that summarizes what is in your résumé. Figure 18-17 shows how I completed this task.	▶ Now type another paragraph that summarizes what is in your résumé. Figure 18-17 shows how I completed this task.	▶ Now type another paragraph that summarizes what is in your résumé. Figure 18-17 shows how I completed this task.
▶ To inspect your HTML and see the result of typing the first two paragraphs of your résumé, click the Code button or pull down the View menu and choose Code to make the HTML Code window appear. Notice how the **\<p\>** start and **\</p\>** stop tags delimit the paragraphs. The **\<p\>** stands for paragraph, and **\</p\>** is the paragraph stop tag.	▶ To inspect your HTML and see the result of typing the first two paragraphs of your résumé, click the Code button to make the HTML window appear. Notice how the **\<p\>** tag appears at the beginning of each paragraph and the **\</p\>** tag appears at the end. The **\<p\>** stands for paragraph, and **\</p\>** is the paragraph stop tag.	▶ To inspect your HTML and see the result of typing the first two paragraphs of your résumé, click the HTML Source tab or pull down the View menu and choose HTML Source to make the HTML Source window appear. Notice how the **\<br\>** tags appear in between the paragraphs. The **br** stands for break. Each time you press Enter to start a new line on the screen, Nvu enters a **\<br\>** code into your HTML.
▶ Click the Design button, and read on.	▶ Click the Normal tab, and read on.	▶ Click the Normal tab, and read on.

I am Professor of Instructional Technology at the University of Delaware. My career goal is to help make multimedia easy enough for everyone to become a creator, not just a consumer, of multimedia. Recently, I have been developing a Web-based educational environment called Serf that makes it possible to create, deliver, communicate, and assess multimedia course content over the Web.

I have been developing multimedia tools and techniques since 1970. This résumé summarizes my life's work according to the following categories, which you can select to find out more:

Figure 18-17   The first two paragraphs of my résumé.

Creating a List

Now that you have created the two introductory paragraphs of your résumé, it is time to create the bulleted list that will serve as your table of contents. Follow the steps in Table 18-8.

Table 18-8 How to create a bulleted list

Dreamweaver	FrontPage	Nvu
▶ Position your cursor in the Dreamweaver window at the end of your second paragraph and press Enter to move down to the point where you want your résumé's bulleted table of contents to begin.	▶ Position your cursor in the Microsoft Front-Page window at the end of your second paragraph and press Enter to move down to the point where you want your résumé's bulleted table of contents to begin.	▶ Position your cursor in the Nvu window at the end of your second paragraph and press Enter to move down to the point where you want your résumé's bulleted table of contents to begin.
▶ Click the ⊟ Bulleted List button; a bullet appears onscreen. Type the first item in your résumé's table of contents.	▶ Click the ⊟ Bulleted List button; a bullet appears onscreen. Type the first item in your résumé's table of contents.	▶ Click the ⊟ Bulleted List button; a bullet appears onscreen. Type the first item in your résumé's table of contents.
▶ To enter another item into the list, simply press Enter at the end of the first item and type your next list item.	▶ To enter another item into the list, simply press Enter at the end of the first item and type your next list item.	▶ To enter another item into the list, simply press Enter at the end of the first item and type your next list item.
▶ Repeat this process to enter as many items as you want to list right now. You can always add more items to your résumé later on.	▶ Repeat this process to enter as many items as you want to list right now. You can always add more items to your résumé later on.	▶ Repeat this process to enter as many items as you want to list right now. You can always add more items to your résumé later on.
▶ To see how your bulleted list appears in a browser, click the 🌐 Preview in Browser button.	▶ To see how your bulleted list appears in a browser, click the 🔍 Preview in Browser button.	▶ To see how your bulleted list appears in a browser, click the ⚙ Browse button.

Figure 18-18 shows how I typed my list, and Figure 18-19 shows the corresponding HTML code. Take a look at the HTML code for your bulleted list. If you have Dreamweaver or FrontPage, click the Code button. If you are using Nvu, click the HTML Source tab.

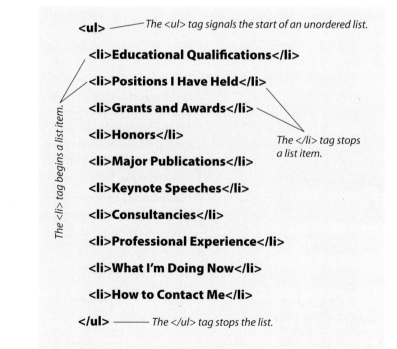

- Educational Qualifications
- Positions I Have Held
- Grants and Awards
- Honors
- Major Publications
- Keynote Speeches
- Consultancies
- Professional Experience
- What I'm Doing Now
- How to Contact Me

Figure 18-18 How I typed my résumé's bulleted table of contents.

Figure 18-19 How the table of contents appears in the HTML code of my résumé.

Undo and Redo

Whenever you make a mistake that you want to undo while editing a document, pull down the Edit menu and choose Undo. If you undo something that you want to redo, pull down the Edit menu and choose Redo.

Microsoft FrontPage has icons for [⤺ ▾] Undo and [⤻ ▾] Redo; FrontPage users can click these icons instead of pulling down the Edit menu.

Horizontal Rules

As you learned in Chapter 16, horizontal rules create neat-looking dividing lines between different parts of a Web page. To insert a horizontal rule after the bulleted table of contents in your résumé, follow the steps in Table 18-9.

It is easy to insert horizontal rules in your documents, and the dividing lines look nice. However, do not give in to the temptation to overuse them! Horizontal rules are best used to separate major sections of your document.

Table 18-9 How to insert a horizontal rule

Dreamweaver	FrontPage	Nvu
▶ In the Dreamweaver window, position your cursor at the end of the list. Press Enter as if you were going to enter another list item.	▶ In the FrontPage window, position your cursor at the end of the list. Press Enter as if you were going to enter another list item.	▶ In the Nvu window, position your cursor at the end of the list. Press Enter as if you were going to enter another list item.
▶ Press Enter again. This ends the list, and puts you into normal text entry mode.	▶ Press Enter again, or pull down the Styles menu and choose Normal. This ends the list and puts you into normal text entry mode.	▶ Press Enter again. This ends the list and puts you into normal text entry mode.
▶ Pull down the Insert menu and choose HTML→Horizontal Rule; the line will appear highlighted on your page. The highlighting means that the line is selected.	▶ Pull down the Insert menu and choose Horizontal Line; the line will appear on your page.	▶ Pull down the Insert menu and choose Horizontal Line; the line will appear on your page.
▶ While the line is selected, you can change the properties of the line by changing the settings in its Properties window, as shown in Figure 18-20. I recommend you choose the Shading option, unless you prefer a plain line instead.	▶ You can change the properties of the line if you want by double-clicking on the line after you enter it; this makes the Horizontal Line Properties dialog appear, as shown in Figure 18-21. The author recommends the default settings, which create a 3D effect.	▶ You can change the properties of the line if you want by double-clicking on the line after you enter it; this makes the Horizontal Line Properties dialog appear, as shown in Figure 18-22. *Note:* If you have trouble double-clicking the line because it is so thin, click the HTML Tags button, then double-click the HR tag. HR stands for horizontal rule.
▶ To see how the line appears onscreen, click outside it to deselect it. If you want to change its properties again, click the line to select it. Notice that the Properties window displays the settings of the object you have selected.	▶ To see how the horizontal line will appear on the Web, click the [icon] Preview in Browser button.	▶ The author recommends you choose the 3-D Shading option, unless you prefer a plain line instead.
▶ To see how the horizontal line will appear on the Web, click the [icon] Preview in Browser button.	▶ To see how the line got inserted in your HTML, click the Code button to make the HTML code window appear. There you will find the **\<hr>** code, which stands for horizontal rule.	▶ To see how the horizontal line will appear on the Web, click the [icon] Browse button.
▶ To see how the line got inserted in your HTML, click the Code button to make the HTML window appear. There you will find the **\<hr>** code, which stands for horizontal rule.	▶ Click the Design button, and read on.	▶ To see how the line got inserted in your HTML, click the HTML Source tab to make the HTML window appear. There you will find the **\<hr>** code, which stands for horizontal rule.
▶ Click the Design button, and read on.		▶ Click the Normal tab, and read on.

Width controls the length of the line.

Width controls the length of the line.

Height controls the thickness of the line.

Height controls the thickness of the line.

Width controls the length of the line.

Check the Shading option for a special effect.

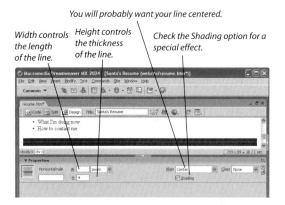

Figure 18-20 Dreamweaver displays the properties of the horizontal rule when the rule is selected.

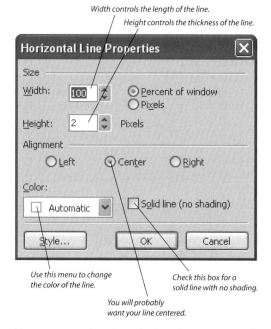

Use this menu to change the color of the line.

Check this box for a solid line with no shading.

You will probably want your line centered.

Figure 18-21 FrontPage displays the properties of the horizontal rule when you double-click the rule.

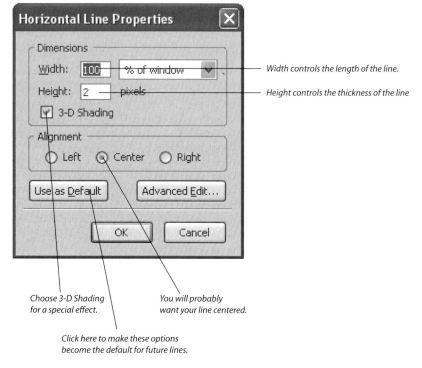

Width controls the length of the line.

Height controls the thickness of the line

Choose 3-D Shading for a special effect.

You will probably want your line centered.

Click here to make these options become the default for future lines.

Figure 18-22 Nvu displays the properties of the horizontal rule when you double-click the rule.

Remember to Save the File

Remember to save your HTML file periodically to prevent accidental loss due to power failures or other accidents. To save the file, click the Save button or pull down the File menu and choose Save.

Inserting a New Heading

Every main section of your résumé should begin with a large-sized heading that identifies what that section is. It is common for Web pages to have a title displayed in the largest-sized heading, **<h1>**, and then use the next smaller size, **<h2>**, for subheads. For example, when you enter the educational qualifications section of your résumé, follow these steps to give it a heading:

- Position your cursor at the start of the education section of your résumé. This location will probably be right after the horizontal line you just inserted.

- Press Enter once or twice to create a little space after the line.

- Type the heading, which in this example will be **Educational Qualifications**

- Pull down the Style menu and choose Heading 2.

To begin a new paragraph after the heading, position your cursor at the end of the heading, press Enter, and begin typing.

Creating Named Anchor Bookmarks

As you create the different sections in your résumé, it will grow too long to fit on the screen all at once. To make it easy for the user to find the different parts of your résumé, you can insert bookmarks known as *named anchors* into your document. Then you can link each item in your résumé's bulleted list of topics to its corresponding bookmark to make it quick and easy for the user to find that section. To create a named anchor bookmark, follow the steps in Table 18-10.

Linking to Named Anchor Bookmarks

Now that you have created a named anchor bookmark, it is time to create a link to the bookmark. When clicked, the link will enable the user to jump quickly to the bookmarked section of your résumé. To create a link to a named anchor bookmark, follow the steps in Table 18-11.

In the HTML window, you will see how the Link tool inserted the following HTML into your document:

<a href="#education">Educational Qualifications</a>

In this code, **a** stands for anchor and **href** stands for hypertext reference. The word in quotes (**#education**) is the name of the bookmark. In HTML hypertext references, bookmark anchor names are always preceded by a pound sign (#).

Now you should test the link. View your résumé with your Web browser. Click on the words *Educational Qualifications* in your résumé. If your browser jumped to the Educational Qualifications section of your résumé, congratulations! If not, repeat these steps, compare your HTML to the samples shown here, and keep trying until you get the bookmark link to work.

Returning to the Table of Contents

Web pages that use named anchor bookmarks often provide a way for the user to return to the table of contents. This return-to-contents capability is created with another named anchor. First, you create a named anchor bookmark at the start of the bulleted list to which

Table 18-10 How to create a named anchor bookmark on a Web page

Dreamweaver	FrontPage	Nvu
▲ To create a bookmark, use the mouse to position your cursor at the spot in the Dreamweaver window where you want the bookmark to be. In this example, position your cursor at the start of the Education section in your document window.	▲ To create a bookmark, use the mouse to position your cursor at the spot in the FrontPage window where you want the bookmark to be. In this example, position your cursor at the start of the Education section in your FrontPage window.	▲ To create a bookmark, use the mouse to position your cursor at the spot in the Nvu window where you want the bookmark to be. In this example, position your cursor at the start of the Education section in your Nvu window.
▲ Click the ![] Named Anchor button, or pull down the Insert menu and choose Named Anchor; the Named Anchor Properties dialog appears.	▲ Pull down the Insert menu and choose Bookmark; the Bookmark dialog appears.	▲ Click the ![] Anchor button, or pull down the Insert menu and choose Named Anchor; the Named Anchor Properties dialog appears, as shown in Figure 18-25.
▲ In the Anchor Name field, type **education**, as shown in Figure 18-23.	▲ In the Bookmark Name field, type **education**, as shown in Figure 18-24.	▲ In the Anchor Name field, type **education**, as shown in Figure 18-25.

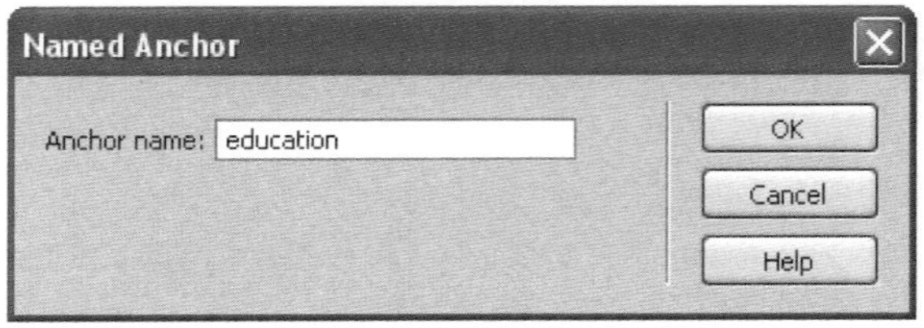

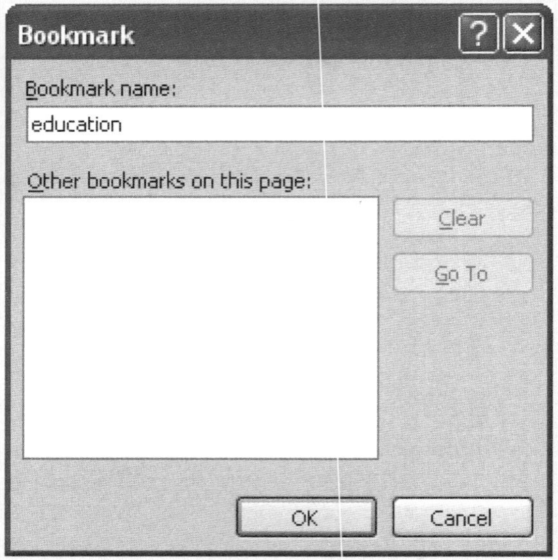

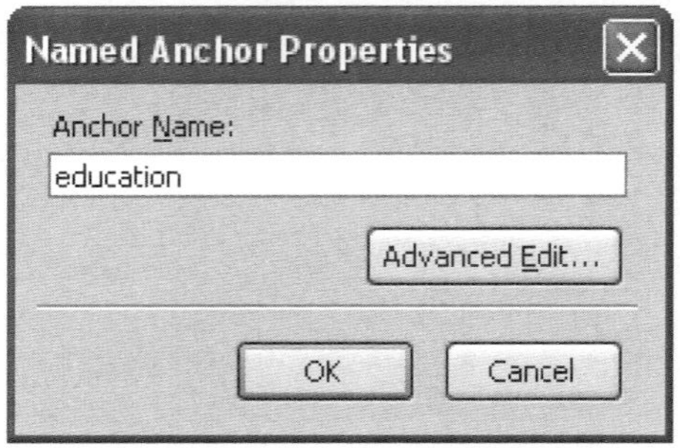

Figure 18-23 Creating the education bookmark in Dreamweaver's Named Anchor dialog.

Figure 18-24 Creating the education bookmark in the FrontPage Bookmark dialog.

Figure 18-25 Creating the education bookmark in the Nvu Named Anchor Properties dialog.

▲ Click OK; the named anchor for the bookmark appears in your document.

▲ Click OK; the bookmark appears in your document.

▲ Click OK; the named anchor for the bookmark appears in your document.

▲ To see how the bookmark got inserted in your HTML, click the Code button. In the HTML Code window, you will see the **<a name="education"></a>** tags that create the bookmark in HTML. The word in quotes is the name of the anchor.

▲ To see how the bookmark got inserted in your HTML, click the Code button. In the HTML Code window, you will see the **<a name="education"></a>** tags that create the bookmark in HTML. The word in quotes is the name of the anchor.

▲ To see how the bookmark got inserted in your HTML, click the HTML Source tab. In the HTML Source window, you will see the **<a name="education"></a>** tags that create the bookmark in HTML. The word in quotes is the name of the anchor.

▲ Click the Design button, and read on.

▲ Click the Design button, and read on.

▲ Click the Normal tab, and read on.

Table 18-11   How to create a link to a named anchor bookmark

Dreamweaver	FrontPage	Nvu
▶ Use the mouse to highlight the text that you want to trigger the link; in this example, position the cursor in your bulleted list right before *Educational Qualifications* and drag your mouse over the words *Educational Qualifications* to select them.	▶ Use the mouse to highlight the text that you want to trigger the link; in this example, position the cursor in your bulleted list right before *Educational Qualifications* and drag your mouse over the words *Educational Qualifications* to select them.	▶ Use the mouse to highlight the text that you want to trigger the link; in this example, position the cursor in your bulleted list right before *Educational Qualifications* and drag your mouse over the words *Educational Qualifications* to select them.
▶ Click the [icon] Hyperlink button; the Link Properties dialog appears.	▶ Click the [icon] Insert Hyperlink button; the Insert Hyperlink dialog appears.	▶ Click the [icon] Insert Link button; the Link Properties dialog appears.
▶ Pull down the Link menu to reveal the named anchors.	▶ Click the Bookmark button at the right side of the dialog to bring up the Select Place in Document dialog.	▶ Click the down-arrow at the right edge of the Link Location field to pull down the menu of choices.
▶ Select the named anchor bookmark you want, which in this example is *education*.	▶ Select the bookmark you want, which in this example is *education*, then click OK to close the Select Place in Document dialog.	▶ Select the named anchor bookmark you want, which in this example is *education*.
▶ Click OK to complete the link.		▶ Click OK to complete the link.
▶ To see how your résumé will appear on the Web, click the [icon] Preview in Browser button. Now the words *Educational Qualifications* should appear in color in your résumé's bulleted table of contents. The coloration denotes hypertext; clicking the colored text will trigger the link.	▶ To complete the link, click OK to close the Insert Hyperlink dialog.	▶ To see how your résumé will appear on the Web, click the [icon] Browse button. Now the words *Educational Qualifications* should appear in color in your résumé's bulleted table of contents. The coloration denotes hypertext; clicking the colored text will trigger the link.
▶ To see how the link got inserted in your HTML code, click Dreamweaver's Code button.	▶ To see how your résumé will appear on the Web, click the [icon] Preview in Browser button. Now the words *Educational Qualifications* should appear in color in your résumé's bulleted table of contents. The coloration denotes hypertext; clicking the colored text will trigger the link.	▶ To see how the link got inserted in your HTML, click the Nvu HTML Source tab.
	▶ To see how the link got inserted in your HTML, click the FrontPage Code button.	

you want the user to return; then you create a return link to that bookmark at the end of each section in your document.

To create a return-to-contents link in the Education section of your résumé, follow the steps in Table 18-12.

Test the link to make sure it works. Clicking on *Educational Qualifications* in the bulleted table of contents should jump to the education section of your résumé. At the end of that section, clicking on *Résumé Contents* should return you to the list of contents.

Linking to Other Pages

There are more than a billion documents on the World Wide Web. You can link your résumé to any document for which you know the URL. For example, if the place where you work or go to school has a home page, you might want to provide a way for the user to navigate there. Follow the steps in Table 18-13.

Table 18-12   Creating a return-to-contents link

Dreamweaver	FrontPage	Nvu
▶ Position the cursor in your Dreamweaver window at the start of the bulleted table of contents in your résumé.	▶ Position the cursor in your FrontPage window at the start of the bulleted table of contents in your résumé.	▶ Position the cursor in your Nvu window at the start of the bulleted table of contents in your résumé.
▶ Create a named anchor bookmark called *contents*—try to do this on your own, but if you need help, follow these steps: ■ Click the 🔱 Named Anchor button, or pull down the Insert menu and choose Named Anchor; the Named Anchor Properties dialog appears. ■ In the Anchor Name field, type **contents** ■ Click OK; the named anchor for the bookmark appears in your document.	▶ Create a named anchor bookmark called *contents*—try to do this on your own, but if you need help, follow these steps: ■ Pull down the Insert menu and choose Bookmark; the Bookmark dialog appears. ■ In the Bookmark Name field, type **contents** ■ Click OK; the named anchor bookmark appears in your document.	▶ Create a named anchor bookmark called *contents*—try to do this on your own, but if you need help, follow these steps: ■ Click the Ⓛ Anchor button, or pull down the Insert menu and choose Named Anchor; the Named Anchor Properties dialog appears. ■ In the Anchor Name field, type **contents** ■ Click OK; the named anchor for the bookmark appears in your document.
▶ Position your cursor at the end of the Educational Qualifications section of your résumé. Insert a new paragraph that contains the text *Résumé Contents*.	▶ Position your cursor at the end of the Educational Qualifications section of your résumé. Insert a new paragraph that contains the text *Résumé Contents*.	▶ Position your cursor at the end of the Educational Qualifications section of your résumé. Insert a new paragraph that contains the text *Résumé Contents*.
▶ Link the words *Résumé Contents* to the *contents* bookmark—try to do this on your own, but if you need help, follow these steps: ■ Drag your mouse over the words *Résumé Contents* to select them. ■ Click the 🖉 Hyperlink button; the Link Properties dialog appears. ■ Pull down the Link menu to reveal the named anchors. ■ Select the named anchor bookmark you want, which in this example is *contents*. ■ Click OK to complete the link.	▶ Link the words *Résumé Contents* to the *contents* bookmark—try to do this on your own, but if you need help, follow these steps: ■ Drag your mouse over the words *Résumé Contents* to select them. ■ Click the 🖳 Insert Hyperlink button; the Create Hyperlink dialog appears. ■ Click the Bookmark button at the right side of the dialog to bring up the Select Place in Document dialog. ■ Select the bookmark you want, which in this example is *contents*. ■ Click OK to complete the link.	▶ Link the words *Résumé Contents* to the *contents* bookmark—try to do this on your own, but if you need help, follow these steps: ■ Drag your mouse over the words *Résumé Contents* to select them. ■ Click the 🖉 Insert Link button; the Link Properties dialog appears. ■ Click the down-arrow at the right edge of the Link Location field to pull down the menu of choices. ■ Select the named anchor bookmark you want, which in this example is *contents*. ■ Click OK to complete the link.
▶ Click the 🌐▾ Preview in Browser button to see how your résumé will appear on the Web.	▶ Click the 🔍 Preview in Browser button to see how your résumé will appear on the Web.	▶ Click the ⚙ Browse button to see how your résumé will appear on the Web.

Table 18-13   How to create a link to a URL

Dreamweaver	FrontPage	Nvu
▶ In your Dreamweaver window, drag your mouse to select the text that you want to link to some other Web page.	▶ In your FrontPage window, drag your mouse to select the text that you want to link to some other Web page.	▶ In your Nvu window, drag your mouse to select the text that you want to link to some other Web page.
▶ Click the 🖉 Hyperlink button; the Link Properties dialog appears.	▶ Click the 🖳 Insert Hyperlink button; the Create Hyperlink dialog appears.	▶ Click the 🖉 Insert Link button; the Link Properties dialog appears.
▶ In the Link field, type the URL to which you want to link; for example, to link to the White House, you would type **http://www.whitehouse.gov**	▶ In the Address field, type the URL to which you want to link; for example, to link to the White House, you would type **http://www.whitehouse.gov**	▶ In the Link Location field, type the URL to which you want to link; for example, to link to the White House, you would type **http://www.whitehouse.gov**
▶ Click OK to complete the link.	▶ Click OK to complete the link.	▶ Click OK to complete the link.

Identifying the Web Page Owner

Netiquette calls for Web pages to end with a few lines of text indicating who owns the page and how to contact the owner. To identify yourself as the owner of your Web page, follow these steps:

- Position the cursor in your Dreamweaver, FrontPage, or Nvu window at the bottom of the document.

- Press ⌈Enter⌉ once or twice to create a little white space.

- Type the following words: **This web page is owned by** *[type your name here].* **My e-mail address is** *[type your e-mail address here].*

Mailto Links

It is customary for Web page owners to include a *mailto link* to their e-mail address to make it easy for you to contact them. When you click such a link, an e-mail window appears, automatically addressed to the Web page owner. For example, consider the Web page owner statement you put at the bottom of your résumé page. Your e-mail address appears there. To provide a mailto link to your e-mail address, follow the steps in Table 18-14.

Character Attributes on Web Pages versus Word Processors

Because the tools in the WYSIWYG Web-page editor look so much like the tools in your word processor, no chapter on Web page creation would be complete without mentioning some caveats regarding things that you commonly do with a word processor but should not do with a Web page editor.

Underlining

In a word-processed document, it is common to underline titles and terms for emphasis. On the Web, underlining normally means that the underlined text is linked as a hypertext. If you want to emphasize something on the Web, therefore, use bolding or italics instead of underlining. To bold or italicize text with your Web page editor, simply drag your mouse over the text to select it, then click the bold button or the italics button. To remove the bolding or italics, drag your mouse over the text to select it again, then click the bold or italics button.

Table 18-14   How to create a mailto link

Dreamweaver	FrontPage	Nvu
▶ In your Dreamweaver window, drag the mouse over your e-mail address to select it.	▶ In your FrontPage window, drag the mouse over your e-mail address to select it.	▶ In your Nvu window, drag the mouse over your e-mail address to select it.
▶ Click the 🖾 Hyperlink button; the Link Properties dialog appears.	▶ Click the 🖾 Insert Hyperlink button; the Create Hyperlink dialog appears.	▶ Click the ⊘ Insert Link button; the Link Properties dialog appears.
▶ In the Link field, type the mailto address to which you want to link; for example, if your e-mail address is SantaClaus@northpole.com, type **mailto:SantaClaus@northpole.com**	▶ In the Address field, type the mailto address to which you want to link; for example, if your e-mail address is SantaClaus@northpole.com, type **mailto:SantaClaus@northpole.com**	▶ In the Link Location field, type the mailto address to which you want to link; for example, if your e-mail address is SantaClaus@northpole.com, type **mailto:SantaClaus@northpole.com**
▶ Click OK to complete the link.	▶ Click OK to complete the link.	▶ Click OK to complete the link.

Another way to emphasize text is to make it larger. To adjust the text size, drag your mouse over the text to select it, then pull down the font size menu and choose the size you want.

Avoid the Pagination Temptation

In a word processor, you can press Enter repeatedly to add white space to arrange the text to fit the size of the printed page. A common mistake beginners make is to try to do the same thing on a Web page. It does not work because there is no guarantee that the user's screen size or window size will fit the one for which you developed your page.

Resist the temptation to press the Enter key repeatedly to add white space in an attempt to create pagination on a Web page. If you really want a new page, create a new Web page and link to it from a hypertext link or a navigational icon. You will learn how to link pages together in Chapter 21. If you really want to control spacing on the screen, the best way to do that is with a table. You will learn how to make tables in Chapter 20.

exercises

1. This chapter got you started creating your Web page résumé. Now you should complete your résumé by adding all the sections you sketched when you designed your résumé at the start of this tutorial. If you have any trouble, refer back to the step-by-step instructions in this chapter for creating new paragraphs, headings, list items, and horizontal rules.

2. Each item in your bulleted table of contents should be linked to its corresponding section in your résumé. Insert named anchor bookmarks at the beginning of each new section in your résumé. Then link each item in your table of contents to the corresponding bookmark in your résumé. Test the links to make sure they work.

3. At the end of each section in your résumé, provide a way for the user to return to your table of contents.

SITUATED CASE PROJECTS
Case 18: Designing a Portfolio

At the end of each chapter in this book, a situated case project provides the student an opportunity to put the chapter's contents to practical use in a workplace situation. Each case has the same number as the chapter in which it appears.

A **portfolio** is a collection of artifacts that document or chronicle the creative works or demonstrable capabilities of a working professional or student aspiring to gain employment in the workplace. If this definition seems broad, that is because almost everyone can benefit from having an online portfolio. In the field of education, for example, accrediting agencies require teacher education majors to keep a collection of artifacts demonstrating different aspects of the aspiring teacher's skills, techniques, experiences, and teaching competencies. Several states require that education majors keep these portfolios online. No matter what line of work you are in, having a well-presented online portfolio of your accomplishments can help when you come up for annual evaluations or when you seek another job. Imagine that your employer has asked you to design a portfolio template for use by your co-workers. To create such a design, follow these steps:

1 Use your word processor to create an outline of the kinds of information that you feel should be collected or contained in a portfolio in your profession.

2 Think about how this information can best be presented online. Try to envision how you can organize it into a set of Web pages that link to each other and make it easy for the user to navigate through the portfolio. The *Interlit* Web site links to a variety of online portfolios. Follow these links to see examples of online portfolios.

3 Each portfolio must have a start page. The start page normally provides demographic information such as the person's name, school or company, and e-mail address. Depending on the nature of your workplace, you may want the person's picture to appear on this page. Type or move to the top of the outline the items that you think should be on the start page.

4 One of the most powerful aspects of an online portfolio is how it can include digitized pictures, audio recordings, and videos of the candidate's artifacts. Make sure your outline includes the kinds of multimedia artifacts typical of portfolios in your field.

5 Portfolios are almost always too large to fit on one page. Instead, there will be a start page that provides links to auxiliary pages representing different categories in the portfolio. Each of these auxiliary pages can link to more subcategory pages. Eventually the links will lead to the artifacts themselves. There are many ways to design such a structure. Be creative, but stay organized. You want to design the portfolio structure so the user will be able to navigate intuitively up and down the various categories and subcategories of the portfolio. Modify your outline so it shows the structure of the categories and subcategories that will be in the portfolio.

6 Underneath your outline of portfolio content, write a brief paragraph describing how the user will navigate from page to page. Remember that you should adopt a navigational scheme that is intuitive and works the same from page to page. The sample portfolios you visited in step (2) provide some examples. Also consider the design of the *Interlit* Web site, which has quick links at the top to items on the page, and navigation buttons at the bottom of each page to take you to the next page, the previous page, the contents of the current page, or the table of contents.

If your instructor has asked you to hand in this assignment, make sure you put your name at the top, then save your portfolio template plan on disk or follow the other instructions you may have been given for submitting this assignment.

19

PUTTING IMAGES ON WEB PAGES

After completing this chapter, you will be able to:

- Download the shareware version of Paint Shop Pro for Windows or Graphic Converter for the Macintosh.

- Capture screens and import images from any software application or from the Web.

- Convert images into a file format suitable for display on Web pages.

- Resize images to fit the layout of a Web page.

- Adjust colors for optimum display performance on Web pages.

- Understand the concept of a transparent GIF.

- Know how to download a utility for creating animated GIFs.

- Paste an image onto a Web page.

- Tile an image onto a Web page.

- Find clip art libraries of banners, icons, tiles, and buttons designed for use on a Web page.

It has often been said that a picture is worth a thousand words. The ease with which you can paste pictures onto Web pages makes it possible to illustrate documents and use images as design elements in the layout of a Web page. Before you can paste a picture onto a Web page, however, you must get it into the proper format for display on a Web page. This chapter provides you with a utility that makes it easy to get images into the proper format. Then you will learn not only how to paste pictures onto Web pages, but also how to create special effects with techniques known as *tiling* and *watermarking*.

Obtaining Images to Use on a Web Page

Canon | Olympus | Sony

Suppose you want to paste your picture onto your Web page résumé, so prospective employers can see what you look like. Before you can paste an image onto your Web page, you need to get the image into a digital format. The simplest way to do this is to have someone take your picture with a digital camera, which creates a bitmap that can be downloaded from the camera to your PC. Canon, Kodak, Olympus, and Sony are just a few of the companies that make digital cameras. To find out what digital cameras are available and how their features compare, follow the *Interlit* Web site links to Digital Cameras.

Kodak | Eckerd Drugs

If you take a picture with a film camera, on the other hand, you will need to have the picture digitized before you can put it on a Web page. Many photo shops, such as Kodak, and mass-market retail stores, such as Eckerd Drugs, give you the option of having a floppy disk or a CD returned along with your prints when you have a roll of film developed. Eckerd Drugs, for example, charges $5.99 extra to get a Kodak Picture CD containing a JPEG digital image of each picture on the film. For more information, follow the *Interlit* Web site links to Eckerd Drugs.

If you have a printed photo that you want to put on a Web page, you can use a scanner to digitize the image. Scanners have dropped in price so much that they have become mass-market consumer items. Sometimes you get a scanner for free when you purchase a new computer. Scanners come with software to digitize printed photographs you can put on Web pages.

On the other hand, if you prefer not to include your picture on your résumé, you may want to enhance the résumé's appearance by including some other graphics. There are many clip-art libraries from which you can download other kinds of graphics by following the procedure you learned for downloading images in Chapter 13. To inspect these graphics, follow the *Interlit* Web site links to clip art.

Preparing Images for a Web Page

Before you can paste an image onto a Web page, you need to ask yourself the following questions:

- Is the image in the correct format for pasting onto a Web page? Images must be in either the GIF or JPEG file format. If the image is not in the correct format, you must convert it into the proper file format:

  ▶ Use the GIF format if the image has 256 colors or less, or if you can live with reducing the color depth of a more fully colored image to 256 colors.

  ▶ Use the JPEG file format if your image has more than 256 colors and you need true color.

  ▶ Use the GIF format if you need one of the colors in the image to be transparent. On Web pages, for example, you will sometimes want the background of the image to be transparent so it can overlay or float on the page.

- Is the image the proper size for your Web page layout? Images that are too large need to be reduced in size with a graphics editor. Many people think they can skip this step and just resize the image with their Web editing software. This does not change the size of the file, however, and the quality will not be as good as when you resize an image with a graphics editor. This is because the browser is told to show the still-large file at a smaller size, but the browser is not as good at resizing images as the graphics editor. If you need to resize an image, therefore, you should do it with a graphics editor. As an added bonus, the smaller file size will save on bandwidth and make the page appear sooner. *Note:* If you have Dreamweaver and you change the size of an image by dragging its handles, the resample icon becomes active. If you click this icon, Dreamweaver will resample the image after warning you this will change the size of the file itself.

- What is the color format of the image? If the image is in 24-bit format (16 million colors), you may want to reduce it to an 8-bit color format (256 colors), which will greatly reduce its file size. Remember that the larger the file size of the image, the longer it will take to download from the Internet.

Happily, there are graphics programs that enable you to do all these things easily on either a Windows or Macintosh computer. In this chapter, you will learn how to use Paint Shop Pro for Windows or Graphic Converter for the Macintosh. Both programs enable you to prepare images to put on your Web pages. In addition to resizing images, you can grab part of an image instead of using the whole picture. You can reduce the number of colors to save disk space and make an image load more quickly over the Internet. You can even apply special effects to the image, such as emboss, chisel, bevel, weave, sharpen, or soften it. More high-end graphics programs that also do these things include Fireworks and PhotoShop. To learn more about graphics tool choices, follow the *Interlit* Web site links to recommended graphics editors.

Paint Shop Pro (for Windows)

Paint Shop Pro is a Windows program for image capture, creation, viewing, and manipulation. Features include painting, photo retouching, image enhancement and editing, color enhancement, graphics format conversion, and color scanner support. More than 30 image file formats are supported, including GIF, JPEG, TIFF, Kodak PhotoCD, BMP, and PNG. You can even browse images on your computer; Figure 19-1 shows how the images appear as thumbnails, which you can double-click to view full-screen.

There is an evaluation version of Paint Shop Pro that you can try out before you buy. You can download it from the Web by following the *Interlit* Web site link to Paint Shop Pro. If you keep using the software for more than 60 days, you must pay the license fee, or the evaluation copy will expire.

The first time you run Paint Shop Pro, you must set up the hot key that you will use to capture graphics. Follow these steps:

- Double-click the ⬤ Paint Shop Pro icon to get Paint Shop Pro running.

- Pull down the File menu and choose Import→Screen Capture→Setup.

Moving your cursor over an image reveals its properties.

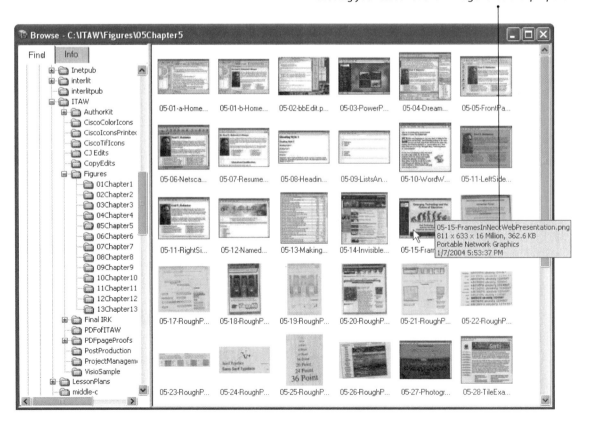

Figure 19-1　Paint Shop Pro contains an image browser and many powerful graphics tools.

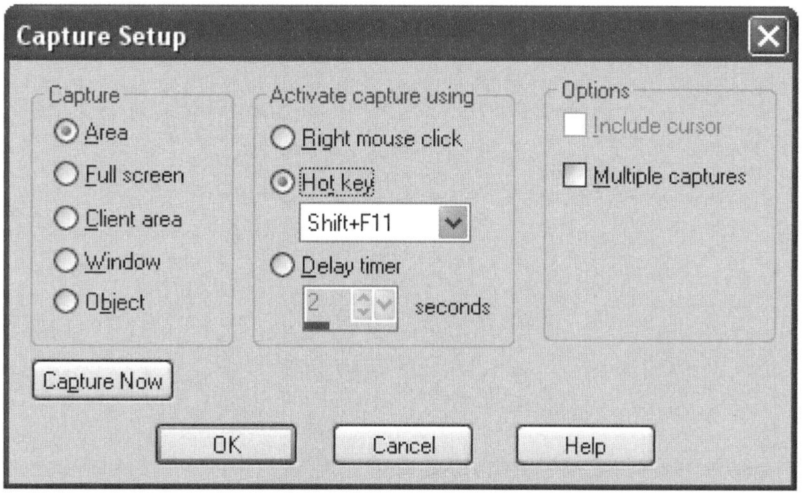

Figure 19-2 The Paint Shop Pro Capture Setup dialog.

- The Capture Setup dialog appears as shown in Figure 19-2.

- Notice how the Capture group lets you set up to capture an area, the full screen, the client area of the current window, the entire current window, or an object. Set it to capture an area.

- In the Activate Capture group, click the option to activate via Hot Key and set the hot key to something you never use in any other application; the author recommends you set the hot key to Shift-F11, which is the hot key this tutorial will use.

- Click OK to close the dialog.

Graphic Converter (for Macintosh)

Macintosh users can do all of the things covered in this chapter with a program called Graphic Converter. It is **shareware,** which means you can try it out before you buy it. To install Graphic Converter, follow these steps:

- Follow the *Interlit* Web site link to Graphic Converter.

- Click the Download option.

- Download the version appropriate for your computer (for most readers, this is the U.S. version, which is in English).

- The download manager will transfer the program to your computer. If the download manager asks you what to do with the file, save it to the desktop.

- When the download is finished, there will be a Graphic Converter DMG icon on your desktop. Double-click the Graphic Converter icon.

- Drag the Graphic Converter program to your Applications folder. To put a quick launch icon on your Dock, drag the  Graphic Converter icon from the Applications folder to the Dock.

- To save disk space, at your option, you may drag the Graphic Converter installation file from your desktop into your trash can. Control-click the trash can and choose Empty Trash to free the disk space.

- Any time you want to start Graphic Converter, simply double-click its icon on your dock.

Capturing Images

A basic skill important to all Web page developers is the ability to capture an image, or part of an image, and save it on the hard drive. You have already learned that if the graphic is on a Web page, and if you are capturing the entire graphic, you can right-click (Windows) or control-click (Macintosh) the graphic and choose Save As to download it onto your hard drive. There are times, however, when downloading will not work. You may want to capture only part of the image, for example, or the image might be in an application that does not support the Save As method of downloading. When the Save As method does not work or will not do what you want, follow the steps in Table 19-1 to capture the image.

Table 19-1 Capturing images to put on a Web page

Windows	Macintosh
▶ Get the program running from which you want to capture a graphic. For example, suppose you want to capture my smiling face. Get your Web browser running and go to www.udel.edu/fth, where my photo appears on my Web page.	▶ Get the program running from which you want to capture a graphic. For example, suppose you want to capture my smiling face. Get your Web browser running and go to www.udel.edu/fth where my photo appears on my Web page.
▶ Get Paint Shop Pro running, if it is not running already.	▶ To capture a rectangular area of an image, press ⌘-Shift-4 and your cursor will change into a crosshair, indicating it is ready to capture something.
▶ Hold down the Alt key and keep pressing Tab until Paint Shop Pro appears. Alt-Tab is a special Windows key for switching among programs running simultaneously on your computer.	
▶ Press Shift-C or pull down Paint Shop Pro's File menu and select Import→Screen Capture→Start; immediately, Paint Shop Pro will disappear.	▶ Drag the crosshair over the area you want to capture. As you drag, a rectangle expands or contracts to show what will be captured when you release the mouse button.
▶ If the image you want to capture is not visible on your screen, hold down Alt and keep pressing Tab until the screen you want to capture appears.	▶ When you release the mouse button, you will hear a clicking sound, indicating that you just grabbed an image.
	▶ Get Graphic Converter running, if it is not running already.
▶ Press the capture hot key (Shift-F11); the cursor turns into a crosshair.	▶ Pull down the File menu and choose Open.
▶ Click on the upper-left corner of the area of the screen you want to capture, and then click the lower-right corner to complete the capture. In this example, you want to click first on the upper-left corner of my smiling face, then click on the lower-right corner.	▶ When the Open dialog appears, use it to look on your desktop for the image you just captured; the image will be called something like Picture 1 or Picture 2, depending on how many images you have captured so far. Double-click the name of the image to open it.
▶ The captured image will now appear in the Paint Shop Pro window. To save the image, pull down the File menu and choose Save As.	▶ The captured image will now appear in the GraphicConverter window. To save the image, pull down the File menu and choose Save As.
▶ In the Save as Type box, select the image format in which you want to save the image. In this example, select CompuServe Graphics Interchange (GIF).	▶ Use the Format menu to select the image format in which you want to save the image. In this example, select GIF.
▶ In the File Name field, type the name you want the image to have. In this example, type **fred**. You do not need to type a filename extension, because Paint Shop Pro will supply one automatically, based on the file type you set in the List Files of Type box.	▶ In the Save As field, type the name you want the image to have. In this example, type **fred.gif**. *Important:* Make sure the filename extension matches the type of file you selected via the Format menu.
▶ Click the Save button to save the file, then pull down the File menu and choose Exit to leave Paint Shop Pro.	▶ Click the Save button to save the file, then pull down the Graphic-Converter menu and choose Quit GraphicConverter.
Note: To capture the full screen or the contents of a window, pull down the File menu, choose Import→Screen Capture→Setup, and set the Capture option accordingly.	▶ If you have OS X, there is a system application called Grab that you can also use to capture windows, regions, or the full screen. Use the Finder to find Grab, then double-click the Grab icon to launch it. Pull down the Help menu and read Grab Help to learn how to use Grab.
	Note: In addition to the ⌘-Shift-4 command that captures a rectangular region of an image, you also can use ⌘-Shift-3 to capture the entire screen or ⌘-Shift-CapsLock-4 to capture the contents of a window.

Converting Images

It is easy to convert images into the proper format for pasting onto Web pages. As noted earlier, the best formats to use are *.gif* if the image has 256 colors or less or *.jpg* for images with up to 16 million colors. To convert an image from one file format into another, follow the steps in Table 19-2.

It is important that when you save the file, you save it in the same folder as the Web page for which it is intended. In this case, if you are making an image for your Web page résumé, save the converted image in your *website* folder. This will simplify the publication process when you transfer your files to the Web in Chapter 22.

Resizing Images

Images may be the wrong size for placement on your Web page. For example, the photo of the author that appears on his Web page résumé was a 640 × 480 image. This would have covered way too much screen space, spoiling the layout of the résumé. Although you can make the image appear smaller by dragging its handles with your Web page editor, this

Table 19-2   How to convert images into the proper format for pasting onto Web pages

Paint Shop Pro (Windows)	Graphic Converter (Macintosh)
▶ Pull down the Paint Shop Pro File menu and choose Open; the Open dialog appears.	▶ Pull down the Graphic Converter File menu and choose Open; the Select a File dialog appears.
▶ In the List Files of Type field, pull down the choices and select the file format of your original image.	▶ Select the image file you want to convert.
▶ Browse to the image and click OK to open it; the image will appear on screen.	▶ Pull down the File menu and choose Save As; the Save As dialog appears as shown in Figure 19-4.
▶ To convert the image, pull down the File menu and choose Save As; the Save As dialog appears as shown in Figure 19-3.	

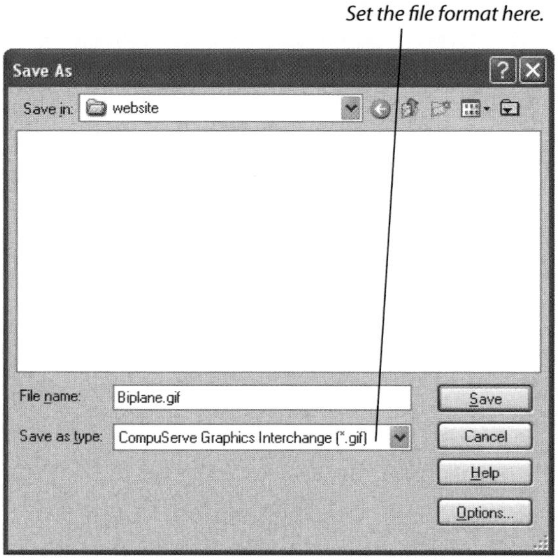

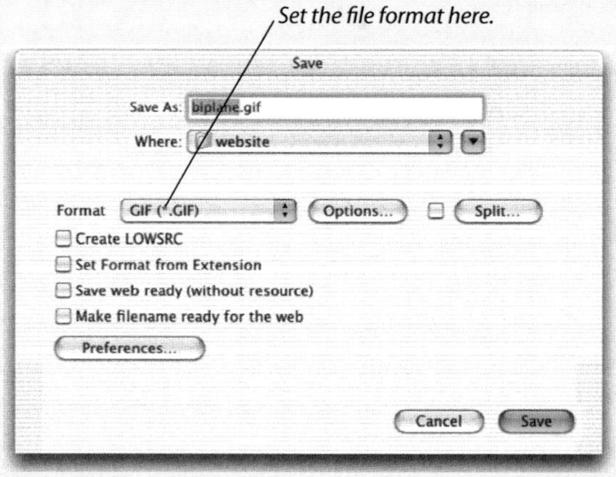

Set the file format here.

Figure 19-4   The Graphic Converter Save As dialog.

▶ In the Save As dialog, pull down the Format menu and choose the format you want (either GIF or JPEG).

▶ Click the Save button to save the file in the folder of your choice (probably your *website* folder).

Set the file format here.

Figure 19-3   The Paint Shop Pro Save As dialog.

▶ In the Save as type field, pull down the choices and select either GIF or JPG.

▶ Save the file in the folder of your choice (probably your *website* folder).

▶ Make sure the name you give the image has the same filename extension as the file format you selected (GIF or JPG).

Table 19-3   How to resize images

Paint Shop Pro (Windows)	Graphic Converter (Macintosh)
▶ Pull down the Paint Shop Pro File menu and choose Open; the Open dialog appears.	▶ Pull down the Graphic Converter File menu and choose Open; the Select a File dialog appears.
▶ In the List Files of Type field, pull down the choices and select the file format of your original image.	▶ Select the image file you want to resize.
▶ Browse to the image and click OK to open it; the image will appear onscreen.	▶ Pull down the Picture menu and choose Size, then Scale; the Scale dialog appears as shown in Figure 19-6.
▶ To resize the image, pull down the Image menu and choose Resize; the Resize dialog appears as shown in Figure 19-5.	

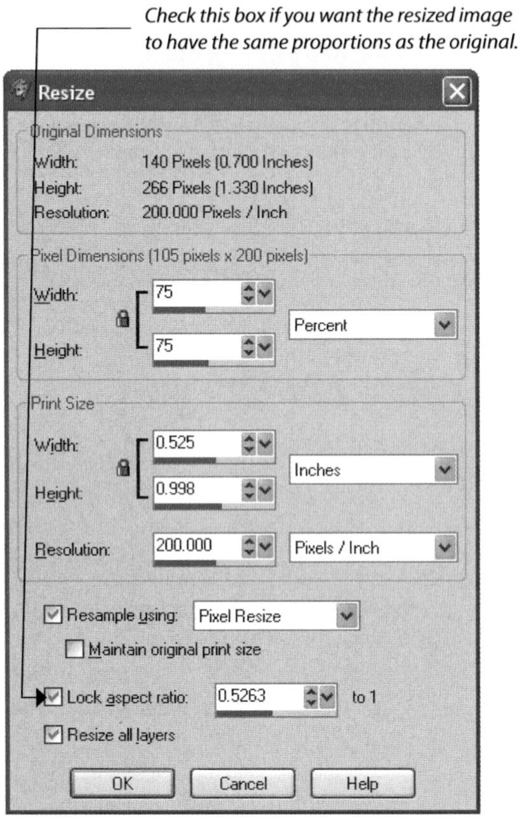

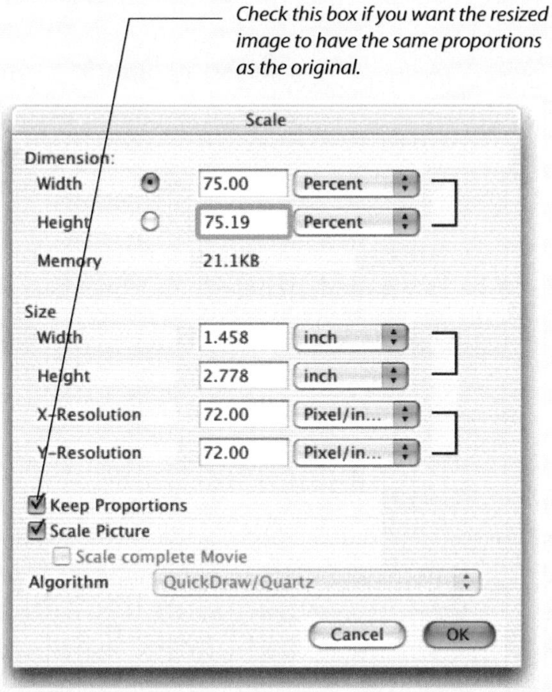

Check this box if you want the resized image to have the same proportions as the original. (Paint Shop Pro)

Check this box if you want the resized image to have the same proportions as the original. (Graphic Converter)

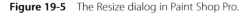

Figure 19-6   The Scale dialog in Graphic Converter.

Figure 19-5   The Resize dialog in Paint Shop Pro.

Paint Shop Pro steps (continued):

▶ Under pixel dimensions, set the width and height you want the resized image to be.

▶ Check the Lock aspect ratio box if you want the resized image to have the same proportions as the original.

▶ Click OK; the resized image appears.

▶ Pull down the File menu and either choose Save to save this file under the same name as the original (this will replace the original file) or choose Save As to save it under another name.

Graphic Converter steps (continued):

▶ Set the width and height you want the resized image to be. You can do this by dimension or size.

▶ Check the Keep Proportions box if you want to maintain the aspect ratio.

▶ Click OK.

▶ Pull down the File menu and either choose Save to save this file under the same name as the original (this will replace the original file) or choose Save As to save it under another name.

does not reduce the file size of the image and therefore consumes more bandwidth than a truly resized image. To truly resize an image, follow the steps in Table 19-3. *Note:* If you are using Dreamweaver, you can also change the size of an image by dragging its handles and then click the ▨ Resample icon to change the size of the file.

Make sure you save the resized file in the GIF or JPEG file format in the same folder as the Web page on which it will appear. If you are resizing an image for your Web page résumé, for example, save the image in your *website* folder.

Color Adjustments

If your image is a logo, icon, or cartoon, you probably do not need the photorealistic colors of an image encoded in 16 million colors (24-bit format). In this case, you should convert the image to 256 colors (8-bit format), which will make it appear three times faster on your Web page because the 8-bit format requires one-third the file space as the 24-bit format. To convert a 24-bit image into an 8-bit image, follow the steps in Table 19-4.

Table 19-4 How to reduce the color depth of an image

Paint Shop Pro (Windows)	Graphic Converter (Macintosh)
▶ Pull down the Paint Shop Pro File menu, choose Open, and open the image, which appears onscreen.	▶ Pull down the Graphic Converter File menu, choose Open, and open the image, which appears onscreen.
▶ Pull down the Image menu, choose Decrease Color Depth, and see if the 256-colors option is active. If it is not active, your image does not need to be reduced in color depth, so close the image and skip the rest of these instructions.	▶ Pull down the Picture menu and choose Colors→Change to 256 Colors, as shown in Figure 19-8.
▶ If the 256-colors option is active, select it; the Decrease Color Depth dialog appears, as shown in Figure 19-7.	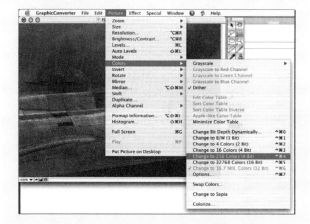 **Figure 19-8** Decreasing the color depth with Graphic Converter.
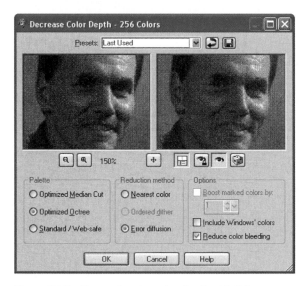 **Figure 19-7** Decreasing the color depth with Paint Shop Pro.	▶ Pull down the File menu and either choose Save to save this file under the same name as the original (this will replace the original file) or choose Save As to save it under another name.
▶ If you choose one of the Optimized palette settings, click the option to Include Windows' Colors. If you are planning to publish this image to the Web, choose Standard/Web-safe.	
▶ Whether to choose Nearest Color or Error Diffusion is up to you. Click OK to close the dialog.	
▶ Pull down the File menu and either choose Save to save this file under the same name as the original (this will replace the original file) or choose Save As to save it under another name.	

Make sure you save the color-converted file in the GIF or JPEG file format in the same folder as the Web page on which it will appear. If you are converting an image for your Web page résumé, for example, save the image in your *website* folder.

Pasting a Picture onto Your Web Page Résumé

You will be happy to discover that pasting an image onto a Web page is a lot easier than preparing the picture to fit the Web page's layout. To paste an image onto a Web page, follow the steps in Table 19-5, which gives you the option of placing the picture on the left or on the right of a paragraph. After you learn to do this, Chapter 20 will teach you how to use tables and layers to position images more precisely on a Web page.

If you have trouble getting the image to position itself exactly where you want it on your Web page, do not worry just now about that or spend time on it right now. In the next chapter, you will learn how to use tables to control more precisely the layout and positioning of text and graphics on your Web pages.

Tiling a Background onto a Web Page

As a final touch, you can add some pizzazz to your résumé. Dreamweaver, FrontPage, and Nvu support a styling element that permits you to set a background image that the browser uses to tile the background. **Tiling** means that the image gets drawn repeatedly across and down the screen until the entire window has been covered. If the image is designed in such a way as to hide the edges when tiled, you get a seamless appearance in the background.

The *Interlit* Web site has a page that contains four images designed for tiling on Web pages. These images appear as follows:

 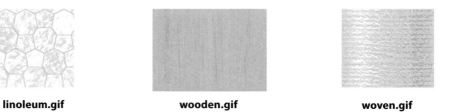

brick.gif   **linoleum.gif**   **wooden.gif**   **woven.gif**

To download one of these images, scroll down to the tile section of Chapter 19 at the *Interlit* Web site. Right-click (Windows) or control-click (Macintosh) the tile you want to download, and choose Save As to download the image. Make sure you save the tile in your *website* folder. Then follow the steps in Table 19-6 to make one of the tiles fill the background of your résumé.

Tiles are nice, but be careful that the pattern in your tiling does not obstruct or interfere with the text on the screen. A good tile provides a subtle backdrop texture that enhances readability. Bad tiles, on the other hand, interfere and make the text harder to read. To conserve bandwidth, tiles should be small, like the ones at the *Interlit* Web site.

To see how the tile was inserted in your HTML, click the Dreamweaver or Frontpage Code button or the Nvu HTML Source tab. In the HTML source code window, you will see how your document's <body> tag styling got modified. Chapter 20 teaches you more about modifying the style of HTML elements onscreen.

Creating Transparent Images

Transparency is a special effect in which one of the colors in a bitmap becomes translucent. Instead of seeing that color, you see through it into the background color or image

Table 19-5 How to paste an image onto a Web page

Dreamweaver	FrontPage	Nvu
▲ Get Dreamweaver running and open the Web page on which you want to paste an image. If you are pasting the image onto your Web page résumé, pull down the File menu, choose Open, and open the file *website\resume.htm*.	▲ Get Microsoft FrontPage running and open the Web page on which you want to paste an image; if you are pasting the image onto your Web page résumé, click the Open File button and open the file *website\resume.htm*.	▲ Get Nvu running and open the Web page on which you want to paste an image; if you are pasting the image onto your Web page résumé, click the Open button and open the file *website\resume.html*.
▲ Position your cursor at the spot on the Web page where you want the picture to appear. For your résumé, position the cursor right before the heading at the top of the document.	▲ Position your cursor at the spot on the Web page where you want the picture to appear. For your résumé, position the cursor right before the heading at the top of the document.	▲ Position your cursor at the spot on the Web page where you want the picture to appear. For your résumé, position the cursor right before the heading at the top of the document.
▲ Pull down the Insert menu and choose Image; the Select Image Source dialog appears, as shown in Figure 19-9.	▲ Click the Insert Picture from File button; the Picture dialog appears, as shown in Figure 19-10.	▲ Click the Insert Image button; the Image Properties dialog appears, as shown in Figure 19-11.

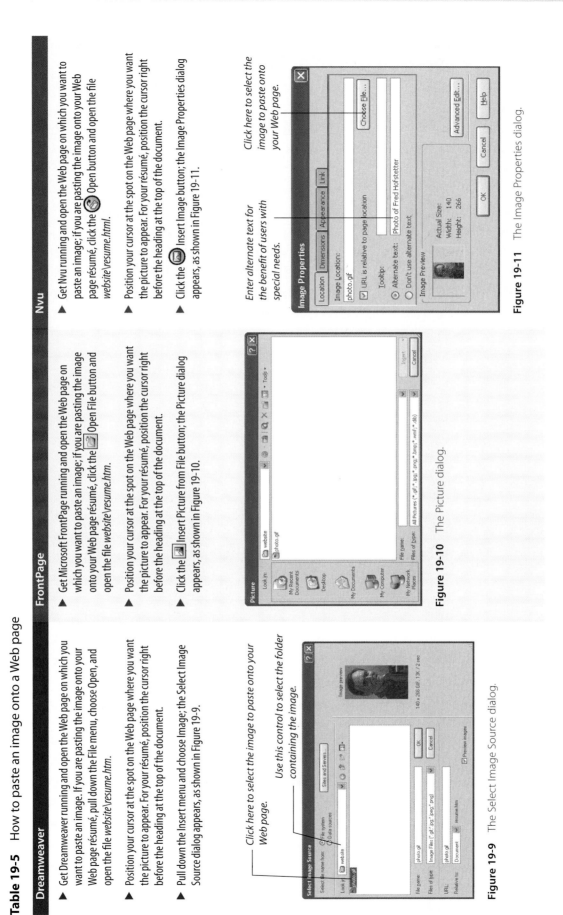

Click here to select the image to paste onto your Web page.

Use this control to select the folder containing the image.

Figure 19-9 The Select Image Source dialog.

Figure 19-10 The Picture dialog.

Enter alternate text for the benefit of users with special needs.

Click here to select the image to paste onto your Web page.

Figure 19-11 The Image Properties dialog.

Table 19-5 *(continued)*

Dreamweaver	FrontPage	Nvu
▲ Use the controls to select the image file you want to appear on your Web page. In this example, I chose my photo, which is *website/photo.gif*.	▲ Select the image file you want to appear on your Web page and click OK. The image now appears on your Web page.	▲ Click the Choose File button and select the image file you want to appear on your Web page.
▲ Click OK to close the Select Image Source dialog. The image appears on your page, and the Properties window displays the image settings.	▲ To make the text flow alongside your image, so your picture appears in the upper-left-hand corner of your résumé, right-click the image and choose Picture Properties to make the Picture Properties dialog appear.	▲ In the Alternate text field, type a description of the image for the benefit of users with special needs who cannot see the picture.
▲ To make the text flow alongside your image, pull down the Align menu in the Properties window and choose Left.	▲ Click the Appearance tab. Pull down the Alignment settings and choose left.	▲ Click the Appearance tab, pull down the Align menu, and choose Wrap to the Right.
▲ Click the ⊙ Preview in Browser button to see how the picture will appear on your Web page.	▲ Click OK to close the Picture Properties dialog. The text should flow alongside your image. If it does not, you did something wrong. Click the Undo button and repeat these instructions more carefully.	▲ Click OK to close the Image Properties dialog. The image should appear on the Web page, and the text should wrap on the right alongside your image. If it does not, you did something wrong. Pull down the Edit menu, select Undo, and repeat these instructions more carefully.
▲ To modify the properties of an image to make the text flow around it differently, or to change other image parameters, click on the image in the Dreamweaver Design window and the Properties window will display the image settings where you can make further adjustments.	▲ Click the ⊙ Preview in Browser button to see how the picture will appear on your Web page.	▲ Click the ✱ Browse button to see how the picture will appear on your Web page.
	▲ To modify the properties of an image to make the text flow around it differently, or to change other image parameters, right-click on the image in the FrontPage window, choose Picture Properties, and the Picture Properties dialog will reappear to let you make further adjustments.	▲ To modify the properties of an image to make the text flow around it differently, or to change other image parameters, right-click on the image in the Nvu window, choose Image Properties, and the Image Properties dialog will reappear to let you make further adjustments.

Table 19-6 How to tile an image onto a Web page

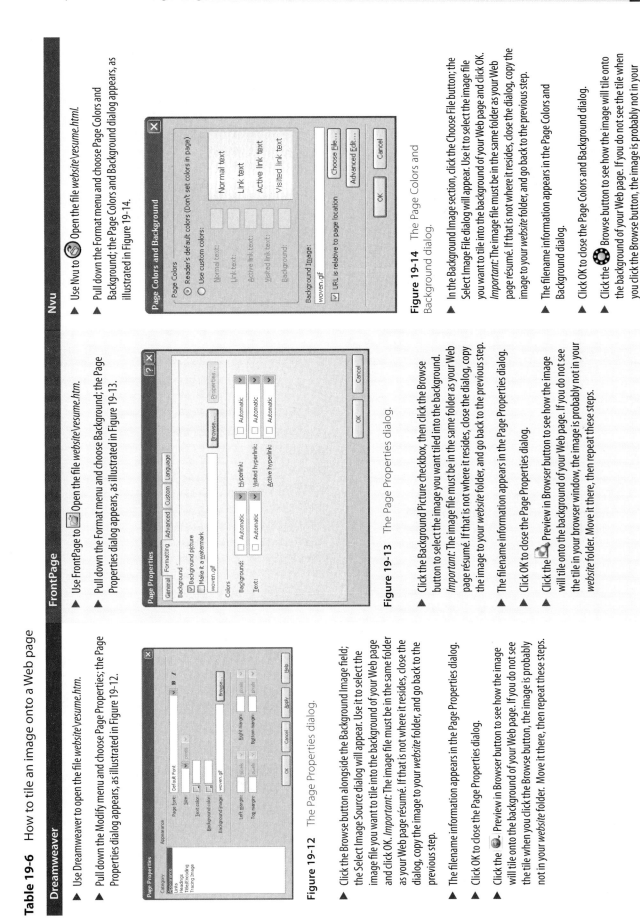

Dreamweaver	FrontPage	Nvu
▲ Use Dreamweaver to open the file *website\resume.html*.	▲ Use FrontPage to ⬚ Open the file *website\resume.htm*.	▲ Use Nvu to ◉ Open the file *website\resume.html*.
▲ Pull down the Modify menu and choose Page Properties; the Page Properties dialog appears, as illustrated in Figure 19-12.	▲ Pull down the Format menu and choose Background; the Page Properties dialog appears, as illustrated in Figure 19-13.	▲ Pull down the Format menu and choose Page Colors and Background; the Page Colors and Background dialog appears, as illustrated in Figure 19-14.

Figure 19-12 The Page Properties dialog.

Figure 19-13 The Page Properties dialog.

Figure 19-14 The Page Colors and Background dialog.

Dreamweaver

▲ Click the Browse button alongside the Background Image field; the Select Image Source dialog will appear. Use it to select the image file you want to tile into the background of your Web page and click OK. *Important:* The image file must be in the same folder as your Web page résumé. If that is not where it resides, close the dialog, copy the image to your *website* folder, and go back to the previous step.

▲ The filename information appears in the Page Properties dialog.

▲ Click OK to close the Page Properties dialog.

▲ Click the ⬤ Preview in Browser button to see how the image will tile onto the background of your Web page. If you do not see the tile when you click the Browse button, the image is probably not in your *website* folder. Move it there, then repeat these steps.

FrontPage

▲ Click the Background Picture checkbox, then click the Browse button to select the image you want tiled into the background. *Important:* The image file must be in the same folder as your Web page résumé. If that is not where it resides, close the dialog, copy the image to your *website* folder, and go back to the previous step.

▲ The filename information appears in the Page Properties dialog.

▲ Click OK to close the Page Properties dialog.

▲ Click the ⬤ Preview in Browser button to see how the image will tile onto the background of your Web page. If you do not see the tile in your browser window, the image is probably not in your *website* folder. Move it there, then repeat these steps.

Nvu

▲ In the Background Image section, click the Choose File button; the Select Image File dialog will appear. Use it to select the image file you want to tile into the background of your Web page and click OK. *Important:* The image file must be in the same folder as your Web page résumé. If that is not where it resides, close the dialog, copy the image to your *website* folder, and go back to the previous step.

▲ The filename information appears in the Page Colors and Background dialog.

▲ Click OK to close the Page Colors and Background dialog.

▲ Click the ◉ Browse button to see how the image will tile onto the background of your Web page. If you do not see the tile when you click the Browse button, the image is probably not in your *website* folder. Move it there, then repeat these steps.

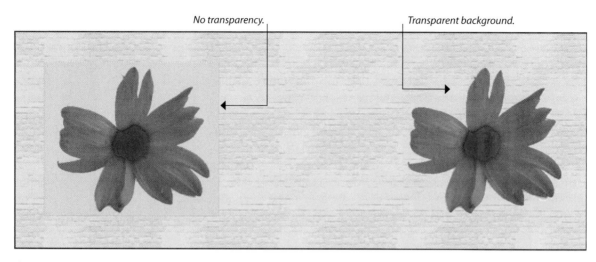

Figure 19-15   Two images overlay a background: one with transparency (right), the other without (left). When the solid yellow color is defined as the transparent color, you see through it into the background onscreen.

Table 19-7   How to create a transparent GIF image

Paint Shop Pro (Windows)	Graphic Converter (Macintosh)
▶ Use Paint Shop Pro to open the image.	▶ Use Graphic Converter to open the image.
▶ Pull down the File menu and choose Save As; the Save As dialog opens.	▶ Click once on the ⬚ Transparency icon to select it as your tool.
▶ Make the Save as Type setting be CompuServe Graphics Interchange (*.gif).	▶ Click once on the image on the color you want to make transparent.
▶ Click the Options button; the Save Options dialog appears.	▶ Pull down the File menu and choose Save As.
▶ In the Save Options dialog, click the Run Optimizer button; the GIF Optimizer dialog appears.	▶ In the Save As dialog, pull down the Format menu and choose the GIF format.
▶ On the Transparency tab, the GIF Optimizer asks: "What areas of the image would you like to be transparent?" Click the option entitled "Areas that match this color."	▶ Click the Save button to save the file in the folder of your choice (probably your *website* folder).
▶ On the image you are saving, click the color you want to be transparent; the color swatch in the GIF Optimizer takes on that color.	▶ *Note:* If you double-click the ⬚ Transparency icon, the Transparent dialog comes onscreen. This dialog shows you the transparent color along with a palette of the image's colors, which you can click to change the transparent color.
▶ Click OK to close the GIF Optimizer.	
▶ Click the Save button to save the file.	

on the screen. Consider the example in Figure 19-15, which shows two images overlaid on a tiled brick background. In the first image, there is no transparency, and the image looks rectangular. In the second image, the yellow pixels are transparent, enabling you to see through them into the background.

To create a transparent GIF image, follow the steps in Table 19-7.

To paste the image onto your Web page, follow the steps that were given previously in Table 19-5. The transparent color in the GIF image will be invisible and the background image or color of the Web page will shine through.

Creating Animated GIF Images

A special feature of the GIF graphics format is its ability to contain animated images. Animated GIFs contain multiple images intended to be shown in a sequence at specific times and locations on the screen. A looping option causes your Web browser to keep showing the frames in the GIF file continually, and, as a result, you see an animation onscreen.

GIF Construction Set

GIF Construction Set

There is a shareware application called the *GIF Construction Set* that Windows users can utilize to create animated GIFs. To download it, click the GIF Construction Set icon at the *Interlit* Web site. For a tutorial on creating animated GIFs, follow the *Interlit* Web site link to the GIF Construction Set.

Animation Shop

Animation Shop

Windows users can also create animated GIFs with Animation Shop, which is part of the Paint Shop Pro software. To run Animation Shop, pull down the Paint Shop Pro File menu and choose Jasc Software Products→Launch Animation Shop.

GifBuilder for Macintosh

GifBuilder

If you have a Macintosh, you can create animated GIF images with GifBuilder. The Gif-Builder software is freeware, which means that it is copyrighted, but you do not have to pay anything to download and use it. Follow the *Interlit* Web site link to GifBuilder.

Clip Art for Web Pages

Clip art is predrawn artwork organized into a catalog or library that you can browse in search of appropriate icons, buttons, banners, backgrounds, tiles, or animated GIFs for your Web pages. Microsoft keeps an extensive clip art gallery, for example, that you can search by genre, topic, and keyword. The *Interlit* Web site links to the Microsoft gallery and several other clip art libraries. Most of these libraries let you freely download and use the graphics on your own personal Web pages. Make sure you check the clip art site's license or copyright policy, however, especially if you are planning to use the clip art in a product that you will be offering for sale. Clip art vendors often require you to pay a special fee for a license that lets you use the clip art in a commercial product.

To download an item of clip art for use on a Web page, you can often simply right-click (Windows) or control-click (Macintosh) the object, and when the quick menu pops out, choose the option to save the graphic on your hard drive. Some clip art sites have special download buttons alongside the images, in which case you click the download button and follow the onscreen instructions. To insert the downloaded graphic on your Web page, following the steps in Table 19-5.

exercises

1. Get on the Web and browse to a screen with an image you would like to capture. Right-click (Windows) or control-click (Macintosh) the image, and when the menu pops out, choose Save As and save the image onto your hard drive. Then get Paint Shop Pro (Windows) or Graphic Converter (Macintosh) running. Pull down the File menu, choose Open, and open the image you saved in the first part of this exercise. If this works the first time, congratulate yourself. Otherwise, make note of any difficulty you encountered and try again. How many tries did it take you to complete this exercise successfully? If you had any trouble, what was the main stumbling block, and how did you overcome it?

2. Get on the Web and browse to a screen with an image you would like to capture. Get Paint Shop Pro (Windows) or Graphic Converter (Macintosh) running. Following the steps in Table 19-1, try the different capture methods you learned in this chapter for grabbing rectangular areas of the screen, windows, or the full screen. Which method is most appropriate for capturing the images you grabbed? Why does that method work better for you than the others?

3. Choose an image that has a lot of detail in it, such as a photograph, and make both GIF and JPEG versions of it. Compare the two images side-by-side and see if you can perceive any difference in the appearance of the files. What difference is there, if any?

4. Take a small image, such as one of the icons found at the *Interlit* Web site, and resize it to 640 × 480. Notice how the resizing process caused the image to become jagged and pixilated. Now take the same small image and enlarge it more gradually. How large can you make it before the distortion renders the image unusable?

5. Take any image and increase its color depth to 16 million colors (24-bit format). Inspect the file's size with the Windows Explorer, or via the Macintosh Finder, and make a note of how large the file is. Now decrease the color depth to 256 colors (8-bit format). Inspect the file's size again. By what percentage has the size of the file decreased? Will this make the file appear more quickly when it gets downloaded from the Internet for display on a Web page?

6. Following the instructions in this chapter, paste your photo onto your Web page, or if you choose not to put your picture on the Web, select some other graphic from the clip art library at the *Interlit* Web site. Experiment with making the text flow along the left or right side of the picture.

7. The *Interlit* Web site contains several images designed for use as tiles on Web pages. Download several of these images and try tiling them onto your Web page résumé. Which tile appears best on your Web page résumé?

8. Both Paint Shop Pro (Windows) and Graphic Converter (Macintosh) contain special effects that can enhance considerably the appearance of an image on a Web page. Use Paint Shop Pro to open a photograph of your choice. Pull down the Colors menu, choose Adjust, and experiment with adjusting the brightness, contrast, and gamma settings. (The gamma settings enable you to correct the difference in color balance between a printed photograph and a computer screen.) With Graphic Converter, pull down the Picture menu and choose Brightness/Contrast. Use the Levels option to adjust the input and output levels of the image. You can adjust black, white, or both.

SITUATED CASE PROJECTS
Case 19: Graphic Design

At the end of each chapter in this book, a situated case project provides the student an opportunity to put the chapter's contents to practical use in a workplace situation. Each case has the same number as the chapter in which it appears.

The adage that a picture is worth a thousand words has never been more appropriate than on a Web page. One could argue that the hypermedia environment adds even more value to the picture, because you can access it quickly when you need it. Being able to find the picture you want quickly may make the image worth a million words when it answers a question or solves a problem for which you need a solution quickly. Imagine that your employer has put you in this kind of a situation. Your school or small company is having budget problems, and your employer has asked you to develop a cost-effective strategy for creating Web site graphics. Get your word processor started and follow these suggested ways of satisfying your employer's request for a graphic design strategy:

❶ There are several good banner and button-making utilities available on the Web. See if you can find a utility that creates banners and buttons in a style compatible with your school or company's look and feel. Follow the Chapter 19 *Interlit* Web site links to banner and button makers. Using your word processor, take notes identifying the names of the sites you visited and report whether you would recommend them for use in your workplace. At the site you like best, create a sample banner and copy it into your report as an example. *Note:* To copy a graphic from the Web into your word processor, right-click (Windows) or control-click (Macintosh) the image and choose Copy. Then go into your word processor, pull down the Edit menu, and choose Paste.

❷ Paint Shop Pro has a button maker built in. If you have Windows, make a sample button with Paint Shop Pro. Copy the button into the report in your word processor and write a paragraph indicating that the button came from Paint Shop. State whether you would recommend using the Paint Shop button maker to make buttons at your school or company Web site.

3 FrontPage has a wide array of themes built in. If you are using FrontPage, you can audition these themes to see if there might be one suitable for use in your school or company. It is also possible to modify the FrontPage themes; if you find one that almost fits, you can fine-tune it. To audition the FrontPage themes, follow these steps:

- In FrontPage, click the ⬜ New Page button to create a new page.

- Pull down the Format menu and choose Theme; the Themes dialog appears.

- In the list of themes on the left, click the theme you would like to see. The theme appears in the window on the right. Repeat this step and look at all the different themes.

- If you see a theme you like, use your word processor to record its name in the report you are writing.

4 The Microsoft Design Gallery is a rich source of graphics for illustrating Web pages. Follow the *Interlit* Web site link to the Microsoft Design Gallery and use the search tools to perform a keyword search for the kinds of graphics needed by your school or company. Use your word processor to add to your report any suitable graphics you may find. Type the graphic's filename, and paste a thumbnail of the graphic into your report.

Note: A thumbnail is a small version of a graphic about the size of the nail on your thumb; hence the term *thumbnail*.

If your instructor has asked you to hand in this assignment, make sure you put your name at the top, then save your graphic design recommendations on disk or follow any other instructions you may have been given for submitting this assignment.

20

USING TABLES AND CSS FOR WEB PAGE LAYOUT

After completing this chapter, you will be able to:

- Explain the role of tables in designing Web pages.

- Use tables to organize Web pages into rectangular regions called cells.

- Flow text and pictures into table cells.

- Recognize the HTML tags that create tables.

- Understand the concept of a cascading style sheet (CSS).

- Define the three kinds of CSS (external, embedded, and inline).

- Use CSS to create colorful stylings and mouseover effects on your Web page résumé.

- Understand the role CSS plays in advanced Web page layout.

● Compare the design of the Web pages illustrated in Figures 20-1 and 20-2. How are they alike? Both contain pictures, and both contain text. How do they differ? Figure 20-1 treats the screen as one large column of information, whereas Figure 20-2 divides the screen into rectangular regions that position the text and graphics in different sections of the Web page. Although both screens convey the same information, you probably will agree that the sectional layout of Figure 20-2 creates a more interesting Web page. This chapter begins by showing how to use tables to arrange information into rows and columns on the screen. Then you learn how to enhance the page's appearance with cascading style sheets (CSS). In the next chapter, you will use tables and CSS to create a unique design for your home page on the Web.

Note: Tables became part of the HTML standard when Version 3.2 was released in 1996. Web pages produced before then were limited to a single column of information.

What Is a Table?

A **table** is a design element that divides the screen into a grid consisting of rectangular regions called *cells*. Into each cell you can enter text or graphics that align with the boundaries of the cell's rectangle. The grid that forms the boundaries of the cells can be either visible or invisible. You normally make the grid visible when presenting a table full of technical information that would be hard to read without horizontal and vertical lines to help the user follow the data across the table. HTML provides control over border thickness, and you can use thin or thick grid lines, depending on the situation.

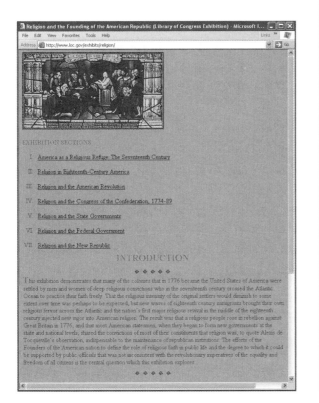

Figure 20-1 How a Web page appears without the use of tables to create rectangular layout regions on the screen.

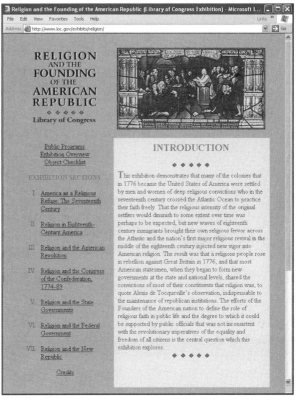

Figure 20-2 Tables create rectangular regions used as design elements in advanced Web page layout.

Why Use Tables on Web Pages?

There are two reasons for using tables on Web pages. The first reason is rather obvious: to present data neatly in rows and columns that help users perceive the order or the relationships in the information. This book uses tables extensively to present complex information in an understandable manner. For example, consider the presentation of HTML tags in Table 17-1. Displaying the tags in column 1 followed by their description in column 2 provides an orderly presentation that enables the user to find a tag in column 1, then read across to its definition in column 2. The grid is visible to help the user read across the table to find the definitions of the different tags.

The second reason for using tables on a Web page is to create advanced layouts consisting of rectangular sections into which you can flow blocks of text or insert graphics. Tables consist of one or more rows of one or more cells. You can adjust the width and height of the cells to create a wide variety of Web page layouts. You can have more than one table on the page or insert a table inside another table, which enables you to create many interesting designs. For example, consider the layout of the Web page shown in Figure 20-3. The layout analysis in Figure 20-4 shows how this page consists of several tables with varying numbers of rows and columns and different cell heights and widths. Notice how the use of multiple tables adds interest to the design of this page. You also can vary the background colors or images in the table cells to create visible regions on the screen.

Creating a Table

It is easy to create a table. If you have Dreamweaver, follow the steps in Table 20-1. If you have FrontPage, follow Table 20-2. For Nvu, use Table 20-3.

Figure 20-3 An advanced Web page design employing multiple tables with varying cell heights and widths.

Figure 20-4 Layout analysis of the tables used to create the Web page in Figure 20-3.

Table 20-1 How to create a table on a Web page with Dreamweaver

▶ Use Dreamweaver to open the Web page on which you want to create a table. If this is your first time through these instructions, you will be creating a table of the world's highest mountains, and you will need a blank Web page to hold the table. Pull down the File menu, choose New, and click the option to create an HTML basic page. Then pull down the File menu, choose Save, and save the page in your *website* folder under the filename *highest.htm*.

▶ If you are not already in Design mode, click the Design button to show the Design view.

▶ Click in the Design window to position your cursor there. If the page is blank, the cursor will go in the upper-left corner of the window, which is where the first element on the page will appear. If the page is not blank, click to position your cursor after the element where you want the table to begin.

▶ Pull down the Insert menu and choose Table; the Table dialog appears, as shown in Figure 20-5.

▶ In the Rows field, enter the number of rows you want this table to have. For this example, enter 7.

▶ In the Columns field, enter the number of columns you want this table to have. For this example, enter 4.

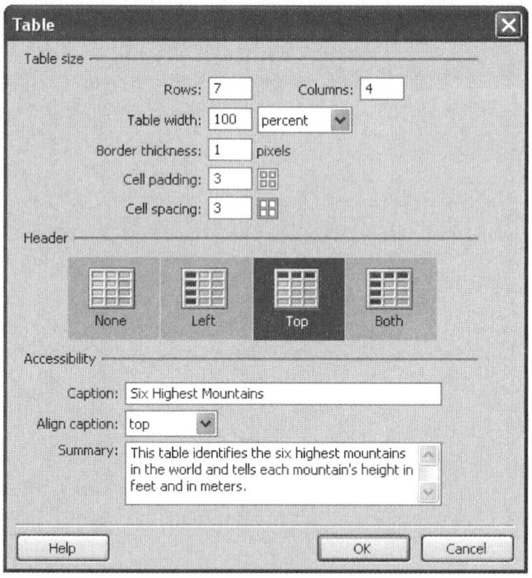

▶ The width setting controls how wide the table will be. You can pull down the menu to make the number you enter set the width as a percentage of the

Figure 20-5 Dreamweaver's Table dialog.

window, or in pixels. If you make this a percentage, the table will scale automatically to fit different screen sizes. If you make this pixels, the table will not scale. Start this table with a width setting of 100 percent, which you can adjust later on.

▶ The Border thickness field lets you define how wide you want the border around the table cells to be drawn, in pixels. If you do not want the table grid to be visible, set the border thickness to 0. For this example, set the border thickness to 1.

▶ In the Caption field, enter the table's caption. In this example, type: **Six Highest Mountains**

▶ Pull down the Align caption menu and choose top; this will make the caption appear on top of the table.

▶ In the Summary textbox, type a summary of what the table contains. The summary is used by accessibility devices to help users with special needs understand the table. In this example, type **This table identifies the six highest mountains in the world and tells each mountain's height in feet and in meters.**

▶ Click the OK button to close the dialog; the table appears onscreen.

Table 20-2   How to create a table on a Web page with Microsoft FrontPage

▶ Use FrontPage to open the Web page on which you want to create a table. If this is your first time through these instructions, you will be creating a table of the world's highest mountains, and you will need a blank Web page to hold the table. Click the New Page button to create the blank Web page, then click the Save button and save the page in your *website* folder under the filename *highest.htm*.

▶ If you are not already in Design mode, click the Design button to show the Design view.

▶ Click in the Design window to position your cursor there. If the page is blank, the cursor will go in the upper-left corner of the window, which is where the first element on the page will appear. If the page is not blank, click to position your cursor after the element where you want the table to begin.

▶ Pull down the Table menu and choose Insert→Table; the Insert Table dialog appears, as shown in Figure 20-6.

▶ In the Rows field, enter the number of rows you want this table to have. For this example, enter 7.

▶ In the Columns field, enter the number of columns you want this table to have. For this example, enter 4.

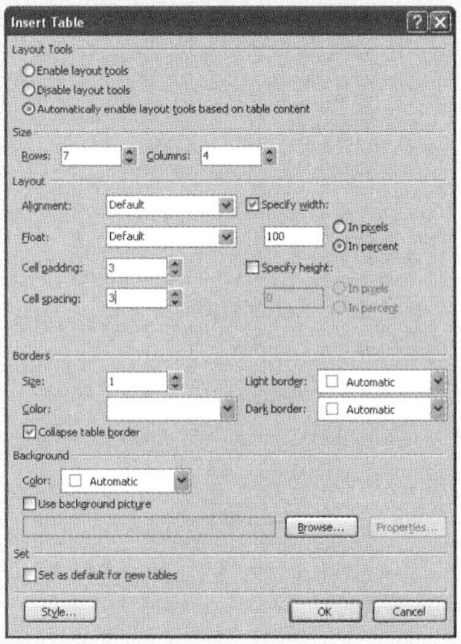

Figure 20-6   The FrontPage Insert Table dialog.

▶ When checked, the Specify Width setting controls how wide the table will be. By clicking the radio buttons below the width field, you can make the number you enter set the width either as a percentage of the screen or in pixels. If you make this a percentage, the table will scale automatically to fit different screen sizes. If you make this pixels, the table will not scale. For this example, specify the width as 100 percent. You will be able to change this later.

▶ The Borders Size field lets you define how wide you want the border around the table cells to be drawn, in pixels. If you do not want the table grid to be visible, set the border to 0. For this example, set the Borders Size to 1.

▶ Leave the rest of the settings at their default values, and click the OK button to close the dialog; the table appears on your Web page.

▶ Click anywhere in the table to position your cursor inside it, then pull down the Table menu and choose Insert→Caption. Your cursor will begin flashing at the center of the caption just above the top of the table.

▶ Type the caption; in this example type **Six Highest Mountains**

Table 20-3   How to create a table on a Web page with Nvu

▶ Use Nvu to open the Web page on which you want to create a table. If this is your first time through these instructions, you will be creating a table of the world's highest mountains, and you will need a blank Web page to hold the table. Click the New Page button to create the blank Web page, then click the Save button. When Nvu asks you to supply a page title, make the title be *World's Highest Mountains*. Then save the page in your *website* folder under the filename *highest.html*.

▶ If you are not already in the Normal view, click the Normal tab to show the Normal view.

▶ Click in the Normal view window to position your cursor there. If the page is blank, the cursor will go in the upper-left corner of the window, which is where the first element on the page will appear. If the page is not blank, click to position your cursor after the element where you want the table to begin.

▶ Pull down the Insert menu and choose Table, or click the Table button to insert a new table; the Insert Table dialog appears. Click the Precisely tab, as shown in Figure 20-7.

▶ In the Rows field, enter the number of rows you want this table to have. For this example, enter 7.

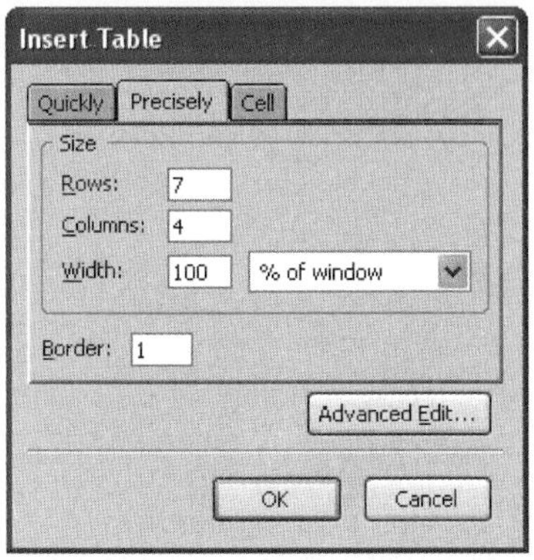

Figure 20-7   Nvu's Insert Table dialog.

Table 20-3   *(continued)*

▶ In the Columns field, enter the number of columns you want this table to have. For this example, enter 4.

▶ The width setting controls how wide the table will be. You can pull down the menu to make the number you enter set the width as a percentage of the window, or in pixels. If you make this a percentage, the table will scale automatically to fit different screen sizes. If you make this pixels, the table will not scale. For this example, specify the width as 100 percent. You will be able to change this later.

▶ The Border field lets you define how wide you want the border around the table cells to be drawn, in pixels. If you do not want the table grid to be visible, set the border to 0. For this example, set the Border to 1.

▶ Click the OK button to close the dialog; the table appears onscreen.

▶ To set the table caption, pull down the Table menu and choose Table Properties to make the Table Properties dialog appear.

▶ Pull down the Caption menu and choose Above Table, then click OK to close the dialog.

▶ Because it is tricky to position your cursor inside the blank caption, click the HTML Source tab and position your cursor in between the **<caption>** and the **</caption>** tags.

▶ Type the caption; in this example, type **Six Highest Mountains**

▶ Click the Normal tab to return to normal editing.

Entering Data into a Table

Once your table has been created, you can enter data into it. Simply click inside the cell into which you want to enter some data, and type what you want to enter. You can move from cell to cell by pressing the Tab key. Pressing Shift-Tab will move you back to the previous cell.

If this is your first time through these instructions, type the information displayed in Figure 20-8 into the table. To change the font, color, size, appearance, or justification of the text in a table, follow the steps in Table 20-4.

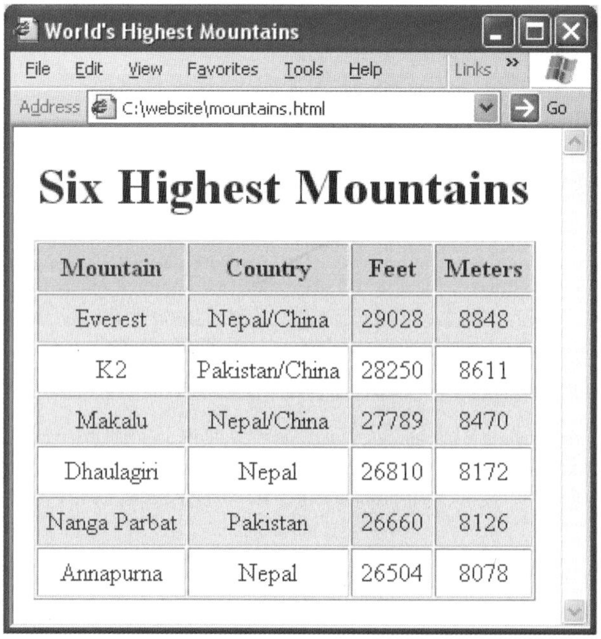

World's Highest Mountains — C:\website\mountains.html

Six Highest Mountains

Mountain	Country	Feet	Meters
Everest	Nepal/China	29028	8848
K2	Pakistan/China	28250	8611
Makalu	Nepal/China	27789	8470
Dhaulagiri	Nepal	26810	8172
Nanga Parbat	Pakistan	26660	8126
Annapurna	Nepal	26504	8078

Figure 20-8   The world's highest mountains. See Table 20-4 to learn how to make your text match the styles in this example.

Table 20-4 How to change text attributes in a table

Dreamweaver	FrontPage	Nvu
▲ Drag your mouse over the text you want to modify, then click the appropriate control in the Properties panel, as shown in Figure 20-9.	▲ Drag your mouse over the text you want to modify, then click the appropriate button on the Formatting toolbar, as shown in Figure 20-10.	▲ Drag your mouse over the text you want to modify, then click the appropriate button on the Format toolbar, as shown in Figure 20-11.

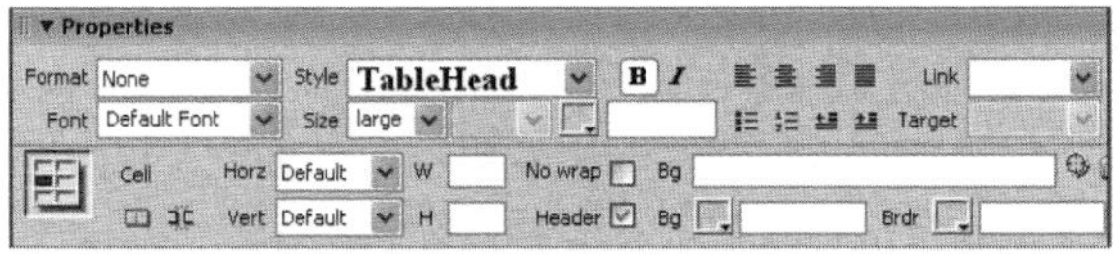

Figure 20-9 Use the Properties panel to modify the appearance of text in a Dreamweaver table.

Figure 20-10 Use the Formatting toolbar to modify the appearance of text in a FrontPage table.

Figure 20-11 Use the Format toolbar to modify the appearance of text in an Nvu table.

Dreamweaver	FrontPage	Nvu
▲ If the Properties panel is not visible, pull down the Window menu and choose Properties.	▲ If the Formatting toolbar is not visible, pull down the View menu and choose Toolbars→Formatting.	▲ If the Format toolbar is not visible, pull down the View menu and choose Show/Hide→Format Toolbar.
▲ For example, to bold the table caption, drag your mouse over the words in the caption to select them and then click the **B** Bold button.	▲ For example, to bold the table caption, drag your mouse over the words in the caption to select them and then click the **B** Bold button.	▲ For example, to bold the table caption, drag your mouse over the words in the caption to select them and then click the **B** Bold button.
▲ To make the words larger, pull down the Size menus and choose the size you want.	▲ To make the words larger, click the **A** Increase Font Size button, or pull down the Font Size menu and choose the size you want.	▲ To make the words larger, click the **A** Larger Font Size button.
▲ Click the Preview in Browser button to see how the table will appear on the Web.	▲ Click the Preview button to see how the table will appear on the Web.	▲ Click the Browse button to see how the table will appear on the Web.

Adjusting the Parameters of a Table

If you want to adjust the parameters of a table after you have created it, follow the steps in Table 20-5.

Inspecting Your HTML

If you inspect the HTML source code of the *highest.htm* file you created in this chapter, you will see how the table begins with the **<table>** tag and ends with the **</table>** tag. Each row of the table begins with **<tr>** and ends with **</tr>**, which stands for table row. Each cell begins with **<td>** and ends with **</td>**, which stands for table data.

Note to Dreamweaver Users	Note to FrontPage Users	Note to Nvu Users
<> Code To inspect your HTML, click the Code tab at the bottom of the window.	**Code** To inspect your HTML, click the Code button at the bottom of the window.	**<HTML> Source** To inspect your HTML, click the HTML Source tab at the bottom of the window.

The typical table uses the table tags in the following structure:

```
<table>
        <tr>
                        <td> row one, cell one </td>
                        <td> row one, cell two </td>
        </tr>
        <tr>
                        <td> row two, cell one </td>
                        <td> row two, cell two </td>
        </tr>
        <tr>
                        <td> row three, cell one </td>
                        <td> row three, cell two </td>
        </tr>
</table>
```

Tables with more cells in a row than this example have more **<td></td>** tags. Tables with more rows add more **<tr></tr>** tags.

Formatting Attributes

Attributes get added to the tags to specify the table formatting. The *border* attribute gets added to the **<table>** tag if the table has a border; for example, if a table has a border thickness of 2, the tag is **<table border="2">**.

Alignment Attributes

The *align* attribute can modify the **<table>**, **<tr>**, and **<td>** tags to control horizontal alignment. Values of the *align* attribute can be *left, center, right,* or *justify,* which means

Table 20-5 How to adjust the parameters of a table

Dreamweaver	FrontPage	Nvu
▶ In the Design view, click once anywhere inside the table, then click the <table> tag in the status bar at the bottom of the Design view. This makes the table settings appear in the Properties pane.	▶ In the Design view, click once anywhere inside the table, then pull down the Table menu and choose Table Properties→Table. The Table Properties dialog appears.	▶ In the Normal view, click once anywhere inside the table, then pull down the Table menu and choose Table Properties. The Table Properties dialog appears.
▶ If the Properties pane isn't visible, pull down the Window menu and choose Properties.	▶ Make the modifications you want, then click the Apply button to preview the change.	▶ Make the modifications you want, then click the Apply button to preview the change.
▶ In the Properties pane, alter the settings you want to change. Note especially whether the table width or height is set for percents or pixels. If you set them for percents, the cells will scale as the user resizes the window. If you set them to pixels, the size is fixed.	▶ Note especially whether the table width or height is set for percents or pixels. If you set them for percents, the cells will scale as the user resizes the window. If you set them to pixels, the size is fixed.	▶ Note especially whether the table width or height is set for percents or pixels. If you set them for percents, the cells will scale as the user resizes the window. If you set them to pixels, the size is fixed.
▶ To cancel a change, pull down the Edit menu and choose Undo.	▶ Click the OK button to make the change, or click the Cancel button to cancel it.	▶ Click the OK button to make the change, or click the Cancel button to cancel it.
▶ To adjust the width of a table, you can click and drag the table's right border. The width of the columns will automatically scale proportionately.	▶ To adjust the width of a table, you can click and drag the table's right border. The width of the columns will automatically scale proportionately.	▶ To adjust the width or height of a table, you can click and drag the table's handles, which are the little squares on the table's corners and on the edges halfway between the corners.
▶ To adjust an individual cell, click in it, then alter the settings you want to change in the Properties pane.	▶ To adjust an individual cell, click in it, then pull down the Table menu and choose Table Properties→Cell. You also can right-click the table cell to pop out the quick menu, and choose Cell Properties.	▶ To adjust an individual cell, click in it, then pull down the Format menu and choose Table Cell Properties. You also can right-click (Windows) or control-click (Macintosh) the table cell to pop out the quick menu, and choose Table Cell Properties.

to double-justify the text. For example, a table cell in which the data is right-justified has the tag **<td align="right">**. The default value is *left*.

The *valign* attribute controls vertical alignment. Its values can be *top*, *middle*, or *bottom*. For example, a table cell in which the data aligns with the bottom of the cell has the tag **<td valign="bottom">**. The default value is *middle*.

To control both horizontal and vertical alignment, you can specify both **align** and **valign** attributes. For example, a table cell in which the data is right-justified at the bottom of the cell has the tag **<td align="right" valign="bottom">**.

Making Data Tables Accessible

Opening Doors to IT

The U.S. government specifies digital age accessibility guidelines in a law known as Section 508, which is part of the Rehabilitation Act of 1973. Rule (g) of the Section 508 Web accessibility guidelines requires that data tables must have clearly identified row and column headers. This requirement applies only to tables that contain data that, in order to be understood, require users to know what specific row or column they are in. Out on the Web, most of the tables are used for page layout. You saw an example of a table used purely for layout in Figure 20-3. Tables that are used purely for layout do not need row and column headers.

The table of the world's highest mountains, on the other hand, is a data table. In order to understand the information in this table, the user must be able to identify the category represented by the row and column of each data cell. Suppose you want to make this table accessible. To define the table headers, you use the HTML table header **<th>** start and **</th>** stop tags. To make the world's highest mountains table use these tags, you would modify the first row of the table as illustrated below. Instead of using the **<td>** and **</td>** tags to create the title cells in the first row, you use the **<th>** start and **</th>** stop tags These table header tags both create a data cell and define it as a table header. The modified code reads as follows:

```
<tr>
  <th>Mountain</th>
  <th>Country</th>
  <th>Feet</th>
  <th>Meters</th>
</tr>
```

For more on Web accessibility guidelines, follow the *Interlit* Web site links to Section 508 and the W3C's Web Accessibility Initiative (WAI).

Putting Images Inside Table Cells

You can insert images inside any table cell. If the image is larger than the cell, the cell will expand to the size of the image, unless you limited the size of the cell to a fixed pixel width or height. To insert an image into a table cell, follow the steps in Table 20-6.

Table 20-6   How to insert an image into a table cell

Dreamweaver	FrontPage	Nvu
▶ In the Design view, click once inside the cell into which you want to insert an image.	▶ In the Design view, click once inside the cell into which you want to insert an image.	▶ In the Normal view, click once inside the cell into which you want to insert an image.
▶ Pull down the Insert menu and choose Image; the Select Image Source dialog appears.	▶ Click the 🖼 Insert Picture from File button; the Picture dialog appears.	▶ Click the ◉ Insert Image button; the Image Properties dialog appears.
▶ Select the image file you want to insert.	▶ Select the image file you want to insert.	▶ Click the Choose File button and select the image file you want to appear on your Web page.
▶ Click OK to close the dialog; the picture will appear inside the cell.	▶ Click OK to close the dialog; the picture will appear inside the cell.	▶ If the cell will include text as well as graphics, click the Appearance tab, pull down the Align Text to Image menu, and choose the alignment option you want to control how the text flows around the picture.
▶ If the cell will include text as well as graphics, right-click the image, choose Align, and select the alignment option you want to control how the text flows around the picture.	▶ If the cell will include text as well as graphics, right-click the image, choose Picture Properties, click the Appearance tab, and choose the alignment option you want to control how the text flows around the picture.	▶ Click OK to close the Image Properties dialog; the picture will appear inside the cell.
▶ Click the 🌐▾ Preview in Browser button to see how the table will appear on the Web.	▶ Click the 🔍 Preview button to see how the table will appear on the Web.	▶ Click the ⚙ Browse button to see how the table will appear on the Web.

Subdividing Table Cells

You can subdivide any table cell by right-clicking the cell and choosing the option to split it. Such a split cell, however, inherits properties from its parent table. To create a subdivision with its own settings, you insert a table inside the cell. Putting a table inside a cell provides another layer of structure on the Web page.

There is no limit to the number of cells you can subdivide. Because subdividing cells enables you to create any conceivable pattern of rectangular regions on the screen, there is no limit to the number of different layouts you can make. Figures 20-12 to 20-15 show layout analyses of Web pages that use subdivided table cells as design elements. As you can see, being able to create tables inside tables makes for some pretty interesting Web pages. To create a table inside a cell, follow the steps in Table 20-7.

In the next chapter, you will apply this method of inserting a table inside a table to create a really cool home page to publish on the Web.

Making Cells That Span More Than One Row or Column

By default, each cell in a table is confined to just one row and column. To vary the layout of a table, you can expand a cell to make it span more than one row or column. To expand a cell to span more than one row or column, follow the steps in Table 20-8.

Note: If you click the source code button to inspect the HTML source code of a table that has a cell spanning more than one row or column, you will notice that the **<td>** tag has *rowspan* and *colspan* attributes. For example, a cell that spans two rows and three columns has the tag **<td rowspan="2" colspan="3">**.

Figure 20-12   This Web page has a table inside a table. This kind of a design lets you create a design structure for one cell that functions independently of the cells in the outer table.

Figure 20-13   Layout analysis of Figure 20-12. Study this analysis to visualize how the tables provide the structure for the page content in Figure 20-12.

Figure 20-14   This Web page is built using one large outer table, a smaller table nested inside that one, and still smaller subtables inside that. Nesting tables in this manner enables you to create any conceivable page layout of content onscreen.

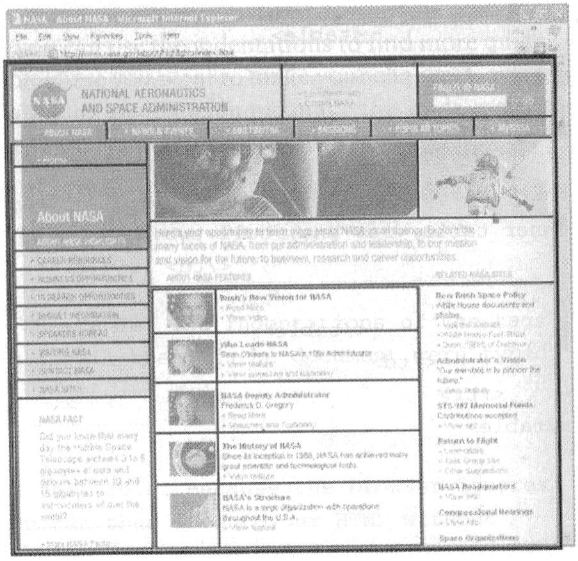

Figure 20-15   Layout analysis of Figure 20-14. Study this analysis to visualize how the tables provide the structure for the page content in Figure 20-14.

Table 20-7   How to subdivide a table cell by inserting a table in the cell

Dreamweaver	FrontPage	Nvu
▶ In Design view, click once inside the cell you want to subdivide.	▶ In Design view, click once inside the cell that you want to subdivide.	▶ In Normal view, click once inside the cell you want to subdivide.
▶ Pull down the Table menu and choose Insert→Table; the Insert Table dialog appears.	▶ Pull down the Table menu and choose Insert→Table; the Insert Table dialog appears.	▶ Pull down the Insert menu and choose Table; the Insert Table dialog appears.
▶ Enter the number of rows and columns you want in the subdivided cell.	▶ Enter the number of rows and columns you want in the subdivided cell.	▶ Click the Precisely tab and enter the number of rows and columns you want in the subdivided cell.
▶ Adjust any other properties you want to modify. For example, if you do not want the grid visible, set the border thickness to 0.	▶ Adjust any other properties you want to modify. For example, if you do not want the grid visible, set the border size to 0. If you do not want any spacing between or around table cells, set the Cell Padding and Cell Spacing to 0.	▶ Adjust any other properties you want to modify. For example, if you do not want the grid visible, set the border thickness to 0.
▶ Click OK to close the dialog and create the table.	▶ Click OK to close the dialog and create the table.	▶ Click OK to close the dialog and create the table.
▶ The newly created table subdivides the cell, providing another grid of rectangles to use as design elements on your Web page.	▶ The newly created table subdivides the cell, providing another grid of rectangles to use as design elements on your Web page.	▶ The newly created table subdivides the cell, providing another grid of rectangles to use as design elements on your Web page.

Table 20-8 How to make a table cell span more than one row or column

Dreamweaver	FrontPage	Nvu
▲ Click once inside the leftmost cell that you want to expand. ▲ Pull down the Modify menu and choose Table→Increase Column Span to make the cell span more than one column, or choose Table→Increase Row Span to make the cell span more than one row. ▲ To delete any unwanted spans created by this process, position your mouse cursor inside an unwanted span, pull down the Modify menu, and choose Table→Split Cell. ▲ Figure 20-16 shows where the Span and Split choices are on the Modify→Table menu.	▲ Click once inside the cell that you want to expand. ▲ Pull down the Table menu and choose Table Properties→Cell; the Cell Properties dialog appears, as shown in Figure 20-17.	▲ Click once inside the leftmost cell that you want to expand. ▲ Pull down the Table menu and choose Join with Cell to the Right. ▲ If you want to span more than one cell, drag your mouse to select the cells you want to span, then pull down the Table menu and choose Join Selected Cells. ▲ To delete any unwanted spans created by this process, position your mouse cursor inside an unwanted span, pull down the Table menu, and choose Split Cell. ▲ Figure 20-18 shows where the Join and Split choices are on the Table menu.

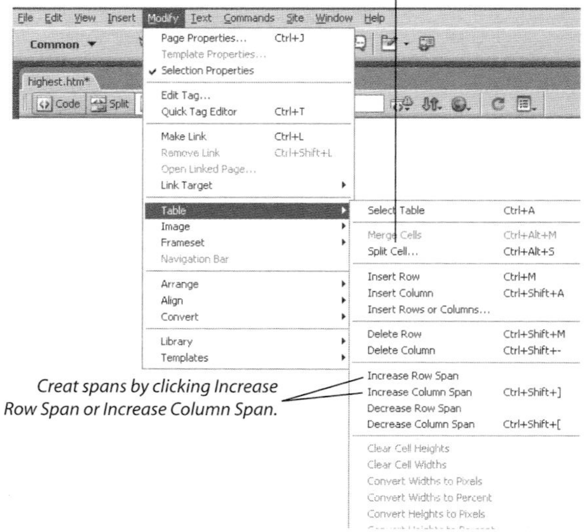

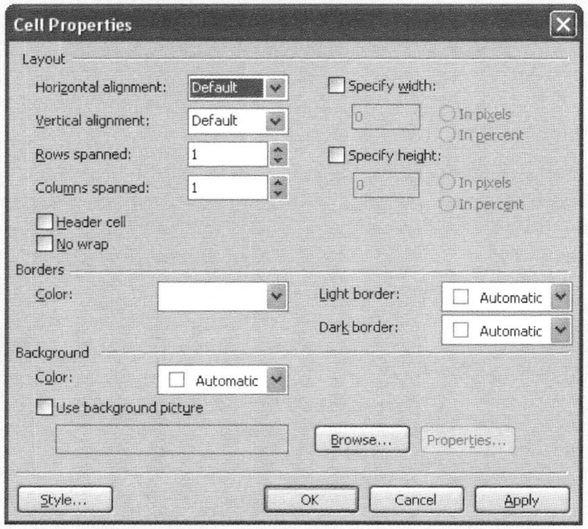

Create spans by clicking Increase Row Span or Increase Column Span.

Subdivide spans by clicking Split Cell.

Figure 20-16 The Span and Split Cell options are on the Dreamweaver Modify→Table menu.

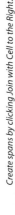

Cell Properties

Layout

Horizontal alignment: Default

Vertical alignment: Default

Rows spanned: 1

Columns spanned: 1

☐ Header cell
☐ No wrap

☐ Specify width: 0 ○ In pixels ○ In percent
☐ Specify height: 0 ○ In pixels ○ In percent

Borders

Color:

Light border:

Dark border:

Background

Color: Automatic

☐ Use background picture

Browse...

Style...   OK   Cancel   Apply

Figure 20-17 The Microsoft FrontPage Cell Properties dialog.

▲ In the Layout group, enter the number of rows and columns you want the cell to span.

▲ Click the Apply button to preview how the cell will appear.

▲ Make any adjustments necessary, and click the Apply button to preview the cell again.

▲ Click OK when you are done formatting the cell.

▲ To delete any unwanted spans created by this process, drag your mouse to select the unwanted spans, then click the right mouse button and choose Split Cells.

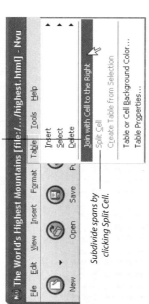

Create spans by clicking Join with Cell to the Right.

The World's Highest Mountains [file:/.../highest.html] - Nvu

File Edit View Insert Format Table Tools Help

New Open Save Pu...

Insert
Select
Delete

Join with Cell to the Right
Split Cell
Create Table from Selection
Table or Cell Background Color...
Table Properties...

Subdivide spans by clicking Split Cell.

Figure 20-18 The Join and Split Cell options are on the Nvu Table menu.

Cascading Style Sheets (CSS)

A **cascading style sheet (CSS)** is a set of rules that define styles to be applied to entire Web pages or individual Web page elements. Each rule consists of a selector followed by a set of curly braces containing the style properties and their values. The selector can be an HTML element, a user-defined style known as a class, or the ID of a specific element on a page. Here are some examples of style definitions that you might find on a CSS:

```
a:link{color: rgb(255,204,0) }
a:visited{color: rgb(153,204,204) }
a:active {color: rgb(102,255,0) }
body
{
        font-family: Garamond, Times New Roman, Times;
        background-color: rgb(51,102,204);
        color: rgb(255,255,153);
}
table
{
        table-border-color-light: rgb(153,255,204);
        table-border-color-dark: rgb(0,0,51);
}
h1, h2, h3, h4, h5, h6{font-family: Verdana, Arial, Helvetica}
h1 {color: rgb(255,204,0) }
h2 {color: rgb(153,255,51) }
h3 {color: rgb(0,255,204) }
h4 {color: rgb(255,204,0) }
h5 {color: rgb(153,255,51) }
h6 {color: rgb(0,255,204) }
```

User-defined style classes begin with a period. ⟶ **.callout { font-size: small }**

ID selectors begin with a pound sign. ⟶ **#slogan { font-family: serif }**

Three Kinds of Cascading Style Sheets

There are three ways of applying cascading style sheets to a Web page: external, embedded, and inline. An **external CSS** keeps all of the style definitions in a separate CSS file, thereby enabling you to use the same style sheet for all the pages in a site. The **<link>** tag tells the Web page what style sheet to use. You normally put the **<link>** tag in the **<head>** section of the Web page. An example of such a **<link>** tag is

<link rel=stylesheet href="MyStyles.css" type="text/css">

An **embedded CSS** is a style sheet that gets copied physically into the **<head>** section of the Web page and applies to the Web page as a whole. The **<style>** start and **</style>** stop tags delimit the embedded CSS, which keeps your formatting rules in a single place in the document, making it easier to maintain. The following embedded CSS, for example, makes the H1 element blue and causes hypertext to change color from blue to red when the user mouses over a link. You can see this blue and red styling in action on my home page at www.udel.edu/fth:

```
<style>
        H1        {color:darkblue; font-family:Arial}
        A:link    {text-decoration:underline; color:darkblue}
        A:visited {text-decoration:underline; color:darkblue}
        A:hover   {text-decoration:underline; color:red}
</style>
```

An **inline CSS** is a style sheet that applies only to one page element, so it gets copied "inline" on the page with that element. The following paragraph element, for example, has an inline style sheet that makes the cheerleading bold, large, and dark green onscreen:

```
<p style="font-weight: bold; font-size: xx-large; color: darkgreen">
Go Eagles!</p>
```

Why CSS Style Sheets Are Called Cascading

More than one style sheet can impact the appearance of an HTML Web page element onscreen. The term **cascading** refers to the manner in which a CSS inherits rules defined by style sheets encountered earlier on the page. If a Web page links to more than one external CSS, for example, the styles defined on each CSS cascade to the next. Further down the cascade, an embedded style sheet can define more style rules. In turn, the embedded style sheet inherits any rules defined earlier on the cascade. Still further down the cascade, inline styles can set rules that apply to individual elements onscreen. An inline CSS can redefine a rule set earlier on the cascade.

If you have Internet Explorer, you can set up an accessibility style sheet that will always be last on the cascade. Seeing-impaired users, for example, can use a style sheet that makes font sizes large and bold. Because this accessibility style sheet is last on the cascade, it can override any styles defined earlier. To set the accessibility style sheet in Internet Explorer, pull down the Tools menu, choose Internet Options, click the Accessibility button on the General tab, and select the option to format documents using your own style sheet. Since this will alter the Web page design, however, you should not use an accessibility style sheet unless you have special needs.

Using CSS to Define the Style of an HTML Tag

After looking at the preceding examples of the three kinds of cascading style sheets, you may worry that learning CSS will be difficult. Fret not, because Dreamweaver, FrontPage, and Nvu have style sheet editors built in. The following exercises will step you through the process of creating style sheets without getting too technical. We begin by creating an embedded style sheet that makes the H1 heading style dark blue. To learn how to do this, follow the steps in Table 20-9.

Note: Sometimes you will see the **<!--** comment start and **-->** comment stop tags around the CSS code in embedded style sheets. The purpose of these comments is to hide the code from older browsers that might otherwise choke on these newer features.

Table 20-9 How to define the style of an HTML tag in a cascading style sheet

Dreamweaver	FrontPage	Nvu
▲ Use Dreamweaver to open the page for which you want to create a CSS. In this example, open the Web page résumé you created in Chapter 18.	▲ Use FrontPage to open the page for which you want to create a CSS. In this example, open the Web page résumé you created in Chapter 18.	▲ Use Nvu to open the page for which you want to create a CSS. In this example, open the Web page résumé you created in Chapter 18.
▲ Pull down the Text menu and choose CSS Styles→New; the New CSS Style dialog appears as illustrated in Figure 20-19.	▲ Pull down the Format menu and choose Style; the Style dialog appears as illustrated in Figure 20-21.	▲ Pull down the Tools menu and choose CSS Editor; the CSS Stylesheets dialog appears.

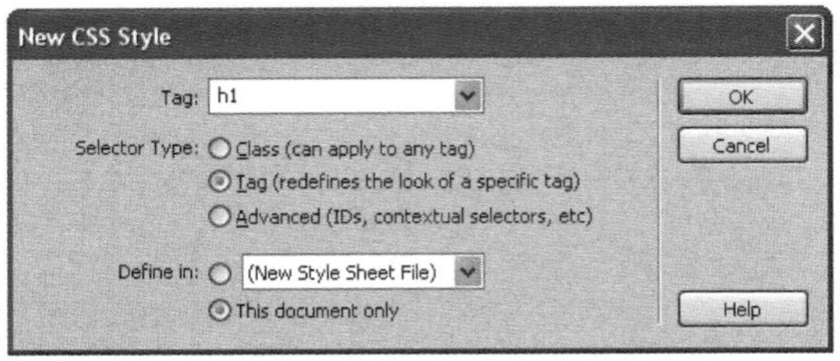

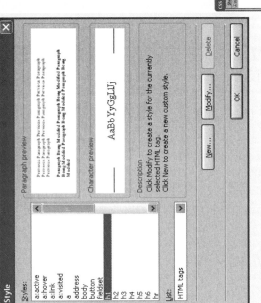

Figure 20-19 Dreamweaver's New CSS Style dialog.

▲ Click the radio button entitled Tag (redefines the look of a specific tag.)

▲ Pull down the Tag menu and choose the tag you want to modify; in this example, select the h1 tag.

▲ If you want to create an embedded CSS, click the option to define the style in this document only; to use an external CSS, click the option to define the style in a style sheet file. In this example, click the option to define the style in this document only.

▲ Click OK; the CSS Style Definition dialog appears. Use it to specify your style settings. In this example, click the Color icon to pop out the color selector. If the color cubes are not showing, click the arrow in the upper-right corner of the color selector, choose Color Cubes, then click to select the color of your choice. I chose dark blue, for which the color code is #003399, as you can see in Figure 20-20.

Figure 20-21 The FrontPage Style dialog.

▲ If the List menu does not say HTML tags, pull down the List menu and choose HTML tags.

▲ In the list of HTML tags, choose the tag you want to modify; in this example, select the h1 tag.

▲ Click the Modify button; the Modify Style dialog appears.

▲ If you want to create an embedded CSS, click the [Style elt.] button; to create an external CSS, click the [Link elt.] button. In this example, click the [Style elt.] button to begin making an embedded style sheet.

▲ You may supply an optional title, and you may specify the type of media to which this style sheet will apply; leave these blank for now, and click the Create Stylesheet button.

▲ Click the Rule button; the New Style Rule pane appears.

▲ Click the option to create a new style applied to all members of type.

▲ In the type field, enter the tag you want to modify; in this example, type h1, as illustrated in Figure 20-23, then click the Create Style Rule button. This click activates the rest of the tabs in the CSS Stylesheets dialog.

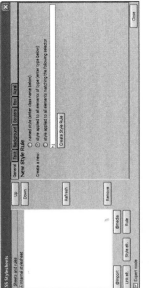

Figure 20-23 The Nvu CSS Stylesheets dialog.

and layout of your home page will project an image on the Web and reflect on the kind of person you are. So you will want your home page to be your best page.

The most original way to create a home page is by **designing** your own custom layout. This takes the most time, but it is the best way to create a Web page uniquely suited to the image you want to project on the Web. You need to be aware, however, that if you come up with a design that is truly unique, it may not be long before other users clone it and create Web pages looking like yours.

Cloning involves the copying of someone else's Web page that you think is worthwhile. While viewing the page, you can easily grab the source code via the browser's view source code option. Since you are copying someone else's design, however, your home page will not be original. Moreover, cloning raises ethical and legal questions with respect to copying other people's work. In the section on cloning, this chapter will address the ethics of cloning someone else's home page.

Home Page Naming Conventions

In the tutorials that follow, you will learn how to create a home page. At the end of each tutorial, when you save your new home page, you will need to give your page a filename. When someone asks for the address of your home page, you will respond with the URL (uniform resource locator) of this file. You see a lot of home page URLs that end with filenames like *home.html* or *welcome.html,* but the coolest home page addresses are the short ones that omit the filename. For example, the author's home page is *http://www. udel.edu/fth* with no filename specified.

Having a cool home page address with no filename in it indicates you understand that when someone visits a Web site folder without specifying a filename, the server looks to see if the folder contains that Web site's default filename, which is often defined as *index.html.* If the default file exists, the server sends it. Since you will want the name of your home page to be cool, this tutorial names the file *index.html.* If your Web server uses some other default filename (such as *default.html*), use that name instead. If you are not sure what default filename your Web server uses, check the guidelines at your Web page hosting site, or ask your server administrator. If you cannot determine the default filename, name your home page something intuitive, such as *home.html.*

The Ethics of Cloning Someone Else's Web Page

If you see a nicely designed page on the Web and you want to make a page with a similar design, it is possible to clone the Web page, make modifications to customize it as you wish, then save the page under your own filename. When cloning Web pages, however, you must observe copyright law and the principles of Netiquette. Refer to the Copyright and Fair Use sections of Chapter 25 and follow the *Interlit* Web site links to Copyright, Fair Use, and Netiquette. If you are sued for copyright infringement, ignorance of these laws is no defense. A common myth is that since the Internet is so freely accessible, everything on the Internet is in the public domain. It just isn't so. You must assume that networked information is copyrighted instead of acting as if it is not. Always ask permission if you have any questions regarding whether your use of the material is a fair use.

How to Clone a Web Page

With the laws of copyright and the principles of ethics in mind, Table 21-1 shows how to create a home page by cloning someone else's page.

Table 21-1   How to clone a Web page

▶ The *Interlit* Web site links to several model Web pages that you can clone and customize to create a page of your own. Follow the *Interlit* Web site link to Web page models and browse to the Web page library of your choice.

▶ Peruse the example pages until you get one onscreen that you would like to use as your home page model.

▶ Pull down your browser's File menu, choose Save As or Save Page As to bring up the Save As dialog, and save the page in your *website* folder.

▶ Use Dreamweaver, FrontPage, or Nvu to open the page you saved in the previous step.

▶ Modify the page by changing the text to say things about you. Delete information you do not want on your home page.

▶ If you want to replace an image on the page with your own custom photo, double-click the image to bring up its Properties dialog, then replace the filename with an image of your own. Chapter 19 provides instructions on how to get your photo into an image file you can use here. Otherwise, if you do not want the image on your Web page, delete the image.

▶ Modify the links in the page so they go where you want. To make a link go somewhere, follow these steps:
  ■ If you are using Ⓙ Dreamweaver, right-click the link and choose Change Link to bring up the Select File dialog. In the URL field, type the Web address of the resource you want to link to.
  ■ If you are using Ⓠ FrontPage, right-click the link, and choose Hyperlink to bring up the Insert Hyperlink dialog. In the Address field, type the Web address of the resource you want to link to.
  ■ If you are using Ⓝ Nvu, double-click on the link to bring up the Link Properties dialog. In the Link location field, type the Web address (URL) of the resource you want to link to.

▶ Study your new home page carefully. Since it came from a model that provided sample information, it may contain unwanted text. Read it very carefully and delete any unwanted text. Make sure the remaining text says what you want.

▶ When someone visits your page, the page title will appear in the browser's title bar. Therefore, you will want this to say something appropriate for your home page. Santa, for example, might make his page title be *Santa Claus the Toymaker*. To give your page a title, follow these steps:
  ■ If you are using Ⓙ Dreamweaver, type the page title into the Title field in the document's toolbar.
  ■ If you are using Ⓠ FrontPage, pull down the File menu and choose Properties to bring up the Page Properties dialog. On the General tab, type the page title into the title field. Click OK to close the dialog.
  ■ If you are using Ⓝ Nvu, pull down the Format menu and choose Page Title and Properties to make the Page Properties dialog appear. Type the page title in the Title field, then click OK to close the dialog.

▶ Click the Save button and save your new home page in your *website* folder. Make the name of your home page be either *index.htm* or *index.html*.

▶ Click the Preview or Browse button to see how your home page will appear on the Web. If you see anything you dislike, use your Web page editor to correct it.

Inspecting the Cloned HTML

Whenever you clone someone else's Web page, you should inspect the HTML code to make sure the page does not contain hidden comments that are derogatory, insulting, obscene, or otherwise inappropriate. It is also possible for the HTML code to contain copyright information about the contents of the page. Click the HTML source code button to inspect the HTML codes. Look especially for <!> tags, which are comment tags that have the form <!*your comment goes here*>. If you find objectionable or unwanted comments in the HTML code, you should remove them. You can delete unwanted codes directly onscreen in the HTML window. Be careful not to create syntactical errors in the

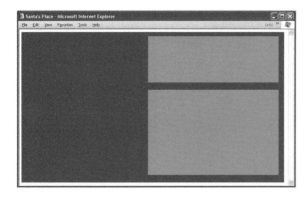

Figure 21-1 Rectangular layout consisting of primary (dark blue) and secondary (light blue) rectangles.

Figure 21-2 Home page created using the layout grid in Figure 21-1.

HTML by deleting a start tag without also deleting its stop tag, or vice versa. When you are done editing, remember to save the file.

Designing a Custom Home Page

The most original way to create a home page is to design your own. By using tables to divide the screen into the rectangles you practiced making in the previous chapter, you can lay out your Web page into different regions on the screen and enter your text and graphics into the different rectangles to create a unique screen layout with a custom look and feel. If you know that all of your users have browsers that support CSS layers, you can use CSS to lay out your page. It may be safer, however, to use tables until all the leading browsers properly support CSS layers.

To create a custom home page using a table-driven layout, think of the page as a grid consisting of primary and secondary rectangles. A primary rectangle is a table cell into which one or more secondary rectangles can be drawn. Secondary rectangles are created by subdividing a cell by inserting a new table into the cell. For example, Figure 21-1 shows a layout grid of primary and secondary rectangles, and Figure 21-2 shows the corresponding home page that was created using this layout.

To create a home page based on a rectangular table-driven layout, follow the steps in Table 21-2 for Dreamweaver, Table 21-3 for FrontPage, or Table 21-4 for Nvu.

Table 21-2 How to create a custom home page with Dreamweaver

- ▶ Pull down Dreamweaver's File menu, choose New, and create a new HTML basic page.

- ▶ Click the Design button to bring up the Design view, then pull down the Insert menu and choose Table to make the Table dialog appear.

- ▶ In the Rows field, enter the number of primary rectangles you want created vertically (i.e., up and down) on the page.

- ▶ In the Columns field, enter the number of primary rectangles you want created horizontally (i.e., left and right) across the page.

- ▶ You will probably want the table grid invisible; to make it invisible, set the Border thickness field to **0**.

- ▶ Click OK to create the table. It will appear shorter than you want, but that is normal, because you have not entered any data into it yet. The cells expand automatically when you enter data into them.

Table 21-2 *(continued)*

- ▶ By default, the vertical spacing of the table cells is symmetrical. If you want to adjust the vertical position of the cell boundaries, click and drag them with your mouse. To make finer adjustments, follow these steps:
  - ■ Click once inside the column whose width you want to adjust; you will see the size settings in the Properties pane. If the Properties pane is not visible, pull down the Window menu and choose Properties.
  - ■ If you want to change the width of the entire column, drag to select the entire column; you will see the column settings in the Properties pane.
  - ■ Adjust the settings as you wish.
- ▶ If your design calls for any of the cells to be subdivided into secondary rectangles, click inside the cell to be divided to position your cursor there, then pull down the Insert menu and choose Table to create the secondary table cells. You will probably want to set the options the same as for your primary table.
- ▶ At any time, you can begin entering your text and graphics into the table cells. Cell height will adjust automatically to the amount of information you enter.
- ▶ Use the Properties panel to set the size, color, style, and appearance of your text.
- ▶ Pull down the File menu, choose Save, and save your new home page in your *website* folder. Make the name of your home page be either *index.htm* or *index.html*.
- ▶ Click the Preview in Browser button to see how your home page will appear on the Web.

Table 21-3 How to create a custom home page with FrontPage

- ▶ Get FrontPage running. If FrontPage has not automatically created a new page for you, click the New Page button.
- ▶ Pull down the Table menu and choose Insert→Table to make the Insert Table dialog appear.
- ▶ In the Rows field, enter the number of primary rectangles you want created vertically (i.e., up and down) on the page.
- ▶ In the Columns field, enter the number of primary rectangles you want created horizontally (i.e., left and right) across the page.
- ▶ You will probably want the table grid invisible; to make it invisible, set the border size to **0**.
- ▶ If you turned the table grid off, you will probably want to set the cell spacing and cell padding to **0**.
- ▶ Click OK to create the table. It will appear shorter than you want, but that is normal, because you have not entered any data into it yet. The cells expand automatically when you enter data into them.
- ▶ By default, the vertical spacing of the table cells is symmetrical. If you want to adjust the vertical position of the cell boundaries, click and drag them with your mouse. To make finer adjustments, follow these steps:
  - ■ Right-click inside the column whose width you want to adjust, then choose Cell Properties to make the Cell Properties dialog appear.
  - ■ Click the Specify Width option and adjust the width as you wish.
  - ■ Click the Apply button to preview the width adjustment.
  - ■ Click OK to close the dialog.
- ▶ If your design calls for any of the cells to be subdivided into secondary rectangles, click inside the cell to be divided to position your cursor there, then pull down the Table menu and choose Insert→Table to create the secondary table cells. You will probably want to set the options the same as for your primary table.
- ▶ At any time, you can begin entering your text and graphics into the table cells. Cell height will adjust automatically to the amount of information you enter.
- ▶ Use the Format toolbar to set the size, color, style, and appearance of your text.
- ▶ Click the Save button and save your new home page in your *website* folder.
- ▶ Click the Preview button to see what your new home page will look like on the Web.

Table 21-4 How to create a custom home page with Nvu

- ▶ Get Nvu running. If it is not already on a new page, click the New Page button.

- ▶ Pull down the Insert menu and choose Table, or click the Table button to insert a new table; the Insert Table dialog appears. Click the Precisely tab.

- ▶ In the Rows field, enter the number of primary rectangles you want created vertically (i.e., up and down) on the page.

- ▶ In the Columns field, enter the number of primary rectangles you want created horizontally (i.e., left and right) across the page.

- ▶ You will probably want the table grid invisible; to make it invisible, set the Border field to **0**.

- ▶ Click OK to create the table. It will appear shorter than you want, but that is normal, because you have not entered any data into it yet. The cells expand automatically when you enter data into them.

- ▶ By default, the vertical spacing of the table cells is symmetrical. If you want to adjust the vertical position of the cell boundaries, click and drag the table's handles with your mouse. To make finer adjustments, follow these steps:
    - ■ Click once inside the column whose width you want to adjust, then pull down the Format menu and choose Table Cell Properties to make the Table Properties dialog appear.
    - ■ If you want to change the width of the entire column, pull down the menu in the Selection group and choose Column.
    - ■ Adjust the size settings as you wish.
    - ■ Click the Apply button to preview the width adjustment.
    - ■ Click OK to close the dialog.

- ▶ If your design calls for any of the cells to be subdivided into secondary rectangles, click inside the cell to be divided to position your cursor there, then click the Table button to create the secondary table cells. You will probably want to set the options the same as for your primary table.

- ▶ At any time, you can begin entering your text and graphics into the table cells. Cell height will adjust automatically to the amount of information you enter.

- ▶ Use the Format toolbar to set the size, color, style, and appearance of your text.

- ▶ Click the Save button and save your new home page in your *website* folder. Make the name of your home page be either *index.htm* or *index.html*.

- ▶ Click the Browse button to see how your home page will appear on the Web.

Linking Your Résumé to Your Home Page

Now that your home page has been created, you can link your résumé to your home page. Because links create webs, this link will form your local Web site. To link your résumé to your home page, follow the steps in Table 21-5.

If your résumé appears when you click the phrase that triggers it on your home page, congratulate yourself, because you have just created a local Web site! If the link does not work, repeat these steps, reading the instructions more carefully. What you have done is to create a link to a local file. A *local file* is a link that resides in the same folder as the page that refers to it. In order for this link to work, both your home page and your résumé must reside in the same folder, which in this example is your *website* folder.

Table 21-5 How to link your résumé to your home page

Dreamweaver	FrontPage	Nvu
▶ Use Dreamweaver to get your home page onscreen.	▶ Use FrontPage to get your home page onscreen.	▶ Use Nvu to get your home page onscreen.
▶ If you have not already entered the text that will trigger your résumé, do so now. In an appropriate place on your home page, enter a phrase such as *Read my résumé to find out about my professional qualifications, career goals, and work experience.*	▶ If you have not already entered the text that will trigger your résumé, do so now. In an appropriate place on your home page, enter a phrase such as *Read my résumé to find out about my professional qualifications, career goals, and work experience.*	▶ If you have not already entered the text that will trigger your résumé, do so now. In an appropriate place on your home page, enter a phrase such as *Read my résumé to find out about my professional qualifications, career goals, and work experience.*
▶ Drag your mouse to highlight the word or phrase that will trigger the link. In this example, highlight *Read my résumé.*	▶ Drag your mouse to highlight the word or phrase that will trigger the link. In this example, highlight *Read my résumé.*	▶ Drag your mouse to highlight the word or phrase that will trigger the link. In this example, highlight *Read my résumé.*
▶ Right-click the highlighted text and choose Make link; the Select File dialog appears.	▶ Click the Insert Hyperlink button to make the Insert Hyperlink dialog appear.	▶ Click the Link button to make the Link Properties dialog appear.
▶ Click to select the file you want to link. In this example, select *website\resume.html* or *website\resume.htm.*	▶ Click to select the file you want to link. In this example, select *website\resume.html* or *website\resume.htm.*	▶ Click the Choose File button and select the file you want to link. In this example, select *website\resume.html* or *website\resume.htm.*
▶ The filename appears in the URL field. Click OK to close the dialog.	▶ The filename appears in the Address field.	▶ The filename appears in the link location field. Click OK to close the dialog.
▶ Pull down the File menu and choose Save to save the file.	▶ Click OK to close the Insert Hyperlink dialog.	▶ Click the Save button to save the file.
▶ Click the Preview in Browser button to see how the link will appear on the Web.	▶ Click the Save button to save the file.	▶ Click the Browse button to see how the link will appear on the Web.
▶ Click the phrase that triggers your résumé to see if it brings up your résumé.	▶ Click the Preview button to see how the link will appear on the Web.	▶ Click the phrase that triggers your résumé to see if it brings up your résumé.
	▶ Click the phrase that triggers your résumé to see if it brings up your résumé.	

Returning to Your Home Page from Your Résumé

Now that you have provided a way for the user to link to your résumé from your home page, it is time to create a link from your résumé back to your home page. While it is possible for users to return to your home page by clicking their Web browser's Back button, it is customary to provide a return link to your home page. Such a return link often appears at the bottom of a Web page, but if the document is lengthy, the return link may appear at the end of major sections. The link to your home page also will come in handy for users who might browse to your résumé some other way, such as through a search engine or via your résumé's URL. Try to create such a return link on your own, but if you need help, follow the steps in Table 21-6.

Now that you have created the return link, you should be able to click back and forth between your home page and your résumé with ease. Try this now. While viewing your home page in your Web browser's window, click the link that goes to your résumé. When your résumé appears, click the link that goes to your home page. Practice clicking back and forth between your home page and your résumé. Congratulations are in order, because you have successfully created a local Web site! In the next chapter, you will learn how to publish this local Web site to the World Wide Web and make your home page and your résumé available to everyone on the Internet.

Table 21-6 How to create a return link to your résumé

Dreamweaver	FrontPage	Nvu
▶ Use Dreamweaver to get your Web page résumé onscreen.	▶ Use FrontPage to get your Web page résumé on screen.	▶ Use Nvu to get your Web page résumé onscreen.
▶ If you have not already entered the text that will trigger your home page, do so now. In an appropriate place on your résumé, such as at the bottom of it or at the end of major sections, enter a phrase such as *Go to my home page.*	▶ If you have not already entered the text that will trigger your home page, do so now. In an appropriate place on your résumé, such as at the bottom of it, or at the end of major sections, enter a phrase such as *Go to my home page.*	▶ If you have not already entered the text that will trigger your home page, do so now. In an appropriate place on your résumé, such as at the bottom of it or at the end of major sections, enter a phrase such as *Go to my home page.*
▶ Drag your mouse to highlight the word or phrase that will trigger the link. In this example, highlight *Go to my home page.*	▶ Drag your mouse to highlight the word or phrase that will trigger the link. In this example, highlight *Go to my home page.*	▶ Drag your mouse to highlight the word or phrase that will trigger the link. In this example, highlight *Go to my home page.*
▶ Right-click the highlighted text and choose Make link; the Select File dialog appears.	▶ Click the Insert Hyperlink button to make the Insert Hyperlink dialog appear.	▶ Click the Link button to make the Link Properties dialog appear.
▶ Click to select the file you want to link. In this example, select *website\index.html* or *website\index.htm.*	▶ Click to select the filename of your home page and make the filename appear in the Address field.	▶ Click the Choose File button and select the file you want to link. In this example, select *website\index.html* or *website\index.htm.*
▶ The filename appears in the URL field. Click OK to close the dialog.	▶ Click OK to close the Insert Hyperlink dialog.	▶ The filename appears in the link location field. Click OK to close the dialog.
▶ Pull down the File menu and choose Save to save the file.	▶ Click the Save button to save the file.	▶ Click the Save button to save the file.
▶ Click the Preview in Browser button to see how the link will appear on the Web.	▶ Click the Preview button to see how the link will appear on the Web.	▶ Click the Browse button to see how the link will appear on the Web.
▶ Click the phrase that triggers your home page to see if it goes to your home page.	▶ Click the phrase that triggers your home page to see if it goes to your home page.	▶ Click the phrase that triggers your home page to see if it goes to your home page.

Case Sensitivity

When you create links to files on the World Wide Web, you need to be careful about when you use uppercase and lowercase letters, because many file servers are case sensitive. The author recommends that you always keep your filenames in lowercase letters. That way, you will never get confused about whether to use uppercase or lowercase when linking to your own files.

You need to be aware, however, that when you want to create a link to a Web address that contains a filename consisting of uppercase and lowercase letters, you must type the filename exactly by observing the uppercase and lowercase letters in the filename.

Spaces in Filenames

You also need to be careful about putting spaces in filenames, because spaces are not permitted in URLs. In order to put a space in a URL, you have to type **%20,** which is the browser's code for a space. If Santa Claus publishes a file to the Web called *My Summer Vacation.html,* for example, and a user wanted to go to it, the user would have to type the URL as follows:

http://www.northpole.com/santa/My%20Summer%20Vacation.html

Save your users the hassle and form a habit of not putting spaces in filenames. Also consider shortening the filename. In this example, Santa might shorten the Web address to http://www.northpole.com/santa/summer.html.

To summarize these pointers regarding filenames, you should (1) keep filenames short so users do not have to type so much, (2) use lowercase to avoid the problems of case-sensitive file servers, (3) not use spaces, and (4) avoid punctuation. If you need to separate words for clarity, use _ or – instead of inserting a space.

Inspecting Your HTML

Click the HTML tab to inspect the HTML code of your home page. Scroll down to the hypertext that triggers your résumé. Notice how the phrase that triggers your résumé appears inside the anchor tags <**a**> and </**a**>, as follows:

<a href="index.html">Read my résumé</a>

As you know, the tag <**a**> stands for anchor, and the attribute **href** stands for hypertext reference.

exercises

These exercises are designed to provide you with more practice creating Web pages via the methods of cloning and designing. Completing these exercises will help you judge when it is best to clone or design your own custom Web page. It all depends on the page's purpose, whether you have a good model to follow, and how much time you have to spend creating the Web page. So you will know how long each method takes, time yourself as you complete each of these exercises.

1. Follow the *Interlit* Web site link to the model Web page library of your choice. Locate a page that has a look and feel appropriate for a club or organization to which you belong. Following the steps in Table 21-1, clone the page and modify it to create a Web page for your club or organization. Remember to time yourself so you will know how long it takes to create a Web page this way. When you save this page, save it in your *website* folder under the name *temp.htm* or *temp.html*.

2. The most creative way to make a Web page is to design your own. Use the table layout method taught in this chapter to create a Web page for your club or organization. When you save this page, save it in your *website* folder under the name *designed.htm* or *designed.html*. Remember to keep track of how long this takes.

3. Compare the results of the previous exercises. Which one took longer to complete? Which was more efficient? Which method—cloning or designing—left you with the better feeling afterward regarding what you created? Why do you think it made you feel that way?

4. You probably like one of the Web pages you created in these exercises better than the others. Create a hypertext or hyperpicture link to it from your home page. If you have trouble, follow the steps provided earlier in this chapter under the section entitled "Linking Your Résumé to Your Home Page," except this time, you will link your club's page to your home page. Also, put a link to your home page on your club's page, so the user will have an easy way to get back to your home page from your club's page. When you are finished, use your Web browser to go to your club's page and test the links to make sure you can go back and forth between your résumé and your club's page with ease.

5. If you are using this book in a class, work with your fellow classmates to create a Web page index of the home pages created in your class. E-mail the URL of this index to your professor and, in the message, tell your professor that you created the index to make grading your Web pages easier.

SITUATED CASE PROJECTS
Case 21: Creating Portfolio Content

At the end of each chapter in this book, a situated case project provides the student an opportunity to put the chapter's contents to practical use in a workplace situation. Each case has the same number as the chapter in which it appears.

Now that you have learned how to create links on your résumé page, you can embellish the page by linking some of the things you have done to examples of the works themselves. If your résumé mentions the title of a paper or an article that you have written, for example, you can link this title to the paper itself. Through this link, a potential employer can click to read your paper and see an example of your writing ability. Similarly, you can link items on your résumé to photographs that document things you have done or show things you have created. If you are a musician, you can provide links to sound recordings that demonstrate your performance skills. Thus, your résumé becomes an online portfolio full of supporting evidence that can help you get a job. To create such a portfolio, follow these steps:

1. In the *website* folder on your hard drive, create a subfolder called *portfolio*. If you need help doing this, refer to Table 6-9.

2. Using the Windows File Manager, My Computer, or the Macintosh Finder, copy into the *website/portfolio* folder the artifacts that your portfolio will comprise. These artifacts can be digital photos, word processor files, spreadsheets, databases, graphical artwork, sound recordings, or any other kind of computer file that you have created.

3. Use Dreamweaver, FrontPage, or Nvu to link the appropriate words or phrases in your résumé page to the artifacts in your *website/portfolio* folder.

4. Some of the items in your *website/portfolio* folder may need to be presented on Web pages of their own that can provide further explanation of the artifact being displayed. If so, use the Web page creation tool of your choice (probably Dreamweaver, FrontPage, or Nvu) to create the auxiliary pages to which the résumé page will link. Save the auxiliary pages in your *website/portfolio* subfolder.

5. On your résumé page, put links to the auxiliary pages created in step (4). Save the résumé page.

6. On the auxiliary pages you created in step (4), put a return link to the résumé; via this link, the user will be able to return to your résumé after viewing the artifacts. Remember to save the pages.

7. Use the Preview in Browser feature to test these pages, follow all the links, and make sure the links work properly. Make any changes that are necessary, save the pages, and test them again. Repeat this step until all the links work properly. Remember that when you test the pages, you may need to click your browser's Refresh button to make the browser load the new version of the page.

If your instructor has asked you to hand in this assignment, copy your *website* folder, including the *website/portfolio* subfolder, onto a disk or follow any other instructions you may have been given for submitting this assignment.

22

PUBLISHING FILES ON THE WORLD WIDE WEB

After completing this chapter, you will be able to:

- Define what it means to publish a file on the World Wide Web.

- Know where to get free Web space for publishing your files.

- Transfer files to your World Wide Web site.

- Inspect the folder of files at your Web site.

- Create folders and maintain a good directory structure at your Web site.

- Rename or delete files at your Web site.

- Edit pages at your Web site.

- Cope with case-sensitive file servers.

- Set the file permission attributes at your Web site.

- Advertise the existence of your Web site.

- Publish a term paper to your Web site.

- Understand what it means to be a WebMaster.

To publish a file on the World Wide Web means to transfer the file into a folder on a Web server so that other people around the world can access the file with a Web browser. Unless your computer happens to be a Web server, you need a way to transfer your files to the Web. This chapter provides you with the knowledge and the tools needed to transfer files from your computer to a World Wide Web file server.

As you work through this chapter, you will publish your home page and your résumé on the Web. Then you will be able to provide access to your Web pages by telling people what URL to go to. For example, suppose your Web server is www.northpole.com and your Web site is located on that server in a Web account named *santa*. Assume further that the default filename on your server is *index.html*. After you complete the exercises in this chapter, the URL of your home page will be http://www.northpole.com/~santa/index.html. Because *index.html* is the default filename, you will be able to shorten the URL and tell users to go to www.northpole.com/~santa to see your home page.

If *index.html* is not the default filename on your Web server, you will use your Web server's default filename instead. If you do not know what the default filename is on your Web server, you should check the guidelines at your Web hosting site or contact your server administrator to find out. If you cannot determine the default filename, you can make your home page have an intuitive name such as *home.html*.

Getting Your Web Space

Before you can publish a file on the World Wide Web, you need to have some file space on the Web to hold your published files. There are three places where you can get file space on the Web. First, your ISP account probably includes a certain allotment of Web space. If you are not sure, check with your ISP. While you are checking, you might want to inquire as to what the limit is and how much it costs if you want to get more space.

Second, your school or workplace may have a Web server on which you can obtain Web space. Check with your supervisor or IT staff to find out the policies for obtaining and using Web space at your school or workplace.

Third, there are sites on the Web where you can get free Web space in return for simply registering at those sites. They give you the free space to keep you coming back to their sites, where you will see commercial advertising that pays for the free space. The free space also may cause ads to be placed on your Web pages, although some sites offer free Web space without putting ads on your Web pages.

Searching Google or Yahoo for the keywords "free FTP Web space" brings up many sites where you can get free FTP Web space.

Your Web Space Address

In order to transfer files to the Web, you need to know the name of your Web server and the path to your file space on that server. If you are using free Web space, you will be given the name of the server and the path to your file space when you register and get your free Web space. Make a note of this information, because it is very important. If you are using Web space from an ISP and you do not know the address of your Web space, contact your ISP and ask the question, "What is the FTP address of my Web space?" If Santa Claus had an AOL account named *Santa,* for example, and he asked AOL for the address of his Web space, the answer would be something like ftp://www.aol.com/santa.

The place where you get your Web space may have instructions for publishing files into it. If the instructions are well written, easy to follow, and work for you, it is OK to follow them instead of the instructions provided in this chapter. You should still read this chapter, however, because it contains a lot of useful tips for publishing and maintaining a Web site.

Note: Sites that offer free Web space normally provide their own upload utility for you to use in publishing files into your Web space. You need to look around the site and read its help page to see if the site also supports FTP. If you use a site that does not support FTP, the parts of this chapter that use FTP may not work for you. If you use a site that supports FTP, everything in this chapter will work for you.

Choosing a Publishing Tool

This chapter covers three approaches to publishing Web pages. You will choose one of these approaches depending on your brand of computer, its operating system, and the Web page development software you are using. The three approaches are (1) publishing files with a Web page editor, (2) using the Windows Explorer to transfer files to your Web site, and (3) maintaining a Web site via FTP software for Windows or the Macintosh.

If you have Windows XP or later, you can use the Windows Explorer to publish your Web site. Using the Windows Explorer is convenient for Windows users who can publish and maintain a Web site using familiar tools that are built right in to Windows. If you do not have Windows XP or later, on the other hand, do not worry. Simply skip to the next part of this chapter, which shows how to publish files to a Web site using FTP software. You will be happy to discover that FTP software is available for both Windows and the Macintosh. Detailed instructions will be provided for installing and using the brand of FTP software that will work on your computer.

Publishing with a Web Page Editor

Dreamweaver, FrontPage, and Nvu have a Web publisher built right in. In order to use it, however, you need to know the FTP address of your Web server, the path to your filespace on that server, and your account name and password. If you do not know this information, check the guidelines at your Web hosting site or contact your server administrator to find out. To publish a Web page with Dreamweaver, follow the steps in Table 22-1. If you have FrontPage, use Table 22-2. If you have Nvu, see Table 22-3.

Table 22-1   How to use Dreamweaver to publish files on the World Wide Web

▶ Use Dreamweaver to open one of the pages you want to publish. In this example, pull down the File menu, choose Open Recent, and open your Web page résumé.

▶ If the Files pane is not already onscreen, pull down the Window menu and choose Files.

▶ In the top left corner of the File pane's toolbar, pull down the menu and choose Manage Sites to make the Manage Sites dialog appear.

▶ Click the New button and choose Site; the Site Definition dialog appears. Figure 22-1 shows that there is a Basic tab and an Advanced tab. The Basic tab features a wizard that makes it easy to configure your site for publishing. If the Basic tab is not already selected, click the Basic tab.

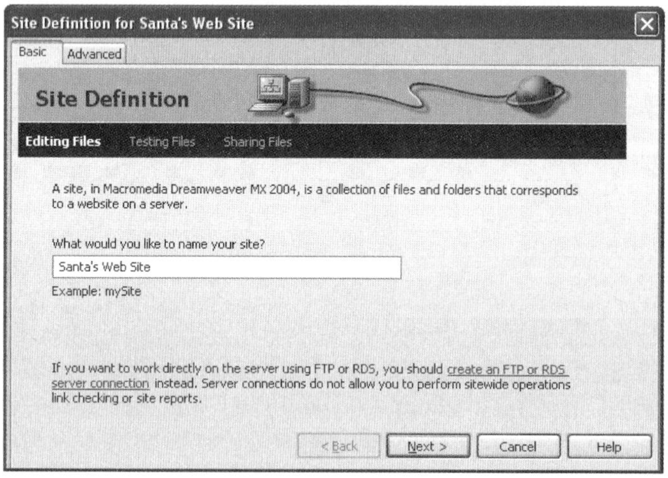

Figure 22-1   The Basic tab of Dreamweaver's Site Definition dialog consists of a wizard that helps you configure a Web site for publishing.

▶ The wizard first asks you to type the name of your site. Type your site's name into the field provided. In Figure 22-1, for example, Santa Claus typed **Santa's Web site.**

▶ Click the Next button to move to the next question, in which the wizard asks whether you want to use a server technology, which defines the scripting language used on advanced Web pages. Answer no because you do not need a server technology right now. You can change this later if you decide to put scripts on the page.

Table 22-1 *(continued)*

▶ Click the Next button. Figure 22-2 shows how the next question asks how you want to work with files during development. Choose the recommended option, which is "Edit local copies on my machine, then upload to server when ready."

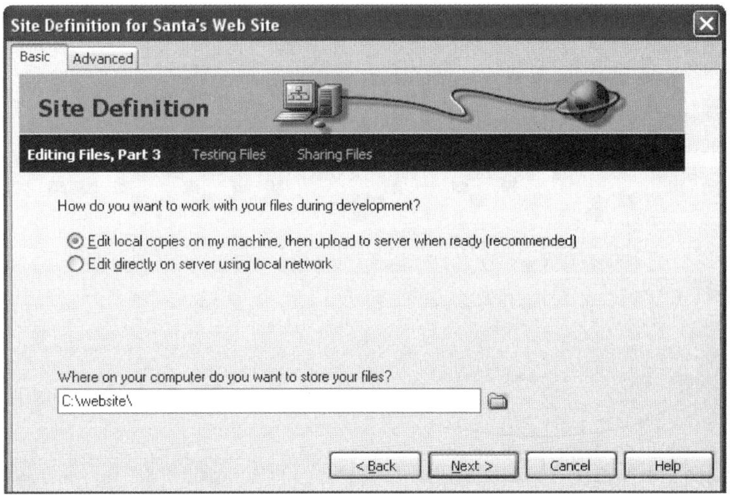

Figure 22-2 Configure your site to edit local copies on your machine, then upload to the Web server when ready.

▶ Under this option, the wizard asks, "Where on your computer do you want to store your files?" Click the ▢ Folder button and select your Web site's local folder. In this example, choose your *website* folder, which is probably located at *c:\website* as illustrated in Figure 22-2.

▶ Click the Next button. The wizard asks, "How do you connect to your remote server?" Assuming you have an FTP account on the remote server, pull down the menu and choose FTP to make the FTP settings appear, as illustrated in Figure 22-3.

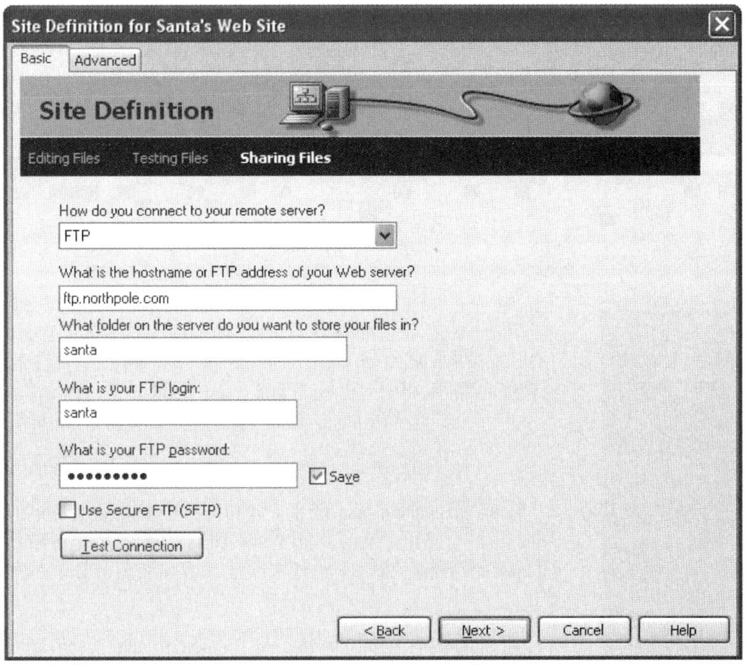

Figure 22-3 When you tell the wizard that you want to use FTP, Dreamweaver displays the FTP settings.

Table 22-1   *(continued)*

▶ In response to the FTP address question, type the FTP address of your Web space. In this example, Santa Claus typed ***ftp.northpole.com***, as illustrated in the second field in Figure 22-3.

▶ In answer to the folder question, type the name of your directory at your FTP site. If your ISP told you to leave this blank, on the other hand, do not enter anything here. Some FTP sites automatically set the directory name based on your login and password info. In this example Santa Claus typed ***santa.***

▶ In the Login field, type your FTP login name; this is often the same as your FTP account name.

▶ If you want Dreamweaver to remember your FTP password so you do not have to type it each time you publish a file, type your password into the FTP Password field. Do not set the Save option, however, if other people besides you have access to your computer.

▶ Click the Test Connection button to test these settings. If you get an error, something is wrong in your FTP settings. Troubleshoot any problems, fix the setting, and click the Test Connection button to make sure the settings work properly.

▶ After you get the Test Connection button to succeed, click the Next button, and the wizard will ask if you want to enable checking files in and out You do this if you are working in a group in which many people may be working on these files. In this example, click *No, do not enable check in and check out.*

▶ Click the Next button one last time; the wizard summarizes your settings and reminds you that you can click the Advanced tab if you need to configure your site further. In this example, click the Done button to close the Site Definition dialog; your site appears in the Manage Sites dialog.

▶ Click the Done button to close the Manage Sites dialog.

▶ Now comes the exciting part: you are ready to publish your site! Figure 22-4 shows that the publishing controls are in the Files pane toolbar.

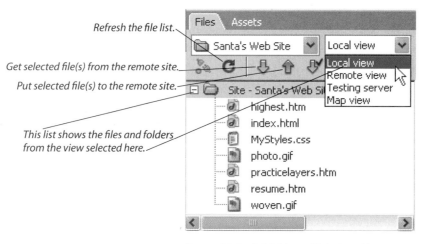

Figure 22-4   Publishing a Web site with Dreamweaver.

▶ Pull down the View menu at the right side of the toolbar, and choose Local view; your local files appear.

▶ Click to select the file or folder you want to publish. In this example, Santa clicked his local Web site folder.

▶ To publish the selected file or folder, click the ⬆ Put File(s) button. In this example, when Dreamweaver asks, "Are you sure you want to put the entire site," click OK.

▶ While the files transfer to your remote Web site, you will see a status dialog onscreen.

▶ After the publishing is done, you can pull down the Files pane View menu and choose Remote view to see the directory of files at your remote Web site.

▶ After you publish a file, always test it by using your Web browser to open the file on your testing server. Make sure the file appears as you intended, and follow any links to make sure they work properly. If you find any mistakes, open the page with Dreamweaver, fix the problems, save the file, then use the controls in Figure 22-4 to republish the page.

Table 22-2   How to use FrontPage to publish files on the World Wide Web

▶ [icon] Pull down the FrontPage File menu and choose Open Site; the Open Site dialog will appear.

▶ Use the Open Site dialog to open the folder containing the Web pages you want to publish. In this example, assuming your hard drive is C, you would type **c:\website** into the Site name field, then click Open.

▶ The first time you do this, FrontPage will ask if you want to add FrontPage information to the folder; click Yes.

▶ Click the [icon] Publish Site button, or pull down the File menu and choose Publish Site; the Remote Web Site Properties dialog appears, as illustrated in Figure 22-5.

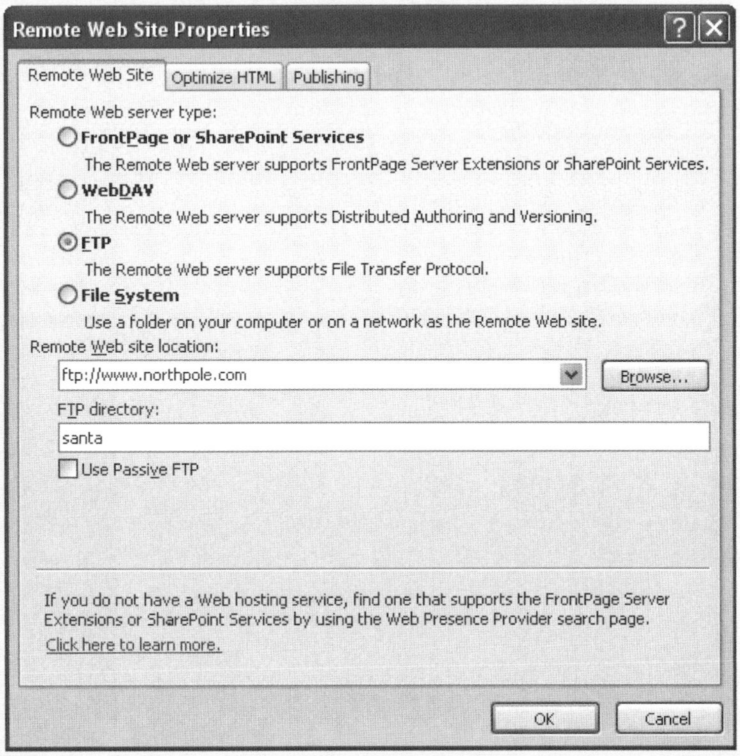

Figure 22-5   The Remote Web Site Properties dialog prompts you to enter the remote Web site settings when you click the FrontPage Publish button.

▶ Click to select the kind of remote Web server to which you are publishing. Depending on the type of server you are using, you will type either the HTTP or FTP address of your Web space into the Remote Web site location field. In this example, Santa Claus is publishing via FTP, so Santa typed his FTP address.

▶ In the FTP directory field, type the name of your directory at your FTP site. If your ISP told you to leave this blank, on the other hand, do not enter anything here. Some FTP sites automatically set the directory name based on your login and password info.

▶ Click OK to close the Remote Web Site Properties dialog.

▶ When the Name and Password dialog appears, type your login name and password, then click OK.

▶ FrontPage will display the two-pane view illustrated in Figure 22-6. In the left pane are the files at your local site. In the right pane are the files at your remote Web site. The first time you try this, the right pane will probably be blank.

▶ To publish a single file from your local site to your remote Web site, click to select the file in the left pane, then click the ➡ Publish Selected Files button in between the two panes.

Table 22-2   *(continued)*

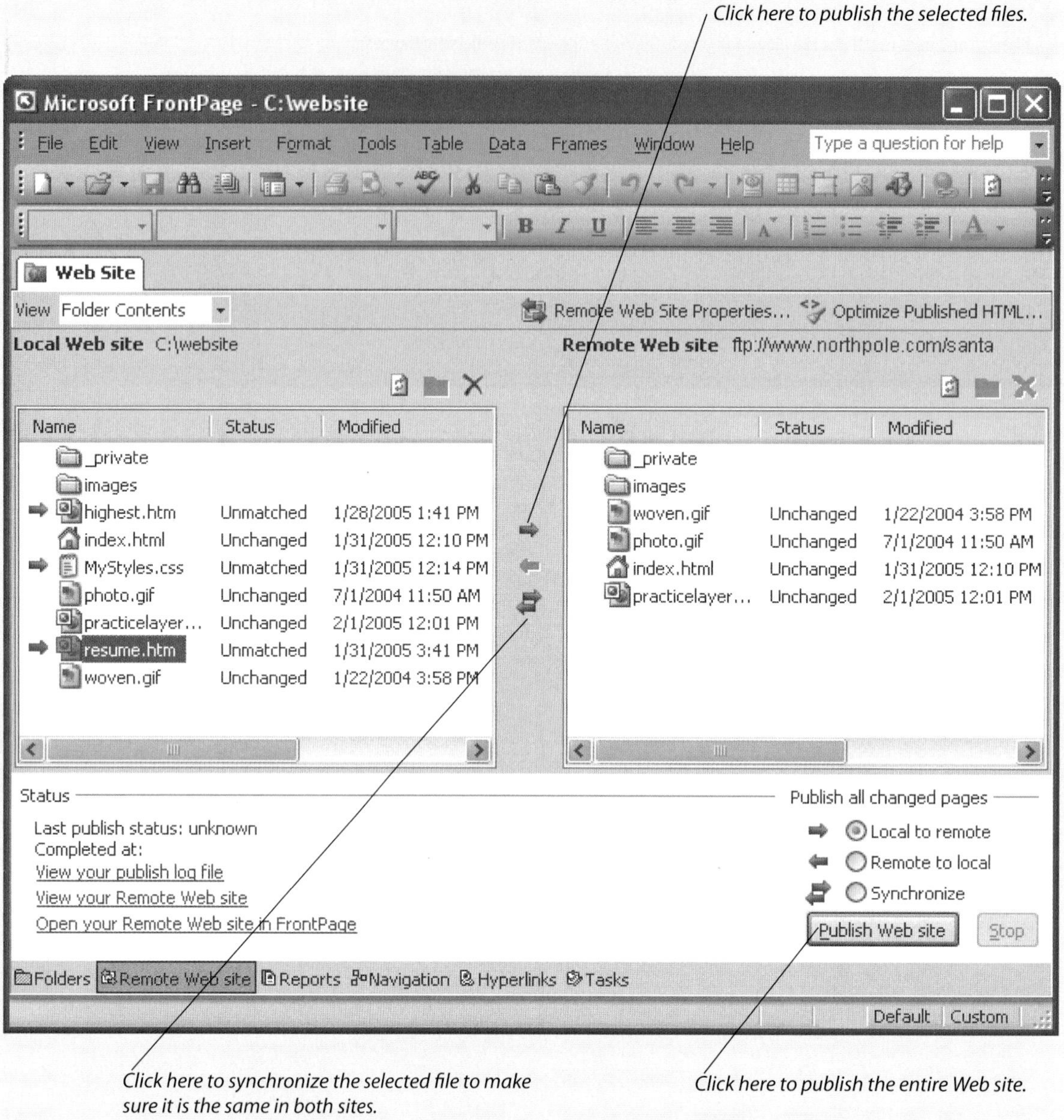

Click here to publish the selected files.

Click here to synchronize the selected file to make sure it is the same in both sites.

Click here to publish the entire Web site.

Figure 22-6   The FrontPage publish window displays your local Web site in the left pane and your remote Web site in the right pane.

▶ To publish the entire Web site, click the Publish Web site button underneath the right pane.

▶ To move a file from the remote Web site to your local site, click to select the file in the right pane, then click the ⬅ Publish from Remote to Local button in between the two panes.

▶ If all goes well, you will see a status dialog informing you of the progress as your files get transferred to the Web. If you get error messages, repeat these instructions carefully.

▶ After you publish a file, always test it by using your Web browser to open the file on your testing server. Make sure the file appears as you intended, and follow any links to make sure they work properly. If you find any mistakes, open the page with FrontPage, fix the problems, save the file, then use the controls in Figure 22-6 to republish the page.

Table 22-3   How to use Nvu to publish files on the World Wide Web

▶ 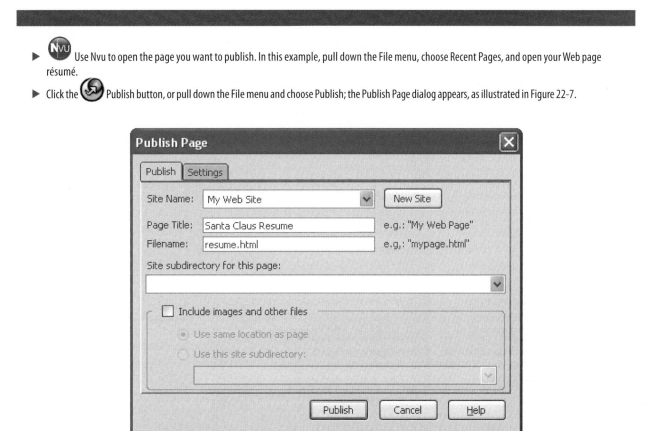 Use Nvu to open the page you want to publish. In this example, pull down the File menu, choose Recent Pages, and open your Web page résumé.

▶ Click the ⟨icon⟩ Publish button, or pull down the File menu and choose Publish; the Publish Page dialog appears, as illustrated in Figure 22-7.

Figure 22-7   The Nvu Publish Page dialog. If the page contains images or multimedia resources that you need to publish, select the option to Include images and other files.

▶ Click the New Site button to create a new remote publishing site. You only do this once per remote site. In the future, you will be able to select the remote publishing site from the Site Name menu.

▶ Clicking the New Site button takes you to the Settings tab of the Publish Page dialog, as illustrated in Figure 22-8.

▶ In the Site Name field, type the site's name. This is the name that will appear on the Site Name menu when you click to publish pages in the future.

▶ In the HTTP address of your homepage field, type the Web address of the site's home page.

▶ In the Publishing address field, type the FTP address of your Web space, as illustrated in Figure 22-8.

▶ In the User name field, type your FTP login name.

▶ In the password field, type your password.

▶ If you want Nvu to remember your FTP password so you do not have to type it each time you publish a file, check the Save Password button. Do not set this option, however, if other people besides you have access to your computer.

▶ To publish image files and other support files along with a page, select the Include Images option that you see in Figure 22-7 on the Publish tab of the Publish Page dialog.

▶ Click the dialog's Publish button to publish the file.

▶ If all goes well, you will see a status dialog informing you of the progress as your file gets transferred to the Web. If you get error messages, repeat these instructions carefully.

▶ After you publish a file, always test it by using your Web browser to open the file on your testing server. Make sure the file appears as you intended, and follow any links to make sure they work properly. If you find any mistakes, open the page with Nvu, fix the problems, save the file, then repeat these instructions to republish the page.

Table 22-3 *(continued)*

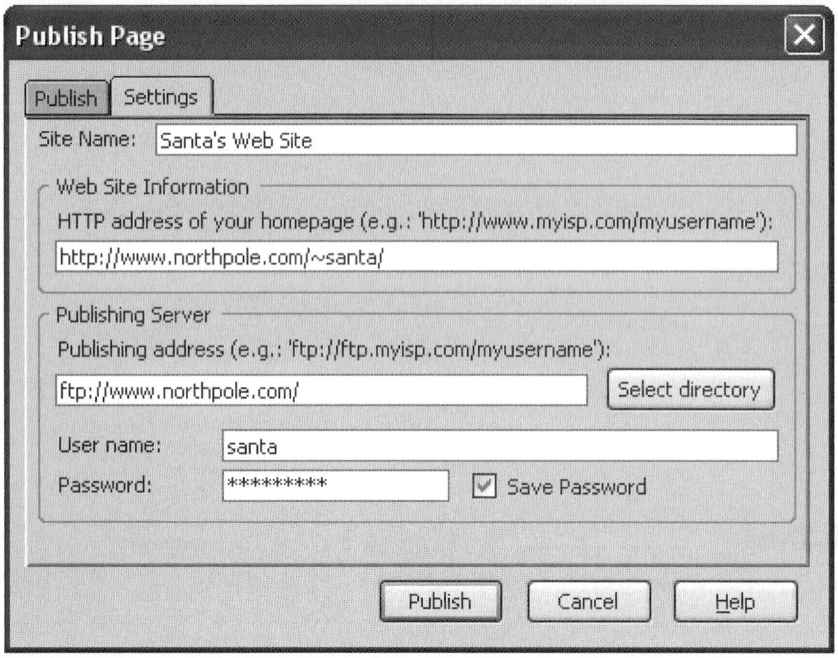

Figure 22-8 The Settings tab on the Nvu Publish Page dialog.

▶ After you publish a file with Nvu, the Nvu Publish button will dim and be inactive on that page. When you change something on the page with Nvu, the Publish button will brighten and you can click it again.

▶ If you ever want to define a new remote publishing site, pull down the Nvu File menu, choose Publish As, click the New Site button, and use the onscreen controls to define the new site.

If your Web page editor's publish feature does not work for you, it may be that your Web server does not allow programs like Dreamweaver, FrontPage, or Nvu to upload files. In this case, you should try one of the other methods for publishing a Web site. The next part of this chapter, for example, shows how to publish a Web site with the Windows Explorer. You also can try publishing your site via the FTP software that is covered later in this chapter. If the FTP software will not work on your server, contact your ISP, who should either be able to help you get one of these methods working or provide you with another method for publishing files to your Web site.

Publishing Files with the Windows Explorer

If you have Windows XP, you can use the Windows Explorer to create a **network place** that maps to the FTP address of your Web site. Once your Web site is mapped as a network place, the site will have a folder icon in the My Network Places section of the Windows Explorer. Then you can use the tools built in to Windows Explorer to copy the files from your local Web site into your public Web space. To learn how to create a network place, follow the steps in Table 22-4. To publish your Web site into that network place, follow the steps in Table 22-5. This process will work regardless of whether you created your pages with Dreamweaver, FrontPage, or Nvu.

Table 22-4   How to create a network place

▶ Click the Windows Start button and choose 🦋 My Network Places. If My Network Places is not on your Start menu, choose All Programs→ Accessories→Windows Explorer, and then click My Network Places.

▶ Figure 22-9 shows how the Windows Explorer displays an option to add a network place. If the Folders option is turned on, click the Folders button to turn it off, because the folders will hide the options on the left.

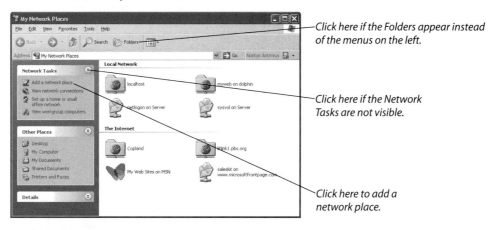

Click here if the Folders appear instead of the menus on the left.

Click here if the Network Tasks are not visible.

Click here to add a network place.

Figure 22-9   The Windows Explorer displays an option to add a network place.

▶ Click the option to add a network place; the Add Network Place Wizard appears onscreen. It will ask you a series of questions. Click Next to continue to the first question.

▶ First, the wizard asks where you want to create the network place. Choose the option to choose another network location, as illustrated in Figure 22-10. Then click Next.

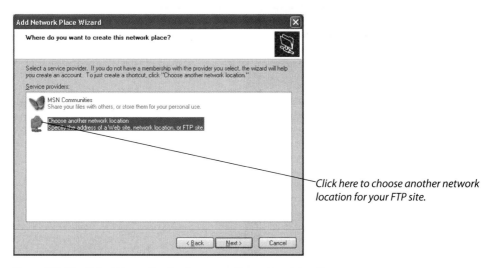

Click here to choose another network location for your FTP site.

Figure 22-10   Select the option to choose another network location.

▶ Second, the wizard asks you to type the address of the network location. Type the FTP address of your Web space, such as ftp://www.northpole. com/~santa and click Next.

▶ Third, the wizard asks if you want to log on anonymously. Uncheck that option and type your account name into the user name field. Santa Claus would type **santa,** for example. Then click Next.

▶ Fourth, the wizard asks you to type a name for the network place. Type a descriptive name, such as **Santa's Web Space,** and click Next.

▶ Finally, the wizard will tell you that you are done and ask if you want to open the network place when you finish. Uncheck that option and click Finish. The Network Place has been created. Now proceed to Table 22-5, which will step you through the process of publishing your Web site into the newly created Network Place.

Table 22-5 How to use the Windows Explorer to publish files into a network place

▶ If My Network Places is not already onscreen, click the Windows Start button and choose My Network Places. If My Network Places is not on your Start menu, choose All Programs→Accessories→Windows Explorer, and then click My Network Places.

▶ Double-click the network place to which you want to publish your files.

▶ When the Log On dialog appears, type your user name and password into the blanks provided and click the Log On button.

▶ Your Web space appears in the Windows Explorer, as illustrated in Figure 22-11.

Figure 22-11 Your Web space appears in the Windows Explorer, where you can copy, paste, delete, and rename files using standard Windows tools.

▶ To publish your local Web site into your public Web space, you can simply copy and paste the files using the standard Windows Explorer controls. Follow the rest of these steps.

▶ Get another Windows Explorer window open by clicking Start→All Programs→Accessories→Windows Explorer.

▶ Expand the file tree to reveal your *website* folder.

▶ Double-click your *website* folder to reveal its contents.

▶ Pull down the Edit menu and choose Select All.

▶ Pull down the Edit menu and choose Copy.

▶ Now click to select the window containing your network place. If you have a hard time finding it, hold down the [Alt] key, and press [Tab] repeatedly while you keep the [Alt] key held down, until your network place icon appears, then release the [Alt] key.

▶ Make sure you are at the place where you want to publish the files. If you want to publish the files into a preexisting folder, for example, click to select the folder.

▶ Pull down the Edit menu and choose Paste. A window will appear showing you the status as the files are copied into your network place.

▶ From now on, you can manage your files at your Web site using the same tools you normally use in the Windows Explorer. Any time you want to go to your Web space, simply click Start→My Network Places, then double-click the icon representing your Web space.

▶ To find out whether your files were published properly, get your Web browser running.

▶ Pull down the File menu, choose Open or Open Location, and type the URL of your home page. For example, if you are Santa Claus, you would type www.northpole.com/~santa.

Table 22-5   *(continued)*

▶ Note that if you named your home page something else besides your Web server's default filename *(index.html)*, you need to include the filename when you type the URL of your home page, such as www.northpole.com/~santa/home.html.

▶ Click OK. If your home page appears, congratulate yourself! Then click the link that triggers your résumé. Try all of the different links on your Web pages and make sure they work OK. Make note of any problems you find. Then fix the problems and republish the corrected Web site. Remember that you can access your Web space at any time by clicking Start→My Network Places, then double-click the icon representing your Web space.

Note: The way to correct a problem in a published Web page is to open the page with Dreamweaver, FrontPage, or Nvu; correct the problem; save the page; then repeat these steps to republish the page.

If using the Windows Explorer to publish a Web site seems too technical, continue on to the next section of this chapter, which teaches you how to use FTP software to maintain a Web site. You may find the FTP software easier to use than the Windows Explorer. After all, the FTP software was invented specifically for the purpose of doing file transfers.

Using FTP Software to Maintain a Web Site

Another way to transfer files to a Web site is to use an FTP program such as Core FTP for Windows or Fetch for the Macintosh. These programs have a graphical user interface that makes it easy to upload and download files, inspect the contents of the folders at your Web site, delete and rename files, and create new folders.

Core FTP

Core FTP is available in both a commercial edition called Core FTP Pro and a freely downloadable version called Core FTP LE that is free for educational use. The abbreviation LE stands for Limited Edition. This book uses Core FTP LE. If you download the free version and like how it works, you may wish to consider upgrading to the professional version, which has even more features. When this book went to press, a single-user Pro license cost $29.95.

Fetch

Created by Dartmouth College, Fetch costs $25 for a single-user license. Students can apply for a free license, as can employees of a public or accredited private school, college, university, or academy; students and parents engaged in homeschooling; and volunteers or employees of a tax-exempt charity, to further the work of that charity. To apply for a free Fetch license, follow the *Interlit* Web site link to Fetch Educational/Charitable License Application.

Installing the FTP Software

To download and install the FTP software, follow the steps in Table 22-6, which provides instructions for installing either Core FTP LE for Windows or Fetch for the Macintosh.

How to Configure a New FTP Connection

The first time you use your FTP software, you will need to configure a new connection for your Web site. This is the connection through which the program will FTP the files that you want to publish to your Web site. To configure a new connection, follow the steps in Table 22-7.

Table 22-6   How to download and install the FTP software

Core FTP LE for Windows	Fetch for Macintosh
▶ Click the link to download Core FTP LE at the *Interlit* Web site.	▶ Fetch is distributed as a BinHex type of self-extracting archive. In order to unpack this archive, you must have StuffIt Expander installed on your Macintosh. If you do not have StuffIt Expander, follow Chapter 13's *Interlit* Web site link to StuffIt Expander and install it.
▶ When the download page appears, click the link to download the free version of Core FTP LE. When your browser asks what folder you want to download the file into, choose the folder you want to put it in. Normally you use your *temp* folder.	▶ Click the link to download Fetch at the *Interlit* Web site.
▶ When the file has finished downloading, click your computer's Start button, choose Run, and use the Run dialog's Browse control to locate the Core FTP LE installation program. You will find this program in the folder where you saved the downloaded file in the previous step. Click the Run dialog's OK button to run the Core FTP LE installation program.	▶ If StuffIt Expander has been installed on your computer, Fetch will automatically self-extract and put a Fetch folder icon on your desktop.
▶ The installation program guides you through the setup; follow the onscreen instructions.	▶ Double-click the Fetch folder icon to open it. You will see the Fetch launch icon. Fetch is now installed.

Table 22-7   How to configure a new FTP connection

Core FTP LE for Windows	Fetch for Macintosh
▶ Double-click the Core FTP LE icon on your Windows desktop to get Core FTP LE running. You can also start Core FTP LE by clicking the Windows Start button and choosing Programs→Core FTP→Core FTP.	▶ Double-click the Fetch launch icon to get Fetch running. If you cannot find the Fetch icon, choose File from the menu, then Find, and do a search for the file containing the word *Fetch*.
▶ The first time you run Core FTP LE, it will ask if you want Core FTP to become your computer's default FTP program. I answered Yes to make Core FTP become the default FTP handler on my computer.	▶ When Fetch displays the New Connection dialog, click the Cancel button to close the dialog.
▶ When the Core FTP window opens, it will display the Site Manager window, which you use to create a new FTP connection. Figure 22-12 shows the settings in the Site Manager window.	▶ Pull down the Customize menu and choose New Shortcut; the Shortcut Editor dialog appears, as shown in Figure 22-13.

Figure 22-13   The Fetch Shortcut Editor dialog.

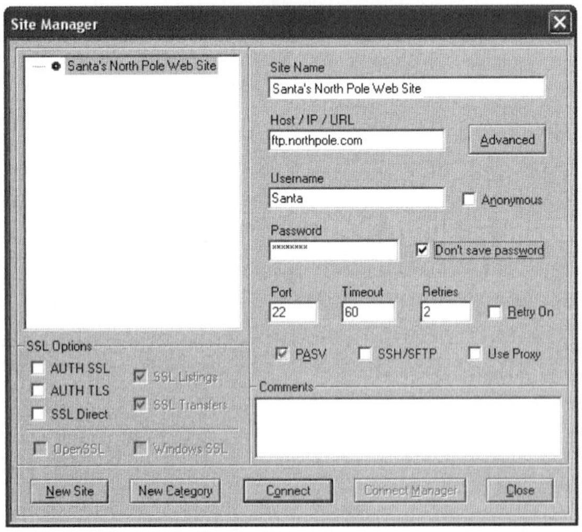

Figure 22-12   When you run Core FTP LE for the first time, you use the Site Manager to configure your FTP connection.

▶ In the Site Name field, type the name of your site. When you make up this name, enter information that clearly identifies your site. Santa Claus, for example, could call his site **Santa's North Pole Web Site.**

▶ In the Name field, type the name you want this bookmark to have, such as **Santa's Web site**

▶ If the type is not already set to Folder, pull down the Type list and choose Folder.

▶ In the Host field, type the domain name of your World Wide Web site, such as www.northpole.com

▶ In the User ID field, type the user ID by which you are known on your Web server; this will probably be the first part of your e-mail address, up to but not including the @ sign

Table 22-7 *(continued)*

Core FTP LE for Windows	Fetch for Macintosh
▶ In the Host/IP/URL field, type the address of your FTP server, such as ftp.northpole.com.	▶ Type your password into the Password field. If you are not using your own computer, you should erase the password field when you are done using Fetch, to prevent another user from accessing your Web site.
▶ If the Anonymous box is checked, uncheck it.	▶ Click OK to save the shortcut.
▶ In the User Name field, type the user ID by which you are known on your Web server; this will probably be the first part of your e-mail address, up to but not including the @ sign.	▶ When the Save dialog appears, give your shortcut a name you will remember, such as **Santa's Web site**
▶ In the Password field, type your password. If you are the only person using this computer, you can let Core FTP remember your password. If other people use this computer, however, you should check the box titled *Don't save password*. When this box is checked, you have to type your password each time you log on to your FTP site.	
▶ If the SSH/SFTP box is checked, uncheck it unless your FTP host supports the secure shell (SSH) or Secure FTP (SFTP).	

How to FTP Files to the Web

Figure 22-14 shows how the Core FTP program has graphical controls that make it very easy for Windows users to FTP a file to your Web site. Figure 22-15 shows the Fetch controls that enable Macintosh users to do likewise.

For example, suppose you want to FTP your home page and your résumé from your computer to your World Wide Web account. Follow the steps in Table 22-8.

How to Delete and Rename Files at a Web Site

Your FTP software provides a way to delete files you no longer want on the Web. It also lets you rename files. To delete and rename files at a Web site, follow the steps in Table 22-9.

Click here to transfer a file from your PC to your Web site. *Click here to transfer a file from your Web site to your PC.*

Click here to transfer a file from your Web site to your PC. *Click here to transfer a file from your PC to your Web site.*

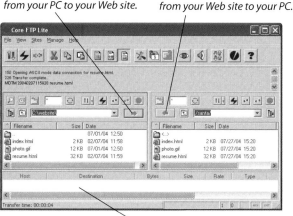

During the transfer, status information displays here.

Figure 22-14 The Core FTP LE program displays folder listings for your local computer and the remote site.

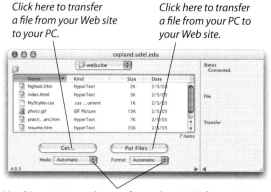

Use this menu to set the transfer mode to ASCII for an HTML file, or binary for graphics, sound, and video files, or leave it set on Automatic to let Fetch decide how to transfer the file.

Figure 22-15 The Fetch program lists the names of the files at your Web site and enables you to upload and download files from the Internet.

Table 22-8   How to FTP files to the Web

Core FTP LE for Windows	Fetch for Macintosh
▶ If you do not already have Core FTP LE running, click the Windows Start button and choose Programs→Core FTP→Core FTP. When the Site Manager window appears, select the site to which you want to connect. Santa Claus, for example, would choose Santa's North Pole Web Site.	▶ If Fetch is not already running, double-click the Fetch icon; the New Connection dialog appears.
▶ At the bottom of the Site Manager window, click the Connect button. Wait a few seconds while Core FTP makes the connection.	▶ In the Fetch New Connection dialog, pull down the Shortcuts menu and choose your Web site's server. Then click OK to open the connection.
▶ The left side of the Core FTP window is the My Computer side, and the right side is the remote computer side. On the left side of the Core FTP window, browse to the folder in which the file you want to transfer resides; in this example, browse to the *website* folder on your hard drive.	▶ When connected to your Web site, the Fetch window will display a listing of the names of the files residing at your Web site.
▶ On the right side of the Core FTP window, browse to the folder to which you want to transfer the files; in this example, that will be the main folder of your World Wide Web account.	▶ To transfer a file to the Web, drag and drop the file from your desktop into the Fetch window.
▶ To transfer your résumé, click once on *resume.html* on the left side of the Core FTP window; then click the → button to transfer the file to the Web. After the transfer completes, you will see your *resume.html* file listed on the right side of the Core FTP window in your World Wide Web folder.	▶ Another way to transfer a file is to click the Put Files button to make the Choose a File dialog appear; select the file you want, click the Choose button, and follow the onscreen instructions.
▶ To transfer your home page, click once on *index.html* on the left side of the Core FTP window; then click the → button to transfer the file to the Web. After the transfer completes, you will see your *index.html* file listed on the right site side of the Core FTP window in your World Wide Web folder.	
▶ To transfer your images, click once on the name of an image on the left side of the Core FTP window; then click the → button to transfer the file to the Web. After the transfer completes, you will see your image file listed on the right side of the Core FTP window in your World Wide Web folder.	
▶ Repeat the previous step for each image you want to publish on the Web. If you click one file and then shift-click another file, you can select multiple files to transfer all at once. To add a single file to a group of selected files, hold down the Ctrl key and click the filename once. You can also transfer files by clicking and dragging them from the My Computer side to the remote-site side of the Core FTP window.	

Table 22-9   How to delete and rename files at a Web site

Core FTP LE for Windows	Fetch for Macintosh
▶ If you do not already have Core FTP Lite running, click the Windows Start button and choose Programs→Core FTP→Core FTP. In the Site Manager window, select the site to which you want to connect, and click the Connect button.	▶ If Fetch is not already running, double-click the Fetch icon; the New Connection window appears.
▶ Click once on the name of the file you want to delete or rename on the remote-site side of the Core FTP window in your World Wide Web site.	▶ In the Fetch New Connection dialog, pull down the Shortcuts menu and choose your Web site's server. Then click OK to open the connection.
▶ To delete the file, click the Delete button. Core FTP will ask if you really want to delete it. Click the Yes button if you really want to.	▶ Click to select the name of the file you want to delete or rename.
▶ To rename the file, click it once to select the name you want to change. Click the name a second time to enter text-editing mode. Type the new filename, or modify the existing name, then press Enter.	▶ To delete the file, pull down the Remote menu and choose "Delete Directory or File."
	▶ Fetch will ask if you are sure you want to delete the file. If you are sure, click Delete.
	▶ To rename the file, pull down the Remote menu and choose Rename Directory or File. Fetch will prompt you to type the new name for the file. Type the new filename, and click OK.

Coping with Case-Sensitive File Servers

Remember that many World Wide Web servers are case sensitive. If your Web server is case sensitive, you need to make sure that the filenames you FTP to the server match the case that you gave them in your HTML source code. For example, the Unix operating system is case sensitive. On a Unix-based server, if an image is named *PORTRAIT.GIF* and your HTML file attempts to access it as *portrait.gif*, you will get a File Not Found error. Folder names are also case sensitive; make sure the case of your folders on the Web matches the case you gave them in your HTML source code.

To cope with case-sensitive file servers, always keep the names of your files and folders in all uppercase or all lowercase letters. Most people use all lowercase, which is what the author recommends you do. You also should avoid typing spaces or special symbols in your filenames and folder names. It is OK to type hyphens and underscores in filenames.

Correcting Problems and Updating Published Web Pages

Sometimes you will need to correct a problem or update information on a Web page that you have published to your Web site. A link might have gone out of date, for example, and you need to update it. Maybe you receive an award and you want to put it on your résumé page. The way to correct a problem or update information on a published Web page is to open the page with Dreamweaver, FrontPage, or Nvu; correct the problem; save the page; and republish it to your Web site. Here are a few pointers to keep in mind when you republish the file:

- In your remote Web site, make sure you put the file in exactly the same folder, and give it exactly the same filename, as the file you are updating.

- Use your Web browser to open the revised page. Since your browser will have cached the previous version of the file, you may need to click your browser's Reload or Refresh button to make your browser read the new version of the file.

- To make your browser refresh everything, including the graphics as well as the text, hold down the Shift button while you click your browser's Reload or Refresh button.

Relative versus Absolute Links

Links on the Web can be relative or absolute. A relative link means that a file has been specified without its complete URL. The browser will look for it in folders related to the current Web page's folder, hence the term *relative*. An absolute link means that the complete URL has been specified.

Suppose that Santa Claus has a folder at his Web site called *wishlist*. In the *wishlist* folder is a file called *danny.html* that contains the list of presents Danny wants for Christmas. On Santa's home page, Santa can link to Danny's wish list either as a relative link or as an absolute link. The relative link would be wishlist/danny.html. The absolute link would be

http://www.northpole.com/~santa/wishlist/danny.html

Because relative links make it easy to work with a Web site on your computer's hard drive, Dreamweaver, FrontPage, and Nvu use relative links when you create links to files relative to the page you are creating. In addition to making it easy to publish the site from your PC to the Web, relative links make it easier to move the site from one Web space to another, should you ever decide to move the site. In order for the relative links to work when you move or transfer the files to the Web, you must maintain a good directory structure on your PC and at your Web site.

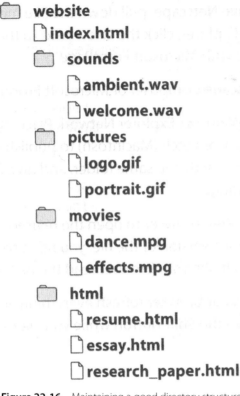

Figure 22-16   Maintaining a good directory structure is important in managing the files at a Web site.

Maintaining a Good Directory Structure

You need to be careful how you create folders and subfolders when you make a local web that you plan to publish on the World Wide Web. Because the links you make to local files are made relative to those files, the directory structure of the local web must be exactly the same as you intend to have out on the World Wide Web. Otherwise, the links will fail when you transfer your local web to the World Wide Web.

Suppose you have lots of HTML files, pictures, sounds, and movies that you plan to mount on the World Wide Web. You should keep them organized in a neat directory structure like the one illustrated in Figure 22-16.

If your files are scattered across multiple folders and multiple drives on your PC, it will be time consuming and tedious to re-create that same directory structure on your World Wide Web server. Troubleshooting problems is more difficult in Web sites that are not well organized. One of the most common causes of links not working, for example, is when you move a file into a different folder after you have already created a Web page that links to it. You can avoid this kind of problem by adopting a good directory structure and adhering to it.

How to Create New Folders on the Web

As the number of files at your Web site increases, you may choose to create folders to help keep your site organized. For example, if you create a series of Web pages related to your work, you might create a folder called *work* to keep them in. The directory structure you create on the Web must mirror the structure of the *website* folder on your PC. If you create a *work* folder at your Web site, then you must also create a *work* subfolder in the *website* folder on your PC. To create a folder at your Web site, follow the steps in Table 22-10.

Table 22-10   How to create a new folder at your Web site

Core FTP LE for Windows	Fetch for Macintosh
▶ If you do not already have Core FTP LE running, click the Windows Start button and choose Programs→Core FTP→Core FTP. In the Site Manager window, select the site to which you want to connect and click the Connect button.	▶ If Fetch is not already running, double-click the Fetch icon; the New Connection dialog appears.
▶ On the remote-site side of the Core FTP window, make sure your current directory is the one in which you want to create a new folder. If it's not, double-click on a directory name to select it, or click the ⬆ Up Directory button to move back a level of directory structure.	▶ In the Fetch New Connection dialog, pull down the Shortcuts menu and choose your Web site's server. Then click OK to open the connection.
▶ Click the ⬛ Make Directory button to open the Make Directory dialog.	▶ In the Fetch directory window, make sure your current directory is the one in which you want to create a new folder. If it's not, double-click on a directory name to select it, or double-click on the two dots at the top of the directory listing to move back a level of directory structure.
▶ Enter the name of the folder you want to create and click OK. *Note:* When you name the folder, avoid special characters and spaces. Instead of a space, you can type a dash or an underscore to represent the space.	▶ From the menu bar, choose Directories, then Create New Directory to make the dialog appear.
▶ Wait for a second or two while the new folder gets created. When Core FTP refreshes the directory listing, the new folder will appear in it.	▶ Enter the name of the folder you want to create and click OK.
▶ If you want to enter the new folder, double-click its icon.	▶ Wait for a second or two, while the new folder gets created. Then Fetch will refresh the directory listing and the new folder will appear in it.
	▶ If you want to enter the new folder, double-click its icon.

Setting the File Permission Attributes

If people are not able to access your files after you FTP the files to the Web, you may need to set the file permission attributes. These attributes determine who is allowed to read and execute your files. You will probably want to set these attributes to let anyone in the world read and execute your files but allow only you to modify or delete them. Core FTP (Windows) and Fetch (Macintosh) make it easy to change the permission attributes. To change the permission attributes of a file with Core FTP, follow the instructions in Table 22-11. If you are using Fetch, follow the steps in Table 22-12.

Promoting Your New Web Site

After you publish your Web site, you will want to let other people know about it. Adding your home page's URL to the signature file of your e-mail software is a quick way of letting everyone to whom you send e-mail know what your Web address is. You also can submit your Web site to the search engines, so your site gets indexed by the Web crawlers. Follow these steps:

- *Yahoo.* At www.yahoo.com, go to the appropriate subject category, scroll down to the bottom of that page, and click the option to Suggest a Site. You will get an online form to fill out and submit. For more info, follow the *Interlit* Web site link to suggesting a Yahoo site.

- *AltaVista.* At www.altavista.com, near the bottom of the page, click the menu option to Submit a Site. Follow the onscreen instructions to submit your site.

- *Lycos.* At www.lycos.com, follow the link to search marketing to learn how you can submit your site through Lycos and its partners.

- *bCentral Submit It!* There is a Web page listing service at www.bcentral.com called Submit It! where you can submit Web pages to about 400 different search engines and indexes. You pay an annual fee for this listing service. A free demo is available. Submit It! is located in the traffic generation section of the bCentral Web site. If you have trouble finding it, follow the *Interlit* Web site link to bCentral Traffic Generation.

Table 22-11   How to change the permission attributes with Core FTP

Core FTP

▶ If you do not already have Core FTP LE running, click the Windows Start button and choose Programs→Core FTP→ Core FTP. In the Site Manager window, select the site to which you want to connect and click the Connect button.

▶ Right-click the file or folder whose attributes you want to change.

▶ When the menu pops out, choose Properties.

▶ The File Properties dialog appears as illustrated in Figure 22-17.

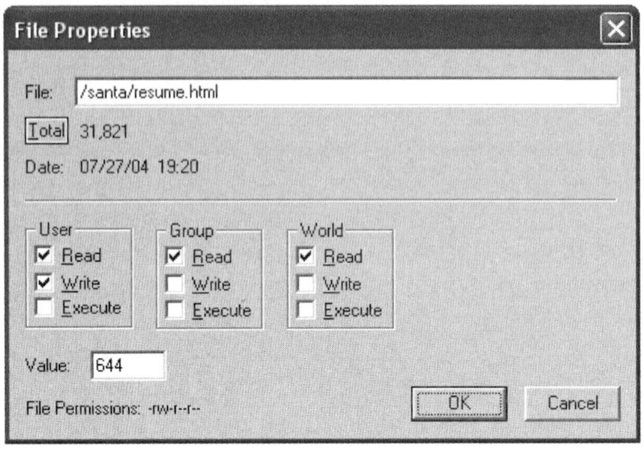

File Properties   ☒

File: /santa/resume.html

[Total] 31,821

Date: 07/27/04 19:20

┌─User──────┐ ┌─Group──────┐ ┌─World──────┐
│ ☑ Read   │ │ ☑ Read   │ │ ☑ Read   │
│ ☑ Write   │ │ ☐ Write   │ │ ☐ Write   │
│ ☐ Execute │ │ ☐ Execute │ │ ☐ Execute │
└───────────┘ └────────────┘ └────────────┘

Value: 644

File Permissions: -rw-r--r--   [OK   ]   [Cancel]

Figure 22-17   The Core FTP File Properties dialog lets you change the file permissions on UNIX hosts.

▶ Check the boxes to let User, Group, and World read your files, but allow only the User to write them. (The user is you!)

▶ Click OK to close the dialog and make the changes take effect.

Table 22-12   How to change the permission attributes with Fetch

Fetch

▶ Get Fetch running, if it isn't already.

▶ Select the file or folder whose permission attributes you want to change.

▶ Pull down the Remote menu and choose Set Permissions to make the Permissions dialog appear, as shown in Figure 22-18.

▶ Check the boxes to let Owner, Group, and Everyone read your files, but allow only the Owner to write them. (The owner is you!)

▶ Click OK to close the dialog and make the changes take effect.

Permissions

Set file/folder permissions to:

	Read	Write	Search/ Execute
Owner:	☑	☑	☐
Group:	☑	☐	☐
Everyone:	☑	☐	☐

Equivalent UNIX™ command : chmod 644

[Cancel]   [OK]

Figure 22-18   The Fetch Permissions dialog lets you change the file permissions on UNIX hosts.

Setting the Metatags

Metatags are extra tags you can add to your Web page to provide extra information about your document. This information does not actually appear onscreen when a user goes to your page. Rather, the metatags reside only in the HTML source code of your Web page. Some of the search engines use a document's metatags to help users search your page via keywords in the metatags. Dreamweaver, FrontPage, and Nvu enable you to set the keywords in your document's metatags. To set the keyword metatags for your Web page, follow the steps in Table 22-13.

Publishing Term Papers with Microsoft Word

Many students who use this book in college courses write a term paper using Microsoft Word. In online courses that use this book, students are often required to publish their paper to the Web. To publish to the Web a paper written with Microsoft Word, follow these steps:

- Pull down the Microsoft Word File menu and choose Save as Web Page. *Note:* If the Save as Web Page option is not visible, click the down arrow at the bottom of the File menu to reveal the rest of the choices.

- When the Save As dialog appears, click the Change Title button; the Set Page Title dialog appears.

- Type the title that you want the published Web page to display in the browser's title bar, then click OK to close the Set Page Title dialog.

- In the File name field, type the filename that you want the published term paper Web page to have. Remember the filename conventions you learned earlier in this chapter and avoid spaces, special characters, and capital letters in the filename.

- Make sure the Save In field is set to save the file in the folder where you want to save the file. In this example, since you are probably going to publish the file to your Web site, set the Save In field to c:\website (if your drive letter is not **C**, replace **C** with your drive letter).

- Figure 22-22 shows how Santa Claus, for example, might set the Save As options to save his term paper as a Web page.

- Click the Save button to save the term paper as a Web page.

- After the term paper gets saved, there will be two new items in your *website* folder. First will be the Web page, which has a *.htm* filename extension; in this example, the filename is *santa-claus-term-paper.htm*. Second will be a folder containing any supporting files, such as any images or illustrations in your paper. The name of the folder will be the filename you chose plus the suffix *_files*; in this example, the supporting folder is named *santa-claus-term-paper_files*.

- Open the *.htm* file of your term paper with a Web browser and scroll up and down through your paper to inspect it. If you find any problems, use Microsoft Word to fix them. Save the file as a Web page, then open it with a browser to check it again. Repeat this step until you get the Web page to read the way you want it.

- Publish your paper and the supporting folder to your Web site. Make sure you copy the folder to the same place you copy the paper. You can do this either with Core _FTP (Windows) or Fetch (Macintosh) or the Windows Explorer Network Place. To use Core _FTP or Fetch, follow the procedure provided

Table 22-13   How to set the keyword metatags in your Web page

Dreamweaver	FrontPage	Nvu
▲ Use Dreamweaver to open the page for which you want to set the keyword metatags.	▲ Use FrontPage to open the page for which you want to set the keyword metatags.	▲ Use Nvu to open the page for which you want to set the keyword metatags.
▲ Pull down the Insert menu and choose HTML→Head Tags→Keywords.	▲ On the File menu, click Properties to bring up the Page Properties dialog.	▲ Click the HTML Source tab or pull down the View menu and choose HTML Source.
▲ When the Keywords dialog appears, type your keywords, using commas to separate the keywords.	▲ Into the Keywords field, type your keywords, using commas to separate the keywords.	▲ Click to position your cursor in the **\<head>** section of the document at a spot where you can insert a new metatag.
▲ If your keywords are *internet, multimedia, web design,* and *publishing,* for example, you would type them as illustrated in Figure 22-19.	▲ If your keywords are *internet, multimedia, web design,* and *publishing,* for example, you would type them as illustrated in Figure 22-20.	▲ As illustrated in Figure 22-21, be careful not to interrupt any tags that might already be in the **\<head>** section.

Separate the keywords by commas.

Keywords

Keywords: internet, multimedia, web design, publishing

OK   Cancel   Help

Figure 22-19   The Dreamweaver Keywords dialog.

▲ Click OK to close the Keywords dialog.

▲ To see how Dreamweaver inserted the keywords into your HTML, click the Code button. In the **\<head>** section of the document, inspect the **\<meta>** tag whose name is *keywords*.

Separate the keywords by commas.

Page Properties

General | Formatting | Advanced | Custom | Language | Workgroup

Location: File:///F:/website/index.html
Title: Fred Hofstetter's Home Page
Page description:
Keywords: internet, multimedia web design, publishing
Base location:
Default target frame:
Background sound
Location:
Loop: 0 ☑ Forever

Browse...

OK   Cancel

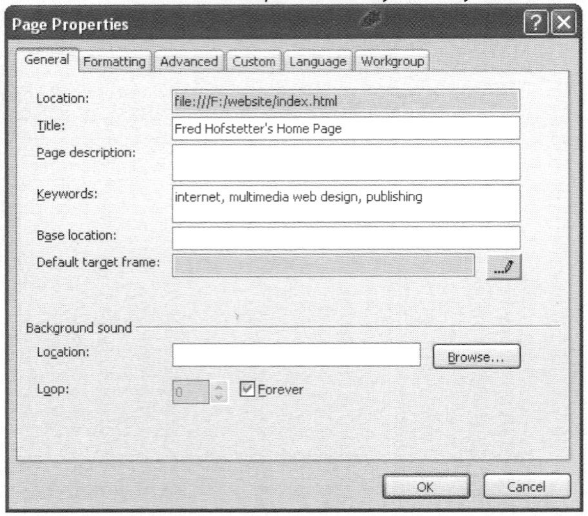

Figure 22-20   The FrontPage Page Properties dialog contains the Keywords field.

▲ Click OK to close the Page Properties dialog.

▲ To see how FrontPage inserted the keywords into your HTML, click the Code button. In the **\<head>** section of the document, inspect the **\<meta>** tag whose name is *keywords*.

Type the keyword metatag on a separate line where it will not interrupt any existing tags.

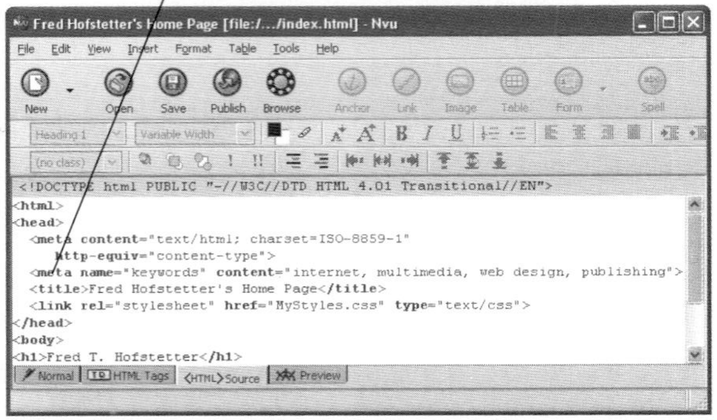

```
<!DOCTYPE html PUBLIC "-//W3C//DTD HTML 4.01 Transitional//EN">
<html>
<head>
<meta content="text/html; charset=ISO-8859-1"
tp-equiv="content-type">
<meta name="keywords" content="internet, multimedia, web design, publishing">
<title>Fred Hofstetter's Home Page</title>
<link rel="stylesheet" href="MyStyles.css" type="text/css">
</head>
<body>
<h1>Fred T. Hofstetter</h1>
```

Figure 22-21   Typing a keyword meta tag into Nvu's HTML Source window.

▲ Type the following metatag, separating the keywords by commas. Replace *keyword1, keyword2, keyword3...* with your actual keywords:

\<meta name="keywords" content="*keyword1, keyword2, keyword3...*">

▲ If your keywords are *internet, multimedia, web design,* and *publishing,* for example, you would type

\<meta name="keywords" content="internet, multimedia, web design, publishing">

Set the Save in field to save the file in your website folder.

Do not use special characters or spaces in the filename; hyphens and underscores are OK.

Click the Change Title button to set the title you want displayed in the browser's title field.

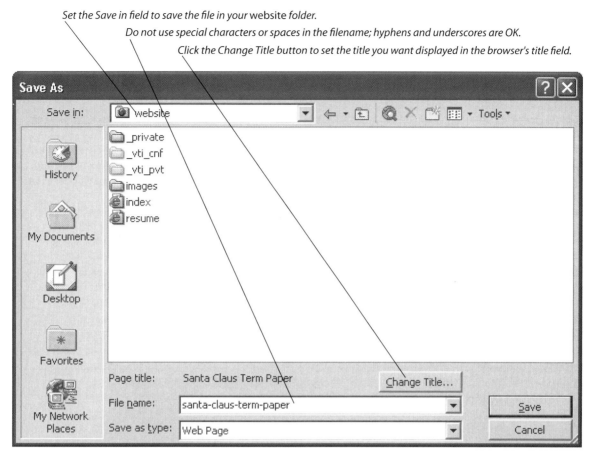

Figure 22-22   The Save As Web Page options in Microsoft Word.

earlier in this chapter in Table 22-8. To use the Windows Explorer, follow the steps in Table 22-4 to create a network place if you have not done so already; then follow the steps in Table 22-5 to publish the term paper and the supporting folder into the network place.

Becoming a WebMaster

Webmastering is an exciting new profession that has emerged along with the World Wide Web. A **WebMaster** is a person in charge of a Web site. The WebMaster keeps track of all the files in the Web site, maintains a good directory structure, and makes sure the links in the Web site work properly. Many commercial Web sites have databases that keep track of customers and orders; the WebMaster either maintains the database or hires the people who maintain it. If the Web site has a lot of custom graphics, the WebMaster may create artwork or hire artists to create it.

CIO

If you found this tutorial easy to complete, you may well have the knack for becoming a WebMaster. To learn more about this new profession, you may be interested in subscribing to *CIO* magazine, which was formerly called *WebMaster* magazine. *CIO* stands for chief information officer, a position at the top of the WebMaster's career path. To apply for a free subscription, click the *CIO* icon at the *Interlit* Web site. See especially the link to Web Professional→WebMaster for position descriptions and job postings.

builder.com

Also linked to the *Interlit* Web site is CNET's builder.com site, which provides access to a wide variety of tools for Web site builders.

exercises

1. Find a few friends who have Web browsers and send e-mail to your friends asking them to try out your new home page and résumé. Be sure to include the URL of your home page so your friends know its address on the Web. Ask your friends to write you back, letting you know how they liked your page and if they had any trouble using it. Ask for comments and suggestions for improving your page.

2. Use your Web browser to get on the Web, go to your home page, and test the mailto link that you put at the end of your Web page when you identified yourself as the Web page owner and provided a mailto link so people can get in touch with you. Click on the link and see if you can send an e-mail message to yourself. If you get a message telling you that your browser has not been configured for e-mail, pull down your browser's Tools→Internet Options or Edit→Preferences menu, find the e-mail settings dialog, and fill in your name and e-mail address. Then click OK and try your e-mail link again.

3. After you complete the steps in the "Promoting Your New Web Site" section of this chapter, see if the search engines find your Web pages. Go to AltaVista, for example, and enter your last name as a keyword. See if AltaVista finds your page. If you have a common name like *Smith* or *Jones,* you will need to be more specific; type your complete name, exactly as it appears on your résumé. Typing your own name into the Web's search engines is known as *egosurfing,* by the way. Try typing phrases from your Web page into the search field as keywords. Be sure to use the advanced search syntax, putting the phrase in quotes, such as "Peter G. Smith's Resume" to make the search engine look for the entire phrase. Now go to Yahoo! and Google to see if they find your Web pages when you type your name as the keyword for a search. Remember that it can take a couple of days for the search engines to begin indexing your material. If the search engines do not find your Web pages right away, wait a couple of days and try again. Finally, reflect on the communication power this process provides. Anyone in the world can publish Web pages and index them into the Internet's search engines. Thus, everyone becomes a provider as well as a consumer of information.

SITUATED CASE PROJECTS
Case 22: Adopting a Publishing Strategy

At the end of each chapter in this book, a situated case project provides the student an opportunity to put the chapter's contents to practical use in a workplace situation. Each case has the same number as the chapter in which it appears.

Being able to publish content quickly to the Web is one of the greatest features of the Internet. As you learned in Chapter 22, there are many ways to do it. Imagine that your employer has asked you to study these methods and recommend which one would work best for your school or company. In formulating such a publishing strategy, consider the following issues:

1 What computer platforms are used in your school or company? Are the computers all running Windows, all Macintosh, or are there multiple operating systems to support?

2 Study carefully the publishing methods presented in Chapter 22. Try all the ones that seem appropriate for the operating system(s) used in your workplace.

3 Use your word processor to prepare a brief essay reporting on the publishing methods you considered. For each method, point out both the advantages and disadvantages you noted.

4 Conclude the essay by stating which method you recommend for use by your school or company.

If your instructor has asked you to hand in this assignment, make sure you put your name at the top of your essay, then copy it onto a disk or follow the other instructions you may have been given for submitting this assignment.

PART SIX
USING MULTIMEDIA ON THE INTERNET

CHAPTER 23	CHAPTER 24
How Web Browsers Do Multimedia	Audio Recording and Embedding

If you can dream it, you can do it.

—Adobe slogan

Multimedia brings Web pages to life with stereo sound, colorful movies, and alluring animations. This part of the book introduces you to multimedia on the Internet. After exploring how Web browsers do multimedia with helper apps, plug-ins, add-ins, applets, and scripts, you will learn how to record audio and add sound to your Web pages.

23

HOW WEB BROWSERS DO MULTIMEDIA

After completing this chapter, you will be able to:

- ■ Understand how Web browsers use plug-ins and add-ins to do multimedia.

- ■ Download and install multimedia plug-ins and add-ins.

- ■ Find hot multimedia Web sites.

- ■ Define Java, understand the concept of an applet, and know where to find tools for creating more dynamic Web pages.

- ■ Define what is meant by the common gateway interface, and understand the server side of Web page development.

- ■ Understand the role of an active server page (ASP) and see how ASP functions in Microsoft's .NET framework.

- ■ Learn how to make a client-side image map.

Multimedia brings Web pages to life with sound, video, and animations. In order to hear the sound or see the video on a Web page, your Web browser must be configured to handle the multimedia resource contained on the Web page. Multimedia is an emerging technology that is undergoing a lot of research and development. As a result of this research, there are a lot of different ways to do multimedia. In the review of commonly found Internet file types in Chapter 12, for example, you learned about several different kinds of audio and video formats.

Web browsers use a clever approach to handling the diversity of multimedia file types. First, the browsers have built-in support for native types of multimedia files. You do not need to do anything special to get these to work, as long as you have a multimedia PC capable of making sound and showing movies. Second, multimedia companies make plug-ins and add-ins that install inside the browser to play their company's brand of multimedia files. Third, some browsers enable you to define so-called helper apps that the browser launches to handle other kinds of multimedia files.

This chapter shows you how to do all three kinds of multimedia browsing. You will learn how to use built-in support and define helpers for file types that are not built in. The *Interlit* Web site will enable you to download the most popular plug-ins and add-ins for handling proprietary multimedia file types. Then you will be ready to visit the world's hottest multimedia Web sites.

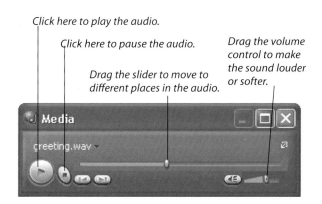

Figure 23-1 Windows Media audio controls.

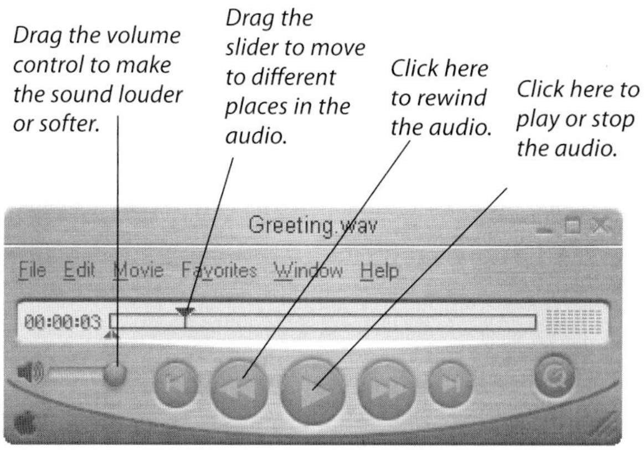

Figure 23-2 QuickTime audio controls.

Built-in Browser Support for Multimedia

The first browsers had no support for multimedia built in. Everything had to be handled through helper apps. Today, the trend is for browsers to contain built-in support for the common multimedia file types. Browser makers accomplish this by obtaining licenses to include in their standard installation file some of the more popular plug-ins you will read about in this chapter.

Audio Controls

Browsers can launch and play audio files. On the Windows operating system, browsers are typically preset to play audio through the Windows Media Player shown in Figure 23-1. If you want to install the latest version, follow the *Interlit* Web site link to Windows Media. To find out whether your browser is configured to use the Windows Media Player, you can simply browse to some audio to find out what application launches to play it. There is an example of an audio file at the *Interlit* Web site. It is a waveform audio file of the author greeting you. To hear this greeting, go to Chapter 23 at the *Interlit* Web site and click the link to the audio greeting from the author. If the Windows Media Player is configured to play your audio, you will get controls like those displayed in Figure 23-1. Another popular player is Apple QuickTime. If your browser is configured to play audio via Apple Quick-Time, the controls will appear as illustrated in Figure 23-2. On the Macintosh, browsers typically play audio via QuickTime.

Video Controls

Browsers can launch and play video files. Under Windows, video files normally get played by the Windows Media Player, illustrated in Figure 23-3. On the Macintosh, video gets played by QuickTime, as shown in Figure 23-4. You can download the latest versions of these video players by following the *Interlit* Web site links to Microsoft's Windows Media Player or Apple's QuickTime plug-in.

Helper Apps

In computer jargon, an **app** is a software application that can make your computer do something. A **helper app** is an application that the browser launches to help it handle something for which a player is not built in. On the Windows operating system, the Internet Explorer uses the Windows filename associations to determine what application will handle multimedia file types. When you trigger the playing of a multimedia file, the

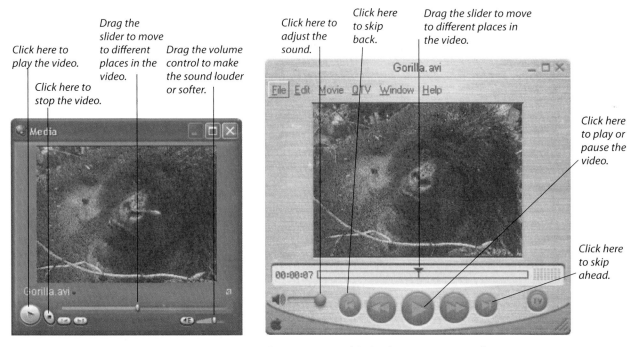

Figure 23-3   Microsoft's Windows Media controller.

Figure 23-4   Apple's QuickTime movie controller.

browser looks to see what application is associated with that type of file on your computer, and the associated app then plays the file. If you have Windows, Table 23-1 shows you how to use the Windows Explorer to inspect or change the filename associations on your computer. If you have a Macintosh, control-click a file's icon and choose Open with Application to see or change the default application handler for that type of file.

Plug-ins and Add-ins

Plug-ins and add-ins are software modules that add functionality to computer applications. There is a subtle and almost trivial difference between the terms **plug-in** and **add-in:** Mozilla calls them plug-ins and Microsoft calls them add-ins. Most people use the terms interchangeably. From now on, this book will call them *plug-ins.*

The advantage of plug-ins over helper apps is that the plug-in usually gives you better integration of the media than the helper app. Plug-ins normally make multimedia play in the browser's window, whereas helper apps often launch a separate window to play the file.

FLASH

Flash is a very popular multimedia plug-in. Disbributed by Macromedia, the Flash player is freely downloadable from www.macromedia.com. According to Macromedia, the Flash player is installed on more than 97 percent of the Internet's end-user computers. Macromedia Flash is so popular, in fact, that the Flash player is built right into the latest browsers.

Web designers create Flash applications with a tool called Macromedia Flash MX Professional. Figure 23-6 shows how this tool uses a timeline metaphor. Authors create rich media content by dragging media objects and behaviors onto the timeline. In addition to creating animated slides, movies, and sound tracks, the latest version lets authors import Adobe PDF documents, design Web forms, and use CSS to create a common style for the Flash plug-in and the surrounding Web page.

Table 23-1   How to inspect or change a Windows filename association

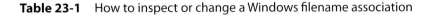

▶ Get the Windows Explorer running, pull down the Tools menu, and choose Folder Options.

▶ Click the File Types tab.

▶ Scroll the list to find the filename whose association you want to see and click once on the filename to select it.

▶ Figure 23-5 shows the setting for an MPEG movie file, for example.

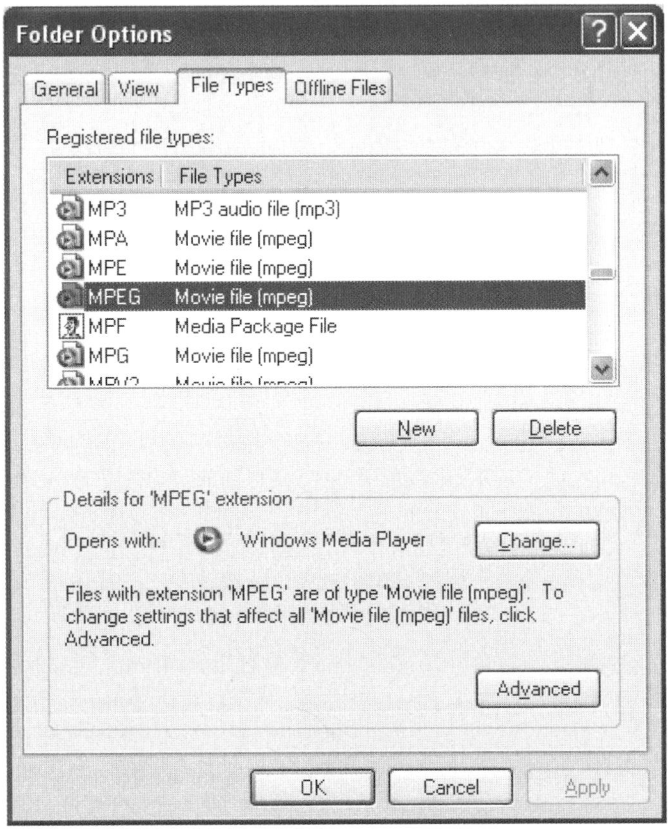

Figure 23-5   Inspecting the filename association of the MPEG file type.

▶ To change the filename association, click the Change button to make the Open With dialog appear.

▶ In the Open With dialog, click one of the recommended programs, or click the Browse button to choose a different program.

▶ Make your changes and click OK. Do not make any changes, however, unless you are sure that the program you are choosing can handle this type of file properly. In this example, the QuickTime player would be a reasonable choice if you wanted to make MPEG movies play in QuickTime instead of the Windows Media Player.

To experience some examples of award-winning Flash applications, follow the *Interlit* Web site link to the Flash Showcase.

BROWSER SUPPORT FOR PLUG-INS

Both Firefox and Internet Explorer have special support for plug-ins. If you have Firefox, you can pull down the Tools menu, choose Options, click Downloads, and

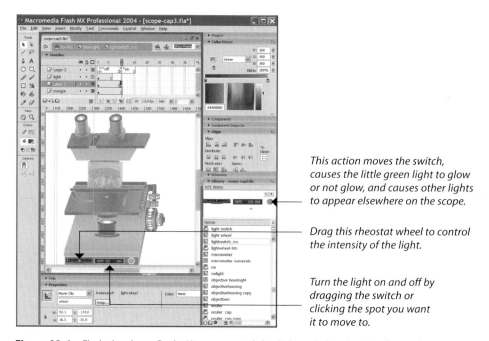

This action moves the switch, causes the little green light to glow or not glow, and causes other lights to appear elsewhere on the scope.

Drag this rheostat wheel to control the intensity of the light.

Turn the light on and off by dragging the switch or clicking the spot you want it to move to.

Figure 23-6 Flash developer Becky Kinney created this light switch animation for use in a microscope simulation at the University of Delaware. You can run this application by browsing to www.udel.edu/Biology/ketcham/microscope/scope.html. To contact Becky, send e-mail to becky@moonlightmultimedia.org. Her company's Web site has a section devoted to "Flash for Educators" at http://moonlightmultimedia.org/f4e, which offers free tools and templates.

then click Plug-ins to find out what plug-ins are installed in your browser. To find out what other plug-ins are available, follow the *Interlit* Web site link to Firefox Central.

If you have Internet Explorer, pull down the Tools menu and choose Windows Update. This takes you to the Windows Update Center, which will take a look around your computer, see what options you have, and give you a list of new items you can add. Especially useful is the notification of new drivers that may be available for devices connected to your computer.

SECURITY RISKS

Every user needs to be aware that whenever you download code that executes on your computer, you run the risk of getting a virus that could cause serious problems on your PC. If you are downloading code from reputable vendor sites, such as Microsoft, Apple, and Macromedia, the chance of your getting a virus is highly unlikely. Downloading code from unknown sources, however, could open the door to trouble.

Even if the code you download is virus-free, it could contain back doors and loopholes through which malicious programmers called *crackers* could send you viruses or cause other problems on your computer. For example, a security hole in one of the major vendor's plug-ins allowed malicious Web page developers to create a movie that could read a user's e-mail messages and upload them to a server, without the user knowing anything about it. Instructions on how to do this were published on the Internet, where any malicious programmer could learn how to do it.

The vendors respond quickly to plug such loopholes by providing fixes called *patches*. To make sure you have the latest patches, follow the *Interlit* Web site link to the download center for your brand of Web browser.

Java

Java is an object-oriented programming language invented by Sun Microsystems. Its main advantage over other programming languages is machine independence. Instead of creating code that can run only on a specific machine (such as a Macintosh or a Windows PC), Java creates an intermediate code that can run on any computer that knows how to interpret it. As a result, Java runs under Windows, Macintosh, Unix, Linux, and many other operating systems, such as the OS9 system used to program set-top boxes for the Internet. Machine independence has made Java the hottest language on the planet. For more information about the Java programming language, follow the *Interlit* Web site link to Java.

Java Applets

Java can be used to create a little application called an **applet** that can be transmitted over the Internet as part of a Web page. Applets can bring Web pages to life in several ways. For example, scrolling tickers can move information across the screen. You can use a mouse to rotate three-dimensional objects that would otherwise appear flat on a static Web page. Active spreadsheets let users manipulate data right on the Web page.

With Java, Web pages can even contain graphics editors that enable users to create their own graphics. Applets can contain games, such as Hangman or Tic-Tac-Toe, or more complex simulations. The Tokamak nuclear reactor simulation, for example, which was featured in Chapter 2 (see Figure 2-11), is a Java applet. To explore a wide range of Web pages that use Java applets, follow the *Interlit* Web site links to Java-enabled Web pages.

JavaScript

Developing applets in Java is time-consuming and requires advanced programming skills. Does this mean Web page programming is beyond the scope of the typical Web page author? No, thanks to **JavaScript,** a client-side, object-based programming language that enables you to make dynamic Web pages without having to become a full-fledged Java programmer. JavaScript has become so popular that virtually all browsers support it, including Internet Explorer, Firefox, Netscape, and Safari. As a result, JavaScript has become the best way for nonprogrammers to create dynamic Web pages that will work in the latest versions of the browsers. There are variations in how JavaScript runs on different platforms, however, so you need to test any scripts you create with any browsers that will be used to execute them.

For more information about the origins and applications of JavaScript, follow the *Interlit* Web site link to the JavaScript Source. There you will find sample code for creating rollovers, graphs, menus, dialog boxes, calendar popups, and layering effects. Figure 23-7

Figure 23-7   A rollover effect created with JavaScript at the Library of Congress. To try this effect, go to **www.loc.gov** and move your mouse over the menu choices. Notice how the photo on the right changes as you mouse over the choices.

shows one of the rollover effects you can create with JavaScript. For even more JavaScript resources, go to www.cnet.com and search for JavaScript.

ActiveX

ActiveX was begun by Microsoft as a way to create and distribute information over the Internet, using existing software applications and data. At first, developers were somewhat reluctant to embrace the ActiveX technology, because it was not an open standard, as was Java. In 1996, Microsoft released ActiveX to the Open Group, an industry consortium experienced in promoting cross-platform technologies. As a result, ActiveX is widely accepted by Windows developers across the industry today.

ActiveX involves three concepts: controls, scripts, and documents. ActiveX controls enable a wide variety of applications and content to be embedded in HTML documents. Through Microsoft's object linking and embedding technology, you can use ActiveX controls to incorporate any supported data type directly into the window of an ActiveX-enabled Web browser such as Internet Explorer. More than a thousand ActiveX controls are available, from multimedia sound and video players, to spreadsheets, charts, graphs, calculators, and paint programs. The Microsoft Internet Explorer itself is an ActiveX control that can be embedded inside other applications. For more information, follow the *Interlit* Web Site link to ActiveX. To see dozens of controls that you can download and use, follow the link to the CNET ActiveX Control Library.

Dynamic HTML

Dynamic HTML is a term invented by Microsoft to refer to the animated Web pages you can create by combining HTML with style sheets and scripts that manipulate Web page elements onscreen. Dynamic HTML makes Web pages dynamic by exposing all page elements as objects. These objects can be manipulated by changing their attributes or applying methods to them at any time. These manipulations also can be triggered by keyboard and mouse events on all page elements.

The definition of the objects and how they can be manipulated is called the **document object model (DOM).** The DOM defines, for example, how text or graphics can be added, deleted, or modified on the fly. Text can change color or size when a user mouses over it. Positioning coordinates can be updated at any time to create animated effects, without reloading the page.

Scripting languages such as JavaScript and Visual Basic Script (VBScript) can manipulate Web page elements dynamically by accessing objects defined in the DOM. To learn more about dynamic HTML, follow the *Interlit* Web site links to Dynamic HTML Central and the Dynamic HTML Web Workshop. JavaScript, VBScript, and Dynamic HTML DOM tutorials are in one of my other McGraw-Hill textbooks, *Advanced Web Design*.

Server-Side Tools

Viewing a Web page on the Internet always involves a client (the browser that requests, downloads, and displays the Web page) and a server (the computer that serves the Web page to the client). After the browser receives the requested Web page from the client, your computer does the work of displaying the text and graphics and enables you to scroll up and down to view the content of the page. No other computer is involved.

There are times, however, when another computer must be used to help a browser process a Web page. Consider the example in Figure 23-8, which displays a Web page with a form that the user fills out to log on to Serf, which is a Web-based e-learning environment. When

Figure 23-8 When a user logs on to the Serf Web-based teaching and learning environment, the browser contacts the Serf server, which validates the password. Illustration provided courtesy of Serfsoft Corp at http://www.serfsoft.com.

the user enters a password and clicks the Logon button, the browser must ask another computer on the Internet to validate the password. For transactions like this between a browser and another computer on the Internet, there is a standard protocol known as the common gateway interface (CGI).

Common Gateway Interface (CGI)

When people typically think of a Web site, they conjure a collection of Web pages that the user can bring onscreen by browsing to the desired page. There are certain sites called gateways, however, that consist of no pages whatsoever. Instead of serving traditional HTML pages, a Web gateway runs a computer application consisting of one or more programs, or scripts, that generate the HTML response the end user sees onscreen. Because the browser displays this HTML as though it were an ordinary Web page, many users are unaware that they are communicating with a Web application as opposed to viewing a traditional Web page.

To provide a standard way for Web gateways to communicate with browsers and other kinds of clients, the National Center for Supercomputing Applications (NCSA) created the **common gateway interface (CGI)** protocol. The CGI protocol defines the manner in which forms data, cookies, and other kinds of information in a Web request get submitted to the program or script that will process and respond to the request. The programs that respond to CGI requests are often referred to as **CGI scripts.** CGI is language neutral, meaning that CGI scripts can be authored in any computer language. Perl and Python are different brands of CGI scripting languages. I write my CGI programs in C# and Java.

The CGI is an open protocol. Any application that can open an Internet socket can implement the CGI interface. The latest version of Flash, for example, supports the CGI. This enables the Flash author to create shows that can display Web forms and interact with users in a browserlike manner. Thus, the Flash author can use the CGI to create a custom Web client that can replace the browser in situations requiring a custom user interface.

Perl

Perl is a machine-independent scripting language developed by Larry Wall, the author of *rn,* which is a popular Unix newsgroup reader. You can create and run Perl scripts under Unix (where Perl was originally developed), as well as under DOS, OS/2, Macintosh, Amiga, and Windows. There is a large public-domain library of Perl scripts that you can download and use freely. The popularity of Perl has led to the release of tools for creating new Perl scripts. For more information, follow the *Interlit* Web site links to Perl. There is also a Usenet newsgroup named *comp.lang.perl.*

Active Server Pages (ASP)

Active Server Pages (ASP) is the premier Microsoft technology for server-side scripting. A typical ASP file consists of a combination of tags and Web-page content, much like you would find in any HTML file. In the midst of this HTML, however, there are script tags. The script start tag is <% and the stop tag is %>. In between those tags comes a script, which can be written in JScript (Microsoft's version of JavaScript) or VBScript. When a browser asks a server to display an ASP page, the server executes any JScript or VBScript on the page before sending the response to the browser. The response contains only the result of executing the script, as opposed to the script itself. Thus, ASP provides programmers with a way to keep their code private, as opposed to JavaScript, which end users can view in the HTML source code of the page.

ASP.NET

The latest version of ASP is called **ASP.NET** (pronounced dot-NET). It consists of a rich library of server-side scripting components that are part of the .NET framework. In addition to writing scripts in JScript and VBScript, ASP.NET allows you to program in C, C++, a new language called C# (pronounced C-sharp), and J# (Microsoft's version of Java). You can still write script in between <% and %> tags on the Web page itself, but ASP.NET lets you do something even more powerful called *code-behind.* Imagine several files full of code that you can call upon from any Web page. Instead of writing code on the pages themselves, you write it in modular files containing reusable objects organized into classes. In ASP.NET, these behind-the-scenes files full of code are called *code-behind files.*

The .NET Framework

The **.NET Framework** is a Microsoft operating system product that significantly enhances the traditional Windows environment. The .NET framework adds thousands of new functions organized into classes of objects that you can use in creating applications. You can use these functions to create ASP.NET Web pages that have an HTML interface, or you can create Web Services that use XML to communicate with other systems and services on the Internet. As an added bonus, the .NET Framework also enables you to develop and publish native Windows applications that run on your PC.

When you install .NET, your computer gets a new runtime environment with a just-in-time compiler. Instead of requiring computer programs to be compiled in advance, the just-in-time compiler can assemble them on demand at the moment they are needed.

In addition to simplifying the development process, this makes it much easier to deploy computer applications over the Web. Microsoft has created a suite of tools called Visual Studio .NET, which is an integrated development environment for creating applications and services. The McGraw-Hill textbook *Advanced Web Design* contains a tutorial on using Visual Studio to create ASP.NET applications.

Client-Side Trends

As HTML continues to evolve and improve, it is becoming possible for Web page authors to handle tasks on the client side that formerly required CGI calls to other computers on the Internet. Image maps are a good example. An **image map** is an invisible layer of hotspots placed over an image onscreen. The hotspots can be rectangular, circular, or polygonal. When the user clicks inside one of the invisible hotspots, the Web browser triggers the object of the link.

In early versions of HTML, using image maps required the use of a CGI call. When the user clicked a hotspot in an image map, the browser sent the coordinates of the mouse click to a CGI program on a server, which told the browser what to do in response to the click. Today's browsers can process image maps locally within the document instead of having to call upon a CGI program for help in handling the mouse click.

Designing an Image Map

If you would like to learn how to create an image map, consider the example in Figure 23-9, which displays a piano keyboard upon which the user is asked to click Middle C. If the user does so, the user will be rewarded. If not, the user will be provided with an appropriate feedback message and a chance to try again. To try this example yourself, follow the *Interlit* Web site link to the Where is Middle C? example.

DEFINING THE MAP AND AREA TAGS

Figure 23-10 shows the HTML code that asks the question presented in Figure 23-9. The <**map**> and </**map**> tags demarcate the beginning and ending of the image map. In between them, you see the <**area**> tags that create the hotspots. Inside each area tag

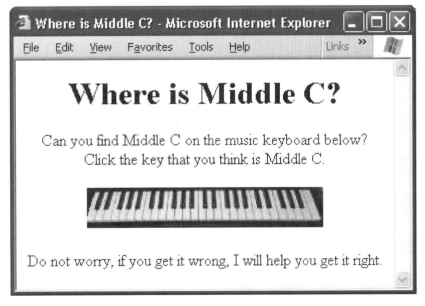

Figure 23-9 The user is asked to click Middle C.

```
middle-c.txt - Notepad
File  Edit  Format  View  Help
<html>
<head><title>Where is Middle C?</title></head>
<body>
<h1 align="center">Where is Middle C?</h1>
<p align="center">
Can you find Middle C on the music keyboard below?<br>
Click the key that you think is Middle C.</p>
<p align="center">
<map name="MusicKeyboard">
<area shape="Rect" coords="0,0,112,32" href="too-low.html">
<area shape="Rect" coords="112,0,116,22" href="correct.html">
<area shape="Rect" coords="112,22,120,32" href="correct.html">
<area shape="Rect" coords="116,0,238,22" href="too-high.html">
<area shape="Rect" coords="120,22,238,32" href="too-high.html">
</map>
<img src="middleC.jpg" border=0 usemap="#MusicKeyboard">
</p>
<p align="center">
Do not worry, if you get it wrong, I will help you get it right.
</p>
</body></html>
```

Figure 23-10   The HTML code that presents the Middle C question.

is a shape attribute and a coord attribute that specifies the x,y coordinates of the links. These coordinates are pixel addresses inside the image. The top-left corner of an image is always pixel address 0,0, which is called the origin. The other addresses are all relative to the origin. The coord attribute has the syntax **coords=x1,y1,x2,y2**. The top-left corner of the area is x1,y1, and the bottom-right corner is x2,y2.

VISUALIZING THE COORDINATES

There are five sets of coordinates in the Middle C image map. Figure 23-11 helps you visualize how these coordinates fit the too-low, too-high, and just-right regions of the music keyboard image.

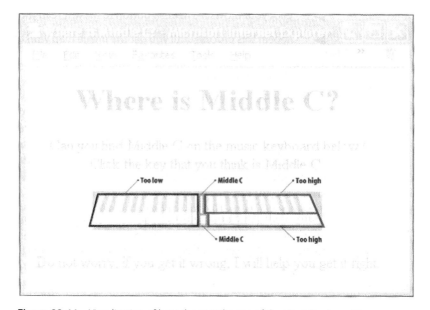

Figure 23-11   Visualization of how the coordinates of the MusicKeyboard image map describe the too-low, just-right, and too-high regions of the music keyboard image.

The first set of coordinates has the HTML encoding of **coords=0,0,112,32**. The format of these coordinates is x1,y1,x2,y2. Therefore, they define an area that goes from 0,0 to 112,32, which is the portion of the keyboard below middle C. When the user clicks there, the too-low link gets triggered.

The second area has the coordinates **112,0,116,22**, thereby specifying a rectangle from 112,0 to 116,22, which is where the top half of Middle C is in the image. The third area has the coordinates **112,22,120,32**, which the bottom part of Middle C comprises. The fourth and fifth areas define the "too high" regions to the right of Middle C.

APPLYING THE USEMAP ATTRIBUTE

Once you have defined an image map with the **<map>** tag, you use the usemap attribute to apply it to any image on the page. The usemap attribute modifies the **<img>** tag that puts the image onscreen. Notice how the image tag in Figure 23-10 has a usemap attribute telling your browser to use the MusicKeyboard map on the middleC.jpg image:

<img src="middleC.jpg" border="0" usemap="#MusicKeyboard">

The syntax of the usemap attribute is **usemap=#*area_name*** where *area_name* is the name you gave the image map in the **<map>** tag's name attribute. When the mouse clicks on one of the areas in the image map, the user follows the corresponding link.

CREATING NONRECTANGULAR AREAS

In the Middle C example, the regions in the image map are all rectangular. Image maps also can contain circle areas. If you wanted a volleyball to be a hotspot, for example, you could make a circle area to do that. The HTML syntax for a circle area is

<area shape="circle" coords="*center-x,center-y,radius*" href="*your_link.html*">

Replace center-x, center-y, *and* radius *with integer values defining the center and size of your circle.*

You can even create polygonal areas with any conceivable shape. On a U.S. map, if you wanted to make the state of Florida trigger something, you could define a polygon the shape of Florida. There is no limit on the number of hotspots or their shape. You can literally create any kind of triggering situation you can imagine. The HTML syntax for a polygonal area is

<area shape="poly" coords="*x1,y1,x2,y2,x3,y3,x4,y4*" href="*your_link.html*">

Replace *x1,y1,x2,y2,x3,y3,x4,y4* with integer values defining the coordinates of each successive endpoint along the polygon. Specify one coordinate for each endpoint. Keep going if there are more than the three sides in this example. The last pair of coordinates should be the same as the first in order to close the polygon.

CREATING AN IMAGE MAP BY CODING

Perhaps the best way of understanding image maps is to create one and see how it functions on your page. There are two basic ways to create an image map: by coding or by drawing. Creating an image map by drawing is a five-step process in which you (1) obtain an image, (2) plot the coordinates, (3) code the map, (4) use the map, and (5) test the map. If you would like to create an image map by coding, follow these steps:

1. *Obtain an image.* In Chapter 19, you learned how to capture and convert images into a format suitable for displaying on a Web page. Following that process, obtain an image upon which you would like to create two or three rectangular hotspots. Save the image in your *website* folder. Remember that the image must have a *.gif*, *.jpg*, or *.png* filename extension.

2. *Plot the coordinates.* Using your graphics editor, figure out the x,y coordinates of the upper-left and lower-right corners of each hotspot you want to make. Most graphics editors will tell you the x,y coordinates as you mouse about the image. Paint Shop Pro, for example, displays the coordinates in the lower-left corner

of the status bar as you move your mouse over the image. Remember that the upper-left corner of the image is coordinate 0,0.

3. *Code the map.* Use your Web page editor to open the page upon which you want to put an image map, and click the Code button or the HTML tab to make the HTML source code appear. After the **<body>** tag, type the following code. When you type this code, substitute your actual coordinates and links for the placeholder values that are italicized in this code sample, which links to your résumé and home page by default:

<map name="MyFirstMap">
<area shape="Rect" coords="*0,0,50,50*" href="*resume.html*">
<area shape="Rect" coords="*0,51,99,99*" href="*index.html*">
</map>

4. *Use the map.* After you create the HTML code for your image map, you can use it on any image on your Web page. In this example, you will apply it to the image you selected in step 1. In Design view, click to position your cursor at the spot on the page where you want the image to appear. In Code view, type the following code, replacing the italicized placeholder values with your actual image filename, width, and height attributes:

<img src="*MyImage.jpg*" border=0 usemap="*#MyFirstMap*"
width="*100*" height="*100*">

5. *Test the map.* Save the file and open it with your browser. Move your mouse over the image and see if the cursor changes shape when you mouse over the hot spots. Click to try those links. If there are any problems, use your Web page editor to make the necessary changes in your HTML, save the file, and test it in your browser. Click your browser's Refresh button to make it read the new version of the file. Repeat this step until you get the image map working, and then congratulate yourself, because image maps enable you to create graphically rich user interfaces onscreen.

CREATING AN IMAGE MAP BY DRAWING

Dreamweaver and FrontPage enable you to create an image map by drawing hotspots on an image in Design view. Creating an image map by drawing is less technically demanding than coding because the Web page editor creates the code automatically when you draw the hotspots. To make fine adjustments in the image map, however, you may need to switch into HTML Code view, where you can tweak the x,y coordinates of the image map's hotspots. To create an image map by drawing, follow the steps in Table 23-2.

To learn more about image maps and tools for creating them, follow the *Interlit* Web site link to the image map tutorial.

Table 23-2   Creating an image map by drawing

Dreamweaver	FrontPage
▶ Use Dreamweaver to open the Web page containing the image upon which you want to draw hotspots.	▶ Use FrontPage to open the Web page containing the image upon which you want to draw hotspots.
▶ Click the Design button to bring up the Design view.	▶ Click the Design button to bring up the Design view.
▶ Click the image to select it; the image settings appear in the Properties inspector.	▶ If the Pictures toolbar is not visible, right-click the image and choose Show Pictures Toolbar.
▶ Click the arrow in the lower-right corner of the Properties inspector to display all of the properties.	▶ On the Pictures toolbar are the rectangular, circular, and polygonal hotspot tools, illustrated in Figure 23-13.
▶ In the Map field, type a unique name for the image map; do not type spaces or special characters.	

Table 23-2 *(continued)*

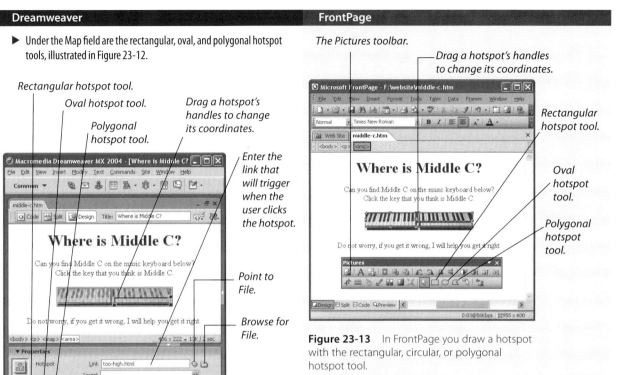

Dreamweaver	FrontPage

Dreamweaver

▶ Under the Map field are the rectangular, oval, and polygonal hotspot tools, illustrated in Figure 23-12.

Rectangular hotspot tool.

Oval hotspot tool.

Polygonal hotspot tool.

Drag a hotspot's handles to change its coordinates.

Enter the link that will trigger when the user clicks the hotspot.

Point to File.

Browse for File.

Figure 23-12 In Dreamweaver you draw a hotspot with the rectangular, oval, or polygonal hotspot tool.

▶ Depending on the shape of your intended trigger, use the rectangular, oval, or polygonal tool to draw the hotspot on the image; the Hotspot Property inspector appears.

▶ In the Link field, type the name of the file to which the hotspot should link, or use the ⊕ Point to File or the 🗀 Browse for File tool to set the link.

▶ To adjust the hotspot's coordinates, you can drag its handles in Design view, or you can make finer adjustments by tweaking the x,y coordinates in Code view.

▶ Click the 🌐▾ Preview in Browser button and click the hotspots to make sure the image map behaves as you intend.

FrontPage

The Pictures toolbar.

Drag a hotspot's handles to change its coordinates.

Rectangular hotspot tool.

Oval hotspot tool.

Polygonal hotspot tool.

Figure 23-13 In FrontPage you draw a hotspot with the rectangular, circular, or polygonal hotspot tool.

▶ Depending on the shape of your intended trigger, use the rectangular, circular, or polygonal tool to draw the hotspot on the image; if you use the polygonal tool, click once to create each side, then double-click to complete the polygon.

▶ When the Insert Hyperlink dialog appears, locate the file to which the hotspot should link, then click OK to close the dialog.

▶ To adjust the hotspot's coordinates, you can drag its handles in Design view, or you can make finer adjustments by tweaking the x,y coordinates in Code view.

▶ If you later need to change the hotspot's link, right-click the hotspot and choose Picture Hotspot Properties.

▶ Click the 🔍 Preview in Browser button and click the hotspots to make sure the image map behaves as you intend.

exercises

1. Go to the multimedia section of the *Interlit* Web site and play the waveform audio recording of the author greeting you. Do you like the audio controls your browser provides to play the greeting? How could the controls be improved? What features do you want in an audio player that your browser's audio controls lack?

2. Go to the multimedia section of the *Interlit* Web site and play the video recording of the author greeting you. Do you like the video controller your browser provides to play the greeting? How could the controller be improved? What features do you want in a video player that your browser's video controller lacks?

3. Flash can make your Web browser do some really neat stuff. Follow the links to the Flash Showcase at the *Interlit* Web site. View some of the demonstrations you will find there. Make a list of the features you find Flash supporting that you have not seen on Web pages without it. What is your favorite Flash feature? *Note:* If you do not have the latest version of Flash, you will be prompted to install it. Go ahead and do so.

4. There is a lot of competition between companies like Netscape, Microsoft, Apple, and Sun Microsystems to come up with the most popular way of distributing applications over the Web. This competition results in requiring you to install support for multiple technologies if you want to take advantage of neat new stuff happening at different sites out on the Web. A good example is the difference between Java and ActiveX. Do you think this kind of competition is good for the industry? Or would it be better for the government to require companies to work together and embrace common standards from the beginning?

SITUATED CASE PROJECTS
Case 23: Creating a Graphical Front End

At the end of each chapter in this book, a situated case project provides the student an opportunity to put the chapter's contents to practical use in a workplace situation. Each case has the same number as the chapter in which it appears.

If you think about what you actually see when you go to a Web site, what appears onscreen is either textual or graphical. Web sites that depend mainly on text, such as keyword search engines, typically have text-based user interfaces. Other sites get more creative and provide you with a visual image to click. You can see an example of a graphical user interface at the Library of Congress Web site at www.loc.gov. Imagine that your employer has asked you to look into the possibility of creating a graphical front-end for your school or company Web site. In developing your recommendation, consider these alternatives:

❶ One way to create a graphical front-end to a Web site is to use an image map. This method is suitable if there is a picture or a graphic that illustrates or contains the objects you want users to click. The author dreams of creating a virtual tour of Fort McHenry, for example, which is located in Baltimore and chronicles the writing of "The Star Spangled Banner." You could snap a wide-angled picture of the fort, put it on a Web page, and use an image map to create hotspots on the doors and windows of the Fort. To look into a window, the user would click it. To enter a room, the user would click its door.

❷ Another way of creating a graphical front end is to use tables to position individual graphics onscreen where you want them. To link the graphics to their intended targets, you use the Hyperlink tool in your Web page creation software. The graphical front end at the Library of Congress uses this kind of table-oriented graphics design. To see where the tables are, use your Web browser to visit www.log.gov, then pull down the File menu and choose the option to save the page. When the Save dialog appears, save the file in your *website* folder. Then open the page with your Web page editor. In Design view or Normal view, you will see the table grid that contains and positions the graphics at the Library of Congress home page.

Use your word processor to write a brief essay describing how your workplace could use image maps. Describe what the images would depict, tell where the hotspots would be, and explain what will happen when the user clicks them. If your workplace has content that lends itself to the use of tables, describe how you would use tables to lay out the content onscreen. If your instructor has asked you to hand in this assignment, make sure you put your name at the top of your essay, then copy it onto a disk or follow any other instructions you may have been given for submitting this assignment.

24

AUDIO RECORDING AND EMBEDDING

After completing this chapter, you will be able to:

■ **Make a waveform audio recording.**

■ **Adjust the quality of a waveform audio recording.**

■ **Explain the difference between sampling rate and bits per sample.**

■ **Reduce bandwidth requirements by converting a waveform audio recording into an MP3 file.**

■ **Link a waveform audio recording to your Web page.**

■ **Embed audio on a Web page.**

● Audio is a great way to begin adding multimedia content to your Web pages. Because every multimedia computer comes with the hardware needed to create waveform audio recordings, you are already equipped to do it.

This chapter steps you through the process of recording waveform audio and linking it to your Web pages. You will learn how to create hypertext and image links that, when clicked, cause your audio to play. You also will learn how to put sound into the background of a Web page, thereby making the sound start automatically when the Web page appears. Then you will learn how to embed an audio recording on your Web page.

Preparing to Make Your First Waveform Audio Recording

Windows comes with a program called the Sound Recorder that enables you to create and edit waveform audio recordings. On the Macintosh, you can use a shareware program called Sound Studio to do likewise. The *Interlit* Web site has a link where Mac users can download Sound Studio.

You can record either from a microphone or from a so-called line output from a tape recorder, audio CD player, or VCR. Your computer has jacks into which you can plug a microphone or a line output. Most computers have two separate jacks: one labeled Mike, the other Line; make sure you plug into the correct jack. If the connectors on your microphone or other audio source do not fit the jacks on your computer, you can purchase the necessary adapters from your local Radio Shack or other electronics store.

Once your audio source is connected, you need to make sure it is selected as the source in the recording section of your computer's sound-mixing software. Follow the steps in Table 24-1 to do that.

Table 24-1 How to select the record sound source

Windows	Macintosh
▶ If there is a sound icon on your Windows taskbar, double-click it to bring up your sound-mixer volume controls. Otherwise, look on your Windows Start menu for a group related to sound or entertainment accessories, in which you should be able to find your sound-mixer volume control software. If you have Windows XP, you can add the sound icon to your taskbar: click Start→Control Panel, double-click Sounds and Audio Devices, click the option to place the volume icon in the taskbar, and click OK.	▶ Follow the *Interlit* Web site link to Sound Studio. Click the link to download Sound Studio. After the file downloads, launch the downloaded file to install it.
▶ Pull down the Options menu and choose Properties; the Properties dialog appears as shown in Figure 24-1.	▶ In the Sound Studio folder, double-click the Sound Studio launch icon to get it running.
	▶ Pull down the Audio menu and choose Input/Output Setup. The Audio Input/Output Setup dialog appears, as illustrated in Figure 24-4.

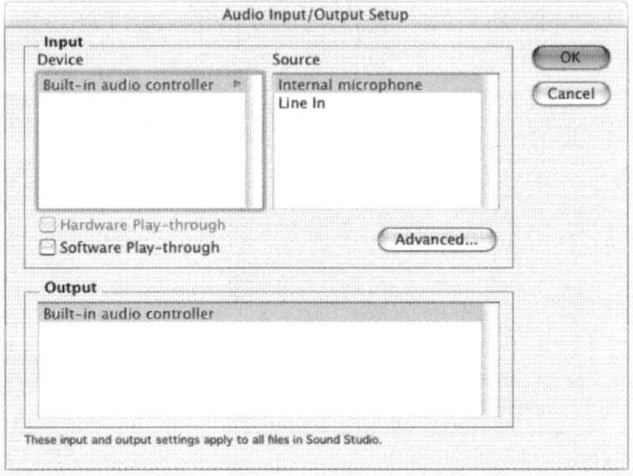

Click here to see Playback settings.

Click here to see Record settings.

Check the sources from which you plan to record.

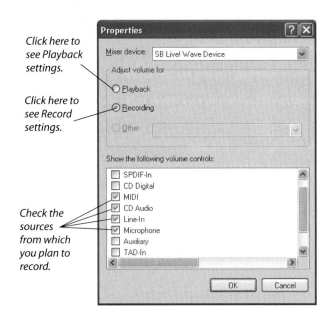

Figure 24-1 The Sound Properties dialog.

Figure 24-4 The Sound Studio Audio Input/Output Setup dialog.

▶ Click the Recording button, if it is not already selected.

▶ The list box identifies the different recording controls on your computer. Make sure the microphone is selected along with any other sound sources you plan to use, so they will show up in the Recording Control window in the next step.

▶ Click OK; the Record Control window appears, as shown in Figure 24-2.

The slider adjusts the record level. It should be up about 90% of the way; increase this if the recording sounds too faint; decrease this if you get distortion.

This box must be checked in order to record from a microphone.

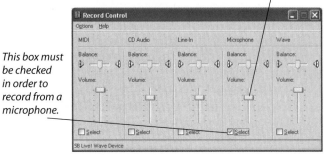

Figure 24-2 The Record Control window.

Table 24-1   *(continued)*

Windows	Macintosh
▶ Make sure the checkbox for the source you are recording is selected. In this example, check the microphone source.	▶ In this example, click Internal microphone to select it as your input source, unless you happen to have an external mike, in which case you should select it instead.
▶ Pull down the Options menu and choose Properties to make the Properties dialog shown in Figure 24-1 reappear.	▶ Click OK to close the Audio Input/Output Setup dialog.
▶ Click the Playback button.	▶ Proceed to Table 24-2 to learn how to make an audio recording.
▶ The list box identifies the different playback controls on your computer. Make sure the play control and the microphone are selected, so they will show up in the Volume Control window in the next step.	
▶ Click OK; the Play Control window appears, as shown in Figure 24-3.	

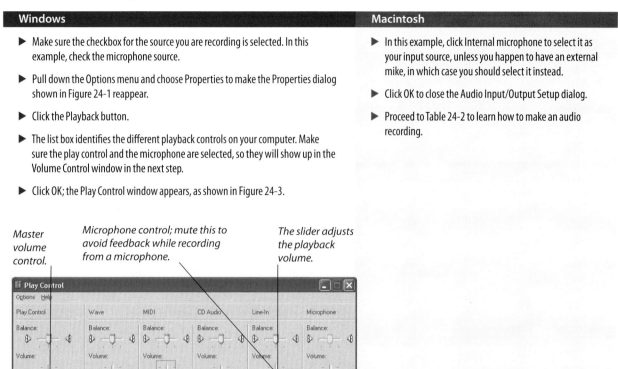

Figure 24-3   The Play Control window.

▶ If you are recording from a microphone, you will probably want to mute the microphone; otherwise, sound from the microphone will feed back through your speakers. Feedback can cause distortion, but it also can create an interesting depth effect if your microphone is not positioned too close to the speakers. The author recommends you mute the mike setting your first time through; later on, you can try making depth effects.

▶ Make sure the master volume control is turned up.

Making a Waveform Audio Recording

Now that have your sound source connected and selected, you can make the recording by following the steps in Table 24-2.

Editing Waveform Audio Recordings

Situations may arise in which you want to edit a waveform audio recording. If you press the Record button too soon, for example, there will be extra sound at the beginning of the recording that you will need to delete. Similarly, if you press the Stop button too late, there will be extra sound at the end that you will want to remove. To edit a waveform audio recording, follow the steps in Table 24-3.

Table 24-2   How to make a waveform audio recording

Windows	Macintosh

▶ To start the Windows Sound Recorder, click the Windows Start button and choose Programs→Accessories→Entertainment or Multimedia→Sound Recorder.

▶ The Sound Recorder appears as shown in Figure 24-5. The green line in the black window is an oscilloscope that shows you the incoming sound wave. When you click the Record button to begin recording, the green line should oscillate as the sound comes in. If the line does not move, your sound source is not active—review the instructions in Table 24-1 to fix the problem.

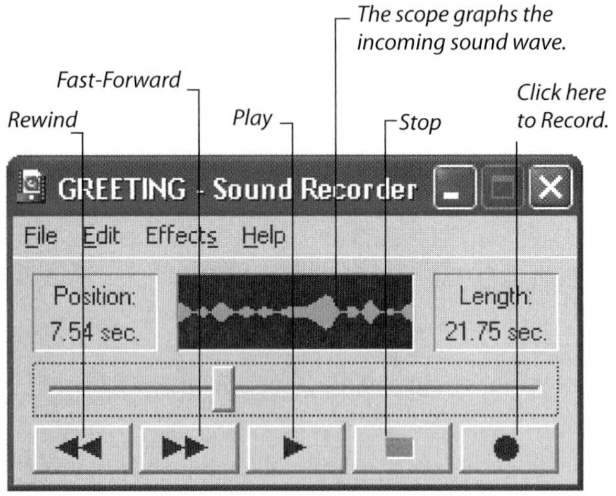

The scope graphs the incoming sound wave.

Fast-Forward

Rewind   Play   Stop   *Click here to Record.*

Figure 24-5   The Windows Sound Recorder.

▶ To begin recording, click the Record button. If you are using a microphone, hold the mike close to your mouth, so your recording will have good presence of sound. Speak in a loud, clear voice.

▶ To stop recording, click the Stop button.

▶ To hear the recording, click the Play button. If you do not hear anything, your sound source is probably not connected properly. Make sure your microphone or line input is plugged into the proper jack and follow the steps in Table 24-1 to select it as the recording source.

▶ To rewind the recording, click the Rewind button.

▶ To save the recording, pull down the File menu and click Save As; the Save As dialog appears. Save the recording in the folder of your choice, such as your *website* folder.

▶ If the recording sounds too faint, you need to adjust the record level; pull down the Edit menu, choose Audio Properties, and turn up the recording level.

▶ If you hear distortion, you need to turn the record level down; pull down the Edit menu, choose Audio Properties, and turn down the recording level.

▶ Get Sound Studio running if it is not already onscreen.

▶ Pull down the File menu and choose New; the New dialog appears, as illustrated in Figure 24-6.

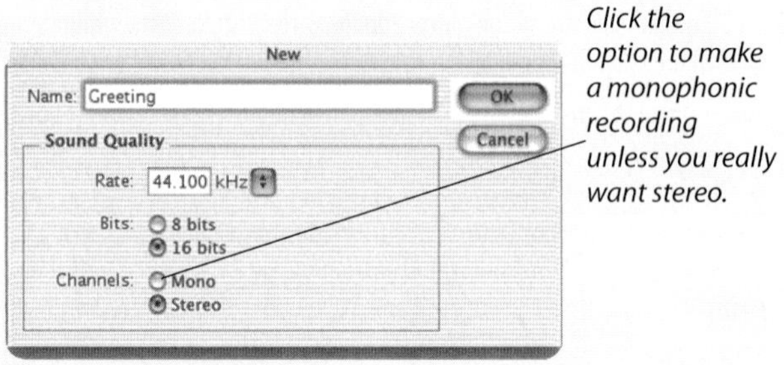

Click the option to make a monophonic recording unless you really want stereo.

Figure 24-6   The Sound Studio New dialog.

▶ In the Name field, type the name you want this recording to have. Then click OK to close the dialog.

▶ The Sound Studio Record window appears as illustrated in Figure 24-7.

Stop

Play

Pause   *Click here to record.*

The graph will display the sound waves you record.

Drag this knob to adjust the playback volume.

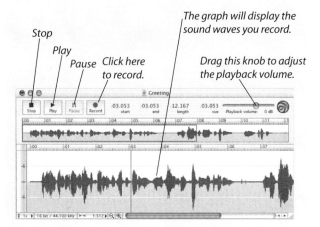

Figure 24-7   The Sound Studio Record window.

▶ To begin recording, click the Record button. If you are using a microphone, hold the mike close to your mouth, so your recording will have good presence of sound. Speak in a loud, clear voice.

▶ To stop recording, click the Stop button.

▶ To hear the recording, click the Play button. If you do not hear anything, your sound source is probably not connected properly. Make sure your microphone or line input is plugged into the proper jack and follow the steps in Table 24-1 to select it as the recording source.

▶ To save the recording, pull down the File menu and choose Save; the Save dialog appears.

Table 24-2 *(continued)*

Windows	Macintosh
▶ It may take you several tries to get a good recording. Keep adjusting the settings and rerecord until you get the result you want.	▶ Pull down the Format menu and choose AIFF, which is the Macintosh audio file format. Both Windows and Macintosh users will be able to play back your AIFF files from the Web.
▶ To rerecord, pull down the File menu and choose New to empty the waveform buffer. If you do not choose New, what you record next will get inserted into the current recording.	▶ Save the recording in the folder of your choice, such as your *website* folder.
	▶ If the recording sounds too faint, you need to adjust the input level. If the Input Levels window is not visible, pull down the Window menu and choose Show Input Levels. Drag the slider to the right to increase the input level.
	▶ If you hear distortion, you need to turn the record level down; in the Input Levels window, drag the slider to the left to decrease the input level.
	▶ It may take you several tries to get a good recording. Keep adjusting the settings and rerecord until you get the result you want.
	▶ To rerecord, pull down the File menu and choose New to empty the waveform buffer. If you do not choose New, what you record next will get inserted into the current recording.

Table 24-3 How to edit a waveform audio recording

Windows	Macintosh
▶ Get the Sound Recorder running if it is not already onscreen.	▶ Get Sound Studio running if it is not already onscreen.
▶ Pull down the File menu, choose Open, and open the waveform audio file you want to edit. If the file is already open, you can skip this step.	▶ Pull down the File menu, choose Open, and open the waveform audio file you want to edit. If the file is already open, you can skip this step.
▶ ▶ Play the file, and make note of the spots at which you want to delete things. You can drag the slider to move quickly to different positions in the recording. The Position counter shows where you are in hundredths of seconds.	▶ ▶ Play the file, and make note of the spots at which you want to delete things. You can use the slider at the bottom of the window to move quickly to different positions in the recording.
▶ To delete the first part of a recording, position the slider at the spot where the good stuff starts, then pull down the Edit menu and choose Delete Before Current Position.	▶ Position your mouse at the spot on the bottom waveform where you want to start deleting. Hold the button down and drag to select the portion of the waveform you want to delete.
▶ To delete the last part of a recording, position the slider at the end of the good stuff, then pull down the Edit menu and choose Delete After Current Position.	▶ Click the Play button to audition the section to be deleted. If you hear something you do not want deleted, adjust the selected area. Repeat this step until the play button sounds only the audio you want deleted.
▶ Play the file to make sure you got what you wanted.	▶ Pull down the Edit menu and choose Clear.
▶ Remember to save the file when you are done editing.	▶ Play the file to make sure you got what you wanted. If you made an error, pull down the Edit menu and choose Undo.
	▶ Remember to save the file when you are done editing.

Adjusting the Quality of Waveform Audio Recordings

Most waveform audio recording software lets you adjust two parameters that govern the quality of a waveform audio recording: sampling rate and bits per sample. Be aware that the higher you set these parameters, the larger your waveform audio file will be.

Table 24-4   The relationship between sound quality and sampling rate

Samples per Second	Sonic Equivalent
6,000	Telephone
15,000	AM radio
37,500	FM radio
40,000	Phonograph records
44,100	Compact disc

Sampling Rate

The **sampling rate** determines the frequency response of the recorded sound. To record frequencies faithfully, your sampling rate must be at least two times greater than the highest frequency you want to record. However, the higher you set the sampling rate, the larger your waveform audio file will be. Since the size of the file increases, do not choose a higher sampling rate than you need because of the increased bandwidth required to transfer the file over the Internet. To help you grasp the relationship between sampling rate and sound quality, Table 24-4 compares different sampling rates to real-world audio devices of differing fidelities.

Bits per Sample

Table 24-5 illustrates how the number of **bits per sample** determines the dynamic range, which determines how much of a volume change you will hear between the loudest and softest sounds in a recording. Waveform audio devices typically give you a choice of 8 or 16 bits per sample. The original MPC standard required that multimedia computers be capable of recording at 8 bits per sample, while the current standard requires 16.

Since file size is determined by multiplying the bits per sample by the sampling rate, you should not choose a higher bits-per-sample setting than required. Try your recording first at 8 bits per sample. Only if that does not provide adequate sound quality should you increase the setting to 16 bits. To help you grasp the relationship between bits per sample and sound quality, Table 24-6 shows the dynamic range equivalents of some real-world sound sources.

Table 24-5   The relationship between bits per sample and dynamic range

Bits per Sample	Dynamic Range	Bits per Sample	Dynamic Range
1	8dB	10	62dB
2	14dB	11	68dB
3	20dB	12	74dB
4	26dB	13	80dB
5	32dB	14	86dB
6	38dB	15	92dB
7	44dB	16	98dB
8	50dB	17	104dB
9	56dB	18	110dB

Table 24-6   Bits-per-sample equivalents of traditional sound sources

Sound Source	Bits-per-Sample Equivalent
AM radio	6 bits
Telephone	8 bits
FM radio	9 bits
Phonograph record	10 bits
Reel-to-reel tape	11 bits
Compact disc	16 bits

Bandwidth Considerations

If you are using the Windows Sound Recorder, you can modify the sound quality settings. Depending on the audio card in your computer, your specific settings may vary, but you should be able to find controls equivalent to the ones described here. If you have Windows XP, pull down the File menu and choose Properties to make the Properties dialog appear. Click the Convert Now button to make the Sound Selection dialog appear, as illustrated in Figure 24-8. Pull down the Name menu and choose CD Quality, Radio Quality, or Telephone Quality to use a preset, or use the Attributes menu to fine-tune the sampling rate and bits-per-sample. Then click OK to close the dialogs. If you have an earlier version of Windows, pull down the Edit menu and choose Audio Properties to make the Audio Properties dialog appear. To adjust the quality, pull down the Preferred Quality menu and choose the setting you want, or click the Customize button to create your own custom settings. Be careful to keep bandwidth in mind, however, because the higher you set the quality adjustments, the larger the file will become, and the longer it will take to download the sound from the Web.

If you are using the Macintosh Sound Studio program, you change the bandwidth settings by pulling down the Audio menu and choosing the option to Resample the sound. The Resample Sound dialog will appear, as illustrated in Figure 24-9.

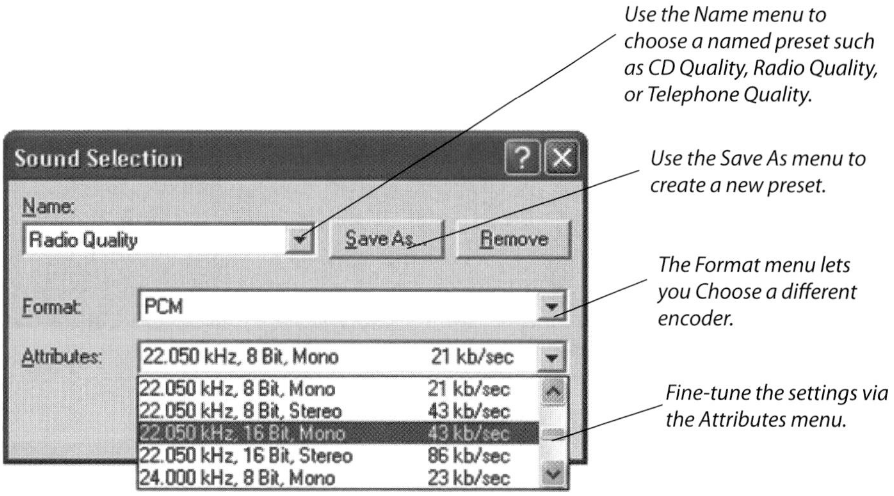

Use the Name menu to choose a named preset such as CD Quality, Radio Quality, or Telephone Quality.

Use the Save As menu to create a new preset.

The Format menu lets you Choose a different encoder.

Fine-tune the settings via the Attributes menu.

Figure 24-8   The Windows Sound Selection dialog.

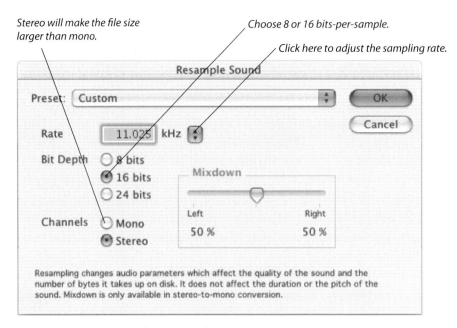

Stereo will make the file size larger than mono.

Choose 8 or 16 bits-per-sample.

Click here to adjust the sampling rate.

Figure 24-9   The Macintosh Sound Studio Resample Sound dialog.

Reducing Bandwidth by Converting Waveform Recordings to MP3 Files

In Chapter 12, you learned how the MP3 audio file format uses one of the MPEG audio compression algorithms to reduce substantially the amount of file space required to store an audio recording. When a waveform audio file is converted into the MP3 format, the resulting file is only about 10 percent as big as the original. Because the file is only one-tenth as large, it requires less bandwidth and will download 10 times faster over the Web.

MUSICMATCH JUKEBOX

If you have Windows, you may be interested in downloading MusicMatch Jukebox, which is one of the more popular MP3 programs (see Figure 24-10). There is a free download that lets you use the program's basic features for free, and a retail version for which you pay a small fee to unleash higher-speed CD burning and ripping. You can download MusicMatch from www.musicmatch.com.

The MusicMatch Jukebox File menu has a feature that lets you convert files from WAV to MP3 and vice versa. Figure 24-11 shows how the File Format Conversion dialog lets you select the file to convert and set the data type of the converted file. MusicMatch also can record audio, either from a CD or from a microphone, and save it in WAV or MP3 format.

The *Interlit* Web site lists other utilities that convert WAV and AIFF files into the MP3 format. Most of these programs are freely downloadable. To peruse them, follow the *Interlit* Web site links to MP3 software and utilities.

Figure 24-10   MusicMatch Jukebox.

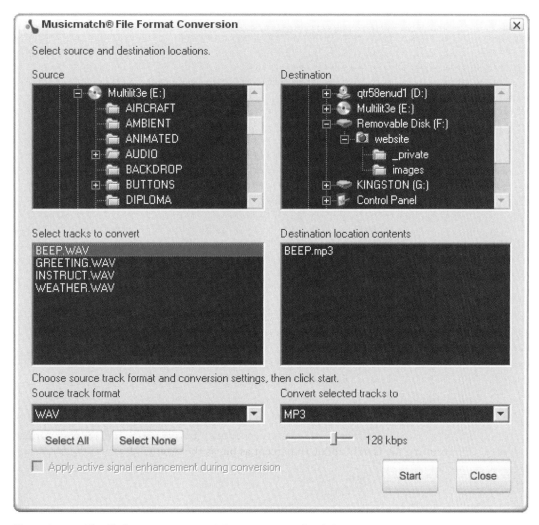

Figure 24-11   The file format conversion dialog in MusicMatch Jukebox.

iTUNES JUKEBOX

On the Macintosh, the popular iTunes Jukebox program can convert audio files to and from a wide range of formats, including AIFF and MP3. To convert a file into the MP3 format, follow these steps:

- Pull down the iTunes menu and choose Preferences to bring up the Preferences dialog.

- Click the Importing button to make the Importing settings appear.

- Use the Import Using setting to choose the MP3 encoder, as illustrated in Figure 24-12.

- Click OK to close the Preferences dialog.

- If the file to be converted is not already in the iTunes library, locate the file in the Finder, then drag the file into the iTunes window.

- Select the file in the iTunes library, pull down the Advanced menu, and choose Convert Selection to MP3.

- Use the Finder to locate the converted file and drag it into the folder of your choice.

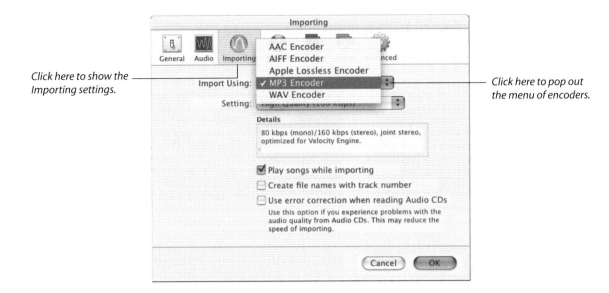

Click here to show the Importing settings.

Click here to pop out the menu of encoders.

Figure 24-12   Selecting the MP3 encoder from the Importing settings in the iTunes Preferences dialog.

Linking Audio to Your Web Page

Now that you have learned how to record audio, the time has come to put it on your Web page. There are two ways to do that. You can either link it or embed it. If you link it, the user will click a hypertext or image link, which will cause your browser to download and play the audio. If you embed the audio, it will be more tightly coupled to your Web page. To link audio to a Web page, follow the steps in Table 24-7.

Table 24-7   How to link sound to a trigger on a Web page

Dreamweaver	FrontPage	Nvu
► Use Dreamweaver to open the Web page to which you want to link some audio.	► Use FrontPage to open the Web page to which you want to link some audio.	► Use Nvu to open the Web page to which you want to link some audio.
► Select the picture or text to which you want to link the audio. Click once on a picture to select it, or click and drag to select some text.	► Select the picture or text to which you want to link the audio. Click once on a picture to select it, or click and drag to select some text.	► Select the picture or text to which you want to link the audio. Click once on a picture to select it, or click and drag to select some text.
► Right-click the highlighted text or image and choose Make link; the Select File dialog appears.	► Click the Hyperlink button; the Insert Hyperlink dialog appears.	► Click the Link button to make the Link Properties dialog appear.
► Click to select the file you want to link.	► Click to select the filename of your wave-form audio file, or type it into the URL field.	► Click the Choose File button and select the file you want to link.
► The filename appears in the URL field. Click OK to close the dialog.	► Click the Save button to save the page.	► The filename appears in the link location field. Click OK to close the Link dialog.
► Pull down the File menu and choose Save to save the file.	► Click the Preview button to test the page. Click the audio link and make sure it plays. If there are any problems, repeat these steps until the audio link works properly.	► Click the Save button to save the modified Web page.
► Click the Preview in Browser button to test the page. Click the audio link and make sure it plays. If there are any problems, repeat these steps until the audio link works properly.		► Click the Browse button to test the page. Click the audio link and make sure it plays. If there are any problems, repeat these steps until the audio link works properly.

Following the steps you learned in Chapter 22, publish the page and the audio file to the Web. Use your browser to click every link on the published page to make sure it works. If any audio link fails to play, follow the steps in Table 24-7 carefully to troubleshoot the problem.

Embedding Audio on a Web Page

To embed audio on a Web page, you use the **<embed>** tag. The **<embed>** tag has parameters that let you preset the volume and the size of the audio controller. You can make the audio autostart, and you also can hide the audio controller. If you hide the controller, however, the user will not be able to turn the audio off. Many people do not like it when Web pages play audio that the user cannot control. Tables 24-8 through 24-10 show how to embed audio on a Web page using Dreamweaver, FrontPage, and Nvu, respectively.

Table 24-8   How to embed audio on a Web page with Dreamweaver

▶ Use Dreamweaver to open the Web page upon which you want to embed some audio.

▶ Click the Design button or pull down the View menu and choose Design.

▶ Click to position your cursor at the spot in the design where you want to embed the audio. If you already have images or text on the page, click the spot where you would like to have the controller appear in relation to the images or text.

▶ Click the Code button and your cursor is positioned at that spot in the code.

▶ Type the following HTML code, replacing *filename.wav* with the filename or URL of the audio file you want to play:

Height and width are optional parameters to control the size and width of the embedded player onscreen.

<embed src="*filename.wav*" volume="100" height="60" width="144">

▶ If you want to make the audio start automatically, include the following parameter prior to the > that ends the **<embed>** tag:

autostart="true"

▶ If you make the audio start automatically, and you want the audio control to be invisible, include the following parameter prior to the > that ends the **<embed>** tag:

hidden="true"

▶ Pull down the File menu and choose Save to save the file.

▶ Click the ⊙▾ Preview in Browser button to test the page. If there are any problems, repeat these steps and troubleshoot until the embedded audio works properly.

Table 24-9   How to embed audio on a Web page with FrontPage

▶ Use FrontPage to open the Web page upon which you want to embed some audio.

▶ Click the Design tab if you are not already in Design view.

Table 24-9   *(continued)*

▶ Click to position your cursor at the spot in the design where you want to embed the audio. If you already have images or text on the page, click the spot where you would like to have the controller appear in relation to the images or text.

▶ Click the HTML tab and your cursor is positioned at that spot.

▶ Type the following HTML code, replacing *filename.wav* with the filename or URL of the audio file you want to play:

Height and width are optional parameters to control the size and width of the embedded player onscreen.

<embed src="*filename.wav*" volume="100" height="60" width="144">

▶ If you want to make the audio start automatically, include the following parameter prior to the > that ends the **<embed>** tag:

autostart="true"

▶ If you make the audio start automatically, and you want the audio control to be invisible, include the following parameter prior to the > that ends the **<embed>** tag:

hidden="true"

▶ Click the 💾 Save button to save the page.

▶ Click the 🔍 Preview button to test the page. If there are any problems, repeat these steps and troubleshoot until the embedded audio works properly.

Table 24-10   How to embed audio on a Web page with Nvu

▶ Use Nvu to open the Web page upon which you want to embed some audio.

▶ Click the Normal tab if you are not already in normal edit mode.

▶ Click to position your cursor at the spot in the design where you want to embed the audio. If you already have images or text on the page, click the spot where you would like to have the controller appear in relation to the images or text.

▶ Click the HTML Source tab and your cursor is positioned at that spot in the code.

▶ Type the following HTML code, replacing *filename.wav* with the filename or URL of the audio file you want to play:

Height and width are optional parameters to control the size and width of the embedded player onscreen.

<embed src="*filename.wav*" volume="100" height="60" width="144">

▶ If you want to make the audio start automatically, include the following parameter prior to the > that ends the **<embed>** tag:

autostart="true"

▶ If you make the audio start automatically, and you want the audio control to be invisible, include the following parameter prior to the > that ends the **<embed>** tag:

hidden="true"

▶ Click the 💾 Save button to save the page.

▶ Click the ⚙ Browse button to test the page. Click the audio link and make sure it plays. If there are any problems, repeat these steps and troubleshoot until the embedded audio works properly.

exercises

1. Record a waveform audio file to welcome people to your home page. Save the file in your *website* folder. Call it *greeting.wav* if you are using Windows or *greeting.aiff* if you have a Macintosh. You will need this file in the next exercise.

2. Link the greeting you recorded in exercise 1 to an image or hypertext on your home page. For example, you could print "Hear me *welcome you* to my site" and make the words *welcome you* trigger the audio greeting. Publish the revised page and the greeting to your Web site. Test the link on the Web to make sure the audio plays properly when a user clicks the link.

3. Embed on your Web page the greeting you recorded in exercise 1. If you have any trouble doing this, review the steps in Table 24-8 (Dreamweaver), Table 24-9 (FrontPage), or Table 24-10 (Nvu). At first, do not include the autostart parameter, so the audio will not start until the user clicks the Play button. Then use the autostart parameter to make the greeting start playing automatically when your Web page appears. Which way do you prefer: autostart or click to start? Do you think it is impolite for a Web page to begin playing audio automatically?

4. Download from the *Interlit* Web site one of the MP3 programs that can convert waveform audio files into MP3 files. If you are using Windows, download MusicMatch Jukebox, for example, or one of the other MP3 programs that can convert WAV files into MP3. If you have a Macintosh, download an MP3 converter for AIFF files. After you download and install the MP3 program, use it to convert to MP3 the greeting you recorded in exercise 1. Then use the Windows Explorer or the Macintosh Finder to inspect the file sizes of the two versions of the greeting. What is the file size of the MP3 file? What is the file size of the original recording? How much smaller is the MP3 version of the file than the original recording? How many times faster, therefore, will the MP3 file download over the Internet?

5. You can add depth, technically known as reverberation, to a waveform audio recording if you let the sound feed back a little through the speakers while you record. You vary the amount of depth by turning the playback volume up or down, and by moving the microphone closer or further away from the speakers. Be careful, however, because you can cause a bad-sounding feedback if you move the microphone too close to the speakers. If your volume is turned up really loud, the feedback could damage your speakers. To experiment with adding depth to your recordings, repeat the steps in Tables 24-1 and 24-2. This time, instead of muting the microphone, turn the microphone on and manipulate the playback volume to create more or less depth. What depth setting makes you sound best?

SITUATED CASE PROJECTS
Case 24: Collecting Multimedia Portfolio Artifacts

At the end of each chapter in this book, a situated case project provides the student an opportunity to put the chapter's contents to practical use in a workplace situation. Each case has the same number as the chapter in which it appears.

Through the process of digitization that has unfolded over the past decade, mass-market consumer devices have become widely available for capturing to the Web any image, sound, or video. It has become possible to digitize anything you can see or hear and publish it to the Web in a worldwide format. This is good news for people creating online portfolios, because it means that the portfolios can contain rich links to multimedia artifacts. Imagine that your employer has asked you to provide a demonstration of how handily a person can add multimedia content to a portfolio. Your task is to digitize a few photos and an audio clip, publish them to the Web, and link them as artifacts to hypertext or image links on a Web page. Follow these steps:

❶ *Collection.* Decide what photographs should appear as artifacts in your portfolio. Think of an audio recording that can be used to document something in your portfolio.

❷ *Photography.* If you cannot find a couple of suitable photos, take some yourself. If you have a digital camera, follow the manufacturer's instructions to upload the photos to your PC. If you do not have a digital camera, get your film developed at Eckerd's or Wal-Mart and check the option to have a Picture Disk returned to you along with your prints.

③ *Audio recording.* If you do not have suitable audio recorded, follow the step-by-step instructions in Chapter 24 to use your computer to make a digital audio recording.

④ *Digitization.* If your audio is not already in digital form, use your computer to digitize it. Chapter 24 describes how to make digital audio recordings. To record from an external source, set the sound source to line input and connect the external source to your computer's audio input jack. If you do not have the proper connector, you can get it from your local Radio Shack or other electronics store.

⑤ *Linking.* Copy the digital artifacts you collected in the previous steps into the *website* folder on your hard drive. Then use your Web page editing software to open the page(s) to which you will be linking these artifacts. Make the links, save the pages, and use the Preview in Browser option to test the links and make sure they work properly.

⑥ *Publication.* Following the publishing strategy you learned in Chapter 22, publish the *website* folder to your Web site. Publishing the entire folder will update everything in that folder at your Web site.

⑦ *Testing.* Use your Web browser to test the multimedia links at your Web site. If possible, test the links on a computer different from the one used to develop them. Try all of the links and make sure they work properly. Make any changes that are necessary, save the pages, and test them again. Repeat this step until all the links work properly. Remember that when you test the pages, you may need to click your browser's Refresh button to make the browser load the new version of the page.

If your instructor has asked you to hand in this assignment, use your word processor to start a new document. Put your name at the top, and provide the Web address of your published pages. Save the file onto a disk or follow the other instructions you may have been given for submitting this assignment.

CHAPTER 25	CHAPTER 26	CHAPTER 27
Societal Issues	Emerging Technology	How to Keep Up and Stay Secure

The best way to predict the future is to invent it.

—Alan Kay, Vice President for R&D, Walt Disney Imagineering

Because the Internet is the communications infrastructure of the 21st century, its future is vitally important. This part of the book introduces you to the many ways in which the Internet will affect your future. You will probably learn about some issues you never thought about. Many of these issues are controversial, and some could shock or even offend you.

The Internet is a publicly accessible resource used by hundreds of millions of people. Like any public resource, its content reflects the people who use it. Unfortunately, not everyone using the Internet is well meaning. Chapter 25 will make you aware of what is bad about the Internet, prepare you to guard against evil, and provide you with a way to voice your opinions about how the Internet should be regulated.

In spite of the bad things done by some hateful users, the Internet is a strategic resource to which everyone needs access. Citizens who cannot access the Information Superhighway will be disenfranchised. This part of the book will make you aware of the equity issues and suggest things you can do to help everyone gain access.

The Internet is growing and changing rapidly. New technologies are emerging that promise to help solve not only the technical issues regarding the Internet, but many of the societal issues as well. For example, declining costs caused by advances in microelectronics will make it possible for more people to become connected, thereby helping to solve the equity problem. Chapter 26 defines and discusses the emerging technologies that are creating new directions for the Internet.

Finally, since the Internet is constantly evolving, Chapter 27 will conclude the book by suggesting ways you can keep up with the new technology. People often ask the author how he keeps up with all the changes in technology. In Chapter 27, you will find out how to use the technology to help you keep up with the changes in technology. Unfortunately, some of these changes include new methods crackers can use to compromise your computer or spy on your Internet activity. Chapter 27 concludes by providing strategies for becoming informed and protected from the latest threats.

25

SOCIETAL ISSUES

After completing this chapter, you will be able to:

- ■ Summarize what is being done to help the technological underclass gain access to the Internet.

- ■ Understand how the Internet threatens your right to privacy, and know what you can do about that.

- ■ Take steps to avoid being stalked on the Internet.

- ■ Exercise the appropriate security measures to protect the privacy of your information on the Internet.

- ■ Understand why protectionists seek to censor certain kinds of material on the Internet.

- ■ Realize how much Internet traffic is pornographic or obscene, and consider who should have access to such material.

- ■ Reflect on the impact of the evil side of technology that is being used to spread electronic hate on the Internet.

- ■ Understand the concept of copyright and fair use in cyberspace, and realize how important it is to exercise your right of Fair Use of electronic resources.

- ■ Define the purpose of a patent and list examples of how some technology companies have abused the patent system.

- ■ Define peer-to-peer (P2P) file sharing and understand the ethical and legal issues involved in P2P sharing of music and video via the Internet.

● As the communications infrastructure for the 21st century, the Internet is the most strategic resource in modern society. But will its true potential be reached? Who will control access? Almost any good thing can be misused; how will the Internet harm society?

Equity, Cost, and Universal Access

As this book goes to press, only 75 percent of Americans have Internet access at home. Although this is up slightly from 66.9 percent in 2000, we still have a long way to go before achieving universal access.

Federal Communications Commission

In 1996, Congress expanded the Universal Service program to cover information technologies. True to its name, the Universal Service program subsidizes the cost of telecommunications in remote and rural areas so the fees paid by end users are roughly compatible. A Link-Up America program helps low-income households pay installation costs, and a Lifeline Assistance program subsidizes their monthly service fees. The National Telecommunications and Information Administration (NTIA) monitors the success of these programs in a series of reports entitled *Falling Through the Net*.

According to these reports, people with high incomes are twice as likely to have access to the Internet. About a third of households earning less than $50,000 have Internet access, while more than two-thirds of households earning more than $50,000 are connected. Whites are more likely to have access to the Internet at home than Blacks or Hispanics have from any location. Black and Hispanic households are half as likely to have home access as Asian/Pacific Islander households. In 2005 the Pew Internet & American Life Project published the results of a demographic survey of Internet users. Table 25-1 shows how the survey detected gaps in Internet usage according to age, ethnicity, community type, household income, and educational attainment.

To understand what needs to be done to achieve universal access, follow the *Interlit* Web site links to the Universal Service Fund, the Digital Divide, *Falling Through the Net,* the Pew Internet and American Life Project, and *A Nation Online.*

Table 25-1   Demographics of Internet users

Gender	
Women	61%
Men	66%
Age	
18–29	78%
30–49	74%
50–64	60%
65+	25%
Race/Ethnicity	
White, non-Hispanic	67%
Black, non-Hispanic	43%
Hispanic	59%
Community Type	
Urban	62%
Suburban	68%
Rural	56%
Household Income	
Less than $30,000/yr.	44%
$30,000–$50,000	69%
$50,000–$75,000	81%
More than $75,000	89%
Educational Attainment	
Less than high school	32%
High school	52%
Some college	75%
College +	88%

Source: Pew Internet & American Life Project, February–March 2005 Tracking Survey, http://www.pewinternet.org/trends/User_Demo_05.18.05.htm. Last updated May 18, 2005. N = 2,200 adults 18 and older. Margin of error is ±2% for results based on the full sample.

How Long Will It Take?

NetDay

In 1995, a grassroots volunteer effort called NetDay launched a national movement to connect the nation's schools to the Internet. From 1996 to 2001, half a million volunteers wired more than 75,000 classrooms in 40 states.

Making it possible for every student to log on from school, however, does not provide equal access to the Internet. Citizens who do not have convenient access outside of school constitute a technological underclass that is seriously disadvantaged in the information society. In California, for example, the Pacific Bell telephone company made plans to provide universal access to all of its customers. In 1993, PacBell announced that it would spend about $15 billion to develop a network that can deliver television and high-speed data services throughout California. Phase one called for wiring 1.5 million homes by the end of 1996; phase two would hook up 3.5 million more by the end of the decade. California's remaining 4 million customers would be wired by 2010 (*New York Times,* 11 November 1993: C4). In 1994, PacBell began replacing copper telephone wiring with fiber optic cables in portions of Orange and Los Angeles counties, San Diego, and the San Francisco Bay area. In 1996, however, the initiative was aborted, and the plan to connect all Californians to the Internet at high speed was waylaid.

Californians were not the only citizens to lose the promise of high-speed connectivity. In 2000, a watchdog organization called the New Networks Institute (NNI) released a report entitled *How the Baby Bells Stole America's Digital Future.* The report reveals that California is just one of many states in which the Regional Bell Operating Companies (RBOCs) failed to deliver on fiber-optic promises. Citizens in Indiana, Ohio, New Jersey, and Texas were similarly shortchanged. The report claims that if the RBOCs had delivered on the promises they made in the early 1990s, 44 million households would already be connected to the Internet via high-speed fiber-optic lines. Instead, only about 500,000 households had fiber-optic access at the turn of the century. In December of 2001, the NNI filed a complaint with the NTIA charging that telephone customers have paid more than $58 billion for broadband services they never received. By the time this book went to press in 2005, that figure had grown to $120 billion. In the meantime, PricewaterhouseCoopers predicts that fiber-optic services will reach an estimated 1.8 million households by 2007 (Hyland, 2004).

For the latest information, follow the *Interlit* Web site link to the New Networks Institute, where you can read the petition filed with the Federal Communications Commission and see how the Computer Professionals for Social Responsibility (CPSR) endorsed the NNI report.

Public Library Internet Access

To provide a way for all Americans to access the Internet, the Bill & Melinda Gates Foundation is working to equip public libraries with hardware, software, and faster Internet connections. Since 1998, the Gates Foundation has given $250 million to buy 47,000 computers at 11,000 public libraries. In 2005, the foundation is giving $11 million in matching cash grants to public libraries in 37 states and the District of Columbia. The goal is to ensure that public libraries can continue to offer patrons free access to technology. Upon receipt of a $416,800 Gates Foundation award, California state librarian Susan Hildreth explained: "We are the first resort for Internet access, particularly in low-income areas. People expect computers to be available at the library, at the highest technological level" (AP/*USA Today,* 13 January 2005).

Privacy

Switchboard

Yahoo! People Search

The U.S. Constitution guarantees every American the right to privacy. The Internet threatens this right. Most users are unaware of how real the threat is. At the very least, your name probably is listed with or without your knowledge at switchboard.com and people. yahoo.com, but the invasions of your privacy can run much deeper.

Break-ins

A lot of data is kept on the Internet at Web sites where people fill out forms and offer sensitive information such as credit card numbers. When Web sites get broken into, this information can be released into the wrong hands. Murphy (2000) tells how credit card information for 26,000 people was hacked from nine e-commerce sites in the United States, Canada, Thailand, Japan, and Britain. One of the 26,000 credit card holders was none other than Bill Gates.

People who break into Web sites are called *crackers*. Under federal law, crackers caught trespassing can get up to a year in prison, five years for stealing money or information of value, and 10 years for stealing classified data.

In 2005, crackers masquerading as legitimate businesses obtained accounts at ChoicePoint, which is a credit reporting agency that contains financial information regarding most Americans. Through the bogus accounts, the crackers obtained the personal data records of an estimated 145,000 consumers. ChoicePoint sent letters informing these consumers of the breach. To protect yourself against the financial harm that can come from this kind of theft, you should routinely check your monthly bank statements and credit card reports for fraudulent charges and review your credit history at least yearly.

Internet Fraud

Internet Fraud Complaint Center

Internet fraud is any situation in which an Internet resource—such as a Web site, chat room, newsgroup, or e-mail—plays a role in communicating false representations to consumers, such as the offering of nonexistent goods or services, in an attempt to transfer funds or goods from the victim into the control of the perpetrator. Because the Internet has become the infrastructure for trade and commerce in the 21st century, the U.S. government wants to keep it as free from fraud as possible. The FBI has therefore partnered with the National White Collar Crime Center to create the Internet Fraud Complaint Center (IFCC), which provides a mechanism for consumers to report Internet fraud and allows for the sharing of fraud data by law enforcement and regulatory authorities. The IFCC develops educational programs aimed at preventing Internet fraud and offers fraud prevention training to local, state, and federal law enforcement agencies.

According to the IFCC, online auctions are the number one source of complaints about fraud on the Internet. The online auction industry, on the other hand, denies that fraud is a serious problem. The leading auction site, eBay, for example, maintains that less than 0.01 percent of its listings results in a confirmed case of fraudulent activity.

To help keep the Internet free from fraud, every user should follow these guidelines:

- Do not assume that everything you read on the Internet is true. If an online offer seems too hard to believe, then don't believe it.

- Do not give out personal information, especially credit card numbers and banking info, without knowing who is asking for it.

- Never provide information if the people requesting the data conceal their identity.

- Report fraud immediately by following the *Interlit* Web site link to the IFCC.

Sniffing Messages on the Internet

When you use the Internet, the information you send and receive gets routed through the gateways and bridges that connect the networks on the Information Superhighway. Each gateway is a computer that can potentially be hacked into. Crackers who hack their way into a gateway can read the messages that pass through it. Intercepting information on the Internet this way is known as **sniffing,** which is the Internet's equivalent of a telephone wiretap.

To protect against the danger of sniffing, you can encrypt your messages. As you learned in Chapter 6, both Mozilla Thunderbird and Microsoft Outlook have encryption options. When someone sniffs an encrypted message, the message will be unintelligible, unless the person who sniffs the message knows the encryption key or can somehow figure it out.

Carnivore

The FBI has a computerized sniffer called Carnivore, which enables the government to monitor e-mail traffic and access other kinds of Internet transmissions including chat rooms, instant messaging, and file transfers. Carnivore is customizable. The FBI can install Carnivore at one or more ISPs and set it to scan the message headers, subjects, or bodies for names, keywords, phrases, and concepts. Copies of suspect messages can be forwarded automatically to the FBI agents working on a certain case.

Whereas Carnivore has been a major concern among privacy advocates, the 9/11 attacks on America led to passage of the USA PATRIOT Act, which broadened federal authority to use Internet surveillance systems including Carnivore and its successors. To learn more, follow the *Interlit* Web site link to Carnivore.

Pretty Good Privacy

One of the ways criminals and terrorists try to evade systems like Carnivore is to use encryption. When a message is encrypted, it cannot be read by someone who does not have the encryption key. An example of an encryption program is Pretty Good Privacy (PGP) by Phil Zimmerman. PGP runs on almost every brand of computer and is the most common way of encrypting e-mail messages in the popular Eudora e-mail package. For more information, follow the *Interlit* Web Site link to PGP. Also written by Zimmerman is PGPfone, which uses a complex algorithm called Blowfish to scramble phone calls made through a computer modem. For details, follow the *Interlit* Web site link to PGPfone. You can download both PGP and PGPfone for free.

Clipper

You can bet the FBI is developing computational methods to figure out the encryption keys needed to decypher PGP and other kinds of encrypted messages. Many firms encrypt their messages, for example, to prevent crackers from sniffing a company's electronic correspondence. The government is concerned that this encryption prevents law enforcement agencies who have court orders from eavesdropping on digital communications.

During the 1990s, the Clinton White House wanted to control the encryption process by requiring that every electronic device contain a **Clipper Chip,** which is an encryption device with a "back door" that allows detectives with the proper access to decipher the messages. In opposition to the White House plan, more than 250 members of Congress cosponsored legislation that would prohibit such back-door devices on computers, and the Computer Professionals for Social Responsibility (CPSR) organized a protest. The Center for Democracy and Technology maintains that Clipper and other back-door technologies violate the Fourth Amendment to the U.S. Constitution, which states that "[t]he right of the people to be secure in their persons, houses, papers, and effects, against unreasonable searches and seizures, shall not be violated." To learn more about civil liberties, privacy legislation, and online activisim, follow the *Interlit* Web Site link to CPSR and the Center for Democracy and Technology.

Cookies

Back in the 1980s, a game called PacMan was popular in video arcades. The game contained magic cookies that, when devoured, made you more powerful. On the Internet, cookies work a little differently, but they are much more powerful. They also pose one of the greatest threats to your privacy.

A **cookie** is a place in your computer's memory where Web sites can store information about you and your preferences. If you buy an audio CD by Britney Spears, for example, the shopping site might create a cookie that remembers you like pop music. The next time you visit the site, it might show you ads for similar pop music titles. Or the cookie might keep track of the screens you visited and use that information to resume where you left off.

Some people have mixed feelings about cookies. On the one hand, cookies can make it very convenient when you revisit a site and do not have to fill in so much information to get where you want to go there. On the other hand, some people dislike information being kept without their knowledge; many browsers never ask if it is OK to keep cookies on your computer. The vendor's assumption is that unless you turn your cookies off, you mean to have them on.

It is possible to turn cookies off, as described in the sections that follow for Firefox cookies and Internet Explorer cookies. If you turn your cookies off, however, some Web sites may no longer act as personable when you visit them, because they will have lost their access to your cookies. Web sites that require you to log on may cease to function at all, because they need cookies to maintain your state from screen to screen after you log on.

For the latest information about cookies, follow the *Interlit* Web site link to Cookie Central, where you can study more details regarding how cookies work technically and why they were invented.

FIREFOX COOKIE SETTINGS

To turn cookies on or off in Firefox, you pull down the Tools menu and choose Options. When the Options dialog appears, click the Privacy button to make the privacy options appear, then click the plus sign next to Cookies. Figure 25-1 shows the cookie settings that appear onscreen. You can choose to accept all cookies, disable cookies, or accept only cookies that get sent back to the originating Web site, which means the site you went to with your browser. The Keep Cookies menu lets you set the option to make your computer ask you every time before storing a cookie.

INTERNET EXPLORER COOKIE SETTINGS

To turn cookies on or off in the Internet Explorer, pull down the Tools menu and choose Internet Options. When the Internet Options dialog appears, as illustrated in Figure 25-2, click Privacy to make the privacy settings appear. To change the cookie settings, drag the slider up or down to increase or lower the cookie level, or click the Advanced button to reveal the Advanced Privacy Settings dialog, shown in Figure 25-3. Notice that there are two kinds of cookie categories, namely, cookies that are stored on your computer's hard disk and per-session cookies that are not stored there. Stored cookies are used by commercial Web sites to keep information about you from session to session on your hard disk. Per-session cookies are kept in your computer's RAM, instead of on your hard disk, and they are used to maintain your state when you log on to a Web site. Web sites that have you log on normally keep information about you on the server, although some of them also keep information in your hard disk cookies.

Clear GIF Web Bugs

Another method used to collect information about you is the so-called **Web Bug.** It can appear either on a Web page or in an HTML e-mail or newsgroup message. Actually *appear* is the wrong term because normally the Web Bug is a single-pixel transparent

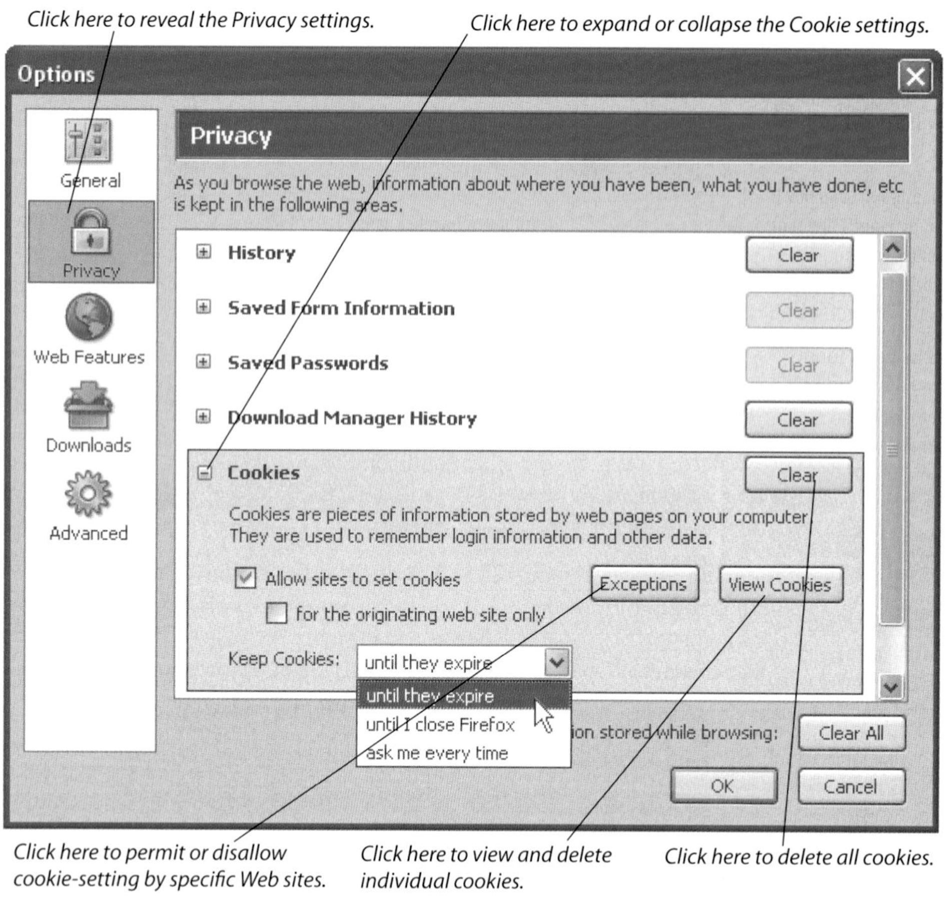

Click here to reveal the Privacy settings. *Click here to expand or collapse the Cookie settings.*

Options

Privacy

General

As you browse the web, information about where you have been, what you have done, etc is kept in the following areas.

Privacy

⊞ **History** — Clear

⊞ **Saved Form Information** — Clear

Web Features

⊞ **Saved Passwords** — Clear

⊞ **Download Manager History** — Clear

Downloads

⊟ **Cookies** — Clear

Advanced

Cookies are pieces of information stored by web pages on your computer. They are used to remember login information and other data.

☑ Allow sites to set cookies   Exceptions   View Cookies

☐ for the originating web site only

Keep Cookies: | until they expire ▾ |

until they expire
until I close Firefox   ion stored while browsing: Clear All
ask me every time

OK   Cancel

Click here to permit or disallow cookie-setting by specific Web sites. *Click here to view and delete individual cookies.* *Click here to delete all cookies.*

Figure 25-1   The Firefox cookie settings are in the Privacy section of the Options dialog, revealed by pulling down the Tools menu and choosing Options.

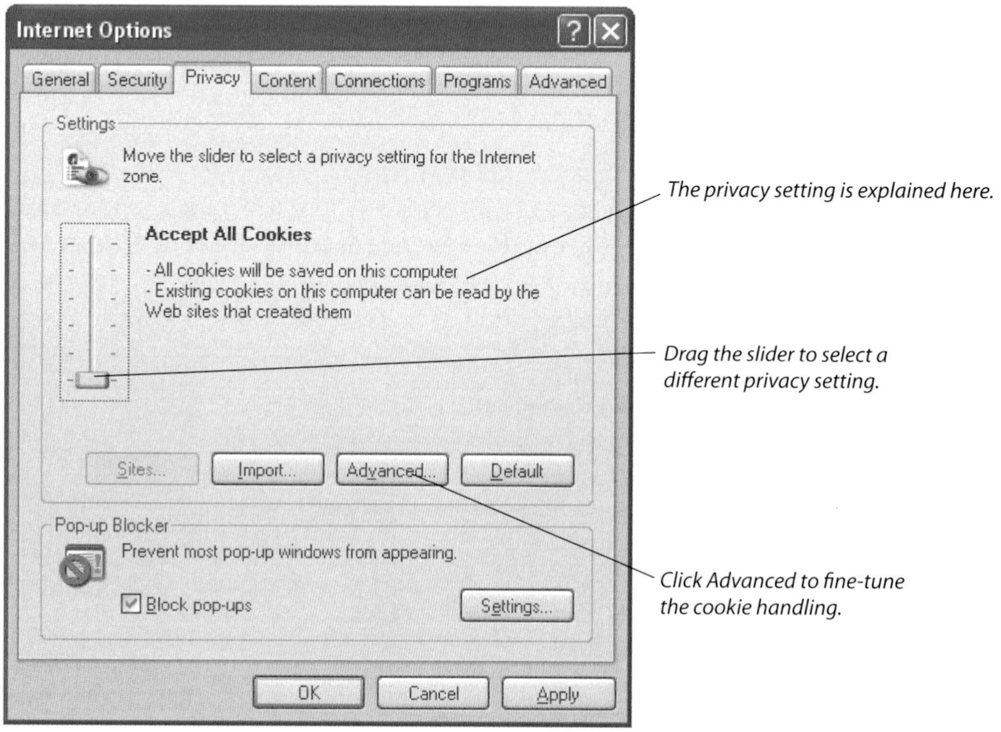

Internet Options   ？ ✕

| General | Security | Privacy | Content | Connections | Programs | Advanced |

Settings

Move the slider to select a privacy setting for the Internet zone.

The privacy setting is explained here.

Accept All Cookies

- All cookies will be saved on this computer
- Existing cookies on this computer can be read by the Web sites that created them

Drag the slider to select a different privacy setting.

Sites...   Import...   Advanced...   Default

Pop-up Blocker

Prevent most pop-up windows from appearing.

☑ Block pop-ups   Settings...

Click Advanced to fine-tune the cookie handling.

OK   Cancel   Apply

Figure 25-2   The Privacy tab of the Internet Options in Microsoft Internet Explorer.

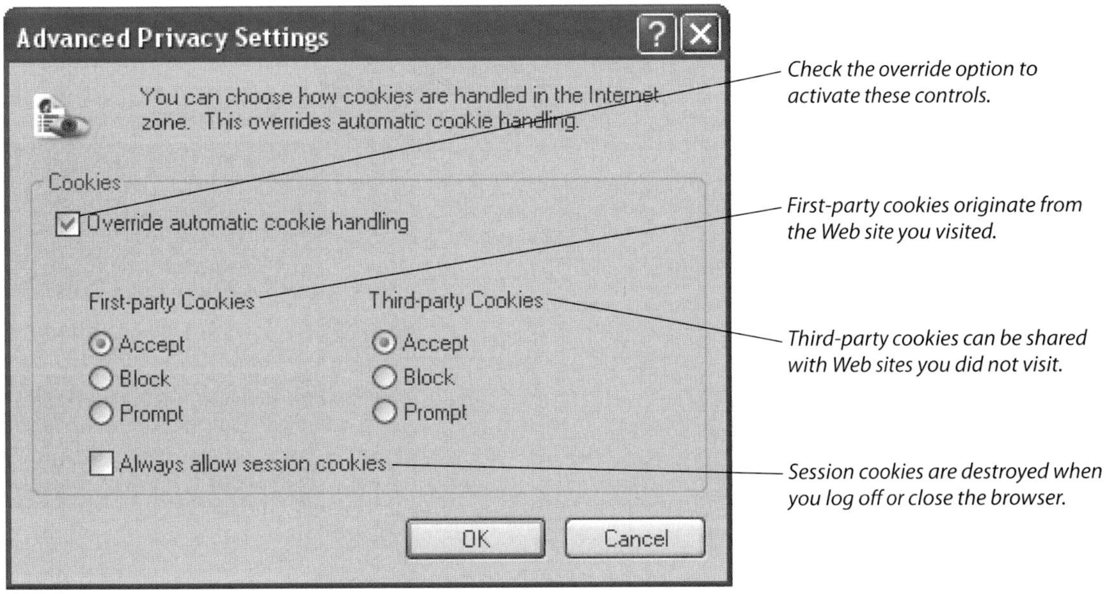

Figure 25-3 The Internet Explorer cookie settings revealed by clicking the Advanced button in Figure 25-2.

GIF image, which you never "see" at all. The purpose of the Web Bug is to inform some third-party advertising site that you read the message or visited a certain Web page. How does the third-party site know this? Because the Web Bug's GIF image resides at that site. When you open an HTML e-mail message or visit a Web page containing a Web Bug, your computer automatically downloads the GIF from the third-party server where the image resides. In the download request, the third-party Web site sees a lot of information including your IP address, the URL of the page you visited, the time you hit the page, and the brand of your browser and operating system. If you have third-party cookies turned on, the value of a cookie stored on your computer also can be sent to the Web Bug server. If the Web Bug appears in an e-mail message, your e-mail address also goes along.

To find out if a certain page contains a Web Bug, wait until the page finishes loading. Then view the source code of the page by pulling down the View menu and choosing Page Source (Firefox) or Source (Internet Explorer). Search the source code for an image tag that has a width of 1 and a height of 1, which indicate the presence of a single-pixel image. If the source of the image that this tag points to resides on a different server than the site you visited, you probably found a Web Bug. *Note:* Web Bugs also can have other sizes and shapes, however, and they need not be invisible.

Advertising agencies use Web Bugs to create a profile of your browsing habits. Over time, you may notice the commercial advertising at Web sites conforming more closely to your personal taste and buying habits. To learn more about Web Bugs and the advertising agencies that use them, follow the *Interlit* Web site link to Web Bugs.

Adware and Spyware

Adware is a form of computer programming that displays commercial advertising in part of an application window or in a popup window that is a child of the application window. Some adware is legitimate and poses no privacy threat. When you download free versions of commercial software applications, for example, ads typically appear onscreen enticing you to purchase a commercial version that is ad-free. There is nothing wrong with this kind of adware if that is all it does.

Because the adware is a program running on your computer, however, it has the ability to collect information about your use of the software. When this is done without your knowledge, the adware becomes a form of spyware.

Spyware is a type of computer program that secretly collects information and can transmit it without your knowledge or use it to display ads or take other actions either in a browser window or in popup windows. If the intent is malicious, the program becomes a form of **malware,** which is a generic term for software born of ill intent. Besides invading your privacy, malware can take over your computer and wreak havoc with your data.

Microsoft has developed software that scans Windows computers for spyware and malware. When this book went to press, Microsoft was distributing it via the Windows Update Service. Apple runs a similar update service for the Macintosh. Chapter 27 concludes this book by teaching you how to use the Windows and Macintosh update services. Follow the *Interlit* Web site link to learn about other brands of adware, spyware, and malware scanners.

Phishing

Phishing is a scam you need to avoid falling for when reading e-mail messages. The term phishing sounds like fishing, which is the metaphor this kind of scam follows. In a phishing scam, you receive an e-mail message (the lure) that appears to come from a legitimate business or financial agency with which you may have registered personal information such as your social security number, bank account, or credit card information. Inside the message is a link (the bait) you are asked to click in order to update or verify this information. When you click the link, it launches a third-party Web site that appears to be legitimate. A Web form prompts you to enter your private information to verify it.

You need to be careful never to fall for such a trick. Never click this kind of link in an e-mail message. Instead, if you want to verify your account information, use your browser to log on to the company's Web site and follow the legitimate process there to check your account settings.

Several times a month, I receive phishing messages that supposedly come from PayPal or eBay, for example. The messages claim that my account will expire if I do not click the link to update my information. Neither PayPal nor eBay would ever ask you to verify personal information in this manner. For more on phishing, follow the *Interlit* Web site link to All About Phishing and the Anti-Phishing Working Group.

Certification

TRUSTe

When you go to a Web site, how can you be sure that it will not make unethical use of information obtained about you? One way is to look for a certificate called a **trustmark.** Companies that have committed to following privacy principles can license a trustmark from an organization named TRUSTe.

Trustmarks are awarded to sites that TRUSTe considers to be safe and secure places to conduct business, education, communication, and entertainment activities. You can trust that the site will not divulge information about you, hence the name TRUSTe.

Trustmarks are served remotely from the TRUSTe servers and are linked to a site's privacy statement, which describes the kind of information a site gathers, what the site does with that information, and with whom the information is shared. For more on trustmarks, follow the *Interlit* Web site link to TRUSTe.

Privacy Legislation

Children's Online Privacy Protection Act

Regardless of what you think about adult rights to privacy on the Internet, almost everyone agrees that children need special protection. The Children's Online Privacy Protection Act (COPPA) went into effect on April 21, 2000. Web site operators who run commercial sites that collect personal information from children under 13 must post their privacy policy, obtain parental consent, get new consent when the site changes the kind of information it collects, allow parents to review personal information collected from their children, allow parents to revoke their consent, and delete information collected from children at their parent's request.

Federal Trade Commission

During the summer of 2000, COPPA was used by the Federal Trade Commission to prevent the bankrupt toymaker ToysMart from selling its customer lists and databases as assets. News of the pending sale prompted a complaint from TRUSTe, which had certified ToysMart's online privacy policy. According to Perine (2000), TRUSTe complained to the FTC that such a sale would violate a ToysMart promise that it would never share names, addresses, credit card numbers, and shopping preferences with a third party.

For more information on COPPA and other privacy legislation, follow the *Interlit* Web site link to COPPA and the Yahoo privacy site.

Platform for Privacy Preferences (P3P)

W3C Platform for Privacy Preferences

With a Microsoft executive saying, "this is unprecedented, but we realized that we need to work together for the common good," Microsoft decided to abandon plans to create its own Internet software privacy standards and endorsed instead the standard proposed by its rival Netscape and Firefly Network, Inc. Part of the World Wide Web Consortium's Platform for Privacy Preferences (P3P), the standard is supported by more than a hundred hardware and software companies, both large and small. It will enable Web surfers to know and control what personal information can be obtained about them during their travels on the Internet.

The first public test of P3P was held on 21 June 2000. More than a dozen Web sites were made P3P-compliant for the event, including AOL, AT&T, IBM, Microsoft, W3C, and the White House. Since then, hundreds of Web sites have adopted P3P. For the latest information, follow the *Interlit* Web site link to the Platform for Privacy Preferences. To see some of the sample privacy policies, follow the link to P3P-compliant sites, choose any one of the sites listed there, and click the link to view its privacy policy.

Center for Democracy and Technology

Center for Democracy and Technology

The Center for Democracy and Technology (CDT) is a nonprofit organization that works to promote democratic values and constitutional liberties in the digital age. The CDT has been instrumental in raising the public's awareness of privacy issues on the Internet. It was the CDT, for example, that conceptualized the P3P and then worked with the W3C to develop it into a worldwide privacy standard. Figure 25-4 shows some of the CDT action

Figure 25-4 Free speech, encryption, and privacy are the hot issues at the Center for Democracy and Technology.

banners. For information about these and other CDT initiatives, follow the *Interlit* Web site links to the Center for Democracy.

Electronic Frontier Foundation

Electronic Frontier Foundation

The Electronic Frontier Foundation (EFF) is a nonprofit civil liberties organization working in the public interest to protect privacy, free expression, and access to public resources and information online, as well as to promote responsibility in new media. When this book went to press, for example, EFF was organizing a protest against using the driver's license as a national ID card, which is one of the 9/11 Commission's recommendations for improving U.S. security.

Some highly respected individuals, including database giant Oracle chairman Larry Ellison, favor a national ID card system in response to the terrorist attacks on America. The EFF, on the other hand, questions how a national ID system can prevent terrorism and believes the risk to privacy outweighs the benefits of such a national ID card. Regardless of how you feel about these kinds of issues, anyone interested in protecting their right to privacy on the Internet should visit the EFF. Follow the *Interlit* Web site link to the Electronic Frontier Foundation. For more information about the proposed national ID card system, follow the link to the National ID Card Action Alert.

Electronic Privacy Information Center

Electronic Privacy Information Center

The Electronic Privacy Information Center (EPIC) is a public-interest research center that was established in 1994 to focus public attention on emerging civil liberties issues and to protect privacy, the First Amendment, and constitutional values. EPIC is a project of the Fund for Constitutional Government. EPIC works in association with Privacy International, an international human rights group based in London, and is also a member of the Global Internet Liberty Campaign and the Internet Privacy Coalition. For more information, follow the *Interlit* Web site link to EPIC. A valuable resource you will find there is the EPIC search engine, which indexes source documents on computer security, cryptography policy, free speech, freedom of information, and privacy.

Sleuthing

Let's face it; when you use the Internet, you leave tracks. Little snippets of information about you litter the Information Superhighway. A social security number here, a phone number there. Here a rèsumè, there a newsgroup message. Someone who is network savvy can put this information together and find out an amazing amount of information about you.

Congressman Frank Horton (1966) predicted the threat of electronic sleuthing in a statement made four decades ago:

> One of the most practical of our present safeguards of privacy is the fragmented nature of personal information. It is scattered in little bits across the geography and years of our life. Retrieval is impractical and often impossible. A central data bank removes completely this safeguard.

Anyone concerned about privacy should be aware of the sleuthing that can be done to find things out about you on the Internet.

Discreet Data Research

Discreet Data Research

Discreet Data Research is a fee-based service that will do electronic sleuthing for you. While the fees are steep, the range of services offered is incredible. You can surf the Discreet Data Research Web site for free to see the kinds of services offered, which fall into the categories of telephone, pager, and voice mail research; missing persons, for finding people who are unintentionally lost; skip tracing, to find people who have intentionally become missing; and "unusual requests" for asking anything else you want to know. To check out the full range of sleuthing services, follow the *Interlit* Web site link to Discreet Data Research.

Stalking

WiredPatrol

On the dark side of the Internet is the danger of being stalked. Someone who is network savvy and knows your name or e-mail address can follow you around virtually on the Internet and harass you by sending unwanted messages and tracking or confronting you in newsgroups and chat rooms. By following the *Interlit* Web site link to WiredPatrol, you can read case studies of chat harassment and e-mail stalking and guidelines on what to do if you get stalked or harassed online.

CyberAngels.org

CyberAngels.org

One of the best ways to protect yourself against stalking is to follow the *Interlit* Web site link to CyberAngels.org, where you will find a wide range of resources for online security, safety, and privacy. CyberAngels also has a Net Patrol, which is a group of volunteers who patrol the Internet looking for child pornography, stalkers, child predators, groups advocating child abuse and pedophilia, hate and bigotry sites, and scam artists. You can even get a personal angel to help you if you get stalked on the Internet.

Security

To protect networks against unauthorized access by users seeking information to which they are not entitled, several steps can be taken. Security measures include passwords, encryption, firewalls, and filters.

Passwords

The simplest form of protection is the **password,** which is an alphanumeric string of characters the user must type in order to gain access. Unless the user knows the password, access to the data is denied. Passwords are not failsafe, however, because it is possible for someone to guess your password. To protect against people guessing your password, choose an unlikely string of characters containing a combination of uppercase and lowercase letters and numbers. Never use your name (or your mother's maiden name, to which passwords are often set initially), and avoid using the names of hobbies or other things people know interest you. As you learned in the section on stalking, it is possible for people to find out things about you, and crackers can use information learned by stalking you to try and guess your password.

Encryption

As you learned in the section on privacy, messages on the Internet can be sniffed. Anywhere along the way from your PC to the server, it is possible that a cracker can hack into the transmission and read your messages. To protect against this, you can encrypt your messages. Both Mozilla Thunderbird and Microsoft Outlook contain built-in encryption capability. Unless the sniffer knows the encryption key, your message remains private.

There is considerable debate regarding national encryption policy. Should individuals have the right to encrypt their messages? Should the government have the right to decipher these communications? To learn more about this debate, follow the *Interlit* Web site link to the Center for Democracy and Technology's Cryptology page, which is dedicated to educating Internet users, policymakers, and the public about the issues surrounding encryption policy. Here you will find background information on the encryption policy debate, including legislation, government documents, and statements by members of Congress and administration officials.

Firewalls

In the housing industry, firewalls are constructed between dwellings in an apartment building to prevent a fire that might break out in one unit from spreading to another. The fire is thereby contained to the domain of the apartment in which it started. On the Internet, firewalls work like that, keeping data from moving outside their domain and preventing access to users from other domains. More specifically, a **firewall** is a combination of hardware, software, and security policies that block certain kinds of traffic from entering or leaving a network, subnet, or individual host computer.

Many corporations use firewalls to keep information on the company's network from being accessible on the public Internet. The company's internal network is known as an **intranet.** The prefix *intra* is a Latin word meaning within. Thus, an intranet is a private network that uses the TCP/IP protocols to provide services within the company's firewall. The firewall can be programmed to allow or disallow different levels of access between the private intranet and the public Internet. The term **extranet** refers to private resources that require users outside the firewall to log on in order to obtain access from the public Internet. To learn more about firewalls, follow the *Interlit* Web site links to How Firewalls Work and Why You Need a Firewall.

WINDOWS FIREWALL

Microsoft has built a firewall feature into Windows XP and recommends that any computer connected directly to the Internet should have the firewall activated. This includes computers that serve as network hubs, to which other computers have been connected, as well as individual computers connected to the Internet through modems, ISDN, DSL, or broadband connections. When you install Windows XP Service Pack 2, it turns the Windows firewall on by default. If you have Windows XP, you can check your firewall settings by following these steps:

- Log on to your computer as the administrator. If you do not have the administrator logon, contact your computer's network administrator. Only the administrator can change the firewall settings.

- Click the Windows Start button, choose Control Panel, and bring up Network Connections.

- When the Network Connections window appears, click the icon of your network connection.

- Under Network Tasks, click Change settings of this connection; the Network Connection Properties dialog appears.

- Click the Advanced tab for the Windows Firewall settings.

- Click the Settings button to see the settings, or click the Network Setup Wizard to let the wizard step you through the firewall setup.

Filters

Filters are sifting algorithms that scan incoming data for certain kinds of content. If you have young children, for example, you would not want them accessing adult content on the Internet. Filters can watch the incoming datastream and block content inappropriate for children. There are two places to run filters: either on the servers that deliver the content or in the clients that receive it.

SERVER-SIDE FILTERING

A good example of the use of server-side filtering can be found in China's educational system. According to the Beijing Education Committee, students were spending too much of their time playing games, talking in chat rooms, and viewing adult content. Less than 50 percent of student time online was devoted to study. To solve this problem, educational software company United Education Limited developed a solution that uses Microsoft's ISA Server software to filter Web content dynamically. ISA stands for Internet Security and Acceleration. The network administrator installs ISA Server on the network hub to filter out unwanted content and accelerate, through caching, access to desirable content. To learn more about ISA Server, follow the *Interlit* Web site links to ISA Server and the Case Study of China's Educational System.

CHILDREN'S INTERNET PROTECTION ACT

In the United States, the Children's Internet Protection Act (CIPA, also known as the CHIP Act) requires that all schools and libraries receiving federal e-rate computing dollars or using Title III funds for computers must implement Internet safety policies by installing filtering technology to block access to objectionable content. Computer funding is withheld from schools that do not conform. Several computer firms produce filtering software that school districts can use to comply with CIPA. To learn more about these products, follow the *Interlit* Web site links to CIPA products and the full text of the CIPA Act.

Citing the First Amendment, three organizations—the Electronic Privacy Information Center, the American Civil Liberties Union, and the American Library Association—challenged in court the constitutionality of the CIPA Act. Based on a lower-court ruling in favor of the libraries, the FCC temporarily suspended the requirement that libraries purchase filtering software. In 2003, however, the U.S. Supreme Court in a 6-3 decision held that public libraries must comply with all portions of CIPA, including filtering software to block objectionable content.

CLIENT-SIDE FILTERING

CYBERSitter

Five-time winner of the PC Magazine Editors' Choice Award in 1997, 2000, 2001, 2003, and 2004, CYBERSitter is an example of client-side filtering that lets parents limit their children's access to objectionable material on the Internet. Parents can choose to block, block and log, or simply notify them when their kids try to access a blocked area. CYBERsitter is password protected and easy to deactivate or reconfigure by the parent. CYBERsitter works with Microsoft, Netscape, and America Online browsers on the full range of Windows computers. When this book went to press, there was no version for the Macintosh. For the latest information, follow the *Interlit* Web site link to CYBERsitter.

There are dozens of other filtering products you can use to block, monitor, or control access to Internet content. To read about these products and download free demos, follow the *Interlit* Web site link to Filtering Tools for Families.

Nationalism and Isolationism

Some countries view technology as a cultural threat and are taking steps to counteract it. In France, for example, there is a law known as the Toubon Law requiring that all advertising in France, while it may be done in other languages, also must appear in the French language. Some people believe that this law applies to the Web. Amrich (1999) tells of a French-speaking reader of *Windows CE Power Magazine,* for example, who wrote a letter to the editor stating, "I am quite disturbed that your webzine is written only in English.

I am in France and we have laws here that requiring [sic] you to display your Internet site in French. You must show honoring of this law to be continued to be allowed to show your site in this country." As this book goes to press, legislation pending approval by the French Senate seeks to amend the Toubon Law by requiring that all Web sites targeted at French consumers must either be in French or have a suitable translation. The law further requires that the sites' error messages also must be in French. For the full text of the law (in French), follow the *Interlit* Web site link to the Toubon Law Internet Amendment.

China has a centrally administered Internet backbone that allows government monitoring of e-mail and other online activities. Special Internet police units administer the network and maintain order. China routinely blocks Web sites deemed politically sensitive or harmful, including Western media outlets and human rights groups. Local portals are forbidden to post news reports from sources that are not controlled by the state. On 3 June 2000, Chinese police in the city of Chengu, for example, arrested Web site operator Huang Qi on suspicion of subverting state power at www.6-4tianwang.com, which was publishing information about human rights problems and corruption in China. His trial ended in August 2001, but the verdict was postponed until 2003. The sentence was five years' imprisonment for subversion and incitement to overthrow the government. Follow the *Interlit* Web site link to find out the status of Huang Qi's imprisonment.

Viewing the Internet as the end of civilization, Iraq under Saddam Hussein denied access to *all* of its citizens. An editorial in the Iraqi government newspaper *Al-Jumhuriya* says that the Internet is "the end of civilizations, cultures, interests, and ethics," and "one of the American means to enter every house in the world. They want to become the only source for controlling human beings in the new electronic village" (AP, 17 February 1997). This viewpoint fails to realize that many of the key Internet inventions came from outside the United States. Packet switching originated in Great Britain, for example, and the Web was invented in Switzerland. According to the arab.net ISP directory: "We can find no Internet Service providers in Iraq. If you know different, then please let us know" (www.arab.net/isp-directory/iraq.html, cited 29 January 2002). When this book went to press, the Iraq button at www.arab.net/isp-directory was not responding. For the current status of Internet connectivity in Iraq, follow the *Interlit* Web site link to Iraqi Connectivity.

The Internet is a worldwide resource in which every country should participate and become a co-inventor. Restricting or denying access to the Internet will severely retard a nation's status in the 21st century. Every citizen in the world should have the right to unrestricted Internet access.

Censorship

Many people are concerned that, in addition to being able to monitor electronic communications that stream across the Internet, network administrators also have the ability to censor them. To what extent and under what circumstances should the government act as a censor on the Information Superhighway?

In a well-publicized criminal trial in Toronto, the Canadian government exercised its right to ban any publicity about the case, lest prospective jurors become biased and the hearings end in mistrial. So the University of Toronto stopped carrying an Internet bulletin board that disclosed banned information about the case. But that did not stop people from distributing the information through e-mail (*Toronto Globe & Mail*, 2 December 1993: A4).

Protecting children from offensive material while providing free range for adults is an ongoing dilemma. There was a lot of controversy, for example, surrounding the Communications Decency Act of 1996, which made it illegal to distribute indecent or offensive materials on the Internet. Ruling that the act violated free speech, a three-judge federal court blocked enforcement of the CDA, describing it as "a government-imposed content-based restriction on speech," in violation of the Constitution. The Justice Department appealed to the

Supreme Court, which overturned the CDA in July of 1997. For the legislative history of the CDA, including analysis by the Center for Democracy and Technology, which opposed it, follow the *Interlit* Web site links to the Communications Decency Act.

Pornography and Obscenity

Too much bandwidth on the Internet is devoted to the transmission of pornographic and obscene sexual content. The JPEG file format, which makes it possible to include beautiful full-color images on Web pages, also can transmit full-color photos of explicit "hardcore" pornography and child pornography. The federal government has been searching and seizing servers that contain such material.

The Supreme Court's 1973 *Miller* ruling gave communities the right to legislate obscenity. To help interpret the laws, Godwin (1994: 58) developed the following four-part test for obscenity:

1. Is the work designed to be sexually arousing?

2. Is it arousing in a way that one's local community would consider unhealthy or immoral?

3. Does it picture acts whose depictions are specifically prohibited by state law?

4. Does the work, when taken as a whole, lack sufficient literary, artistic, scientific, or social value?

Distributing such materials over the Internet raises some difficult issues. For example, while an erotic picture might not be immoral in the community where it was uploaded, it may very well be considered obscene in the place it gets downloaded. Screen-capture utilities make it easy to take things out of context; who can prevent users from circulating an image devoid of the supplementary material that made it legitimate? Moreover, children can easily access materials over the Internet that were intended for adults.

The U.S. child protection laws forbid any pornographic images that use children, whether or not they meet Godwin's obscenity test. Individuals convicted can be fined up to $100,000 and imprisoned up to 10 years. For example, as the result of a nationwide FBI investigation of online pornography, a distributor of child pornography was sentenced to five years in prison for sending sexually explicit photos of children via his America Online account (*Tampa Tribune,* 24 February 1996: A6). In 2005, a federal court judge sent an Alabama man to prison for 30 years for possessing, receiving, and producing child pornography found on his computer, and for offering this material in Internet chat rooms (AP/WKRN News, 17 February 2005).

Canada's best-known computer science school, the University of Waterloo, banned from its campus five Internet bulletin boards dealing with violent sex out of concern that the bulletin boards' contents break laws on pornography and obscenity (*Toronto Globe & Mail,* 5 February 1994: A1). In the last three months of 2004, China closed more than 12,000 Internet cafés to create what the Xinhua News Agency refers to as a "safer environment for young people in China" (AP/*Washington Times,* 14 February 2005). To prevent pornographic pictures from being taken in the first place, Saudi Arabia banned camera-equipped cell phones so they would not "spread vice in the Muslim community" (*The Age,* 4 October 2004).

Internet Content Rating Association

The Internet Content Rating Association (ICRA) has created an open, objective, content-rating system called ICRA. It provides users with information about the level of sex, nudity, violence, vulgarity, or hate-motivated language in software games and Web sites. Authors use an ICRA labeling tool to create metadata tags containing the ICRA settings for a Web site. Parents and teachers can set the level at which to block offensive content with an Internet Explorer add-in called ICRA*filter.* A password gives parents access to areas blocked from children. To learn how to set the level at which content will be blocked, follow the *Interlit* Web Site link to ICRA.

Prejudice and Hatred

Unfortunately, the world contains many insecure individuals who, for some sick reason, feel superior by defaming people based on race or ethnic origin. Not only does the Internet reflect the hatred that exists in society, but it provides bigots with a wider audience and a new way to hide while defaming people.

Anti-Defamation League According to the Anti-Defamation League, electronic hate is the dark side of technology. Anti-Semites have so taken to the medium, for example, that the 2003 Audit of Anti-Semitic Incidents contains an entire section on anti-Semitism and the Internet. One of the reasons why bigots prefer the Internet is because they can spew their hatred with little chance of being identified. The 2003 Audit warns that Internet sites not only can spread hateful propaganda, but they also can serve as an impetus for anti-Semitic incidents by distributing fliers that can be downloaded and printed. After speaking out about Mel Gibson's film *The Passion of the Christ,* the ADL received a barrage of hate e-mail that was not counted in the audit. For more information about hate and the Internet, follow the *Interlit* Web site links to the Anti-Defamation League and the Audit of Anti-Semitic Incidents. See especially the Internet hate filter and the article on racists, bigots, and law on the Internet.

In September of 1998, Rishi Maharaj was walking in his Queens, New York, neighborhood when two men shouting racial epithets set upon him with baseball bats. They said they wanted to beat up an Indian, and they beat the Indo-Caribbean youth until he lost consciousness. After the attack, with a broken jaw held together by a steel plate, Maharaj helped launch a Web-based campaign seeking to hasten the approval of federal hate crimes legislation. To learn more about Web-based initiatives to combat hate crimes, follow the *Interlit* Web site link to the Civil Rights Coalition for the 21st Century.

Chat Room Decency in MOOs, MUDs, IRCs, and MUSHes

In her fascinating book *Life on the Screen,* Sherry Turkle (1995) describes what it is like to participate in multiuser domains (MUDs), virtual spaces in which you can navigate, strategize, and converse with other users. Turkle views MUDs as a new kind of parlor game and a new form of community that lets people generate experiences, relationships, identities, and living spaces that arise only through interaction with technology. One of the dangerous aspects is how participants can take on extremely antisocial roles as stalkers, rapists, or murderers. For example, Turkle tells of a virtual rape:

> One MUD player had used his skill with the system to seize control of another player's character. In this way the aggressor was able to direct the seized character to submit to a violent sexual encounter. He did all this against the will and over the distraught objections of the player usually "behind" this character, the player to whom this character "belonged." Although some made light of the offender's actions by saying that the episode was just words, in text-based virtual realities such as MUDs, words *are* deeds. (Turkle, 1995: 15)

Parents need to be aware of the dangers of MUDs because young people are especially susceptible. Discussing childhood encounters with Net sex, Turkle warns:

> Parents need to be able to talk to their children about where they are going and what they are doing. This same commonsense rule applies to their children's lives on the screen. Parents don't have to become technical experts, but they do need to learn enough about computer networks to discuss with their children what and who is out there and lay down some basic safety rules. The children who do best after a bad experience on the Internet (who are harassed, perhaps even propositioned) are those who can talk to their parents, just as children who best handle bad experiences in real life are those who can talk to an elder without shame or fear of blame. (Turkle, 1995: 227)

SafeKids.Com

Parents need to be aware of the danger of adults posing as children in chat rooms. For a good set of rules for safe conduct, follow the *Interlit* Web site link to SafeKids.Com and NetSmartz.org.

Monitoring Online Conversations with ChatWatch

A ChatWatch feature is in the BeAware monitoring program by software producer Ascentive. ChatWatch enables parents to record their children's instant-messaging chats much like a VCR records a television program. After the chat has been recorded, parents can view frequent screen shots of the conversations, search IM logs for keywords, and view full-text transcripts of the dialog. According to Ascentive CEO Adam Schram, monitoring software like ChatWatch is more effective than filtering, because "filters give you too many false positives and negatives—they block breast-cancer sites but not all porn sites" (*The Wall Street Journal,* 11 December 2001). For more information, follow the *Interlit* Web site link to BeAware with ChatWatch.

Copyright

Article I, section 8 of the U.S. Constitution grants Congress the power "To Promote the Progress of Science and useful Arts, by securing for limited Times to Authors and Inventors the exclusive Right to their respective Writings and Discoveries." Congress used this power to pass the Copyright Act of 1976, which defines and allocates rights associated with "original works of authorship fixed in any tangible medium of expression, now known or later developed, from which they can be perceived, reproduced, or otherwise communicated, either directly or with the aid of a machine or device" (17 U.S.C. § 102). This means that all of the downloadable elements presented in Chapter 12 ("Commonly Found Internet File Types") of this book—including illustrations, text, movies, video clips, documentaries, animations, music, and software—are protected by copyright. There are stiff penalties for copyright offenders. If a company is sued for civil copyright infringement, for example, the penalty ranges up to $100,000 per software title. If the company is charged with a criminal violation, the fine goes up to $250,000 plus up to five years in prison. The stakes are high because the Software & Information Industry Association (SIIA) reports that its members lose more than $12 billion annually due to software piracy. That is why the SIIA sues organizations that pirate commercial software or circumvent copyright protection, resulting in millions of dollars in fines. Whenever you plan to publish a Web page on the Internet, you must make sure you have the right to use every object in it. To learn about recent actions taken against copyright infringers, follow the *Interlit* Web site link to the SIAA.

Although Web pages, like any other form of writing, are considered to be copyrighted by default, in order to be fully protected, you should register a copyright for your Web pages. To copyright a Web page, include the following copyright notice on the page, replacing *xx* by the current year:

Copyright © 20*xx* by your_name_goes_here. All rights reserved.

Although this notice legally suffices to protect your copyright, it is also a good idea to register the copyright with the U.S. Copyright Office. If someone infringes your copyright and you take legal action to defend it, copyright registration can help your case. To register a copyright, follow these steps:

- Go to the U.S. Copyright Office Web page at www.copyright.gov. In the section on how to register a work, choose literary works.

- Read the instructions for registering a literary work. Notice how the instructions tell you that computer programs and databases are considered to be literary works for copyright purposes.

- You will see a link to download either the long or the short version of form TX. Read the instructions that explain which form to use, and download the form you need.

- Complete the application form and make a copy to retain in your files.

- Mail the application along with a printout of the work and the $30 registration fee to the Library of Congress, Copyright Office, 101 Independence Ave., S.E., Washington, D.C. 20559-6000.

If you want a receipt, have the Post Office mail your application "return receipt requested." It will take several weeks for the Library of Congress to process your application and send you the registration number. For more information, follow the *Interlit* Web site link to the U.S. Copyright Office.

Fair Use

Fair Use is a section of the U.S. Copyright Law that allows the use of copyrighted works in reporting news, conducting research, and teaching. The law states:

> Notwithstanding the provisions of section 106 [which grants authors exclusive rights], the fair use of a copyrighted work, including such use by reproduction in copies or phonorecords or by any other means specified by that section, for purposes such as criticism, comment, news reporting, teaching (including multiple copies for classroom use), scholarship, or research, is not an infringement of copyright. In determining whether the use made of a work in any particular case is a fair use the factors to be considered shall include:
>
> 1. the purpose and character of the use, including whether such use is of a commercial nature or is for nonprofit educational purposes;
>
> 2. the nature of the copyrighted work;
>
> 3. the amount and substantiality of the portion used in relation to the copyrighted work as a whole; and
>
> 4. the effect of the use upon the potential market for or value of the copyrighted work.

INTERPRETING FAIR USE FOR EDUCATION

To summarize the Fair Use law for education, one may shorten its first paragraph as follows: ". . . the fair use of a copyrighted work for . . . teaching (including multiple copies for classroom use) . . . is not an infringement of copyright." The difficulty arises from interpreting the four tests, which are intentionally left vague, as the law goes on to state: "Although the courts have considered and ruled upon the fair use doctrine over and over again, no real definition of the concept has ever emerged. Indeed, since the doctrine is an equitable rule of reason, no generally applicable definition is possible, and each case raising the question must be decided on its own facts."

THE FAIR USE GUIDELINES FOR EDUCATIONAL MULTIMEDIA

To help educational institutions interpret the Fair Use law with regard to multimedia and the Internet, the Consortium of College and University Media Centers (CCUMC) spearheaded the creation of the *Fair Use Guidelines for Educational Multimedia*. The committee that created these guidelines consisted of representatives from print, film, music, and multimedia publishing companies who spent many months discussing and debating Fair Use issues with representatives from educational institutions. Professor Lisa Livingston, director of the Instructional Media Division of the City University of New York, chaired the committee, and well-known copyright attorney Ivan Bender (who died too young in 1996) was retained to advise on legal issues. As a member of this committee, I can attest to the rigor of the process.

The *Fair Use Guidelines for Educational Multimedia* are linked to the *Interlit* Web site. They specify what is fair for students as well as for teachers. I encourage you to study these guidelines carefully and use them to exercise your right of Fair Use. Also linked to the *Interlit*

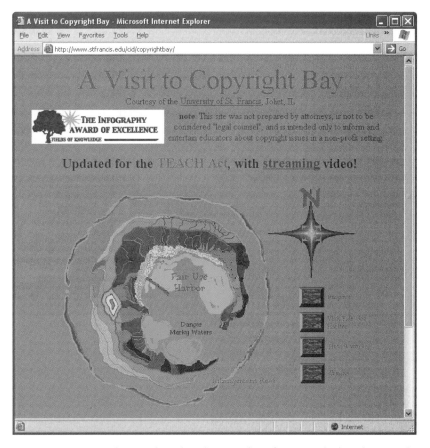

Figure 25-5 Copyright Bay is based on the metaphor of a Fair Use harbor. The metaphor stems from the belief that the Fair Use guidelines provide a "safe harbor" within which multimedia users can exercise the right of Fair Use.

Source: http://www.stfrancis.edu/cid/copyrightbay/fairuse.htm.

Web site is Copyright Bay, which uses the metaphor of a harbor, as pictured in Figure 25-5. Clicking the bay's links brings up tutorials on the Fair Use issues illustrated in the harbor.

World Intellectual Property Organization (WIPO) Treaties

Because the Web is worldwide, any company conducting business online must consider the international ramifications of its e-commerce activities. As described at www.wipo.org, the World Intellectual Property Organization (WIPO) is in charge of administering 23 treaties comprising an international intellectual property (IP) system. When this book went to press, 179 countries belonged to WIPO, including the United States, which is a major stakeholder in this attempt to protect intellectual property rights throughout the world. To resolve conflicts, there is a WIPO Arbitration and Mediation Center. If someone in a WIPO member country infringes the copyright of someone in another member country, WIPO provides a mechanism for that infringement to be prosecuted in both countries. For the latest, follow the *Interlit* Web site link to WIPO.

Digital Millennium Copyright Act (DMCA)

In 1998, the Digital Millennium Copyright Act (DMCA) was enacted into law in the United States. One of the primary purposes of this complex act was to bring the United States into conformance with the World Intellectual Property Organization (WIPO) treaties. The DMCA includes

- New rules prohibiting the circumvention of Technological Protection Measures (TPM), with stiff penalties for infringers.

- Prohibition of the removal from a copyrighted work of information related to ownership, copyright, and licensing.

- Limitation of liability of online service providers if someone using their service infringes a copyright.

- Promoting distance education over digital networks while maintaining an appropriate balance between the rights of copyright holders and the needs of teachers and students making fair use of copyrighted works.

TEACH Act

In late 2002, the **Technology Education and Copyright Harmonization (TEACH) Act** was signed into law. This act extends the concept of Fair Use beyond the classroom to "anytime, anywhere" distance learning courses; permits educational institutions to use "reasonable and limited" portions of audiovisual works and sound recordings in distance learning courses without needing to request permission; and permits educators in certain instances to digitize and make Fair Use of works that are not already available in digital form. The TEACH Act also clarifies a point that has been in dispute since the passage of the DMCA, namely, that the temporary "buffer" copies created on networked file servers to transmit content over the Web also are covered under the exemption.

While extending the concept of educational Fair Use to digitally transmitted works, the TEACH Act also requires that the transmitting institution must ensure that the performance can only be received by students who are enrolled in the course. To learn more, follow the *Interlit* Web site links to the TEACH Act and the TEACH Act primer.

Patents

The U.S. Patent and Trademark Office defines the term **patent** as the granting to an inventor of a property right for an invention to exclude others from making, using, offering for sale, or selling the invention in the United States or "importing" the invention into the United States. The purpose of the patent is to provide the inventor an opportunity to profit from the invention for a reasonable period of time (i.e., 20 years) before the patent expires. It is the responsibility of the inventor to enforce the patent if someone infringes it. Monetary penalties awarded in patent infringement suits can range into the tens of millions of dollars. Therefore, companies need to be careful not to infringe the patents of others. In a patent suit, ignorance is no defense. All patents are online, and you can search them at www.uspto.gov.

What causes problems in the computer industry is when a company applies to patent an invention for which there is prior art, meaning that the so-called invention preexisted. There have been several cases in which computer companies have fooled the patent office into granting patents for technology that preexisted. When these cheaters began suing other companies for infringing, there was such an industrywide outcry that the patent office overturned the patents. The danger is that in less high-profile cases, it may cost a company less to pay for the right to use the mistakenly issued patent rather than to undergo the lengthy legal proceeding needed to overturn the patent.

Compton's Multimedia Search Patent

One of the most blatant cases of patent abuse occurred when Compton's announced at the 1993 Fall COMDEX convention that they had been awarded a patent that would require all multimedia developers to pay them royalties. As Compton's CEO Stanley Frank said, "We helped kick start this industry. We now ask to be compensated for our investments. We will do whatever it takes to defend our patent."

The Compton's patent is very broad. It covers any type of computer-controlled database system that allows a user to search for mixed media that includes text with graphics, sound, or animation. Compton's did not limit their claims to CD-ROM products; they also claimed rights to any type of database involving interactive TV or the Internet. Thus, the patent includes the searching of product catalogs that contain text and graphics advertising products for e-commerce purposes.

Compton's demanded that all multimedia developers pay back royalties of 1 percent of net receipts from sales before June 30, 1994, and 3 percent thereafter. To say the least, developers reacted negatively to Compton's demands. Some suggested that users should burn all Compton's CD-ROMs and refuse to purchase future titles from any company that would try to force such a Machiavellian proviso on the multimedia industry. As a result of public hearings held by the U.S. Patent and Trademark Office to review its handling of software patents, the Compton's patent was rescinded, and the patent office initiated reforms that include publicizing patent applications, hiring software specialists as examiners, revamping the examiner bonus program so it does not encourage superficial review, and requiring more information about patent applications before decisions are made. In fairness to the government, industry leaders like Compton's (who know better) should stop trying to profit from patenting prior art; instead, they should concentrate on improving their products and moving the industry forward.

Unisys GIF Patent

Unisys owns the patent on the compression scheme used in the GIF file format, which is one of the most popular image formats in the world. In 1994, Unisys decided to begin charging developers a licensing fee for using the GIF file format. This resulted in a backlash of harsh opposition from developers and users who felt Unisys had acted unfairly, and Unisys backed down. Toward the end of the 20th century, Unisys began to try again to charge for the use of GIF images. Unisys asked all WebMasters to pay $5,000 if their Web site uses one or more GIF images created by a program that is not licensed by Unisys to use GIF images.

By trying a second time to make users pay for something they thought was free, Unisys caused another uproar among GIF users and developers who, instead of paying the $5,000 fee, began converting their graphics to the PNG format. PNG stands for Portable Network Graphics, a file format created largely in response to the Unisys patent fiasco. The World Wide Web consortium's PNG Web site refers to the format as "… a patent-free replacement for GIF" (www.w3.org/Graphics/PNG, cited 26 February 2005). PNG is the graphics format I used when making the screen captures that illustrate this book.

In the meantime, the U.S. version of the GIF patent happily expired on June 20, 2003.

Eolas '906 Patent

In 2003, Microsoft was ordered to pay $520 million for allegedly infringing U.S. patent number 5,838,906 issued to the University of California, which formed a company named Eolas to handle the licensing. The so-called Eolas '906 patent covers the technology used by browsers to launch automatically the appropriate applet or plug-in to display embedded content, such as a Flash animation, within a hypermedia document. When Eolas won the $520 million settlement against Microsoft, the World Wide Web Consortium (W3C) asked for a review of the patent. The W3C provided evidence that the Eolas patent was based on prior art and therefore should be overturned. The W3C further pointed out that enforcing this patent could cause "substantial economic and technical damage to the operation of the World Wide Web." As this book goes to press, the U.S. Patent and Trademark Office is reevaluating the Eolas '906 patent. By the time you read this, the patent will hopefully be overturned. For the latest, follow the *Interlit* Web site link to the Eolas FAQ. To read the patent itself, go to www.uspto.gov and search for patent number 5,838,906.

I believe that the actions taken in these kinds of patent cases by Compton's, Unisys, and Eolas are unethical and self-defeating. In the Compton's and Eolas examples, technologists were taking advantage of the U.S. Patent and Trademark Office by obtaining patents for prior art of which the patent office was unaware. Unisys, on the other hand, appears to have waited until its GIF technology spread throughout the world before enforcing the patent in an attempt to cash in on its widespread adoption. In all three cases, I believe that the technologists working within these companies knew that this kind of activity was unethical. Corporations need to be more honest and up-front if the patent system is to function as intended. The purpose of the patent system is to give an inventor an honest period of time in which to profit from an invention. High-tech companies are not acting in the best interests of the Internet when they abuse the patent system in order to rip people off.

BlackBerry Patent Fight

BlackBerry

BlackBerry is the popular wireless e-mail device pictured in Figure 25-6. Although most of BlackBerry's three million owners use the device in the United States, the main BlackBerry relay server is located in Waterloo, Ontario, where the Canadian firm Research In Motion (RIM) invented and patented the technology. As this book goes to press, a patent fight continues over a claim by Arlington, Virginia-based NTP, a patent-holding company, that the BlackBerry device infringes on 16 claims of five NTP patents. A U.S. court in Virginia agreed that BlackBerry infringed on 11 claims, but RIM maintains (amongst other arguments in its defense) that U.S. patent laws have no jurisdiction in Canada. EarthLink, an ISP that supplies the BlackBerry service to many U.S. customers, has filed a "friend of the court" brief supporting RIM's position. In addition, the United States Patent and Trademark Office has now corroborated RIM's original defense of patent invalidity and rejected 100 percent of the claims in four out of the five patents and is expected to rule on the fifth patent soon. At stake are millions of dollars in royalties that NTP believes it is owed because RIM is using the technology to make huge profits south of the 49th parallel.

The Canadian government has also stepped into the case on the question of jurisdiction, and the outcome will be important in determining the international boundaries of the U.S. Patent System in cyberspace. For the latest news, follow the *Interlit* Web site link to the BlackBerry Patent Fight.

Internal high-performance antenna.

Convenient phone button to quickly access the phone application and mute/unmute calls.

Integrated speaker.

LED indicator notifies users when new information has arrived.

USB port enables data loading and battery charging.

Thumb-operated trackwheel allows for quick navigation.

Easy access to e-mail, data, Web, phone, and organizer.

Full-color screen.

Phone dial pad.

33-key QWERTY keyboard allows for two-handed thumb typing.

Integrated microphone.

Figure 25-6   The BlackBerry Wireless Handheld. The BlackBerry 7250 shown here integrates e-mail with cell phone, text messaging services, Web browsing, and enterprise applications.

Peer-to-Peer (P2P) File Sharing

Music is one of the greatest pleasures in life. Because people enjoy listening to music, the selling of audio on compact discs has become a mass-market industry. This industry has been threatened, however, by **peer-to-peer (P2P)** file-sharing systems. Using software called a *ripper,* people can insert a commercial audio CD into their computer's CD-ROM drive and convert the songs on the CD into MP3 files. P2P file sharing systems then make these files available to other users. The problem is that the other users have not paid for the CD.

The first P2P music file-sharing system on the Web was Napster, which was invented by 19-year-old Shawn Fanning and 20-year-old Sean Parker in September 2000. Napster became so popular, particularly among college students, that the bandwidth devoted to music file sharing clogged many campus networks. Napster grabbed a lot of headlines as the Recording Industry Association of America (RIAA) sued and the courts ordered Napster to shut down until it could demonstrate the ability to keep its users from transmitting illegal copies. Napster was particularly vulnerable because it kept a central directory of the music files residing on the disk drives of P2P users that were sharing them. More difficult to catch are the users of Gnutella, which is a peer-to-peer file-sharing system in which there is no central directory. Instead of keeping a central directory on the Web, Gnutella establishes direct links between its users.

Gnutella supports the sharing of all kinds of files, including movies. The growing popularity of Gnutella threatens the movie industry. Because there is no central directory in Gnutella, many Gnutella users assume they are anonymous and therefore safe from detection when they share illegal copies of movies. Behind the scenes, however, the Gnutella user's IP address is associated with each file transfer. In a criminal proceeding, courts can order an ISP to identify the name of the user associated with an IP address.

You need to be aware of how illegal it is to share copyrighted songs and movies over the Internet. In a felony conviction in 2005, for example, an 18-year-old University of Arizona student caught uploading digital copies of recently released movies and music was fined $5,400 and sentenced to three months in prison, three years' probation, and 200 hours of community service. The court ordered the student to take a copyright class and stop making illegal use of P2P file sharing (AP/kvoa.com, 17 February 2005).

The songs and movies you buy are for your personal use. It is both unethical and illegal for anyone besides the copyright holder to transmit them over the Internet. It is unethical because it deprives the artists of being paid for their work. It is illegal because it fails the Fair Use law's fourth test, which requires you to consider "the effect of the use upon the potential market for or value of the copyrighted work."

Since 2003, Napster has been running a legitimate music downloading business with a million tracks available at napster.com for a monthly subscription fee of $14.95. Other legitimate music downloading services that cater to Windows users include MusicMatch, which has a library of about 800,000 songs and prices its downloads at 99 cents each at musicmatch.com; and Wal-Mart, which sells downloads for 88 cents. Apple's iTunes service at www.itunes.com works on both Windows and Macintosh platforms and offers more than a million songs and a large selection of audio books. The cost is $10 per album or 10 songs.

The FCC, meanwhile, has ruled that all equipment capable of receiving digital broadcasts must be able to read the **broadcast flag,** which is a tiny amount of data sent in a digital television broadcast to prevent the video from being recorded in its high-definition format. The goal is to prevent people from recording HDTV broadcasts that could be subsequently distributed illegally through P2P file sharing. By the time you read this, retail digital television equipment will probably incorporate the broadcast flag technology, although there are some legal challenges that may delay it. Follow the *Interlit* Web site links for the latest on the Broadcast Flag, Napster, Gnutella, and P2P file sharing.

exercises

1. The White House has promised the public that everyone will have equal access to the Information Superhighway. Do you believe that everyone will have equal access, or do you feel that uneven access to the Internet will create a technological underclass in our society? What do you see as the major obstacles that must be overcome to provide equal access for everyone?

2. Where do you stand on the issue of privacy and encryption technology? Do you believe that every citizen should have the right to use any encryption scheme he or she pleases? Should the government have the right to decipher encrypted messages under court order to eavesdrop on electronic communications among criminals? To help answer these questions, follow the *Interlit* Web site links to Privacy.

3. Find the cookies folder on your computer. If you have Windows, you can find the cookies folder by clicking the Start button, choosing Find, and doing a file search for the key word *cookie*. If you have a Macintosh, you can do a file search by clicking the Apple icon in the upper left corner of the screen to pull down the menu, then choose Sherlock or Find File, and search for files containing the word *cookie*. Inspect your cookies file(s). What information do your cookies contain about the history of your activity at commercial Web sites? Did you realize this kind of information was being kept? Do you think companies should be permitted to collect this kind of information about you? Why or why not?

4. Since 1995, Discreet Data Research has operated a Web site where people can find out information about you that is normally considered to be private or confidential. Follow the *Interlit* Web site link to Discreet Data Research and check it out. While there, peruse the different stalking services and investigative links. Do you think any of the Discreet Data Research services should be illegal? If so, which ones? Why do you believe they are improper?

5. Do you agree that the University of Waterloo was justified in banning obscene bulletin boards from its network? Should obscene bulletin boards be banned from the Information Superhighway altogether?

6. Has a government regulation ever prevented you from accessing services you felt you had a right to? For example, when the FCC ruled that cable companies were no longer permitted to rebroadcast FM signals, the author's community lost its cable access to National Public Radio and several other FM stations. Since we live in an area too remote for good FM reception, we became disconnected from these important stations. Have you had a similar experience? If our government cannot regulate access to a simple FM radio station, how will it ever manage an Information Superhighway?

7. Follow the *Interlit* Web site links to the *Fair Use Guidelines for Educational Multimedia*. Read the guidelines and reflect on whether the resources at your Web site adhere to the guidelines. Have you done anything at your Web site that is not a Fair Use? If so, have you obtained the necessary copyright permission to use the material?

SITUATED CASE PROJECTS

Case 25: Developing a Privacy Policy

At the end of each chapter in this book, a situated case project provides the student an opportunity to put the chapter's contents to practical use in a workplace situation. Each case has the same number as the chapter in which it appears.

It is important for every school and company to develop a privacy policy and publicize it at their Web site. This is important for legal as well as ethical reasons. If someone files a lawsuit because information they provided confidentially at your site became public, for example, it can be important to the court whether you published at your site a privacy policy stating how you would treat information collected at your site. It is also just plain unethical to mislead users by collecting information under the guise of confidentiality and then distributing that information to others. Imagine that your employer, who intends to be up-front with users, has asked you to develop a privacy policy to link to the home page of your school or company Web site. Follow these steps:

1 To familiarize yourself with the form and substance of privacy statements typically posted at school and corporate Web sites, follow the Chapter 25 *Interlit* Web site links to sample privacy statements.

2 Using your Web page creation software, create a draft privacy statement as an HTML page for use at your workplace Web site.

3 It may help you to visit the privacy statement generator linked to the *Interlit* Web site. This generator is a wizard that will step you through the process of creating a privacy statement.

4 Save the privacy statement in the *website* folder on your hard drive.

If your instructor has asked you to hand in this assignment, make sure you put your name at the top of your privacy statement, then copy it onto a disk or follow any other instructions you may have been given for submitting this assignment.

26

EMERGING TECHNOLOGY

After completing this chapter, you will be able to:

- Explain the methods being used to speed up the Internet, and know how to avoid consuming unnecessary bandwidth when you use the Net.

- Prepare yourself to take advantage of the real-time wireless communications technologies that are emerging.

- Reflect on the human interface and the role that personal digital assistants (PDAs) will play in the future of the Internet.

- Understand how artificial intelligence makes it possible for people to make more efficient use of the Internet.

- Know what bots can do for you on the Information Superhighway.

- Define HDTV and consider the role digital television will play in the future of the Internet.

- Explain how digital hubs are connecting home entertainment devices into wireless Ethernet networks.

Because the Internet is the communications infrastructure of the 21st century, its future is vitally important. From a technological standpoint, this future promises to be bright indeed, because of some exciting new technologies that are emerging. Newly emerging technologies follow a cycle that includes (1) invention, (2) prototyping, (3) proof of concept, (4) productizing, and (5) manufacture. It often takes many years for an emerging technology to achieve widespread use in the marketplace. One reason why this takes so long is because consumers have a hard time seeing the benefit. As Bane and McMahon (1994: 89) describe the problem: "Customers are typically incapable of understanding the value of a new technology until they actually experience it. Microwave ovens, for example, were a kitchen curiosity and a perceived health hazard in the 1970s, but they are now found in 87 percent of U.S. homes."

A problem particularly related to information technologies is the rapid rate of change. Any PC you buy this year, for example, will be considered outdated in just a year or two. The computer will still do the job for which you purchased it, but newer models will be faster and more fully featured. Ira Fuchs, vice president for research in information technology at the Andrew W. Mellon Foundation, articulates this problem with a principle that has become known as Fuchs's law: "The time to acquisition is longer than the time to obsolescence" (*Chronicle of Higher Education*, 28 March 1997).

This chapter will introduce you to emerging technologies that promise to improve the Internet substantially in coming years. Then the next chapter, which deals with how to keep up with changes in technology, will provide you with ways of tracking the progress of these inventions as they emerge. In the end, you will be prepared to take advantage of these innovations sooner rather than later.

Improving the Infrastructure

You have undoubtedly experienced some problems with the Internet's physical transport layer. Network delay is the most obvious problem. You click a hypertext trigger to go to a Web site, and you wait, and you wait, and you wait. Sometimes it seems like WWW stands for World Wide Wait. The delays can be particularly long if the transmission carries multimedia content.

Multimedia MBONE

IP Multicast Initiative

MBONE stands for Multicast Backbone. It is a network of computers on the Internet specially designed for the transmission of simultaneous live video and audio broadcasts. In a traditional packet-switched network, if you send a video to four different people, four identical copies of the information are sent over the network. Multicasting the video over the MBONE sends only one copy of the message and replicates the information only at branch points in the network.

As the television, telephone, and computer industries continue to converge, real-time audio and video will grow in importance on the Internet. Look for IP multicasting on the MBONE to have a significant impact on the Web in the years ahead.

Connecting to the MBONE requires that your Internet service provider (ISP) have special routing and switching equipment. Follow the *Interlit* Web site link to Multicasting and the MBONE for a technical description of how the MBONE works.

Streaming Media Networks

Streaming media network (SMN) vendors are applying MBONE concepts to bring uninterrupted audio and video streams to end users. For example, iBeam is an SMN that uses satellites to feed streaming media directly to servers located at or near local ISPs. Akamai is another SMN that locates streaming media content on server farms that are physically closer to an ISP network than the streams would normally be on the public Internet. Akamai refers to these locations near the ISP as the "edge" of the Internet. Relative to the users connected to that local ISP, the local Akamai server is on their edge of the Internet. In Europe, an SMN named Servecast has built a similar edge delivery network.

Figures 26-1 and 26-2 illustrate the difference between a typical MBONE multicast network and an edge delivery system. In Figure 26-1, streams move across the MBONE and eventually reach their ISPs, who distribute them over the quintessential "last mile" to end users. The further an ISP is located from the primary server, the longer the delay. In Figure 26-2, edge servers mirror the content on the primary source server. Multimedia streams get delivered more efficiently because the edge servers are located physically closer to the ISPs. In many cases, SMNs locate their servers within the local ISP's server farm. To learn more about this emerging SMN technology, follow this book's Web site links to Streaming Media Networks.

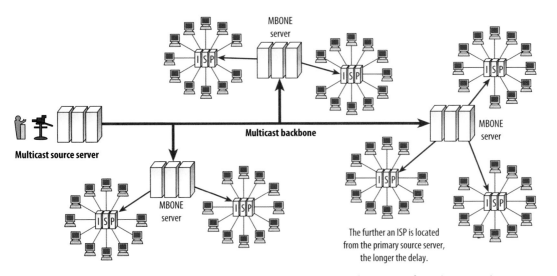

Figure 26-1 On the MBONE, audio and video streams propagate across the Internet from the server that initiates the broadcast.

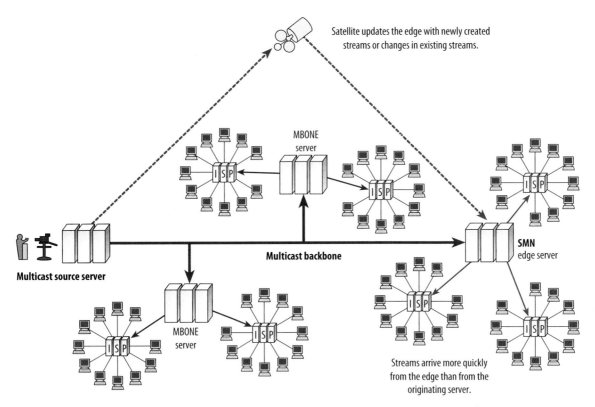

Figure 26-2 Streaming media networks locate so-called edge servers that contain mirror copies of multimedia content; thus, an ISP can get a stream started faster from the edge server than from the original source server of the webcast.

Internet2

A consortium of more than 200 universities is leading a project called **Internet2.** The goal is to create a higher-speed version of the Internet that revolves around a high-speed connection point called the *Gigapop.* Strategically placed throughout the network, Gigapops guarantee high-speed bandwidth between universities, schools, and companies that are implementing the Internet2 standards.

Internet2 uses three protocols to provide high-speed transmission and guaranteed bandwidth:

- Resource Reservation Protocol (RSVP) permits a user to reserve bandwidth from the workstation to the network host computer.

- Internet Protocol version 6 (IPv6) is a packet-delivery protocol that lets the user assign priority to certain kinds of information. You may want your Web search traffic to have a higher priority than your e-mail traffic, for example, so your searches get completed faster.

- Multicast uses IP tunneling and multithreading to increase multimedia throughput.

The K20 project extends Internet2 participation to all levels of education, from K-12 (pre-college) to 16 (college) and 20 (doctoral level study)—hence the name, K20. To find out the current status, follow the *Interlit* Web site link to Internet2.

Wireless Communications

In the 20th century, most Internet use occurred at the end of a wire or cable that connected the user's computer to the Internet. Today, emerging wireless technologies are enabling mobile users to remove the tether.

Figure 26-3 Motorola's MPX 200 Smartphone runs the Windows Mobile operating system, bringing the Internet literally into the palm of your hand.

Cingular Wireless, for example, offers Internet service on the Motorola Smartphone pictured in Figure 26-3. In addition to letting you make ordinary phone calls, the Smartphone provides you with access to e-mail and a mobile Web browser with which you can do online shopping; get news, weather, sports, and stock quotes; make flight reservations and check arrival times; and even trade online. ActiveSync software synchronizes your phone with personal information managers such as Microsoft Outlook or Lotus Notes. You can read e-mail via your wireless phone from AT&T WorldNet, AOL, or Yahoo! mail services. To learn more about the wireless phone's features, follow the *Interlit* Web site link to Smartphone. For more about new products that enable you to access the Internet without needing a conventional telephone line or network cable, follow the *Interlit* Web site links to Wireless Design and Development.

BLUETOOTH

Bluetooth is an emerging standard for high-speed wireless communications. All of the major telecomm vendors and computer companies are supporting it, including Ericsson, IBM, Nokia, 3COM, Lucent, Microsoft, Motorola, Apple, Toshiba, Agilent, Tektronix, and Intel. Bluetooth enables the synchronization and exchange of information between mobile computers, telephones, portable handheld devices, and the Internet. Bluetooth transmits a short-range radio signal intended to replace the cables connecting electronic devices. It offers wireless connections to LANs, the public switched telephone network, and the Internet.

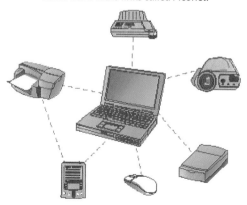

Bluetooth

Bluetooth devices communicate via short-wave radio links called Piconet.

Figure 26-4 Bluetooth-enabled devices can communicate with up to seven devices at once.

Figure 26-4 depicts how a Bluetooth-enabled device, such as a PC, can communicate with up to seven devices at once. Because Bluetooth communicates over radio frequencies (RF), it does not need the line-of-sight required by infrared devices. There is a wide array of applications in home automation, security systems, network access in public places, and wireless headsets. You can even buy a jacket with Bluetooth technology built in for making telephone calls whenever you walk within range of a Bluetooth hub. Manufactured by German clothing firm Rosner, the so-called mp3blue jacket features MP3 controls on the left sleeve, a hands-free microphone and headphones in the collar, and a Bluetooth gateway for mobile phones. Woven electrically conductive fabric connects devices within the jacket. When you wash the jacket, however, you must remember to remove the electronics module.

The Bluetooth specification is available royalty-free at www.bluetooth.com. To learn more, follow the *Interlit* Web site links to Bluetooth and the Bluetooth tutorial.

Wi-Fi

Wi-Fi Alliance

Wi-Fi is the industry trade name for products based on the IEEE 802.11 specification for wireless local area networking. The Wi-Fi Alliance is a nonprofit international association that formed in 1999 to certify interoperability of these products. When this book went to press, the Wi-Fi Alliance had 205 member companies from around the world, and 1,500 products had received Wi-Fi certification.

Wi-Fi networks operate over a radius of up to 300 feet, depending on local conditions and equipment. Wi-Fi access points are called HotSpots. When you bring a Wi-Fi-equipped computer or PDA into the range of a HotSpot, you can tap into the network, which uses 128-bit encryption to keep your data secure. Unless you are at a FreeSpot, you must have a Wi-Fi provider account in order to connect. There is a FreeSpot directory that lists Wi-Fi hotspots offering free wireless Internet access. FreeSpot locations include hotels, coffee shops, restaurants, shopping malls, airports, and downtown business districts. To learn more, follow this book's Web site links to Wi-Fi and the FreeSpot directory.

IP Telephony

VoIP

Imagine making a long distance telephone call from your PC without having to pay toll charges. Imagine a virtual help desk that brings a live person on screen to help when you have trouble using your computer. Imagine being able to place a phone call to your computer and remote-control your PC via voice commands. Microsoft's Telephone Application Program Interface (TAPI) is enabling Windows users to do all these things and more by converging the public switched telephone network (PSTN) with Internet Protocol (IP) telephony. IP telephony converges voice, video, and data into a common Internet protocol, effectively collapsing three networks into one. Using TAPI, a Web site can have a push-to-talk button that instantly establishes a Voice over IP (VoIP) link, for example, between the user at a microphone-equipped PC and a customer service representative at a Web site.

TAPI is evolving as the technology progresses and Microsoft adds more features. For example, Microsoft is developing a telephone markup language that will enable Web pages to contain telephony tags. This will enable Web site developers to create pages to which users can dial up and talk over the phone. Speech recognition will be used to translate the user's voice into commands that the browser will use to surf the Web. Speech synthesis will render the Web's response as a voice that the user will hear in reply. For more on the future of TAPI, follow the *Interlit* Web site link to Microsoft Internet Telephony. To learn more about the telephony markup language, follow the link to the World Wide Web consortium's Voice Browser activity.

As Internet telephony services emerge, traditional telephone companies are scurrying to get on the VoIP bandwagon, because VoIP calls cost about 80 percent less than traditional long distance. In the summer of 2004, for example, Verizon began offering its VoiceWing VoIP services a year earlier than planned in an attempt to head off a similar venture by broadband cable rival Comcast. By the time you read this, Comcast will be selling cable-based VoIP services in 20 markets. The cost is $54.95 monthly for unlimited local and long distance calling, three-way calling, caller ID, voice mail, and call waiting. A modem enables customers to plug in multiple phones throughout the home using traditional telephone jacks. Comcast cable or Comcast Internet customers get a discount to $44.95; customers with both Comcast cable and Internet service get a discount to $39.95. To learn more about VoIP availability, follow the *Interlit* Web site link to the directory of Internet telephony service providers.

Personal Digital Assistants

Personal digital assistants (PDAs) are portable, handheld computers that you can take with you to work, school, or anyplace where a PC might come in handy. You can easily synchronize a PDA with your personal computer and take almost any information with you, such as your address book, calendar, and key Web sites. If you have enough memory in your PDA, you can even download music and videos to view while you are away from your PC. There are two main families of PDAs: Windows CE and Palm. Both have taken on exciting new capabilities as PDA technology continues to emerge.

Windows CE

Microsoft Windows

Windows CE is a compact modular version of the Microsoft Windows operating system designed for use on consumer electronic devices. If you know how to use Windows, you know how to use Windows CE. Consider, for example, the user interface on Toshiba's PocketPC. As illustrated in Figure 26-5, you use the Windows Start button to choose programs, which include special pocket versions of Microsoft Office apps—MS Word, MS Excel, and MS Schedule—as well as e-mail, Pocket Windows Media, Pocket MS Reader, and the Pocket Internet Explorer Web browser. Instead of using a mouse, you choose things on screen with a stylus via Microsoft's pen computing interface.

One of the advantages of using Windows CE is that it contains modular versions of the Microsoft Windows application programming interfaces. Windows CE supports TAPI, for example, which was described above in the section on Internet telephony. If you have a PDA that runs the Phone Edition of Windows CE, you can use that PDA to connect to the Internet. If your PDA and your cell phone both have Bluetooth, for example, your PDA can use your cell phone as a wireless modem to dial up to the Internet. To learn more about these emerging technologies, follow this book's Web site links to Windows CE and the PocketPC Web site.

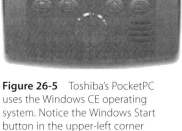

Note: PocketPC is the trade name for palm-sized PDAs based on the Windows CE operating system.

Palm OS

Palm

Palm, Inc., has traditionally been the market leader in personal digital assistants. Palm established its early lead by being first to market, in 1996, with an operating system developed specifically for a small-sized device. Palm

Figure 26-5 Toshiba's PocketPC uses the Windows CE operating system. Notice the Windows Start button in the upper-left corner of the screen.

handhelds began as personal organizers designed to make people's lives easier through built-in programs including a date book, address book, note-taker, and to-do list. Today the Palm OS offers Internet connectivity enabling people to access all kinds of information, from stock quotes for investors to driving instructions for travelers. Figure 26-6 illustrates how the latest model has Wi-Fi connectivity built in.

When this book went to press, however, the Palm OS was losing market share. Palm's 70 percent market share in 2000 had slipped to about 30 percent in 2005, while Windows CE rose to 48 percent. Windows enthusiasts feel that the PocketPC will begin to sell even better as larger memories and faster processors permit Windows CE to work more like the familiar desktop computer. This will not necessarily make PocketPCs outsell Palm devices, however, because the challenge is not so much trying to make Windows run on a PDA as it is figuring out what works best on a PDA. Look for an exciting

Figure 26-6 The Palm OS combines built-in personal productivity programs with Internet connectivity.

competition between the PocketPC and the Palm OS in the years ahead. For the current status, follow this book's Web site links to Palm OS, PocketPC, and CNET's comparative reviews of the different brands of PDAs that are available today.

Smart Watches

MSN Direct

In the comics, Dick Tracy wore a watch sporting the ultimate in PDA functionality. In reality, it is difficult to pack that much functionality into a wristwatch. Microsoft's MSN Direct service offers a Smart Watch that shows how far wrist technology has progressed so far. Through a three-step process, you can select information you want to receive on your Smart Watch:

1. Choose a watch from the showcase of Smart Watches from well-known watch manufacturers such as Swatch, Fossil, and Tissot.

2. Use a Web browser to register your watch, activate the service, and select the information you want to receive from the MSN Direct Web site.

3. News, stocks, weather, sports, showtimes, messages from your MSN Messenger contacts, and your Outlook calendar appointments are encrypted and delivered straight to your watch via FM radio signals.

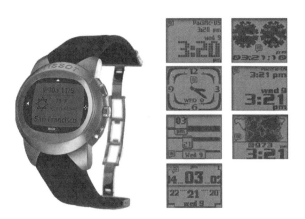

Figure 26-7 shows the Tissot High-T, which is a Swiss-made Smart Watch with a touch screen. To learn more about smart watches, follow the *Interlit* Web site link to MSN Direct.

Figure 26-7 The Tissot High-T is a Smart Watch with a Touch Screen. Six alternate faces come with the watch. More faces are downloadable from the Tissot Web site at www.tissot.ch.

Artificial Intelligence

Artificial intelligence (AI) is for real. It is not just a theoretical science for researchers. As handheld technologies reduce the size of computers, for example, AI researchers are developing more effective ways for people to use them. Featured here are several AI technologies that promise to improve your use of the Internet in years to come.

Voice Recognition

Many people do not type very fast, and even those who do wish there were an easier way to enter information into a computer. Voice recognition is rapidly emerging as a solution to this problem. Apple Speech Recognition, for example, is a product that lets developers incorporate speech recognition into any Macintosh application. Among the first to take advantage of this new technology was the *Star Trek Omnipedia* CD-ROM from Imergy, a voice-activated guide to a galaxy of Star Trek facts, characters, and movies. Imergy was amazed at how accurate the recognition is, even for phrases like "Denibian Slime Devil." Apple Speech Recognition enables the application developer to define how many words are active and to build custom vocabularies or language models. Apple Speech Recognition is built into Mac OS X. To learn more, follow this book's Web site link to Apple Speech Recognition.

Dragon NaturallySpeaking

On the Windows platform, IBM's speech division is dueling with Dragon Systems, and all users will benefit from the resulting breakthroughs. The IBM product is ViaVoice, and the Dragon product is NaturallySpeaking. Both products can recognize tens of thousands of words, and they are trainable, meaning that you can teach them new words. Applications include voice-controlled Web surfing, legal dictation, environmental control systems, and word processing by persons with physical disabilities, such as repetitive stress injuries. ViaVoice is also available in Macintosh and Linux versions. For more information, follow this book's Web site links to ViaVoice and NaturallySpeaking.

Text-to-Speech Conversion

In Chapter 9, you learned about a virtual chat environment, which is called the Palace on the Internet. If you have a Macintosh, Apple's text-to-speech extension enables you to hear the conversations as well as see them onscreen in the cartoon talk balloons. Called Plain-Talk, Apple's text-to-speech product can speak in Mexican Spanish as well as English.

On the Windows and Unix platforms, IBM has a product called DirectTalk, which is a text-to-speech system for building interactive voice response systems. There is also a library of DirectTalk JavaBeans for use in creating Java applications that can talk. Chant Corporation makes a SpeechKit consisting of speech synthesis and text-to-speech components that developers can use when developing Web sites with C/C++, Delphi, Java, JavaScript, VBScript, or Visual Basic. For more information about text-to-speech technology, follow this book's Web site links to PlainTalk, DirectTalk, and the Chant SpeechKit.

Foreign Language Translation

WebSphere

IBM's WebSphere Translation Server can translate Web pages, e-mail, and chat from English into a host of languages, including French, Italian, German, Spanish, Chinese, Japanese, and Korean. It also can translate into English from French, Italian, German, and Spanish. Translation speeds range from 200 to 500 words per second. Slot grammars are used to parse complex sentences that might fool less capable translation engines. Idiomatic expression handling can be fine-tuned for specific domains and contexts.

Foreign language translation technology is used at the Google.com search engine, which has language tools that can translate English-language Web pages into German, French, Italian, Portugese, or Spanish, and vice versa. In addition to these languages, the search site at AltaVista.com adds Chinese, Japanese, Korean, and Russian. To learn more, follow this book's Web site links to Google language tools, AltaVista translator, slot grammars, and the IBM WebSphere Translation Server.

Image Recognition

Virage

If you have ever tried to find a specific image in a database, you know how difficult it is to locate an image via keywords. Virage has developed software that can compare images with a visual template, which is how the human brain recognizes images. The Virage software reduces the image into a one-kilobyte file called a feature vector, which is based on the placement, color, and texture of shapes in the image. You search for images by describing the visual properties of what you are seeking. Virage's product, which is called VIR for Visual Image Recognition, is protected by U.S. Patent 5,893,095. The VIR Image Engine has been licensed for use in databases from Oracle, Informix, Sybase, Object Design, and Objectivity.

VIRAGE VIR PATENT

U.S. Patent and Trademark Office

You can read any patent by going to the U.S. Patent and Trademark Office at http://www.uspto.gov and following links to perform a patent search. To read the Visual Image Recognition (VIR) patent, follow these steps:

- Use your Web browser to open the site www.uspto.gov.

- Follow the link to perform a patent search.

- Under issued patents, choose the option to search via patent number.

- When the search form appears, type the following patent number into the blank: 5,893,095

- Click the button to perform the search and view the patent.

Bots

Bots, short for robots, are software applications programmed to act as intelligent agents that go out on the network to find or do things for you. You tell a bot what you want, and it worms its way through the Internet, finding all the relevant information, digesting it, and reporting it to you succinctly.

Likening them to robotic librarians, Krol (1996: 418) refers to bots as ". . . software worms that crawl from source to source, looking for answers to your question. As a knowbot looks, it may discover more sources. If it does, it checks the new sources too. When it has exhausted all sources, it comes crawling home with whatever it found."

The *Interlit* Web site links to several bot repositories. At FerretSoft, for example, you will find search utilities for locating Web pages, utilities, e-mail addresses, files, chat channels, phone numbers, and news. At BotSpot you will find bots that can help you shop, invest, learn, research, and game. StreetPrices, MSN eShop, Priceline, mySimon, and BottomDollar are online shopping sites that use agents to help you find the best prices. For books, an interesting bot is AddALL, because you can see it working for you when you click to compare prices. Also linked to the *Interlit* Web site are the Software Agents Group and the Multi-Agent Systems Laboratory.

Digital Television and Video

Computer technology is creating fundamental changes in the way televisions are made and videos are distributed. Almost everyone reading this book will be purchasing one of the new TVs during the next few years. Because the new TV signal is digital, computer data and Web pages can be transmitted along with the television broadcast to enhance the user experience. By the end of the decade, this convergence will enable most users to surf the Internet and watch TV on the same high-resolution display screen.

High-Definition Television (HDTV)

HDTV

The new digital television signal is called **HDTV,** which stands for **high-definition television.** HDTV is intended to replace NTSC as the television standard for the United States. HDTV is based on four technologies:

- MPEG digital video compression.

- Transmission in packets that will permit any combination of video, audio, and data.

- Progressive scanning for computer interoperability up to 60 frames per second (fps) at 1920 × 1080 pixels.

- CD-quality digital surround sound using Dolby AC-3 audio technology.

During the 1990s, the major television studios began recording shows in HDTV so reruns can be broadcast in HDTV when the standard changes. To find out how many television stations are broadcasting in HDTV today, follow this book's Web site link to HDTV, where you can perform an HDTV search by zip code.

How soon will your analog TV become obsolete? The FCC had planned to order all analog TV transmitters off the air in the year 2006, but Congress lobbied to delay that until most Americans have either new HDTV sets or digital adapters for their older analog sets. There is a lot of intrigue involved in the rollout of high-definition television. To find out the current status of HDTV, follow this book's Web site link to *Current* newspaper's briefing on digital television.

MPEG Digital Video

Motion Picture Experts Group

MPEG stands for **Motion Picture Experts Group,** which is the name of the ISO standards committee that created this digital video standard. MPEG compresses video by using a discrete cosine transform algorithm to eliminate redundant data in blocks of pixels on the screen. MPEG compresses the video further by recording only changes from frame to frame; this is known as *delta-frame encoding.* MPEG is emerging as the digital video standard for compact discs, DVD, cable TV, direct satellite broadcast, and high-definition television. MPEG is the standard for the DirecTV system. Direct satellite broadcasts have become so popular as an alternative to videotape that Blockbuster has begun selling DirecTV in its home video stores. For the DirecTV dealer nearest you, follow this book's Web site links to DirecTV.

MPEG also is being used to bring digital video to handheld wireless devices. The PocketTV movie player, for example, can play MPEG movies on certain models of Windows CE PocketPCs, including Casio's Cassiopeia, HP's Jornada, and Compaq's iPAQ line of pocket computers. Due to the present-day memory limitations of handheld computers, different versions of MPEG are being worked on to enable movies to play on devices that have different bandwidth and memory capabilities. A special version of MPEG is being created, for example, to permit video streaming over wireless connections to the Internet. For more information, follow this book's Web site links to MPEG and PocketTV.

MSN TV Internet Receiver

The MSN TV Internet Receiver is one of the hottest set-top boxes on the planet, and emerging technology promises to keep it that way. The set-top box is a device that essentially combines your telephone with the video signal on your TV or VCR. When you start up the MSN TV Internet Receiver, it dials up to your Internet service provider. Figure 26-8 shows how you see the Web pages on your TV screen. As depicted in Figure 26-9, a cleverly designed hand control lets you do one-thumb surfing on the Internet, but to really take advantage of all the features, you need to use the wireless computer keyboard that comes as part of MSN TV.

Figure 26-8 MSN TV connects your telephone to your TV for access to the World Wide Web and e-mail.

Figure 26-9 MSN TV comes with a set-top box, a computer keyboard, and a universal remote that features "one-thumb" surfing.

In order to use the MSN TV receiver, you must subscribe to the MSN TV service. The MSN TV service provides access to MSN Messenger, MSN News, and Hotmail. Your mail messages can include pictures and audio clips, and you can build personal Web pages. There is a $10 per month discount if you already have an ISP; otherwise, you use MSN as your ISP.

Through products like MSN TV, you can see how emerging technology is integrating the television, the telephone, and the computer into a networked supermedium. Withrow (1993) credits technology prophet George Gilder with coining the phrase **telecomputer** to describe such a device.

Microsoft TV

Fiber Optic Service

Microsoft is continually enhancing its digital television products. In 2005, Verizon announced that it will use Microsoft TV technology to provide digital television services through Verizon's Fiber Optic Service (FiOS). The FiOS TV service includes an interactive program guide, HDTV, digital video recording, and video on demand. Verizon's announcement followed similar Microsoft TV deals with SBC and BellSouth.

Microsoft TV lets you record your favorite shows without a VCR, pause live television, create your own TV program lineup, and instantly replay anything you see on TV. Everything you watch is digitally recorded onto a digital video recorder that uses an internal hard drive to record up to 35 hours of your favorite shows. You can make your own slow-motion instant replays during sporting events. You also can participate in interactively enhanced TV programs such as *Who Wants to Be a Millionaire, Judge Judy, Wheel of Fortune,* and *Jeopardy!* To learn more about Microsoft's digital television offerings, follow this book's Web site links to Microsoft TV.

Digital Hubs

Start thinking of your home PC not so much as a personal computer, but rather as a **digital hub** that will eventually coordinate all of the electronic devices in your home. According to a 2004 eMarketer survey, 72 percent of U.S. adults are interested in having a digital hub at home. Very aware of this trend, Microsoft created a digital hub version of Windows, called Windows XP Media Center Edition, which a dozen leading brands are using as the operating system for their digital entertainment hubs. Apple also is working to position the Macintosh as the center of your home entertainment system.

In 2004, a digital hub called the Moxi Media Center won an Emmy for Best TV User Interface Design. Its inventor is Moxi founder Steve Perlman, who created WebTV back in the 1990s and sold it to Microsoft for $425 million in 1997. As the digital hub technology evolves, it will be interesting to watch how the Moxi competes for market share with Windows Media Center PCs and the Macintosh.

Features that you will see emerging in digital hubs over the next few years will include

- Wireless transmission of multimedia objects to devices located at various places in the house. This will enable you to play, for example, music stored on a PC in your study on the surround sound system in your family room.

- Distribution of video streams from the digital hub to receivers located in different parts of the house. While Dad watches *Monday Night Football,* Mom can watch *Absolutely Fabulous* and the kids can watch the Discovery Channel.

- Print photos taken by your digital camera without having to plug anything in.

- Download music into your PDA or other portable listening device.

- Upload a movie from your camcorder, edit the movie on the PC in your den, and play the movie on the HDTV set in the living room.

- Capture images from wireless cameras located about the house and out in the yard so you can see your house over the Web when you are not at home.

- Page you if someone jumps or falls into your swimming pool when it is supposed to be closed.

- Provide remote control of all home appliances and electronic devices, both inside the house when you are home and via the wireless Web when you are away.

To quote the Apple digital hub Web site, these are the kinds of features that will "make your digital lifestyle possible." To learn more about digital hubs, follow this book's Web site links to Windows XP Media Center, Moxi, and Apple digital hubs.

exercises

1. Follow the *Interlit* Web site links to Voice Recognition and explore the material you find there. Then reflect on how voice recognition might help make computers easier to use. What ways can you think of? How would you use voice recognition in your daily life? How long do you think it will take before the common mass-market retail computer can do voice recognition without requiring special hardware and software to be installed?

2. Follow the *Interlit* Web site link to BotSpot and peruse the range of intelligent agents available there. Which one of the bots would be most useful to you in your daily life? Name the bot, describe what it does, and tell why it would be useful for you.

3. Follow the *Interlit* Web site link to BotSpot and look for bots that could improve the efficiency of your school or workplace. Name the bots, describe what they do, and tell how they could make things better at work or school.

4. Go to your local television store and ask to see a demonstration of HDTV as compared to NTSC. Can you see the difference in quality between an HDTV picture and a standard NTSC television signal? How much do HDTV sets cost? Are you willing to pay that much to get one, or will you wait for the price to come down? How many of your friends have HDTV sets?

5. Go to your local computer store and ask to see demonstrations of a PocketPC running Windows CE and a Palm device running the Palm OS. Compare the Windows CE to the Palm OS operating systems. Were you able to launch programs from the Windows Start button on the Pocket PC? Do you feel that is more intuitive for a Windows user than the custom interface on the Palm OS, or does the Palm interface work better for a handheld device? What was the nicest feature you found on the PocketPC? What did you find to be the best feature of the Palm OS? If you had to choose one over the other for use in your school or workplace, which family of PDA would you recommend: one of the PocketPCs based on Windows CE or a Palm device running the Palm OS? Give at least three reasons why you chose this particular brand.

6. Go to your local computer store and ask for a demonstration of the leading brand of PDA, such as a PocketPC or a Palm computer. Use the stylus to write a message onscreen. How well does the PDA recognize your handwriting? Do you have to alter your style of writing, or can the PDA recognize your natural handwriting style? Tell what brand and model of PDA you used for this.

7. Go to your local computer store and ask for a demonstration of the Tablet PC. Use the pen to write a message onscreen. How well does the Tablet PC recognize your handwriting? Does the Tablet PC do better than the PDA you tried in exercise 6? Tell what brand and model of Tablet PC you used for this exercise.

8. Go to your local computer store and ask for a demonstration of the Tablet PC. Do you think it works well enough for use in your school or workplace? Give at least three reasons for or against using the Tablet PC in your school or workplace. Also tell what brand and model of Tablet PC you used for this exercise.

9. Go to your local computer store and ask for a demonstration of Windows XP Media Center Edition. Imagine what it would be like using this at home to coordinate your audio and video entertainment devices. Give three reasons why you would or would not want to use Windows XP Media Center Edition as the digital hub in your home.

10. Go to About.com and do a search for "emerging technology." What new technologies do you find listed at the About site that were not discussed in this book? Which ones merit inclusion in the next edition?

SITUATED CASE PROJECTS
Case 26: Adopting a PDA Platform

At the end of each chapter in this book, a situated case project provides the student an opportunity to put the chapter's contents to practical use in a workplace situation. Each case has the same number as the chapter in which it appears.

As you learned in Chapter 26, the PDA market is divided into two camps: PocketPC and Palm. The operating systems are very different, as is the software needed to use these devices. Because of these differences, most schools or companies will probably choose to adopt one or the other instead of trying to support them both. Imagine that your superior has asked you to recommend which PDA platform your school or company should adopt. In developing this recommendation, consider these issues:

❶ The marketplace for PDAs is volatile. From 2000 to 2005, for example, Palm's market share dropped from over 70 percent to about 30 percent of the market for personal digital assistants, while Windows CE rose to 48 percent. Use the search engines to find the latest reports on PDA market share.

❷ Consider the extent to which your co-workers use Windows. If they are diehard Windows users, for example, they may prefer the PocketPC platform due to the familiarity of the Windows user interface.

❸ Get personal experience with both operating systems before you make a recommendation. You can try them in the PDA departments at Circuit City, Best Buy, OfficeMax, Staples, or Office Depot, plus many other retail stores.

❹ Functionality should be your guiding light in deciding on a PDA platform. Consider the applications that are available on the various brands and match these applications up to the daily tasks faced by your co-workers.

Use a word processor to write a brief essay telling what PDA you recommend and why. Report the brands of PDA you considered. Discuss the relative pluses and minuses of the PocketPC and Palm platforms as they relate to daily activities in your workplace. If it seems necessary to support both the PocketPC and the Palm, state the reasons why this will be necessary. Also in this report, state what the current market share is for the Palm versus the PocketPC brands of PDA. If your instructor has asked you to hand in this assignment, make sure you put your name at the top of your PDA recommendation, then copy it onto a disk or follow any other instructions you may have been given for submitting this assignment.

27

HOW TO KEEP UP AND STAY SECURE

After completing this chapter, you will be able to:

- Keep up with the changes that are occurring on the Internet.

- Join listservs that will e-mail you periodic summaries of the latest Internet news.

- Bookmark Web sites that announce and explain changes in technology.

- Peruse catalogs for new products that may interest you.

- Subscribe to free magazines that review and compare the new products.

- Read books that will extend your knowledge of computers, multimedia, and the Internet.

- Subscribe to Internet security bulletins that alert you of the latest security threats and recommend measures you can take to thwart them.

- Configure Windows and Macintosh computers to receive automatic software updates that install the latest security patches.

Computer technology is advancing so rapidly that even the so-called expert sometimes feels overwhelmed by the fast pace of change. Never has a field had so many new inventions happening so rapidly, with so much hype surrounding the new product announcements. How can you see through the hype when you consider purchasing new technology? How will you know what model of computer to buy, what software to use, and how best to connect to the Internet?

Happily, you can use the technology to keep up with what is new. This chapter provides you with a list of recommended listservs, Web sites, catalogs, periodicals, and books. These recommendations are succinct and strategic; instead of providing you with a list so long that you would not know where to start, this chapter provides you with a short list of the most strategic ways to keep up with changes and advances in technology.

Safeguarding your computer is one of the most important aspects of keeping up with changes in technology. This chapter concludes by telling you how to stay informed of the latest security threats and keep your computer updated so you can minimize the chance of having a cracker spoil your journey along the Information Superhighway.

Listservs and E-mail Newsletters

Table 27-1 recommends listservs that will send you periodic e-mail messages to keep you up to date with what is happening in technology. At the InfoWorld site, there are several newsletters from which to choose, depending on your interests and the level of detail you want.

Table 27-1   Recommended listservs and e-mail newsletters

Name of Listserv	What the Listserv Does	How to Subscribe
InfoWorld	Summarizes news about the Internet and emerging technologies	Go to subscribe.infoworld.com, click the e-mail newsletter button, and follow the onscreen instructions.
TOURBUS	Provides a virtual tour of the best Internet sites and tools	Go to www.tourbus.com and follow the onscreen instructions to subscribe.
Netsurfer Digest	Reviews the latest hot spots on the Internet	Go to www.netsurf.com/nsd, click the Subscribe button, and follow the onscreen instructions.
LockerGnome	Technology reviews, press releases, hot downloads, MP3 releases, and separate newsletters for Windows, Linux, and OS X fanatics	Go to www.lockergnome.com and follow the onscreen instructions to subscribe.

Catalogs

Computer Shopper

One of the best catalogs for people considering computer purchases is the *Computer Shopper*. It is filled with new product announcements, evaluations, advertisements, technology reviews, and shopper's guides to computer peripherals, input/output devices, and modems. You will find the *Computer Shopper* on the magazine rack of most newsstands. It is very popular, and new editions come out monthly. Although the *Computer Shopper* is called a magazine, it looks and feels more like a catalog, which is why it is listed here as a catalog. To subscribe, follow the *Interlit* Web site link to *Computer Shopper*. You also can search the catalog online at ZDNet; follow the *Interlit* Web site link to ZDNet Shopper to search the catalog online.

There are also Web sites where you will find annotated lists of computer products for sale, including multimedia PCs, peripherals, and networking. Table 27-2 lists the recommended technology catalogs on the Web.

Periodicals and Web Sites

Listed here are periodicals that will help keep you updated on the new technology. Most of these periodicals are free and appear monthly, either in a printed magazine or an ezine delivered via e-mail. These periodicals also have Web sites where you can search for information by keyword and read extra material that expands on the monthly edition.

Table 27-2   Technology Catalogs on the World Wide Web

World Wide Web Address	What You Will Find There
www.cnet.com	Hardware and software catalog presented in the context of the latest technology news and trend analysis, special reports, hardware and software reviews, and numerous download indexes that provide you with access to the Web's freeware and shareware programs.
www.compusa.com	Searchable Web site catalog of a leading chain of computer stores featuring a wide range of products including Windows and Macintosh hardware and software, peripherals, cameras, mobile devices, and supplies.
www.microsoft.com/catalog	Microsoft product catalog, including product categories and an alphabetical list of product names.
store.apple.com	Apple's online store for Macintosh hardware and software.

Internet World

Internet World

A good source for the latest news about the Information Superhighway, *Internet World* features articles about new trends on the network, advertises Internet addresses of new online resources, reviews books about the Internet, and presents profiles of the key companies, people, and products that impact the Internet's growth and development. Penetrating analyses probe legal, social, and ethical issues. Labs educate users and buyers about important new Internet products and technologies for home and business. Job announcements list employment opportunities across a broad range of technologies. Subscriptions are free. To get a subscription, follow the *Interlit* Web site link to *Internet World* and click to create a new account.

G4

G4

G4 is a combination Web site and cable television channel devoted to technology and video games. The Web site complements the show and provides more in-depth coverage of technologies and issues discussed live on TV. Programming includes product reviews, breaking industry news, celebrity interviews, and insider opinions. You will find G4 on the Web at www.g4tv.com, where you can subscribe to daily or weekly newsletters. If your local cable carrier does not have G4, you can find it on the DirecTV or Dish Network satellite services.

Wired

Wired

Wired is an award-winning monthly magazine that captures the excitement and the substance of the digital revolution. The best writers and designers in the world help you identify the people, companies, and ideas shaping our future. Reviews of the latest gadgets and gizmos appear with feature stories and interviews of people who are working furthest out on the edge of pioneering the Internet. To subscribe, follow the *Interlit* Web site link to *Wired*.

T.H.E. Journal

T.H.E. Journal

T.H.E. stands for Technological Horizons in Education. *T.H.E. Journal* appears monthly; each issue contains application highlights and dozens of new-product announcements. Each year, *T.H.E. Journal* publishes special supplements from vendors like IBM, Apple, and Compaq.

T.H.E. Journal is free to qualified individuals in educational institutions and training departments in the United States and Canada. To subscribe, follow the *Interlit* Web site link to *T.H.E. Journal,* where you also will find an online version that lets you download product demos, search back issues, and read articles that did not appear in the printed journal. Online features include the Infrastructure Supplement, a Road Map to the Web for Educators, and a review of presentation products and a database of their manufacturers.

Technology & Learning

Technology & Learning

Technology & Learning is published monthly, except in December and the summer months. Targeted primarily at precollege educators, it reviews software, advertises grants and contests, contains vendor supplements, articulates classroom needs, reviews authoring tools, and has a Q&A section to answer questions about technology and learning. Plus it has great cartoons.

To apply for your free subscription, follow the *Interlit* Web site link to *Technology & Learning,* where you also will find an online version that lets you search software reviews.

Classroom Connect

Classroom Connect

An excellent Web site for teachers, parents, and students is Classroom Connect. It develops Web-based curriculum projects and professional development programs for K-12 educators. At the Classroom Connect Web site, you can purchase subscriptions to Connected Newsletter, which matches state and national education standards to topics in social studies, science, language arts, and mathematics; Connected University, which provides just-in-time professional development courses that help teachers sharpen their teaching with technology skills; and Connected Tech, a Web-based instructional program that teaches students technology skills within the context of the core curriculum. You also can subscribe to Classroom Connect's extensive catalog of curriculum materials and Internet guides. To find out more about these materials and sign up for a free trial subscription, follow the *Interlit* Web site link to Classroom Connect.

Campus Technology

Campus Technology

Formerly known as *Syllabus* magazine, *Campus Technology* informs the higher-education community on how technology can be used to support teaching, learning, and administrative activities. Each issue includes feature articles, case studies, product reviews, and profiles of technology use at the individual, departmental, and institutional level. Regular features cover multimedia, distance learning, the Internet, quantitative tools, publishing, and administrative technology. A variety of multiplatform technologies are covered, including computers, video, multimedia, and telecommunications.

Campus Technology is published monthly. In the United States, subscriptions are free to individuals who work in colleges, universities, and vocational/technical schools. To subscribe, follow the *Interlit* Web site link to *Campus Technology*.

Internet Booklists

There are more than a thousand books about the Internet. You can search for them by topic or keyword at amazon.com and barnsandnoble.com, where you can buy the books online. Hogan Productions maintains an online catalog of computer and Internet books that you can read online, most of them for free. There is also an online booklist called "The Information Superhighway: A Bibliography of Its Past, Present, and Future" that contains a very good list of Internet books. Follow the *Interlit* Web site links to peruse these and other booklists.

Staying Secure

In order to enjoy your journey on the Information Superhighway, you must protect your computer from crackers who are continually devising new methods of attacking the Internet. If you do not have a virus scanner, get one from a leading antivirus company such as Norton or McAfee by following the antivirus links in Chapter 6 of the *Interlit* Web site. Check the settings to make sure your virus scanner is configured to scan all incoming files and messages, and make sure the virus definition's auto-update service is turned on.

Viruses are not the only way crackers can attack your computer, however. You also must use your computer's firewall to block other kinds of attacks that can come from the Internet. If you have Windows, click the Windows Start button, choose Control Panel, and click Windows Firewall to check the settings. If you have a Macintosh, pull down the Apple menu, click System Preferences, choose Sharing, click the Firewall tab, and click Start if the firewall is not running.

Microsoft Windows Update Service

Microsoft runs a **Windows Update Service** that can automatically download the latest security patches to your computer. You can configure the service to install the patches right away or notify you when the patches are ready to install. To configure the Microsoft Windows Update Service, follow these steps:

- Log on to your computer as the administrator. Only the administrator can configure the Windows Update Service.

- Click the Windows Start button, go to Control Panel, and double-click System to bring up your computer's System Properties window.

- Click the Automatic Updates tab. Figure 27-1 shows how the configuration settings appear onscreen. To enable automatic updating, check the box alongside the option Keep my computer up to date.

- The settings let you choose one of three service levels. The first level notifies you before downloading any updates. The second level downloads the updates automatically but notifies you before installing them. The third level downloads and installs the updates automatically.

- Click OK when you are done configuring the settings.

Besides configuring Windows Update to run automatically, you also can force it to run manually at any time. To run Windows Update manually, follow these steps:

- Click the Windows Start button and choose Help and Support to bring the help center onscreen.

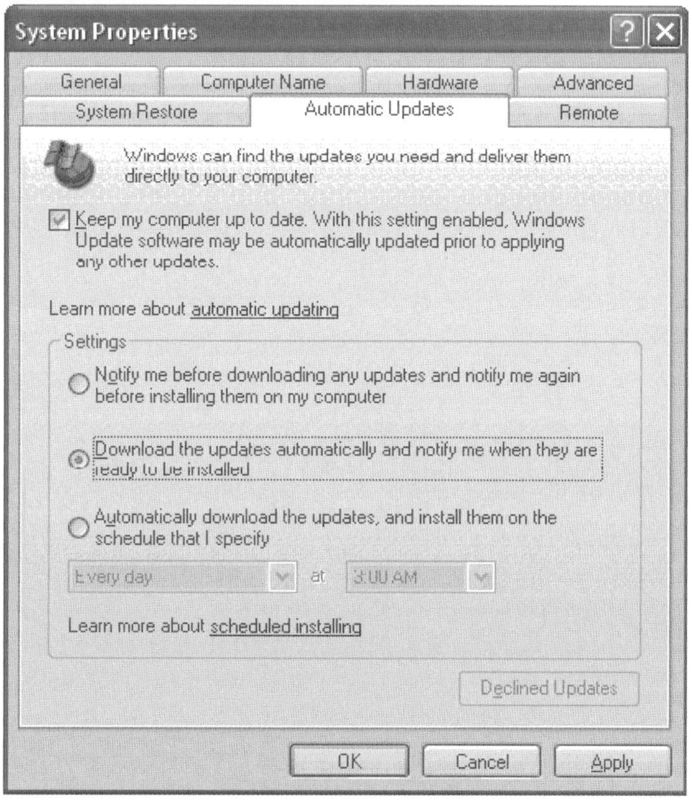

Figure 27-1 You configure the Windows Update settings on the Automatic Updates tab of the System Properties window that you bring onscreen by choosing System from the Windows Control Panel.

- Follow the link to Windows Update. When the Windows Update screen appears, follow the link to scan for updates.

- After scanning for updates, the Windows Update service will display a list of (1) critical updates that are very important for you to install, (2) operating system updates, and (3) driver updates. Follow the onscreen instructions to review the updates and choose the ones you want installed on your computer. By definition, you should always install the critical updates, because they patch serious bugs and security holes that make your computer vulnerable to attack.

Macintosh Update Service

The Macintosh has a software update service that can automatically download the latest security patches to your computer. These updates cover OS X as well as applications manufactured by Apple Computer. You can configure the service to install the patches right away or notify you when the patches are ready to install. To configure the Macintosh Update Service, follow these steps:

- Pull down the Apple Menu and choose System Preferences.

- Pull down the View menu and choose Software Update; the Software Update Preferences panel appears as illustrated in Figure 27-2.

- Select the option to automatically check for updates.

- Choose the interval you prefer (daily, weekly, or monthly) from the popup menu; I recommend you choose daily.

- Click the Check Now button if you want to check for updates now, and follow the onscreen instructions to install the updates.

Figure 27-2   Configuring the Macintosh software update settings. I recommend you choose the daily update setting.

Figure 27-3 The Microsoft Subscription Center lets you set your Newsletter Preferences. Follow the link to Newsletter Subscriptions to bring up the newsletter choices in Figure 27-4.

Figure 27-4 Check the boxes alongside the newsletters to which you want to subscribe and then click the Update button. To find out more about a newsletter, click its plus sign.

Microsoft Security Newsletters

For millions of end users and server administrators that have the Windows operating system, subscribing to one or more of the Microsoft Security Newsletters is an excellent way to keep up with Microsoft's security strategies and guidance. To subscribe, follow these steps:

- Go to www.microsoft.com/technet/security/secnews/newsletter.htm and follow the link to subscribe to a newsletter. The link is in the footer at the bottom of the page.

- When the Passport screen appears, log on via your Passport credentials. If you do not have a Passport, follow the onscreen instructions to get one. *Note:* Passport is Microsoft's online authentication service.

- The Microsoft subscription center appears as illustrated in Figure 27-3. Follow the link to Newsletter Subscriptions.

- Figure 27-4 shows how you can subscribe to a wide range of newsletters. Server administrators and IT staff should subscribe to the Microsoft Security Notification Service, which provides detailed technical information on security issues. Other users should subscribe to the Microsoft Security Newsletter.

- Check the boxes alongside the newsletters to which you want to subscribe and click the Update button.

- If you later decide to unsubscribe, repeat these steps, uncheck the boxes alongside the newsletters you want to stop, and click the Update button.

Macintosh Security Newsletter

Apple maintains a Macintosh security support page at www.apple.com/support/security. One of its recommendations is that Macintosh users should subscribe to the Security-Announce mailing list, which will send you product security news from Apple Computer. To subscribe, follow these steps:

- Use your browser to go to lists.apple.com.

- Click the option to view the lists on this site; the list of available lists appears.

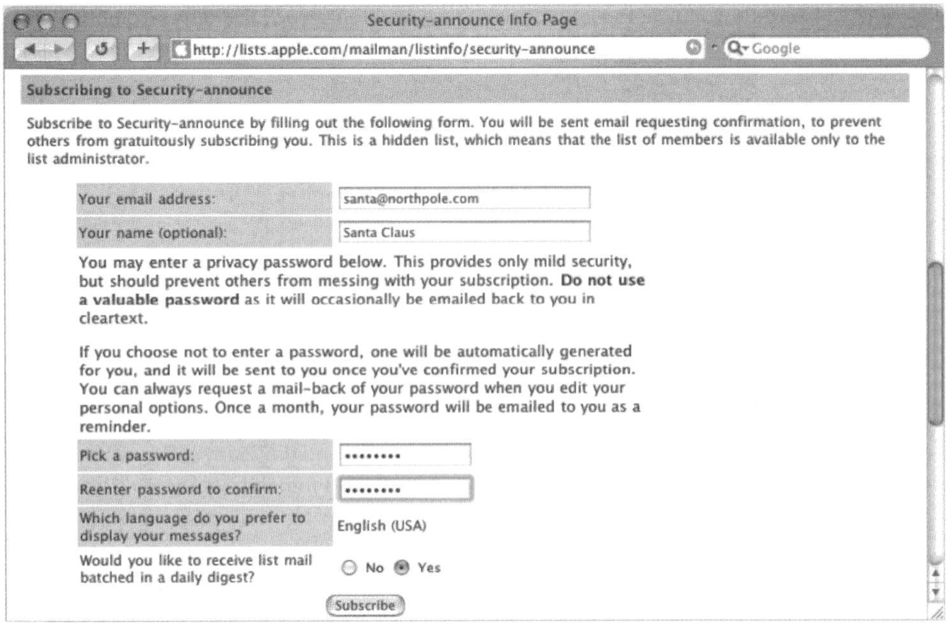

Figure 27-5   The Apple Security-announce subscription form. I recommend that end users choose the daily digest mode to limit to a maximum of one per day the number of messages you may otherwise receive.

- Scroll down the list and click Security-announce; the Security-announce list information appears.

- After you read this info, scroll down the page to reveal the subscription form illustrated in Figure 27-5.

- When you fill out the form, unless you are a network administrator, I recommend you choose the daily digest mode, which will reduce to a maximum of one per day the number of messages you may otherwise receive.

- Click the Subscribe button to join the list.

Enjoying the Journey

If you follow the security advice provided in this chapter and (1) install a virus scanner and keep your virus definitions up to date, (2) use a properly configured firewall, (3) subscribe to the operating system's software update service, and (4) read and heed the security newsletter for your brand of operating system, you can stay reasonably protected from attacks that can otherwise spoil your journey on the Information Superhighway. Having warned you and advised you, I want to end this book on a positive note. To borrow a metaphor from Disneyland, the Internet is an E-ticket ride. Stay safe and enjoy the journey!

exercises

1. Subscribe to all of the listservs recommended in Table 27-1. As you begin receiving information from the listservs, you will develop a feel for which ones you like best. After a few weeks of comparing the messages you will receive, you can unsubscribe from the listservs you no longer want. Which listserv did you find most useful? How did it help you the most?

2. Subscribe to the free printed version of *T.H.E. Journal*. For the first few months, when you receive the printed magazines, also visit the journal's Web site at www.thejournal.com. How do you prefer reading the journal: on the Web or in print? What are the advantages and disadvantages of print versus electronic media? Did you find

anything helpful at the Web site that was not printed in the magazines? Which medium makes it easier for you to find things in back issues: the printed journal or the Web site? If you were forced to read the journal only in one form, which would you choose: the printed edition or the electronic version?

3. Go to your local newsstand and have a look at the latest issue of the *Computer Shopper*. What new products do you find listed there that you did not already know about? Do you think it would be practical to subscribe to a magazine so large? Would you enjoy receiving such a magazine each month? Now visit the online version of the *Computer Shopper* by following the *Interlit* Web site link to ZDNet Shopper. Compare how the product information is organized at the ZDNet Shopper Web site to the way the materials are presented in the printed version of the catalog. Which medium—printed or online—would you prefer for your computer shopping? Why do you feel that way?

4. Follow the instructions provided in this chapter to subscribe to the security newsletter for your brand of operating system. Read carefully the security messages you receive. In your opinion, what is the most dangerous security threat discussed in these messages? Give the name of the threat, summarize the risk it poses, and tell what action you plan to take in order to protect your computer from this mode of attack.

SITUATED CASE PROJECTS

Case 27: Publishing an Electronic Magazine

At the end of each chapter in this book, a situated case project provides the student an opportunity to put the chapter's contents to practical use in a workplace situation. Each case has the same number as the chapter in which it appears.

Now that the most commonly used e-mail clients support the sending and receiving of mail in HTML format, you can use a combination of the Web and e-mail to publish a pretty slick-looking electronic magazine. Imagine that your employer has been receiving such ezines from some of your competitors. Your employer wants you to create a sample issue showing what an ezine might look like for your school or company. To create such an ezine, follow these steps:

1 In the *website* folder on your hard drive, create a subfolder called *ezine*. If you need help doing this, refer to Table 6-9.

2 Use the Web page creation tool of your choice (probably Dreamweaver, FrontPage, or Nvu) to create the sample issue of your ezine. Use the HTML tables you learned in Chapter 20 to lay out your ezine with a magazine-looking style. Save the result as an HTML page in your *website/ezine* subfolder.

3 Following the publishing techniques you learned in Chapter 22, publish the *ezine* folder to your Web site.

4 If you are using Thunderbird as your mail program, pull down the Tools menu, choose Options, click Composition, and make Forwarded Messages be sent inline instead of as attachments.

5 To test the ezine and make sure it will work properly when distributed via e-mail, send yourself a copy by following these steps:

Firefox	Internet Explorer
▶ Use Firefox to open the Web page you want to send as an ezine.	▶ Use Internet Explorer to open the Web page you want to send as an ezine.
▶ Pull down the View menu and choose Page Source.	▶ Pull down the File menu and choose Send→Page by Email.
▶ When the source code window appears, pull down the Edit menu and choose Select All, then pull down the Edit menu again and choose Copy.	▶ When the mail window appears, type your e-mail address in the To field.
▶ Close the Page Source window.	

(continued)

(continued)

Firefox	Internet Explorer
▶ Pull down the Firefox Tools menu and choose New Message.	▶ Fill in the subject line with a topic such as **ezine test.**
▶ When the Compose window appears, type your e-mail address in the To field.	▶ If a horizontal rule and some extra white space appear in the message body at the top of the page, delete them.
▶ Fill in the subject line with a topic such as **ezine test.**	▶ Click the Send button to send the message.
▶ Click to position your cursor in the body of the message.	
▶ Pull down the Insert menu and choose HTML.	
▶ When the HTML window appears, click Ctrl-V to paste the HTML into the window.	
▶ Click the Insert button to insert the HTML.	
▶ Click the Send button to send the message.	

6 E-mail the ezine to the listserv you created in Chapter 7. To do this, follow the same process as you did in step (4), except address the message to the mailing list instead of to yourself. Because you are a member of that listserv, you will know this works OK when you receive your copy of the ezine from the listserv.

7 If you encounter difficulties and need to troubleshoot problems, follow the *Interlit* Web site link to the ezine tips.

If your instructor has asked you to hand in this assignment, make sure you put your name at the top, then save it on disk or follow any other instructions you may have been given for submitting this assignment.

Appendix A
Internet Toolkit for Windows and Macintosh

● Listed here is a collection of the tools used in this book. All of these tools can be downloaded or ordered from the *Interlit* Web site. Follow the *Interlit* Web site link to Appendix A, Internet Toolkit.

Web Browsers

Name of Package	Windows	Macintosh
Firefox	Yes	Yes
Internet Explorer	Yes	No
Safari	No	Yes

Animated GIF Tools

Name of Package	Windows	Macintosh
Animation Shop	Yes	No
GIF Construction Set	Yes	No
GifBuilder	No	Yes

HTML Translators

Name of Package	Windows	Macintosh
Microsoft Word	Yes	Yes
WordPerfect	Yes	Yes

FTP Software

Name of Package	Windows	Macintosh
Core FTP	Yes	No
Fetch	No	Yes

Web Page Editors

Name of Package	Windows	Macintosh
Dreamweaver	Yes	Yes
Microsoft FrontPage	Yes	No
Nvu	Yes	Yes

Waveform Audio Recording Software

Name of Package	Windows	Macintosh
Sound Recorder	Yes	No
Sound Studio	No	Yes

Graphics Editors and Converters

Name of Package	Windows	Macintosh
Paint Shop Pro	Yes	No
GraphicConverter	No	Yes

Appendix B
Situated Case Projects

At the end of each chapter in this book is a special section containing a situated case project. These projects are called situated because they present the student with real-world problems. The student imagines being employed in a small company or school that is planning how to use the Internet to improve daily operations. After completing each chapter, the student applies its content to solving a real-world need or problem related to the use of information technology in the workplace. The case projects are optional and need not be done in sequence. For a quick course about the Internet, the case projects can be skipped. Longer courses can use some or all of the cases to deepen understanding by immersing students in the solution of real-world problems in the workplace. Listed here is an index of the progressive case projects.

Situated Case Projects

Appendix C
Basic Windows and Macintosh Tutorials

Throughout this book, instructions have been provided on how to perform basic Windows and Macintosh tasks. Experienced users will not need these tutorials, but beginners will find them helpful. To make it easy for both students and instructors to find these basic Windows and Macintosh tutorials, this appendix lists the names of the tutorials and tells where to find them.

Title of Tutorial	Windows	Macintosh
How to use a vertical scroll bar	Table 4-2	Table 4-2
How to resize and position a window	Table 4-5	Table 4-5
How to hide and reveal a window	Table 4-6	Table 4-6
How to create a file folder	Table 6-9	Table 6-9
How to create a plain text file	Table 6-10	Table 6-10
How to start a program if its icon is not visible	Table 13-4	Table 13-4

Glossary

5.1 Surround Sound Dolby Digital surround sound; the nomenclature 5.1 describes the speaker configuration, which has five speakers (left-front, center-front, right-front, left-rear, and right-rear) plus one subwoofer for low bass sounds.

10BaseT Ethernet baseband wiring standard that uses category 5 twisted-pair telephone wiring to deliver networking speeds up to 10 Mbps. *See* CAT 5.

10/100BaseT Ethernet wiring standard that can run at 10 or 100 megabits per second over category 5 twisted-pair telephone wiring. *See* 10BaseT.

10GbE Ethernet wiring standard that uses fiber optics to push Ethernet into speeds ranging up to 10 gigabit per second (Gbps). The prefix giga means billion; 10 Gbps is therefore 10 billion bits per second.

absolute positioning A cascading style sheet feature that enables you to position page elements precisely onscreen based on x,y coordinates.

account A subscription with an Internet service provider that provides the basic Internet services of e-mail, listserv, newsgroup, FTP, telnet, and the Web.

Active Server Pages (ASP) Microsoft's technology for including on Web pages little programs called scripts that execute on the server and render dynamic output on the page that gets sent to the user.

ActiveX A technology invented by Microsoft that enables a wide variety of applications and content to be embedded in Web pages and other computer applications.

add-in *See* plug-in.

ADSL Asynchronous DSL; *see* DSL.

address book In an e-mail program, an index of the e-mail addresses you want to keep for future use, thereby avoiding the need to look up a person's e-mail address every time you want to send e-mail.

adware A form of computer program that displays commercial advertising in part of an application window or in a popup window that is a child of the application window. Some adware is legitimate and poses no privacy threat. *See also* spyware; malware.

alt attribute In Web accessibility, an attribute that provides alternate text for a nontext element, such as an image.

animated GIF A graphic that contains multiple images intended to be shown in a sequence at specific times and locations on the screen.

APA style The bibliographic style guidelines developed by the American Psychological Association (APA).

app A software application that can make your computer do something.

applet Written in Java, a little application that can be transmitted over the Internet as part of a Web page. *See* Java.

Archie Search tool for finding files available on the Internet via FTP servers. *See* FTP.

archive Container into which one or more files has been compressed to save space and packed into a single file that can be transmitted easily over a network.

ARPANET A packet-switched network invented in 1969 by the Advanced Research Projects Agency (ARPA) of the United States Department of Defense. Its goal was to support military research about how to build a network that could continue to function in the midst of partial outages that could be caused by bomb attacks.

ASCII American Standard Code for Information Interchange; the file format of a plain text *(.txt)* file.

ASP.NET A powerful version of ASP that lets you create code behind the Web page on so-called code-behind pages that can be part of complete applications. Users interact with these pages from the browser window, which becomes the Web application's display surface. *See* Active Server Page (ASP).

avatar An icon or representation of a user in a shared virtual reality.

AVI Audio/video interleave; a video file format in which audio frames are interleaved with the video. The sound track plays without interruption because the audio always takes priority. Then the computer shows as many frames of video as it has time to process.

bandwidth The volume of information per unit of time that a computer, person, or transmission medium can handle.

bits per sample In waveform audio recording, the dynamic range setting, which determines how much of a volume change you will hear between the loudest and softest sounds in the recording.

bits per second (bps) The unit of measurement in which modem speed is often expressed. *See* Kbps.

blog A Web-accessible log written by an individual who wants to chronicle activity related to a given topic that is often personal.

Bluetooth An emerging standard for high-speed wireless communications that enables the synchronization and exchange of information between mobile computers, telephones, portable handheld devices, and the Internet. Bluetooth transmits a short-range radio signal intended to replace the cables connecting electronic devices.

Bobby A comprehensive Web accessibility tool that can analyze a single page or an entire Web site, expose barriers to accessibility, make recommendations for necessary repairs, and encourage compliance with existing guidelines. *See* Web accessibility.

body The section of the Web page that comes after the **<body>** start tag but before the **</body>** end tag.

bookmark In a browser, a pointer to a favorite Web page that enables you to jump directly to that page, without having to navigate the Web to get there. In an HTML file, a named anchor to which a hypertext reference can link.

Boolean Named after the 19th-century mathematician George Boole, a form of algebra in which all values reduce to either TRUE or FALSE. The Boolean operators AND, OR, and NOT are widely used in computer programming and in search engines to construct queries that narrow a search to find precisely what you are looking for.

boot record virus A type of virus that spreads through malicious code that runs from the boot record of the startup device when the computer boots.

bot Short for robot; a software application programmed to act as an intelligent agent that goes out on the network to find or do things for you.

broadband Network connection that carries multiple channels of information over a single cable.

broadcast flag A tiny amount of data sent in a digital television broadcast to prevent the video from being recorded in its high-definition format.

browse *See* surf.

browser *See* Web browser.

business to business (B2B) An e-commerce model describing transactions that occur when companies conduct business electronically between themselves.

business to consumer (B2C) An e-commerce model that occurs when an end user buys something from a company's online storefront.

cable modem Network adapter used to connect PCs to TV cables in neighborhoods where cable TV companies offer Internet services over TV cables. The term *broadband* is used to refer to this type of connection that carries multiple channels of information over a single cable. *See* broadband.

cache Location on a user's hard disk where the browser keeps copies of the most recently visited Web sites when you surf the Web.

caching server A server that speeds access to resources by making a local copy of resources requested from the network so Web content and other kinds of documents and files can be served more quickly to subsequent users who request the same resources. Only if the date on the original document changed will the caching server download a fresh copy of the requested resource.

Carnivore An FBI surveillance system that can scan the Internet's e-mail traffic looking for key words and phrases related to terrorist plots and criminal investigations.

cascading The manner in which a CSS inherits rules defined by style sheets encountered earlier on the page.

cascading style sheet (CSS) A set of rules that define styles to be applied to entire Web pages or individual Web page elements.

CAT 5 Category 5 unshielded twisted-pair (UTP) wiring commonly used for Ethernet LANs. The outer sheath contains four twisted pairs in which the wires in each pair are twisted four times per inch.

cell padding The amount of white space that the browser puts inside the borders of the cells in a table.

cell spacing The amount of space that the browser puts between the borders of the cells in a table.

CGI Common gateway interface; the protocol that enables the Web page author to link buttons, fields, and controls on a Web page to programs on a server that can process them.

CGI script A computer program that responds to a CGI request. *See* CGI.

chat Synchronous form of real-time communication that enables people to converse with one another over the Internet. As you type a message on your computer keyboard, the people you are chatting with see what you type almost immediately, and you can simultaneously see what they type in reply.

client   The computer or software program that receives information from a server on the Internet.

client-server computing   A network architecture in which computers exchange information by sending it (as servers) and receiving it (as clients).

clip art   Predrawn artwork organized into a catalog or library that you can browse in search of appropriate icons, buttons, banners, backgrounds, tiles, or animated GIFs for use on Web pages.

Clipper Chip   An encryption device with a "back door" that allows government agents with the proper access to decipher the messages.

cloning   The copying of someone else's Web page that you modify to create a page of your own. *See* designing.

CMS style   The bibliographic style guidelines developed by the University of Chicago Press and published in a book called *The Chicago Manual of Style*.

common gateway interface (CGI)   The protocol that browsers use to communicate with server-side scripts to send and receive data across the Internet. The CGI protocol defines the manner in which forms data, cookies, and other kinds of information in a Web request get submitted to the program or script that will process and respond to the request. *See* CGI script.

convergence   The process of unification that digitalization causes by enabling all of the world's traditional ways of communicating to work over a common communications medium on the Internet. *See* digitalization.

cookie   A place in the computer's memory where browsers can store information about the user to maintain your state as you click through a site and to retain information about you between visits. Persistent cookies are stored on the user's hard disk; per-session cookies are stored in RAM.

customer to customer (C2C)   An e-commerce model that enables online users to bypass the storefronts and pay each other directly for goods or services that people want to sell to each other.

default page   The Web page that appears onscreen when you visit a Web site without requesting a specific document. The default page is often the home page of the company or person who owns the site. *See* home page.

delta-frame encoding   A video compression technique that records changes from frame to frame instead of recording a full frame every time.

designing   Creating an original home page uniquely suited to the image you want to project on the Web. *See* cloning.

digital divide   The barriers faced by people who do not have adequate access to the Internet.

digital hub   A multimedia computer that can distribute audio/video streams to Ethernet receivers located in different parts of the house.

Digital Millennium Copyright Act (DMCA)   Legislation enacted into law in the United States in 1998 in order to bring the United States into conformance with the World Intellectual Property Organization (WIPO) treaties. *See* WIPO.

digital subscriber line (DSL)   Broadband method of connecting to the Internet over existing telephone lines. *See* broadband.

digitalization   The process of encoding messages into a digital format that can be transmitted over the Internet.

direct connection   An Internet connection that is always on, such as Ethernet, ISDN, cable modem, DSL, and satellite connections.

DirecTV   A satellite service that uses MPEG to deliver more than 175 channels of digital TV programming throughout North America. *See* MPEG.

div tag   In HTML, the <div> start and </div> stop tags create structural divisions onscreen. <div> is an abbreviation for division.

DMCA   *See* Digital Millennium Copyright Act.

DNS   *See* domain name system.

DOCTYPE declaration   A line of code at the top of a file that identifies the XML schema that defines the tag structure of the document.

document object model (DOM)   The official W3C structural definition of the objects, methods, and properties that comprise documents on the World Wide Web.

domain   Everything after the hostname in a fully qualified domain name. *See* fully qualified domain name (FQDN).

domain name system (DNS)   The protocol that translates a fully qualified domain name (*e.g.,* www.loc.gov) into the numeric IP address (*e.g.,* 140.147.249.7) needed to route information across the Internet.

dotted quad notation   The format of an IP address that has four 8-bit bytes separated by periods. *See* domain name system (DNS).

DSL   Digital subscriber line; a type of digital telephone connection that can send data at speeds up to 2 million bits per second.

DVD   Digital versatile disc; an optical storage medium that uses CD-size discs (120mm diameter) to store 4.7 GB (gigabytes) per layer, which is seven times more than a CD can hold. Dual-layer DVDs can hold 8.5 GB on a single side, with 17 GB on a double-sided, dual-layer disc.

dynamic HTML A term invented by Microsoft to refer to the animated Web pages you can create by using the DOM to combine HTML with style sheets and scripts that bring Web pages to life. *See* document object model (DOM).

e-commerce The integration of digital communications, data management, and security capabilities that allows organizations to exchange information related to the sale of goods and services.

EFF The Electronic Frontier Foundation, a nonprofit civil liberties organization working in the public interest to protect privacy, free expression, and access to public resources and information online, as well as to promote responsibility in new media.

electronic data interchange (EDI) The computerized exchange of business information between trading partners over computer networks.

electronic mail (e-mail) The most often used Internet service in which electronic mail messages queue up in your Inbox, and you read and respond to the messages at your convenience. Many users read their electronic mail several times a day.

e-mail client The software used to receive, read, and respond to electronic mail messages.

e-mail signature A block of text that automatically gets appended to the e-mail messages you send.

embedded audio Audio that's built in to a Web page, as opposed to being linked to it.

embedded CSS A style sheet that gets copied physically into the head of the Web page and applies to the Web page as a whole.

embedded video Video that's built in to a Web page, as opposed to being linked to it.

emoticon A character combination that, when turned sideways, conjures a facial expression. The most common form of emoticon is the smiley :) that conveys a happy facial expression.

encryption The process of encoding a message with symbolic substitutions, secret patterns, and algorithms so the message cannot be deciphered by anyone who does not have the encryption key.

Ethernet The high-speed network invented in Bob Metcalfe's Harvard Ph.D. thesis in 1973 that fueled the explosion of local area networks (LANs) throughout academia and industry. Ethernet works by detecting the data collisions that can occur when two or more devices use a data channel simultaneously. A device waits a random amount of time after detecting a collision and attempts to resend the message. If the data collide again, the device waits twice as long before resending the message.

Ethernet hub An Ethernet multiport repeater, also known as a concentrator.

eXtensible Markup Language *See* XML.

eXtensible Stylesheet Language (XSL) An XML dialect that Web designers use to specify the styling, layout, and pagination of the structured content in an XML document for some targeted presentation medium, such as a Web browser, a printer, an eBook, a screen reader, or a handheld device.

external CSS A kind of style sheet that keeps all of the style definitions in a separate CSS file, which you include in a Web page at runtime by using the <link> tag to apply the style sheet to the page.

extranet Network resources, such as Web sites, that are beyond the public's reach and require authorized users to do something extra, such as type a logon name and password, in order to obtain access. An extranet enables authorized users to access an intranet from outside its normal boundaries. *See* intranet.

ezine An electronic magazine periodically distributed to users who subscribe to it.

Fair Use A section of the U.S. Copyright Law that allows the use of copyrighted works in reporting news, conducting research, and teaching.

FAQ Frequently asked question; also, a list of frequently asked questions and their answers.

file infector virus Malicious code that attaches to individual files, which propagate primarily via e-mail attachments. *See* virus.

file permission attributes Settings that determine who is allowed to read, write, and execute your files.

firefighter A peacemaker who works to diminish flames on the Internet. *See* flame.

Firefox An enhanced Web browser built upon open source code from the Netscape Navigator browser.

firewall A combination of hardware, software, and security policies that block certain kinds of traffic from entering or leaving a network, subnet, or individual host computer.

FireWire Apple trade name for the IEEE 1394 high-speed serial technology also used under Windows for connecting to a computer multimedia peripherals such as DV (digital video) camcorders and other high-speed devices like hard disk drives and printers.

flame   To send an e-mail message intended to insult or provoke; also used as a noun to refer to the insulting e-mail message.

Flash   Freely distributed by Macromedia, a multimedia plug-in that is installed on more than 97 percent of the Internet's computers. *See* plug-in.

folder   On a hard disk, a place where computer files get stored; file folders provide a way to organize the files on a computer.

frame   On a Web page, a window in a document that often has its own scroll bar; provides a way for a Web page to display more than one document simultaneously.

freespot   Hotspot offering free wireless Internet access in selected hotels, coffee shops, restaurants, shopping malls, airports, and downtown business districts. *See* hotspot; Wi-Fi.

FTP   File Transfer Protocol; the method used to transfer files from one computer to another over the Internet. FTP can be used as a verb as well as a noun.

fully qualified domain name (FQDN)   A complete DNS address that has the format hostname.registered-domain-name.top-level-domain. *See* domain name system (DNS).

Gbps   Gigabits per second. *See* gigabit.

GIF   The Graphics Interchange Format; one of the most popular graphics formats for transferring images over the Web.

giga   A billion; abbreviated G, as in GB, meaning a billion bytes, which is also called a *gigabyte.*

gigabit   A billion bits; giga means billion.

Gigapop   High-speed connection point strategically placed throughout the Internet2 network in order to guarantee high-speed bandwidth between universities, schools, and companies that are implementing the Internet2 standards. *See* Internet2.

graphics accelerator   A computer chip or circuit card that helps your PC process the specialized calculations required for 3D imaging.

HDTV   *See* high-definition television.

head   The section of a Web page that goes in between the <head> and </head> tags.

heading   The title of a section or subsection of a document. In HTML, there are six heading styles numbered from H1 to H6.

helper app   An application that the browser launches to help it handle something for which a player is not built in.

hertz (Hz)   Vibrations or cycles per second.

high-definition television (HDTV)   A digital television signal intended to replace NTSC as the television standard for the United States. HDTV is based on four technologies: (1) MPEG digital video compression; (2) transmission in packets that will permit any combination of video, audio, and data; (3) progressive scanning for computer interoperability up to 60 frames per second (fps) at 1920×1080 pixels; and (4) CD-quality digital surround sound using Dolby AC-3 audio technology.

home page   On the Web, the page that you define as your browser's take-off point or start page.

horizontal rule   A Web page element that creates a neat-looking dividing line between different parts of a Web page.

host   The computer that provides a service, such as a bulletin board, chat room, or MUD, to which other computers connect. *See* MUD.

hot word   Hypertext link. *See* hypertext.

hotspot   Wi-Fi access point. *See* Wi-Fi; freespot.

HTML   Abbreviation for hypertext markup language, which is the standard format used for hypertext documents on the Web. *See* markup; Web page.

HTML editor   An editor that lets you create Web pages by working directly with the HTML tags.

HTML translator   A tool that can convert an existing document into the HTML format. Microsoft Word, Excel, Access, and PowerPoint have HTML translators built in.

hub   The device that serves as the center of a star network topology. In IEEE 802.3 Ethernet networks, a hub is an Ethernet multiport repeater, also known as a concentrator.

hypergraphic link   A pictorial hotspot you click to trigger events linked to images on the screen.

hypertext   A term coined by Ted Nelson in 1965 to describe text that has been linked. When you view a hypertext and click a word that has been linked, your computer launches the object of that link. The links give the text an added dimension, which is why it is called hyper.

hypertext link   One or more words that you click to trigger the events that are linked to the text. Synonymous with hot word. *See* hypertext.

hypertext reference (href)   An HTML attribute that indicates where the link will go when clicked.

Hypertext Transfer Protocol (HTTP)   The protocol that transfers hypertext Web pages across the Internet.

ICANN   The Internet Corporation for Assigned Names and Numbers that is in charge of the assignment of domain names, IP address numbers, and protocol parameter and port numbers.

IETF   Internet Engineering Task Force, the official working group that develops standards and specifications for Internet protocols and services.

IM   *See* Instant messaging.

image map   An invisible layer of triggers placed over an image on the screen. The triggers can be rectangular, circular, or polygonal. When the user clicks inside one of the invisible triggers, the Web browser triggers the object of the link.

information warfare   An electronic invasion of a nation's computer networks intended to disable the networks and give the aggressor a strategic advantage during wartime.

inline CSS   A style sheet that applies only to one page element, so it gets copied "inline" on the page with that element.

instant messaging (IM)   A real-time communication protocol that lets you send and receive instant messages over the Internet. IM can be used as a verb as well as a noun. You put onto a buddy list the names of the users who are permitted to contact you. Only the people on your buddy list can IM you.

Integrated Services Digital Network (ISDN)   The digital telephone system that the regional Bell companies are installing in most of the United States. The Basic Rate Interface (BRI) service of ISDN is 144 Kbps, made up of two 64-Kbps data channels and one 16-Kbps control channel. The Primary Rate Interface (PRI) service uses 23 data channels and a 64-Kbps control channel to boost the data rate to 1,544 Kbps (1.544 Mbps).

Internet   A worldwide connection of more than 285 million computers that use the Internet Protocol (IP) to communicate.

Internet2   A higher-speed version of the Internet that revolves around a high-speed connection point called the Gigapop that connects members of a consortium of research universities working in partnership with industry and government to create the faster network.

Internet Engineering Task Force (IETF)   The organization that defines the Internet architecture protocols through a request for comments (RFC) process. The maturity states that an RFC moves through on its way to becoming a standard are called (1) Proposed, (2) Draft, and (3) Internet Standard.

Internet Explorer (IE)   The Microsoft Web browser that ships as part of the Windows operating system.

Internet fraud   Any situation in which an Internet resource—such as a Web site, chat room, newsgroup, or e-mail—plays a role in communicating false representations to consumers, such as the offering of nonexistent goods or services, in an attempt to transfer funds or goods from the victim into the control of the perpetrator.

Internet Message Access Protocol (IMAP)   An e-mail protocol designed for situations in which you want the mail to remain on the server, instead of being delivered physically to your PC. This enables you to read your mail from different computers.

Internet Protocol (IP)   The addressing system that TCP uses to transmit packets over the Internet. As defined by RFC 791, the Internet Protocol (1) determines the best path for routing the packet on to its destination address, (2) addresses the packet accordingly, and (3) fragments the packet if it is too long for the network segment. The critical importance of these tasks earned IP its place in the name of the TCP/IP protocol suite. *See* IP address; TCP/IP.

Internet service provider (ISP)   A networking company that connects you to the Internet and provides you with Internet services, including access to the World Wide Web, e-mail, listserv, chat, and newsgroups.

intranet   A network that uses the TCP/IP protocols to provide private services within an organization whose computers are not publicly accessible on the Internet. Intra is a Latin word that means within.

IP address   Four numbers separated by periods. The numbers are 8-bit bytes that range in value from 0 to 255. The smallest address is 0.0.0.0 and the largest is 255.255.255.255. The number of IP addresses this scheme allows is 256^4, which is 4,294,967,296.

IRC   Internet Relay Chat, a worldwide "party line" network that allows one to converse with others in real time in chat rooms on the Internet.

ISDN   Integrated Services Digital Network, the digital telephone system that is being installed by regional Bell companies in most of the United States, as well as in other countries.

ISP   Internet service provider, a type of company that sells Internet access.

Java   An object-oriented programming language that can be used to develop applications and applets that will run on any computer on which the Java virtual machine (VM) has been installed. *See* applet.

JavaScript   A client-side, object-based programming language that enables you to create dynamic Web pages without having to become a full-fledged Java programmer. JavaScript runs client-side in the browser without requiring any server-side processing. *See* Java.

Joint Photographic Experts Group (JPEG) Image format named after the standards committee that formed it. Intended to become a platform-independent graphics format, JPEG is arguably the best choice for publishing full-color photographs on the Web.

Kbps Kilobits per second. *See* kilobit.

kilo A thousand; abbreviated K, as in KB, meaning a thousand bytes, which is also called a *kilobyte.*

kilobit A thousand bits. Kilo means thousand. *See* kilo.

Knowbot A software application programmed to act as an intelligent agent that goes out on the network and finds things for you.

layout The relationship among the design elements that appear onscreen, including headings, paragraphs, horizontal rules, lists, images, backgrounds, bookmarks, links, special characters, tables, and frames.

legacy browser An old version of a Web browser possibly used by people who have not upgraded to the latest version.

license A permission to use a good or a service provided by a third party who owns the good or provides the service.

link A hotspot that, when selected, triggers the object of the link. You select the link by clicking on the word or picture that triggers it.

Linux Developed by Linus Torvalds, an open source operating system that mimics the form and function of UNIX on an independently developed platform. *See* UNIX; open source.

list item tag The <li> start and </li> stop tags that mark an item in an ordered or unordered list.

listserv A mailing list service that enables users to send a message to a particular mailing list, which e-mails a copy of the message to each member of the list. Listserv stands for list server.

local area network (LAN) The connection of two or more computer devices for the purpose of networking within a relatively small area, such as a home, school, or departmental office building.

local Web site A folder on the user's PC containing files and resources to be published to the Web.

lossless A kind of graphical file compression in which none of the original information in the image gets lost in the compression/decompression process.

lossy A kind of graphical file compression in which some of the image data can become lost, depending on how much compression is used when the image gets saved.

lurk To participate in a conversation on the Internet without responding to any of the messages.

lurker One of the silent majority in an electronic forum who posts occasionally or not at all but reads the group's postings regularly.

Macintosh OS X The UNIX-based operating system on Macintosh computers. *See* UNIX.

mailto A link that, when clicked, opens a new message window addressed to the person identified in the link.

malware Generic term for software born of ill intent. Besides invading your privacy, malware can take over your computer and wreak havoc with your data. *See* spyware; adware.

markup The special codes, called *tags,* that mark up a text in the Web's HTML file format, controlling how the text will flow onto the screen and automatically arrange itself with respect to pictures and other screen design elements.

MBONE Multicast backbone, the network of computers on the Internet specially designed for the transmission of simultaneous live video and audio broadcasts.

Mbps A million bits per second. *See* megabit.

mega A million; abbreviated M, as in MB, meaning a million bytes, which is also called a *megabyte.*

megabit A million bits. *See* mega.

metasearching The searching of searching, which you perform with a metasearch engine that invokes the other search engines automatically, synthesizes the results, and reports back with a single integrated list of hits.

MIDI *See* Musical Instrument Digital Interface.

MILNET The military network that formed when the military segment separated from the Internet in 1983.

MLA style The bibliographic style guidelines developed by the Modern Language Association (MLA).

MMOG Massively multiplayer online game.

MMORPG Massively multiplayer online role-playing game. Also known as RPG.

modem A combination of the terms *mo*dulate and *dem*odulate, which describe how your computer sends and receives digital information over analog phone lines. The device that performs this modulation and demodulation is called a modem.

MOO MUD, Object-Oriented. A MUD in which participants can own objects that have properties and behaviors. *See* MUD.

Mosaic The world's first graphical Web browser, which was released by the National Center for Supercomputer Applications (NCSA) in 1993.

MP3 MPEG audio layer 3, an audio file format that uses an MPEG audio codec to encode (compress) and decode (decompress) recorded music; MP3 can compress a CD audio track into a substantially smaller-sized file requiring significantly less bandwidth (about 10 percent) to transmit over the Internet without degrading the original sound track's quality.

MPEG Motion Picture Experts Group, the name of the ISO standards committee that created the digital video file format known by the same name (MPEG).

MUD Multiuser dimension, also multiuser dungeon; a synchronous multiuser communication environment that enables participants to take on a persona and create virtual worlds out of their own imaginations.

multicast backbone (MBONE) A network of computers on the Internet specially designed for the transmission of simultaneous live video and audio broadcasts. Instead of sending multiple copies of these transmissions, multicasting sends only one copy of the message and replicates the information only at branch points in the network.

multimedia The use of a computer to present and combine text, graphics, audio, and video with links and tools that let the user navigate, interact, create, and communicate.

multimedia streaming *See* streaming.

MUSH Multiuser shared hallucination. A text-based MUD. *See* MUD.

Musical Instrument Digital Interface (MIDI) A low-bandwidth music synthesizer file format that consists of a stream of codes that tells your computer when to turn notes on and off, how loud to make them, what instrument should make the sound (such as trumpet, flute, or drum), and whether to bend the notes or add other special effects.

named anchor An anchor tag with a name to which a hypertext reference can link, thereby creating a bookmark in the midst of a Web page.

Net Synonym for Internet. *See* Internet.

.NET Framework A Microsoft operating system product that adds thousands of new functions organized into classes of objects that can be used in creating applications.

Netiquette Internet etiquette, which is the observance of certain rules and conventions that have evolved in order to keep the Internet from becoming a free-for-all in which tons of unwanted messages and junk mail would clog your Inbox and make the Net an unfriendly place to be.

Netscape Corporation formed in 1994 by some of Mosaic's developers. *See* Mosaic.

Netscape Navigator The Web browser in the Netscape software suite. *See* Netscape.

network The connection of two or more digital devices for the purpose of communicating, transferring, or obtaining data.

network access point (NAP) A junction that provides direct access to the traffic on a network.

Network Interface Card (NIC) The physical network component that contains the jack into which you plug the connector on a network cable.

network operating system The software that adds to a computer the functions required for connecting computers together for the purpose of networking.

network place In the Windows operating system, a shortcut to shared resources and folders on your network, Web, and FTP servers.

networking The act of communicating over a network. *See* network.

newsgroup One of Usenet's many discussion groups; *see* Usenet.

NSFNET Created by the National Science Foundation (NSF) in 1986, a backbone that connected the nation's five supercomputer centers at high speed.

object In computer programming, a self-contained entity consisting of properties and methods enabling you to do something programmatically.

object-oriented A style of programming in which applications are constructed from reusable code segments known as objects that several programs can share.

open source Software for which the source code is available to the general public free of charge. Anyone can download the source code, use it freely, and make enhancements.

ordered list A Web page element in which the items in a list are numbered automatically.

packet Also known as a datagram, a container for a segment of the data that comprise a message, plus a header containing protocol information and addressing.

packet filter In a firewall, a filter that inspects the headers of all incoming and outgoing packets and blocks transmissions based on certain source or destination ports or IP addresses, thereby enabling the firewall to stop attacks waged on specific ports and block access to malicious or forbidden sites. *See* firewall.

page title Created by the <title> tag in the head section of the document, the name that will appear in the browser's title bar when people visit your Web page on the Internet.

paired tag An HTML tag format that consists of a start tag and a stop tag.

password   A secret word that a user must enter to gain access to a secured resource, such as an e-commerce Web site that requires users to log on to access their accounts.

patent   The granting to an inventor of a property right for an invention to exclude others from making, using, offering for sale, or selling the invention in the United States, or "importing" the invention into the United States, for a reasonable period of time (i.e., 20 years) before the patent expires.

PDA   Personal digital assistant; a portable, handheld computer that you can take with you to work, school, or anyplace where a PC might come in handy. You can easily synchronize a PDA with your personal computer and take almost any information with you, such as your address book, calendar, and key Web sites.

PDF   Portable document format; created by Adobe, a file format for sharing digitized documents in such a way that they can be viewed on any computer platform.

peer-to-peer (P2P)   A network architecture in which each workstation has equal responsibilities.

Perl   A scripting language used especially for creating CGI programs on CGI servers. *See* CGI.

personal portal   A Web site that lets users set preferences that make the portal show the kinds of information the user wants to see, and hide what the user is not interested in. *See also* portal.

phishing   The act of sending an e-mail message that appears to come from a legitimate business or financial agency. The e-mail message lures the user into clicking a link (the bait), which takes you to a Web site where the scam artist prompts you to fill in personal information such as your social security number, credit card information, and bank account.

plaintext   The text and nothing but the text. *See* ASCII.

plug-in   A software component that adds functionality when installed into an existing computer application. The advantage of plug-ins over helper apps is that the plug-in usually gives you better integration of the media than the helper app. Plug-ins normally make multimedia play in the browser's window, whereas helper apps often launch a separate window to play the file. *See* helper app.

PNG   *See* Portable Network Graphics.

Pocket PC   The trade name for palm-sized PDAs based on the Windows CE operating system. *See* PDA.

point size   A unit of measure that indicates how high the text is. In print media, a point is one-seventy-second (1/72) of an inch. On a typical computer screen, a point is about the height of a single pixel. Due to different-sized monitors, the actual size of the text will vary somewhat, depending on the physical height of the screen.

Portable Network Graphics (PNG)   An image format created by the World Wide Web consortium to replace the patented GIF format. *See* GIF.

portal   A Web site whose purpose is to provide access to other Web sites and services on the Internet.

Post Office Protocol (POP)   An e-mail protocol invented for the purpose of delivering mail post-office style from the server to your PC.

POTS   Plain old telephone service.

PPP   Point-to-point protocol; the communications software that permits computers to connect to the Internet via ordinary telephone lines and a modem.

Pretty Good Privacy (PGP)   Invented by Phil Zimmerman in 1991, a data integrity system that uses encryption, data compression, and digital signatures to provide for the secure transmission of e-mail messages and other kinds of store-and-forward file systems.

property   An attribute of an object that has a value. *See* object.

proportional font   A font in which the fat letters such as m and w take up more space than thin letters such as l and i.

proxy server   A computer that serves as an intermediary between client workstations and the external network.

public key infrastructure (PKI)   A certificate authority system that assigns to each user a digital certificate containing a key pair consisting of a public key and a private key. The person sending a message uses the public key to encrypt the message, while the person receiving the message uses the private key to decrypt it. *See* encryption.

QuickTime   Apple's brand of multimedia. Originally for the Macintosh only, QuickTime is now one of the finest cross-platform tools available for multimedia creation and delivery. The free QuickTime player plugs in seamlessly to Microsoft Internet Explorer, and it works on Windows as well as Macintosh computers.

Rich Site Summary (RSS)   An XML format for syndicating the content of a Web site in a form that can be registered with an RSS publisher to which other sites can subscribe in order to access the RSS feed and display its content onscreen.

ripper   Software used to create an MP3 file from an audio CD. *See* MP3.

routing   The process conducted by the Internet Protocol in determining the optimal network path over which the packets will be sent.

RPG   *See* MMORPG.

RTSP   Real-time streaming protocol; a method and a standard for streaming audio and video over the Internet.

Safari   The default Web browser that ships with every new Macintosh.

sampling rate   In waveform audio recording, the setting that determines the frequency response of the recorded sound.

scripting   The act of writing little computer programs that can enhance the appearance and functionality of a Web page.

scroll bar   A control that lets you move the contents of a window up or down to reveal more information.

seamless   The appearance of a background tile when its bitmap replicates itself up and down the screen in such a way that you cannot perceive the edges of the bitmap or detect a regular interruption in the pattern caused by the edges of the bitmap not fitting against each other smoothly. *See* tiled background.

self-extracting archive   An executable file that, when executed, automatically extracts the files that are contained in the archive.

serif   A decorative line stemming at an angle from the upper and lower ends of the strokes of a letter.

server   A computer that is devoted primarily to sending information in response to requests from client computers. *See* client; client-server computing.

shareware   Software you can download for free, try out for a limited time period (usually 30 to 60 days), and then, if you decide to keep using it, pay a reasonable fee (usually $29 to $39) to the vendor to purchase the software.

Shockwave   The plug-in that makes it possible for a Web browser to play multimedia sequences created with Macromedia Director, Authorware, and Flash. *See* plug-in.

shouting   On the Internet, typing a message ALL IN CAPITAL LETTERS to add emphasis; almost always, this is considered in bad taste and should be AVOIDED.

signature file   A block of text that automatically gets appended to the e-mail messages a person originates, intended to identify the sender by providing information such as your name, address, telephone number, and home page Web address.

single tags   HTML tags that function on their own with no stop tag.

sniffing   Intercepting information as it moves across the network; the Internet's equivalent of a telephone wiretap.

spam   Unwanted messages posted to newsgroups or sent to a list of users through e-mail. The term can be used as either a verb or a noun. To spam means to send unwanted messages to a list of users on the Internet. Likewise, unwanted messages that you receive are called *spam*.

spider   A robot that searches the Web continually, organizing what is found into a hierarchical directory of topics. When you conduct a subject-oriented search, the search engine searches this directory and provides you with a list of items related to your topic.

spyware   Type of computer program that secretly collects information and can transmit it without your knowledge or use it to display ads or take other actions either in a browser window or in popup windows. If the intent is malicious, the program becomes a form of malware. *See* malware.

Standard Generalizable Markup Language (SGML)   The parent markup language from which HTML was derived.

start tag   The first of the two tags in a paired tag. *See* paired tag.

stop tag   The last of the two tags in a paired tag. *See* paired tag.

streaming   The digital transmission of a real-time feed from an audio or video source, encoded in such a way that the media can begin playing steadily without making the user wait for the entire file to download to his or her computer.

subdomain   In the domain name system, a division of a domain. *See* domain name system.

surf   To browse a communications medium in search of interesting stuff, especially on the World Wide Web.

Surround Sound   *See* 5.1 Surround Sound.

table   A design element that provides a way of dividing the screen into rectangular regions into which you can lay out text and graphics on a Web page.

tags   Markup codes that determine how the text will flow onto the screen, whether it will contain pictures and where they will appear, and what will happen when the user triggers items linked to the document.

target   A named location on a Web page intended to provide the user with a quick way to jump around among the various topics on a Web page.

TCP/IP   The Internet's protocol suite, which takes its name from the Transmission Control Protocol (TCP) that manages the physical transmission of the packets and the Internet Protocol (IP) that handles addressing and routing.

Technology Education and Copyright Harmonization (TEACH) Act   Legislation that redefines the terms and conditions under which accredited, nonprofit educational institutions may use copyrighted materials in distance education without permission from the copyright owner and without payment of royalties.

telecommuting The act of working from home, using computers, dialup modems or broadband network connections, and fax machines to perform work that formerly required a person to travel physically to work.

telecomputer A term coined by technology prophet George Gilder to refer to the merging of the television, the telephone, and the computer into a networked supermedium.

telephone modem *See* modem.

teleworker Someone who works by telecommuting. *See* telecommuting.

telnet Terminal emulation protocol that enables users to log on to remote host computers over the Internet.

three-letter acronym (TLA) Shorthand method of reducing the amount of keyboarding required to write a message, such as FYI (for your information).

tile To draw an image repeatedly across and down the screen until the entire window has been covered. *See* seamless.

tiled background A graphical effect created with a tile. *See* tile.

Token Ring A type of high-speed network that passes data in tokens that move around the network in a ring.

top-level domain (TLD) The highest level of the domain name system, including the well-known domains of .com, .gov, .org, and .net., as well as the country codes typically used for domains outside the United States.

TOURBUS One of the most popular listservs on the Internet, providing you with a biweekly tour of the most interesting and informative sites on the Internet.

Transmission Control Protocol (TCP) On the Internet, the protocol that establishes and manages the connection between the computers that are exchanging data, numbers the packets on the sending computer, reassembles the packets on the receiving computer, and ensures that all of the data are intact with no omissions or duplications. *See* TCP/IP.

transparency A special effect in which one of the colors in a bitmap becomes translucent. Instead of seeing that color, you see through it into the background color or image on the screen.

Trojan A malicious application that masquerades as a desired object that you download knowingly to your computer.

Trojan horse *See* Trojan.

trustmark A seal demonstrating that a Web site complies with best practices for privacy defined at www.truste.org.

UNIX Invented by Bell Labs in the early 1970s, an operating system that supports the full range of networking services, including both client- and server-side components. *See* Linux; Macintosh OS X.

unordered list A list in which the items are bulleted instead of numbered.

URL Uniform resource locator; a global address that uniquely identifies the location of resources on the World Wide Web, including hypertext documents, pictures, sounds, movies, animations, and application software.

USA PATRIOT Act Signed into law in October 2001 in the aftermath of the 9/11 attacks on America, legislation that gives the U.S. government wide latitude in using Internet surveillance systems including Carnivore and its successors.

USB Universal Serial Bus; a popular way of connecting to your computer peripherals such as digital cameras, scanners, printers, fax machines, zip drives, and optical mice.

Usenet A distributed bulletin board system hosting more than 10,000 newsgroups.

videoconferencing The use of real-time video and audio streaming to enable people conversing over the Internet to be able to see and hear each other. *See* streaming.

virus Malicious or unwanted code that installs itself on your computer without your knowledge by hiding inside other programmed objects. Viruses are dangerous because they can consume all of the memory on your computer, destroy data, and spread across the network to other computers that are connected to yours.

Voice over IP (VoIP) A real-time telecommunication technology that is converging the public switched telephone network (PSTN) with IP telephony.

VRML Virtual Reality Modeling Language; a standard and a file format that enables Web designers to add dimensions, texture, and lighting to Web pages.

W3C *See* World Wide Web Consortium.

Web *See* World Wide Web.

Web accessibility The capability that results from the process of making it possible for users with special needs to receive, understand, and navigate content that people without disabilities can process in lieu of such special assistance.

Web Accessibility Initiative (WAI) Begun in 1997, the Web's official efforts to achieve accessibility. *See* Web accessibility.

Web browser Software that enables you to use your computer to surf the Web and download texts, pictures, sounds, databases, software applications, and movies to your computer. *See* surf.

Web Bug A single-pixel transparent GIF image, which you never "see" at all, that informs some third-party advertising site that you read the message or visited a certain Web page.

Web Content Accessibility Guidelines (WCAG) Web accessibility standards consisting of 65 checkpoints organized under 14 general guidelines created as part of the Web Accessibility Initiative. *See* Web Accessibility Initiative.

Web page An HTML file stored at a Web site where users can view the page with a browser. *See* Web browser.

Web server The stand-alone computer or server component that responds to HTTP requests from browsers and other kinds of Internet clients, including media players and handheld devices. Because Web servers use the HTTP protocol, they are also called HTTP servers. *See* Hypertext Transfer Protocol (HTTP).

Web site The place on the Web where persons or companies store their collections of Web pages, images, audio files, videos, and any other files used in conjunction with their Web pages.

WebCam Popular term for a videoconferencing camera designed for use on the World Wide Web.

Webcasting The simultaneous broadcast of a live event over the Web.

WebMaster The person in charge of a Web site.

WebTV A settop box that accesses the Internet via your telephone and displays its output through the video input on your TV or VCR; on startup, the WebTV automatically dials up to your local WebTV Internet service provider, and you see the Web pages on your TV screen.

what you see is what you get (WYSIWYG) A kind of editor that lets you create Web pages by typing your text directly onscreen, where it appears exactly as it will look on the Web. To change a font, size, color, or other text attribute, you select the text you want to change, then click a button or icon that makes the change. You do not need to know the HTML codes, which the WYSIWYG editor inserts automatically as you click the controls.

whiteboard A computer program that enables remote users to share a common screen across the network; Microsoft's LiveMeeting, for example, combines a whiteboard with audio- and videoconferencing.

Wi-Fi Trade name for products based on the IEEE 802.11 specification for wireless local area networking. Wi-Fi networks operate over a radius of up to 300 feet, depending on local conditions and equipment. *See* hotspot, freespot.

Windows CE A compact modular version of the Microsoft Windows operating system designed for use on consumer electronic devices. *See* PocketPC.

Windows Update Service An online Microsoft security service that can automatically download the latest security service that can automatically download the latest security patches to your computer and, depending on the configuration settings, install the patches right away or notify the user when the patches are ready to install.

Wireless Application Protocol (WAP) A protocol for translating Web pages into a format appropriate for display on mobile phones, thereby making it possible for mobile telephone users to access the Internet.

Wireless Markup Language (WML) The syntax followed by the Wireless Application Protocol in formatting Web pages for display on mobile telephones. *See* Wireless Application Protocol.

World Intellectual Property Organization (WIPO) An international organization in charge of administering 23 treaties comprising an international intellectual property system.

World Wide Web A networked hypertext system that allows multimedia documents to be shared over the Internet without requiring people to travel anywhere physically in order to obtain the information. *See* hypertext.

World Wide Web Consortium (W3C) Located online at www.w3.org, the organization that coordinates the research and development of new standards and features for the Web.

worm A special kind of virus that can propagate across the Internet and infect other computers without hiding inside other objects or attaching itself to other programs. *See* virus.

WWW World Wide Web; *see* World Wide Web.

WYSIWYG What you see is what you get; a type of software that lets you edit a document such as a Web page via graphical controls instead of requiring you to learn HTML codes. *See* HTML.

XHTML The eXtensible Hypertext Markup Language, which is a reformulation of HTML in XML. *See* XML.

XML A simple, self-describing markup language that enables computers to read and understand the structure of different kinds of documents and to exchange data across different operating systems, software applications, and hardware configurations without requiring any human intervention.

z-index In absolute positioning, an attribute that tells the browser the order in which to display objects that overlap. *See* absolute positioning.

zip file An archive into which one or more files has been compressed to save space and packed into a single file that can be transmitted easily over a network. *See* self-extracting archive.

Bibliography

Most of the resources used in this book are online references linked to the *Interlit* Web site. Listed here are the scholarly citations and some print-only resources you will not find at the Web site. For the hundreds of online references, follow the links at the *Interlit* Web site.

American Electronics Association. "U.S. High-tech Workforce Surges to 5 Million," *AEA News Release* [online], 17 May 2000. http://www.aeanet.org/aeanet/aeacommon/displaystartlink. asp?file=/aeanet/pressroom/pradet0000_nationalcyberstates051700.htm (accessed 8 August 2000).

Amrich, Denise. "The Internet, Legality, and You," *Windows CE Power Magazine* [journal online], August 1999. http://www.cepower.com/issuesprint/issue199908/ceeditorial0899. html (accessed 29 August 2000).

Bane, P. William, Stephen P. Bradley, and David J. Collis. "Colliding Worlds," Harvard Business School Colloquium, 5–7 October 1994. Revised March 1995.

Bane, P. William, and Debra B. McMahon. "Learning to Grow: The New Marketing Challenge in Telecommunications," *Mercer Management Journal,* vol. 2 (1994): 83–92.

Bergman, Michale K. *The Deep Web: Surfacing Hidden Value*. Bright Planet, July 2000. http://www.completeplanet.com/Tutorials/DeepWeb/index.asp (accessed 19 August 2000).

Berners-Lee, Tim. "Information Management: A Proposal," *CERN* [online], March 1989. http://www.w3.org/History/1989/proposal.html (accessed 3 February 2002).

BizReport. "Nortel: eBusiness to Grow by 86 Percent Annually," *BizReport,* 31 January 2000. http://www.bizreport.com/news/2000/01/20000131-4.htm (accessed 27 July 2000).

Bloomberg News. "EarthLink, MindSpring Complete Merger," *Bloomberg News* [online], 4 February 2000. http://news.cnet.com/news/0-1004-200-1543009.html?tag=st (accessed 8 August 2000).

CAUCE. "Cauce Does the Math—Why Can't the Marketing Industry?" *CAUCE* [online], 15 May 2001. http://www.cauce.org/pressreleases/math.shtml (accessed 4 January 2002).

Cheskin Research. *Trust in the Wired Americas*. Redwood Shores, CA: Cheskin Research, July 2000. http://www.cheskin.com/think/studies/trust2.html (accessed 9 February 2002).

Cyber Dialogue. "Telecommuting Boosted in 1998 by Internet & Economy," *Cyberdialogue* [online], 28 October 1999. http://www.cyberdialogue.com/resource/press/releases/1998/ 10-28-sb-telecommuting.html (accessed 29 July 2000).

eMarketer. "Online Advertising," *eMarket eReports* [online], 1 August 2001. http://www. emarketer.com/ereports/advert_onl/ (accessed 8 December 2001).

Friedman, E. A., J. D. Baron, and C. J. Addison. "Universal Access to Science Study via Internet, *T.H.E. Journal* (June 1996): 83–86.

Godwin, Mike. "Sex and the Single Sysadmin: The Risks of Carrying Graphic Sexual Materials," *Internet World* 5, no. 2 (March/April 1994): 11–13.

Horton, Frank. *The Computer and the Invasion of Privacy: Hearings before the Special Sub-committee on Invasion of Privacy of the House Committee on Government Operations.* 89th Cong., 2d Sess. 6 (1966).

Hyland, Thomas. "The Global Outlook for Internet Advertising and Access Spending, 2003–2007." *re: Business* (June 2004). http://www.pwcglobal.com/extweb/newcolth.nsf/docid/1670AFF327F223E385256E9900608E1D (accessed 23 February 2005).

Kathman, David. "The Merger Express of 1999." *Morningstar* [online], 1 January 2000. http://news.morningstar.com/news/ms/specialreports/99endmergers.html (accessed 29 July 2000).

Krol, Ed, adapted by Bruce Klopfenstein. *The Whole Internet: User's Guide & Catalog*, Academic Edition. Sebastopol, CA: O'Reilly & Associates, Inc., 1996: 418.

Kulik, Chen-Lin C., and James A. Kulik. "Effectiveness of Computer-Based Education in Colleges." *AEDS Journal* (Winter/Spring 1986): 81–108.

_____. "Effectiveness of Computer-Based Instruction: An Updated Analysis." *Computers in Human Behavior* 7 (1991): 75–94.

Kulik, Chen-Lin C., James A. Kulik, and Barbara J. Shwalb. "The Effectiveness of Computer-Based Adult Education: A Meta-Analysis." *Journal of Educational Computing Research* 2, no. 2 (1986): 235–52.

Kulik, James A. "Meta-Analytic Studies of Findings on Computer-Based Instruction" in Eva L. Baker and Harold F. O'Neil, Jr. (eds.) *Technology Assessment in Education and Training*. Hillsdale, N.J.: Lawrence Erlbaum, 1994.

Kulik, James A., Chen-Lin C. Kulik, and Robert L. Bangert-Drowns. "Effectiveness of Computer-Based Education in Elementary Schools." *Computers in Human Behavior* I (1985): 59–74.

Lee, Lydia. "RealAudio Goes Mainstream: SDK in Beta," *NewMedia* (October 7, 1996): 30.

Murphy, Dave. "Hackers Get Bill Gates' Credit Card," *ITinfo* [online], 26 March 2000. http://trainonline.org/itinfo/2000/it000326.html (accessed 28 August 2000).

Nelson, Theodore H. "The Hypertext," *Proceedings of the World Documentation Federation*, 1965.

Perine, Keith. "ToysMart Settles with FTC," *The Standard* [online], 21 July 2000. http://biz.yahoo.com/st/000721/17051.html (accessed 28 August 2000).

Pew Internet & American Life Project. "Internet: The Mainstreaming of American Life." *Trends 2005*, pp. 54–69. http://www.pewinternet.org/pdfs/Internet_Status_2005.pdf (accessed 10 March 2005).

Raymond, Eric S., ed. New Hacker's Dictionary. Third edition. Boston: MIT Press, 1996.

Rohde, Laura. "European Online Sales Doubled in 1999," *The Standard* [online], 24 November 1999. http://www.thestandard.com/article/display/0,1151,7873,00.html (accessed 27 July 2000).

Saunders, Christopher. "Study: Pop-Under Ads Can Backfire," *NewMedia* [online], 2 August 2001. http://www.newmedia.com/nm-ie.asp?articleID=2900 (accessed 16 December 2001).

TeleWork America. "Research Results," *ITAC* [online], 2001. http://www.telecommute.org/twa/twa2000/research_results_summary.shtml (accessed 16 December 2001).

TNS Interactive. *Global eCommerce Report 2001* [online]. Available from http://www.tnsofres.com/ger2001/.

Turkle, Sherry. *Life on the Screen: Identity in the Age of the Internet*. New York: Simon & Schuster, 1997.

UCLA Center for Communication Studies. "The UCLA Internet Report: Year Two" [online], 29 November 2001. http://www.ccp.ucla.edu/pages/internet-report.asp (accessed 27 January 2002).

Verton, Dan. "DOD Pushing Forward on Internet Disconnect," *Federal Computer Week* [online], 26 April 2000. http://www.fcw.com/fcw/articles/2000/0424/web-dod-04-26-00.asp (accessed 8 August 2000).

Wimpsett, Kim. "Who Says You Can't Get Something for Nothing?" *CNET Review* [online], 11 July 2000. http://home-internal.cnet.com/internet/0-3765-7-2198531.html?tag=st. cn.sr1.ssr.cn_isp (accessed 16 November 2000).

Withrow, Frank. Guest editorial in *T.H.E. Journal* 21, no. 2 (September 1993): 10.

Image Credits

Figure	Credit
1-2	Reprinted by permission of Robert Hobbes Zakon, www.zakon.org. Contributions insure future availability and maintenance of the timeline. Information is available at http://www.zakon.org/robert/internet/timeline/contributions.html.
1-4	Screen shot reprinted by permission from Microsoft Corporation. Copyright © 2005 Microsoft Corporation. All rights reserved.
Timeline	Courtesy of Xerox.
Timeline	National Museum of American History, Behring Center. © 2004 Smithsonian Institution.
Timeline	Courtesy of Apple Computer, Inc.
Timeline	Courtesy Microsoft® Corp.
Timeline	Courtesy of the Computer History Museum.
Timeline	Courtesy of Apple Computer, Inc.
Timeline	Courtesy of IBM Corporate Archives.
Timeline	Courtesy of IBM Corporate Archives.
Timeline	Courtesy Microsoft® Corp.
Timeline	Courtesy of palmOne, Inc.
Timeline	Courtesy of Apple Computer, Inc.
Timeline	Courtesy Microsoft® Corp.
Timeline	Courtesy of Apple Computer, Inc.
Timeline	Courtesy Microsoft® Corp.
2a	Reprinted with permission of the Counsel of Better Business Bureaus, Inc., Copyright 2003.
2-4	Copyright © 1995–2005 DNC Services Corp.
2-5	Screen capture provided courtesy of the Republican National Committee. © 2005 Republican National Committee.
2-10	Real Time Data Projects in science education at the Center for Improving Engineering and Science Education at Stevens Institute of Technology. http://www.k12science.org/realtimeproj.html.
2-12	Copyright © 2005 Journey North. All rights reserved.
4-5	Mozilla Firefox™ is a trademark of the Mozilla Foundation.
4-6	Navigation Buttons reprinted by permission from Microsoft Corporation. Copyright © 2005 Microsoft Corporation. All rights reserved.
4-7	Screen capture reprinted by permission of Miami Herald Web site.
4-10	© 2005 Cable Network News, LP, LLLP. All rights reserved. Used by permission of CNN.
4-15	© 1995–2005 Musée du Louvre.
4-19	Copyright © 2005, reprinted by permission of the New York Stock Exchange.
4-20	Copyright © 2005 The NASDAQ Stock Market, Inc. Reprinted with permission.
4-21	Image courtesy of *The Weather Channel*®.
4-24	The MapQuest.com logo is a registered trademark of MapQuest, Inc. The MapQuest trademarks and content are used with permission.
4-25	Information courtesy of The Internet Movie Database (http://www.imdb.com). Used with permission.
4-26	© 2005 About, Inc. About and About.com are registered trademarks of About, Inc.
5-1	© Copyright 1992 Computer Ethics Institute.
Table 5-1	Source: Eric S. Raymond, (ed.), THE NEW HACKER'S DICTIONARY, 3rd Ed. MIT Press, ISBN: 0-262-68092-0.
8-11	Screen shot reprinted by permission from Microsoft Corporation. Copyright © 2005 Microsoft Corporation. All rights reserved.
8-12	Google™ is a trademark of Google Inc.
8-15	Mozilla Thunderbird™ is a trademark of the Mozilla Foundation.
9-1	Copyright © 1998–2005 ICQ Inc. All rights reserved.
9-7	MSN® Logo reprinted by permission from Microsoft Corporation. Copyright © 2005 Microsoft Corporation. All rights reserved.
9-14	Used with Permission from CNET Networks, Inc. Copyright © 1995–2005 CNET Networks, Inc. All rights reserved.
10-2	©2005 National Cable Satellite Corporation.
10-3	©2005 National Cable Satellite Corporation.
10-4	© 2005 National Cable Satellite Corporation.
10-4	Real logo is a trademark of Real Networks, Inc.
10-5	© Copyright NPR® 2005. This material is used with the permission of NPR Inc. Any unauthorized duplication is strictly prohibited.
Table 25-1	Pew Internet & American Life Project, February–March 2005 Tracking Survey, http://www.pewinternet.org/trends/User_Demo_05.18.05.htm. Last updated May 18, 2005.
25-5	Reprinted by permission of Glen Gummess, Janet Agnew, and Michael Hudson. © 2000.
25-6	Courtesy of Research in Motion (RIM).
26-3	Courtesy of Motorola Inc.
26-5	Courtesy of Toshiba.
26-6	Courtesy of palmOne, Inc.
26-7a	Courtesy of Tissot US.
26-7b	Courtesy of Tissot US.
26-9	Courtesy of Microsoft Corporation.

Index

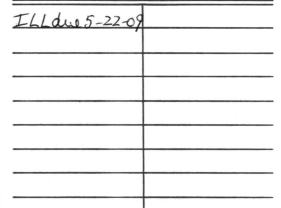

DATE DUE

ILL due 5-22-09

WITHDRAWN